INNOVATIVE STRATEGIES FOR COMPETITIVENESS AND SUSTAINABILITY IN GLOBAL BUSINESS ENVIRONMENTS

INNOVATIVE STRATEGIES FOR COMPETITIVENESS AND SUSTAINABILITY IN GLOBAL BUSINESS ENVIRONMENTS

Chief Editor

Kamal Kishore Sharma

Editors

Atul Kumar Agarwal
Jitender Bhandari

KALPAZ

ISBN: 978-93-5128-148-1

First Published, 2015

Published by

Kalpaz Publications
C-30, Satyawati Nagar,
Delhi-110052
Ph. : 9212142040
E-mail: kalpaz@hotmail.com

Printed at: G. Print Process.

Cataloging in Publication Data—DK
Courtesy: D.K. Agencies (P) Ltd. <docinfo@dkagencies.com>

Innovative strategies for competitiveness and sustainability in world business environments / [editors], Atul Kumar Agarwal, Jitender Bhandari.
pages cm
Includes bibliographical references.
ISBN 9789351281481

1. International trade. 2. India—Commerce. 3. Technological innovations—Economic aspects. 4. Technological innovations—Economic aspects—India. 5. Competition, International. 6. Sustainable development. 7. Sustainable development—India. I. Agarwal, Atul Kumar, editor. II. Bhandari, Jitender, editor.

DDC 382 23

Contents

ACCEPTED PAPERS

About the Editors

Chief Editor - Dr. Kamal Kishore Sharma- Professor and Dean

Dr. Sharma is an acclaimed strategic thinker, institution builder, team leader with distinguished abilities in directing, coordinating and motivating large cross-functional teams.

He is a Fellow (PhD) of IIM Ahmedabad and MBA (Marketing and Financial Management) from Institute of Management Studies, Ajmer University. In a rich career span of 24 years from a management trainee in 1989 to a young CEO at an MNC subsidiary abroad and later with consulting and academics, he has worked with a prestigious range of organizations viz. Public Sector (SAIL-Bokaro Steel), Indian Civil Services (Indian Railways Traffic Service), MNC (ArcelorMittal) and reputed Indian Universities (IIMA, CEPT, EDI). He was instrumental in setting up the Adani Institute of Infrastructure Management (AIIM) at Ahmedabad. He has been duly felicitated with coveted awards and recognition through his career and has excellent teaching ratings.

Dr. Kamal did his Doctoral Thesis in area of Public Policy Management in Indian Energy and Environment sector. He has published papers and presented at National and International seminars and workshops. He has a keen interest in academic institution building, entrepreneurial platforms and his research interests revolve around building simulation platforms and case writing on business strategies. He is a regular member of the US based Strategic Management Society (SMS).

Editor – Dr. Atul Kumar Agarwal - Professor

Dr. Agarwal has done his PhD (Central University) in Rural Marketing, M.Phil. (Mgt.), M.B.A., M.S.W. He is an avid researcher, prolific writer and an academician of repute. He has also competed short term course on

Industrial organization and policy contemporary theory and practices at IIT-Kanpur. He has attended and presented research papers in National and International Conferences at leading Institutions and published more than dozen research papers and articles in peer-reviewed journals and magazines. His research interest areas include Innovation and Knowledge Management, Brand Management, Advertising, Sales and MIS, Services Marketing, Rural Marketing etc.

Dr. Agarwal has worked at various managerial levels with organizations of great repute like Alkem Laboratories Limited, Unimarck Pharma India Limited, CEPL etc., before debuting into Academics. He has worked with IMS Unison University-Dehradun, Mody Institute of Technology and Sciences (MITS-Rajasthan, Deemed University), Kanpur Institute of Technology (KIT-Kanpur), PSIT/PSITCOE- Kanpur at Professor and HOD level, currently serving at Ansal University-Gurgaon (NCR) India as Professor and Chairperson–Marketing Management in School of Management Studies-Ansal University Gurgaon, India. He has conducted MDPs (Management Development Programs) at Grasim Industries Limited, Ultrapure Technologies Limited, Ordinance Factory - Dehradun, and also authored two books on 'Marketing Management' and 'Data Base Management Systems' by Sun India Publication–New Delhi, also written many study materials for Distance Learning Programme of Pondicherry University (Central University), had been a member of Study Material Preparation Editorial Board in IMS Dehradun.

Editor: Dr. Jitender Bhandari – Associate Professor

Dr. Bhandari is UNCTAD trained economist presently working as Associate Professor and Area Chair-Economics and International Busines in School of Management Studies at Ansal University, Gurgaon, India. He specializes in International Economics, International Business, Managerial Economics and other related subjects. He has earned his PhD in Economics from Kumaun University, Nainital. Dr. Bhandari has also completed a Refresher Course/Training Programme (21days) on "International Trade Theory and Policy-Modeling and Methodology" which was held at Department of Economics, University of Allahabad under the United Nations Conference for Trade and Development (UNCTAD) (India), Department for International Development (DFID) (UK) and Ministry of Commerce (GOI) Programme, "Strategy and Preparedness for Trade and Globalization in India." Dr. Bhandari has been appointed as the founder Editor of Ansal University Business Review, the flagship journal of Ansal University. In addition, Dr. Bhandari has been nominated as the editorial member of (i) Journal of Economics and Economic Education Research (JEEER), Allied Academies, North Carolina, USA (ii) Journal of International Business Research (JIBR). Allied Academies, North Carolina, USA. He has also written many research papers which have been published in refereed journals and conference proceedings. Dr. Bhandari has been invited by ASSOCHAM in various conferences as speaker He is member of Indian Economic Association and Academy of International Business (India Chapter). Recently.

Dr. Bhandari was conferred with "Senior Educator and Scholar Award" by National Foundation for Entrepreneurship Development, Coimbatore, Tamilnadu on Teacher's Day 5th September 2014.

International Advisory Committee

- Dr. Frina Albertyn, Professor and Head, School of Business, Eastern Institute of Technology, New Zealand.
- Prof. Paulo Barcellos, Director, Foreign Academic Relations, University of Caxias do Sul, Brazil.
- Prof. Caroline Stern, Distinguished Professor, Ferris State University, Big Rapids, MI, USA.
- Dr. Pius J Egbelu, Distinguished Professor, New Jersey Institute of Technology, USA.
- Dr. Marilyn M. Robitaille, Director, International Programs, Tarleton State University, Texas, USA.
- Prof. Jit Sharma, Chair, Department of Civil Engineering, Lassonde School of Engineering, York University, Canada.
- Prof. Andrew Maxwell, Director, Bergeron Entrepreneurs in Science and Technology (BEST), Lassonde School of Engineering, York University, Toronto, Canada.

Review Committee:

- Dr. Manmohan Rahul – Professor, School of Management Studies, Ansal University.
- Dr. Puja Chhabra Sharma- Professor, School of Management Studies, Ansal University.
- Dr. Atul Kumar Agarwal - Professor, School of Management Studies, Ansal University.
- Dr. Jitender Bhandari – Associate Professor, School of Management Studies, Ansal University.
- Dr. Tania Shaw - Associate Professor, School of Management Studies, Ansal University.
- Dr. Pratika Mishra – Assistant Professor, School of Management Studies, Ansal University.

- Dr. Indu Prabha Pathak - Assistant Professor, School of Management Studies, Ansal University.

Editorial Committee

- Dr. Indu Prabha Pathak, Assistant Professor, School of Management Studies, Ansal University.
- Ms. Aparna Sethi, Assistant Professor, School of Management Studies, Ansal University.
- Mr. Sumeet Malik, Assistant Professor, School of Management Studies, Ansal University.
- Mr. Navdeep Barwal, Assistant Professor, School of Management Studies, Ansal University.
- Ms. Neetu Jora, Assistant Professor, School of Management Studies, Ansal University.

Preface

Ansal University has a legacy of over two decades and is dedicated to providing advanced quality of education with a futuristic approach and a strong focus on trans disciplinary learning. Taking this strong tradition forward, it gives me immense pleasure to introduce our efforts at organizing and hosting the International Conference "Innovative Strategies for Competitiveness and Sustainability in Global Business Environments (ISCSGBE)", on March 26-27, 2015 at Ansal University Campus, Gurgaon.

This conference aims at examining innovation, competitiveness and shifts in business strategies with a regional and global perspective. The discussions focus on the impact of globalization on innovation, competition, and business environment sustainability activities. In our endeavor, we have received around 55 papers, out of which 40 papers are being published in this edited book. We have also included 11 invited papers from across the globe. The contents and coverage of the papers presented is spread across the sphere of business opportunities, emerging markets, strategy, innovation and challenges in international markets.

In reference to the globalization, more regional business clusters are emerging with technological innovations, which are triggering global competition. The policy makers and business strategists are thence searching new theoretical frameworks to understand the underlying dynamics of this global reshuffling of production and marketing activities of firms and how this business dynamics will affect innovation and competitiveness of firms. This conference discusses various perspectives of market growth and development of emerging firms in the global context and examines the impact of innovation and technology adoption on business growth and competitiveness.

We extend our heartfelt thanks to the core organizing committee for their extensive and appreciable team efforts. We are grateful to our

Hon'ble Chancellor, Shri Sushil Ansal for his motivation and support. We extend our gratefulness to Prof. Raj. S. Dhankar, Vice Chancellor, Ansal University, Gurgaon, India for providing us the necessary thought leadership and support in organizing this conference. We are also indebted to our distinguish International Advisory Committee for constant support.

We deeply acknowledge with humble gratitude all the valuable intellectual contributions of our authors that forms part of this conference proceeding.

The conference is the culmination of a successful team work by all faculty members of the School of Management Studies, Ansal University.

Dr. Kamal Kishore Sharma

Chief Editor and Conference Chair

Dr. Atul Kumar Agarwal

Editor and Conference Convenor

Dr. Jitender Bhandari

Editor and Conference Co-Convenor

List of Contributors

Aditi Nath, Assistant Professor, Department of Social Work, Assam University: Silchar (A Central University).

Ajay Mittal, Head-Training (North and West Region) Birla AMC Mumbai.

Amarjeet Kaur Malhotra, Visiting Professor, Valparaiso University USA. (2)

Ankita Saxena, Lecturer, Anand Engineering College.

Anu Singh Lather, Professor, University School of Management Studies, Guru Gobind Singh Indraprastha University, Delhi.

Aparna Sethi, Assistant Professor at Ansal University, Gurgaon.

Ashamayee Mishra, Research Scholar, Department of Business Administration, Sambalpur University.

Ashutosh Kumar, Professor, Amity Business School, Amity University, Gurgaon, Haryana.

Asif Ali Syed, Assistant Professor, Department of Business Administration, Faculty of Management Studies and Research, Aligarh Muslim University.

Asma Khan, Research Scholar, Department of Business Administration, Faculty of Management Studies and Research, Aligarh Muslim University.

Bhavya Soni, Assistant Professor, R.A. Podar Institute of Management, FMS-University of Rajasthan.

Deepali Dabas, Ph.D. Scholar, School of Management Studies, Ansal University, Gurgaon.

Dipankar Saha, Research Scholar, Calcutta University.

Ekta Pandey, Assistant Professor, School Of Management Studies, Ansal University, Gurgaon.

Esha Jain, Assistant Professor, School of Management, G.D. Goenka University.

Gaurav Jain, Senior Manager, Birla AMC, Mumbai.

Gaurav Wadhwa, Student, BBA, School of Management Studies, Ansal University, Gurgaon.

Gesty Ernestivita, Islamic University Kadiri, Kediri, East Java, Indonesia. (1)

Harold Andrew Patrick, Professor, Institute of Management, Christ University, Bangalore.

Harsh Purohit, Dean WISDOM, Banasthali Vidyapith University, Rajasthan.

Hemant Sharma, Professor, Department of Business Administration, Amity University, Gurgaon, Haryana.

Indu Prabha Pathak, Assistant Professor, School of Management Studies, Ansal University, Gurgaon.

Jitender Bhandari, Associate Professor, School of Management Studies, Ansal University, Gurgaon.

Jyoti Sharma, Research Scholar School of Management Studies, Ansal University, Gurgaon.

Kanika Mahajan, Student - MBA Ansal University, Gurgaon.

Kashmira Patel, Student, MBA (Healthcare), School of Management Studies, Ansal University, Gurgaon.

Kumkum Mukherjee, Professor and Head, MHRM, IISWBM.

M.S. Khan, Head/Coordinator-MBA Programme, School for Management Studies, Babasaheb Bhimrao Ambedkar University.

Manish Madan, Associate Professor, Rukmini Devi Institute of Advanced Studies.

Monika Khurana, Assistant Professor, Ansal University, Gurgaon.

Narinder Tanwar, Associate Professor Department of Management Studies, B.S. Anangpuria Institute of Technology and Management, Faridabad.

Neelam Vohra, Associate Professor, Ansal University, Gurgaon, Haryana.

Neetu Jora, Assistant Professor, School of Management Studies, Ansal University, Gurgaon.

Nidhi Chowdhry, Associate Professor. School of Management Studies, Ansal University, Gurgaon.

Pratibha Kumari Singh, Research Scholar Ansal University, Gurgaon.

Priyanka Anand, Research Scholar, School of Management Studies, Ansal University, Gurgaon.

Puja Chhabra Sharma, Professor, School of Management Studies, Ansal University, Gurgaon.

Pulkit Gupta, Student, BBA, School of Management Studies, Ansal University, Gurgaon.

R.B. Solanki, Assistant. Professor, DBRAU (Delhi University, Delhi).

R.C.S. Rajpurohit, Professor, Department of Business Administration, Faculty of Commerce and Management Studies, Jodhpur, Rajasthan.

Rachna Madan, Ph.D. Scholar, School of Management Studies, Ansal University, Gurgaon.

Rachna Madan, Ph.D. Scholar, School of Management Studies, Ansal University, Gurgaon.

Rajeev Srivastava, Head and Associate Professor IMS Unison University, Dehradun.

Rajiv Kumar, Assistant Professor, Haryana School of Business, Guru Jambheshwar University of Science and Technology, Hisar, Haryana.

Rajiv Kumar, Assistant Professor, Haryana School of Business, Guru Jambheshwar University of Science and Technology, Hisar, Haryana, India.

Ravi Dutt, Research Scholar, Banasthali Vidyapith (Rajasthan).

Rupa, Research Scholar, Haryana School of Business, Guru Jambheshwar University of Science and Technology, Hisar, Haryana, India.

Sambhavna Dogra, Student, MBA, School of Management Studies, Ansal University, Gurgaon.

Sana Rehman, Junior Research Fellow, UGC, EAFM Department, University of Rajasthan.

Sarbani Chowdhury, Clinical Psychologist, (INDIAN AIR FORCE), Visiting Faculty, Ansal University, Gurgaon.

Sharadindu Pandey, Assistant Professor Gautam Buddha University, Greater Noida, U.P.

Shashi Shekhar Gautam, Assistant Professor, Hindustan College of Science and Technology, Mathura.

Shashi Shekhar Gautam, Assistant Professor, Hindustan College of Science and Technology, Mathura.

Shefali, Research Scholar, Guru Gobind Singh University, Dwarka.

Shefali, Research Scholar, Guru Gobind Singh University, New Delhi.

Shikha Sharma, Professor, Amity University Rajasthan, Jaipur.

Shilpa Jain, Assistant Professor, University School of Management Studies, Guru Gobind Singh Indraprastha University, Delhi.

Shivani Dubey, Research Scholar, Ansal University, Gurgaun, IMS Ghaziabad.

Shivani Khandelwal, Student, MBA (Healthcare), School of Management Studies, Ansal University, Gurgaon.

Subhabrata Dutta, Professor and Head Department of Social Work, Assam University: Silchar.

Suman Dahiya, Assistant Professor at Ansal University, Gurgaon.

Sumeet Malik, Assistant Professor. School of Management Studies, Ansal University, Gurgaon.

Sunayana Jain, Associate Profesor, Ghaziabad.

Tania Shaw, Associate Professor, School of Management Studies, Ansal University, Gurgaon.

Tanuja Singh, Research Scholar, School for Management Studies, Babasaheb Bhimrao Ambedkar University, Lucknow.

Vidhu Gaur, Assistant Professor, MDI, Gurgaon, Haryana.

Vijita Singh Agarwal, Associate Professor, Guru Gobind Singh University, Dwarka.

Vinitaa Agrawal, Professor, Amity University Rajasthan, Jaipur.

Vinod Kumar, Research Scholar, Haryana School of Business, Guru Jambheshwar University of Science and Technology, Hisar, Haryana.

Yukti Bajaj, Assistant Professor, School of Management Studies, Ansal University, Gurgaon.

Yukti Bajaj, Assistant Professor, School Of Management Studies, Ansal University, Gurgaon.

INVITED PAPERS

1

Comprehend India's Commitment in WTO

R.C.S Rajpurohit & Ashutosh Kumar

Abstract

The formation of World Trade Organisation is an important milestone in the history of international trade. It registered its existences in Jan. 1995. GATT in its initial stage covered only goods. Later, it included agriculture and textile in the fold of multilateral trade negotiations while WTO dealt with the different aspects such as investments, services, and intellectual property rights in particular. The main objective of WTO is the liberalisation of world trade. Member countries are required to apply fair trade rules covering commodities, services and intellectual property. WTO also encourages development and economic reforms among the increasing number of developing countries.

India is a signatory to the WTO agreement executed at Marrakech in 1994 and has made national commitment in respect of market access for all goods. The present study is an effort to highlight India's those commitments under the major headings like, Bindings, Quantitative restrictions, Anti dumping and safeguards, Technical barriers to trade and sanitary and phyto-sanitary measures, Intellectual property, The general agreement on Trade in Services (GATS), Trade related investment measures (TRIMS), Environment, Information technology agreement (ITA), Global electronic commerce and Agreement on agriculture.

The study is ended with comments regarding India's commitment on WTO.

Key Words: WTO, Bindings, GATS, TRIMS, ITA, GATT

JEL: M1

(I) Introduction

The formation of World Trade Organisation is an important milestone in the history of international trade. Installed as comprehensive dispute settlement machinery with a wider sphere covering international trade in both goods and services, it contains the single most important set of governing rules.

WTO is a permanent organisation which has been established on the basis of an international treaty approved by participating countries.

The WTO is embodied with five specific functions: —

1. To administer and implement multilateral trade agreements and legal instruments negotiated in connection with the Uruguay round.
2. To provide a forum for multilateral trade negotiation.
3. To administer the rules and processes related to dispute settlement.
4. To review national trade policy mechanism.
5. To assist IMF and IBRD for establishing coherence in universal economic policy determination.

WTO, being an improved edition of GATT, reiterates the objectives of GATT and as such improves the general discipline to clarify the provisions with a greater precision, and to prescribe the procedures for their implementation.

It is inferred from "Marrakech" Declaration, that the agreement made during Uruguay round would provide a strong base to the economy and lead to more free-trade, investment, employment and income growth to not only the developed nations but also to developing nations, like India. The WTO is the culmination of Uruguay round results and successor to GATT.[1]

The Uruguay round of GATT (1986-93) gave birth to World Trade Organisation. The members of the GATT signed on an agreement of Uruguay round in April 1994 in Morocco for establishing a new organisation named WTO.

While GATT comprised only trade in goods, WTO was designed to cover several new areas viz, services, investment and intellectual property rights. GATT in it's initially stage covered only goods. Later, it included agriculture and textile in the fold of multilateral trade negotiations. The basic principle behind these agreements was to provide free trade system among member's countries.

The main objective of the WTO is the liberalisation of world trade. Member countries are required to apply fair trade rules covering commodities, services and intellectual property. The Uruguay Round also commits the members to lowering of tariffs on industrial goods, abolition of import duties on a variety of items, progressive abolition of quotas on garments and textiles, reduction of trade-distorting subsidies and import barriers, agreements on intellectual property and rules for civil aviation, telecommunications, financial services and the movement of labour. The WTO also encourages development and economic reform among the increasing number of developing countries and countries with economies in transition participating in the international trading system. The WTO operates a limited number of technical assistance programme, related to training recognised the need to protect the environment and to promote sustainable development.

(II) Objective of the Study

The objective of the present article is to highlight commitment of India in relation to WTO and to offer comments in this regard.

(III) India's Commitment in WTO

India is a signatory to the WTO agreements executed at Marrakech in 1994, and has made national commitments in respect of market access for all goods. Mainly India has made following commitments in respect to WTO:

1. Bindings: India so far has bound 67 per cent of all its tariff lines. Earlier it was mere 6 per cent. For non-agricultural goods, with a few exceptions, ceiling bindings of 40 per cent *ad valorem* on finished goods and 25 per cent on intermediate goods, machinery and equipment have been undertaken. In textile, reduction has completed over a period of 10 years, ending on December 31st 2004. Under the agreement on agriculture except for new items, India's bound rates range from 100 to 300 per cent and no commitment have been made regarding market access, reduction of subsidies or tariffs. Necessary action is being taken to fulfill India's commitments to reduce tariffs to the bound levels by March 1, 2005 in respect of non-agricultural and non-textile items. The only subsidies are in the form of exemption of income tax on profits from export sales and subsidies on costs of freight on export shipment of certain products like fruit, vegetables and floriculture products.

2. Quantitative Restrictions (QRs): As per the legal documentation, by 1 April 2001, no quantitative restrictions shall exist in respect of any goods imported into India. This shall apply to agricultural as well as consumer goods, which are presently restricted for imports. In 1997, India offered a phase-out schedule for 2,700 items on which import restrictions were being retained on balance of payments grounds and would be lifted by 2004, in three stages. The phase out schedule was accepted (with negotiations) by the EU and other trading partners, but was disputed by the US at the WTO. India lost the dispute and accepted 1 April 2001 as the final date for eliminating quantitative restrictions on all items of the list and, on 1 April 2000 opened all these items for imports, as committed.

3. Anti-dumping and Safeguards: Dumping means disposing off unwanted goods, such as rubbish, in a place other than the home ground. Thus when a company sends unsaleable goods to a foreign market at a low price, we say that dumping is taking place. Thus excess sugar production in Brazil sent to a market like India is said to be dumped. Anti-dumping and countervailing duties are imposed under the Customs Tariff Act 1975 and the rules made there under.

These Act and Rules are in consistent with GATT accord on anti-dumping and countervailing duties. The designated authority strictly follows the time limits and the procedures prescribed under the Indian laws/GATT Agreement. As dumping cases are augmenting, a proposal to establish Directorate General of Anti-Dumping and Allied Duties for speedy disposal of such cases, by the Government of India, was put in.

India applies anti-dumping duties using the provisions of the WTO Agreement on Dumping, in cases where abnormal price exceeds the landed price in India by more than the minimal margin of 2 per cent and the volume of dumped goods exceeds 3 per cent of domestic market from a single origin, or 7 per cent in case of more than one origin. India's anti-dumping legislation does not consider the consumer interest aspect and is based on industrial representations alone. As a result, anti-dumping actions can be initiated even when the Indian market prices are higher than international levels because of a monopoly or dominant Indian player's intervention.

India introduces, Section 8(B) of the Custom Tariff Act, 1975 to impose safeguard duties as per the provision of the World Trade Organisation agreement on safeguard. Such duties may be applied in respect of any item whose import volumes exceed the preceding 3 year average by more than 25 per cent or whose average CIF price falls below the preceding 3 year average by more than 10 per cent.

Despite this, WTO rules were imposed even on goods that may have a very meager share on our total imports thus, leading to discrimination. For imposition of safeguard duties, The Director General of Safeguards has been appointed to consider complaints received form domestic industry suffering injury from the increased import.

4. Technical Barriers to Trade and Sanitary and Phytosanitary Measures: India is also committed, under the Agreement on Technical Barriers to Trade and Sanitary and Phytosanitary Measures, to set up and govern national standards and technical regulations, keeping in view the basic percepts of MFN, National Treatment and Transparency. Being signatory to the Agreement on Technical Barriers to Trade and that on Sanitary and Phytosanitary measures India is trying to bring there standards to that of international levels.

In India, health and safety regulations are compulsory for several products. The Bureau of India Standards (BIS) responsible for formulating and setting national standards had harmonised Indian standards with international standards for the last decade. Till today about 3,500 Indian standards have been harmonised with ISOTEC and EC standards/regulations.[2]

5. Intellectual Property: In case of Intellectual Property, India has committed to amend its intellectual property right legislation in conformity with the TRIPS Agreement. As a developing country, India has a 5-year transitional period for a number of these changes and an additional 5 years to extend product patent protection to areas of technology not protected so far. However, for some, notably Articles 70.8 and 70.9 [3], India's obligations became effective with the signing of the WTO Agreement; India has not yet passed legislation to do so. [4] Those countries that failed to provide product patent in certain areas could delay the provisions of product patents for another five years. However, they have to provide Exclusive Marketing Rights for products, which obtain patents after January 1, 1995. As per the obligations under the WTO agreement, the Patents (Amendments) Act, 1999 was passed in March 1999 to provide for EMRs. In respect of plant varieties, a decision has been taken to put in place a ***sui generic*** system as it is seeming to be in our national interest.

India has made commitments in 33 activities, (total 161) as compared to an average of 23 activities for developing countries. The foreign direct investment regime has been liberalised to attract foreign investment in the services sector. India aims to encourage greater inflow of FDI in those sectors in which such investment could generate greater benefits. India has also committed to allow automatic approval of up to 25 per cent foreign equity participation (compared with the present policy of 49 per cent) in the area of voice telephone services. While developed countries have surplus capital to invest, the majority of the developing countries have excess of skilled, semi-skilled and unskilled workers. India is at advantage to have large pool of well-qualified professionals capable of providing services abroad. As developed countries have a comparative advantage in exporting capital-intensive services, similarly developing countries have a comparative advantage in exporting labour intensive services involving movement of persons. To this, India have taken up a number of related issues, such as recognition of qualifications, economic needs tests (ENTs), administrative procedures relating to visas, mutual recognition agreements (MRAs), social security contributions. Our objectives in service negotiations has been to offer entry to foreign service providers in which entry was considered to be most advantageous for us in terms of capital inflows, technology and employment.

6. The General Agreement on Trade in Services (GATS): One area where India has real chance of becoming a super power is services. The General Agreement on Trade in Services covers a wide range of service activities.[5] Being a active participant in the Uruguay Round, India negotiated for certain commitments like business, communication, construction work for civil engineering, financial, health-related and social, and tourism services.

In this order, India's commitments are for 33 activities in which foreign services providers will be allowed to enter. The choice of activities is reported to have been guided by considerations of national benefit, viz., and impact on capital inflows, technology and employment.

7. Trade Related Investment Measures (TRIMs): India has already notified the TRIMs maintained by it. It has been eliminated by 1.1.2000. India allows foreign direct investment to varying levels of foreign equity participation, ranging from 24 to 100 per cent, depending on whether the sector is given priority. India has opened all the sectors of the economy to foreign investment other than the areas of national security viz, defence, railways and atomic energy and also the insurance sector. Foreign investment in the small-scale sector is restricted to 24 per cent foreign equity participation.

8. Environment: So far concerned to environment, India has adopted an eco-labeling scheme applicable to 15 groups of products ranging from soaps and detergents to food additives, textiles, leather and food products. Although the ecomark has not found many takers so far yet, environmental awareness is gradually spreading among Indian firms, particularly those engaged in exports.

The WTO, and the growing international demand for free trade, is a direct threat to environmental quality, especially in the less developed countries." What we need today is a complete reversal of the argument about trade and the environment. Neither trade nor the environment is limited to the economic realm. These are issues that have to be politically and ethically debated. The environment is not an issue that can be assessed in economic measure alone, most ostensibly not within the ambit of trade negotiations. As a matter of global strategy, all groups negatively affected by recent trade regimes have good reasons to unite politically irrespective of whether they are developed or less developed countries. Farmers and fishermen, cottage and small scale industries, need to work out mechanisms for sustainably managing their landscapes and ecosystems without jeopardising their present and future livelihoods and compromising environmental quality."[6]

9. Information Technology Agreement (ITA): India joined as a participant to Information Technology Agreement on 1 April 1997 after analysing the complete implications of the proposed agreement. The agreement covered, computers, telecommunications equipment, semiconductors, and semiconductor manufacturing equipment, software, and scientific instruments. Its offer included zero rates on 217 items at the HS six-digit level by the year 2005 (i.e. tariffs have to be brought down to zero on 95 lines by the year 2000, on 4 tariff lines by 2003, on 2 tariff lines by 2004 and on the balance 116 tariff lines in the year 2005). India is committed to phase out the import tariffs on the products covered by the ITA as scheduled. At the same time, India has also raised the issue during plurilateral discussion that if the global information technology infrastructure is to be strengthened, the rules for movement of skilled persons working in this sector should also be liberalised.

10. Global Electronic Commerce: India made a comprehensive intervention on Electronic Commerce at the Special Session of the WTO General Council in September 1990 and is taking active part in the work programme on E-Commerce which is going on in the TRIPs council, the Committee on GATS and the Committee on Trade and Development of the WTO.

11. Agreement on Agriculture: Agriculture sector is a source of more than 2/3 of the population and contributes 30 per cent of GDP in India. AOA of WTO recognises free and market oriented trading system in agriculture. The only commitment India has undertaken is to bind its agricultural tariffs. Developing countries are to reduce their bindings by simple un-weighted average of 24 per cent with a minimum of 10 per cent for each tariff line over a period of ten years (1995-2004). India has indicated tariff bindings of 100 per cent on primary agricultural goods and raw commodities like wheat, rice, milk and cream etc. 150 per cent on processed agro-commodities like cotton, etc. In India wheat and rice are staple foods and hence their imports can be restricted. India's prevailing agricultural tariffs are well within the bound rates.

(IV) Comments

In GATT one talks of free market and free trade but in reality the developed nations are following protectionist's policies. The history of GATT reveals that whenever newly industrialised nations have challenged the competitive strength of the developed countries, they have immediately strike back by imposing both tariff and non-tariff barriers. Today after getting hold on the world economy by the inclusion of Agriculture, TRIPs, TRIMs and Services they have started talking of labour clauses, tomorrow they will talk of environment and then human rights etc. Anyhow they wish to restore their affluence and create more jobs and that too in the name of free trade. This is ridiculous.

When the Uruguay round concluded in March 1994 and the World Trade Organisation (WTO) was established, what would be the next round of negotiation was left unresolved. The Uruguay round of negotiation of the GATT was ostensibly about framing new rules in order to spur the growth of world trade. In actual fact, the Uruguay Round was about the search for new markets by the industrial countries.

India's response during Uruguay round negotiations was never adequate. Therefore, the acceptance of the final agreement raised the controversy regarding the wisdom of remaining a part of multilateral trading arrangement. Despite liberalisation of various policies and procedures, India has so far been unable in the face of a highly competitive international business environment. The size and content of India's export basket has remained almost the same over the past four decades. As a result, with the signing of the final agreement, India has entered into a maples web without a compass.

Similar problems were seen in other areas as well viz, intellectual property rights (TRIPS). While China has adopted product patents to derive benefits from the emerging multilateral trade regime, India is still debating on the merits and demerits of process and product patents. The country has yet to respond strategically to the impending realities of multilateralism. Agriculture and skilled manpower has to be advantageously used. There has to be a substantial environment in production and productivity. A viable welfare system for India's labour and changes in labour policies is still due. Quality of labour and products will have to get urgent priority. Consumer sovereignty and consumer protection is yet to get its due recognition. Moreover, a greater transparency in the tariff system is needed. It must be realised that delays in these areas would only mean gradual corrosion of the little gains that have been made in a liberalised regime

To survive, and emerge strong, in the post GATT multilateral trading arrangement, we will have to be fully conscious of our strengths and weaknesses in future negotiations. We should build on our strengths and overcome our weaknesses to the fullest extent possible. We should shed our egotism of having always been right and accept our mistakes. Only such a sensible approach will help us bridge the gap in our preparations and avoid future mistake.

Thus, in order to integrate into an increasingly interdependent and highly competitive global market, India will have to shed it passively and undergo a profound process of economic transformation. The process would, no doubt, involve some trade-offs in maintaining a social consensus in support of economic reforms. India will have to review the sequencing of basic reform measures such as stabilisation, structural change, and private sector development.

Mr. R.K. Khurana of the India international center has rightly summed up the position: "The consensus, however, is that the Uruguay round has been a game in which the more powerful nations lay down the rules. Unfortunately, India is not one among the powerful trading nations and it is, therefore, doubtful if the country could have achieved anything significantly more than what our negotiations have managed". [7]

References

- Yadav, Singh Subash: WTO and its impact on Indian agriculture; Yojana (A Development working) VOL.45. Dec. 2001.
- A brief guide to the WTO for small business, published by FISME, sponsored by SIDBI.
- Trade Policy Review; India: 998. p.26. Articles 70.8 refers to the obligation of a member country that does not presently provide patent protection for pharmaceutical and agricultural chemical products to provide a means by which patent applications for these products can be filed and to apply the criteria for patent ability as laid down in the Agreement from this date. Article 70.9 requires that the subject of the patent application referred to in 70.8 shall be granted exclusive marketing rights for a period of five year after obtaining marketing approval in the country.
- Trade Policy Review; India: 1998. p. 27. According to the authorities, although the legislation has not been padded by parliament, India has provided a means to receive patent applications for pharmaceuticals and agricultural chemicals through administrative instructions. A panel decision followed by an Appellate Body decision concluded that India's administrative instructions were inconsistent with Article 70.8(a) of the TRIPS Agreement, and that by failing to have mechanism in place to provide for the grant of exclusive marketing rights effective from the date of entry into force of the WTO Agreement.
- The Trade Policy Review; India: 1998. p. 152. WTO secretariat has divided these activities into 12 sectors: business services; communication services; construction and related services; distribution services; educational services; environmental services; financial services; health-related and social services; tourism and travel-related services; recreational, cultural and sporting services; transport services; and other services not included elsewhere.
- Mishra, Harindra Kishor: Impact of WTO on Indian economy. Ed. by G.K. Chadha: WTO and the Indian economy, Deep and Deep Publishers, 2003, p.104.
- Khurana, R.K.: Some Synthesising Thoughts,*Op.* eit., p.51, ed. By Datt, Rudar and Sundaram, K.P.M, 2000, p.801.

2

Sudoku of Perceived Service Quality and Service Loyalty

Hemant Sharma

Abstract

It is easy to observe from the previously made studies that concept of service loyalty is relatively little explored. Only a few studies attempt to conceptualise service loyalty and to probe into its antecedents. However, despite these few attempts, customer loyalty still remains a vital issue to researchers because of its significance in service marketing. In most of the literature, service loyalty has often been incorporated as a dependent variable in service quality models, nevertheless the exact relationship of the service quality - service loyalty has remained a mystery as the result of limited conceptualisations and contradictory empirical results. Most studies that have examined the service quality-service loyalty relationship focused on one specific industry only, limiting the generalisation of the results. In this paper, researcher examines the relationship between service quality and different dimensions of service loyalty across four different service industries. This paper is structured as follows. Firstly, this discusses the existing literature on key conceptual issues. Secondly, subsequent discussions on the results of an investigation designed to provide a multi-sector insight on the relationship between service quality and service loyalty. Finally, it concludes with the managerial implications of the results.

Key words: perceived service quality, service loyalty, preference loyalty, hospitals

Introduction and Review of Literature

In the earlier researches made in 1970s, customer loyalty was approached predominantly from a behavioural perspective. Jacoby and Chestnut (1978) observe that in these studies the focus was on interpreting patterns of repeat purchasing in primarily panel data as a manifestation of loyalty. As Day (1969) criticised the behavioural approach for a number of reasons and Bass (1974) found that stochastic components (i.e., randomness that could not be explained) occur in repeat purchasing patterns, researchers began to question the adequacy of using behaviour as a measure of loyalty. It became clear that the consumer's disposition to re-buy is an essential element of loyalty (Gremler and Brown, 1996). Jones and Sasser (1995) consider that customer loyalty is "a feeling of attachment to or affection for a company's people, products, or services". Therefore, Dick and Basu (1994) supplemented the behavioural approach with the concept of relative attitude which reflects the degree to which the consumer's evaluation of one service dominates that of another. They assume that true loyalty only exists when repeat patronage coexists with a high relative attitude. Hence, customer loyalty is approached as an attitudinal construct. Attitude denotes the degree to which a consumer's disposition towards a service is favourably inclined (Azjen and Fishbein, 1980). This is reflected, for instance, in the willingness to recommend a service provider to other consumers or the commitment to re patronise a preferred service provider (Gremler and Brown, 1996; Jain *et al.,* 1987; Pritchard, 1991). Based on a favourable attitude towards a service provider, customers may develop preference loyalty.

Previous literature also favours cognition as a significant parameter of loyalty. In its cognitive sense, service loyalty may be considered as a conscious evaluation of the price/quality ratio or the willingness to pay a premium price. Lee and Zeiss (1980) and Oliver (1996) reveal that cognition is predominant in service loyalty. Berger and Mitchell (1989) disclose that in the case of services, direct experience through the service encounter increases information acceptance and use in repurchase decisions. In nutshell, customers will make an explicit comparison between what they pay and receive.

Hirschman (1970) argued that a customer, who is not satisfied, has basically two options to a negative (service) experience: either discontinue the relationship or communicate dissatisfaction. Hence, it is justified to view service loyalty as a multi-dimensional construct comprising of the three dimensions as: preference loyalty, price indifference loyalty and dissatisfaction response. In the previously made studies, perceived service quality is often considered as a prerequisite for service loyalty and loyalty is included in models as an outcome variable. However, these studies provide varied results pertaining to the relationship between service quality and service loyalty.

Therefore, the present study will examine this relationship more closely in the next section.

There are many studies that have examined the relationship between service quality and customer preference loyalty. Boulding *et al.* (1993) studied the elements of repurchasing and willingness to recommend and revealed positive relationships between service quality and repurchase intentions and willingness to recommend. Cronin and Taylor (1992) focused solely on repurchase intentions and found that service quality did not have a significant (positive) effect on repurchase intentions. Dabholkar and Thorpe (1994) disclose that customer satisfaction with a store has a positive impact on intentions to recommend that store to the others. Zeithaml *et al.* (1990) reported a positive relationship between service quality and the willingness to pay a higher price and the intention to remain loyal in case of a price increase. Day (1984) found that following a negative experience, most of the customers simply remain inactive and do not undertake any action. Further, Beardon *et al.* (1979) and Yi (1990) argue that responding to dissatisfaction is negatively related to the level of service quality.

In fact, most of the studies made so far, connecting service quality, satisfaction and behavioural intentions have been organised only in the context of one specific service setting. For instance, Rust and Zahorik (1993) studied service quality perceptions to consumer loyalty in banking, Crosby and Stephens (1987) explored loyalty in the insurance industry and Kelley *et al.* (1993) investigated customers' patronage in retail industry. Theoretically, the individualistic nature of each service setting does not permit the generalisation of previous research findings with regard to behavioural intentions. Cronin and Taylor (1992) report considerable differences with regards to the relationship between satisfaction and repurchase intentions between the four service industries of banking, pest control, dry cleaning and fast food. Likewise, Parasuraman *et al.* (1994) found industry differences with regards to the service quality- behavioural intentions link. Therefore, it becomes imperative to adopt a cross-sectional perspective to enhance the knowledge about the development of service loyalty. Further, there are many studies that relate customer satisfaction and loyalty. Fornell (1992) give a new concept of "elasticity per industry" which means consequences of service quality in terms of loyalty differ per industry. He also concludes that the relationship between customer evaluations and loyalty across industries is "neither linear nor simple".

As per the previous studies, another significant variable of service loyalty may be switch over cost. It is defined as the cost involved in changing from one service provider to another (Porter, 1980). In addition to objectively measurable monetary costs, switching costs can also be related to time and psychological effort involved in facing the uncertainty of dealing with a new service provider. In literature, it has been argued that the costs of switching providers tend to be higher for services than for goods. Previous studies mainly including (Anderson and Fornell, 1994; Dick and Basu, 1994; Fornell, 1992; Gremler and Brown, 1996) which suggest that the degree of switching cost may have an impact on customers' loyalty in an industry. Furthermore, switching costs are sometimes used as a proxy for market structure or the level of customer perceived uncertainty. For instance, Quinlan (1991) reveals that for some services (e.g. fast food restaurants, retailers) switching costs are low for the mass of "anonymous" customers, for instance as a result of the fact that there are ample suppliers and "the inherent inability to differentiate on some valuation criterion" (Barnes and Cumby, 1995). In contrast, switching costs for services that are intrinsically difficult to evaluate, or for which there is only a limited number of suppliers (legal services, management consulting and medical services), are high (Brown and Swartz, 1989; Patterson and Johnson, 1993).

In the next section, some hypotheses have been developed on the complex relationship between perceived service quality and service loyalty.

Development of Hypotheses

According to available literature, researcher assumes a positive association between service quality and preference loyalty and service quality and price indifference loyalty and a negative relationship between service quality and dissatisfaction response. It is assumed that both service quality and the type of industry will determine the different forms of loyalty. Furthermore, cross-sectional variation is expected with regard to the relationship between perceived service quality and service loyalty for different types of service industries on the basis of relative switching costs involved for service customers. This leads to the following hypotheses:

H_{1a}: There is no significant relationship between perceived service quality and preference loyalty.

H_{1b}: There is not significant relationship between perceived service quality and price indifference loyalty.

H_{1c}: There is not negative relationship between perceived service quality and dissatisfaction response.

H_2: The level of preference loyalty, price indifference loyalty and dissatisfaction response is a function of service quality and type of industry.

Methodology Used

Data are gathered from the respondents in Delhi and NCR region by means of personal interviews on the basis of a structured questionnaire containing the questions on service quality, service loyalty dimensions and switching costs with regard to four different service industries including hospitals, theatres, fast food and supermarket. According to Zeithaml *et al.* (1996), total 13 items of behavioural intention are identified (refer Table I). Each item is accompanied by a seven-point scale ranging from 1 = not at all likely to 7 = extremely likely. Moreover, the items are adapted to specific characteristics of the service industries investigated. A unidimensional measure of perceived service quality relating to an evaluation of the core service is used with a seven-point scale ranging from 1 = completely disagree to 7 = completely agree (Strandvik and Liljander, 1994).

A total of 750 usable questionnaires are gathered randomly by trained personnel. Every seventh customer leaving the premises of a particular service provider is invited to participate in the present study. Only those people have been included in the survey; who have used the particular service within the last one month to ensure a latest evaluation of service quality and service loyalty. The number of respondents for each service provider was: Hospitals 200, theatres 150, fast food restaurants 200 and supermarkets 200.

Descriptive Analysis

In connection with perceived service quality, the mean scores are as follows: hospitals; 9.23 (std.dev 1.02), theatres; 8.52 (std.dev 1.34), fast food; 8.05 (std.dev 0.92), supermarkets; 9.23 (std.dev 1.69). Further analysis reveals that there is a significant differences between mean service quality scores ($F = 46.56$; $p < 0.001$) across service industries. Besides, mean score for switching costs are also calculated as: hospitals; 9.34 (std.dev 2.56), theatres; 9.06 (std.dev 2.05), fast food; 2.67 (std.dev 1.86), supermarkets; 1.87 (std.dev 0.83). Analysis reveals that these scores for switching cost significantly differ ($F = 39.56$; $p < 0.001$) across service industries.

Subsequently, to support the three dimensional pattern as derived on the basis of theory, researcher goes for factor analysis on the items pertaining to service loyalty. Factor analysis is run using Principal Component Analysis method with Varimax rotation. As one can see in Table 1, the analysis shows that a three dimensional structure could be identified. Items with factor loading higher than 0.04 are shown in the table. Total 58.45 per cent variations are explained with the revealed factor structure. Thus, empirical analysis supports the theoretical construct of this study. Further, Reliability analysis of these three factors namely preference loyalty, price indifference and dissatisfaction response yields the value of the coefficient alpha 0.87, 0.68 and 0.71 respectively. These values are quite acceptable.

Table 1: Dimensions of service loyalty

Factor Description	*Cronbach's alpha*	*Factor loading*	*Total variation explained (%)*
Preference:			
1., Recommend to someone who seeks your advice	0.87	0.9178	58.45
2. Encourage friends and relatives to do business with		0.8856	
3. Do more business within the next few years		0.8634	
4. Say positive things about to other people	0.7965		
5. Consider your first choice to buy ... services	0.7498		
6. Do less business within the next few years (–)	0.7149		
Price Indifference:			
7. Pay a higher price than competitors charge for the benefits you currently receive	0.68	0.7945	
8. Continue to do business with if its prices increase somewhat		0.7636	
9. Take some of your business to a competitor that offers (–)		0.6934	
Dissatisfaction response:			
10. Complain to other consumers if you experience a problem with ...'s service	0.71	0.6247	
11. Complain to external agencies, such as consumer organisations, if you experience a problem with ...'s service		0.5278	
12. Complain to employees if you experience a problem with ...'s service		0.4180	
13. Switch to a competitor if you experience a problem with ...'s service (–)		——	

Hypotheses Testing

Researcher decides to go for regression analysis to test hypotheses 1 and 2. Regression analysis is performed with perceived service quality as a predictor variable and each of the three loyalty dimensions namely preference loyalty, price indifference and dissatisfaction response as a dependent variable. Table 2 depicts the regression equation in model 1. Further, in order to take into account the effect of industry, researcher uses a set of multiple dummy variables. In this analysis, hospital is used as a reference group or intercept for the other service industries because the highest mean service quality score was obtained for hospitals. The value of the regression coefficient for the reference industry signifies the effect on the particular loyalty factor for hospitals. Remaining regression coefficients predict the impact of different types of service industries compared with the reference industry (hospitals). Subsequently, in order to assess the effect of multiple dummy variables on the model, researcher applies incremental F-test for change. It is evident from table 2 that multiple dummy variables contribute significantly to the model by comparing the values of R^2 for models 1 and 2. By including the multiple variables, value of R^2 increases from 0.5327 to 0.5886. It is easy to note in table 2 that perceived service quality contributes positively to explaining preference loyalty.

On this basis, hypothesis H_{1a} *can be rejected. For the reference industry, hospital, there is a significant positive relation between perceived service quality and preference loyalty.* It can also be noted that other industries excluding supermarkets differ significantly from the reference industry i.e hospital. For instance, in case of theatres, the impact of perceived service quality on preference loyalty is stronger as compared to hospitals and supermarkets, while for the remaining service industries the impact of perceived service quality on preference loyalty is smaller. Thus, it may be concluded that, for instance, that the same level of service quality results in a relatively higher level of preference loyalty for theatres than for hospitals and supermarkets. The significance of the incremental F-test indicates that incorporation of different types of industries, along with perceived service quality, contributes significantly to explaining preference loyalty.

Table 2: Regression results of perceived service quality and preference loyalty

Variable	*Industry*	*B*	*β*	*t*	*p*
Perceived service quality		0.7134	0.6587	19.645	0.0001
	Hospital (reference)	1.698		8.56	0.0001
	Theatres	0.4634	0.6803	3.98	0.0265
	Fast food	-0.4731	-0.8945	-4.73	0.0076
	Supermarket	-0.2904	-0.6021	-1.793	0.0834

Model 1	Model 2
$R^2 = 0.5327$	$R^2 = 0.5831$
Adjusted $R^2 = 0.5318$	Adjusted $R^2 = 0.5819$
$F = 578.63$ ($p < 0.0001$)	$F = 102.05$ ($p < 0.0001$)
	F change = 8.586 ($p < 0.0001$)

As far as price indifference loyalty is concerned, it is obvious from table 3 that perceived service quality contributes positively to explaining price indifference loyalty. *Therefore, it seems to be justified to reject the hypothesis* H_{1b}. The impact of perceived service quality on price indifference loyalty is the strongest for hospital; the reference industry. For the fast food and supermarkets, there is a comparatively small impact of perceived service quality on price indifference loyalty. But for the theater, the impact of service quality on price indifference loyalty is comparatively high. As far as, incorporation of different types of industries along with perceived service quality in the regression model as dummy variables is concerned, the significance of the incremental F-test (F change = 34.754, $p < 0.0001$) indicates that it contributes significantly to explaining price indifference loyalty.

Table 3: Regression results of perceived service quality and price indifference loyalty

Variable	*Industry*	*B*	*B*	*t*	*p*
Perceived service quality		0.06123	0.4621	11.6423	p < 0.0001
	Hospital (reference)	4.0764		10.9302	p < 0.0001
	Theatres	-0.9861	-0.2437	-4.8530	p < 0.0061
	Fast food	-1.8374	-0.5328	-11.065	p < 0.0001
	Supermarket	2.2943	-0.5102	-11.326	p < 0.0001

Model 1	Model 2
$R^2 = 0.2437$	$R^2 = 0.4231$
Adjusted $R^2 = 0.2340$	Adjusted $R^2 = 0.4212$
$F = 231.33$ ($p < 0.0001$)	$F = 120.05$ ($p < 0.0001$)
	F change = 34.754 ($p < 0.0001$)

In order to gauge the impact of service quality on the third dimension of loyalty i.e., dissatisfaction response, researcher again goes for regression analysis. The results have been summarised in table 4. It is easy to observe from table 4 that there is no significant relationship between perceived service quality and dissatisfaction response. *On this basis, hypothesis* H_{1c}*: there is no significant relationship between service quality and dissatisfaction response, has to be accepted.* However, cross-sectional differences between industries can be observed. For instance, hospitals and fast food industries, the relationship between perceived service quality and dissatisfaction response is relatively higher.

As in above analysis, researcher incorporates types of industries as dummy variable and results advocate that there is significant differences across the industries in relation to all three loyalty dimensions namely preference loyalty, price indifference loyalty and dissatisfaction response loyalty.

Therefore, hypothesis $\boldsymbol{H_2}$ *can be accepted. Undoubtedly, service loyalty is a function of service quality and industry type.*

Table 4: Regression results of service quality and dissatisfaction response loyalty

Variable	*Industry*	*B*	*β*	*t*	*p*
Perceived service quality		-.1364	-0.0961	-1.428	0.4942
	Hospital (reference)	6.2352		14.730	< 0.0001
	Theatres	0.6936	1.076	2.3630	0.2431
	Fast food	0.8941	0.2041	4.7508	< 0.0001
	Supermarket	0.4752	0.0893	1.9499	0.0677

<u>Model 1</u>	<u>Model 2</u>
$R^2 = 0.0437$	$R^2 = 0.0553$
Adjusted $R^2 = 0.0425$	Adjusted $R^2 = 0.0532$
F = 7.1436 (p = 0.0584)	F = 8.201 (p < 0.0001)
	F change = 7.754 (p < 0.0001)

Conclusion

In the present paper, researcher has made an attempt to focus on two important aspects of service industry. Firstly, explore the various dimensions of service loyalty and secondly, finding out relationship between perceived service quality and service loyalty. The results of present study suggest that there are three important dimensions of service loyalty namely; preference loyalty, price indifference loyalty and dissatisfaction response loyalty. Moreover, it is revealed that there is a positive relationship between perceived service quality and preference loyalty and price indifference loyalty. No significant relationship between perceived service quality and dissatisfaction response has been found. This may be because of the fact that dissatisfaction response is linked particularly to an incident or a specific attribute of service (like a complaint handling procedure) instead of an overall evaluation of the quality of the core service. Further, study investigates the influence of industry type on the perceived service quality-service loyalty relationship. It is discovered that the impact of service quality on preference loyalty generally varies per industry. According to Fornell (1992), these findings from one industry cannot be generalised to other industries. Thus, there seems to be a "loyalty-elasticity" across service industries.

Limitation of Study

Like many others, the present study is also not without the limitations. Acknowledgement of these limitations provides the new directions for future researcher to explore the researched issues. *Firstly*, there seems to a pressing need to further develop and refine the scale that has been used to measure service loyalty. Particularly, more number of items should be included to the dissatisfaction response dimension in order to enhance the reliability of this portion of scale. *Secondly*, it is suggested to future researchers to incorporate multiple measures of the relevant constructs in order to increase the number of items. *Thirdly*, this study takes into account only behavioural intentions that are an inadequate substitute for actual behaviour (Keaveny, 1995). Therefore, it would be good for further researchers to take into account actual (re)actions of consumers to perceived service quality. *Fourth*, as this study uses only cross sectional data that were collected at one moment in time, therefore, relationships between service quality and service loyalty reported in this paper are tentative only. There is a need to explore it using longitudinal research (data collection over multiple time periods) so that exact causal nature may be established. *Lastly*, this study takes into account only four industries. Future studies may relook at link between service quality-behavioural intentions by including more number of service industries in the sample. Besides above, availability of time, money and limited knowledge of researcher has been the natural constraints of the present study.

References

Anderson, C.H. (1986), "Hierarchical moderated regression analysis: a useful tool for retail management decisions", *Journal of Retailing,* Vol. 62, pp. 186-203.

Anderson, E.W. and Fornell, C. (1994), "A framework for comparing customer satisfaction across individuals and product categories", *Journal of Economic Psychology,* Vol. 12, pp. 267-86.

Andreasen, A.R. (1985), "Consumer responses to dissatisfaction in loose monopolies", *Journal of Consumer Research,* Vol. 12, pp. 135-41.

Boulding, W., Kalra, A., Staelin, R. and Zeithaml, V. (1993), "A dynamic process model of service quality: form expectations to behavioural intentions", *Journal of Marketing Research,* Vol. 30, pp. 7-27.

Brown, S.W. and Swartz, T.A. (1989), "A gap analysis of professional service quality", *Journal of Marketing,* Vol. 53, pp. 92-8.

Dabholkar, P.A. and Thorpe, D.I. (1994), "Does customer satisfaction predict shopper intentions", *Journal of Consumer Satisfaction, Dissatisfaction and Complaining Behaviour,* Vol. 7, pp. 161-71.

Fornell, C. (1992), "A national customer satisfaction barometer: the Swedish experience", *Journal of Marketing,* Vol. 56, pp. 6-21.

Guiltinan, J.P. (1989), "A classification of switching costs with implications for relationship marketing", in Childers, T.L., Bagozzi, R.P. *et al.* (Eds), *AMA Winter Educators' Conference: Marketing Theory and Practice,* Chicago, IL, pp. 216-20.

Jain, A.K., Pinson, C. and Malhotra, N.K. (1987), "Customer loyalty as a construct in the marketing of banking services", *International Journal of Bank Marketing,* Vol. 5, pp. 49-72.

Jones, T.O. and Earl Sasser, W. (1995), "Why satisfied customers defect", *Harvard Business Review,* Vol. 73 No. 6, pp. 88-99.

Keaveney, S.M. (1995), "Customer switching behaviour in service industries: an exploratory study", *Journal of Marketing,* Vol. 59, pp. 71-82.

Oliver, R.L. (1996), *Satisfaction. A Behavioural Perspective on the Consumer,* McGraw Hill, New York, NY. Olson, J.C. and Jacoby, J. (1971), "A construct validations study of brand loyalty", *Proceedings of the American Psychological Association,* Vol. 6, pp. 657-8.

Patterson, P.G. and Johnson, L.W. (1993), "Disconfirmation of expectations and the gap model of service quality: an integrated paradigm", *Journal of Consumer Satisfaction, Dissatisfaction and Complaining Behaviour,* Vol. 6, pp. 90-9.

Parasuraman, A., Zeithaml, V.A. and Berry, L.L. (1994), "Reassessment of expectations as a comparison standard in measuring service quality: implications for further research", *Journal of Marketing,* Vol. 58, pp. .111-24.

Porter, M.E. (1980), *Competitive Strategy; Techniques for Analysing Industries and Competitors,* Macmillan, New York, NY.

Reichfeld, F.W. and Sasser, W.E. (1990), "Zero defections: quality comes to services", *Harvard Business Review,* Vol. 68 No. 5, pp. 105-11.

Rust, R.T. and Zahorik, A.J. (1993), "Customer satisfaction, customer retention, and market share", *Journal of Retailing,* Vol. 69, pp. 193-215.

Zeithaml, V.A., Parasuraman, A. and Berry, L.L. *et al.* (1990), *Delivering Quality Service:*

Balancing Customer Perceptions and Expectations, The Free Press, New York, NY.

Zeithaml, V.A., Berry, L.L. and Parasuraman, A. (1996), "The behavioural consequences of service quality", *Journal of Marketing,* Vol. 60, pp. 31-46.

3

Managers Leadership Strategies and its Influence in Information Technology Organisations

Harold Andrew Patrick

Abstract

Today, leaders need to transition from leading and supporting to transforming, reshaping and impacting growth and development by unconventional ways. Their approach work and interaction with followers needs a reorientation. Leader effectiveness is contingent on the diagnosis of the situation, magnitude and direction of influence and the strategies adopted to achieve impact. Literature suggests that need for power and influence of leaders actually creates value and benefits most organisations. Researchers (e.g., Clements and Washbush, 1999) opine that there is a general illusion among leaders that their behaviours are always well intended to benefit the organisation. 515 employees using a stratified random sampling technique from leading IT (Information Technology) companies were surveyed. Leadership Strategies and Impact on others developed by Cooke (1996) was adopted with permission for data collection. IT managers preferred to use prescriptive leadership strategies more often than restrictive strategies in IT organisations. The leadership strategies had a constructive impact on IT employees. The detail findings, conclusions, implications and suggestions for further research have been discussed in the full length paper.

Key Words: *Leadership strategies, Leadership impact, Prescriptive strategy, Restrictive strategy, Constructive impact, Passive/Defensive impact, Aggressive/Defensive impact.*

Introduction

Indian information technology has come a long way since the starting from the 1990's. It has grown from US $ 150 million in 1991-92 to US $ 50 Billion in 2009-10. Most of its success has been attributed to accessibility of low cost technical resources, skilled manpower, lower salary, and project execution from India. Profit revenue was based on the number of projects executed and the number of resources deployed. The biggest challenge is not just attaining growth but to sustain it. Mohandas Pai and K. Dinesh of Infosys who resigned from the board opined that Infosys should prepare for a challenging future and for this leadership is most vital. The new leader behaviour needed to achieve this future rests with younger, more autonomous and a freeing climate for innovation and creativity. Mr Pai said that Infosys has become conservative and succession requires more transparency. The sacking of two CEO's by Wipro chief and appointing T.K. Kurien as new head are all indicators that Indian IT organisations to grow and sustain need a new leadership climate to inspire the workforce to voluntarily and creatively add value. This paper investigates the most frequently adopted leadership strategies and how it impacts employees.

Organisations goal achievement is highest when all employees successfully contribute their knowledge. The value of leadership is a vital antecedent to the quality of organisational and managerial behaviour, since leadership involves exert influence. The ability to inspire confidence and support among employees who are the bedrock for achievement organisational goals is leadership. Leaders have many employees to lead and leverages power to affect others behaviour in goal attainment. Managers must know how to lead as well as manage, Kotter (1990). Employees willingly follow leaders because they want to, not because they have to which makes leadership different from management. Managerial behaviour in information technology organisations is affected by leadership behaviour. Empowering practices by leader include providing a positive emotional atmosphere, rewarding and encouraging in visible and personal ways, expressing confidence, fostering initiative and responsibility, and building on success, praising initiative, and practicing super leadership, Conger (1989).

Literature Review

IT organisations need to create an appropriate leadership culture for non-linear growth. Hunter et al (2011argue that the pursuit of innovation requires a unique leadership approach one that may not be currently captured by traditional views of leadership. Creativity and innovation and how leadership effects team creativity has are researched by Reiter-Palmon (2011). Managing the innovative process and the dynamic role of leaders and how their cognition and social behaviours need to adapt to effectively and efficiently manage innovation, Stenmark et al (2011). Transformational leadership positively influences advice network density in teams and that advice network density serves as a mediating mechanism linking transformational leadership to team performance, Zhang and Peterson (2011). Empowering leadership climate was related to psychological empowerment climate, Wallace et al (2011). Yaffe and Kark (2011) explored the importance of leading by personal example by investigating leader OCB and group OCB. Servant leadership influenced team performance through affect-based trust and team psychological safety, Schaubroeck et al (2011). Boies et al (2010) found that team potency and trust were positively related to shared transformational leadership and negatively related to passive avoidance leadership. Sosik and Cameron (2010) proposed that leaders first create an ascetic self-construable that derives from character strengths and virtues and then project this self image through idealised influence, inspirational motivation, intellectual stimulation, and individualised consideration behaviour. Gentry et al (2011) found the biggest gaps among generations in leading employees, change management, and building and mending relationships. Colbert and Witt (2009) found that goal-focused leadership moderates the relationship between conscientiousness and job performance and that person-organisation goal congruence mediates this moderated relationship. Most of the recent literature review emphasises the fact that leaders need to create and engage in freeing, autonomous, interdependent and prescriptive leader behaviour which creates the right climate for employees to be more able, willing, agile and ready to engage in meaningful and innovative behaviours at the workplace especially knowledge workers in the IT organisations.

Need and Rationale for the Study

There are no Indian studies in the IT context that has pegged the leadership strategies and what type of impact these strategies have on IT employees. The study gains importance to see if the climate is right for growth in the Indian IT firms. Business in India (2009) has predicted that the Indian I.T sector is a fast growing, developing and maturing sector and contributes 5.9 per cent to the country's GDP and export earnings. This article investigates leadership strategies adopted and its impact in the IT context and intends to add to the field of behavioural sciences. It is also an earnest attempt to highlight the relevance and importance of leadership to management, individual, and organisational effectiveness. The present study adds to literature gap where the impacts of leadership strategies are investigated. The study also provides insights in the knowledge worker psyche for increasing leadership effectiveness in IT organisations operating in India.

Method

Sample Size and Technique

515 IT employees working in Indian, Indian multi national and multinational IT companies were surveyed. Stratified random sampling technique was used to draw respondents from three levels of management (senior, middle, and junior levels). The inclusion criterion was that only employees with minimum 12 months work experience with the present company and has worked with the reporting manager for a minimum 12 month were eligible to respond to the questionnaire.

Measure Employed

Robert A. Cooke's (1996) *Leadership/Impact®* instrument. **Leadership Strategies[ii] and Impact on Others[iii] Dimensions -** A standardised instrument *Leadership/Impact®* Cooke's (1996) was adapted with permission; it is a description by others inventory. The inventory has two sub scales - Impact on others and Leadership Strategies. Subscale I Impact on others: Impact on others had 96 statements for Constructive and Defensive impact. The inventory uses a five-point scale (1 = Not at all; 2 = To a slight extent; 3 = To a moderate extent; 4 = To a great extent; 5 = To a very great extent). This measures the influence of leaders with respect to Constructive behaviours (32 statements) the specific Constructive behaviours (32 statements that can be promoted by leaders are Achievement (8 statements), Self-Actualising (8 statements), Humanistic/Encouraging (8 statements), and Affiliation (8 statements). The Passive/Defensive behaviours (32 statements) that can be attributed to leaders are Approval (8 statements), Conventional (8 statements), Dependent (8 statements), and Avoidance (8 statements). The Aggressive/Defensive behaviours (32 statements) that can be promoted by leaders are Oppositional (8 statements), Power (8 statements), Competitive (8 statements) and Perfectionist (8 statements). Subscale II Leadership Strategies: Leadership strategies had 60 statements for Restrictive and Prescriptive strategies. The inventory uses a five-point scale (1 = Never; 2 = Rarely; 3 = Sometimes; 4 = Often; 5 = Always).

Cronbach's Alpha reliability was 0.88 for Impact on others scale and 0.93 for Leadership strategies scale.

Respondent Profile

60 per cent of the respondents were junior level executives, 28 per cent were middle level managers and 12 per cent were senior managers. 80 per cent of the respondents were male and 20 per cent female. 52 per cent of the respondents were below between 21 - 25 years of age, 24 per cent were between 26 30 years of age, 16 per cent were between 31 35 years and 8 per cent were in the age group 41 45 years. 72 per cent of the respondents were unmarried, 24 per cent married, 4 per cent divorced or widowed. 28 per cent of the respondents had one year of work experience, 36 per cent 1 3 years, 8 per cent 3 5 years, 8 per cent 5 7 years, 12 per cent 7 9 years and 8 per cent had above 9 years work experience.

Results and Discussion

H1: Prescriptive leadership strategies adopted by managers will have a positive influence on constructive impact and Restrictive leadership strategies will have a negative influence on constructive impact on employees in IT organisations.

Table 1: Indicating (coefficients) step-wise multiple regression of Constructivea leadership impact on leadership strategies adopted.

Leadership Strategiesa	*Unstandardised Coefficients*		*Standardised Coefficients*	*t*	*Sig*
	B	*Std. Error*	*Beta*		
Prescriptive leadership strategy	.691	.038	.715	18.122	.000**
Restrictive leadership strategy	.247	.034	.220	7.243	.000**

* Significant at the 0.05 level. ** Significant at the 0.01 level.

aFrom *Leadership/Impact®* Feedback Report by R.A. Cooke, Human Synergistics.

It was found that Prescriptive and Restrictive leadership strategies significantly influenced Constructive impact. Prescriptive leadership strategy had the strongest influence followed by Restrictive leadership strategy. Together these two variables explained 98.5 per cent (R Square = .985) of the variation in the Constructive impact on respondents. The hypothesis was partly accepted as restrictive strategies had a constructive impact. This indicates the cancelling effect of the leader behaviour in IT organisations. It was found that prescriptive and restrictive leadership strategies are adopted interchangeably and almost equally in IT organisations. As data was collected during recession it could be possible that both restrictive as well as prescriptive leadership strategies has a constructive impact on IT employees. However in normal circumstances this will be a rare phenomenon.

H2: Restrictive leadership strategies adopted by managers will have a positive influence on defensive impact and Prescriptive leadership strategies will have a negative influence on defensive impact on employees in IT organisations.

Table 4: Indicating (coefficients) step-wise multiple regression of Passive/ Defensivea leadership impact on leadership strategies adopted.

Leadership Strategiesa	*Unstandardised Coefficients*		*Standardised Coefficients*	*t*	*Sig*
	B	***Std. Error***	***Beta***		
Restrictive leadership strategy	1.059	.042	1.143	25.028	.000**
Prescriptive leadership strategy	-.258	.047	-.323	-5.452	.000**

* Significant at the 0.05 level. ** Significant at the 0.01 level.

aFrom *Leadership/Impact*® Feedback Report by R.A. Cooke, Human Synergistics. Copyright © 2008 by Human Synergistics International. Adapted by permission.

It was found that Prescriptive and Restrictive leadership strategies significantly influenced Passive/Defensive impact. Restrictive leadership strategy had the strongest influence followed by expert Power base. Prescriptive leadership strategy had a Negative influence on Passive/Defensive impact. Together these two variables explained 96.5 per cent (R Square = .965) of the variation in the Passive/Defensive impact on respondents.

Table 5: Indicating (coefficients) step-wise multiple regression of Aggressive/Defensivea leadership impact on leadership strategies adopted.

Leadership Strategiesa	*Unstandardised Coefficients*		*Standardised Coefficients*	*t*	*Sig*
	B	***Std. Error***	***Beta***		
Restrictive leadership strategy	1.037	.056	1.133	18.471	.000**
Prescriptive leadership strategy	-.339	.051	-.430	-6.697	.000**

* Significant at the 0.05 level. ** Significant at the 0.01 level.

aFrom *Leadership/Impact*® Feedback Report by R.A. Cooke, Human Synergistics. Copyright © 2008 by Human Synergistics International. Adapted by permission.

It was found that Restrictive, Prescriptive leadership strategies significantly influenced Aggressive/Defensive impact. Restrictive leadership strategy had the strongest influence. Prescriptive leadership strategy had a Negative influence on Aggressive/Defensive impact. Together these variables explained 96.2 per cent (R Square = .962) of the variation in the Aggressive/Defensive impact on respondents.

The hypothesis was accepted as restrictive strategies influenced defensive behaviours and prescriptive strategies negatively influenced defensive behaviours of employees in IT organisations.

Implications

In the new people-economy, today's organisational credo is increasingly 'It knows therefore it is.' People drive organisations to success or failure. People as a resource have gained paramount importance in most CEOs' comments and annual reports. Organisations today are service oriented and operate is a turbulent and fast changing environment. Knowledge workers not only drive these organisations, they are its key resource. In the words of Drucker (2001) 'Every knowledge worker in modern organisation is an "executive" if, by virtue of his position or knowledge, he is responsible for a contribution that materially affects the capacity of the organisation to perform and to obtain results. Therefore there is a need for new methods that will make the improvements in knowledge-worker productivity that will be required in the 21st century.

Drucker (2001) identifies these six major factors for knowledge-worker productivity in the future. 1. The knowledge-worker's question is "What is the task?" 2. Knowledge-workers have to manage themselves and have autonomy. 3. Continuing innovation has to be part of the work, the task and the responsibility of knowledge workers. 4. Knowledge work requires continuous learning, and continuous teaching by the knowledge worker. 5. Productivity of the knowledge worker is not primarily a matter of quantity of output. Quality is at least as important. 6. Knowledge workers must be treated as "assets" rather than a "costs". They must prefer to work for the organisation, over all other opportunities. The results of the present study indicates a more conservative and traditional way of leading in IT organisations and this may stifle and scuttle the non-linear growth. IT Managers today apart from guiding and directing need to in some way engage in transforming, shaping or influencing the organisational context of members and the ways in which they approach their work and interact with one another.

Leaders in information technology organisations have many potent techniques for increasing effectiveness. Most tools are built around strategy, skills and behaviours that are significantly linked in research to leadership performance. IT leaders need to define and introduce practices for integration and solving problems of the critical organisational sub units. They should courageously introduce and strengthen a culture that articulates constructive and active norms and expectations from employees. IT Leaders need to encourage employees to imbibe behaviours that are achievement oriented, engage in cooperative actions that emphasise personal and organisational growth and development. The outcomes of such behaviours are enhanced performance, increased personal satisfaction and lesser work stress. Being visionary and future oriented and promoting psychological empowerment and productivity increases the likelihood of drawing out the best in people and a sustained long-term performance. By being open to feedback and investing effort in self and organisation development, younger leaders need to be promoted to higher levels. Increase understanding and awareness of managers of how their leadership strategies impact employees by providing continual feedback. Increase leader understanding about the degree to which they engage in Prescriptive and Restrictive strategies and its affect on employee work behaviour. IT leaders must be equipped to have a significant influence on the cognitive, behavioural and performance of their followers. They need to intentionally and unintentionally, directly and indirectly motivate and drive employees to behave in certain effective ways. Constructive impact is helpful in meeting higher order needs for growth and satisfaction, whereas Passive/ Defensive impact leads to self protective ways and Aggressive/Defensive impact to forceful ways. This is a way forward in infusing non-linear growth in IT organisations. This will also ensure voluntarism on the part of organisational members to engage in behaviours of innovativeness and efficiencies to add value as a way of life.

Conclusion

This article reinforces the criticality of centrality of leadership strategies and its impact and how they affect knowledge workers work attitudes and behaviours in the IT context. Leaders engaging in Prescriptive leadership strategies will experience constructive impact on employees and restrictive leadership strategies will have a defensive (passive/aggressive) impact in IT organisations. IT organisations need to create a culture that reinforces and sustains prescriptive leader behaviours in their employees so that they may be able to leverage its benefits and IT leaders can confidently choose non-linear methods for growth and sustainability of Indian IT organisations.

Notes

- *Leadership/Impact*® is a registered trademark of Human Synergistics International.
- All *Leadership/Impact*® leadership strategy descriptions: From *Leadership/Impact*® Feedback Report by R.A. Cooke, Human Synergistics. Copyright © 2008 by Human Synergistics International. Adapted by permission.

- All *Leadership/Impact®* style names and descriptions: From *Leadership/Impact®* Feedback Report

References

- Bass, B.M., (1990). Bass and Stogdill's Handbook of Leadership: Theory, research, and managerial applications. New York: The Free Press.
- Boies, K., Lvina, E., and Martens, M. L. (2010). Shared leadership and team performance in a business strategy simulation. Journal of Personnel Psychology, Vol. 9(4), 195-202.
- Colbert, A.E., and Witt, L. A. (2009). The role of goal-focused leadership in enabling the expression of conscientiousness. Journal of Applied Psychology, vol. 94(3), May, 790-796.
- Conger, J.A. (1989). Leadership: The art of empowering others. The Academy of Management Executive, 33, 17-24.
- Cooke, R.A. (1996). *Leadership/Impact®*. Plymouth, MI, USA: Human Synergistics International.
- Cooke, R.A. (2008). *Leadership/Impact®* Feedback Report. Plymouth, MI, USA: Human Synergistics International.
- Drucker, P. F. (2001). Management Challenges for the 21st Century. Reprint by Harper Collins Publishers.
- Gentry, W.A., Griggs, T.L., Deal, J.J., Mondore, S.P., and Cox, B.D. (2011). A comparison of generational differences in endorsement of leadership practices with actual leadership skill level. Consulting Psychology Journal: Practice and Research, Vol. 63(1), March, 39-49.
- Hunter, S.T., Thoroughgood, C.N., Myer, A.T., and Ligon, G.S. (2011). Paradoxes of leading innovative endeavours: Summary, solutions, and future directions. Psychology of Aesthetics, Creativity, and the Arts, Vol. 5(1), February, 54-66.
- Kim, W.C., and Mauborgne, R.A. (1992). Parables of leadership. Harvard Business Review, 70(4), 123-128.
- Kotter, J. P. (1990). Force for Change: How Leadership Differs From Management. New York: Free Press.
- Reiter-Palmon, R. (2011). Introduction to special issue: The psychology of creativity and innovation in the workplace. Psychology of Aesthetics, Creativity, and the Arts, Vol. 5(1), February, 1-2, Abstract.
- Schaubroeck, J., Lam, S.S., and Peng, A.C. (2011). Cognition- based and affect-based trust as mediators of leader behaviour influences on team performance. Journal of Applied Psychology, March, Abstract.
- Sosik, J.J., and Cameron J.C. (2010). Character and authentic transformational leadership behaviour: Expanding the ascetic self toward others. Consulting Psychology Journal: Practice and Research, Vol. 62(4), December, 251-269.

- Stenmark, C. K., Shipman, A. S., and Mumford, M. D. (2011). Managing the innovative process: The dynamic role of leaders. Psychology of Aesthetics, Creativity, and the Arts, Vol. 5(1), February, 67-80, Abstract.
- Wallace, J. C., Johnson, P. D., Mathe, K., and Paul, J. (2011). Structural and psychological empowerment climates, performance, and the moderating role of shared felt accountability: A managerial perspective. Journal of Applied Psychology, March, Abstract.
- Yaffe, K., and Kark, R. (2011). Leading by example: The case of leader OCB. Journal of Applied Psychology, March, Abstract.
- Zhang, Z., and Peterson, S. J. (2011). Advice networks in teams: The role of transformational leadership and members' core self-evaluations. Journal of Applied Psychology, April, Abstract.

Other Sources

- Ramamurthy Prakash B, How can Indian IT companies achieve non-linear growth? http://www.slideshare.net/raamam/how-can-indian-it-companies-achieve-nonlinear-growth-5543715.
- Shivani Shinde, Wipro to sharpen focus on non-linear growth/Business Standard , February 12, 2010, http://www.business-standard.com/india/news/wipro-to-sharpen-focusnon-linear-growth/385483/.
- Shivani Shinde, IT companies may take time for non-linear growth / Mumbai August 12, 2009, 1:10 IST http://www.business-standard.com/india/news/it-companies-may-take-time-for-non-linear-growth/366731/
- Srikant Suddekunte, Non-linear growth for IT service providers, www.expresscomputeronline.com Weekly Insight for Technology Professionals, 11 June 2007 http://www.expresscomputeronline.com/20070611/management03.shtml.
- Premji springs a surprise, sacks two joint CEOs - Deccan Herald 22 Jan 2011.
- Two executives quit Infosys - Deccan Herald 27 Apr 2011.
- Infosys has become conservative: Mohandas Pai, P S Balakrishnan, April 19, 2011 (New Delhi) NDTV, http://www.ndtv.com/article/profit/infosys-has-become-conservative-mohandas-pai-150331
- The NASSCOM - McKinsey report 2005 on India's IT industry.

4

e-Waste Management: A Case Study of HCL Technologies Using SAP-LAP Analysis

Rajeev Srivastava

Abstract

The amount of e-Waste is growing very fast in India. There are many sources for this growing volume of e-Waste. Software industries are also one of the major sources of the growing volume of e-Waste. These Software industries are not only purchasing bulk amounts electronic equipments, but also replace them very rapidly due to frequent changes in technology. In this paper one of the Software industries was selected for the study. The main objective of the case study was to understand the process of e-Waste management in an organisation. The SAP - LAP methodology was used for the case analysis. From the analysis, variables were identified which influence the effective e-Waste management in an organisation.

Keyword: *e-Waste Management, SAP-LAP, Software Industry, HCL Technologies.*

Introduction

Sushil, (2000) has recommended SAP-LAP methodology as a formal analysis methodology for examining a case. This methodology consists of two phases- SAP analysis and LAP analysis. In SAP analysis, case is described through three basic components which are Situation, Actor, and Process (SAP). In LAP analysis case is studied through Learning, Action and

Performance. The main purpose of using SAP-LAP framework here was to understand the fundamental questions about the effective e-Waste management in an organisation. These fundamental questions were: know what, why and how (Divedi, 2005). The steps of the SAP - LAP methodology to understand the effective e-Waste management in an organisation are:

Situation:

- What is the status of e-Waste management in an organisation?
- Why e-Waste should be managed effectively by the organisation?
- How the status of e-Waste management can be improved in an organisation?

Actors:

- Who are the actors involved in the management of e-Waste?
- What they will get by effective e-Waste management?
- Why they will be benefited by effective e-Waste management?

Process:

- What is the current process of e-Waste management?
- How the present process can be changed?
- What are the key processes covered under the effective e-Waste management?

Learning:

- What is the learning from current e-Waste management system?
- How the effective e-Waste management is going to affect the existing process?
- How actors are affected by effective e-Waste management?

Action:

- What should be done for the effective e-Waste management?
- Who will play the major role in the effective e-Waste management?
- What should be done for enhancing the effective e-Waste management?

Performances:

- How the performance can be enhanced by the effective e-Waste management?
- What are the stakeholder aspects of performance?
- How to measure the performance?

Field studies were conducted to understand the process of e-Waste management in an organisation. In the field studies, information was gathered through structured and unstructured personal interviews with the senior managers and Software developers of HCL Technologies. They explained about the organisation and the management of e-Waste in their organisation. In the interview process the valuable observations were made which helps in the SAP-LAP analysis. Some basic information was gathered from the website of the HCL Technologies. After gathering the information from different sources, it was compiled for the further analysis. The flow diagram of the case study is given in Figure 1.

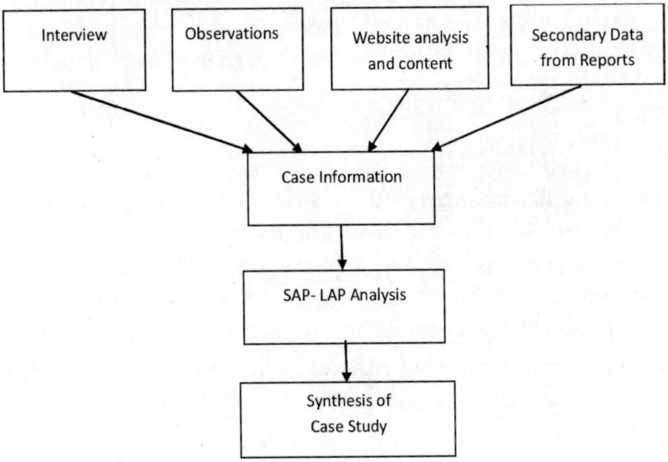

Figure 1: Methodology for Case Study

Selection of Organisation for Case Study

By field survey, experts' opinion and literature study, it was found that in service sector Software Industries are using huge amount of electronic equipments like computer, servers, printers, scanners and due to market demand and use of latest technologies they are more frequently removing their old electronic equipments. Hence, one top organisation HCL Technologies from Software Industries was selected for the study on the basis of convenience.

Organisation Profile of HCL Technologies

HCL Technologies (HCLT) is a leading global IT services company. Its inception into the global landscape after its IPO in 1999, HCL (Hindustan Computer Limited) focuses on 'transformational outsourcing', underlined by innovation and value creation, and offers integrated portfolio of services including software-led IT solutions, remote infrastructure management, engineering R&D services and BPO. HCLT leverages its extensive global offshore infrastructure and network of offices in 26 countries to provide holistic, multi-service delivery in key industry verticals including Financial Services, Manufacturing, Consumer Services, Public Services and Healthcare. HCLT, along with its subsidiaries, had consolidated revenues of US$ 3.5 billion (Rs 16,034 cores), as on 30 June 2011 (on last 12 months basis).

Global Operations

Australia, Belgium, Brazil, China, Czech Republic, Denmark, Finland, France, Germany, Hong Kong, India, Indonesia, Israel, Italy, Japan, Malaysia, Mexico, Netherlands, New Zealand, Norway, Poland, Puerto Rico, Qatar, Saudi Arabia, Singapore, South Africa, Sweden, Switzerland, UAE, United Kingdom, USA.

Responsible Business

During the financial year 2010-11, on a consolidated basis, HCLT revenues for the year 2010-2011 stood at US$ 3.5 billion registering a growth of 31.1 per cent over the previous year. HCLT recruited 9,572 (gross) and 3,626 (net) employees for FY 2011 and the current work force strength at global level is 77,046. The new customers added are 70 and the total number stands at 467.

Unique Green Datacenter services framework has powered HCLT to deliver cost and energy savings to their customers, some of which are as follows:

- 15-40 per cent savings through Data Center Consolidation and Virtualisation.
- 10-15 per cent savings from Data Center Asset re-build and buy out.
- 10-15 per cent savings due to Rack Optimisation in Datacenter.
- 4-10 per cent savings by installing best-in class power equipments in the Datacenter.
- 7-15 per cent savings due to efficient Air conditioning architecture within the Datacenter.

Fostering Innovation

HCLT have created multiple channels and opportunities, especially for Halite's and research and academic communities for participating, contributing and developing ideas that benefit society and the environment. Including FY 2011, HCLT have filed for 62 patents and have received 49 patents in technical and business areas. More than 2000 HClite's works in 150+ solution areas to enable customers around the globe. HCLT Intellectual Property Management Services incubates new ideas and help Halite's transform into innovators.

HCLT is committed to achieve health and safety by:

- Ensuring the health and safety of their employees, contractors, visitors and others affected by their operations, aiming to eliminate all work-related injuries and illnesses.
- Establish Health and Safety strategies that optimally utilise resources and prevent pollution to conserve and preserve the environment and ensure the long-term sustainability.
- Meeting all applicable Health and Safety laws of the land, regulations and other requirements which relate to Health and Safety aspects and hazards.
- Managing Health and Safety like any other critical business activity.
- Providing a framework for setting and reviewing Health, Safety and Environmental objectives and targets.
- Adopting Health and Safety practices at par with global standards using latest technologies to ensure continual improvement of Health and Safety management and performance.

HCLT, as a corporate entity, is committed to protect and conserve the natural environment in their operations and services, for meeting their current and future requirements. The company is also committed to control and improve environmental performance with respect to significant environmental aspects of the organisation's products, services and/or activities. The Company aims to provide a healthy and safe work environment, optimise the use of energy and natural resources like Land, Air and Water etc. It is committed to Continual Improvement and enhancing the Environmental Management System to include the following:

- Prevention of Pollution
- Compliance of Environmental Laws and Regulations promulgated by the Central and State Governments
- Assessing and minimising impacts of business activities on environment by
- Optimising or minimising power and energy consumption, reducing carbon
- Footprints, conserving natural resources and promoting Green Initiatives.

HCL Technologies Organisation profile is given in Table 1:

Table 1: Organisation Profile: HCL Technologies

Parameters	*Features*
Year of Establishment	1999
Corporate Headquarter	HCL Technologies, A-9, Sec.3, Noida, U.P. India.
Corporate Offices	26 Countries
Services	Software-led IT solutions, remote infrastructure management, engineering R&D services and BPO.
Domains	Financial Services, Manufacturing, Consumer Services, Public Services and Healthcare
Patents in technical business area	49
No of employees	2000 plus

SAP-LAP Analysis

The case was analyses applying Situation - Actor - Process, Learning - Action - Performance (SAP - LAP) framework to understand the e-Waste management process of HCL Technologies. The situation was the opportunities and threats that HCL Technologies were confronted with. Learning issues were explored and action was recommended. Finally, the impact of suggested actions on situation, actor and process were highlighted.

Situation:

A field study was conducted to understand the situation of the HCL Technologies. In the process of the field study, interaction was made with the top management and the employees of the organisation. Unstructured and structured questions were asked for understanding of e-Waste management process. It was found that computer and other electronic equipments like printer, Server etc. are being used in software development and maintaining different types of databases.

The organisation also has the online presence through the website www.hcltech.in. Since the organisation main focus is developing quality software and other IT related services, many of the employees are aware about the e-Waste impacts on environment and health. Even the top management was also very much interested in the effective e-Waste management because they understand their responsibility towards the environment and health. The organisation understands the need for effective e-Waste management. Further it was found that they devise a process for effective e-Waste management in their organisation. The situation of the organisation is summarised below:

- The organisation came into global landscape after its IPO in 1999.
- The computer was used in development center, data center and other IT related services.
- The company has the online presence through the website www.hcltech.in
- Many employees were aware about the effective e-Waste management.
- Even the top management was also very much interested in the effective e-Waste management because they feel that their responsibility towards the environment and health.
- The organisation has already recognised the need for effective e-Waste management.
- Further company has already devised a process by which the effective e-Waste management can be implemented.

Actor:

The top management of the company feels that they will be much benefited if the effective e-Waste management implemented in their organisation. After globalisation the company was facing the international competition therefore the quality is the most important for the growth of the organisation. In this way the top management was positively towards the effective e-Waste management in the organisation. The company provides additional training to the employees involved in the management of e-Waste. The actors of effective e-Waste management in the company are summarised below:

- The top management of the company influences the effective e-Waste management.
- The company is positive towards the effective e-Waste management.
- The employees involved in e-Waste management were trained time to time.

Process:

It was found that in organisation, e-Waste management is operated in the efficient manner with the main focus on effective e-Waste management. All elementary works are being carried out. The company is basically selling his old computers and other electronic devices to authorised recycling vendors. The present process could be improved if institute focus on buying energy efficient and upgradeable electronic devices and sale discarded electronic devices only to authorised recycling or collection centers of e-Waste. So we can say that here was a potential for effective e-Waste management in the institute. The existing process of effective management of e-Waste in the company is summarised below:

- The company was operating in the efficient manner.
- All elementary works were done.
- The company is basically selling his old computers and other electronic devices to authorised recyclers only.
- The present process could be improved if institute focus on buying energy efficient and upgradeable electronic devices and sale discarded electronic devices only to authorised recycling or collection centers of e-Waste.
- There was a potential for implementing the effective e-Waste management in the company.

Learning:

Literature study suggests that the effective e-Waste management leads to the safe environment and the health of people thus leads to a good public image of the organisation. Right now the company was in the middle stage of the effective e-Waste management and improvement is still required. There could be many reasons which hinder the effective management of e-Waste by the company. The company already is using energy efficient and low carbon dioxide producing devices. The company understands that by effective e-Waste management, they can safe environment and health and will be able to make a broader global presence. The learning from the existing process of effective e-Waste management in the institute is summarised below:

- Effective e-Waste management suggested by the HCL Technologies for a safe environment and health.
- Right now the company was in the middle stage of the effective e-Waste management and improvements are still required.
- There could be many reasons which hinder the effective e-Waste management by the company.
- The company understands that by effective e-Waste management they can safe environment and health and will be able to make a broader global presence.
- Effective management of e-Waste will give competitive advantage to the company.

Actions:

The top management needs to be more focused towards effective e-Waste management. Effective management of e-Waste is one of the strategic decisions for the company. Organisational structure needs to be redefined for the effective e-Waste management. Sometimes the employees were reluctant towards the effective e-Waste management. Their counseling may be done to explain the importance of effective e-Waste management. Training of the employee will also make them more familiar about the hazardous nature of e-Waste. Separate fund may be dedicated to the effective e-Waste management in the company. The suggested actions to be taken are summarised below:

- The top management needs to be more focused towards effective e-Waste management.
- Organisational structure needs to be redefined for the effective e-Waste management.
- Employee counseling and training should be done for the effective management of e-Waste.
- Separate fund may be dedicated to the effective e-Waste management in the company.
- Training of the employee will also make them more familiar towards the hazardous nature of e-Waste.

Performance:

Effective management of e-Waste has been implemented by the organisation of many developed countries. It was found that after the effective e-Waste management, their performances have improved. The performance can be measured by the number of factors like good public image, reuse and reduce of electronic devices etc. It will benefit the owner in terms of the good public image and better resource utilisation. The company will also be able to reduce cost of IT products by effective management of e-Waste. Implementation of effective e-Waste management across the value chain will enhance the company's ability to deliver better image to its customers. Effective e-Waste management of e-Waste implementation will improve by:

- Effective management of e-Waste has enhanced the performance of organisations in many countries.
- The performance can be measured by the number of factors like good public image, reuse and reduce of electronic devices etc.
- It will benefit the owner in terms of the good public image and better resource utilisation.

- The company will also be able to reduce the cost of IT by the effective management of e-Waste.
- Effective management of e-Waste across the value chain will enhance the company's ability to deliver better image to its customers.

Conclusion

The organisation was focused towards quality software development and IT services. The top management of the company feels that they will be benefited, if the effective e-Waste management implemented in the organisation. However, there was a potential for effective e-Waste management in the company.

Literature study suggests that the effective e-Waste management leads to enhance the public image of the organisation. Effective management of e-Waste is implemented by the organisations of many developed countries. It was found that after the effective management of e-Waste by the organisation, their performance has improved. It will benefit the owner in terms of good public image and better resource utilisation. The company will also be able to cut the cost of IT products by the effective e-Waste management. Effective management of e-Waste across the value chain will enhance the company's ability to deliver better image to its customers. Keeping this in view, it is suggested to implement effective e-Waste management by the company.

Reference

- Dwivedi, R. (2005). *E-Business Transformation and Stakeholder Flexibility: A study of Manufacturing Industry in India*. Ph.D Dissertation, Indian Institute of Technology Delhi (India).
- http://www.hcltech.in (accessed September 2012).
- Sushil (2000). SAP-LAP Models of Enquiry. *Management Decision*, 38 (5), 347-353.

5

Health Service: Management for Ageing People

Vidhu Gaur

Abstract

What criteria should be followed to decide if one is 'young' or 'old'? A physically 'old' person can be 'mentally' young and vice versa. We cannot stop physical ageing, but we can stop to age mentally, and may even reverse it, and become 'childlike.' We get to know our inner world. We begin to realise the futility of projecting ourselves with too much make-up and begin to enjoy life again. The paper shows that longevity requires a strong cohesiveness between the body, the mind, and most importantly, the spirit. The spirit, being a direct connection to God's energy, is an ever-present source of vitality. The body is a tool that enables us to interact on this physical plane of existence. The mind permits to learn and better ourselves which is a tremendous aid in connecting the spiritual and the physical sides of ourselves. The strength, power and efficiency of old age are to benefit others with the treasure of experience.

Key Words: *Art of Relaxation, Meditation, Middle Ageing, Elder Ageing, Liberation.*

Introduction

Ageing is the single greatest challenge facing our society today. Recent breakthroughs have demonstrated that it is possible to combine a long life with the absence of age-related disease. Scientists at the forefront of this research will explain the science of slower ageing and will consider the ethical issues surrounding the field and the challenge of developing a true preventative approach for age-related disease and degeneration. Recent European research indicates that the physical body can have a long, productive, and relatively healthy existence. What is surprising is that the studies show that longevity requires a strong cohesiveness between the body, the mind, and most importantly, the spirit.

The spirit, being a direct connection to God's energy, is an ever-present source of vitality. The body is a tool that enables us to interact on this physical plane of existence. The mind permits to learn and better ourselves which is a tremendous aid in connecting the spiritual and the physical sides of ourselves. Everyone has a different symbolic picture that comes to their mind's eye when they hear the word. The variance of these individualistic references is based on the belief process we were taught as children and our life experiences. Sometimes a new reference may be stronger than an older reference and the belief structure and the identification changes. Sometimes the identification with the word spiritual remains throughout life.

But, as we are doing all of these things we have to acknowledge the fact that life is moving us forward in time and that we have created the word, concept and identification associated with aging. Being old is a relative circumstance; when one is ten years old, someone who is forty seems ancient. Unfortunately we have a tendency to carry that youthful relativity throughout life. When we reach forty, or whatever magic number we have attached to the concept of being old, we identify with that, begin to think and feel old and equate it to uselessness, lack of vitality and our own mortality. In our concept of 'age' we need to learn to embrace the physical, mental, and spiritual changes that naturally occur in all of us, male or female. We need to approach age with new definitions that don't reflect maintaining adolescence. We need to alter the labels we have created that identify the concept getting older. We need to learn to respect the time we have spent on this earth and the lessons we have learned. We need to accept ourselves and not fear a wrinkle, lost hair or extra pound. We also need to appreciate the physical body as a transitional vehicle for the spirit which is everlasting. There is no doubt that each and every human will undergo changes. They are perpetual from birth. There is no need to fear or deny them. But, there is a need to understand, welcome and involve ourselves in these transitions. We have worked hard to reach the levels we have attained and the knowledge we have garnered through the experiences of living and we have every right to expect and demand the reward of joy as we age.

The question is: What would make life happy and liberating? We need to define our lives, our spirituality. Naturally, the older we get, the more we understand our vulnerabilities, and the more we want to discover our attachment to the Divine. Many don't even begin a spiritual search until they have raised a family, conquered the business world and finally found the time to do some inner exploration. But, it is never too late or too early to explore one's personal relationship with Creation.

Four simple ingredients to ward off the effects of aging: (1) stress management skills, (2) interests and exercise, (3) strong relationships, and (4) humor.

Stress Management

Physical stress occurs when the body is over taxed. It can be very functional, but it drains energy and nutrients from the body. Mental stress is an external negative influence, a toxic emotion that the body relates to as physical stress. Stress management is a must in today's hectic reality. Duke University conducted a five year study that concluded that mental stress is far more dangerous to the heart than physical stress and way we respond to mental stress is a strong predictor of whether or not a person may be vulnerable to heart disease. Our physical body and our spirit know that we, as a whole being, require tranquility to achieve optimum performance on any level. Neither the mind nor the body can function at peak levels when stress rules our lives. There are many ways to lessen or control stress. Meditation is one of them, but it is important that each person find their own way of relieving this toxic reaction called stress.

Interests and Exercise

Interests in life maintain the body, the mind and the spirit. It keeps you going, thinking and producing. Retiring doesn't mean retiring from life. Age should allow us to live life. If a person is doing, he/she is using all forms of the energy that make up his/her being. Keeping the mind and body active, help the energy flow from the spirit.

Strong Relationships

Strong relationships are very vital to our success as individuals and as a community or society. It doesn't matter if the relationship is with a spouse, child, parent or best friend. We all need people to interact with on a regular basis. It is extremely important to have people around us that we can depend on to be there when we need them. Whether it's a borrowed shoulder for a good cry or just someone that will share an afternoon tea and listen to a day's worth of problems, a close friend or family member can heal in a myriad of ways that prescriptions can't. It means letting our walls down, sharing our feelings and listening. We all have a tendency to think our personal problems are the most important. That's because so much of our world is based on each of us as individuals. We are no longer communally centered groups and because of our individuality, we have lost much of our listening ability. But listening to a friend can teach us about ourselves. Are their problems similar? How do they deal with the kids, the job, the boss or the house? Is something they are doing capable of making our life easier? So lower those protective walls a bit.

Humor

A belly laugh after dinner helps the digestion. Watching a comedy can lower blood pressure. Sharing a funny story with an acquaintance can form a bond of friendship. The lists of physical and mental aspects of ourselves that effected by humor and laughter is endless. What does humor do for the spirit? When the body and mind are functional, the energy of the spirit is free flowing. If we can incorporate these four simple ingredients into our lives, we can each be less stressed, productive, congenial and happy for a long, long time.

Art of Relaxation

In our present life we carry with us an unnecessary load of worries, fears, anxieties and excitements which none will say are unnecessary, as they have become part of the price we have to pay in our present day life for all its vaster wealth, larger trade, greater production and world-wide contracts. But we need not allow that load to crush us; in spite of them we can learn to steel our shoulders and straighten our backbone. And this technique is to "Be Quiet". At least for ten minutes each day let us try to be totally relaxed, not only in body, but also in both our mind and intellect. Allow the body to sit in total relaxation. The more successfully the mediator can relax, the more he can easily withdraw all his extra attention from his physical structure. Even when the relaxation is to a degree successful, one can experience an embracing joy and peace within oneself as a cool arbor against the blasts blowing from the deserts of agitated mind.

Benefits of Meditation

The benefits of meditation are endless and certainly deserve our contemplation and consideration. Many successful business people, celebrities and sports professionals practice and enjoy the benefits of meditation. Numerous businesses promote and provide help and assistance to their staff with the benefits of meditation courses and because of this they gain an advantage over their competitors and create more profit.

Research has scientifically proven that meditation is a safe and simple way to balance our physical, emotional, and mental state and its countless values have been known and practiced for thousands of years. More and more doctors promote the benefits of meditation to cure many stress related illnesses. Everyday most of us experience stress in many different ways. Normally life threatening situations trigger off the stress response which enables us to act without contemplation and deliberation and survive intense situations using fast reflexes. When our bodies are exposed to a sudden threat we respond with the characteristic fight or flight reaction which is known as an adrenaline rush. When adrenaline and other hormones are released from the adrenal glands the pulse races, blood pressure increases, our breathing becomes faster and the blood flow to the muscles increases. If we are in extreme danger these reactions are of great assistance and gain to us. We have inherited this survival response from our ancestors who faced many life threatening situations every day. The same response is now triggered in our daily lives when we are in a traffic hold up or someone irritates us at work or we simply break a cup. If we do not confront the situation we end up being in a permanent state of stress.

1. **Happiness**: Meditation can help us to cultivate a real abiding happiness. Meditation allows us to be in tune with our inner self. When we live in the heart we can experience a sense of oneness with others, this brings a happiness that does not depend upon outer events.

2. **Inner Peace**: Most people would like to experience more inner peace in their lives; at times peace feels an elusive quality because our lives are so hectic. Meditation teaches us how to switch off from the noise of the mind; we no longer give importance to the teeming thoughts which fly through our mind. Through meditation we can gain a clear state of mind; this is the secret of feeling a real inner peace.

3. **Health Benefits**: There have been numerous studies showing a link between meditation and improved physical health. Meditation is a practical solution to relieve stress. When we relieve stress we help to reduce our blood pressure and heart related diseases.

4. **Simplicity**: Meditation helps to simplify our lives. When we live in the mind we can feel life is nothing but teeming problems and worries. Through learning to meditate we find we can get joy from appreciating the simplicity of life. "Meditation simplifies our outer life and energises our inner life. Meditation gives us a natural and spontaneous life, a life that becomes so natural and spontaneous that we cannot breathe without being conscious of our own divinity." — Swami Chinmyananda

5. **Living in the Present**: When we analyse the thoughts that go through our mind we find that many of them are dealing with the past or present. We are either fearful of the future or ruminating on the past. However by dwelling on the past or future, it means we are unable to live in the present moment. When

we meditate we are completely in the here and now. Meditation teaches us to appreciate life as it is; we learn to value our present circumstances.

6. **Better Relations with Others**: Often we can have minor conflicts with other people because we dwell on minor faults of the other person, whether it is justified or not, it is a common source of unhappiness and division. Meditation teaches us to give no importance to minor thoughts. When we meditate powerfully we develop a sense of oneness with other people; we naturally look to their good qualities. Their minor faults seem unimportant.

7. **To discover a real sense of whom we are**: Our intellectual mind can seek to discover the answer to many questions, but the one question of who am I? Always remains unanswered. To discover our real self; to be aware of our own soul we have to go beyond the mind. It is in meditation that we can become aware of a living spiritual presence. When we find this we feel a new purpose in life.

One of the most important benefits of meditation is how it releases stress from our bodies. Meditation practiced regularly will lead us to a deeper level of relaxation and contemplation. If we want to be free of constant worry, pressure and stress the benefits of meditation can give us a life that is calm, peaceful, happy and relaxed. Even ten minutes of meditation a day will help alleviate stress. Some of the benefits of meditation are:

1. Reduces anxiety attacks as it lowers the levels of blood lactate.
2. Builds self confidence.
3. Increases serotonin which influences moods and behaviour. Low levels of serotonin are associated with depression, headaches and insomnia.
4. Enhances energy, strength and vigor.
5. Helps keep blood pressure normal.
6. Reduces stress and tension.
7. Creates a state of deep relaxation and general feeling of wellbeing.
8. Helps with P.M.T.
9. Increases concentration and strengthens the mind.
10. Helps reduce heart disease.
11. Helps with weight loss.

If we practice regularly, the benefits of meditation will promote a sense of calm and control, we'll feel far more relaxed and happy. Our ability to concentrate will be greater. We won't become stressed about things and we'll feel more peaceful and relaxed about everything. One of the greatest benefits of meditation is learning to go with the flow and things that used to irritate us before simply become insignificant.

Taking Care of Ourselves

Are we our own friend? Do we know how to love ourselves? If so, we are already taking good care of ourselves. The better we take care of ourselves the more we will appreciate the other people in our life. When we were born we had caretaker, usually our mother, whose job was to care for our physical and emotional needs. Our only way to ask for help was to cry; our mothers quickly learned what our cries meant the need for changing, holding, feeding etc. Gradually we learned words, and then how to put those words together to ask for what we wanted and needed. If we had good parenting and our needs were met in a loving way, we were then able to care more and more for ourselves, until finally we could leave our parents' home and make a home for ourselves and our own children.

In some people, however, the transition from total dependence to complete independence is interfered with by various outer and inner disruptions. Such people never learn to care for themselves as much as they need to and they may forever be looking for some "good mommy" who will appear miraculously and take care of them for the rest of their lives. Some people in their seventies, eighties or nineties who are perfectly able to care for themselves do not do this because they want a fairy godmother to bring them what they need. In theory, miracle mothers could appear but in fact this is not likely! The reality is that whatever our early parenting deficiencies, we all need to learn to take good care of ourselves right now. We need to be our own best friend. Here are five ways to do that:

1. Eat for health: Many people eat to eat, eat to have something to do, eat because its mealtime, eat because they are bored, or eat without being aware that they are eating. Eating for health is different. Food is for our bodies' nourishment, growth and strength. If we eat "funny" food, junk foods and non-foods, if we fill our stomachs with salt, sugar, caffeine, additives, preservatives and fats, we can expect to have aches and pains and a dwindling supply of energy. If, on the other hand, we eat well-balanced meals along with an adequate supplement of vitamins, minerals, and amino acids we can more likely expect healthy tissues, strong muscles and feelings of well being. It is unfortunate that many physicians have little knowledge of nutrition. It is also unfortunate that many food faddists frighten us into balanced, dangerously lopsided diets. But sound nutritional information is nevertheless available.

2. Move your body: Twenty minutes of continuous exercise is such things as walking, swimming, running or biking is considered to be ideal for most adults if such exercise is done three to five times a week. Nothing contributes to pain, stiffness and atrophy as much disuse. So the rule is "keep moving as much and as long as one can". Even if we are at an irreversible point and even if we are in a wheelchair, you can still do some isometric exercise with our hands, feet or hand.

3. Rest: Most people will agree that a good night's sleep is part of a sensible lifestyle. The number of hours people sleep is widely variable. Some get along quite well on a few hours of sleep; others need eight hours or more. Sleep researchers have found that the quality of sleep is as essential as the amount of sleep, and the most people seem to find what is best for them. Sleeping at night is accepted as a good idea by almost everyone, but researchers have found frequent resistance to their suggestion that people have a midday rest. Nevertheless, a midday rest is a wonderful way to break up the day's activities and allow our bodies to wind down before continuing the afternoon and evening program. It is not self-indulgent or lazy to have a midday rest. It is a way of being refreshed, of preventing over-tiredness, and of gaining renewed energy for the rest of the day.

4. Have fun: According to one psychological study we all have three internal ego structures (Parent, Adult, and Child). One parent function tells us what's right and wrong- the dos and don'ts which take care of us and makes it available to us when we need it, rather like a computer data bank and processor. The child function is our feelings and among other things is the fun-loving part of us, the simple, accepting, trusting, free part. When we are growing up, this part of our child is sometimes squashed by older people who are intent on making us into responsible, obedient, hardworking, good adults. Somewhere along the way, the happy, free, fun-loving child gets lost. We become responsible, obedient, hardworking and good grown-ups, and we may also become over-serious, guilty, depressed and unhappy. Taking good care of us includes recovering our lost child and learning again how to have fun. It is never too late to start to find your lost child. Here's how:

(a) Make a fun list. List everything we have ever wanted to do. Don't think about it. Just like it.

(b) Give ourselves permission from our caring parent to do anything on that list is not going to hurt us or anyone else. Try as many things as we want to and keep doing them until we see what is really fun for us now.

(c) Add to our list as we think of other possibilities or see other people doing things we would like to try. If in our head you hear comments like "Don't be childish," "You've acting silly," "What will people think?" tell that voice to stop talking and replace it with another voice that says, "I like to see we have fun," "we deserve to play," "It's great to see us so happy."

(d) Find other people to play with us. They have been waiting to ask them to have fun with us. Here are some ideas from fun lists: Buy an ice cream cone, Wear socks that don't match, Go barefoot through the grass or sand, Learn to bike, swim, play tennis, sail, Play Bridge, or a musical instrument. Join a group to do clay modeling, ceramics, or other art forms, Sit in a shopping mall and make silly remarks to yourself about people who look funny to you, Make faces at yourself in your bedroom mirror, Soak in a hot bathtub with only candlelight in the room and music playing in the background, Try new hairstyles.

5. Checkups: If we are willing to take good care of ourselves, we can often prevent bodily distress. Some physicians suggest that we care for ourselves by having a yearly or every other year physical checkup after we reach the age of forty. Such checkups can often forestall serious illness because they make it possible to solve simple problems in early stages. If there is a physical problem, we need to know of it as soon as possible and take care of it. Eating for health, moving, resting, relaxing and having fun will prevent many physical problems; regular physical checkups will often prevent more serious illnesses.

The Final Years

Few of us want to think about the final years of our lives. We want to believe we will live forever. Often this is true even of people whose lives have been difficult or who are in great distress. Despite our strong will to live, we cannot escape the final stages of our lives. We have identified three stages of ageing:

- Early ageing: a period of renewed energy.
- Middle ageing: our world of renewed energy.
- Elder ageing: increased dependency.

Many people find it easy to live happily in the years of early ageing. This paper offers help for those in middle and elder ageing so that these stages may also have meaning and joy. Commenting on middle ageing, the period from retirement to mid or late seventies, we hear many people say, "I've never had it so good!" Job responsibilities are over and children are grown. For many people this is a time for travel, for studying in adult programs at universities or Elderhostel, for reviewing life, for saying goodbye to self-destructive behaviour, and for enjoying what is called "golden age". If there is no devastating illness during this time, if finances allow us to meet daily expenses and still have something left over for fun and travel, if we have lived our earlier years with a fair degree of insight and honesty, if we love the past, enjoy the present, and are courageous about tomorrow, then this will be a wonderful segment of our life.

This period of the middle ageing years comes to a close usually in our late seventies, sometimes in the mid-eighties. We have lived in the ten to fifteen year period immediately following our retirement or mid-sixties; now another change takes place. Travel is less frequent and some of us seem not interested in traveling at all unless it is absolutely essential. We have the feeling of having been everywhere, or if we have never been anywhere we feel that going is just too much effort. Organised activities hold less interest than they did, although we may occasionally be part of a class, or activity group. At this time some of us move from our own homes into retirement communities or into homes of family members or even into group homes with surrogate families. Our world grows a little smaller.

Given these inner changes of mind and heart which have led to changes in outer activity, the period of the late seventies to late eighties can still be one of rich meaning and joy. Riding bicycle, singing old songs in tenor voice, walking, making friends, creative writing, gardening, laughter, comedy movies etc are healthy outer activities.

Conclusion

Our second innings start when we retire from 'active' work life. Retirement brings with it a mixed feeling. The feeling could be that of leisure and freedom or boredom and isolation. Retirement may change our attitude towards ourselves as well as others. It may affect our identity and relationship. Some think we are no longer 'useful.' In the mid of last century retirement was seen as rest, by the 80's it had become a reward, and by the 90's leisure became the predominant choice. In the present setting the idea of 'extended period of leisure' is not the choice of many; people want to practice 'active ageing'. And this is possible, thanks to healthier lifestyle and new opportunities. In the present Indian sociological view, the word retirement conjures a vision of being useless or of spending one's limited remaining days on a porch in a rocking chair. Too often we feel all used up; like we can no longer contribute to the very society that has labeled us 'old'. But one shouldn't lose heart. Experiencing and living life should become limitless when we age. Ageing should be liberating. Life can begin at 60. Timeless joys of ageing includes: deepening connection with our own Being, realising our oneness with all creation, seeing the light in all people, blessing and encouraging others, loving our body more fully, dare to think of immortality, dare to be fit. We need to define our lives, our spirituality. Naturally, the older we get, the more we understand our vulnerabilities, and the more we want to discover our attachment to the Divine. Many don't even begin a spiritual search until they have raised a family, conquered the business world and finally found the time to do some inner exploration.

References

- Gulati, S. Kumar and Sudhir, K. Jain. "Formal and Informal Care of the Elderly: Emerging Economic and Business Issues for India," 6th International Conference on Contemporary Business 2012, Souvenir p. 36.
- Chinmayananda, Swami. "Meditation and Life," Mumbai: Central Chinmaya Mission Trust, 2006, pp. 3-13.
- Chinmayananda, Swami. "Hinduism at a Glance," Mumbai: Central Chinmaya Mission Trust, 2006, pp. 3-12.
- Radhakrishnan, S. "Eastern Religions and Western Thought," Delhi: Oxford University Press, 1988, pp. 351-382.
- Morrison, Ruth and Radtke, D. Dridan. "Ageing with Joy," Mumbai: Better Yourself Book, 1999, pp. 63-115.
- Kaehr, Shelley. "The Life You Deserve," Bhopal: Indra Publishing House, 2010, pp. 62-72.
- Kabra, R. Narain. "Symphony of Life," Jaipur: Raj Publishing House, 2004, pp. 44-50.
- World Health Organisation, *Active ageing*, Geneva, WHO, 2001.
- Walker, A., 'A strategy for active ageing', *International Social Security Review*, Vol. 55, No.1, 2002, pp.121140.
- Professor Richard Faragher, University of Brighton/uploadedImages/Royal_ Society/Events/Events_Diary/couple.JPG2010-05-11T:2010-05-11T:
- htpp://www.spiritualnow.com/authors/20/Richard-Pettinger.

6

Level of IT Implementation and Contextual Factors: A Case Survey of BPR Projects

Sharadindu Pandey

Introduction

IT implementation and BPR implementation are closely related (Markus and Benjamin, 1997). However, IT implementation projects may or may not have process reengineering component. Venkatraman (1994) argued that level of IT implementation may be of five types viz. localised exploitation, internal integration, business process redesign, business network redesign and business scope redefinition. Out of which, first two may be categorised as non-BPR and remaining three may be as BPR involving IT implementation. As more and more organisations have been implementing BPR and IT, one need to understand the implementation related aspects of these efforts.

Aubert et al (2008) mention that past researches on IT implementation had mostly been focusing on individual level acceptance of IT. As the IT implementation is done at the project level so the future studies should undertake the project framework. They further mention that antecedent variables of IT implementation are either given or freely chosen by management decisions. So we need to have research basis of antecedent variables of IT implementation. Some of these antecedent variables may be managerial factors, institutionalisation of implementation process, and organisational aspects.

Organisational implementation research is one of the corner stone of the core business process research (Sidorova and Isik, 2010). Terziovski, Fitezpartick and Neill (2003) attempted to explore the successful predictors of BPR implementation. They determine that 30 per cent of variance in organisation performance is due to practices of BPR. Organisations ambition to implement the IT/BPR project substantially differ. So there is a requirement of matching organisational characteristics and scope of IT/BPR project. This 'management of matching' is a critical success factor in reengineering projects (Huzing, Koster and Bouman, 1997). Recently Margherita and Petti (2010) indicated that effective introduction of IT/BPR requires the understanding at four levels. These aspects are related to strategy, people, process and enabler's level. The enabler's level include organisational and technological facilitators. Our understanding about the significance of various enablers according to the level of IT/BPR implementation is not much clear.

Literature Review

Handerson and Venkatraman (1993) discuss about the internal and external contexts of strategy-IT alignment. Internal context is concerned about organisational variables and external context is about the environmental forces. Tae Kyung sung and Others (1998) further studied BPR implementation in Korean enterprises and identified 20 critical factors. They broadly categorised them as Strategic, Organisational, Methodological and Technological factors. Ting, Shu-Ping, De-Hai and Jin (2009) studied corporate culture and BPR implementation. They also studied the role of contextual factors like ownership of enterprise and size of enterprise. They classified enterprises in to two types; State owned and non-state owned. Government projects are also likely to suffer from the bureaucratic impediments. Government projects may further lower the level if IT implementation due to employee resistance, vertical structure, excessive regulation, lack of communication from top management and many others. On the contrary, government projects generally being large sized in nature may invoke higher level of IT implementation (with BPR).Ting, Shu-Ping, De-Hai and Jin (2009) further mention that state owned and non-state owned types are no different on mission, consistency and involvement dimensions of corporate culture, but adaptability plays bigger role in BPR implementation in non-state enterprise than state enterprise. They also studied the scale of enterprise as Small (less than 300 employees), Medium (301 to 2000 employees) and Large (over 2000) employees). Subsequently they concluded that there is no obvious difference in above three scales of enterprise on mission, consistency and involvement dimensions, Adaptability plays more positive role in implementing BPR in small organisation rather than medium and large organisations. Adaptability may affect the level of IT implementation. So it would be interesting to learn how scale and ownership of enterprise differ between low and high BPR involving IT implementation. Following hypothesis can be proposed:

H1: The level of IT implementation (with or without BPR) is significantly associated with Government and Private form of ownership.

H2: The level of IT implementation (with or without BPR) issignificantly associated with the size of the organisation.

Kuruppuarachchi (2000) performed a literature review on IT implementation and organisation factors. He identified two categories; employee related factors and implementation related factors. He suggested that employee reaction to the IT implementation may differ as per their position in the organisational hierarchy. Employee who feel the need of job security may view the technology as threat. On the other hand, the employee whose level of Job involvement is high regardless of their level in the hierarchy will be positive about technology implementation. Attaran (2004) further suggested that employee resistance to change is one of the most serious barrier for BPR implementation. Later on Shen and Chou (2009) indicated that non-BPR companies seek more involvement from their employees rather than BPR companies. It may be interesting to learn whether degree of employee involvement may create difference in low and high level of IT implementation. Cultural factors are equally crucial for attaining BPR success. Wang (2007) suggests that before the enterprise carries out BPR efforts, culture of enterprise revolving around BPR has to be tested and evaluated. Employees enterprise and social values which is the major component of the culture may affect the decision to choose the degree of IT implementation. Based on above discussion, hypothesis can be proposed as follows:

H3: The level of IT implementation (with or without BPR) is significantly associated with the degree of top level involvement

H4: The level of IT implementation (with or without BPR) is significantly associated with a degree of bottom level involvement

H5: The level of IT implementation (with or without BPR) is significantly associated with the degree of cultural constraints.

Another major factor affecting the decision of IT implementation is environmental related challenges. Afshar and Sepehri (2006) mention that BPR works best in rather stable environment. They further elaborate that project oriented firms where each project is different and resource recombination is quite frequent, BPR may not work. It may be interesting to know whether level of IT implementation is significantly different across fast, slow and standard cycle markets. Shen and Chou (2009) studied the difference of the success factors in BPR and non-BPR companies and noted that funds and resources for these projects are always limited. They also mentioned as one of their interesting findings that these factors are not industry specific.

H6: The level of IT implementation (with or without BPR) is significantly associated with the fast, standard and slow cycle market.

H7: The level of IT implementation (with or without BPR) is significantly associated with the level of financial commitment.

H8: The level of IT implementation (with or without BPR) is significantly associated with the industry sectors viz. manufacturing, services and technology.

Project related variables may also determine about level of IT implementation. Deloittee (1994) suggested nine BPR obstacles, and identified narrow project character as one of the barrier. Abdul-Hadi, Al-Sudairi and Alquahtani (2005) ranked the barriers on the basis of the strength. Out of the 29 barriers, they identified using external consultant in the project as tenth important barrier. Braganza and Myers (1996) explains that use of external consultancy is not for IT implementation but for skills transfer. They maintain that the BPR implementation job is primarily in the hands of steering group or BPR champion. Literature is not much clear about level of IT implementation and the use of external of internal consultancy.

H9: The level of IT implementation (with or without BPR) is significantly associated with the scope of implementation viz. corporate, division and functional.

H10: The level of IT implementation (with or without BPR) is significantly associated with the use of internal or external consultant.

BPR projects are different to the non-BPR projects on the basis of risk taking nature also. Presence of the risk may lead practitioners to choose incremental approach of IT implementation rather than big-bag or one-go approach. Heygate (1993) located different BPR projects as the degrees of radicalness. He attempted to develop a continuum involving single process redesign, multiple process redesign, single major business process change and, subsequently, multiple integrated business model change. Level of IT ambition also varies from quick hits to total commitment to become the world leader. However, Braganza and Myers (1996) remarks that Heygate (1993) appears to confuse radical with risks. Presence of so many barriers may be summed as level of complexity. Braganza and Myers (1996) unravel this confusion and pooled the factor into low and high difficulty areas. They consider external consultancy, process modeling tools and reducing headcount as low difficulty areas, whereas; culture change, changing role and functions, changing reporting lines and identifying tangible benefits as high difficulty areas. Difficulty as can be conceptualised as project complexity. It may be seen whether level of complexity significantly different in BPR and non-BPR projects involving the use of IT. The discussion leads to following propositions.

H11: The level of IT implementation (with or without BPR) is significantly associated with the scale of project implementation viz. one-go or incremental.

H12: The level of IT implementation (with or without BPR) is significantly associated with the the degree of project complexity.

Methodology

The present study employ case survey methodology to statistically test and identify the patterns across case studies. The procedure suggested by Larsson (1993) is used. He suggests that the basic procedure of case survey is to (i) select a group of existing case studies relevant to chosen research questions (ii) Design a coding scheme to systematic covert the qualitative information in to quantifiable variables (iii) Using multiple raters to calculate inter-rater reliability, and (iv) Statistically analyse the coded data. For collecting the case sample, all major sources were explored. The data bases like Proquest ABI/Inform complete, EBSCO, (Business Source complete), Emerald, IEEE (electronic library), ACM digital library, JSTOR, Springer, Sage and Oxford were searched. Other sources of case like ECCH (European Case Cleaning House), anonymous case available on company websites, dissertations, conference proceedings and teaching cases were also checked. Case containing at least some information related to the research questions were included in case sample. As Yin (1984) indicated some of his reservation to achieve theoretical and statistical generalisation, however, Larsson (1993) suggested that the case survey researcher can control the secondary selection of the cases to be included in the sample. The suitability of the case survey approach also depends upon the nature of the research questions. The information availability regarding the chosen contextual variable is generally reported in most of the case studies.

Out of 142 potentially suitable cases, only 50 were included for the present study. Thus the case acceptance rate was 35.21 per cent. Majority of the selected studies are from published sources which adds in the credibility of the information. Authors him self and one independent rater analysed all the cases. The rating was performed using the coding scheme developed by the author. Inter-rater reliability is calculated using Cohen's kappa coefficient. Categorical scale is used to investigate all the research questions. The value of Kappa coefficient ranged from 0.39 to 1.00. Calingo (1989) suggested that approximately two third of agreements can be considered as satisfactory reliability. 10 out of 12 measurement reported kappa higher than two third of agreements which shows the high reliability of the rating procedure. Hypothesis are tested using Fisher exact test. The test is used for categorical data. Fisher test exactly calculated the deviation from the null hypothesis. Null hypothesis can be rejected where p- value comes out be less than 0.025 (for 2 tail test) at 5 per cent significance level. Fisher test is preferred over chi-square test where sample size is smaller. Case studies being the sample unit, which is further subjected to availability and suitability resulted the smaller sample size. The limitation required the use of Fisher test. The Fisher test is supposed to be conservative. Actual significance level may be higher than nominal level. Yates (1984) proposed to use mid-p values to get over the conservativeness of Fisher test. Actual significance level of the mid-p value is more close to the nominal level. Simple logistic regression was also used to further analyse the data. The technique is suitable to predict binary categorical outcome. IT implementation without BPR and IT implementation with BPR were two outcomes. The study analysed how much the contextual variables predict these two outcomes. The logit model also overestimates the odds ratio when sample size is less than five hundred. This overestimation might not have any effect on the interpretation of the results. As this is much less than the standard error of the estimate. Intercept is the point on Y-axis (log odds) crossed by the regression line when X=0. Slope is the rate at which predicted log odds increases (or decreases) with each successive units of X.

Results and Analysis

The first hypothesis is tested for the statistically significant associated between ownership types whether Government or private and Level of IT implementation. As indicated in table 1, H1 is rejected. 2-tails p-value is very high (0.99) and mid value is slightly less than this (0.86). Both of these values comfortable comes in acceptance zone. By using the logit model, we can predict whether ownership type can affect level of IT implementation. The overwhelming value of r-square (see table 2) shows the full predictability between the criterion and outcome variables. Similarly alternative hypothesis H2, H3, H4, H5, H7, H8, H10, H11, H12 also rejected. That means level of IT implementation (with or without BPR) is not significantly associated with size of the organisation, degree of top level involvement, degree of bottom level involvement, degree of cultural constraints, level of financial commitment and industrial sector. However, result was significant for H6 and H9. This means the level of IT implementation (With our without BPR) is significantly associated with fast, standard and slow cycles of market. In addition, level of IT implementation has also the significant relationship with scope of implementation i.e. corporate, divisional and functional. The logit model indicates that R-square was high (>0.50) for form of the ownership, size of the organisation, market cycles, financial commitment, and industry sector, use of consultants and scale of project. It was lower (<0.50) for top level involvement, bottom level involvement, cultural constraint, scope of project and project complexity (Refer table 2). For determining the inter-rater reliability, Cohen's kappa coefficient is calculated. For many of the parameters, substantial to perfect agreement is found (See Table 3). Only for financial commitment and use of consultant, the inter-rater agreement is lower.

Conclusion and Implication

The results show that IT projects involving BPR is associated with market cycle and scope of implementation. Remaining parameters are not found associated. The use of the BPR including IT implementation is high in fast and standard cycle markets. As Afshar and Sepehri (2006) mention that BPR works best in stable environment, the results indicate that BPR is less used in stable environment. Further the results indicate that scope of the project is associated with level of IT implementation. It reaffirms the findings of Deloittee (1994) that narrow project character is barrier of BPR. The study has not got significant association with ownership type i.e., Govt. or private. The finding is similar to the traditional notion that employee resistance and culture may be hurdle in level of IT implementation but scope of the government projects pacifies the restraining factors. Academic literature was not much clear whether involvement of external or internal consultants is associated with level of IT implementation. This study shows that there is no association with level of IT implementation and use of internal or external consultants. The current study quantitatively synthesises the use of BPR and common practices. It may insights to the practitioners who have any pre-notion about any of the factors affecting BPR implementation.

Bibliography

- Aubert, B.A. et al (2008). A multi-level, multi-theory perspective of information technology implementation. *Information Systems Journal*, 18 (1), 45-72.
- Huizing, A., Koster E., Bouman, W. (1997). Balance in business reengineering: an empirical study of fit and performance. *Journal of Management Information Systems*, 14 (1), 93-118.
- Margherita, A and Petti, C (2010). ICT-enabled and process-based change: an integrative roadmap, *Business Process Management Journal*, 16 (3), 473 491.
- Markus, L.M. and Benjamin, R.I. (1997). The magic bullet theory in IT-enabled transformation. *Sloan Management Review*, 5568.
- Sidorova, A and Isik, O. (2010). Business process research: a cross-disciplinary review. *Business Process Management Journal*, 16 (4), 566 597

- Terziovski, M.E., Fitzpatrick, P. and O'Neill, P. (2003) Successful predictors of business process reengineering (BPR) in financial services. *International Journal of Production Economics*, 84 (4), 23-32.
- Venkatraman, N. (1994). IT-enabled business transformation: From automation to business scope re-definition. *Sloan Management Review*, 35 (2), 73.

7

Developing Innovative Red Flags for Preventing Frauds in Health Insurance

Ajay Mittal & Gaurav Jain

Overview

Fundamentally insurance is a risk distribution system that requires the accumulation of liquid assets in the form of reserve funds which are in turn available to pay loss claims. Insurance companies generate a large steady flow of cash through insurance premiums. Steady cash flow is an important economic resource which is very attractive and easily diverted. Large accumulations of liquid assets make insurance companies attractive for *take over* and *loot* schemes. All Insurance companies even public sector giant insurance companies are under great pressure to maximise the return on investment, thus making them vulnerable to fraudulent schemes. Hence need arises for robust Fraud Risk Management culture across insurance industry.

Research Design

Starting with basics by giving insight on General Health insurance frauds first, research aims towards analysing trends associated with Health Insurance frauds and developing innovative red flags to prevent different types of fraudulent activities to create a road map for fighting against frauds since "It is Fraud to Conceal Fraud".

It is important to note that a red flag does not necessarily prove fraud; even the presence of several indicators does not mean fraud has occurred. However it is very important to understand Red Flags associated with frauds to combat frauds and develop innovative system and controls.

Research Methodology

Why Does Fraud Occur?

There are generally three factors that influence the commission of fraud. To understand why fraud occurs, we can use a model called The Fraud Triangle. It is a model developed by Dr. Donald Cressey, a criminologist whose research focused on fraudsters. According to Dr. Cressey, there were three factors that were present when an ***ordinary*** person committed fraud. These are:

- Pressure
- Opportunity
- Rationalisation

Let's decipher above phenomenon with a help of recent example of Bernard Madoff's Fraud. (In March 2009, Madoff pleaded guilty to 11 federal felonies and admitted to turning his wealth management business into a massive Ponzi scheme that defrauded thousands of investors of billions of dollars) his fraud can be dissected into the components of the Fraud Triangle.

Pressure - (Panic Redemptions of the 1987 Crash) Madoff said in an interview that In the eighties he saw consistent returns of 15 per cent-20 per cent,a time when the Dow Jones Industrial Average went from 800 to 2,722 from 1980 to its peak before the crash of 1987 (a growth rate of about 15 per cent compounded a year). So Madoff could have invested in an index fund and done as well as anyone. But the sell-off associated with the crash (redemptions) and the slow recovery (low returns) put pressure on Madoff. That's when Madoff borrowed from investor capital to pay out redeeming investors and began falsifying results showing big returns. Those returns became the advertising he needed to get more investors/victims.

Opportunity (Nobody Asked Questions) Many large investment banks like UBS, Credit Suisse and Banco Santander saw Madoff's returns and wanted to invest. However, Madoff refused to disclose the means by which he was maintaining his consistent returns. The banks, according the Madoff, never pushed further for more information beyond the false return statements that they had received. In reality, Madoff was taking the money, sticking it in treasuries yielding 2 per cent and started printing false statements showing holdings in stocks yielding far more. Funding from sophisticated investors began to flow to Madoff.

Rationalisation (Everyone was greedy) From the beginning, Madoff seemed doomed to make a mistake thinking that Wall Street was rigged against the little guy. Thoughts of "getting even" seemed to be deeply rooted in his initial view of the financial market. Madoff said he put up warning signs to potential investors who pursued him to invest their money. The warnings, that investing is risky and could lead to losses, was enough of a disclosure to get permission to take more money into the scheme.

While Madoff's despicable act is not to be debated, a look at the Opportunity portion of the fraud triangle provides us a glimpse at where the Securities and Exchange Commission and professional investment institutions could have done more to catch Madoff earlier. Most of us are not interested in what mad thoughts drove Madoff to steal or justify the theft, but what could have been done to prevent it .Trying to understand the rationalisation or pressure Madoff faced to justify his actions will be debated for years but those answer are sure to only spark more questions.

Most vulnerable to Frauds is Insurance Industry as easy to find Opportunity to make money by paying small premiums, pressure is always there on selling brokers and easy for fraudsters to rationalise their behaviour. Insurance Industry can do very little about other 2 factors that is Pressure and Rationalisation of Fraudster behaviour but certainly can do a lot in preventing Opportunity for frauds. Hence research paper aims to provide insight on prevalent Health Insurance Frauds and developing innovative ways to see red flags to prevent and detect Insurance Frauds.

Health Care Fraud

Health Insurance is the fastest growing industry in India. However it is badly affected by the menace of fake claims. Health care fraud is usually committed against private and public insurance companies (Medicare/ Medicaid) by providers, subscribers, non-subscribers masquerading as subscribers, insured groups, claims processors, insurance company employees, brokers, and agents. Providers commit most of the acts because they have greater access to the claims system than others. While most health care providers are honest and ethical, some are involved in billing abuse and fraud. In some cases, non-medical professionals create fraudulent medical facilities and bill for services that were never rendered. Medical fraud and abuse does not just hurt the workers' compensation system—it can hurt the injured insured person, as well.

Like all other industries, insurance is susceptible to both internal and external fraud schemes. External health care fraud is perpetrated by outsiders against the company. The two main types of external fraud schemes are those committed by providers (such as doctors, institutions, and inter-mediatory agencies) and claim fraud by the insured. **The largest amount of fraud is in health care, more so in developed countries but such fraudulent activities catching up in India too and that was the reason why most of the hospitals are now not accepting Cash less facilities.** Even PSU insurance companies stopped the cashless facility in select private hospitals, alleging over-billing by them. Hence need was felt to uncover some of the Health Care fraudulent activities in detail and developing Innovative Red Flags to prevent Health Insurance Frauds.

In India, statistics are also alarming. **According to the survey conducted two years back by one of the leading TPA the number of false claims in the industry is estimated at around 10-15 per cent of total claims. The report suggests that the Health care industry in India is loosing approximately Rs.600 crores on "false claims" every year.** So to make health insurance viable there is a need to focus on eliminating or reducing fraudulent claim

From the data Collected on Claims Settled during 2010-11 we draw below interesting Inferences:

- **15 per cent in number accounting for 22 per cent in claim paid amount did not have hospital stay information**
- Lengths of stay 'Less than 1 day' and '3 days' had considerable chunks both in number and paid amounts of claims.
- **23 per cent in number accounting for 15 per cent in claim paid amount were paid for hospital stay 'Less than 1' day.**
- **54 per cent in number accounting for 40 per cent in claim paid amount were paid for hospital stay '0-3' days.**
- 67 per cent in number accounting for 55 per cent in claim paid amount were paid for hospital stay '0-10' days.
- 18 per cent in number accounting for 23 per cent in claim paid amount were paid for hospital stay beyond 10 days.

Before moving ahead lets also take a look at Claims data of two years where increase was phenomenal in Claims:

	Average Claimed (in %)		*Proportionin (in %)*		*Increase in average claimed amount for 2009-10 in comparison with 2007-08 (in %)*
Disease Name	**2007-08**	**2009-10**	**2007-08**	**2009-10**	
Arthropathies	1,36,354	1,47,401	10.10	7.60	7.49
Blood Diseases	95,992	1,07,944	0.70	0.54	11.07
Circulatory	1,53,349	3,56,505	28.04	44.95	56.99
Digestive	75,694	79,564	10.01	7.35	4.86

Ear	65,841	68,066	0.49	0.41	3.27
Endocrine	1,05,843	1,03,402	3.02	1.69	-2.36
Eye	60,137	57,168	1.94	1.83	-5.19
Infections	88,200	83,301	4.40	2.74	-5.88
Injury	88,039	94,284	11.03	7.99	6.62
Neoplasm	96,287	1,03,566	10.83	8.27	7.03
Nervous	1,10,135	1,28,055	2.34	1.96	13.99
Pregnancy	56,148	57,820	4.42	4.19	2.89
Respiratory	85,237	92,019	3.67	3.23	7.37
Skin	78,747	78,477	0.91	0.68	-0.34
Urology	72,023	77,455	8.11	6.57	7.01
Total	**98,101**	**1,34,550**	**100**	**100**	**27.09**

Inferences:

- The Claim Severity has increased in all cases except for Endocrine, Eye, Infections and Respiratory diseases.
- The increase is very high for Circulatory disease i.e. 56.99per cent.
- **Overall 27.09 per cent increase in the claim severity for the year 2009 10 compared to 2007-08.**

Common Health Insurance Frauds:

Agent Fraud: Nearly all insurance companies use the services of a broker or agent external to the firm. Unfortunately, the best interests of the insurance company are not always served. Several schemes have been identified which can be classified as fraudulent.

Phony Groups: Agents will set up bogus companies in order to sell health insurance to individuals at group rates.

Phony or Nonexistent Policies: Rather than going to the trouble of setting up a bogus company, many agents will sell a phony policy, and take the money and run.

Medical Underwriting Fraud: The broker will write a policy knowing that the client has pre-existing conditions that would prevent acceptance for coverage.

Eligibility Fraud: A broker may seek to add ineligible family members, friends, or associates to a group policy by representing them as eligible policyholder.

Switching Policies: This scheme involves the agent telling the customer that he is obtaining one policy, taking the premium for that policy, and then buying instead a cheaper policy with less coverage. The agent then pockets the difference.

Provider Fraud: Provider fraud is a fraud perpetrated by a medical practitioner, medical supplier, or medical facility on patients or customers in order to increase their income by illicit means.

A greater potential for fraud exists with providers since they have the availability of more sophisticated equipment, such as computers, to use in generating bills. Providers possess greater knowledge of medical/dental techniques, medical procedures, terminology, etc., that would not be questioned by claim-handling personnel. More insurance companies are contracting with providers for direct billing, leaving the patient out of the loop. In addition, patients are usually reluctant to accuse physicians of wrongdoing since they rely on the provider's continued services, and when providers submit to fraudulent practices, they forgive any out-of-pocket expenses the patient should incur.

Developing Innovative Red Flags to Prevent Provider Fraud

System at Claims Department can alert Claims settlement team in case of:

- Pressure for rapid adjudication of claims.
- Threats of legal action for delay in making payments.
- Frequent telephone inquiries on claim status.
- Assertive providers who demand same-day claim payment and special handling.
- Charges submitted for payment with no supporting documentation available (x-rays, lab results).
- Individual provider using P.O. box as return addresses.
- Insured's address on claim form is the same as provider.
- Routine (not specialised) treatment for patients living more than 150 miles from the provider.
- Referring physician and provider of service in same Professional Corporation.
- Medical records that have been altered.
- Medical records that have additional information attached that would make an apparent noncovered service now covered.
- Missing pages of medical records that would cover the period of time you are reviewing.

Fraud by the Medical Staff

In addition, employees of providers also have an opportunity to steal and cover up theft of cash. They can submit fraudulent claims for their patients and divert the payments to themselves. If they are covered under insurance, they can also use their own contract to submit fraudulent claims. For many employees, care rendered by their employer (doctor) to them or their family is free, but claims may be filed and assignment not accepted.

Another scheme involves the provider's office calling in prescription drugs for their "patients" to pharmacies. Once the drugs are picked up they can be sold. For example, in a case involving collusion between a medical staff employee and an elderly lady in a retirement community, the elderly lady had developed a business selling the drugs purchased from the employee to her friends and neighbors in her community. If the employee is in collusion with an insured, the fraudsters can collect not only from the sale of the drugs, but also from the proceeds of insurance claims.

Kickbacks in the Health Care Industry

Kickbacks relating to the health care industry can come from several sources. The medical community is facing competition that it has not faced in the past, and monetary offers to prospective patients have been difficult to refuse. For example, in a South Florida community, incentives such as free transportation to medical facilities, shopping centers, refreshments, and the like are common.

Examples of kickbacks are:

- Payment for referrals of patients
- Waiver of deductible and co-payments
- Payment for insurance contracts
- Payment for vendor contracts

Payments to Adjusters

In order to get a claim settled quickly, an insured, or someone operating on his behalf, may bribe adjusters or other claims-handling personnel to approve or speed up payment of a claim.

Inflated Billings

Health care billings can be inflated by providers as well as insured. The following are some of the most common fraud schemes encountered by investigators and claims approvers:

- Alterations
- Adding services
- Code gaming

Alterations

Altering valid claims can be accomplished using a pen or a photocopier. Common alterations are:

- Altered claim forms/super bills
- Amounts changed
- Date of service changed
- Name of patient changed
- Altered financial ledgers

For example, a prescription/medical bill can be altered by placing an additional number in front of the amount charged. The date of service can be altered so that it becomes a covered expense rather than one which was incurred prior to being eligible for coverage. The individual submitting a claim changes the name on the bill from a noncovered family member to one that is covered under the contract.

Detection

- Computer programs can be developed which identify excessive charges for prescription or medical services above an acceptable level.
- There is a machine that can identify any alterations, erasures, change of ink, or whiteouts on the original bill prior to paying the claim. This is important in today's environment in which original bills, Cheques, etc., are destroyed as soon as they are microfilmed to minimise storage space for record keeping.
- Train the adjusters to look for obvious alterations when processing claims.

Adding Services

This scheme involves adding on services never rendered to dates of actual services. In these cases, the verification process is the same as the procedures listed under the alteration process.

Insured Fraud

Insured may attempt to perpetrate a fraud by submitting fictitious claims forms:

- Multiple surgeries
- Multiple office visits
- Foreign claims—patient supposedly goes out of the country and falls ill
- Noncovered dependents

Doctor/ER Shopping

Excessive drug claims for controlled substance drugs. Patient "shops" for controlled substance drugs. One physician doesn't know that the other has prescribed the drug. In addition, the patient may shop for drugs in emergency rooms complaining of soft tissue injuries, sprains, and strains.

Misrepresentation on Application

Failure by insured to list all prior medical conditions or group to list medical conditions of employees.

Third-Party Fraud

This category involves an unauthorised use of an insured's identification card by another known person or unknown person. The insurance company is usually notified by the insured once they receive a benefit statement work sheet for services rendered.

Death of Insured

The primary insured passes away; however, the beneficiary does not notify the insurance carrier and continues to submit fictitious claims on medical expenses after the death of the insured.

Investigation Tips

- Determine how the insured lost his/her card. If stolen, the police should be contacted to determine if the crime was reported. A copy of the police FIR report should be obtained.
- Obtain an actual description of the cardholder so that identification can be made of the impostor who used the card improperly.
- Visit the providers or medical doctors to obtain any information to identify the perpetrator.

Criminal Rings

Individual criminals infiltrate mailrooms and are able to obtain copies of legitimate bills submitted to providers. They subsequently establish a mail drop point or rent an office and begin submitting false claims to insurance companies by creating fictitious tax identification numbers. Since the claimants are genuine, insurance companies will normally pay these bills.

Collusion

Collusion is the most difficult insurance fraud to detect since several people are involved in committing the fraud. Usually cases of this nature are disclosed by accident or by a tip received from someone who may have been involved and has had a falling-out. Any time a fraud is committed by an insured; there is no question on the part of the perpetrator as to the intent to obtain funds to which he or she is not entitled. However, it is also extremely difficult to detect this type of fraud.

Detection

- Excessive billings report may show that a provider is submitting large amounts of expenses. In addition, the claimant requests substantial payments to be made to him/her rather than the provider.
- Explanation of benefits if submitted to the provider will probably generate some reaction from the provider. If substantial, at the time that Form is submitted to the provider, there may also be comments by the provider.
- Periodically management should compare the membership/enrollment file to the Social Security file to determine if the insurance company is paying claims on deceased insured. The membership file also may be compared to the file from the vital statistics department to search for divorced policyholders.

Foreign Insured

A foreign insured submits phony information that the primary insured passed away. For the last month he/she was hospitalised in a foreign hospital and a sizable bill was mailed to the carrier for payment.

Recommendations:

- The claim file should be reviewed to determine if the charges are legitimate.
- Determine if the medical language appears to be proper by comparing samples of bona fide claims.

- It may be necessary to submit a letter to the attending physician to determine if the charges are correct.
- Through law enforcement contacts, it may be necessary to obtain information regarding the legitimacy of the claim.
- Check the style of the date. In many foreign countries, dates are listed with the day first, then the month and year, e.g., 07/01/04 would be 7 January 2004. If the U.S. style of dating is used (month/day/year), it may indicate a fraudulent claim.

Detection of External Fraud

- Misspelled medical/dental terminology.
- Unusual charges for a given service.
- Similar handwriting by the claimant and the provider of service.
- Typed, not printed bill heads.
- Bills with irregular columns.
- Unassigned bills that are normally assigned, such as large hospital or surgical bills.
- Typed or handwritten hospital bills.
- Drug receipts from the same pharmacy but on different colour paper.
- Erasures or alterations.
- Lack of any provider's signature on a claim form.
- Absence of the provider's medical degree, i.e., "Dr. Rakesh Moyal" instead of ". Rakesh Moyal, M.D."
- An illegible provider signature on the bill submitted or the signature does not match the one on file.
- Surgeries that don't have other related services such as hospital charges.
- Physician's specialty does not agree with diagnosis.
- Services billed do not agree with diagnosis.
- Impossible or unlikely services.
- Photocopied bills.
- Other indicators that a claim approver or investigator should be aware of that could result in identifying a possible fraud:
    - Pressure by a claimant to pay a claim quickly.
    - Individuals who hands deliver their claim insist on picking up their claim cheque.
    - Threats of legal action if a claim is not paid quickly.
    - Anonymous telephone call inquiries regarding the status of a pending claim.

- Identical claims for same patient in different months or different years.
- Dates of service just prior to termination of enrollment or just after enrollment.
- Services billed that do not appear to agree with the medical records.
- Billing for services or equipment which are clearly unsuitable for the patient's needs.
- Foreign claims listing charges or providing bills in Indian Currency when that isn't the currency of that country.
- Multiple foreign claims for same subscriber.
- Multiple foreign claims from same physician/ hospital.

Fraud by Medical Institutions

Fraud schemes perpetrated by institutions and their employees include those commonly used by doctors and other providers. However, the more common schemes in which hospitals are primarily involved include:

- Filing of false cost reports
- Billing for experimental procedures
- Improper contractual and other relationships with physicians
- Revenue recovery firms to (knowingly or unknowingly) bill extra charges

Other Common Red Flags of Possible Healthcare Fraud

- The medical treatment is inconsistent with injuries originally alleged by injured worker.
- The medical provider attempts to influence injured workers to seek treatment outside of medical provider network.
- The injured worker undergoes excessive treatment for soft tissue injuries.
- The doctor's billing records are inconsistent with the treatment, as reported by the injured worker.
- The injured worker is unable to define the medical ailments listed on the claim form.
- The injured worker can not physically describe the treating physician or building.
- The medical billing does not coincide with medical records or reports.

- The injured worker reports seeing a doctor for very brief time, but billings indicate a lengthy visit.
- The injured worker's description of the treatment indicates that non-medical personnel rendered the medical treatment.
- The injured worker lives far from medical facility, yet receives frequent treatments.
- The medical provider prescribes similar DME (durable medical equipment) on the first or second visit.

Conclusion

Managing fraud is one of the most challenging and costly realities, which insurers, government, different regulatory authorities and society cannot afford to overlook. There is a need for participation of the honest stakeholders to jointly address the most burning issue in financial services industry. All the insurers need to join hands and form a committee for tackling fraudulent claims. Similar to the Health Insurance Portability and Accountability Act of 1996 (HIPAA) of United States of America, which established health care fraud as a federal criminal offense with punishment of up to 10 years of prison in addition to significant financial penalties, there is a need to introduce similar sort of act for the Indian market. **All these efforts towards fraud detection and control are not a full proof mechanism but an innovative attempt towards minimising the same; towards the growth of the insurance industry.**

"Fraud and falsehood only dread examination. Truth invites it."

—***Samuel Johnson***

References

1. **Websites** :
    - Google.com,
    - Wikipedia.com,
    - Moneylife.in,
    - Healthcarespace.blogspot.com
    - ACFE.com
    - www.irda.gov.in
2. **Others** :
    - International Fraud Examiners Manual (Association of Certified Fraud Examiners).

8

Rural Products and Marketing in North–East India: Initiatives of Social Entrepreneurships

Subhabrata Dutta & Aditi Nath

Abstract

Micro enterprise, Self-help Groups (SHGs) and small cooperatives are increasing in rural areas as social entrepreneurs by the support of the government directly and indirectly for the improvement of the rural economy. But Small-scale rural producers in India are often limited by the markets within their reach. It has found that many SHGs and village industries though produced good products but fail to sustain due to lack of marketing opportunities of their products. This study conducted in 'Barak Valley', the southernmost part of Assam state in North-East India which is composed of three Districts. This area is socio economically remains backward. But many rural products mainly made up of natural resources are available here due to availability of forest based raw materials. Basically, SHGs, Individual/family entrepreneurships and small cooperatives are contributors of rural products. Availability of bank loan and training opportunities as well as the demand of rural made products fostered them. But there is a gap exists between the producer and the customers. Producers are facing acute crisis in selling of their products and rolling back the money into business. Many models of social entrepreneurships are upcoming in north-east which should be studied to formulate a policy for the promotion of social entrepreneurship for the north-east region.

Key Words: *Rural Products, Social entrepreneurship, SHGs, Marketing.*

Introduction

India lives in Villages. Since independence special attention was given for the development of rural life and infrastructure with various policies and programmes. Entrepreneurships, especially the social entrepreneurships has been encouraged and promoted for the development of rural economy. Many individuals pursue a business activity because alternative options for work are limited or non-existent; by having the option to engage in self-employment they are able to take care of themselves and their families. According to emerging body of literature the phenomenon of "social entrepreneurship", which is about people starting and developing new initiatives where the value of the (local, regional) society is put before the value of the individuals leading these initiatives. Policy makers are increasingly attempting to implement policies supporting social entrepreneurship, especially in areas where governments are forced to cut budgets and unemployment has been increasing; hence the idea is that entrepreneurs come up with the solutions to societal challenges.

Micro enterprise, Self-help Groups (SHGs) and small cooperatives (in fisheries, sericulture etc) are increasing day by day by the support of the government directly and indirectly for the improvement of the rural economy to reduce poverty, unemployment and to promote women empowerment in rural areas.

Modern communities demand many goods and services. In seeking to satisfy these needs, manufacturers, merchants and professional workers apply their skill and energies. Now-a-days human needs are dynamic. As soon as one is satisfied yet another replaces it to continue the never-ending spiral of satisfactions.

There was always a demand of a category of products which are simple, natural, indigenous, less chemical or less harmful and bear a sense of beauty. These are basically rural products made by using natural resources and with a price which can be afforded by general people. For example, products made of jute, *Tarecotta*, *Khadis* etc.

Social Entrepreneurial Activity in North Easter Region

While most of India has seen slowly rising social entrepreneurial activity for about a decade now, the NER has been considered as the black-hole for business and enterprise. The limited organised networks for social enterprises, the sustained conflict, geographical isolation, militarisation and migration have led to a drying up of investments, and the lack of economic and social development in the region. This is despite the richness of natural resources in the region, presenting a huge opportunity for investment, and the growth of enterprise in the region.

There is little entrepreneurial activity in North East but there is potential to develop it based on the natural resources available locally. Sending semi-processed goods from the north-eastern part of the country to the industrially better developed regions across India is not restricted to incense sticks. Anthurium flowers grown in Mizoram are exported, again via Bangalore. Another traditional activity common across the region is handloom weaving. While the hidden talents stored in the North East have recently been highlighted through a range of platforms, set up mostly by civil society actors, the market in the North East however comes with its challenges. With cheap Chinese import having flooded the market, as well as lack of demands for local products, local artisans are slowly losing ground. For example a local woman would buy a shawl from an artisan only once-this will last her for a whole life time. There is no steady need for local handicrafts in this region. Thus these products emerging from a tradition of arts and crafts have less value within the region, as compared to the rest of the country and for that matter, the world. To allow local entrepreneurs to reach such emerging markets, there needs to be a significant thrust towards the development of a relationship between the rest of the country and people from this region. Such a long-term relationship will not only lead to the creation of a dependable market place for local artisans and entrepreneurs but will also help in creating employment opportunities among the masses.

Rural Products

Mr. Mani Shankar Aiyar (Union Minister for Panchayati Raj) told in a conference that, there is tremendous scope for production and marketing of large- scale rural products in India. It will be an unending list of the products produced by the rural people with a simple mechanism. Few products may be of use of low cost mechanics specially the food items like jelly, jam, bread, pickle, and noodles etc. Sometimes, the traditional rural products are now being produced as a new one with the help of simple technology. For example, leaf-made plate which was very simply arrangements of leafs are now made better and getting the look of a plate. As day by day the social enterprises, like the rural industries, self-help groups are increasing besides the traditional enterprises like, sericulture, pottery etc, the time is not far away that the electronic goods will be added to the list and so on (in few semi-urban areas such products are already developing).

If we look towards the history of community development in India with the efforts of *Sriniketan* experiment in 1921 initiated by Rabindranath Togore, it was found that the emphasis was laid on the use of community resources and rural products made of by the people by themselves. Rural products are the ways towards the achievement of self-reliance of an individual and the rural community itself.

Marketing of Rural Products

Marketing *means the performance of business activities that direct flow of goods and services from producer to consumer or user*. Marketing is more than the selling. Selling is generally concerned with the plans and tactics of trying to get consumer to exchange what he has and what you have. Marketing is primarily concerned with the much more sophisticated strategy of trying to have what the consumer wants. Selling focuses on the needs of the seller but marketing on the needs of the buyer. Selling is preoccupied with the seller's need to convert his product into cash; marketing with the idea of satisfying the needs of the customer by means of the product as well as the whole cluster of customer value satisfactions associated with creating, delivering and finally consuming the product. In a nutshell, it can be said that a market-minded firm tries to create value satisfying goods and services that customers will want to buy.

Problems of Marketing

Rural products are basically being sold out either in the near-by townships, mela or in different exhibitions. But it is not enough for the huge products. It is true that few products have made possible to get some dent into large markets, but majority are far way from such reality.

It has been found from different studies, report and news that social entrepreneurs in rural areas are financially poor and they face problem of selling their products. Small-scale rural producers in India are often limited by the markets within their reach. It has found that many SHGs and village industries though produced good products fail to sustain due to lack of marketing opportunities of their products and hence close down their units though there were enough demands and customers of those products. May be either it is not reaching to the customers or a market place where customers can get in touch of the products. It means there is an absence of link between the producers and the customers. It can not be said that the products item are less value-oriented. It has been observed in some cases, that though the rural producers / artisans / micro entrepreneurs are good in carrying out production/ manufacturing activities, they find it difficult to market their products sustainably on their own. Marketing has always been a problem for rural producers/ manufacturers. It means that products are in an isolated zone beyond the true customers. It has been already discussed above that now-a-days rural producers are making products which are in demand too. Specially, the food items are in heavy demand. Mr. Raghuvansh Prasad Singh (former Union Rural Development Minister, GOI) said that while the world was looking at the Indian market, there was no market for the rural products within the country.

Initiatives for Marketing

Small-scale rural producers in India are often limited by the markets within their reach. In the past, they have been unable to sell directly to urban consumers, and instead their products have been bought up by middlemen. The example of 'Gram Shree' or 'wealth of villages' exhibitions are important which have provided an urban marketplace for rural artisans to sell their products, at the same time receiving practical advice on marketing from experts. The organisers of the exhibition, the Council for the Advancement of People's Action and Rural Technology (CAPART) have also helped producers to negotiate contracts with large customers directly without going through wholesalers.

The initiative and efforts of Rural Business Hub (RBH) is a unique effort of the government considering the socio-political conditions of the country. RBH is a *Public-Private-Panchayat* partnership to improve the locally available resources and skills to produce goods that could be marketed nationally and internationally. It sought to bring village blocks into the commercial main stream through product and process development and to develop synergies with other rural schemes like the Bharat Nirman Pura. The local village panchayats or blocks would act as facilitators. According to Mr. Aiyar, RBHs would ensure easy access to market through branding, provide value addition products through technology inputs from experts and increase productivity by adding effective quality and cost management to dovetail with the centrally sponsored schemes. He also emphasised that rural industry would be successful if it was started with the consent of villagers and the Gram Sabha. The Government would also help to promote these industries through the RBH. Knowledge coupled with the involvement of locals would create an effective rural and urban marketing link.

On the other hand, Non-Government Organisations (NGOs) solely are playing very crucial roles in the process of development initiatives in the social sector all over the country. Government of India has been realised the critical role played by the NGOs and assigned them a place of prominence in implementation of developmental and impact-making programmes/activities. There are plethoras of examples of NGOs helping local people in setting up their enterprises. In the era of globalisation competition is increasing and the NGOs need to be more proactive in order to market rural products effectively.

A Case Study in Barak Valley of Assam

Barak Valley:

'Barak Valley' is the southernmost part of Assam in North-East India. Barak Valley is composed of three Districts, namely, Cachar District, Karimganj District and Hailakandi District.

Geographical Locations of the districts:

Cachar district is bounded on the north by Borail and Jayantia Hill ranges, on the south by the state of Mizoram, on the east by Manipur and on the west by sister districts of Karimganj and Hailakandi and also Bangladesh..

Kaimganj District is bounded on the north by Bangladesh and Cachar district, on the south Tripura, Mizorm on the East Hailakandi and on the West Bangladesh and Tripira.

Hailakandi district is bounded by River Barak and Cachar district in the North & East, Mizoram State in the South & East and Karimganj district in the west. The inter-state border is stretched over 76 KM in the south east.

Socio-economic condition of Barak Valley:-

The socio economic condition of Barak Valey remains backward with lack of major establishment in the valley and the developmental scenario of Barak Valley is not very bright. Geographical remoteness from the main part of the country coupled with poor communication and other instrumental facilities are the major factors behind the low level of development.

Three districts of the Valley at a Glance:

Subject	*Cachar*	*Karimgang*	*Hylakandi*
Area	37861.1 sqkm	1809 sqkm	1,32,700 Hcr (Forest Area 74115 Hcr)
Rural Population	10,96,161	934,126	4,98,787
Urban Population	1,19,224	73,850	44,085
Total Population	12,15,385	10,07,976	5,22,978
Major Language	Bengali	Bengali	Bengali
Occupation	Agriculture and Plantation, Cultivation, Fishing, Farming, Forestry, Oil and natural gas exploration.	Agriculture and Plantation, Cultivation, Fishing, Farming, Forestry, Oil and natural gas exploration.	Agriculture, Cultivation, Fishing, Farming, Forestry, Oil and natural gas exploration.

Raw materials Available	Mineral, Agro based materials, fruits (Banana, pineapple, betaluts etc), Bamboo, Oil and natural gas.	Mineral, Agro based materials, fruits (Banana, pineapple, betaluts etc), Sugarcane Bamboo, Oil and natural gas.	Mineral, Agro based materials, fruits (Banana, pineapple, betaluts etc), Oil and natural gas.

Study on Rural products and Problems in the Valley:

In Barak Valley, the rural products are being produced by mainly three categories of social entrepreneurs- Namely:

- SHGs
- Individual/ Family Entrepreneurship
- Small Cooperatives

A small study was conducted with the objectives of:

1. to know the types of products which are being produced at rural areas
2. to identify their source of finance
3. to study the problems, specially marketing problems

Sample and tools of data collection:

We interacted with 10 SHGs, 10 individual/family entrepreneurs and five small cooperatives. So it was total 25 samples from three groups. These samples are from 15 villages of six Panchayats from three districts (Valley). Snow ball sampling method was used to reach such selected categories of group.

An interview schedule was developed consisting of 20 questions considering the objectives. Statistical software SPSS was used to convert the raw data into meaningful information. 'Frequency distribution' and 'Cross Tabulation' was done to conclude on the basis of objectives.

Results and Discussions:

The Products of social entrepreneurs in this region are mainly made up of natural resources available at the area. The main raw materials are jute, bamboo, wood, mushroom, fruits (orange, pineapple, banana etc) and local fish. So majority of the rural products are based on such easy access of raw materials. The main products can be categorised as below.

1. Jute- bag
2. Carpet
3. Embroidery

4. Apparel Manufacturing
5. Various Dolls
6. Finished warm woolen products
7. Products made of cane and bamboo.
8. Fruit juice, Jam, Pickle & Papad
9. Mushroom based product
10. Sital Pati
11. Pottery and flower.
12. *Thela* and Rickshaw parts manufacturing
13. *Sidal* making (fish based)
14. *Agarbati* stick
15. Candle

Source of financial Support:

The table below shows that all SHGs (10) and all Cooperatives (five) are getting financial support directly from the bank, where as five out of 10 (50 per cent) Individual /family entrepreneurs are receiving financial assistance from the bank and two of them (20 per cent) are from the NGOs. Three entrepreneurs are not getting any support either from Bank or NGOs. They are self-dependent in that direction.

Category	*Source of financial Support*			*Formal Training*	
	Bank	*NGOs*	*No Support*	*Taken*	*Not Taken*
SHGs	10	—	—	10	—
Entrepreneurs	5	2	3	10	—
Cooperatives	5	—	—	4	1

The above table also depicts that all SHGs, all entrepreneurs and four out of five (80 per cent) cooperatives have undergone formal training for making their respective products. Small Industries Service Institute (SISI), Jana Siksha Sansthan (JSS), Rajib Gandhi Open Institute and other private institutions has provided such skill-developing training.

It was also revealed that the members of cooperatives and SHGs and the entrepreneurs themselves had some skill and knowledge of their respective product before taking any training. They expressed that they have been benefited by obtaining formal training.

Problems:

The social enterprises of this valley are facing different similar problems in running their business. All of them are facing the following problems:

- Poor Infrastructure and Communication
- Financial arrangements and support (enough finance, finance in time and availability in regular interval)
- Turbulent Political environment
- Lack of training and skill
- Disaster and natural calamities
- Inadequate market linkage
- Unemployment and migration
- International borders

Besides these, SHGs and Small Cooperatives face the problems of coordination and adjustments among the members.

According to the members, all three categories of enterprises, selling of products and rolling back the money is most vital in the business and they are facing acute crisis in this area. They have to earn, Repayment of loan (revolving fund) and again purchase of raw materials to run the business are solely dependent on the sell out of their products. Members have also felt that there is a need of receiving feedback of their product to make change according to the need of the people to satisfy the customer. None of them have used any formal methods for advertisement. One member said, "We don't have that much of sophistication to spend money on formal advertisement, though there is a need". In the study, it has been found that people are using the following methods for selling and marketing their products.

- Direct door to door selling in towns and sometimes at villages
- Through shops in near-by towns
- In mela, especially at the Gandhi mela, Netaji mela of the Valley and other different melas as per suitability of the products.
- Through different exhibitions
- Through selling stores (one Entrepreneurs and two Cooperatives have their own shops)

On the above methods they mainly depend for marketing of their products and results are much beyond their satisfaction. On many occasions it takes three to four time to sell the products than production. Such incidents forced them to take help and depend on middlemen to sustain their business with lot of discomfort and sometimes with exploitations and humiliations.

To allow local entrepreneurs to reach the emerging markets, there needs to be a significant thrust towards the development of a relationship between the rest of the country and people from this region. Such a long-term relationship will not only lead to the creation of a dependable marketplace for local artisans and entrepreneurs but will also help in creating employment opportunities among the masses

Concluding Discussions and Suggestions

If we go by opinion of the members of the rural enterprises, it can be said that economic conditions of the valley, the availability of raw materials and the opportunities of training have forced rural people to become an entrepreneur and to prepare home based products with the help of simple technology. Even getting financial support by the bank is also available, though there is difficulty. Moreover, there are demands of such products or on the other hand, people depend on those but there is a gap between the producer and the customers. There are also many instances, where SHGs have closed down after making it products for the first time and this is due to lack of marketing.

Suggestions:

Keeping the findings as well as limitations in mind we can suggest the following for the betterment of the marketing strategy of the rural products:-

First of all, The Government will have to facilitate an ecosystem where business practices can occur smoothly and without hassle for the social entrepreneurs. Despite several attempts by the Government and planning commission to enhance the rural economy and business, the current strategy has led to a distribution oriented, politically led economic process and not the efficiency led process envisioned.

Secondly, Panchayati Raj Institutions (PRIs) should play the prime role in this direction. The involvement of PRIs so far is not up to the mark as it should be. Gram panchayat (GP) should play the leading role in this direction as it will be closer to the producers and their problems could be assessed. Anchalik Pachayats (Block level) and Zilla Parishad will act on the basis of the need identified by the Gram Panchayat. So far GPs' role is very negligible as expressed by the respondents. So the responsibility of looking after the promotion of social entrepreneurs in this region which is one of the prime sources of income generation should be entrusted with the Panchayat.

NGOs as well as professional social workers who are playing role in formation of social enterprises especially, SHGs and financing the rural producers should look after the marketing part of these products. They can play a facilitator's role to carry the products to the different shops in market, arrange exhibitions, special *melas*, expos, and making advertisement about the products in various camps they are organising. The strategy of social marketing could be utilised for the rural products.

With the efforts of formation of social enterprises and financing the entrepreneurs, steps should be taken by the responsible bodies for the promotion of training (the integral and essential part of such business) which is somehow not up to the mark. So, more emphasis should be made for providing training for skill and knowledge development. Knowledge related to marketing especially regarding the opportunities and possibilities of the need and sells of their products should be imparted through such trainings.

There are few examples of market-oriented initiatives in the north-east region. For example, the work of *Pranjal Baruah* and *Rakhee Choudhary.* Pranjal's Mushroom Development Foundation works closely with mushroom farmers in Assam, putting them in control of their produce through his land-to-lab strategies, training and support, thereby creating 'mushroom entrepreneurs.' Not only is he creating livelihood opportunities for thousands of unemployed youth and landless farmers in Assam, he is also developing a whole new market for mushroom consumption.

Similarly, Rakhee works closely with Assamese women, revitalising the weaving industry in the region. With weaving being the second largest economic activity in Assam, she organises women weavers into cooperatives, connecting them directly to the market. She builds entrepreneurial skills in these women, and encourages them to deliver quality products to the market. The weaver entrepreneurs she has trained then train others, thus creating groups of entrepreneurs across the region. Thus, she also advances an industry that has great cultural significance for the people of the North East.

Therefore, the current need is to evaluate these models through full-fledged research by the professionals to study the existing products, conditions of the producers (skill, availability of raw materials, finance etc.) and problems and opportunities of social enterprises and accordingly and see how they can be made relevant for all eight states of the North-east. By bringing all the stakeholders together and evolving a comprehensive road map for development, the North-east can become the new hub for social enterprise in the country.

References

- Desai, V. (1983), *Organisations and Management of Small Scale Industries*, Himalay Publishing House, Mumbai.,
- Dutta, S. (2008), Institutional Support for Women Entrepreneurship, in *Women Speak*, by Ghosh, B. and Dutta,S. (Ed.), Mittal Publications, New Delhi.

- Dutta, S. (2002) Poverty Alleviation Programme in India: A Realistic Appraisal, *Man and Development*, Vol. XXIV (2).
- Dutta, S. (2006), *Democratic Decentralisation and Community Development Programme in India,* paper presented at the ICSD Conference in June 2006, in Warsaw, Poland.
- Narasaiah, M.L. and Margaret B.D. (1999), *Small Scale Industry*, Deep Deep Publication, New Delhi.
- Rao, S.L. (1989), Innovative Marketing Strategies: Small Enterprises Fight Large Established Companies, *Economic and Political Weekly*, August 26, pp.127-130.
- www.cachar.gov.in.
- www.silchar.com.
- http://articles.economictimes.indiatimes.com/2008-12-15/news/27731509_1_incense-sticks-young-entrepreneurs-unit.
- http://india.ashoka.org/changing-face-north-east-india.
- http://www.intellecap.com/sites/default/files/publications/GIZ_North_East_LR_2.pdf.

9

Role of Instagram in Social Media Marketing

Gesty Ernestivita

Abstract

Businessmen claimed to be easier to market its products through Instagram. Instagram is an online mobile photo sharing, video sharing and social networking service that enable its users to take pictures and videos, and share them on a variety of social networking platforms. The purpose of Instagram marketing is to build community, to create a series of connected, creating communication, credibility, sell, increasing followers that mean increasing customers also. There are some advantages in doing Instagram marketing activities, like: increased engangement, building trust and personality, increase in traffic, gaining a competitive advantage, reaching target market, and free advertising. Instagram Marketing has the following ways to increase number of followers: publish the product, use hastag, follow and followback the customer, link with another social media, and join in SFS (Shoutout for Shoutout).

Keywords: *Instagram, Social Media Marketing*

Introduction

In the current modern society, Social Media channels are commonly used in order to connect people together throughout the world using the Internet. Whether it is through social networks, forums, blogs or media sharing websites, people can now have a conversation online, also called interactive dialogue, with anybody and on any subject, permitting them to share their experiences and valuable information. Looking on a business perspective, it goes without saying that Social Media Marketing has offered a large variety of new opportunities for companies to promote their brand, products and services. One of the social marketing with largest users is Instagram. Instagram has quickly become one of the web's top photo sharing services. After six month launch, the company passed two millions user marks and announced the launch of their API. Instagram adding 130,000 registered users per week. Instagram's 2.2 million users upload 3.6 million new photos per week, means about 6 photos per second. The chart below shows weekly new user additions since Instagram's launch.

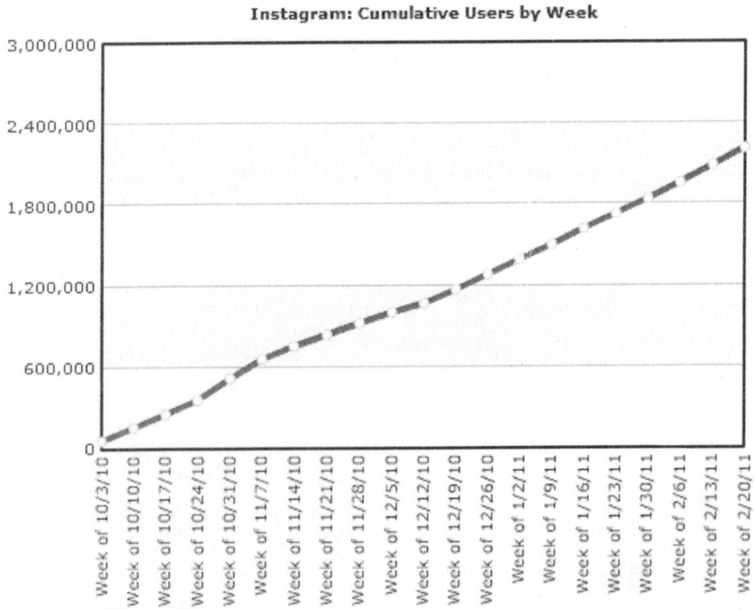

Source : RJ Metrics

The fact about the huge number of users, Instagram become one of the most favourite social media which is used by online bussiness people as a media for online marketing.

Social Media

Social Media is enganging with consumers online. According to Wikipedia, social media is internet based tools for sharing and discussing information among human beings. Social media is all about networking and networking in a way that espouses trust among parties and communities involved. Any website which allows user to share their content, opinions, views and encourages interaction and comunity building can be classified as a social media. Some popular social media sites are: Facebook, YouTube, Twitter, Pinterest, and Instagram.

The meaning of term 'social media' can be derived from two words which constitute it. Media generally refers to advertising and the communication of ideas or information through publications/channels. Social implies the interaction of individuals within a group or community. Taken together, social media simply refers to communication of individuals through specific medium or tool. Wikipedia has a general definition of term: Social Media is the democratisation of information, transforming people from content readers into content publishers. It is the shift from a broadcast mechanis to a many to many model, rooted in conversations between authors, people, and peers. Social media uses the "wisdom of crowds" to connect information in a collaborative manner. Social media can take many different forms, including internet forums, message boards, weblogs, wikis, podcast, pictures, and video. social media are media for social interaction, using highly accessible and scalable publishing techniques. Social media used web-based technologies to turn communication onto interactive dialogues (Sisira Neti, 2011).

Evans (2008:37) defines social media as "participatory online media where news, photos, videos and podcasts are made available via social media web sites via submission and are normally accompanied by a voting process to make via media items become more popular". Social media are thus characterised by the content trail they leave on social media sites and also by the voting process that represents the perceptions of the users of particular content. Another definition is the one formulated by Daugherty, Eastin and Bright (2008:1), who refer to social media as "user generated content created or produced by the general public rather than by paid professionals and primarily distributed on the Internet". Social media are unique in that they are 'media rich' and empower users to share their opinions, insights, experiences, content and contacts with their friends and family through multiple content forms. Similar to multimedia, social media allow for multiple content forms such as text, audio, still images, animation, video and other interactivity content forms. At the same time, users are able to learn more about favourite products and brands (Charton, 2007). Social media further focus on messaging while having huge potential to distribute content to a large number of people (Social networking goes mobile, 2007).

Social media are not a new phenomenon, but popular social network sites such as Facebook, MySpace and Twitter have made social networking more accessible to the masses. Currently, thousands of sites are related to social media. According to the social comparison theory developed by Festinger (1954), human beings compare their opinions and abilities with others because of a drive to evaluate themselves. This theory reinforces the perception that people in general enjoy social networking because of a need to look externally to assess and judge their own opinions and to see how they compare to the online group. Later work on the social comparison theory includes the suggestion that people search for other people with whom to compare themselves in order to validate themselves. In the absence of real comparison, for instance, in a virtual reality context, people are tempted to construct a social reality in which they are the 'star' players (Suls and Wheeler, 2000:34).

Social Media Marketing

Traditional marketing messages alone are no longer enough to build an organisation's brand and organisations therefore now also consider using social media. There are numerous definitions of social marketing. According to Evans (2008:13), social media marketing is an application of social media in that it uses natural conversation strategically to benefit the organisation. Cosme (2008) explains social media marketing as "establishing relationships between companies and current and/or potential customers, and tapping into the power of peer-to-peer influence". The nature of social media provides a unique opportunity to complement an organisation's traditional marketing activities along with other new media opportunities. It is therefore an extension of online marketing but focuses more on social media content and communities (Cosme, 2008). Social media marketing provides new ways for organisations to interact with their target audience and to encourage customers to spread the message for the brand (Charton, 2007). It furthermore creates a 'richer' understanding of customers' needs by 'tapping into customers' intelligence' through having access to their conversations (Mullins, 2008).

According to Wikipedia, Social Media Marketing is the process of gaining website traffic or attention trough social media sites (Facebook, Twitter, Pinterest, Path, Instagram, Etc). Social media marketing programs usually center on efforts to create content that attracts attention and encourages readers to share it accross their social networks. The resulting electronic word of mouth refers to any statement consumers share via internet (e.g., web sites, social networks, instant message, news feeds) about an event, product, service, brand or company. When the underlying message spreads from user to user and presumably resonates because it appears to come from a trusted, third-party source, as opposed to the brand or company itself, this form of marketing result in earned media rather than paid media.

Social Media Marketing is marketing that focuses on people, not products (Diamond, 2008). The products can be presented by the company with as many qualitative features and promotional tools as possible, but what really matters is the comments and appreciations left by the customers. People provide the content, and this is the reason why Social Media Marketing is so scary and challenging for marketers. They do not control the marketing content anymore. Negative word-of-mouth can be spread worldwide in a couple of minutes only. With the explosion of Internet-based messages transmitted through the Social Media, they are now a main factor in influencing many aspects of consumer behaviour, such as awareness, consideration, information gathering, opinions, attitudes, purchasing decisions and post-purchase evaluation. International marketers need to recognise the power and critical nature of the conversations being hold by consumers using Social Media. Consequently, the ability of influencing the crowd effectively is the main quality needed by the marketing team (Evans, 2008).

Also, what is important about Social Media Marketing is that marketer can listen, track and measure what is shared on the Social Media Sites in order to improve the offered message and adapt it more to the customers' needs. Thanks to the Social Media analytics and metrics available, the impact of Social Media on a company's marketing strategy can be measured and evaluated relatively easily.

Instagram Marketing

Nowadays, online business people promote their product not only by content article but also use pictures as marketing media. The growth of digital technology gets faster and makes online business people easier to create high quality picture to promote their products. one of it of course to optimise the role of Instagram which is become one of the most popular platforms that will enable you to leverage the power of this shift and also one of the best and most used photo sharing platforms with over 150 million users.

Instagram is an online mobile photo sharing, video sharing, and social networking services that enable its users to take pictures and videos, and share them on a variety of social networking platforms, such as Facebook, Twitter, Tumblr, and Flickr. A distinctive feature is that it confines photos to a square shape, similar to Kodak Instamatic and Polaroid images. Users can also apply digital filters to their images. The maximum duration of video is 15seconds. Instagram added hastag feature to help users discover both photographs and each other. Instagram encourages users to make tags both specific and relevant, rather than tagging generic word like "photo" to make photographs stand out and attract like-minded Instagram users. There are over 55 million photos shared on Instagram everyday which is another great reason why business needs to utilise this platform.

There are some reasons why Instagram can generate for bussiness, and these are the key benefits of using Instagram:

1. *Increased Engagement*

Depending on the quality of the post, branded updates on Facebook and Twitter are sometimes overlooked by the user. However this isn't true for Instagram users; having an active Instagram account with useful and interesting content can earn you crazy levels of engagement with your audience. Latest study Forrester found that Instagram content generates 58 times more engagement per follower than Facebook and 120 times more than Twitter.

2. *Building Trust And Personality*

With branded content being more popular for generating engagement, one of the key benefits of Instagram is that it can help you build trust. People buy from people and Instagram will help you to create that emotional connection with your audience. The great thing here is that it allows you to share the day-to-day experiences of your business in an informal and casual way therefore giving a personal feel to your business. Behind the scene photos and employee images tend to rank well on Instagram, especially if you're a specific service provider. Such photos can make your company more attractive and trustworthy which in turn can have a positive effect on your bottom line.

3. *Increase In Traffic*

Although you can not add clickable links to every Instagram update you publish, Instagram can be a powerful source of traffic. Plus with the higher levels of engagement than on Facebook and Twitter, creating and maintaining a strong profile could be hugely beneficial for your site's visibility.

4. *Gaining A Competitive Advantage*

There is still far less competition on Instagram than on Facebook or Twitter. An American Express survey showed that only 2 per cent of small businesses are currently embracing Instagram, giving them an advantage over their competitors. Plus the businesses that incorporate Instagram into their marketing strategy will more likely reach their target audience far easier than with Facebook or Twitter where the competition is much bigger.

5. *Reaching Target Market*

If you're targeting people born from 1980 to the early 1990s (the so called millennial) then Instagram is the place to be as over 37 per cent of people in this age group use Instagram (Source: JennsTrends) So if you want to reach and connect with the under 30 crowd you should definitely create an Instagram account. Having said that, Instagram doesn't only work for youth-focused brands like Red Bull, brands like Ford and General Electric are gaining a great level on engagement on their Instagram profiles.

6. *Free Advertising*

The great thing about Instagram is free advertising. You can showcase your products and services in action which generates huge exposure. It gives you a chance to show off more of what you have to offer.

There are some ways to increase the number of customer by using Instagram:

1. Publish the products, Instagram is the best mobile application to publish best quality picture in a second. Online business people can use the advantage of Instagram to publish their product trough good picture. The picture should be interesting and creative, because the best quality picture will make the customers visit regularly the Instagram account.
2. Use hastag, the using of hastag not only in Twiter and Pinterest. Instagram also used hastag. This features make Instagram a powerful tool for enganging with people. Hastag is an excellent way to follow conversatiobs within your niche and discover customers who'd be interested with certain brand. In business, the using of hastag in every picture caption can help buyer to search product through search result and use many hastag as possible because this will help to identify Instagram influencers within your online shop and begin growing your Instagram follower.
3. Follow and follow back the customer Instagram account, do marketing research through email or another social media of your customer to search whether they have Instagram account or not. If your customers have Instagram account, just follow them. This strategy is one of the ways to promote your Instagram business account and increase the number of follower. Do not forget to follow back the customer who follow your business account, this strategy will also make the customer respect and buy or rebuy your product.
4. Link your Instagram account with another media social like Facebook, Twitter, Pinterest, Flickr and as many as social media you have.
5. Join SFS (Shoutout for Shoutout), known in early 2013 and booming in April 2014, it is the way how online bussiness people promote each other account on Instagram especially for online shop. Usually, if a seller has different product they promote other seller product in their account and conversely. SFS is an effective and free way to increase

the number of followers, we can promote our product in other account by joining SFS member.

Conclusion

There are six benefits by using Instagram as Social Media marketing: increased engangement, building trust and personality, increase in traffic, gaining a competitive advantage, reaching target market, free advertising.

There are some ways to increase the number of costumers or followers in Instagram: publish the products, use hastag, follow and followback the customer, link with another social media, join SFS (Shoutout for Shoutout).

Nowadays, Instagram is a social media with large number of users around the world, about 2.2 million users. Because of this reason Instagram is the best Social Media which can be used as a media to promote products.

For Social Media Marketing, Instagram can be used as a media to share their photo products, testimonial to build trust, and promote their shop by using hastag or SFS (Shoutout for Shoutout) and another advatage. For costumers, Instagram offers various products from many trusted online shops account so its make you easily find what products you need in various price and quality and it is also can be used as a means to get to know more of the products offered by the company events and promotions offered by the company to its customers.

References

- Assaad, Waad. Gomez, Jorge Marx. (2011). *Social Network in Marketing (Social Media Marketing) Opportunities and Risks*. International Journal of Managing Public Sector Information and Communication Technologies Vol.2, No.1. Germany: Oldenburg.
- Cahyono, Darmawan Budi. (2013). *Penggunaan Facebook Sebagai Media Pemasaran Online*. Surabaya: Universitas Katolik Widya Mandala.
- Diamond, S. (2008), *Web Marketing for Small Businesses: 7 Steps to Explosive Business Growth*, Sourcebooks Inc., Illinois.
- Evans, D. (2008). *Social media marketing: an hour a day*. London: Wiley.
- Evans, M., Wedande, G., Ralston, L. and Van't Hul, S. (2001). *Consumer interaction in the online era: some qualitative insights*. Qualitative Market Research: An International Journal, 4, (3), 150159.
- Festinger, L. (1954). *A theory of social comparison processes*. Human Relations, 7, (2), 117- 140.

- Neti, Sisira. (2011). *Social Media and Its Role in Marketing.* International Journal of Enterprise Computing and Bussiness Systems ISSN, Vol 1 Issue 2.
- Suls, J. and Wheeler, L. (Eds). (2000). *Handbook of social comparison: theory and research.* New York: Plenum.
- TC du Plessis. (2010). *Theoritical Guideliness for Social Media Marketing Communication.* Communicare: Volume 29.
- Charton, D. (2007). *Why social networking matters for SA marketers.* Retrieved March 25, 2009, from http://www.marketingweb.co.za.
- Cosme, G. (2008). *Social media: an introductory guide for your business, organisation or agency.* Retrieved March 3, 2008. From http://www.ginocosme.com/downloads/Introductionto-Social-Media.pdf.
- Koozai. (2014). *6 Bussiness Benefits Using Instagram.* Retrieved February 20, 2015. From: http://www.koozai.com/blog/social-media/6-key-benefits-using-Instagram-business/
- Mullins, J. (2008). *Effective Marketing for Web 2.0.* Retrieved February 20, 2015. From: http://www. bizcommunity.com.
- Social networking goes mobile. (2007). Retrieved February 20, 2015. From: http://www.marketingweb. co.za.
- UKM, Bisnis. (2013). *Tips Sukses Menggaet Konsumen Melalui Instagram.* Retrieved February 20, 2015. From: http://bisnisukm.com/tips-sukses-menggaet-konsumen-melalui-Instagram.html.

10

Sustainable Growth in VUCA Times: HR Perspective

Anu Singh Lather & Shilpa Jain

Abstract

This paper will be analysing the importance of sustainable growth for an organisation in today's world and the impact VUCA components have on the same. In order to achieve sustainable growth within the organisational boundaries a structure and culture that incorporates Employee Engagement, which would ensure a close connect between employees. The goal of Employee Engagement can be achieved by Talent Management (Retaining and developing the talent pool of the company), Succession Planning (Preparing employees to fit into higher and more demanding positions) and finally transforming Top Management to Top Leaders by keeping them motivated. It also becomes significant in this regard to add and expand the scope of a few processes already being followed in most firms. Behavioural Assessment for instance, should be used even after the recruitment stage to study the behavioural competencies of employees. Reinforcement and increasing the impact of team building exercises is of value in this respect. Lastly the creation of a spirit of Interpersonal Sensitivity among the organisation members would inaugurate a culture devoid of internal conflicts, full of trust and cooperation in the company. The final result is a workplace where employees Accept each other despite the prevailing differences, Appreciate each other for their skills and qualities, Adapt to one another and finally Accelerate each other's as well as the organisation's performance.

Key Words: *Sustainable Growth, VUCA.*

Sustainable Growth can be described as a growth rate an organisation can achieve, realistically without facing difficulties. It forms a basis for fundamental management activities and increases the firm's credibility which in turn leads to higher negotiating powers with financial partners. Apart from this, the organisation can be sure of forming a strong and favourable brand image, making it an employer of choice. Sustainable growth is hence not just an added advantage, but an indispensable prerequisite for an organisation to define as well as secure its future success.

But strategic leaders are frustrated today because of anticipation of what will happen next have became a challenge. The volatility and speed of change is so high that it seems like you are thrown in turbulent waters. In fact, the last decade was so chaotic that in its cover story, *Time* magazine labeled it "the decade from hell." This work environment is termed as VUCA (**Volatility, Uncertainty, Complexity, Ambiguity**)" a term coined by US Army War College as a shorthand notation for the ever evolving, fast changing and uncertain scenario of global business.

Volatility	*Uncertainity*	*Complexity*	*Ambiguity*
•The ripeness for explosive change. The dramatically escalating rate and speed of change. •The associated risks of instability and flux. •It impacts the organization by causing fear, risk-aversion, and "back-to-basics" reactions.	• Prediction is impossible. Lack of clarity about current and future outcomes. • Uncertainity causes paralysis through a tendency to invest excessive-and futile-efforts on data analysis.	• The intricate relationship of systems and their parts. • Complexity causes a desire to look for scapegoats or black and white solutions that are usually erroneous.	• Complexity causes a desire to look for scapegoats or black and white solutions that are usually erroneous. • Abiguity induces doubt, distrust and hesitancy, and impedes decision making and change

Figure 1: Showing the Explanation of VUCA work environment

Source: http://www.zeislerassociates.com/VUCA.html

In VUCA environment, there are numerous, faster, and impactful changes which leave the practices designed for predictable times ineffective. So the BIG question and challenge for human resource managers becomes, "how do you effectively hire, develop, place, and retain individuals and leaders in the volatile environment where literally everything changes in months rather than years?"

In order to maintain a sustainable growth rate from the human resource perspective, an organisation needs to set up a framework where there is

Employee Engagement. Employee engagement would ensure that all the members of the organisation are connected with each other just like they would be in a family. The aim hence, is to establish a **behavioural, cognitive and affective** connect among not only the management and the lower level staff, but also within staff functioning at the same level of the firm. An organisation that comprises employee engagement would automatically not only be able to achieve higher productivity, but also the development of an organisational culture wherein there are significantly less conflicts and employees are not eager to leave the organisation.

A key concept that comes into play when the establishment of a close knit firm is talked about is "**Talent Management**". Talent Management, as defined by Derek Stockley is "A conscious, deliberate approach undertaken to attract, develop and retain people with the aptitude and abilities to meet current and future organisational needs." Talent management is the management and creation of best talent within the organisation in order to succeed in this hypercompetitive business world. Best of the talent is kept within the organisation and the rest of the talent is always developing in an efficient manner. Talent management solves various purposes for a firm. It ensures the retention of top talent, so that it does not lose out to its competitors. It also assists in making early and better professional development decisions. Organisations can assess on the basis of value creation and talent, which employees it should bet its resources on. A proper analysis of each individual's skill set ensures that the "Right person is doing the Right job".

Multinational organisations across the world are adopting talent management strategies. Facebook, for instance views employees as a high value asset. It just doesn't provide incentives, but premium quality incentives, such as exquisite food to its employees. Indian Corporations are also adopting these varied talent management strategies to come at par with their global counterparts. Tata Consultancy Services for example implements certain talent management practices such as Investment into learning and development to build their skills and competence; Career planning; employee engagement and work culture with an open door policy.

A comparative study on talent management practices adopted by US companies and Indian companies has however revealed that even the best of Indian companies are not engaging in significant talent management strategies. These are Collaboration and Innovation, Transparency and Openness, Unique Problem Solving Practices, Choice of project, Flexi Working Hours, Work from Home and Work Life Balance.

Another key ingredient in building up a competent and efficient organisational culture, devoid of VUCA elements, is "**Succession Planning**". Succession Planning is a systematic and effective way to develop talent for the top level of management. It is basically a method by which employees functioning at a lower level become prepared to replace someone at the succeeding level. This is usually undertaken for key positions in the firm. Succession planning ensures that crucial positions of the organisations are filled by competent individuals who not only have the requisite skill sets but also a developed self which is competent enough to satisfy the given role. It also aids the development of a culture where employees trust the top management and are convinced that their growth is on the organisational agenda. Conflicts relating to "Why or how" someone else got chosen to occupy a given position are avoided this way. As a consequence of all this, a Symbiotic relationship is established in the company.

To survive in a VUCA world, organisations should not only hire and develop agile leaders but also create an **organisational culture** that rewards innovation, agile behaviour, and calculated risk-taking. Performance management systems should reflect VUCA Prime values of Vision, Understanding, Clarity and Agility. A key to the best rewards systems in a VUCA environment is to not be rigid and to offer successful leaders rewards that appeal to them the most—in other words, be adaptable and agile. The organisational culture that promotes and rewards agile leaders will begin to perpetuate itself and attract and retain the type of innovative and agile talent that businesses today are seeking. It will also provide businesses a competitive advantage in our ever-changing global marketplace—which is the ultimate VUCA environment (Lawerence, 2013). For example Olam a global supply chain managing organisation has seen its organisation double in size every three years and attributes that growth in large part to the entrepreneurial abilities of a select cadre of managers known as the global assignee talent (GAT) pool. Other important factors in its rapid organisational growth have been creating a coaching culture and encouraging the use of peer-to-peer support to encourage debate around business challenges. Ernst and Young have developed a strong coaching culture to improve performance and differentiate itself from its business rivals in Asia.

In any given organisation, there is a significant focus on the building up of a motivational spirit among the employees; however the need of the hour is to additively build up a motivated top management. The requirement is to bring about this transformation: "**Top Management Top Leaders**". It is a given that employees envision their future in their managers and get inspired by them. However there are fewer inspirations available to top level managers. It is therefore important to strike the correct chord in order to give them what they would want by assessing their needs. MSSL (Motherson Sumi Systems Ltd), an Indian organisation that is a leading manufacturer of Auto ancillary parts adopts a policy of keeping their management "**Absolutely Pampered**". The idea is not to just give them what they need, but what they can dream of. From luxury gift items to fully sponsored luxurious trips across the globe, the firm goes that extra mile to ensure that their crucial and best talent stays with them. Apart from material comforts and world class experiences they also ensure their managers get enough decision making powers. All these factors impart managers with a greater will to excel in their work and exceed in what is expected from them. The organisation developed is hence holistically enthusiastic to work with zeal.

At the organisational level, it is imperative to lower attrition rates and conflicts within the organisation in order to attain sustainable growth. The reason for that is that with every employee who leaves the organisation, leaves a great amount of talent and potential performance. The cycle continues and with a high attrition rate the organisation is back to its original position. The idea is to improvise and extending a few processes already implemented in the organisation.

Behavioural Assessment that is done at the recruitment stage with the agenda of screening potential employees is an effective process, but it must be extended to the post recruitment stage as well to screen employees on behavioural competencies required in future managers. The absence of these competencies should be checked by undertaking soft skills and behavioural training sessions. Currently firms are adopting team building exercises in order to improve communication, establish interdependence and trust, but what is noteworthy is that these exercises must not be competitive and employees are not made to work against each other but with each other. It is of equal substance that while these programs start with a lot of gusto, their impact on employees is questionable. Undertaking these sessions requires time, effort and cost. If the results do not last for a relevant time, they are of no use. Hence there must be endeavours to reinforce the same skills into them from time to time to have a continuous impact. Apart from team building exercises and behavioural assessments, organisations must undertake in-depth, extensive and ongoing training programs that assist employees in developing an '**Interpersonal Sensitivity**' for each other.

The goal of this pursuit is to make employees understand each other in an efficient manner, and to perceive their views, opinions, competencies in a more thoughtful way. A family system is the best example for comprehending the concept of interpersonal sensitivity. All members are cherished for their qualities but none is ridiculed for faults or failures. There is a constant attempt by one member to help the other to nurture and develop. There is no spirit of unhealthy or harmful competition which is what makes functioning so smooth. With this view, the **5 A's** that are needed to develop among the organisation's employees are : **Accept** (The thought to accept one another despite differences that are inherent or self created), **Appreciate** (The spirit to recognise one another and respect one another despite those accepted differences), **Adapt** (To mould oneself to adjust according to the differences prevailing with other employees in order to FIT perfectly in the organisation), **Accelerate** (To assist each other in developing as individuals and progressing in their careers, such that the organisational growth is boosted) and finally to **Accomplish** (To achieve not only the organisational goals but the goal of being a true human being that generate the feeling of accomplishment.

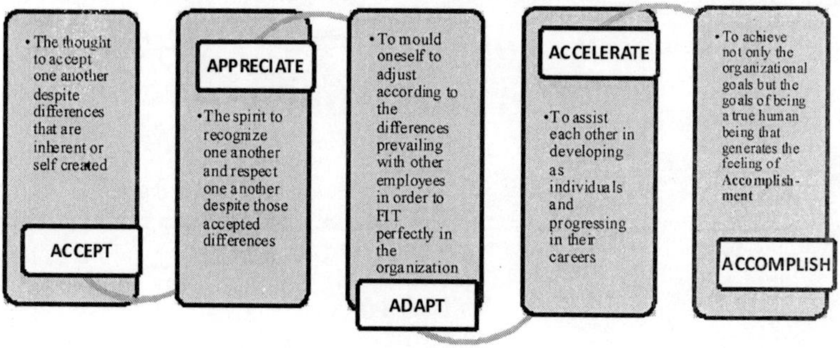

References

- Ashton, C., and Morton, L. (2005). Managing Talent for Competitive Advantage: Taking a systematic Approach to Talent Management. *Strategic HR Review*, *4* (5), 28-31.
- Berger, L., and Berger, D. (2004). *The Talent Management Handbook.* New York.
- Bhatnagar, J. (2007). Talent management strategy of employee engagement in Indian ITES employees: key to retention. *Employee relations*, *29* (6), 640-663.
- Coulson-Thomas, C. J (2012) *Talent Management 2, a quicker and more cost-effective route to the high performance organisation*, Policy Publications, Peterborough.
- Lawerence, K. (2013). Developing Leaders in VUCA environment. UNC Executive Development, 2013.
- Oladapo, V. (2014). The Impact Of Talent Management On Retention. *Journal of Business Studies, 5* (3).

Acknowledgement: Special thanks to Prarthana Wadhwa MBA IInd year Student, University School of Management Studies, Guru Gobind Singh Indraprastha University for her dedicated effort towards compilation of ideas of authors.

11

VISTA: An Innovative and Integrated Teaching Model

Amarjeet Kaur Malhotra

Abstract

The objective of this study is to examine the effect of an integrated teaching approach that combines technology, case studies, industrial visits and traditional chalk and talk method. This study was conducted in United States of America for a course on Managerial Accounting. The study introduces a teaching model named ***'VISTA'.*** *This model was tested with the help of experiments carried over two groups namely treatment and controlled groups. The performance of the treatment group, who were taught using this model VISTA was compared with the performance of a control group who were taught using only traditional methods. A Pre-test and a post-test were conducted on the experimental group while the control group had only a post-test. A Mann-Whitney test was used to ensure homogeneity and also to assess the level of the groups' prior knowledge. The proposed model has been tested by the author and her colleague independently and has proved very effective in both the cases. The study concludes that an integrated teaching model works better than depending either too much on technology or using only chalk and talk pedagogy.*

Key Words: *Teaching Pedagogy, Integrated Approach, VISTA Model, Chalk and Talk Method.*

Introduction

There have been many calls, especially in the United States, to improve the teaching of accounting since teaching is too much focused on only financial accounting rules and entry level jobs. Many challenges in effective teaching of accounting have been identified in different studies and have been used here as basis for problem identification. Accounting is often regarded as one of the tough subjects for students in universities, especially at undergraduate level. The teaching/learning process of this subject demands high attention on the part of faculty/instructors combined with hard work on the part of students every semester (Myint Thein, 2006). Lack of industry/work exposure of students to being able to correlate and connect with discussion is the biggest challenge against effective learning. Another problem with teaching of managerial accounting is that most of the students take managerial accounting before cost accounting courses probably due to curriculum design. Historically speaking, management accounting developed from cost accounting only in late 1940s which was the starting point of introduction to management accounting in business schools' curricula to the present day (Boer, Germain B., 2000). Even if the students have learned financial accounting and some basic cost accounting, the problem is that the students tend to forget them at the time they take managerial accounting course (Adams at el., 1999).

Not only have this, for many years the methods used to teach accounting been criticised. There have been numerous calls to incorporate real-life work skills rather than emphasising the memorisation of technical rules (Elliott, 1991; Maher, 2000; Boer, 2000; Burnett, 2003; Dillon, 2004; Kiger, 2004). This criticism propelled accounting educators/researchers to carry action research to test alternative approaches to the accounting teaching. A good number of researches emphasised upon the intensive use of technology, whereas another good number still supports only the traditional chalk and talk method. Myint (2006) concluded that there is always a flux over the use and limitations of computer-assisted system in class rooms. This is also evaluated in contrast to traditional chalk and talk method of teaching.

An intensive literature review reveals that unfamiliarity with Practical world; non-motivating/ stimulating teaching pedagogy; lack of required background knowledge of financial and cost Accounting; memory retention, uncertainty about majors; faulty curriculum design; high standards of evaluation; lack of interest or competency of teacher are the biggest challenges for effective learning in accounting. Of all the challenges Instead, this paper will focus on **pedagogy part** and related matters.

The remainder of this paper is organised in five sections. Section 2 talks about the related literature review. Section 3 describes the model VISTA and the learning activities used. Section 4 explains the research method used for this study followed by section 5 on Results and discussion. Finally, conclusions of the study and suggestions for future work are presented in Section 6.

Literature Review

Researchers in accounting education have examined and reported the use of many distinct techniques. Paisey and Paisey (2004) presented a comprehensive analysis of accounting education research which was published between 1992 and 2001. They concluded that more attention should be paid to the effect of instructional strategies, and the specific educational context within which those strategies were implemented, on learning outcomes. It was concluded by Sharma (1997) that altering accounting students' learning approaches would require altering the learning context to one that encourages understanding rather than reproduction of information. Leveson (1999), and Lancaster and Strand (2001) reported positive student responses, but they did not find significant difference in student performance when they experimented with forms of the cooperative learning format in teaching accounting courses. Possible explanations of these results could be deficiencies in the method of performance assessment, the special nature of the accounting courses, and lack of instructor/faculty training in using active learning techniques. Watson *et al.* (2003) argued that the use of technology in the assessment of student learning remains important area for future accounting education research while addressing the impact of educational technology on accounting students' performance.

Results from experiments with the use of various forms of educational technology in teaching accounting courses seem to indicate that accounting students have a positive attitude towards the use of technology and that using computer technology, at the minimum, will not harm their academic performance (Basile and D'Aquila, 2002; Dowling *et .al.*, 2003; De Lange *et. al.*, 2003; Fry and Love, 2004; and Kalbers and Rosner, 2003).

According to Fry and Love (2004) there is a need for the accounting instructors to reflect on their teaching strategies when using a Virtual Learning Environment if the benefits expected are to be realised. Kalbers and Rosner (2003) went a step further when they concluded that the real benefits of integrating modern technology in teaching may not be easy to measure over the short term. On the integration of active learning techniques with technology, Rainsbury and Malcolm's (2003) analysis revealed that students' reactions were positive to such techniques. They also reported that students with a non-

English background participated more when using an electronic discussion board. Boland *et al.* (2004) concluded that students who speak English as a second language prefer a computer-assisted learning environment. Leveson (1999), Lancaster and Strand (2001) experimented with different forms of the cooperative learning methods in teaching accounting courses and reported a positive response by students, but no significant difference in student performance. This was probably because of lack of effective evaluation criterion.

Myint Thein (2006) concluded that the use of multi-media equipment is attractive and effective to some extent but it should not jeopardise the initiative of instructor and students as well as face to face interactive teaching/ learning process. There are a number of studies that support multi-media or computer-assisted teaching over traditional teaching (Jensen and Sandlin 1992, Alavi 1994, etc).

Beets and Lobingler (2001) conducted an experiment and concluded that students in their project performed no differently on examinations and daily quizzes among different pedagogical approaches of chalkboard and computer projected software. Researches also indicates that using technology does not detract from student performance (Sherrod *et al.*, 2000; Becker and Haugen, 2004; Moss *et al.*, 2003) and that students' reactions to it are positive (Efaw *et al.*, 2004).

Objectives of the Study

The author believes that combining various techniques of active learning with the available educational technology to teach management accounting courses in a more coherent manner will provide students with a better opportunity to acquire and retain the accounting knowledge, and gain the analytical and problem solving skills expected from accounting graduates. This study examines the effects of such an integrated teaching approach on students' performance. The author call this approach as "Integrated Teaching Approach" which aims:

To examine the effect of proposed teaching model named VISTA that combines active learning activities, traditional chalk and talk method with that of modern educational technology (such as Blackboard and laptop computers) on student performance.

Research Method

This study is based on experimental style. The experimental design involved a treatment group and a control group which were selected from the academic year 2014. The groups were similar in terms of the mean class size, student GPA, gender, and English language skills. The control group received the traditional approach (TA) only, while the treatment group received the integrated approach (IA). The TA involved one way instructor-centered teaching using chalk and talk method. The IA combined various active learning activities with the use of modern educational technology. This learning environment was used for the treatment group only for the complete course material.

Data was collected that indicated student performance (i.e., test results). The class tests, marked out of 10, were used as indicators of student performance throughout the experiment. The test results of each test for the treatment group and control group were collected separately and then used for comparison. The performance of the group of students who were taught using integrated teaching model VISTA was compared with the performance of a control group who were taught using only traditional methods.

Homogeneity among the treatment and control groups of students was checked using a Mann-Whitney test. The purpose of this test was to make sure that the results of the experiments are not affected by any significant differences in the prior knowledge level of the treatment and control groups. Mean scores were calculated to compare the effect of the two learning approaches (TA and IA through VISTA) on student performance, using the relative values of the test scores of the treatment group.

The university is laptop-based and uses 'Blackboard' VLE software. All classrooms are equipped with wireless internet. All students have personal laptops. The student population consists of a majority of students who speak English as a first language with a small minority of international students. The teaching and assessment in all courses is in English. Class duration is 75 minutes, twice a week. Both the author and her colleague have taught this course several times before implementing this integrated approach. Both have long teaching experience and have attended several training workshops.

The integrated learning model was designed to change the students' learning style and encourage a deeper style of learning. The intention was to make it clear to the students that surface learning was not enough to pass the course and that the teaching methodology for this course would be different. This was achieved by communicating the distribution of grades to the students in advance through syllabus.

The Integrated Teaching Model-VISTA

This section introduces the VISTA model and discusses the justification for all the variables of this model.

Table 1: An Integrated Teaching Model- VISTA

V	**Make them** VISIT—Industry, Shop floors, Retail stores etc for understanding costs, cost behaviour and organisational structure. Attach grades to visit.
I	**Make Them** **INTERESTED**—Attach grades to visit, Report on Visit, assignments or quiz based on the visit and study material **(PPT) already uploaded on Blackboard** or shared on e-mail.
S	**Make Them** **STUDY**—Use **Flipped Classroom for selected topics** by asking them to solve some problems based on the self study and practice and add it as grading criteria. Encourage **exploring on internet** to find real world examples.
T	**Make Them** **THINK—Put Questions** from what they studied from the posted PPT and encourage others to vouch or challenge. Randomly ask them to present the **lecture/discussion summary to increase participation** and grade it. Use Marker/chalk to solve questions on the board while prompting them to answer next step.
A	**Make Them** **ANALYTICAL**—Use **Serial Case.** Encourage them to **quote examples** to help them correlate better. Ask them to visualise the usefulness of the concept in real business. **Internet based group homework assignment** can work very well.

Justification of the Model

This model has been suggested based upon the intensive literature review and the personal teaching experience of the researcher. Here is a mention of a few of studies which helped me in proposing this model:

- Maher (2000) mentions that more and more educators include field trips and field studies in their management accounting classes thereby increasing students' understanding of real-world problems. Thereby, visit to industry/workshop/retail store etc. has been proposed in this model. Grades were attached to this activity to make them interested in the activity since it has been concluded by many studies that grades work as one of the most effective motivators.
- In this context, White (1998) suggests asking the students to play specific roles in class when evaluating more technical and complex cases. As an example, he suggests one student to play the role of the corporate controller, while another to play the divisional manager, and let them engage in a budget negotiation. I have gone step further and

have proposed the incorporation of 'Flipped Classroom' technique but only for a few selected topics and not for the whole syllabus. This will make them study in advance.

- Another variation of team work with cases is an experimentation of serial-case pedagogy in the introductory managerial accounting course by the California State University in the early 1990s (Adams et al, 1999). White (1998) also suggests that students who studied cases in teams felt that their time in the classroom was well spent. This is what has propelled the researcher to incorporate the use of small serial cases instead of lengthy and bulky cases. This make students think and become more analytical in their learning.
- There are a number of studies that support multi-media or computer-assisted teaching over traditional teaching (Jensen and Sandlin 1992, Alavi 1994, etc). Boland *et al. (2004) pointed out that students who* speak English as a second language prefer a computer-assisted learning environment. That is why a reasonable use of power point presentations and the availability of study material on the Blackboard have been suggested. But, it is essential to propel them to think so the author has suggested the use of traditional chalk and talk method to solve practical problems on the board which helps students to think about the next step of the solution.

Result and Discussion

This section reports and evaluates the results obtained from a comparative analysis of the two teaching approaches. The objective here is to analyse and discuss the effects of the traditional learning and integrated learning on student performance.

Homogeneity between the Treatment and Control Groups

This is very important for this kind to study to ensure that both, the control group and treatment group are homogeneous as far as their prior knowledge is concerned. A Mann-Whitney test was used to ensure homogeneity and assess the level of the groups' prior knowledge. Table 2 presents the results for the performance of the treatment and control groups using the same learning environments before conducting any experiments. The result shows no significant differences (p = 0.289) between the mean scores of the two groups. This indicates that homogeneity in prior knowledge existed between the two groups.

Table 2: Homogeneity between the Treatment Group and the Control Group

Control Group	*Treatment Group*	*Descriptions*
5.25	5.00	Mean
1.90	2.85	Standard Deviation
1	1	Minimum
8	9	Maximum
0.289		**Nonparametric P Value***

*The Nonparametric value has been derived using Mann-Whitney Test.

The Effect of two Teaching Approaches on Students' Performance

Table 3 reports the results of performance of both the groups using the two different learning environments: the traditional learning approach (control group) and the integrated approach (treatment group). One explanation for this result is that moving from the traditional approach to a more interactive approach motivates students to interact, think and analyse thus improving their performance. The results agree with the findings of Dowling *et al.* (2003) that students scored higher marks on their midterm and final exams when a hybrid, flexible approach was used compared with a traditional face-to-face approach. In addition, because this integrated approach involves appropiate use of technology, these results may also be considered to be in agreement with that of Moss *et al.* (2003) that the use technology improves the learning environment and results in enhancing student performance. These results are also consistent with those of Lovata (1986), Lightbody (1997), and Kern (2002) regarding hands-on techniques. The integrated approach seems to have increased overall student comprehension and their ability to retain and recall knowledge.

Table 3: Comparative Performance of the Control Group and the Treatment Group

Description	*Control Group*	*Treatment Group*
Highest Score in the Class	89	98
Class Average	69	80
Lowest Score in the Class	**49**	**62**

Coclusion

This paper focuses only on the pedagogy part of teaching managerial accounting, leaving curriculum part and detail discussion on qualification of instructors, which may need separate study. The proposed model **'VISTA'** has been suggested based on experiments carried over controlled and treatment groups. Moreover, international teaching experience of the author combined with literature review has also helped extensively. VISTA stands for make them (students) **Visit; Interested; Study; Think and Analytical.** An integrated teaching model works better than depending too much on technology or using only chalk and talk pedagogy. This integrated model will lead to effective learning as was concluded by Sharma (1997) that altering accounting students' learning approaches would require altering the learning context to one that encourages understanding rather than reproduction of information. Further research can be conducted including student workloads, the effects of class timing and personal circumstances of the students and the results of the study can be tested with the help of some more effective statistical tools.

References

- Adams, Steven J., Lea, Richard B., Harston, Mary E. (1999). "Implementation of serial-case pedagogy in the introductory managerial accounting course". *Issues in Accounting Education Vol. 14, No. 4.*
- Alavi, M., (1994). "Computer-mediated collaborative learning: An empirical evaluation". *MIS Quarterly. 1994, June, 159-174* (quoted by Beets and Lobingler, 2001).
- Boer, Germain B., (2000). "Management Accounting Education: Yesterday, Today, and tomorrow". *Issues in Accounting Education Vol. 15, No. 2.*
- Boland, G., S. Sugahara, and S. Gregor (2004). "Web usage by the first year undergraduate accounting students: the effects of language background and individual differences". *AFAANZ Conference Proceedings, Alice* Springs, July.
- Essam Moustafa, Khaled Aljifri (2009). "Enhancing Student Performance in Managerial Accounting: A Laptop-Based Active Learning Approach". *The Accounting Educators' Journal,* Vol. XIX, pp. 111-125.
- Jensen, R.E., and Sandlin, P. K., (1992). "Why do it? Advantages and dangers of new waves of computer-aided teaching/instruction".
- Kalbers, L.P. and R. Rosner (2003). "An investigation of the emerging trend towards a laptop requirement for accounting majors in the USA", *Accounting Education, 12(4): 341-372.*
- Lancaster, A.S., and Strand, Carolyn A., (2001). "Using the Team-Learning Model in a Managerial Accounting Class: An Experiment in Cooperative Learning". *Issues In Accounting Education Vol. 16, No. 4.*

- Leveson, L. (1999). "Small group work in accounting education: an evaluation of a programme for first-year students". *Higher Education Research and Development, 18(3): 361-377.*
- Maher, Michael W., (2000). "Management Accounting Education at the Millennium". *Issues In Accounting Education Vol. 15, No. 2.*
- Paisey, C. and N.J. Paisey (2004). An analysis of accounting education research inAccounting Education: an international journal 1992-2001, *Accounting Education*, 13(1): 69-99.
- Sharma, D. (1997). "Accounting students' learning conceptions, approaches to learning, and the influence of the learning-teaching context on approaches to learning". *Accounting Education, 6(2): 125-146.*
- Thein Myint (2006). "Teaching Managerial Accounting: A Discussion on Pedagogy". *ABAC Journal Vol. 26, No. 1 , pp.31 - 40.*
- White, Lourdes Ferreira, (1998). "Motivating students to become more responsible for Learning". *College Student Journal Vol. 32, No. 21.*

ACCEPTED PAPERS

12

And the Tick Tick Stops for Ever... (Case on Closing Down of HMT Ltd.)

Aparna Sethi & Suman Dahiya

Abstract

Indian watch Industry is one of the fastest growing markets in the world. But nowadays it is in the news due to different reason. And that is the failure of one of the leading watch maker company - HMT (Hindustan Machine Tool). The company has been facing financial issues for many years. HMT was leading brand since 1953 in India. The market scenario changed with an entry of Titan in October 1987.

However once the market leader in mechanical watches, HMT lost its market share primarily due to very strong competitors. It could not change its product as the preference of the customers which changed over time and bad work culture.

However due to the severe financial crisis (nearly Rs 24 crore in 2012-13) faced by the HMT, it would be shutting shop after over fifty years in business. Even the company has no funds to pay the salaries to the employees.

This case outlines strategic changes required for sustainability of an organization.

Keywords: *Watch industry, HMT, strategic changes, sustainability, crisis and restructuring.*

1. History

India attended independence in 1947. Prime Minister Pandit Jawaharlal Nehruji led the era with the strong vision of self-reliant India. This initiated initiatives in agriculture, industry and infrastructure. Panditji's had a vision to sensitize the time consciousness among the Indians and he believed that India also had a capability to manufacture precision components. In 1961, Government of India assigned the job to HMT due to its capability, name and fame amongst the public sectors.

HMT set up a watch manufacturing Unit at Bangalore in collaboration with M/s Citizen Watch Co., Japan in 1961. The Company was converted into a Public Limited Company on May 13, 1977. As the first manufacturer of Wrist watches in the country, HMT successfully captivated the entirely new precision manufacturing technology for mass production, and assembly of micro sized components.

This tryst with 'firsts' continued and led to launch of India's first Automatic Day-Date watch , first Quartz watch , first Braille watch, first Ana-Digi watch. The first batch of Hand Wound Wrist Watches was released by the Hon'ble Prime Minister Pandit Jawaharlal Nehru.

2. Environment Analysis

An environment of a product comprises both macro and micro environment. Macro environment are Political, Economic, Socio cultural and Technical (PEST). Micro environment consist Competition, consumer behavior, supply chain etc.

HMT being in public sector always had support of government. It was a leading brand in mechanical watches. HMT had major trouble with bad work culture and had faced challenges with distribution channels. Authorized retailers started projecting themselves as wholesalers and this result in losing control over pricing.

HMT also faced tough competition with brands like Titan, Swatch, and Timex. HMT was unable provide after sale service to existing customer which result in lack of trust in consumers. HMT could not gauge change in customer's preferences which changed over time.

2.1 SWOT Analysis

Table 1

Strength	Weakness
Mechanical Watches: HMT was the market leader in mechanical watches. **Strong Brand Image:** HMT had a very strong brand image. It has excellence of trustworthiness. **Training capability:** It had superior training facility. (Association with Citizen Japan for formal training). **Industrial Relation:** Company had a very good industrial relation. **Ample Asset:** It had land, building and machinery. **Government Support:** The Company has government support. **Manufacturing Capacity:** In-house capacity to manufacture 60 lakh dials, 26 lakh cases annually (2002- 2003).	**Research and development Design:** No importance and consideration to novel design. **Vendor Policy:** HMT lost control over vendors. Some of the authorized retailers started acting as whole sellers. **Organizational Culture:** Lack of team moral and scarce motivational Strategies/ reward/punishment. **Market audit:** No regular market audit was being conducted by the company to take track the market happenings. **Promotion:** Insufficient advertisement, promotion which led to highlight the distinctiveness of HMT quartz design. **Centralization:** The centralization of decision making lead to lack of faster response to the market.
Opportunities	**Threats**
Diversification of Product: HMT could have focused on anadigi, digiana, multifunction, digital stopwatch, alarm etc. **Export:** International market was never tapped. It was stick to single customer segment. It did not expand and launched for different customers profile or watches for different moods (e.g., formal, casual etc.) **Sales Distribution:** HMT could have developed good retailers of different brands with big distribution networks to display and sell some newly launched models (jewel watches etc.) **Novel Product:** It could have hired professional designers to design new models of the watches based on customer preferences.	**Competitor:** Titan, Timex, Citizen Swatch etc were the biggest threats. **New Model:** Many luxury and varieties of watches were competing in the market nowadays. **Age-old Design style:** HMT's product is quite old fashioned when other brands are manufacturing innovative and attractive products.

Opportunities
Market Insights: Conducting market survey would have help to judge market dynamics.
Retail Store: Attractive retail store would have led to more footfalls.

Table 2 2.2 Marketing Mix of HMT Watches

Product	Price
Few Designs as compared to competitors. HMT has only 40 odd variants of four basic designs compared to competitor line, Titan which has 70 watches in its ranges with better looks and designs. **Less emphasis** on product research and development. **Underestimation of Quartz** watches segment and not able to be leader in this segment. **Scant attention** to aesthetics and packaging of its watches.	**Premium pricing for quartz segment:** HMT positioned the quartz watches as the space age generation watches and charged high prices for this category. **Price change didn't work:** In less than a year the company had to reduce the price and followed lifestyle advertising to justify the still higher price of the quartz, however even this backfired as consumers were not convinced of the differentiation between the quartz and other HMT watches.

Place	Promotion
Didn't strategize its established marketing network according to growing competition and new market trend like downtrend of mechanical watches & the growing market for the quartz watches. **Retailers not interested in HMT's home grown products** as a result it had to sell through its 13 branch offices for Machine tool equipment. **Did not take advantage of FERA:** as it could have taken in a limited way by offering service agencies to about 50 watch key retailers as a way of expanding its selling reach. **HMT's selective retailer policy** began going against it in mid 80's.	Though HMT's advertising was distinctive and did cater to the lifestyle segment, it **failed to communicate the uniqueness** of HMT's quartz design vis-à-vis other HMT watches. **Delay in Promotions:** Because of centralized decision making even the decisions on the campaigns for specific products were delayed leading to the time lag and responding to market changes.

Place
Some of the authorised retailers started acting as wholesalers without officially being appointed so. **The retailer margins provided by HMT were 2 per cent** less than what its most prominent competitor, Titan, was offering to the retailers.

2.3 Product Life Cycle of HMT Watches

Table 3

Introduction	Growth	Maturity	Decline
1960s	**1970s**	**1980s**	**1990s**
In July of 1961, one hundred employees of HMT Watches went to the Citizen factory in Tokyo and learned every aspect of manufacturing watches for one year. **Production of watches began in 1962**, with first batch released by then Prime Minister Nehru. With it's brands like 'Janata', 'Pilot' and 'Sona'	**In 1972,** HMT expanded its watch manufacturing capacity with a set up alongside the Bangalore Factory to manufacture additional watches. **In 1975,** factory further expanded to manufacture Main Spring, Hair spring and Shock absorber components. It expanded its production facilities with **two additional factories**, one in Tumkur, near Bangalore, and another in Ranibagh in Northern India.	**HMT has produced over 110 million** watches since the 1960s. **HMT dominated the Indian market until the late 1980s** with inexpensive mechanical watches . **HMT watches had enjoyed 70% market share** during 1980s. **The watch model, Kanchan,** used to sell at a premium in the grey market at Rs 1,000, when its legal price was Rs 700.	In 1990s came an onslaught of **quartz watches from Titan,** a subsidiary of Tata Corporation. **Market share dwindled** as Titan and Timex introduced trendy quartz watches. It **started incurring losses** since the year 2000. **Incurred huge loses of** upto Rs. 242.47 Crore in 2012-13 from Rs. 224.04 Crore.

3. Current Status

3.1 Clarification received by Bombay Stock Exchange - India dated 23rd September 2014 is as follows:

The Exchange had sought clarification from HMT Ltd with respect to the media report titled and quote; HMT watches may stop ticking soon and quote;

appearing in Business Standard on September 12, 2014. HMT Ltd replied as under; As regards the newspaper advertisements we do not have any details either on the source of their information or its authenticity. However, in this regard, we would like to inform you that HMT Watches Limited, a wholly owned Subsidiary of HMT Limited, is an Unlisted Company. The Company has been incurring cash losses since last 15 years as can be seen in our Annual Reports submitted to you and other stakeholders from time to time. The Company is on budgetary support for payment of Salaries and Statutory Dues since for over the past 10 years. The present Manpower of the Company is 1045 with an Annual wage bill of around Rs. 45 Crores. In view of the above and with the aim of reducing recurring costs, the Ministry had directed the company to formulate an attractive VR/VS Scheme to its employees in discussions with the employees and union/association. A scheme for downsizing of man power has been prepared based on the direction of DHI, and after due approval of the Board and has been submitted to the Government for its examination and necessary action.

4. Why Did the Tick Tick Stop?

Ignorance

"Learning and innovation go hand in hand. The arrogance of success is to think that what you did yesterday will be sufficient for tomorrow." — ***William Pollard***

HMT was branded as "timekeepers to the nation". But the HMT could not realize the market trends. In 1987, Titan entered in the market with the range of Quartz watches. At the beginning Titian made huge investment in advertising. Indian consumer who was always obsessed with style, and which was going abroad (Dubai and Singapore) to get good watches, swiftly exposed an incredible collection of stylish quartz watches and HMT found itself on greasy ground, for the first time.

But instead of relishing the stylish range of Titan product, loyal consumers of HMT went back to the outlets. But they were disappointed to see no stock available. HMT's greatest stoppage was its failure to mark the trend that Quartz was going to rule the Indian markets. The company's top management rejected Titan's passion with Quartz and continued to open plants to manufacture mechanical watches!

Not cosmetic Enough

Till 1991, HMT led the Indian watch market with almost 90 per cent market share for three decades, with the punch line of *'Desh ki Dhadkan'*. Post LPG (liberalization, privatization, and globalization) Indian market flooded with imported watches.

HMT was futile to recognize that a watch was no longer a time-keeping machine. It was becoming a fashion accessory for both men and women. Customers were sought after an elegant and stylish product to match and express their style. Aesthetics play a significant role in marketing. Titan, in four years, became the foremost watch manufacturer.

HMT positioned as a reputed but bulky mechanical watch maker. Titan, on the other hand, established as 'Today's watch manufacturer', with sleek watch models.

Production out of Time

Even when HMT tried to sustain its image with promotions for brand new watch models, there were reports that the promoted new model would be in short supply at stores.

It was production, again, which stumbled up financially. Former CMD N Ramanujan says, "Everything was going smoothly for HMT, which was a public-sector jewel, till 1989-90. It went into losses when production at its Srinagar factory stopped. It had to face working capital shortage as it had to feed around 500 employees without any production. This led to its downfall." The government rejected the transformational plan he projected and this led to accumulate losses.

The net losses for 2013-14 stood at Rs 233.08 crores, compared to Rs 242.47 crores in the previous year. The scarcity of working capital, attrition of trade channel and high cost of borrowings exaggerated it the most terrible. The yearly wage bill of the company stood at Rs 35-40 crores.

People Management

Around 1,105 employees at the company's three factories and corporate head office are a worried lot as they will no longer be "keeping time to the nation". During the zenith of its operations in 1991-92, it had over 8,000 employees and reported it's highest-ever sales of around Rs 300 crores. Starting 1994, however, it started its slide, and despite a restructuring in 1999, never recovered from red territory. In 1986, the company faced another major setback when about 350 of its best engineers left for Titan Watches, a Tata company and the new kid on the block with sleeker designs and aspirational value. Also, political intervention at every level, including appointment and promotion of employees, affected its functioning and demoralized staffers. HMT lacked Internal Marketing Concept in its HR approach and even failed to induct fresh blood into the organization.

5. Conclusions

HMT was never big on innovation. Lack of innovation has resulted that at one point enjoyed a 90 per cent market share of the watch market in India. The days of monopoly will be over sooner than one can imagine, organizations need to keep on innovating. It began building mechanical watches and could not foresee shifting market trends as the competitors started to forcefully push Quartz Analog watches. Technology is reckless. Companies need to keep on updating technology to sustain in the market. Lack of discipline and commitment are also to blame for the sad demise of HMT. In spite of having adequate managerial talent and training facilities, there was a lack of skilled employees that HMT faced. An absence of team spirit and urge to innovate contributed a lot to HMT's failure.

It is vital to keep the employees motivated not just towards personal goals, but also organizational goals. Motivational strategies such as reward and punish should be adopted. It also failed to create a suitable distribution channel for a product firm. Whether it is a website or a customer product, cautious efforts needs to be invested in design and aesthetics, as the customer today is highly discerning. Insufficient cost control system was set up by HMT. The wage bill and manufacturing costs were increasing. Frequent cost auditing needs to be conducted. HMT was unsuccessful to diversify. It could have diversified into different watch categories like analog-digital, multi-function, digital, stop-watch, alarm clocks, etc. It did not tap the export market too. It is more significant than ever to stay appropriate to your audience. HMT Quartz was positioned to be a prime product and targeted to the new Indian young man. But the high pricing meant it was to be afforded by only the middle age well off purchaser.

Teaching Notes

1. The purpose of the case is to make the students aware about importance of innovation for sustainability in today's business world. - "Change is constant and inevitable"
2. The issue involved in the case are about ignore competition and its effects on the business and market share of the company.
3. The case would be first given for individual reading and then for 15 min the case can be discussed in groups of 4 to 5 students.
4. The case can be taught along with the concepts like ways to overcome the crises and surviving strategies in organizations and marketing mix analysis.
5. The students can come prepared with topics of prevailing crises in

Indian watch industry and other factors related to watch industry in detail.

6. Cross reference can be made taking into account the strategies used by the local, national and international players to capture the slipping market of the falling organization.

References

- http://timesofindia.indiatimes.com/business/india-business
- http://www.business-standard.com
- http://www.thehindubusinessline.com
- http://articles.economictimes.indiatimes.com
- http://forbesindia.com
- http://hmtindia.com/
- http://www.bbc.com/news/world-asia-india
- http://www.business-standard.com/article/beyond-business/time-comes-to-a-stop-114091901229_1.html
- http://economictimes.indiatimes.com/articleshow/45171480.cms?utm_source = content ofinterest &utm_ medium = text & utm_ campaign = cppst

Annexure 1

hmt WATCHES — *Annual Report 2012-2013*

PERFORMANCE HIGHLIGHTS

(` in Lakhs)

	2012-13	2011-12	2010-11	2009-10	2008-09	2007-08	2006-07	2005-06	2004-05	2003-04
OPERATING STATISTICS										
Sales	**1106**	1024	882	1054	1352	1514	3688	2184	2354	2692
Other Income *	**180**	975	790	1087	371	618	3498	7710	306	939
Materials	**200**	353	253	434	357	551	1288	926	653	891
Employee Costs	**5884**	7406	12503	5599	5343	5426	4934	5793	4285	4274
Other Costs	**1572**	873	1379	1539	1995	1952	11968	3622	3872	5858
Depreciation	**54**	83	92	109	123	155	195	245	252	352
Earnings before Interest	**-6424**	-6716	-12576	-5774	-6401	-5816	-11405	-314	-7309	-8102
Interest	**17823**	15688	12798	11061	9982	8864	8161	7269	6144	5379
Earnings/(Loss) before Tax	**-24247**	-22404	-25374	-16835	-16383	-14680	-19566	-7583	-13453	-13481
Taxation	-	-	-	-	22	15	15	17		
Net Earnings	**-24247**	-22404	-25374	-16835	-16405	-14695	-19581	-7600	-13453	-13481

Source: HMT Watches Ltd Annual Report 2012-13

Annexure 2

Balance Sheet of HMT ------------------ **in Rs. Cr.** ------------------

	Mar '14 12 mths	*Mar '13 12 mths*	*Mar '12 12 mths*	*Mar '11 12 mths*	*Mar '10 12 mths*
Sources Of Funds					
Total Share Capital	1,420.35	760.35	760.35	760.35	760.35
Equity Share Capital	760.35	760.35	760.35	760.35	760.35
Share Application Money	443.74	443.00	443.00	443.00	443.00
Preference Share Capital	660.00	0.00	0.00	0.00	0.00
Reserves	-725.71	-812.92	-667.54	-585.35	-506.11
Networth	1,138.38	390.43	535.81	618.00	697.24
Secured Loans	31.55	111.27	109.41	143.72	254.65
Unsecured Loans	52.78	420.92	346.15	454.99	366.26
Total Debt	84.33	532.19	455.56	598.71	620.91
Total Liabilities	**1,222.71**	**922.62**	**991.37**	**1,216.71**	**1,318.15**

Application Of Funds

	Mar '14 12 mths	*Mar '13 12 mths*	*Mar '12 12 mths*	*Mar '11 12 mths*	*Mar '10 12 mths*
Gross Block	139.42	139.33	139.76	136.48	136.39
Less: Revaluation Reserves	0.00	0.00	0.00	0.00	0.00
Less: Accum. Depreciation	111.11	107.73	104.70	100.40	96.93
Net Block	28.31	31.60	35.06	36.08	39.46
Capital Work in Progress	0.00	0.00	0.00	2.60	0.82
Investments	763.90	765.56	765.56	765.56	765.56
Inventories	43.43	32.99	56.14	28.36	29.00
Sundry Debtors	30.96	35.30	64.54	72.49	68.64
Cash and Bank Balance	43.74	4.53	3.62	1.61	2.69
Total Current Assets	118.13	72.82	124.30	102.46	100.33
Loans and Advances	559.30	613.23	581.90	550.90	624.66
Fixed Deposits	0.00	0.00	0.00	2.22	1.69
Total CA, Loans and Advances	677.43	686.05	706.20	655.58	726.68
Deferred Credit	0.00	0.00	0.00	0.00	0.00
Current Liabilities	147.94	495.53	442.26	167.55	142.56
Provisions	98.99	65.04	73.20	75.54	71.81
Total CL and Provisions	246.93	560.57	515.46	243.09	214.37
Net Current Assets	430.50	125.48	190.74	412.49	512.31
Miscellaneous Expenses	0.00	0.00	0.00	0.00	0.00
Total Assets	1,222.71	922.64	991.36	1,216.73	1,318.15

Contingent Liabilities	13.74	17.71	33.92	8.09	10.52
Book Value (Rs)	0.46	-0.69	1.22	2.30	3.34

Source : *Dion Global Solutions Limited*

Annexure 3

Profit & Loss account of HMT ------------------ **in Rs. Cr.** ------------------

	Mar '14 12 mths	*Mar '13 12 mths*	*Mar '12 12 mths*	*Mar '11 12 mths*	*Mar '10 12 mths*
Income					
Sales Turnover	78.44	99.42	159.56	202.55	194.94
Excise Duty	0.00	0.00	0.00	1.61	1.48
Net Sales	78.44	99.42	159.56	200.94	193.46
Other Income	305.18	47.56	46.58	48.61	53.36
Stock Adjustments	8.77	-22.26	27.95	-0.90	-12.23
Total Income	392.39	124.72	234.09	248.65	234.59
Expenditure					
Raw Materials	67.00	53.65	121.18	137.35	120.83
Power & Fuel Cost	4.78	4.40	4.74	4.44	3.97
Employee Cost	90.30	70.70	74.99	83.71	67.62
Other Manufacturing	0.00	0.00	0.00	0.20	0.07
Expenses					
Selling and Admin Expenses	0.00	0.00	0.00	17.29	20.11
Miscellaneous Expenses	105.69	17.22	21.42	7.87	6.62
Preoperative Exp Capitalised	0.00	0.00	0.00	0.00	-4.62
Total Expenses	**267.77**	**145.97**	**222.33**	**250.86**	**214.60**

	Mar '14 12 mths	*Mar '13 12 mths*	*Mar '12 12 mths*	*Mar '11 12 mths*	*Mar '10 12 mths*
Operating Profit	-180.56	-68.81	-34.82	-50.82	-33.37
PBDIT	124.62	-21.25	11.76	-2.21	19.99
Interest	14.34	104.03	89.55	79.08	68.61
PBDT	110.28	-125.28	-77.79	-81.29	-48.62
Depreciation	3.40	3.55	4.40	3.87	3.92
Other Written Off	0.00	0.00	0.00	0.00	1.87
Profit Before Tax	106.88	-128.83	-82.19	-85.16	-54.41
Extra-ordinary items	-1.08	-16.56	-0.02	5.92	1.50
PBT (Post Extra-ord Items)	105.80	-145.39	-82.21	-79.24	-52.91
Tax	18.61	0.00	0.00	0.00	0.00

Reported Net Profit	87.21	-145.38	-82.20	-79.24	-52.91
Total Value Addition	200.77	92.31	101.14	113.51	93.77
Preference Dividend	0.00	0.00	0.00	0.00	0.00
Equity Dividend	0.00	0.00	0.00	0.00	0.00
Corporate Dividend Tax	0.00	0.00	0.00	0.00	0.00
Per share data (annualised)					
Shares in issue (lakhs)	7,603.50	7,603.50	7,603.50	7,603.50	7,603.50
Earning Per Share (Rs)	1.15	-1.91	-1.08	-1.04	-0.70
Equity Dividend (per cent)	0.00	0.00	0.00	0.00	0.00
Book Value (Rs)	0.46	-0.69	1.22	2.30	3.34

Source : *Dion Global Solutions Limited*

13

Role of Financial Inclusion in Socio-Economic Development in Rural India

Ravi Dutt & Harsh Purohit

Abstract

Financial inclusion is the most important initiative of the Government of India, and the RBI is focusing on providing banking facilities to the poor even in unbanked areas. Even after 60 years of independence, a large section of Indian population still remains unbanked. In India out of 19.9 Crore households, only 6.82 crore households, have access to banking services. As far as rural areas are concerned, out of 13.8 crore households in India, only 4.86 crore households have access to banking services. In urban areas only 49.52 per cent of households have access to banking services. Over 41 per cent of adult people in India do not have bank account. It is in this context the term "financial inclusion" gains importance and it is defined as the process of ensuring access to financial services and timely and adequate credit needed by vulnerable groups such as weaker sections and low-income groups at an affordable cost. Financial Inclusion makes people, especially the poor, commended with economic opportunitiesto the rural India where a signification portion of the population are suffering from poverty, inequality, unemployment, illiteracy and superstition. Since socio-economically rural residents are the most vulnerable portion of the society, it is the ethical, moral and social responsibility for the Government to ensure that the downtrodden common mass of the country receive protection from the risk of misspelling by the unscrupulous financial intermediaries. This research paper is an attempt to discuss the role of financial inclusion to ensuresocio-economic development so that the poverty may be reduced in India.

Key Words: *Financial Services, Socio-Economic Development, Poverty, Inclusive Growth.*

Introduction

Financial inclusion is emerging as the new paradigm of economic growth andthe main focus of financial inclusion in India is to promote socio-economic development and generating employment in rural areas for the rural population. Financial inclusion has an important role to play in promoting economic growth and reducing poverty. Despite finances being a necessity, a large section of people mostly in the rural areas are not aware of the art of managing the hard earned money to make it grow, so that it stands by them in their hours of need. Due to their financially ignorance, they are also prone to falling in the hands of greedy money lenders.

Financial inclusion refers to the strategies adopted to reach banking activities and its benefits to the unbanked areas; it is a drive to bring the underprivileged people into the mainstream. However, the connotation of the term financial inclusion does not restrict itself to credit alone; it also includes generating financial awareness, knowledge about banks and banking channels, facilities provided by banks and the advantages of treading the banking route. Besides, it also entails the task of educating people and making them financially literate. In the absence of financial literacy, very few conduct banking transactions and even few receive credit from formal financing channels.

Millions of people across the country are thereby denied the opportunity to increase their earning capacity and entrepreneurial talent and continue to struggle with their limited resources. Many countries are employing ûnancial inclusion as an important part of their strategies to achieve inclusive growth. Inclusive growth has recently become one of the world's most important policy goals. Governments, development partners, and economists have given attention to inclusion in economic and social life, including universal access to education, health care, social security, clean water and sanitation, and affordable transport and electricity,

"We recognise that financial inclusion is a key driver for economic development at national level and economic empowerment at an individual level. It's a human right of the modern age." — David Lewis, Former Lord Mayor of the City of London, at a seminar in Mumbai in 2007.

Objectives

1. The paper aims to study the concept of financial inclusion.
2. To study the current scenario of financial inclusion in socio-economic developmentin Rural India.
3. To highlight the measures taken by the Government of India and RBI for promoting financial Inclusion.

Research Methodology

The Methodology used for the proposed study is based on secondary data available from several research articles prevalent in the different reputed national and international journals in the sphere of financial inclusion.

Literature Review

A perusal of literature on finance and economic development reveals that the earlier theories of development concentrated on labour, capital, institutions, etc., as the factors for growth and development. There have been numerous researches analysing how financial systems help in developing economies. A great deal of consistency exists among economists regarding financial development prompting economic growth. Many theories have established that, financial development creates favourable conditions for growth through either a supply leading or a demand-following channel. According to Rajan and Zingales (2003), development of the financial system contributes to economic growth.

- The RBI Governor, Raghuram Rajan, on taking office in 2013, stated the urgent need for broad-based and diversified growth to combat poverty. He also recognised ûnancial inclusion as the most important pillar for equitable and sustainable growth and expanding access to micro, small, and medium-sized enterprises (MSMEs), the poor, and the remote and underserved areas of the country. Addressing capital and financial infrastructure needs of both households and businesses is an important part of the RBI's goals (Rajan 2013).
- The examination of ûnancial access began with the All-India Rural Credit Survey in the early 1950s. The survey indicated that farmers borrowed Rs. 7.5 billion in 19511952, with moneylenders accounting for 70 per cent of that total, and commercial banks providing less than 1 per cent (Pradhan 2013).
- Financial access differs between rural and urban areas but both areas are under-serviced. Financial inclusion nationwide is 36 per cent, with urban residents slightly higher at 45 per cent and rural residents at 32

per cent (RBI 2013; CRISIL 2013).3 Thus, the majority of urban residents are also excluded and as urban areas continue to expand, it will be important to build access in these areas. The approach of financial inclusion since 2004 has been to focus on rural areas and a more equitable strategy is needed.

Socio-Economic Development through Financial Inclusion: Historical Perspective

The financial sector in ensuring equitable and sustainable development was realized quite early in the post-independence period and there was a focus on channelling credit to the neglected sectors of the economy and weaker sections of the population. Increasing access to credit for the poor has remained a core concern for India's planning architecture, in its fight against poverty. Having recognized the social and economic imperatives of broader financial inclusion early, the policy makers set about finding innovative ways to empower the poor.

Starting with the nationalization of banks (1969/1980), outlining priority sector lending requirements for banks,introduction of the Lead BankScheme, establishment of Regional Rural Banks (RRBs-1975-76), Service Area Approach (1989) and Self-Help Group-Bank Linkage Programme (1989-90), all these initiatives were taken with an underlying objective of taking banking services to the masses and making them participate in the developmental process of the economy.

The financial sector reforms, set in motion in the 1990s, saw the focus shift to strengthening financial institutions and bringing in new players to infuse competitiveness, with the ultimate objective of achieving enhanced financial access, greater efficiency and improved consumer satisfaction. These initiatives, undoubtedly, had a positive impact and resulted in some improvement in access of banking services to remote parts of the country.

However, since these initiatives lacked a structured and coordinated approach, the developments were rather skewed with few regions witnessing better financial access and inclusion than others. The skewness in financial development across regions could mainly be attributed to poor polices as well as inadequacy of Governance framework. The lack of formal structure and effective co-ordination in the financial inclusion initiatives, thus, contributed to regional disparities in growth and economic prosperity.

Role of Govt. of India and RBI in Promoting Financial Inclusion

India has been proactive in pursuing a strategy of equitable development through the efforts of the Government of India and the Reserve Bank of India

(RBI) to broaden financial inclusion. With over 1.2 billion citizens and a rapidly developing country, India has put financial inclusion at the forefront of the political and socio-economic agenda. As the world's second-largest developing country, India has focused on poverty reduction as a central goal of development policy since independence in 1947.

Financial inclusion is the most important initiative of the Government of India,The RBI's approach to financial inclusion has been a "structured, planned and integrated approach" is focusing on providing banking facilities to the poor even in unbanked areas. The financial inclusion survey conducted by the World Bank team in India between April and June 2011 revealed that India lags behind developed and many developing countries in bank account penetration, but is much closer to the global average when it comes to borrowing from formal institutions.

There has been little reform in the past five years of public sector banks but reforms have occurred in the private bank sphere. Prior to becoming RBI Governor, RaghuramRajan wrote a report where he outlined the next generation of reforms for India's financial system (Rajan 2008). The report laid the groundwork for regulatory changes to the financial system to promote growth and social inclusion. The report highlighted the need for competition to spread finance, such as the licensing of new banks including foreign ones.

Now as Governor, RaghuramRajan has been speeding up the process of financial sector reforms. Most notable is the 2013 Licensing of New Banks in the Private Sector (RBI 2013c). As a result, in April 2014, the RBI approved licenses for two new small banks. This is the first time in over a decade that new banks have been allowed to enter the banking systemthe bank-led model has also reformed the way banks pursue and promote financial inclusion. Through the Reach pillar, the RBI has refocused the banks to:

1. Simplify branch authorization to address the uneven spread of bank branches and allow branches in areas of less than 100,000;
2. Use FIPs to expand the branch network and encourage the use and sustainability of accounts with small balances; and
3. Expand into unbanked rural areas with the RBI mandating that 25 per cent of new branches be in unbanked rural areas and that small intermediary structures are opened between the base branchand the unbanked villages (Joshi 2014a).

The RBI roadmap for banks was to provide banking services in every village with a population over 2,000 by March 2013 and the target of reaching 74,414 previously unbanked villages was achieved. The second phase will cover villages with a population less than 2,000 by March 2016. About 490,000 such unbanked villages have been identified and allotted to banks.

In table-1 given data for India is for 2012 and reveals the bank branch penetration per adult and per 1,000 square kilometres. The penetration level of ATMs is also given.

Table 1: Access to and use of Financial Services

Commercial bank branches per 1,000 km^2	33.17	Commercial bank branches per 100,000 adults	11.38
ATMs per 1,000 km^2	32.67	ATMs per 100,000 adults	11.21
Outstanding deposits with commercial banks (% of GDP)	68.64	Outstanding loans from commercial banks (% of GDP)	54.24
Deposit accounts with commercial banks per 1,000 adults	1,042.48	Loan accounts with commercial banks per 1,000 adults	151.06
Household deposit accounts with commercial banks per 1,000 adults	892.49	Household loan accounts with commercial banks per 1,000 adults	23.54

ATM = automated teller machine; GDP = gross domestic product; km^2 = square kilometer.

Source: International Monetary Fund. Financial Access Survey Database. http://fas.imf.org/ (accessed 22 July 2014)

Financial Inclusion is a Key Driver of Socio-Economic Growth and Poverty Alleviation

Inclusive financial sector development makes two complementary contributions to poverty alleviation; firstly financial sector development is a driver of economic growth which indirectly reduces the poverty and inequality. Secondly an appropriate, affordable, financial service for poor people can improve their welfare. They are complementary because financial inclusion enables the previously excluded to connect to the formal economy and contribute to economic growth, while economic growth facilitates the inclusion of more people in the economy and in the financial system.

Financial inclusion is the most recent item to be added explicitly to the social inclusion agenda and promotes the need for access among all segments of society to a range of financial services at affordable cost. Financial services and financial development stimulates economic growth by increasing the rate of capital accumulation by improving the efficiency. Financial inclusion provides an opportunity to small firms, farmers and low-wage earners to break out of the poverty trap both through lowering the risk of exploitation as well as improving their education and employment opportunities.

In such a scenario, financial inclusion holds special significance for India, as majority of the Indian population resides in rural areas. Besides, bringing progress and prosperity in the rural areas, it also augurs well for the overall economic development of a country like India. It allows poor households to save and manage their money in a secure manner, decreases their exposure to economic shocks in the form of drought, floods or any calamity of the kind which affects people dependant on agricultural activities.

Financial Inclusion Plans 2013-2016

FIPs provide an opportunity to promote financial inclusion. The 2013 RBI review of FIPs recognized the following needs:

Increasing Reach

- Ensuring coverage of all unbanked villages in next 3 years
- Increasing rural branches
- Opening of bank accounts for all eligible individuals

Increasing Transactions

- Leveraging direct benefit transfers
- Delivery of credit products through business correspondents
- Hassle free emergency credit (that is, automatic overdraft)

Human Resources Structure

- Banks to review human resources policy in view of financial inclusion requirements
- Consider appointing a separate cadre of staff for cost optimization

Fine-tuning the Business Correspondents Model

- Stabilizing the business correspondents delivery model
- Encouraging innovations in remittances model
- Review of cash management for these operations

Spreading Financial Literacy

- Implementing a national strategy for financial education
- Creating a dedicated website
- Organizing financial literacy camps (Chakrabarty 2013a)

The FIPs focus on reaching the most excluded portions of society and increasing financial education, while providing suitable products. The use of UID linked bank accounts will also help reduce the financial gap for millions of Indians.

The first year of the new FIP 20132016 are summarized in Table 2 with the key points as follows :

Table -2 Financial Inclusion and Access Progress

No. of Scheduled Commercial Banks				Basic Savings Bank Deposit Accounts Opened			
Mar 2006		Mar 2013		Mar 2010	Mar 2013	Mar 2014	
68,681		102,343		73.45	182.06	242.96	million
No. of Rural Branches				**Expansion of the ATM Network**			
Mar 2006	Mar 2010	Mar 2013	Mar 2014	Mar 2010		Mar 2013	
30,572	33,378	40,837	46,126	60,153		114,014	
No. of Villages Covered				**Rural ATMs**			
Mar 2010	Mar 2013	Mar 2014	Population	Mar 2010		Mar 2013	
27,353	74,414	n/a	>2,000	5,196		11,564	
26,905	65,234	183,993	<2,000				
Total Bank Outlets				**Kisan Credit Cards Issued***			
Mar 2010	Mar 2013	Mar 2014		Mar 2010	Mar 2013	Mar 2014	
67,964	268,454	383,804		24.31	33.79	39.94	million
Bank Outlets by Business Correspondents (BC)				**General Credit Cards Issued**			
Mar 2010	Mar 2013	Mar 2014		Mar 2010	Mar 2013	Mar 2014	
34,316	227,617	337,678		1.39	3.63	7.43	million

ATM = automated teller machine.

*for small farmer credit requirements

Source: Compiled by author based on Joshi (2014a, 2014b).

Jan- Dhan Yojana-2015

Most significant move in the recent times came only weeks ago when Prime Minister Narendra Modi announced the launch of ambitious Rs. 1 lakh crore financial inclusions plan called Prime Minister's Jan-Dhan Yojana. The programme envisages a bank account for 150 million Indians by August 2018.

Making the announcement from the ramparts of historical Red Fort, Modi proposed an overdraft facility of Rs. 5,000 for each account and a repay debit card with inbuilt accident insurance cover of Rs. 1 lakh. The overdraft will be backstopped by a Credit Guarantee Fund. Incidentally, it was a pleasant surprise to see banks opening as many as 1.5 crore bank accounts on the very first day of the launch of the scheme on August 28, 2014.

Finance Minister Arun Jaitley's maiden budget also aimed at giving a significant push to financial inclusion in the country. The Union Budget 2014-15 reiterated the commitment to set up differentiated banks such as "payments banks" and said the RBI would roll out a framework for issuing licences to such banks.. In the Budget, the FM also announced setting up of a Financial Inclusion Mission, which would "particularly focus to empower the weaker sections of the society, including women, small and marginal farmers and labourers." As part of the mission, the FM proposed to open two bank accounts for each household in the country. A similar move was suggested by the Mor committee, which had recommended the creation of a free Aadhaar-linked bank account for every Indian by end 2015.

Improvement in Rural Financial Inclusion

The situation of financial inclusion, particularly in rural areas, has improved significantly although more time is needed to fully evaluate the effectiveness of recent changes. More diversified financial providers and products have promoted the development of rural financial inclusion. In the past ten years, the significant increase in the number and diversity of banking institutions involved in rural areas has dramatically improved rural financial services.

The last decade has witnessed the rapid development of financial inclusion in rural India. New policies, regulations, and measures put into practice have significantly improved financial inclusiveness by increasing access to financial services. There is a huge potential in the construction of an inclusive financial system. The final goals of developing financial inclusion are to allocate funds more effectively and promote the sustainable development of the rural economy.

Financial inclusion is not sufficient and needs to be improved. While financial inclusion has been promoted, efforts need to be made so the weakest can access basic financial services.

The Figure 1 shows (1) banking outlets in villages increased from 67,694 to nearly 384,000 (2) 12,700 rural branches were opened (in contrast to the closure of 1,300 rural branches in the previous two decades).

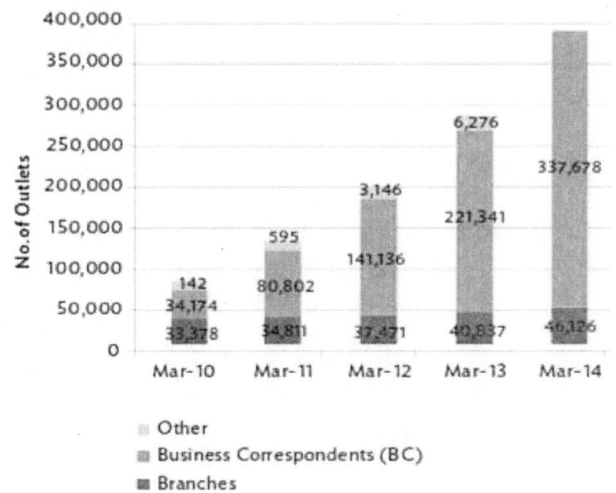

Source: Joshi (2014b).

Figure 1: Bank Outlets in Villages

Financial inclusion is not sufficient and needs to be improved. While financial inclusion has been promoted, efforts need to be made so the weakest can access basic financial services. About 450 million people don't have any deposit account and most of them live in rural and remote areas. The financial product and service requirements of MSEs and households are far from satisfied, despite a significant increase in the number of such products and services available. In addition, very few financial institutions serve the poorest with financial services they urgently need, such as microcredit. In the field of agricultural insurance, more services are needed.

Recommendations

The study, upon analysing and drawing inferences from the study, recommends the followings:

1. Better access to credit by the poor enables them to pull themselves out of poverty by investing in their human capital and microenterprises, thus reducing aggregate poverty.
2. Financial liberalisation can affect the reduction of inequality through indirect channels such as higher labour demand and higher wages for lower income groups.
3. Branch expansion into rural unbanked locations can significantly reduce poverty, mediated by increased deposit mobilisation and credit disbursement by banks in rural areas.
4. Bank branch expansion can also alleviate poverty by decreasing unemployment and enabling existing business owners to continue their operations rather than becoming wage earners or unemployed.

Conclusion

Financial inclusion enables improved and better sustainable economic and social development of the country It is proven fact that financial inclusion & financial literacy is an effective way for "Poverty Alleviation". The objective of financial inclusion is to meet the expectation of the unbanked and excluded, yet silent mass of our population are untouched. Poverty continues to dominate socio-economic development in India over the last six decades. The ongoing reforms attach great importance to poverty alleviation. Despite being one the fastest growing economies of the world, India is still a home to one-third of the world's poor.

India has adopted financial inclusion as an essential pillar of the national strategy for reducing the rising income disparity between rural and urban areas, having easy access to various financial services by poor, vulnerable, and less privileged people and it is the essential objective of socio-economic development of rural India.

References

- Prasann Kumar, (2014), Microfinance — A Tool for Socio - Economic Development in Rural India.
- Special Report | 4 September 2014 Financial Inclusion: Reaching the unbanked.
- Sayantani Banerjee, Greeshma Francis, (year) Financial Inclusion and Social Development Website: www.ijsrm.in ISSN (e): 2321-3418.
- Reserve Bank of India (2006) "Economic growth Financial Deepening and Financial Inclusion" speech by Rakesh Mohan, deputy Governor of RBI, November, 2013.
- Asian Development Bank (ADB). 2014. India. http://www.adb.org/countries/ india/main (accessed 29 July 2014).
- Financial Inclusion Insights. 2014a. Digitised Government Payments in India: Qualitative Study. Developed with support from InterMedia and the Bill and Melinda G-ates Foundation- April.
- Demirguc-Kunt, A., L. Klapper, and D. Randall, (2013), World Bank Global Findex Database—Financial Inclusion in India. World Bank and Gates Foundation
- Government of India (GoI). 2013. Annual Report 2012-13: Micro, Small and Medium Enterprise. New Delhi: Ministry of Micro, Small and Medium Enterprises.
- Financial Inclusion in Asian Country-Surveys.
- Social Harmony Sarkar A.N. (2013), "Financial Inclusion Part-II: Fostering Sustainable Economic Growth in India", The Banker, Vol. VIII, No. 5, pp. 32-40.
- K.C. Chakrabarty (March 21, 2014.) Inclusion, Growth and Governance-Issues and Reserve Bank of India at the 35th SKOCH Summit in New Delhi.
- Verma Priyanka, Singh Anupam (2014) Financial Inclusion in India: Panacea or Mirage to Rural Economic Development Financial Inclusion for Reviving Growth: Success Stories, Challenges and the Road Ahead" CII Report.

14

To Stress Test or Not: A Question Faced by Banks

Neetu Jora

"You can't really know what you are made of until you are tested."
—O.R. Melling

Abstract

Stress tests attracted a great deal of attention in 2009, as the worst global financial crisis since the Great Depression has left many banks and financial institutions severely under-capitalised. However, the question whether the existing stress testing practices are sufficient and robust to cope with rapidly changing circumstances, still needs to be answered.

Looking at the state of economy today, it makes sense that instead of doing financial projection on a "best estimate" basis, a company or its regulators may do stress testing where they look at how robust a financial institution or a financial instrument is. An essential part of the stability and efficiency of a financial system depends on those facets of the banking system, which are based on prudential regulation and effective supervision.

This paper is intended to study and review and the most representative features of stress exercises. It also explains the origin of stress testing, its scope, its worldwide implications, methodology, complexity and risk profile of the system under examination. A general conclusion is than there by drawn.

Key words: *Banks, Financial, Stress test Basel committee, Financial regulators, Risk Management.*

Introduction

In today's era of liberalization and globalization ,when there are extreme challenges on the shoulders of banks and financial institutions, who are to deal with more and more complex problems on a daily basis, stress testing is inevitable. Today, it makes sense that instead of doing financial projection on a "best estimate" basis, a company or its regulators may do stress testing where they look at how robust a financial institution or a financial instrument is. A stress test, is an analysis or simulation designed to determine the ability of a given financial instrument or financial institution to deal with an economic crisis.

A bank stress test in particular is a simulation based on an examination of the balance sheet of that institution or in other words it is a thorough analysis which is conducted under unfavorable economic scenarios to determine whether a bank has enough capital to withstand the impact of adverse developments. The focus is on key risks such as credit risk, market risk, and liquidity risk. It aims to answer questions like:

- What if a borrower fails to repay a loan or otherwise meet a contractual obligation?
- What if you experience losses due to factors that affect the overall performance of the financial markets, from movements in market prices?
- What if a given security or asset cannot be traded quickly enough in the market to prevent a loss or make the required profit?

Stress tests can either be carried out:

- internally by banks as part of their own risk management, or
- by supervisory authorities as part of their regulatory oversight of the banking sector.

The results of stress tests depend on the assumptions made in various economic scenarios, which are described by the International Monetary Fund as "unlikely but plausible."

USE

Large international banks began using internal stress tests in the early 1990s.Tests attracted a great deal of attention in 2009, as the worst global financial crisis since the Great Depression left many banks and financial institutions severely under-capitalized.In 1996, the Basel Capital Accord was amended to require banks and investment firms to conduct stress tests to determine their ability to respond to market events. However, up until 2007, stress tests were typically performed only by the banks themselves, for internal self-assessment. Beginning in 2007, governmental regulatory bodies became interested in conducting their own stress tests to insure the effective operation of financial institutions. Since then, stress tests have been routinely performed by financial regulators in different countries or regions, to insure that the banks under their authority are engaging in practices likely to avoid negative outcomes. In India, legislation was enacted in 2007 requiring banks to undergo regular stress tests. In October 2012, U.S. regulators unveiled new rules expanding this practice by requiring the largest American banks to undergo stress tests twice per year, once internally and once conducted by the regulators. Starting in 2014 midsized firms (i.e., those with $1050 billion in assets) are also being required to conduct Dodd-Frank Act Stress Testing.

The financial crisis re-affirms the need for macro stress testing to assess banks vulnerability. The Global Financial Stability Report of International Monetary Fund, (IMF, 2009), proposed that identifying and dealing with distressed assets, and recapitalizing weak but viable institutions and resolving failed institutions are the two important priorities which directly relate to non-performing assets (NPAs). In 2009 The Reserve Bank of India (RBI) announced that the Indian banking system is resilient to the shocks from high NPAs.

- These tests are meant to detect weak spots in the banking system at an early stage, so that preventive action can be taken by the banks and regulators.
- Stress testing models typically allow not only the testing of individual stressors, but also combinations of different events.
- They are the window to banks' financial health in crisis situations.
- They emphasis on adequate, risk adjusted determination of capital as has been further enhanced by modifications to banking regulations such as Basel II.
- It also facilitates internal and external communication and helps senior management understand the condition of the bank in the stressed time.
- Stress testing outputs are used by a bank in decision making process in terms of potential actions like risk mitigation techniques, contingency plans, capital and liquidity management in stressed conditions, etc. It was, therefore, included as an important element of risk management framework and capital planning in the Basel Committee on Banking Supervision (BCBS) document titled 'An International Convergence of Capital Measurement and Capital Standards: A Revised Framework' known as Basel II.
- Stress testing should form an integral part of the internal capital adequacy assessment process (ICAAP), which requires banks to

undertake rigorous, forward looking stress testing that identifies severe events or changes in market conditions that could adversely impact the bank.

- Play an important role in the communication of risk within the bank and external communication with supervisors to provide support for internal and regulatory capital adequacy assessments.

Stress Tests Worldwide

In March 2013, the Financial Policy Committee (FPC) recommended that regular stress testing of the UK banking system should be developed to assess the system's capital adequacy. On 16th December 2014, the Bank of England published the results of the first concurrent stress test. The 2014 UK stress test explored vulnerabilities stemming from the UK household sector, in particular, reflecting the Financial Policy Committee's assessment of the main domestic risks to financial stability. The Bank of England set out in April 2014 the details of the UK scenario for the stress tests that the eight major UK banks and building societies would undertake. This built on the common, EU wide exercise co-ordinated by the European Banking Authority (see further information below about the EBA exercise).

The EBA Exercise

In April 2014, the EBA announced the key elements of the 2014 EU-wide stress test that will be conducted on a wide sample of EU banks. The objective of the EU-wide stress tests was to help supervisors assess the resilience of financial institutions in the European Union to adverse market developments. This exercise aimed at ensuring consistency and comparability of the outcomes across all banks based on a common methodology, scenarios and accompanied by a consistent disclosure exercise. Four major UK banks participated in the common, EU-wide test in 2014. For results see Statement on EBA stress test publication. Regulators asked banks in Shanghai to conduct stress tests related to their real estate loans, Reuters reported, citing a notice issued by the China Banking Regulatory Commission's office in the city.

The CBRC also asked for continued monitoring of risks stemming from loans taken out by major property companies outside of Shanghai, according to the report. Kaisa Group Holdings Ltd. (1638) failed to make an interest payment due Jan. 8, putting the Shenzhen-based company at risk of becoming the first real estate company in China to default on its U.S. currency debt. Chinese banks' bad-loan ratio jumped the most in at least a decade in the fourth quarter amid a slowdown in the world's second-biggest economy.

In 16 December 2014,The Bank of England announced the results of the first concurrent stress testing exercise of the UK banking system. Alongside the stress test publication, the Bank of England also published its Financial Stability Report, which sets out the Financial Policy Committee's (FPC) assessment of the outlook for the stability and resilience of the financial sector, and the Systemic Risk Survey, which quantifies and tracks market participants' perceptions of systemic risks.

The eight banks and building societies tested as part of this exercise were Barclays Bank, Co-operative Bank, HSBC Bank, Lloyds Banking Group, Nationwide Building Society, Royal Bank of Scotland, Santander UK and Standard Chartered.

There was substantial variation across the banks and building societies in terms of the impact of the stress scenario. From an individual-institution perspective, the Prudential Regulation Authority (PRA) Board judged that this stress test did not reveal capital inadequacies for five out of the eight participating banks, given their balance sheets at end-2013 (Barclays, HSBC, Nationwide, Santander UK and Standard Chartered). The PRA Board did not require these banks to submit revised capital plans.

Projected CET1 capital ratios in the stress scenario

	Actual (end 2013)	*Minimum Stressed ratio (before the impact of 'strategic' management actions)*	*Minimum Stressed ratio (after the impact of 'strategic' management actions)*	*Actual (latest, Q2 or Q3 2014)*
Barclays	9.1%	7.0%	7.5%	10.0%
Co-operative Bank Plc	7.2%	-2.6%	-2.6%	11.5%
HSBC Bank Plc	10.8%	8.7%	8.7%	11.2%
Lloyds Banking Group	10.1%	5.0%	5.3%	12.0%
Nationwide Building Society	14.3%	6.1%	6.7%	17.6%
Royal Bank of Scotland	8.6%	4.6%	5.2%	10.8%
Santander UK	11.6%	7.6%	7.9%	11.8%
Standard Chartered Plc	10.5%	7.1%	8.1%	10.5%

(a) The minimum CET1 ratios shown in the table do not necessarily occur in the same year of the stress scenario for all banks. (b) Actuals are in Q2 2014 for the Co-operative Bank plc, Santander UK plc and Standard Chartered Bank Group; Q3 2014 for Barclays Group, HSBC Holdings PLC, Lloyds Banking Group, Royal Bank of Scotland Group; and September 2014 for Nationwide Building Society. (c) As a result of Nationwide's different reporting date, the Bank used an estimated 4 April 2014 balance sheet as the start point of the stress-testing analysis. This results in the difference between the CET1 ratio quoted in this table and that reported in Nationwide's annual accounts.

Regulators devise hypothetical future adverse economic scenarios to test banks. These established scenarios are then given to the banks in their jurisdiction and tests are run, under the close supervision of the regulator. They evaluate if the bank could endure the given adverse economic scenario, survive in business, and most importantly, continue to actively lend to households and business. If it is calculated that the bank can absorb the loss, and still meet the minimum bank capital requirements to remain in active business, they are deemed to have passed. For example, in the U.S. in 2012, an adverse scenario used in stress testing was all of the following:

- Unemployment at 13 per cent
- 50 per cent drop in equity prices
- 21 per cent decline in housing prices.

List of Bank Stress Tests

This list covers formal bank stress testing programs, as implemented by major regulators worldwide. It does not cover bank proprietary, internal testing programmes.

Asia

1. Monetary Authority of Singapore
    - Annual Industry-Wide Stress Testing exercise (usually around Q1)
2. International Monetary Fund
    - 2011 and 2012 stress testing of Japan banks, Financial System Stability Assessment Update (FSAP)
3. China Banking Regulatory Commission
    - 2011 CARPLES risk indicators framework

Europe

1. Financial Services Authority
    - 2008 Stress and scenario testing CP08/24
    - 2009 Stress and Scenario Testing Feedback on CP08/24
2. European Banking Authority
    - 2010 European Union bank stress test
    - 2011 European Union bank stress test
    - 2014 European Union bank stress test

- The stress test was part of the Comprehensive Assessment by the European Central Bank.

Americas

1. Federal Reserve System
    - 2009 Supervisory Capital Assessment Program (SCAP)
    - Note: *there was no 2010 stress test in the USA*
    - 2011 Comprehensive Capital Analysis and Review (CCAR)
    - 2012 Comprehensive Capital Analysis and Review (CCAR)
    - 2013 Comprehensive Capital Analysis and Review (CCAR)
    - 2014 Comprehensive Capital Analysis and Review (CCAR)
    - 2015 Comprehensive Capital Analysis and Review (CCAR)
2. Central Bank of Brazil (Portuguese: Banco Central do Brasil)

Conclusion

In the light of what has been discussed and observed, it can be concluded that stress testing is inevitable and this is the reason it has become increasingly widespread. However, the question whether the existing stress testing practices are sufficient and robust to cope with rapidly changing circumstances, is still needs to be answered. That is why stress testers commonly refer to regulatory stress tests as a walk in the park, a kiss in the dark!

References

- Bank Of England. (2014). Bank of England announces results of UK stress test. (Press release).Retrieved from http://www.bankofengland.co.uk/publications/Pages/news/2014/169.aspx
- http://www.bloomberg.com/news/2015-01-26/shanghai-cbrc-seeks-stress-test-on-property-loans-reuters-says.html
- Bank stress test. (n.d.). In *Investopedia.* Retrieved February 13, 2015, from http://www.investopedia.com/terms/b/bank-stress-test.asp
- Stress test (financial). (n.d.). In *wikipedia.* Retrieved February 13, 2015, from http://en.wikipedia.org/wiki/Stress_test_(financial)
- Bank of England. (2014). 2014 stress testing. (Press release). Retrieved from http://www.bankofengland.co.uk/financialstability/Pages/fpc/stresstest.aspx
- European Banking Authority.(2014). EBA publishes 2014 EU-wide stress test results test. (Press release). Retrieved from http://www.eba.europa.eu/-/eba-publishes-2014-eu-wide-stress-test-results
- List of bank stress test.(n.d.). In *wikipedia*. Retrieved February 13, 2015, from http://en.wikipedia.org/wiki/List_of_bank_stress_tests

15

Management of Workforce Diversity: A Global HR Practice

R.B. Solanki, Shashi Shekhar Gautam & Ankita Saxena

Abstract

Due to the enhanced rate of globalization, privatization and liberalization we can view the change at our workplace also, gone were the days where the people of same age, same professional qualification, same experience and same religion come together to work in an organization. Now day's females are also working in the equal ratio with males. Workforce diversity means similarities and differences among employees in terms of age, cultural background, physical abilities and disabilities, race, religion, gender, interpersonal relationship and sexual orientation. No two humans are alike. People are different in not only gender, culture, race, social and psychological characteristics but also in their perspectives and prejudices. Society had discriminated on these aspects for centuries. Diversity makes the work force heterogeneous. Due to globalized scenario, employing diversified workforce is a necessity for every organization but to manage such diversified workforce is also a big challenge for management. This paper critically analyses the workforce diversity, the problems which employees are facing due to diversified workforce like communication, resistance to change etc and its management through strong and effective leadership. The researchers after examining the literature and various research papers, concluded that workforce diversity is strength for any organization but people still stick to their views related to caste, religion etc and so consider diversity as a problem but effective and global leadership can increase the productivity because a strong link exists between leadership and diversity. Leadership is about empowering people; bringing out the best in others. Organizations can bring out the best in people by making them feel accepted, respected and connected. When people feel good about themselves and the organization, they perform better individually and as part of a team, resulting in an organization that performs better. These are the same objectives and desired results of diversity strategies. A sustainable advantage of globalization depends on the skills and abilities of a leader who can manage diversity and implement increasingly complex business strategies. Effective workforce diversity management is a key to global business success. Global leaders should be aware and appreciate the diversity they face in leadership practices. Finally the researchers have suggested some techniques for the problems which employees are facing due to diversified workforce like soft skills training, including communication, interpersonal skills and leadership skills. These are the skills that foster the kind of inclusion where everyone, regardless of who they are or where they come from, feels they are an integral member of the organization and encouraged to fully participate. Using leadership skills to promote these simple values can have an incredible impact in creating an environment where everyone, regardless of who they are, where they were born or their educational background, feels welcomed and supported. This is an important key not only to managing diversity, but to retaining all employees because human resource is an important asset for any organization. Capital and physical resources, by themselves, cannot improve efficiency or contribute to an increased rate of return on investment.

Keywords: *Diversity, Leadership, Workforce, Productivity, Globalization*

Introduction

The world is becoming smaller every day. The Internet, mass media, telecommunications and mass transportation have all contributed to the shrinking of international market. Because of these technologies, there is a continuing requirement for companies to address the needs of a very diverse market so that they can be competitive. Companies must now ask themselves what they can do to increase the number of customers for which they serve while determining the needs of these customers. This business process makes diversity an important part of a company's growth and operation.

As companies are becoming more and more diverse it's becoming more and more crucial for companies to understand and manage it. The people of different background, races, religion creates diverse workforce. There is an importance of having diverse workforce to provide better performance. There are perspectives of managing the diverse workforce, which require organization leaders and managers of being responsible of attaining better diverse workforce.

Jackson *et al.* (1995) define diversity as the presence of differences among members of a social unit. Today, the workforce is more diverse in terms of gender, race, ethnicity, national origin an comprises people who are different and share different attitudes, needs, desires, values and work behaviours as noted by Rosen and Lovelace (1991). Greenberg (2004) also defines workplace diversity refers to the variety of differences between people in an organization including race, gender, ethnic group, age, personality, cognitive style, tenure, organizational function, education, background and more. The U. S National Partnership for Reinventing Government (NPR) Diversity Task Force in conjunction with the US Department of Commerce in their sponsored benchmark study of diversity (2007) defined diversity as including all the characteristics and experiences that define each of us as individuals. It is clear from these definitions that most scholars concur on the definition of workforce diversity. The main sources of diversity include age, race, gender, ethnicity (culture) and education although there are other sources of diversity like personal demographics; knowledge, skills, and abilities; values, beliefs, and attitudes; personality and cognitive and behavioral style; and organizational demographics. Diversity can be defined as a mixture of people with different group identities within the same social system (Fluery, 1999). Diversity includes factors such as race, gender, age, colour, physical disability, ethnicity, etc. (Kundu and Turan, 1999). Companies have decided to incorporate diversity and consider it as essential part of their business strategy (Hayes and Mandez, 1997; Palich and Gomez, 1999) for keeping and gaining market share, reducing costs, increasing productivity and improving quality of management (Morrison, 1992) etc., as business case.

In western countries, there has been a strong drive for maintenance and management of diversity in organizations. A number of studies, reviews, laws, regulations and programs have been advocated in this line. Our Indian organizations contain employees from diverse groups also. However we have not paid much attention towards this. Recruitment of employees belonging to diverse backgrounds is not sufficient to improve those employees' health as well as organizational health. There should be something else to enable people to perform optimally as per their potential. This something else is managing diversity: managing diversity in such a way as to get from a heterogeneous workforce the same productivity, commitment, quality and profit that we got from the old homogeneous workforce (Thomas, 1990).

As we enter the 21st century, a fundamental shift is occurring in the world economy. We are moving towards a world in which barriers to cross border trade and investments are tumbling, perceiver distance is shrinking due to advances in transportation and telecommunications technology in short we can say that day by day the world is becoming a global village due to globalization. In this interdependent global economy, an American might drive to work in a car designed in Germany that was assembled in Mexico, components made in the United States and Japan that were fabricated from Korean steel and Malaysian rubber. From Indian perspective also, the world has now recognized India as one of the prime economic driver in the global scenario. Various companies are coming India to explore this opportunity. In order to survive in this type of cut throat competitive world the organizations have to hire an effective an efficient workforce that can handle such competitive environment. Employing diversified workforce is a very essence for each and every organization. In the current scenario the organizations that employ quality and competitive workforce regardless of their age, attitude, language, gender, religion, region can only compete at the marketplace. Human resource is an important asset for any organization. Capital and physical resources, by themselves, cannot improve efficiency or contribute to an increased rate of return on investment. On the basis of above statement, researcher has prepared the following model.

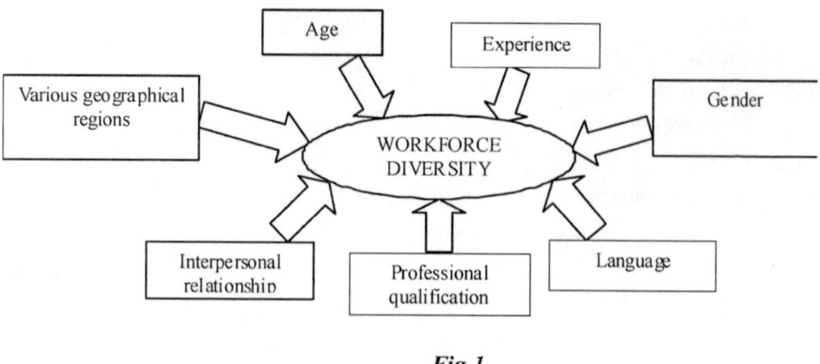

Fig.1

It is through the combined and concerted efforts of people that monetary or material resources are harnessed to achieve organizational goals. But these attitudes, efforts and skills have to be sharpened from time to time to optimize the effectiveness of human resources and to enable them to meet greater challenges. Without employees the organization cannot move an inch. Therefore the management of this resource is also an important issue. Human resource management is concerned with managing 'human aspect' of the organization in such a way that organizational objectives are achieved along with employee development and satisfaction. When the organizations employ human resource having different age, gender, perception, attitude, caste, religion, region then it will be very difficult for the management as well as for the employees to manage and adjust with that environment. To manage diversified workforce is a big challenge for any organization.

Diversity to us means all aspects in which people differ from one another. This includes both the visible and relatively easily demonstrable personal characteristics such as gender, age and ethnicity, as well as the less visible personal characteristics, such as competencies, needs and wants, work styles and character traits. Each employee has his or her own, unique combination of such characteristics. Another definition describes diversity as creating high performing organizations through valuing and using all the talents of employees of different groups. Regardless of how diversity is defined, it is an issue that is sweeping the nation. If the corporate society does not address the issue by learning how to manage diversity, they will fail. "It is very helpful to suggest that diversity is not so much an end in itself as it is a condition of our society and the condition of the World in which we live." Frank Wong Vice President for Academic Affairs University of Redlan.

Each and every individual is different from each other because of their different religion, educational background to which they belong, age and also the perception that forms there personality. When different types of people in terms of thinking, perception, generation come together to work at the same place then definitely a situation may come where all these different types of people may not agree at the same point. At that point of time it is going to affect the interpersonal relationship among people. The researcher has taken some aspects which are a part of diversity among workforce they are age, gender, experience, professional qualification and the employees coming from various geographical regions. Any organization's main motive is to earn profit, for that management wants productive employees in their organization. For every organization, employees are considered as an asset or resources, because they come with skills, knowledge, talent which is scarce in nature. Therefore organizations want to employ such manpower which is productive in nature and every organization wants optimum utilization of available resources. That is why the researcher wants to identify impact of workforce diversity on productivity. The researcher has chosen certain parameters of work force diversity like age, nowadays the government banks are creating new vacancies for young generation by introducing certain schemes like voluntary retirement scheme etc. Privatization is increasing at a fast speed therefore number of private banks is also increasing at a fast speed. Even youngsters are coming into private and public sector banks. Next parameter is gender, gone were the days when the workplace was meant for males only, nowadays females are working in different sectors. Today, hiring diversified workforce is the very essence for every organization to compete in this cut throat competitive world regardless of their language, educational background, experience and geographical region which creates diversity at workplace and can affects their interpersonal relationship which is ultimately going to affect the productivity of an organization.

Workforce Diversity includes the obvious differences we see when we look around: race, gender, sexual orientation, national origin, religion, age and ethnicity. But it's also the less obvious traits, the subtle differences that often register with us unconsciously such as, socioeconomic status, marital status, educational background, language, accent and appearance. We all have something that makes us unique, some special ability or talent that we bring to the table that differentiates us from our colleagues. That's diversity at its best.

Due to the increased rate of globalization, privatization and liberalization we can view the change at our workplace also, gone were the days where the people of same age, same professional qualification, same experience and same region were working in an organization. Now day's females are also working in the equal ratio with males. Therefore the researcher is focusing over these critical aspects of diversified workforce that affects interpersonal productivity of an organization. Next aspect that affects working of an employee is language. People may speak different languages at work place because of different geographical region to which they belong. Due to which the people may find some problem. Employees coming from various geographical regions with their different mindset create contradiction among employees. Gender discrimination is also a major problem at Indian workplace.

Cordial interpersonal relationship among the employees is one of the major ingredients for smooth functioning of an organization. Organization is a network of people who work together to achieve some common objective and if this network has some loopholes then it would be very difficult for any organization to achieve those objectives effectively.

Need of Diverse Workforce

Workforce diversity is a necessity for clarity and efficiency of all organizations. In order to make this work, strategies must be put into place to make the each organization become a multicultural, diverse workplace. This process begins with managers but must include assistance from employees within the corporation.

In today's global market, diversity is a must. Traditional barriers are being broken down, and for many companies cross border trade is essential for the company's success and growth. A decade ago Japan, Europe and North America were responsible for over 80 per cent of global commerce, but new markets are opening up throughout the world and these have brought increased opportunity and also competition. In addition, rapid developments in technology such as the Internet have made new markets accessible to even the smallest of companies.

We believe that diversity is not just a nice thing to do but is also good for business. This belief is re-enforced if we see the benefits that (research shows) diversity can bring, as illustrated below: (Source: Business for Social Responsibility)

Changing Customer Base: For companies to remain competitive in the global economy, the composition of their workforce must reflect their changing customer and market populations. Companies with a diverse workforce are better able to market their products and services to an increasingly diverse market population.

Enhanced Financial Performance: Several studies have demonstrated that effective diversity programs are linked to the company's financial performance: A 1997 study by the University of Houston found that companies with diversity programs performed better than those without such programs.

Reduced Turnover: Anecdotal evidence from companies shows that attention to diversity can lead to reduced turnover.

Improved Productivity: Anecdotal information from several companies - including Intel, DuPont, General Motors, Inland Steel and Pitney Bowes - shows that a more diverse and team-based workforce helps generate new ideas and increase revenues.

Increased Job Satisfaction and Employee Morale: The Families and Work Institute's "1997 National Study of the Changing Workforce" reports that, when looking at a range of issues including equal opportunities for advancement, lack of discrimination, and respect, "employees in supportive workplace environments are the most satisfied with their jobs," and "employees whose workplaces are supportive and responsive to their individual needs are the most loyal."

Decreased Vulnerability to Legal Challenges: Companies that have established diversity programs and management systems to address and resolve potential discrimination and harassment issues are less vulnerable to lawsuits and penalties.

Enhanced Reputation: A company's ability to be known as a great place to work with an open and inclusive environment can enhance its reputation in the marketplace.

Diversity Hiring is a Competitive Advantage

Sourcing people from a diverse background is an essential part of a successful employment strategy. Workers who vary in age, gender, ability, sexual orientation, socioeconomic background or culture, ethnicity and language make a positive contribution to an organization's workforce; they are an asset to company culture and bottom line. And a diverse workforce brings innovation and creative solutions to an organization "outside the box" An effective corporate diversity program is a powerful way to gain competitive advantage and stand apart from your competitors.

The most successful companies have successfully integrated workforce diversity into their corporate vision. They provide mentorship, networking and career development opportunities. They create, update and execute regular inclusiveness training. They establish in-house diversity councils and committees, and assign leadership roles. They target for hire those diverse groups in which their research shows they are lacking. And they adapt their interviewing and hiring criteria as necessary to ensure opportunities are available to everyone.

Top managers often say that their company's people are its most important asset. In a tight job market and a global economy a company that puts people first - regardless of their race, religion, gender, age, sexual preference, or physical disability - wins.

Companies, especially big multinational players which have to deal with these changes, are growingly forced to react. Employees, once a homogenous group in many countries, are increasingly diverse and need to be integrated within and into working environments. Diversity can present an immense source of opportunities but it can also mean the opposite, a big threat.

Diversity management is a managerial approach in response to these trends and can help companies to effectively and efficiently manage their personnel diversity, i.e., personnel made up of diverse and multifaceted people. The text argues that a diverse workforce can be regarded as an instrument of sales promotion, a marketing tool to induce customers to buy certain products or services.

To be successful at creating workforce diversity program involves attracting and retaining the highest quality individuals in the talent pool. For the HR professional it means looking beyond obvious recruitment methods and venues for good people, then learning how to manage human potential sensitively. It requires an ever-increasing awareness of how people from different backgrounds deal with authority, communication, overall business etiquette, and relate to their communities of affiliation.

Promoting workforce diversity is a process that takes place in many stages and on many levels. It requires HR professionals first to recruit a competent and qualified staff, then to accommodate individual needs within the context of the work team and the organization.

In today's world of cultural diversity, our business can't thrive unless we implement a workforce diversity initiative. Besides tapping into the unique abilities and talents of people from different backgrounds, we can improve our image in the community by opening up a place of business to anyone regardless of race, color, gender, ethnicity, sexual orientation and disability.

Advantages and Disadvantages of Workplace Diversity

Diversity is beneficial to both associates and employers. Although associates are interdependent in the workplace, respecting individual differences can increase productivity. Diversity in the workplace can reduce lawsuits and increase marketing opportunities, recruitment, creativity, and business image. In an era when flexibility and creativity are keys to competitiveness, diversity is critical for an organization's success. Also, the consequences (loss of time and money) should not be overlooked.

Having inside information on how to communicate and what a community wants in a product is a great asset. A multicultural company can penetrate and widen their markets with the knowledge of political, social, legal, economic, and cultural environments. Further, having someone within the organization who can negotiate and speak the language of the country is a very valuable asset to the corporation.

Despite the powerful advantages possessed by the multicultural organization, diversity is nevertheless not a panacea and not without its drawbacks. With the benefits of diversity come organizational costs. Too much diversity in problem-solving groups can be dysfunctional. Diversity increases ambiguity, complexity, and confusion. Diverse organizations may have difficulty converging meanings, may find it hard to reach a single agreement, and have difficulty agreeing on courses of action.

Homogeneous groups often outperform culturally diverse groups, especially where there is a serious communication problem. Heterogeneous work teams often under-perform homogeneous teams because they do not allow each member to make a special contribution to the work effort. Cross-cultural training is necessary to enable culturally diverse groups to live up to their potential and overcome communication difficulties.

With all of the positive aspects that multiculturalism brings a company, there are a few disadvantages. Many people feel threatened by working with people of a different age, sex, or culture. First, there is an increase in the cost of training. This increase comes from costs associated with seminars, programs and lectures given to promote diversity in the corporation. These types of training are given to all levels of staff within the organization (Outtz, James L, 2004). They teach employees how to accept the personalities and ideas or thoughts of others. These programs also teach one how to deal with conflicts and prejudice in a professional and civil manner.

In the absence of effective diversity management, culturally diverse workgroups may have certain dysfunctional outcomes such as miscommunications, longer decision times, lower member morale and lower team cohesiveness than culturally homogeneous workgroups. The negative consequences of diversity can reduce creativity and innovation, problem solving, and workgroup cohesiveness. As a result, these negative consequences can reduce market share, profitability, and achievement of organizational goals. (Outtz, James L, 2004)

With having more diverse work environment organization can produce better performance. It is important for the companies to know diversity and how to handle the issues relating to it. Also the need of the diverse workforce is getting more not only because there are different people but also because they can produce better results with having different types of people working. Leaders in the organizations should learn diversity (differences of gender, age, sex and religion in their work environment and also to communicate will between them) and how to manage it effectively.

As workforce demographics shift and global markets emerge, workplace diversity inches closer to becoming a business necessity instead of a banner that companies wave to show their commitment to embracing differences and change. Employees reap tangible and intangible benefits from workplace benefits, not the least of which include respect from co-workers and business gains.

Challenges of Workforce Diversity

Managing diversity is one of the most important challenges faced by managers and their organizations. In today's work environment, co-workers are likely to be of different gender, age, religion, cultural background, race and ethnicity. They also differ in terms of lifestyle, choices available, perspectives, attitudes, value system, beliefs, behaviors, expectations, skills and experiences. These issues are not just about discriminatory practices but they modify the nature and demands placed on leadership and management and bring into prominence the concept of diversity. How well or how prepared managers are able to invest in the concept of diversity will impact not just on work issues but also on sensitivity to customer's needs, legal compliance, business' ethical issues, profitability and even social cohesion. Taking full advantage of the benefits of diversity in the workplace is not without its challenges. Some of those challenges are:

Communication - Perceptual, cultural and language barriers need to be overcome for diversity programs to succeed. Ineffective communication of key objectives results in confusion, lack of teamwork, and low morale.

Resistance to change - There are always employees who will refuse to accept the fact that the social and cultural makeup of their workplace is changing. The "we've always done it this way" mentality silences new ideas and inhibits progress.

Implementation of diversity in the workplace policies - This can be the overriding challenge to all diversity advocates. Armed with the results of employee assessments and research data, they must build and implement a customized strategy to maximize the effects of diversity in the workplace for their particular organization.

Successful Management of Diversity in the Workplace - Diversity training alone is not sufficient for an organization's diversity management plan. A strategy must be created and implemented to create a culture of diversity that permeates every department and function of the organization.

Review of Literature

This study tries to assess the impact of diversity on productivity of the organization. From past years many researchers have studied different aspects of workforce diversity and its impact over organizational productivity and various other areas not only at all India level but at international level. The various findings of past researches were of great help for the researcher to sort out the different factors to be used in the study. This review also helped in finding out the differences between the past researches and the current research on the same topic. Let us look at glance on the earlier researches.

Meaning of Diversity

"Searching for Common Threads: Understanding the Multiple Effects of Diversity in Organizational Groups "Milliken and Martins (1996), opines that diversity appears to be a double-edged sword, increasing the opportunity for creativity as well as the likelihood that group members will be dissatisfied and fail to identify with the group. **"Traits, Expectations, Culture and Clout: The Dynamics of Diversity in Workgroups" McGath, Berdahl and Arrow (1995)** conceptualized workplace diversity by developing a five cluster classification. This often cited categorization is as follows: demographic characteristics such as age, ethnicity, gender, sexual orientation, physical status, religion and education; task-related knowledge, skills and capacities;

values, views and attitudes; personal, cognitive and attitudinal styles; Status in the organization such as one's hierarchical position, professional domain, departmental affiliation and seniority.

Cultural Diversity

"Cultural diversity and negotiations A global perspective" Prof. Rajesh Asrani. In the first part of this paper the researcher tries to explore the meaning of culture, role of culture in finding global opportunities and second part has a major emphasis in understanding the dynamics of successful international business negotiations and strategies that work in the current multi cultural business arena. This paper give some suggestions on appropriate behavior coupled with acculturation, assimilation & maintenance of the new culture **Cultural diversity : "implications for workplace management" Donatus I. Amaram (Nov.4 2007).**In this study the researcher has focused over the effects of cultural diversity on organizational behavior and the advantages & disadvantages of culturally diversified workforce, he says that diversified workforce comes with different advantages like wider labor pool, best suited to serve the diverse external clientele, competitive advantage, creative problem solving etc as well as certain challenges like high turnover and absenteeism, serious communication issues among employees which gives rise to conflicts. Further the researcher has concluded that in order to manage diversified workforce effectively, the management has to show the paradigm change by changing the traditional human resource policy into new by implementing non- hierarchical, decentralized and flat organizational structures.

Need of Workforce Diversity

"Critical review of literature on workforce diversity" Ongori Henry & Agolla J. Evans (27 June, 2007) the author says that implementing diversified workforce in an organization is very much important in today's scenario because of increased globalization. The diversified workforce comes with both advantages as well disadvantages and in order to make the organization competitive it is important to manage the diversified workforce effectively, by evaluating the benefits of workforce diversity in their organization , by identifying the conditions which would enhance the workforce diversity in their organizations and by nurturing, cultivating & appreciating the diverse workforce. **"Managing Human Resources" (Carrel, 2006).** The increased diversity in the workplace converges with the increased use of teams in the workplace through clusters of attributes like personal demographics; knowledge, skills, and abilities; values, beliefs, and attitudes; personality and cognitive and behavioral style; and organizational demographics. Diversity recognizes the unique barriers of race and gender among others while at the same time creating a work environment that values the diversity that all employees bring to the organization. Thompson and DiTomasso in Ellis and Sonnenfield (1994) also argue that a multicultural management perspective fosters more innovative and creative decision making, satisfying work environments, and better products because all people who have a contribution to make are encouraged to be involved in a meaningful way this in turn yields more information, more points of view, more ideas and fewer reservations.

Challenges Due to Diversified Workforce

"Workplace diversity" Josh Greenberg (2004). In this article the author has defined the workforce diversity as a variety of differences between people in an organization. The diversified workforce in an organization affects interactions among the employees because diversity not only involves how people perceive themselves but how they perceive others. The author further says that the organizations employing diversified workforce faces lot of challenges like communication problem, resistance to change among employees, implementation of diversity in the workplace policy, successful management of diversity in the workplace etc but the organizations also enjoys certain benefits like larger pool of ideas and experiences, variety of solutions to problem in service, sourcing and allocation of resources. **"Challenges of leading a diverse workforce" Janice R.W. Joplin and Catherine S. Daus (1997).** In this paper the author emphasizes that various companies are focusing over capitalizing the skills of a diverse workforce but they have to face many challenges like diverse opinion, lack of empathy, differences in perception, lack of participation. Further the author has concluded that these challenges can be faced by effective leadership style instead of implementing traditional methods. **"Workplace Diversity: Benefits, Challenges and Solutions" Greenberg (2004)** according to the author, major challenges are communication, resistance to change, and implementation of diversity in the workplace. **"Workforce America Managing Employee Diversity as a Vital Resource" Loden and Rosener, (1991)** the author argues that an important barrier that affects full integration of ethnic employees is the issue of poor communication or lack of it by failure to overcome the various barriers to communication.

Interpersonal Relationship and Diversity

"Interpersonal Relationship between Teachers and Students: An Intercultural Study on Chinese and Australian Universities" by Suxian Zhan This paper investigates the differences in interpersonal relationship between teachers and students at Chinese and Australian universities. The results indicate that cultures, ideology and gender have a great influence on the perceptions of interpersonal relationship between teachers and students, particularly from the Chinese perspective; the significance of this relationship goes beyond the setting of current teaching and learning and strengthens further in a wider social context. **"Interpersonal Relationships in a Global Work Context" Jeffery Sanchez-Burks and Michal E. Mor Barak (2005)** the researcher has discussed one's perceptions, values, and behavior in such situations reflect deep-seated beliefs about the nature of interpersonal work relationships. He further emphasized that to understand and manage these differences requires understanding the nature of cultural diversity and how it influences relational and communication styles.

Managing Diversified Workforce

"Driving Diversity Management in India: HR's Alienation" Ashok Chanda (Dec 2006). In this article the author says that workforce diversity is a hot and burning issue in every organization of current scenario. Every human resource manager has to take care in managing this diversity and finally he concluded that there is a lack of awareness towards diversity management approach, the manager don't have sufficient knowledge and competency to manage diversified workforce. **"Culture assessment in a cross country deal" Kulin Patel and Anuradha Sriram (Oct 2010)** in this article the author explore the role of managing diversified workforce in the case of mergers and acquisitions. The author said that the merger and acquisitions among the organization is just like a marriage which means that the compatibility among the employees of both the organizations having different cultures is most important for this the culture assessment of both the organizations is necessary. **"Global Human Resource Management Maneuvering Cultural Currents" K Mallikarjunan (2007)** in this the author is saying that each and every individual is different, every body is having their own perception, attitude and thoughts and to manage such type of different individuals require a specific skill because of the complexities involved in this process. **" Culture Compatibility The Way Forward" Radha Mohan Chebolu (2007)** in this article the author says that the culturally diversified workforce is really competent but to manage such a talent is not an easy task it requires such a leader that have an organizational vision and an attitude that are line in culture. **"Nurturing Cultural Diversities A Leadership Challenge" Arpita Saha (2007)** in this article the author says that due to the increased globalization the world is shrinking day by day. Hence the organizations have to recruit cross cultural employees but it is very difficult for the employees to adapt and adjust with a new environment and culture. At this point of time a manager can play a very important role like a leader by providing the employees with training, interactive sessions so that they come to know about the rituals, dressings, mannerisms, food habits of different people. **"Best Practices for Managing Organizational Diversity" by Patricia A. Kreitz (29 January 2008).** In this paper the author says that in today's scenario the organizations are facing diversity challenges from many areas like demographic changes in the workforce and customer populations, combined with globalized markets and international competition. The researcher focuses over the ways to manage diversity strategically. Further the researcher added that successful diversity management requires HR managers to possess skills in leadership, organizational development, change management, psychology, communication, measurement, and assessment.

Gender Diversity

"Changing labor-force gender composition and male female income diversity in Singapore" Pundarik Mukhopadhaya (June 2001). In this paper the author tried to explore employment trends by gender among the various organizations of Singapore due to the increasing educational level female labor-force participation rate has increased. Further the author said that in the absence of proper childcare facilities and availability of part time work majority of women aged 35 or more remain outside the workforce, and this has further hampered their ability to find work. The government has mainly used policies, to encourage women back to the labor force. To encourage married women to rejoin the workforce, since 1978 foreign maids has been permitted to enter Singapore to help in domestic chores and caring of children. ***"Diversity management: A new organizational paradigm"* Gilbert, Stead, and Ivancevich (1999)** found that women who were hired in organizations that valued diversity were found to be qualified for the job that they held; however, the affirmative action label stigmatized women regardless of job type. The creativity of teams that were homogeneous on a series of attitude measures was compared against teams with heterogeneous attitudes. Problem solution creativity was judged on originality and practicality. Results indicated that as long as the team members had similar ability levels, the heterogeneous teams were more creative than the homogeneous ones (Cox & Blake, 1991).

Racial and Ethnic Diversity

"Racial and ethnic diversity and organizational behavior: a focused research agenda for health services management" Janice L. Dreachslina, Robert Weech-Maldonadob, Kathryn H. Dansky (2004). In this research paper the researchers have predicted a three leg stool model in order to reduce racial and ethnic disparities at workplace. The model is: Public policy: to ensure a legal and regulatory environment designed to eliminate disparities in access and health status; clinical practice: to ensure patient satisfaction and loyalty and improve treatment outcomes through the cultural competence of clinicians; and organizational behavior: to ensure that leadership, staff, and the culture of the health services organization represents and values the communities they serve. Further the authors have concluded that the third leg that is organizational behavior is the most effective tool to manage diversity at workplace because by implementing these management practices it is going to give positive outcomes on individual, group and organizational levels.

Diversity and Productivity

"The role of workplace flexibility in managing diversity" Hall and Parker, (1993) says that good workforce diversity practices in the area of human resources are believed to enhance employee and organizational performance. Diversity brings the value of different employee perspectives and varied types of contribution especially when organizational members increasingly reflect the diverse custom base of the organization. This provides a way in which organizations can understand, and therefore meet, their customer needs. Following the same line of argument, **Allen and Montgomery (2001)** say that for an organization to succeed, its strategies must consist of managing change, establishment of appropriate diversity management policies and procedures and target diversity related competencies. **"The Diversity Directive" Hayles and Mendez, (1997)** this study shows a strong correlation between good diversity practices and profits as diversity allows increased creativity, a wider range of perspectives, better problem definition, more alternatives and better solutions. Managing workforce diversity refers to a comprehensive managerial process for developing an environment that works for all employees. **"The Diversity Directive" Hayles and Mendez (1997)** add that even recent studies have shown a strong correlation between good diversity practices and profits. **"Racial Diversity, Business Strategy, and Firm Performance" Richard (2000)** examined firm wide business strategies as a variable in determining the relationship between diversity and performance. **"Human Resources Diversity in Ideal Organizational Types and Firm Performance Employing the Concept of Equifinality" Richard (1999) and Richard & Johnson (2000)** espoused human resource practices as possible contextual factors that influence the diversity performance link.

Need of the Study

Managing diversity in the workplace should be the concern of every organization. In order to survive, a company needs to be able to manage and utilize its diverse workplace effectively. Managing diversity in the workplace should be a part of the culture of the entire organization (Anderson, 2012).Valuing and recognizing diversity is imperative in order to maintain competitive advantage. Diversity management practices enhance productivity, effectiveness, and sustained competitiveness. Organizations that promote and achieve a diverse workplace will attract and retain quality employees and increase customer loyalty (Cox, 1994). The focus on differences in individual characteristics leading to inequality has posed the challenge of achieving unity in diversity and harnessing that diversity to improve employee performance. Failure to manage diversity in terms of race, gender, level of education, profession, ethnic affiliation, religious affiliation often leads to differences in promotions, pay, training, turnover, mutual acceptance, job satisfaction and other forms of inequality (Tilly, 1998; Reskin, 2003). However, the challenges that organizations face in promoting teamwork with employees from diverse cultural background, age, gender, race, education religion and harmoniously directing their efforts towards the achievement of organizational goals and objectives, still shows that there is much to be done in terms of the improvement of workforce diversity management strategies.

The findings of the study will be of great significance in offering guidelines to address the current challenges in Human Resource Management and Development and ultimately enhance employee performance in organizations. The research will help the managers by expanding the literature in the management of workforce diversity to improve employee performance for competitive advantage of their various organizations. It will also enable practicing Human Resource Managers in organizations to remain relevant amidst the contemporary challenges by putting in place programmes for managing workforce diversity and employing strategies for management of workforce diversity in their organizations to get better employee performance. To the researchers, it will pose a challenge to be proactive in the search for solutions to the contemporary HRM challenges and also enrich the limited body of knowledge on workforce diversity. This study will be of benefit to the organizations by improving the benefits from unity in diversity, be it in terms of knowledge, cultural, gender, racial among others. This includes improvement of employee performance and consequently, the overall performance of the organization. The implementation of the proposed workforce diversity management policies and strategies shall also be of great benefit to the organizations in giving it a competitive edge over other organizations. The research shall benefit the employees in terms of improved interpersonal relationships, mutual understanding, and mutual acceptance of each other regardless of the various differences. Although some researchers may have already carried out other such-like studies in other parts of the world, this study brings uniqueness in terms of a different political, economic, socio cultural, technological, and legal environment.

Statement of the Problem

Diversified workforce is the latest and current trend in every organization today. Due to the culturally diversified workforce in some or the other way, people are facing lot many problems at the workplace. As if the diversified workforce may experience less cooperation from some of their colleagues but to achieve the organizational goals each member must be effective in terms of its functioning in the particular department. However, firing is not the solution. A strong link exists between leadership and diversity. Leadership is about empowering people; bringing out the best in others. You bring out the best in people by making them feel accepted, respected and connected. When people feel good about themselves and the organization, they perform better individually and as part of a team, resulting in an organization that performs better. These are the same objectives and desired results of diversity strategies. A sustainable advantage of globalization depends on the skills and abilities of a leader who can manage diversity and implement increasingly complex business strategies. Effective workforce diversity management is a key to global business success (Okoro, 2012). Global leaders should be aware and appreciate the diversity they face in leadership practices.

Findings

After critically examining the literature and various research papers from different authors related with workforce diversity, it has been found that: An organization's major objective is to earn profit and to enhance its productivity, no doubt that almost all the authors are saying that employing diversified workforce is the very essence in today's scenario but to manage such a diversified workforce is a big challenge in front of the management. Hiring diversified workforce will definitely leads to improved productivity, but may prove to disaster if not managed properly because not only the management but employees are facing various problems due to diversified workforce like language problem (which is acceptable and is not due to thoughts of the employees), attitude clashes, and difference in perceptions, which is directly related to human behavior. Further taking diverse workforce as a problem employees felt that they are more comfortable and in tune with the people of their own caste, creed, religion etc which leads to discriminatory behavior and unhealthy relations in the organization. The problem do not ends here it continues with the thought of the employees that they form informal groups only with the employees of their own culture which ultimately affects the productivity of any organization and shows that there will be lack of organizational citizenship behavior due to such thoughts.

Suggestions

After considering all the findings in the research it becomes a compulsion for the researchers to suggest, the ways to handle the shortcomings found during the survey. It is really a big matter of concern for all HR professionals as one side we say that we should include new trends in HR policies and on the other hand, the latest trend like workforce diversity is treated as a problem. However, this problem can be solved by adopting various policies like encouraging the use of common language in the organization among the employees, by conducting various **motivational and mentorship programs,** by keeping the channels of communication open among the employees and employers, by encouraging employee participation.

- Encouraging the use of common language in the organization among the employees
- By conducting various **motivational and mentorship programs**
- By keeping the channels of communication open among the employees and employers
- By encouraging employee participation
- Accepting all differences and integrating all ideas
- Treating all employees with dignity and respect
- Promoting collaboration with others and building effective working relationships.
- By using leadership as a way to foster and maintain diversity
- Further one should accept the fact it is not the matter of culture in fact it is the matter of quality.

Therefore, for improving productivity, quality has to be maintained and not thrown out. In order to create a true environment of inclusiveness, however, training is not enough it is merely the beginning. Soft skills training, including communication, interpersonal skills and leadership skills, is also essential. These are the skills that foster the kind of inclusion where everyone, regardless of who they are or where they come from, feels they are an integral member of the organization and encouraged to fully participate. The soft skills training that I find most desired and has the biggest impact on diversity is leadership training for leaders of all levels. Using leadership skills to promote these simple values can have an incredible impact in creating an environment where everyone, regardless of who they are, where they were born or their educational background, feels welcomed and supported. This is an important key not only to managing diversity, but to retaining all employees.

References

- Arpita Saha, (2007) *"Nurturing Cultural Diversities A Leadership Challenge"* HRM Review.
- Asmita Jha, (2009) *"Need for Cross-Cultural Management"* HRM Review ICFAI University Press.
- Ashok Chanda, (Dec. 2006) "Driving Diversity Management in India: HR's Alienation" HRD News Letter Issue 9.
- Bonnie Daily, Art Whatley, Steven R. Ash and Robert L. Steiner, (1996) *"The effects of a group decision support system on culturally diverse and culturally homogeneous group decision making" Information and Management 30 281-289.*
- Dr. Karine Schomer (2007) *"Workforce diversity in India and the U.S."*
- Eleanor v. Iaudicina *"Managing workforce diversity in government: an initial assessment"* (1995).
- Public Administration Quarterly, Vol. 19, No. 2 , pp. 170-192.
- Emiko Magoshi a, Eunmi Chang, *"Diversity management and the effects on employees' organizational commitment: Evidence from Japan and Korea"* (2008).
- Janice R.W. Joplin and Catherine S. Daus (Aug 1997) *"Challenges of leading a diverse workforce"* The Academy of Management Executive (1993-2005) Vol. 11, No. 3.
- Jennifer J. Dose, Richard J. Klimoski, (1999) *"The diversity of diversity: work values effects on formative team processes"* Human Resource Management Review Volume 9, Number 1.
- Josh Greenberg, (2004) *"Workplace diversity"*.
- Joyendu Bhadurya. E. Joy Mightyb, Hario Damarb, (1 June 1999) *"Maximizing workforce diversity in project teams: a network flow approach"* Omega 28 (2000) 143±153.
- K Mallikarjunan, (June 2007) *"Global Human Resource Management Maneuvering Cultural Currents"* HRM Review.
- Kulin Patel and Anuradha Sriram, (Oct 2010) *"Culture assessment in a cross country deal"* Human Capital Vol.14, No .5.
- L.M. Prasad, Organizational behavior, Sultan Chand and Sons, New Delhi (2007).
- Marie-Élène Roberge , Rolf van Dick, (2010) *"Recognizing the benefits of diversity: When and how does diversity increase group performance?"* Human Resource Management Review 20 (2010) 295308.

- Ongori Henry and Agolla J. Evans (27 June, 2007) *"Critical review of literature on workforce diversity"* African Journal of Business Management, pp. 072-076
- Patricia A. Kreitz, (29 Jan 2008) *"Best Practices for Managing Organizational Diversity"* The Journal of Academic Librarianship, Vol. 34, No. 2, pages 101120.
- Prof. Rajesh Asrani *"Cultural diversity and negotiations a global perspective"* HRM Review.
- Pundarik Mukhopadhaya, (June 2001) *"Changing labor-force gender composition and male female income diversity in Singapore"* Journal of Asian Economics 12 (2001) 547568.
- Radha Mohan Chebolu, (2007) *"Culture Compatibility The Way Forward"* HRM Review.
- Ronald J. Burke, Eddy Ng, (2006) *"The changing nature of work and organizations: Implications for human resource management"* HRM Review 16, pp. 86-94.
- Saumya Goyal, (Aug. 2009) *"Diversity at Workplace"* HRM Review.
- Sharbari Saha, Dewpha Mukherjee Patra, (2008) *"Cross-cultural Issues Intricacies and Ignarance"* HRM Review ICFAI University Press.

16

The Impact of Creativity and Emotional Intelligence on Employee Motivation in a Multigenerational Workplace

Deepali Dabas & Puja Chhabra Sharma

Abstract

In today's highly competitive corporate environment, powerful employee motivation is very important to the success of any organization. In ancient times, management was essentially logical and practical and employee's emotions were not considered. It is important for an organization to recognize that employee motivation goes beyond reward system for multigenerational workforce. At present employees need to be connected with their work emotionally, mentally and physically in order to deliver outstanding performance. In motivating today's employee, organizations have to capture their minds and charm their heart, which can be achieved by assimilating emotional intelligence and skills of creativity. Emotional Intelligence is a key driver to creativity wherein becoming a key for a business success. Emotional intelligence and creativity equip employees with skills to turn challenges of generational differences into positivity. Emotionally intelligence and creative employee enable their organization to offer an environment that develops and motivates employees despite of generational differences at workplace.

This paper discusses the implications of creativity and emotional intelligences by outlining how these skills can enable organization to cultivate cultures that enhance employee motivation. The paper focuses on existing cases from the literature emphasizing that creativity and emotional intelligence impact motivation in a multigenerational workplace. Thus, this paper gives a message to organizers to develop their organizations.

Keywords: *Creativity, Emotional Intelligence, Employee Motivation, Multigenerational Workplace.*

Introduction

Worldwide countries are striving to sustain in a highly competitive environment. An organization may have managers with a great number of technical skills and good education. But can they entirely relate to other managers and employees? Can they motivate employees to be productive at workplace? Presently, employee retention challenges are common to managers regardless of the company's size, technology and market focus (Manzoor, 2011). One superlative challenge is the management that has remarkable variations in positions and goals due to generational differences (Glass, 2007).

A multigenerational workplace is very important for the growth of any organization. The advantage of working in a multigenerational workplace outpace the challenges involved (Hughes, 2011). But one the most important question is how to keep employees motivated at multigenerational workplace? Answer lies in the fact that organizations need to find ways to make the use of their creativity and emotional intelligence. Additionally, they need to find more ways to face the challenges of fast developing multigenerational workplace (Gladwell and Dorwartet al., 2010).

In today's competitive world, employee's motivation in multigenerational workplace is one of the major challenges to most of the organizations. Innumerable literature provides mechanisms that organizations can accommodate to keep their multigenerational workplace motivated. There is no formula to keep employees motivates at workplace as every organization offers a distinctive workplace to their employees. Therefore, organizations must focus on the ways of increasing motivation that meet employee's needs. Managers also need to be sensitive of employee's motivational factors.

Creativity

Creativity is a concept which we use in our everyday conversation. Creative people admire creative objects and things around. Over the past few years' creativity has become very popular in both business and academic world. Potoènik and Zhou, (2014, p. 2) integrative definition of creativity at workplace as the "process, outcomes, and products of attempts todevelop and introduce new and improved ways of doing things. The creativity stage of this processrefers to idea generation Creativity can occur at the level of the individual, work team, organization, or at more than one of these levels combined but will invariably result in identifiable benefits at one or more of these levels of analysis".

There is a great need for organization to be creative these days to the extent that their environment is unforeseeable, threatening or unstable(Roni Reiter-Palmon, Jody J. Illies, 2004). In a chaotic environment, unpredictable change in technology, heightened competition and more and more managers are realizing the importance that employees should be encouraged to be creative at workplace (Shalley and Gilson, 2004). The organizations must understand the behavior of the employees and create a culture which motivates employee's creativity. Suggestion system is one of the most useful way to obtain and utilize employee's creative ideas. Management team must motivate their employees to think out of the box creatively and participate in the suggestion system with full zeal (James Fairbank, Spangler, Scott, 2003).

Nair and Gopal (2010) in their study concluded that creativity is mental ability to produce novel and useful ideas by group of individuals working together or by individuals therefore, it is very important for organization competitiveness and long term survival. The primary aim of creativity is to resolve, clarify and provide best solutions and to improve the ability of the organization at all levels (Nair and Gopal, 2011, p.144).The ability of organization to nurture creativity highly depends on organizational culture. Nair and Gopal (2011), in their study quoted that such a culture is built incrementally by providing incentives, providing facilities, conducive work atmosphere, and leadership. Good leadership impacts followers ability to generate new ideas and question, which is achieved by leaders displaying qualities such as support, empathy, consideration which help to overcome the fear of challenging the status quo (Gong, Huang and Farh, 2009) the study by Gong, Huang and Farh (2009) concluded that there exists a positive relationship between creativity and performance while the Hon (2012) in his study examined the role of intrinsic motivation in shaping environment conductive to creativity.

Kao (2001), in his study stated that an individual's creativity can be enhanced by the organization through several ways, namely:

- Creating an organizational structure that is open and decentralized.
- Support the culture that encourages creative experiments
- Encouraging the behavior of trial and error
- Publishing a success story
- Emphasizes the role to become a champion

- Freeing failure
- Powerful communication at all levels
- Provide the resources which are necessary stimulate the emergence of new initiatives
- Provide a good support system for any success
- Developing a culture that is willing to risk
- Minimizing administrative intervention
- Give freedom to the evaluation
- Eliminate the *deadlines*
- Assign responsibility of new activities.

Emotional Intelligence

Daniel Goleman attributed the concept of emotional intelligence to general public and the academia in 1995 through his book *Emotional Intelligence: Why it can matter more than IQ*. Emotional intelligence as defined by Goleman (2006) is the ability to understand, identify, use and manage one's as well as other's emotional states effectively. This involves a process that leads to the use of those feelings to plan, motivate and achieve. Emotional intelligence can be used as a phrase that refers to the ability to manage, recognize and influence one's and as well as other's emotions (Keating and Harper et al., 2013). Consequently, emotional intelligence can be defined as an interconnection between thinking and feelings; Chopra and Kanji (2010) put emotional intelligence in a very simple terms as an individual's self-perceived ability of their emotional abilities.

There are four important clusters of emotional behaviors as outlined by Goleman and Boyatzis (2008); self-management, self-awareness, social awareness and relationship management. Nonetheless, Emmerling and Boyatzis (2012) quoted that emotional intelligence is best accepted as a competency. According to the trait-based model (Petridges and Pita et al., 2007) emotional intelligence can be defined as an individual's perception of their own emotional capabilities, and encircle behavioral complexion and self-perceived emotional skills.

Emotional Intelligence impact organizational effectiveness in number of ways:

- Teamwork
- Employee Commitment
- Job Satisfaction

- Innovation
- Creativity
- Efficiency and Productivity
- Quality of Service
- Development of Talent

Diggins (2004) concluded that Emotional Intelligence is one of the most important key to effective performance. According to Brown and Brooks (2002) "an understanding of emotions both our own and those of other people play a major role in organizational life."

Goleman (1995) in his book justified that emotional intelligence could be a good success predicator of job performance and leadership ship ability than IQ. These justification further led to more academic researches and studies exploring the concept in later years (Petrides and Pita et al., 2007, Antonakis and Ashkanasy et al., 2009, and O'Boyle and Humphrey et al., 2010). In addition, studies also showed that emotional intelligence plays a major role in the organization, motivation and direction of human activities (Chopra and Kanji, 2010). Employees who have a greater level of emotional intelligence display a better skills in people oriented services such as sales, management, recruiting and customer service (Antonakis and Ashkanasy et al., 2009). Recent studies showed that emotional intelligence is highly important in development of human potential, effective leadership, teamwork, Creativity and innovation (Chopra and Kanji, 2010). Employee intelligence helps employees to manage stress, it is important for enhanced teamwork and cooperation as it helps an individuals to learn in relationships. Ability to work together is completely affected by one's emotions and this requires an ability to connect and integrate in relationships at workplace. One may get the job because of skills and experiences but its only emotional intelligence which will determine how well one will succeed in an organization.

Employee Motivation

The English dictionary defines motivation 'as the reason(s) an individual has for acting or behaving in a particular way'. Motivation is important for an organization to succeed in a competitive environment. Employees are one of the most important assets of any organization, managers must understand the process of motivation in order to motivate their employees to utilize their efforts toward organizational objectives.

Devadass (2011) defined Employee Motivation as a set of intrapersonal and environmental forces that impacts employee's work related attitude. Consequently, employee motivation can be seen to cuts across many disciplinary barriers such as human resource management, economics, psychology, sociology and organizational behavior. In an attempt to grow effective job performance amongst employee, management team struggle to execute effective employee motivation policies (Guillen and Saris, 2009). Manzoor (2011) clarify that motivating employees to perform best even in difficult situations is one of the most important challenges faced by managers. Workplace are changing rapidly these days, employee motivation stay pivotal survival plan for many organizations. When employees are motivated by the managers, they become optimistic and responsive to the organizations objective and goals and can successfully direct their talent towards achieving them (Manzoor, 2011).

Previous studies have shown that monetary rewards had a significant impact as a motivational technique. In management science, Fredrick Taylor featured money to have an extraordinary effect to motivate and maintain employees towards higher productivity and performance. With time, organizations have started using most extrinsic rewards (bonuses, increase pay and promotion) as one of the tool to encourage performance and maintain high level of motivation among employees (Ali and Ahmed, 2009). Suggestion system is also one of the technique used these days to motivate employees to think out of the box and give them opportunity to participate in decision making process. (Fairbank, J. F. and Williams, S. D., 2001). Employees who bring new experiences and ideas should be acknowledged and rewarded to make knowledge sharing a reality that supports creativity and innovation in the organization (Popadiuk, Choo, 2006, Pluskowski, 2002). Nohriaand associates in their study defined a new model of employee motivation. In this model they declared that managers try to increase employee motivation by satisfying the four fundamental emotional drives; that is the drive to bond, the drive to acquire, the drive to defend and the drive to comprehend (Nohria and Groysberg et al., 2008). At the same time, Rukhmani (2010) concluded that motivation is entirely a leadership behavior that comes from the employees wish to do what is right for the organization as well as for the people. In addition, theories of transformational leadership concluded that managers and employees foster one another to a higher levels of motivation (Rukhmani and Ramesh et al., 2010). Many studies and models have quoted that employee motivation is an intricate and sophisticated subject. Additionally to this, in multigenerational workplace where monetary rewards are considered to be less effective in keeping employees motivated whereas younger generations are driven by growth in their career (Wong and Gardiner et al., 2008). Eventually, empowerment and recognition are playing an important role in strengthening employee motivation in today's multigenerational workplace (Manzoor, 2011).

Multigenerational Workplace

Most of today's multigenerational workplaces constitute four different generations of employees, namely Traditionalist, Baby Boomers, Generation X and Generation Y (Gladwell and Dorwart et al., 2010). With four generations working together, business owners, management teams and employees are struggling to bridge the gap. Considering the needs of employees ranging in age from 18 to 80, and motivating such a distinct workforce, are not easy tasks. Multigenerational workplaces can bring out the worst and the best of their employees and the organization (Bennett and Pitt et al., 2012). Therefore, it is important for managers to understand the core values and attitudes of each generation to effectively impact the generation's satisfaction in such a distinct workplace (Gladwell and Dorwart et al., 2010). One of the most important effect of multigenerational workplace is that it can lead to increased productivity among the employees and eventually to a successful organization.

There are four primary generational groups in workforce, each with similarities such as income bracket and age and has been greatly influenced by demographic trends, cultural phenomena and by a combination of events:

The Traditionalists: Also known as the World War II Generation and the Greatest Generation, Traditionalists were born before 1946. Traditionalist contribute to the workplace in many ways including dedication, commitment, loyalty, knowledge and perseverance. They view work as a privilege, they are reserved, modest to disagree with other employees and are uncomfortable with conflict (Murphy, 2007).

Baby Boomers: Born between 1946 and 1964 and 81 million strong, they prefer to stay with the same organization for years. Their core values include advancement and recognition, work long hours, and have plans for their retirement age, retirement savings and investments.

Gen X: Born between 1965 and 1980. The first generation to accept computer and internet, they are independent and entrepreneurial, have changed several career with different companies and tend to be constructive and result oriented.

Millennials (Gen Y): Born between 1980 and 1995, they represent the youngest generation in the workplace. They are tech smart and are engaged with social media through internet and their smart gadgets. Highly educated and need immediate feedback about their performance.

Next Step conducted a research and interviewed over 3,000 clients in 2008 and found out that organization faces challenges when working with different age groups.

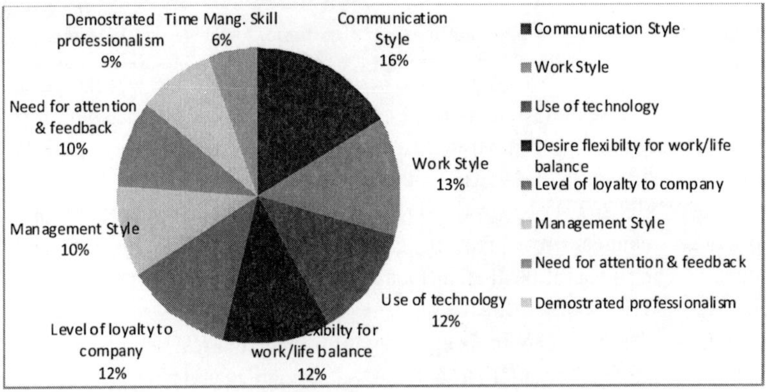

Source: Next Step, 2008

A victorious multigenerational workplace understands the challenges and the dynamics of generational differences and uniqueness and is able to design a space that sanctions knowledgeable skills and effective communication across the generations (Hughes, 2011). With centuries of experience, the older generation attracts wisdom to the younger generation, who in turn attracts new ideas and skills. Nevertheless, challenges of cooperation and communication within the generations are perceivable on a daily basis in a multigenerational workplace (Glass, 2007). Hughes (2011) further concluded that despite the challenges of meeting the needs of its multigenerational workforce, a company creates an exceptional opportunity in its overall business success.

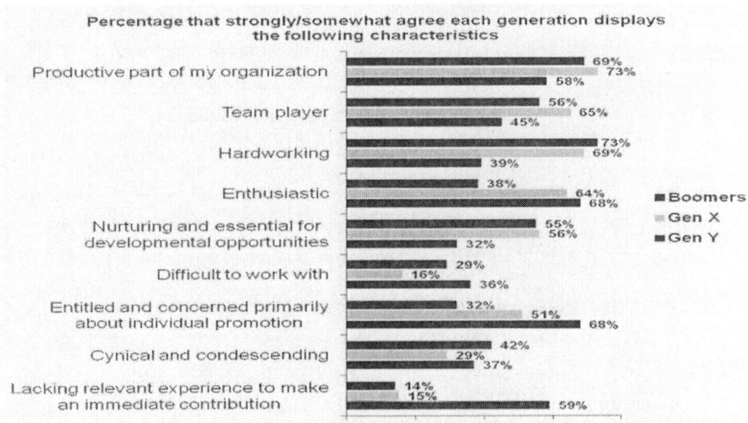

Source: Online Generations Survey, Ernst and Young, June 2013.EY's online generations survey of more than 1,200 US, cross-company professionals includes evenly split responses from managers and non-managers in three select generations Gen Y/ millennials: currently ages 18-32; Gen X: ages 33-48; and baby boomers: ages 49-67.

Different Research studies show that employees from distinct generations need different management strategies when it comes to retaining, recruiting and motivating employees and managers (Glass, 2007,Hudges, 2011, Bennett and Pitt et al., 2012). To productively run a motivated multigenerational workforce, mangers must take into consideration the distinct attitudes and values of each generation that influence different generation at workplace (Gladwell and Dorwartet al., 2010). Understanding what makes each generation's talent tick is important for optimizing an organization's culture. For organizational leaders and HR it is important to understand, recognize and acknowledge the similarities and differences among the generations regarding leadership qualities when it comes to development of leadership programs for current and upcoming leaders, for example (see Figure 1).

Generation	***Assets in Workplace***	***Leadership Preference***
Traditionalists Born 1922-1945 Ages 63-86.	Hard working, loyal, detail-oriented, stable, focused, emotional maturity.	Fair, clear, direct, and respectful.
Baby Boomers Born 1946-1964 Ages 44-62	Team perspective, dedicated, experienced, dedicated, Knowledgeable.	Treat as equals, mission defined, warm and caring, Democratic approach.
Generation X Born 1965-1980 Ages 28-43	Independent, creative, adaptable, willing to challenge.	Direct, genuine, informal, competent, flexible, results-oriented, and supportive of learning opportunities.
Millennials Born 1981-2000 Ages 8-27	Optimistic, tenacious, able to multitask Technologically smart, driven to learn and grow, socially responsible, team-oriented.	Motivational, positive, collaborative, organized, achievement-oriented.

Source: AARP, 2007, Sabatini Fraone, J., Hartmann, D., and McNally, K. (2008), Zemke, R., Raines, C., and Filipczak, B. (2000).

Interestingly, nearly all challenges within a multigenerational workplace are related with the more traditional differences of ethnicity and gender (Rathman, 2011). Management team think that there are great number of differences among generations in terms of employee motivating factors. Nevertheless, studies have shown that different generations at workplace have more in common than the previous literature shows. Studies have also shown that employees are motivated by equally alike things in the workplace (Wong and Gardiner et al., 2008).

(I) Objectives

- To study the impact of creativity on employee motivation in a multigenerational workplace.
- To study the impact of emotional intelligence on employee motivation in a multigenerational workplace.

(II) Variables

Independent Variable

- *Creativity:* Creativity is mental ability to produce novel and useful ideas by group of individuals working together or by individuals.
- *Emotional Intelligence:* The capacity to be aware of, control, and express one's emotions, and to handle interpersonal relationships judiciously and empathetically.

Dependent Variable

- *Employee Motivation:* Employee Motivation is a set of intrapersonal and environmental forces that impacts employee's work related attitude.
- *Multigenerational Workplace:* Generation is defined as "a group of individuals born and living contemporaneously who have common knowledge andexperiences that affect their thoughts, attitudes, values, beliefs, and behaviors." Multigenerational workplace is when four generations work together.

(III) Discussion

It is not something new that workplaces have generational differences, but the immensity of these differences is new and constitute unique challenges for the organizations. Today's multigenerational workplaces need that organizations value and understand diversity in order to get benefit from it ultimately, the need to feel respected cuts through all generations. In current scenario, the needs of employees are remarkably changing and organizations are in a regular search of motivation.

A common assessment of employee motivation at workplace displayed that organizations accept employees from every generation. In a multi-generational workplace, a one-size-fits-all approach to employee's motivation hardly produces the desired results (Wong and Gardiner et al., 2008). Some of the common approaches that led many organizations to maintain a motivated workforce include provision of sharing rewards, work-life balance, offering benefits, engaging employees with customized rewards and building lasting relationships through effective communication (Gladwell and Dorwart et al.,

2010). These approaches have positive effect in establishing a successful employee-employer relationships. Regardless of the positives of these approaches, the frequently changing workplace demographics mean that managers still facing the problems and challenges of building an extraordinary workplace cultures where motivation and creativity are employee- driven.

Emotional Intelligence has come out to be one of the significant skill that managers can efficiently use in informing successful retention, recruitment and motivation skills within an organization (Sharma, 2012). In a multi-generational workplace, employees normally tend to see things differently depending on individual's mindset and perspective. Emotional intelligence help the multigenerational workforce the ability to identify and recognize social cues and respond accordingly in a way that makes evident their empathy of others' aspect or mindset (Emmerling and Boyatzis, 2012). Managers who have a high level of emotional intelligence can easily recognize the needs of their employees and respond them efficiently. Thus, emotional intelligence is one of the important factor in predicting a manager's work efficiency. Managers who possess a certain level of emotional intelligence are able to make time for their employees. By doing this they have a great awareness of their team's needs. Moreover, it authorizes them to provide their employees with regular feedback that help the employees to improve their performance in the organization. Emotional Intelligence is inestimable to a multigenerational workplace in that it increases job satisfaction, employee productivity and leadership competency furthermore, it creates mutual employee-employer relationship which increases employee's level of commitment towards an organization.

Creativity is becoming increasingly significant for the development of the 21st century knowledge society. Creativity has always been at the heart of human endeavor. Associated to innovation, which creates unpredicted value, it is now recognized as central to organizational performance. Creativity in services, products, procedures and processes is now more important than ever before. It is equally requires in the established organization, the public organization and the new venture. The figure given below shows that creative thinking skills are important part of creativity but that expertise and motivation are also equally important. Managers in organization can influence the first two but doing so is time consuming and expensive. They make a more successful difference by increasing the intrinsicmotivation of personnel. To manage for creativity in ways that keep employees stratified, they have five keys (1) the challenge they give to employees to stimulate minds (2) the freedom they offer around to minimize hassle, (3) the way they design groups from all ranks, (4) the incentives and encouragement should include recognition and rewards and (5) the organizational support. Mangers must be motivated to do things for their employees and create positive environment.

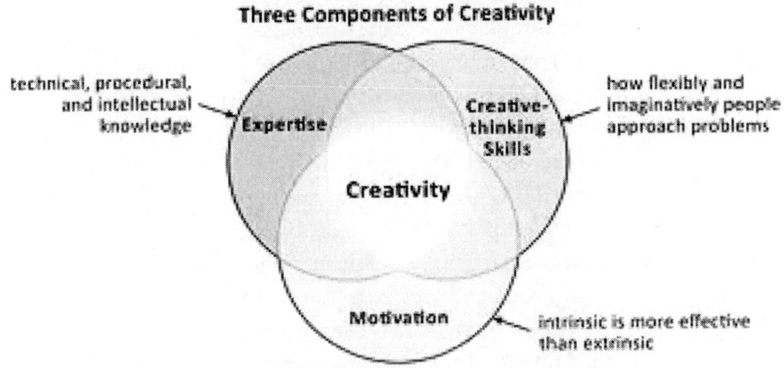

Source: Teresa Amabile. 1998. How to Kill Creativity. Harvard Business Review. September October: 7687.

Organizations that incorporate both creativity and emotional intelligence as a part of their culture can very effectively use their employee's potential and have a great experiences. When both creativity and emotional intelligence are being valued in multigenerational workplace there is so much variety, everyone's ideas and thoughts are respected and valued, teamwork is strengthens and destructive behaviors are controlled. Giving employees space and freedom is an extract of what makes organizations successful and productive. Employees feel engaged and empowered when they have a choice to make. An organization which provide their employees with choices will attract talented employees no matter their generational differences. In spite of the generational differences, employees are motivated by new challenges, increased responsibility and interesting work which are intrinsic motivating factors over the commonly assumed extrinsic factors.Motivation of employee is directly dependent on an individual's way of perceiving things around. Creativity and emotional intelligence help existing generations at workplace to value, respect and understanding each other and be creative at their workstation in spite of their vast differences in goals and perspective. Both these concepts help managers effectively achieve their important role of influencing how employees interact.

Conclusion

In present days business scenario survival of an organization completely depends on advancement. Creativity and emotional intelligence plays an important role and improve the productivity of an organization. There are lot of methods, techniques and systems used by the organization in order to increase their growth, profit and advancement in today's competitive world. Organizations continue to struggle to find the most successful way to keep employees motivated in a multigenerational workplace. Employees from different cultures and different generations are changing the lifestyle of workplace. The well liked notion is that generational difference at workplace lead to difference in the level of motivation and personality. Security of job and immersion to work are motivational drives that cut across all generations in today's workplace. Therefore, it is very important for managers to possess a high level of emotional intelligence and creativity, as these skills will help them to deal with individual differences regardless of generations. Managers who possess both emotional intelligence and creativity find it very easy to turn difficult challenges of generations to positives. Clearly, emotional intelligence and creativity have the ability to positively impact employee with outcomes such as self-efficacy, positive work attitude, leadership ability and job satisfaction. When employees with different backgrounds come on one stage they learn to be cooperative, creative and innovative. The result from this variety in the workplace is that employees learn how to communicate effectively and generate ideas that normally creates high impact. Given such diverse outcomes creativity and emotional intelligence become a very important factor for employee motivation in a multigenerational workplace.

Recommendations

This study adds to the growing body of research and literature that emphasizes on the impact of creativity and emotional intelligence on employee motivation in multigenerational workplace. The study recommends that there is a great need to rebuild employee work environment in order to stimulate creative behavior among employees. There is a great need to challenge existing patterns of thinking and assumptions in order to empower emotional intelligence and creativity. There is also a great need for organizations to rebuild atmosphere of creative work and engagement for their employees. Managers need to foster actions that leads to high productivity and they should also evaluate every management practice and reflect on how that affects the performance of their employees with careful assessment. It is essential for the managers to foster environment which inspires their employees to think out of the box and beyond the routine duties and tasks. Requesting for employee views and involving them in decision making at all level is important in shaping up creative environment. An organization should spend more on resources in training employee's creativity and emotional intelligence. Organizations which have creativity and emotional intelligence development programs and aimed to enhance creativity and emotional intelligence competencies of their employees have observed more powerful change in effectiveness of employee. Further, steps should be taken to improve supervisor and subordinate relationship, management should provide an opportunity to their employees which will result in effective communication at all levels. Management should make sure that employees implement their creative ideas through activities such as team building. Employees should be rewarded for their creative ideas. At the time of recruitment and selection process, management should include creativity test and emotional intelligence test which can be done with the help of questionnaires, this would help management to identify the right candidate for their organization who have a high level of commitment which in return will change the overall culture of the organization.

Referrences

- AARP. (2007). *Leading a multigenerational workforce.* Washington, DC: Author.
- Ali, R. and Ahmed, M.S. (2009). The impact of reward and recognition programs on employee's motivation and satisfaction: an empirical study. *International Review of Business Research Papers*, 5 (4), 270—279.
- Antonakis, J., Ashkanasy, N.M. and Dasborough, M.T. (2009). Does leadership need emotional?
- Intelligence? *The Leadership Quarterly*, 20 (2), 247-261.
- Bennett, J., Pitt, M. and Price, S. (2012). Understanding the impact of generational issues in the workplace. Facilities, 30 (7/8), 278—288.
- Brown, R. and Brooks, I. (2002). Emotion at work: identifying the emotional climate of night nursing, *Journal of Management in Medicine*, 16 (5), 327-44.
- Chopra, P. K. and Kanji, G. K. (2010). Emotional intelligence: a catalyst for inspirational leadership and management excellence. *Total Quality Management*, 21 (10), 971-1004.
- Devadass, R. (2011). Employee's motivation in organizations: an integrative literature review.
- *International Proceedings of Economics Development and Research*, 10.
- Diggins, C. (2004). Emotional intelligence: the key to effective performance and to staying ahead of the pack at times of organizational change. *Human Resource Management International Digest*, 12 (1), 33-5.
- Emmerling, R.J. and Boyatzis, R.E. (2012). Emotional and social intelligence competencies: cross cultural implications. *Cross Cultural Management: An International Journal*, 19 (1), 4-18.

- Fairbank, J.F. and Williams, S.D. (2001), Motivating Creativity and Enhancing Innovation through Employee Suggestion System Technology. *Creativity and Innovation Management*, 10, 68–74.
- Gladwell, N.J., Dorwart, C.E., Stone, C.F. and Hammond, C.A. (2010). Importance of and satisfaction with organizational benefits for a multigenerational workforce. *Journal Of Park And Recreation Administration*, 28 (2), 1—19.
- Glass, A. (2007). Understanding generational differences for competitive success. *Industrial and Commercial Training*, 39 (2), 98—103.
- Goleman, D. and Boyatzis, R. (2008). Social intelligence and the biology of leadership. Growth: *Journal of the Management Training Institute*, 36 (2), 52-55.
- Goleman, D. (2006), Social Intelligence: The New Science of Social Relationships, New York, Bantam Books.
- Goleman, D. (1995). *Emotional Intelligence.* New York: Bantam Books.
- Gong, Y., Huang, J.C., and Farh, J.L. (2009). Employee learning orientation, transformational leadership, and employee creativity: The mediating role of employee creative self-efficacy. *Academy of Management Journal*, 52(4), 765-778.
- Guillen, L. and Saris, W.E. (2009). *Making sense of managerial competencies: a motive-based approach.* INSEAD Working Paper.
- Hon, A.H.Y. (2012). *Shaping Environments Conductive to creativity: The Role of Intrinsic Motivation.* DOI: 10.1177/1938965511424725
- Hughes, L.W. (2011). Managing the multigenerational workforce: from the GI generation to the millennials. *Leadership and Organization Development Journal*, 32 (6), 648-651.
- Keating, R.J., Harper, S.C. and Glew, D. J. (2013). Emotional intelligence dilutes the toxins. Industrial Engineer, 45 (6), 30.
- Manzoor, Q. (2011). Impact of employee's motivation on organizational effectiveness. *EuropeanJournal of Business and Management*, 3 (3), 36-44.
- Murphy, S. (2007). Leading a Multigenerational Workforce. Washington, D.C.: AARP.
- Nair, K.K., and Gopal, R.R. (2010). Advocating Different Paradigms: Relevance of Workplace Creativity. *SIES Journal of Management*, 7(2), 142-150. Available at: http://search.ebscohost.com/login.aspx?direct=true&db= buh&AN=84409567&site=ehost-live
- Nohria, N., Groysberg, B. and Lee, L. (2008). *Employee motivation: a powerful new model.*

- Harvard Business Review, 86 (7/8), 78.
- O'boyle, E.H., Humphrey, R.H., Pollack, J M., Hawver, T.H. and Story, P.A. (2011). The relation between emotional intelligence and job performance: a meta-analysis. *Journal of Organizational Behavior,* 32 (5), 788-818.
- Petrides, K.V., Pita, R. and Kokkinaki, F. (2007). The location of trait emotional intelligence in personality factor space. *British Journal of Psychology*, 98 (2), 273-289.
- Popadiuk, S. and Choo, W.C. (2006), Innovation and knowledge creation: How are these concepts related?" *International Journal of Information Management*, 26, 302-312.
- Rathman, V. (2011). Four Generations at Work. Offshore, 71(7), 10-11.
- Reiter-Palmon, Roni and Illies, Jody J. (2004) "Leadership and creativity: Understanding leadership from a creative problem-solving perspective". *Psychology Faculty Publications.* Paper 31.
- Rukhmani, K., Ramesh, M., and Jayakrishnan, J. (2010). Effect of Leadership Styles on Organizational Effectiveness. *European Journal of Social Sciences*, 15 (3), 365-369.
- Sabatini Fraone, J., Hartmann, D., and McNally, K. (2008). *The multigenerational workforce: Management implications and strategies for collaboration* [Executive Briefing Series]. Boston:Boston College Center for Work and Family.
- Shalley, C.E., Gilson, L.L., Blum, T.C. (2009). Interactive effects of growth need strength, work context, and job complexity on self-reported creative performance. *Academy of Management Journal*, 52, 489-505.
- Sharma, R. (2012). Measuring social and emotional intelligence competencies in the Indian context. *Cross Cultural Management: An International Journal*, 19 (1), 30-47.
- Wong, M., Gardiner, E., Lang, W. and Coulon, L. (2008). Generational differences in personality and motivation: do they exist and what are the implications for the workplace? *Journal of Managerial Psychology*, 23 (8), 878-890.
- Zemke, R., Raines, C., and Filipczak, B. (2000). *Generations at work: Managingthe clash of veterans, boomers, Xers andnexters in your workplace.* New York: American Management Association.

17

Human Resource Management: As it Stands Today and the Impediments Facing the HR Managers in the Current Scenario

Vinitaa Agrawal and Shikha Sharma

Abstract

Over the last few years, Human Resource Management has evolved as one of the important functional area of management. Traditionally human resource management was known as personnel management which was a part of the mechanistic organization having high degree of centralization, formalization, bureaucracy and low flexibility, which in early 1970's became Human Resource Management, as a part of the organic structure characterized by its cross functional nature, low formalization, flexible and decentralized. Today, Human Resource Management is considered as a strategic partner in the business having convergence with the business strategy and which is proactive having an impact on the firm's performance and effectiveness.

As the scenario stands, today's Human Resource Managers are facing enormous challenges thrown before them by the turbulent business environment, global business world, information technology up gradation, socio-economic and cultural shifts which in turn makes it very pressing on the HR managers to prove the role of HR as a strategic partner of the business through cost reduction, higher performance in terms of improved productivity and profits and delivering meaningful and measurable results.

In this backdrop the current paper tries to examine the current trends and challenges facing the HR managers. The major trends and the challenges which will be discussed in the paper are to include evaluation of HR as a function, increased HR competencies, technology driven HR, impact of social networking, talent management, leadership in pipeline, HR outsourcing etc.

Key Words: *Human Resource, Competencies, Outsourcing, Social Networking*

Introduction and Review of Literature

Over the last few years Human Resource Management has evolved as one of the important functional area of management. Traditionally human resource management was known as personnel management which was a part of the mechanistic organization having high degree of centralization, formalization, bureaucracy and low flexibility, as also studied by, Ulrich 1996; Huselid, Jackson and Schuler 1997, that, traditionally, organizations maintained HR staffs that consisted of very different categories of employees. Some positions were administrative or transactional in nature – focused on routine transactions such as benefits administration or payroll. Others focused on narrow areas of technical expertise. In early 1970's it became Human Resource Management, as a part of the organic structure characterized by its cross functional nature, low formalization, flexible and decentralized. Today Human Resource Management is considered as a strategic partner in the business having convergence with the business strategy and which is proactive having an impact on the firm's performance and effectiveness. As studied by Fransis and keegan, 2006, HRM is attempting to move away from the "routine administration of personnel management into a "business partnership model, ultimately contributing to the productivity and financial performance of the firm. Keegan, 2006, drawing on the work of Ulrich, 1997, recognize that two possible roles for HR managers are that of "business partner" and "employee champion."

Therefore, HR has moved from very tight hierarchical systems to open, flat and flexible systems where employees look forward for an open work environment, informal relationships, quality of work life and better work life balance so that they can work with zeal, enthusiasm, trust, equability and openness.

After recovery from economic recession, organizations have realized that quality human resources seem to have become an important base with which organizations have to respond in the emerging environment. People are the most important critical success for any organization. According to Pfeffer, 1994, Firms have increasingly recognized the potential for their people to be a source of competitive advantage. Authors argue that the people management function has come of age and that, increasingly, one primary difference between the average and the best organizations will be how effectively and efficiently they manage their human capital, Burack and Miller, 1976; Foulkes, 1975; and Meyer, 1976. According to Baron and Kreps, 1999, human capital is a key and by all accounts increasingly important part of the resource-base of firms. Human resources have been called the "key ingredient to organizational success and failure."

To cope up with the ever growing market and socio-economic changes the business organizations has to seriously pay attention to three key areas for its success i.e., creating an environment where people skills are developed, better placements of systems to utilize the skill set and finally a very strong reward and recognition system.

As the scenario stands, today's Human Resource Managers are facing enormous challenges thrown before them by the turbulent business environment, global business world, information technology up gradation, socio-economic and cultural shifts which in turn makes it very pressing on the HR managers to prove the role of HR as a strategic partner of the business through cost reduction, higher performance in terms of improved productivity and profits and delivering meaningful and measurable results.

Methodology and Objective

The methodology adopted for the entire exposition is on the basis of deductive reasoning. In a way, the exposition is based on exploratory work but it is theoretical in a sense that its issues have not been studied in the empirical setting. The purpose of this research is to acquire deeper insight in to the major challenges, trends and the impediments facing the HR managers in the present day context. The entire exposition is supported by relevant literature review. So, the study is exploratory in nature.

In the above backdrop the current paper tries to examine the current trends and challenges facing the HR managers. The entire exposition has been prepared on the basis of the upcoming HR trends and challenges. The exposition mainly addresses the current issues that are most relevant for the HR managers today. At the same time it focuses upon the importance of all these issues along with the challenges faced by the managers for implementing them. A few issues the paper deals are to mention, measuring the HR performance, increased HR competencies, use of social networking sites, performance based incentives, use of technology, HR as a strategic partner etc.

Recent HR Trends Vis a Vis Challenges

1. HR for HR's Sake and Measuring its Own Performance: An assessment of the performance of the HR function has become very crucial as they have to demonstrate the bottom-line contribution of the HR function through, for example, reduced turnover. HR is responsible to demonstrate the function's role in organizational effectiveness. The challenge lies in the fact that firm's performance measures are quantitative and financial whereas the HR practices are intangible and also the impact of external factors makes it difficult to isolate the impact of HR on firm's performance. As per the studies conducted by Delery and Doty, 1996; Guthrie, 2001; Huselid, 1995, Much of the research has demonstrated statistically significant relationships between measures of HR practices and firm profitability. But according to Wright and Gardner, 2002, while these studies have been useful for demonstrating the potential value created through HR practices, they have revealed very little regarding the processes through which this value is created.

2. Increased HR Competencies- Multi-Skilled HR: The traditional HR was mainly responsible for data management and administrative work but today HR professionals need variety of skills to be effective in the dynamic environment. Business acumen, financial awareness, analytical skills, change agent, and relationship builder. Also HR today is not only HR's responsibility but line managers are also supposed to assume the role of HR manager. Hence, HR as become more of a generalist functions as against an excluded function. According to a study conducted by Dave Ulrich, Wayne Brockbank, Dani Johnson, and Jon Younger, 2009, HR professionals are expected to play new roles, and to be able to play those roles, they need new competencies.

3. Performance is the Key and Therefore Performance Based Incentives: Performance has been now taken as a crucial and critical factor for determining the rewards and therefore organizations are focusing upon devising better performance measures to match the business requirement. Organizations are also focusing upon high performers to be identified, retained and rewarded. Gone are the days where employees continued inspite of ordinary of poor performance and it was difficult for the organizations to get rid of these employees and had to carry the back log. According to a study conducted by Arold D. Stolovitch, Richard E. Clark, and Steven J. Condly, 2002, Quota-based incentive measures work best. Programs that reward performance based on meeting or exceeding goals generate the most positive results. But at the same time, the literature also suggests that the results of performance incentives are not always positive. Martinez (2003) points out that individual performance rewards are often more discouraging than encouraging to staff. Therefore, the implementation of performance based incentive system poses challenge before the management. They can "introduce tensions and grievances whenever achievements of outcomes is the responsibility of a team rather than an individual responsibility, or wherever rewards are highly substantial or insignificant relative to the salary package" (Martinez 2003: 212).

4. HR as a Strategic Business Partner: The traditional view of HR as administrative support has been replaced by an increasing focus on HR adding value as a strategic and business oriented function, Hope-Hailey et al., 1997. This emergence of strategic human resource management includes a proactive management of people with the intention of aligning HR processes with the business goals within the organization, Boxall et al., 2007. Hence, in today's competitive scenario, HR has to work as a strategic business partner through generating strategic capability by ensuring that the organization has the skilled, committed and well-motivated employees it needs to achieve sustained competitive advantage and by delivering meaningful and measurable results. HR has to provide a unified framework with is integrative and contingency based. HR is no longer an enabler function; it is now emerging as a business partner. According to a study conducted by Wright, 2008, the human resource business partner role depends on acceptance by line managers which in turn requires a profound knowledge of the business, ability to influence decisions as well as strong communicative and interpersonal skills, which poses a challenge before the management.

5. Talent Management and Leadership in Pipeline: Right talent is the need of the hour. HR has to make sure that they have the right people available with them at any point of time through two means. The first, by developing a strong and sustainable talent pool within the company and the second, by ensuring that the right talent is injected from the market when required. For the talent management to be effective and to decide the leadership in pipeline, it should be routed through Competency Mapping, Talent Pool Creation, Assessment Development Centre, Individual Development Plan, Job Rotation and Succession Planning.

6. Social Networking: For Sourcing, Maintaining and Retaining: As organizations and recruitment firms prepare for the upswing ahead, they are increasingly focusing their efforts on establishing a strong online presence. These include developing interactive websites and posting advertisements in job forums and job boards to increase brand awareness online. There is also a rise in the use of numerous social networks in order to get promising leads on potential applicants. Social networking websites are no longer used for personal purposes but also for hiring, business marketing and promotions.

7. Diverse and Multicultural Workforce: Over the past few years the composition of workforce has changed drastically in terms of increased involvement of women employees, as also diversity in terms of multicultural workforce. Though there are many advantages of a diverse workforce in terms of addressing opportunities and facing business challenges as it provides more practical, innovative solutions along with enriching the working styles but at the same time diverse workforce also poses challenge before the management. Organizations need to manage the diverse workforce with openness, transparency, enhanced communication, respect, equality, simplicity and try to create innovative cross functional teams and maximize the value of multicultural teams.

8. Technology Driven HR: The growth and advancement of technology has given an edge to HR managers in managing their tasks efficiently and in a cost effective manner. Ulrich, 1997, mentions that the use of human resource information technology provides value to the organization and raise HR professionals' status in the organization. According to Sunil Goel, director, GlobalHunt India earlier, HR function was just confined to a facilitating function; where one of the roles was to support administration activities. Now, with the passage of time, HR function has become an integral business function and technology here is playing a pivotal role. "Technology is enabling HR in efficiently managing human resources by ensuring the right resources are available with the right skills at the right time," says Deepak Shetty, director HR, Philips Innovation Campus (PIC).

9. Human Resource Outsourcing: Human resource outsourcing has gained momentum over the last couple of decades as it reduces cost and enhances productivity. Outsourcing enables a business to pay more attention to its specialized functions as against those functions that can be outsourced at a cheaper price along with benefits of domain expertise, best practice and process. Over the last decade, the HR function and the delivery of HR services has been significantly altered by the trend toward outsourcing. While the practitioner literature has offered a number of reasons for this trend, important questions remain regarding why these trends in outsourcing have emerged. Equally important, given that HR outsourcing models are still developing, much change is expected in how HR outsourcing will be used across different sectors of the economy (Brian S. Klaas 2008). Although HR outsourcing may be increasing, there is substantial variation in how firms are responding to this controversy (Csoko, 1995). While some firms may make little use of HR outsourcing, others rely heavily on the use of outside vendors to provide HR activities, ranging from routine administrative tasks (Jamrog et al., 1997). One of the biggest challenges in off shoring HR services is communicating across varied and diverse cultures. While outsourcing HR services reduces cost and increases efficiency, cultural barriers may often interfere in understanding the client requirements. HR outsourcing has an undeniable appeal to organizations. Apart from cost savings, this is the best-known reason for companies to outsource (Davidson, 2005).

10. Employee Engagement: HR should ensure that the employees are committed, and have tremendous pride and job ownership. This should be routed through excellent work environment, celebrating events and festivals, communication, fun and joy at work etc. In the highly competitive world as the employees are under continuous pressure, the engagement activities should act as a stress buster and help the employees in keeping high morale. According to Bassi and Mc Murrer, 2007, new age organizations are increasingly recognizing the importance of Human Capital Management in organization development. A key aspect of human capital management is employee engagement.

Employee Engagement Initiatives can contribute directly to the business by attracting and retaining the right talent. The quote 'the taste of pudding is in eating' rightly applies to the engagement activities. The effectiveness of engagement activities is only known after studying the attrition data. If the attrition is on the decline then the initiatives are effective. Further, the low attrition directly contributes to the positive business results.

11. Knowledge Management: According to Peter Drucker, *"The Knowledge Society will become far more competitive than any society we have yet known. There will be no poor countries; there will be only ignorant countries. Thus the competitive position of every country, industry, institution and individual will depend on the ability to harness and capitalize on Knowledge."*

Today for any business to grow and sustain, intellectual and system capabilities and skills are the most important resources as compare to physical assets. Effective leadership and executive skill lies in a fact that how these capabilities can be managed, utilized and converted in to products and services. Key HR processes like Corporate Education, Performance Management and Nurturing culture have a very significant role in the development of the knowledge-based enterprise.

12. Employer Branding: Brand building is not only required for products and services it's become equally important for HR to market the organization to the prospective employees through long term planning and employer branding. HR need to create the image of the organization as a 'great place to work' in the minds of current employees and key stakeholders in the external market as according to Sutherland, Torricelli and Karg, 2002, in organizations skilled employees are hard to attract and difficult to retain and it become critical to business success. The employer branding is used for corporate image building.

13. Work Life Balance: Work-life balance is a vital issue in the field of human resource management and it has got an important bearing on the organizational growth and employee's positive perceptions. In today's fast-paced society, human resource professionals seek options to positively impact the bottom line of their companies, improve employee morale, retain employees with valuable company knowledge, and keep pace with workplace trends. In the 1980s and 1990s, companies began to offer work-life programs. While the first wave of these programs was primarily to support women with children, today's work-life programs are less gender-specific and recognize other commitments as well as those of the family.

With the advancement of technology and changing workplace dynamics, the line between one's work and personal life is narrowing rapidly, thus making the struggle between striking the right chord between office duties and familial commitments a day-to-day affair for many people. Individuals experience more conflict between work and personal life as they continue to pursue the quality of life that they need (Casper et al., 2011). Thus, successfully balancing work and family life is one of the major challenges facing current individual workers, Halpern, 2005.

Conclusion

To conclude, the authors feel that the present day HR is a lot different and challenging as compared with the way it was looked upon traditionally. The authors tried to comprehend the major trends vis a vis challenges facing the HR managers in the current day context. The issues discussed are vital issues in the field of human resource management today and they have got an important bearing on the organizational growth and employee's positive perceptions.

The entire exposition is theoretical in nature but through this exposition, the author expects the future researchers to undertake researches in the empirical setting of the society for their practical feasibility and fair success.

References

- Baron, J.N., and Kreps, D. M. 1999. Strategic Human Resources: Frameworks for General Managers. New York: John Wiley.
- Bassi, L., and McMurrer, D. (2007).Maximizing Your Return on People. Harward Business Review. March, pp 115-23
- Boxall, P., Purcell, J. and Wright, P. (2007). Human Resource Management: Scope, Analysis, and Significance. In: Boxall, P., Purcell, J. and Wright, P. (eds.) The Oxford Handbook of Strategic Human Resource Management. Oxford University Press: UK, pp. 1-16.
- Burack, E.H. and E.L. Miller "The Personnel Function in Transition." California Management Review 18 (1976), 32-38.
- Casper, W.J., Harris, C., Taylor-Bianco, A. and Wayne, J.H. (2011), "Work-family conflict, perceived supervisor support and organizational commitment among Brazilian professionals", Journal of Vocational Behavior, Vol. 79 No. 3, pp. 640-652.
- Dave Ulrich, Wayne Brockbank, Dani Johnson, and Jon Younger, 2009, Human Resource Competencies: Rising to meet Business Challenge, RBL group.

- Foulkes, F.F. "The expanding Role of Personnel Function." Harvard Business Review, 1975, 53, 71-84.
- Francis, H. and Keegan, A. (2006), The changing face of HRM: in search of balance, Human Resource Management Journal, 16, 3,231-249.
- Halpern, D.F. (2005), "Psychology at the intersection of work and family: Recommendations for employers, working families, and policymakers", American Psychology, Vol. 60, No. 5, pp. 397-409.
- Harold D. Stolovitch, Richard E. Clark, and Steven J. Condly, Incentives, Motivation and Workplace Performance, Incentive Research Foundation, 2002.
- Hope-Hailey, V., Gratton, L., McGovern, P., Stiles, P., and Truss, C. (1997). A chameleon function? HRM in the '90s. Human Resource Management Journal,7(3), pp. 5-18.
- Martinez J. 2003. Assessing Quality Outcome and Performance Management. In P Ferrinho and M DelPoz (Eds.), Towards a Global Health Workforce. Antwerp: ITG Press.
- Martinez J. and T. Martineau. 2001. Introducing Performance Management in National Health Systems: Issues on Policy and Implementation. IHSD Issues Note, 1–11.
- Pfeffer J. (1994). Competitive Advantage through People: Unleashing the Power of the Workforce, Boston: Harvard Business School Press.
- Sutherland, M.M., Torricelli, D.G., and Karg, R.F. (2002):"Employer of choice Branding for knowledge Workers," South African Journal of Business Management, 33 (4), pp. 13-20.
- Ulrich, D. (1997). Human Resource Champions: The Next Agenda for Adding Value and Delivery Results. Harvard Business School Press.
- Unnati Narang, *the effect of the global financial contagion on HR trends, policies and lesson drawn there from*, October 28, 2009, PMhttp://timesascent.in/article/
- Wright, C. (2008). Reinventing human resource management: Business partners, internal consultants and the limits to professionalization. Human Relations, 6 (8), pp. 1063-1086.

18

Does Employee Spirituality Affect Their Innovative Thought and Creative Action in the Workplace? A Study on Service Industry Professionals in Kolkata

Dipankar Saha and Kumkum Mukherjee

Abstract

The concept of spirituality is traditionally concerned too abstract in nature. However, in recent times there seems to be a spurt of interest in the area of spirituality, as the available research has found some positive impact of spirituality on individual creativity and innovation, a critically important aspect for organizational success. Spirituality tends to enhance creativity (Krishnakumar and Neck, 2002) to a considerable extent as it helps people maintain emotional stability and handle stress, two important factors in finding innovative solutions. Organizations with stronger sense of spirituality appear to enable employees to exercise stronger values and ethical beliefs in their workplace and empower them to show more creativity and flexibility at work (Mitroff and Denton, 1999). The present study therefore has made an effort to measure and quantify the level of individual spirituality and to probe further to identify the possible impacts of the same on workplace creativity and innovation, a factor considered imperative for organizational success, particularly in today's highly competitive environment. More specifically, the aim of the present research is to find out whether there exists any possible relationship between employee spirituality and their level of innovation and creativity in the workplace. The study was conducted on employees engaged in service industry operating in Kolkata (n=50). Standardized questionnaires on spirituality and innovation and creativity were administered individually on each of the respondents of the study. The data of the present study seem to indicate the presence of a moderately strong and positive relationship existing between employee spirituality and their creative thinking and innovative actions in the work place.

Key words: **Spirituality, Creative thought, Innovative action, Emotional Stability, Stress, Organizational Success.**

Introduction

Importance of creative thought and innovative action on organizational effectiveness

In today's competitive business world creativity and innovation is required for firms that want to stay ahead of the race. Creative thinking and innovation adds value to each and every department of management. It is helpful in finding out different ways of marketing a product, new ways of motivation, new ways of production etc. Creativity and innovation gives an opportunity to explore new ways of getting the business done in a more professional manner adding to both profitability and competitive edge. An organization where creativity and innovation is given its due employees generally try to find out new ways to solve older problems. The staff should be trained with innovative techniques which makes the business stronger and enables the employees to compete in the present day competition. Creativity and innovation remains vital aspects for the success of the organization and it is fast becoming a challenge for organizations benefiting not only the organization but also its people. It has been accepted that creativity and innovation leads to competitive advantage and adds to profit. It is up to the company to take up the challenge of creativity and innovation. When the company innovates it makes its customers happy. Creativity and innovation also increases the size of the business. When the company innovates it is able to create a space for the future where there will be minimal competition for the firm. When one innovates it creates exclusive customer base which also leads to increased market share.

Factors that may possibly inhibit employee's creative thought and innovative actionTop of Form

Turmoil, anxiety, stress, emotional instability in the minds of the employees erodes employee's creativity. Familiar emotional blockages such as anger, fear, restlessness, hate, and love can act as barriers. Creativity and innovation is also hampered by external environment such as colleagues, friends, spouses, or children, or by pressures from other firms. More permanent emotional blocks include chronic sources of insecurity and anxiety such as fear of failure, fear of being different, fear of criticism or ridicule, fear of rejection, fear of supervisors, timidity, or a shaky self-esteem (Davis, 1999).

Effects of reduced employee creative thought and innovative action

Reduced employee creative thought and innovative action leads to lower employee contribution, lower productivity hence lower profits. Reduced creativity and innovative action leads to reduced job satisfaction, which leads to deviant workplace behavior that further leads to increased attrition rates. Reduced creativity also leads to reduces workplace motivation among employees. Reduced creativity and innovation leads to reduced competitive edge.

Old habits, inability to adapt to change, and beliefs create an obstacle to new ideas and take a toll on creative and innovative actions. No creativity halts the progress of the firm and company remains where it is. Lack of innovation and creativity brings in negativity in all aspects of management which leads to lack of faith among employees and the next big idea might be stopped. Employees might feel disinterested in the day to day operations. Some employees may feel displeased and may not like the work environment which does not promote innovation and creativity.

Spirituality

Spirituality is an individual, personal thing. It is a "feeling of interconnectedness". The respondents expressed that believing in God is spirituality and most of them believed in a higher power. Workplace spirituality is not performing religious practices or going into jungles or hills but it recognizes that employees have an inner life a soul that should be nourished to get the best out of them. Organizations should encourage a spiritual culture that recognizes the inner self of employees which gives meaning to their work and helps them to stay connected with other employees in the organization. Organizations should take a balanced approach which gives rises to balanced workplaces and therefore, this paper makes an attempt to understand the theoretical perspective of workplace spirituality and its impact on creative thought and innovative action. Workplace spirituality has become important since the late 1990's, as human resource standards are on the rise and somewhere a relaxed mind is needed in business practices. Employees use various ways to inculcate spirituality. Prayer, meditation, utterance of a powerful name, and asceticism are applied to attain almost all form of spiritual development. Uttering upon a word or thinking thoroughly about it can lead to creative and innovative insights. Numerous philosophers and prophets have used the above mentioned process.

Many poets used to develop their creativity by observing the nature or world and then coming back and thinking upon it using their own perceptions. Spirituality allows an employee to know oneself in a way like never before as compared to others. It helps employees to have a relaxed mind and think about important issues. Miller says that self-awareness leads to openness to intuition, emotions, insights, purpose and values. Hall says you are to "listen to your heart."

Literature Review

In this modern age with so much competition, complexities among firms and a globalised economy requires the introduction of spirituality within the organization so that the employee's hearts will expand and become creative and innovative. Staude (2005) says that spirituality is a transformational process through which the different aspects of life are integrated (physical, emotional, occupational, intellectual and rational) i.e., spirituality involves a connectedness to oneself, others, nature and to a larger meaning or presence which is strongly associated with creativity. Gull and Doh (2004) claims that workers who find meaning in their work activities perform more responsibly, ethically, collaboratively and creatively at work. Employees who incorporate their spirituality and values into their work show increasing personal satisfaction and job commitment (Dehler and Welsh, 1994; Reave, 2005); become creative and innovative.

In the words of Leigh (1997), workplace spirituality starts with the acknowledgement that employees do not bring only bodies and minds to work, but also their hearts, souls, creativity, talents and unique spirit. Spiritual activities benefit all aspects of management because they focus on creativity and innovation. The Sloan Management Review article concludes, "We need to integrate spirituality into management. No organization can survive for long without spirituality and soul." Miller states, "It is too late to argue whether spirituality belongs in the workplace or doesn't. Our spiritual values go to work with us, and it's time to express them consciously."

Organizations should encourage managers and staff to develop their own spirituality which will help them in their creative process. Researchers such as (Rahimi, 2011) says that workplace spirituality may lead to benefits such as increased creativity, honesty and confidence, developed feeling of personal evolution, increased organizational commitment, improved organizational citizenship behaviors, improved attitudes of staff toward their job and also decreased decisions to absenteeism. Researchers such as (Tischler, 2002) have said that by addressing the spiritual side of human experience organizations help reduce stress, enhance creativity. Market value of rms is moving toward more and more intangible resources (Henson, 2003). New ways of competitive advantage are being found out in the form of creativity (Basadur, 1992); Woodman, 1993), innovation (Cho and Pucik, 2005), tacit knowledge (Nona and Takeuchi, 1995), and, interestingly, spirituality (Mitroff and Denton, 1999).

Research performed at University of Southern California's Marshall Graduate School of Business by Professor Ian Mitroff (Mitroff, 1999) shows that organizations which see themselves as spiritual have employees who, (1) perceive their organizations as being significantly more profitable; and, (2) report that they can bring significantly more of their complete selves to work, especially their creativity and intelligence.

Aim of the Present Study

The aim of the present study is to probe whether there exists any possible relationship between employee spirituality and their creativity in the workplace, expressed in terms of creative thought and innovative action. More specifically, the present study has made an effort to measure individual spirituality and determine the possible impact of the same on their workplace creativity and innovation.

Hypotheses of the Present Study

H_0: There is no correlation between the individual spirituality and creative thought and innovative action of employees in the workplace.

Methodology

Sample: Employees engaged in service sector industry operating in Kolkata were selected as the sample of the present study (n=50) by the method of purposive sampling.

Description of the Sample

Exhibit 1: Age Distribution of the Respondents

Age (in years)	*Percentage of Respondents in Each Category*
20-29	62
30-39	16
40-49	8
50-59	14

Figure 1: Age Distribution of the Respondents

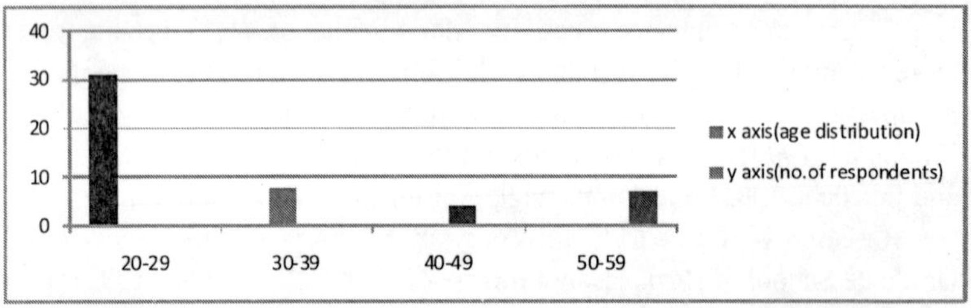

The majority of the respondents are young in age as 62 per cent of them belong to the age group of 20-29 years with only 22 per cent of the respondents above the age of 40.

Exhibit 2: Percentages of male and female

Gender	*Percentage*
Male	92
Female	8

Figure 2: Male and Female Distribution

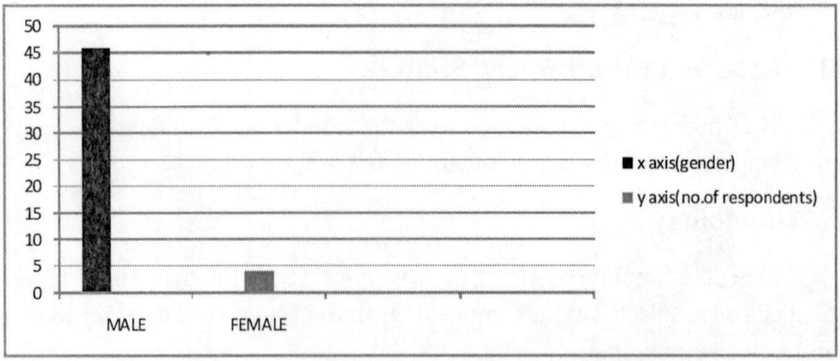

The majority of the population is being dominated by the males with only 8 per cent of the respondents being female.

Exhibit 3. Percentages of married and unmarried

Marital Status	*Percentage*
Married	40
Unmarried	60

Figure 3: Percentages of the married and unmarried lot represented in a pie chart

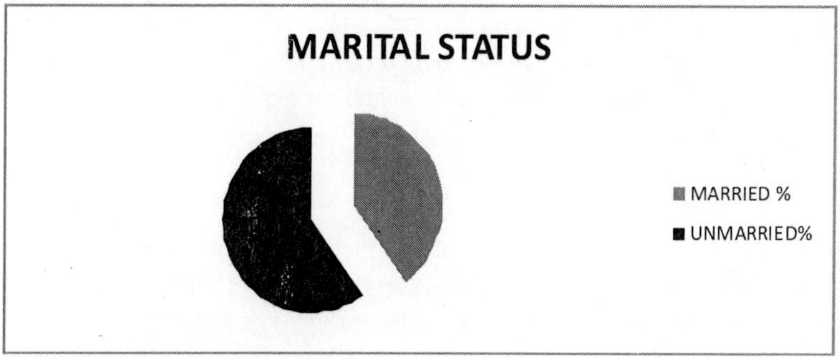

The majority of the respondents are unmarried with 40 per cent being the married lot.

Exhibit 4-Educational qualification distribution along with their percentages

Educational Qualification	*Percentage*
Graduate	56
Post Graduate	32
Professional	12

Figure 4: Educational qualification distribution of the respondents

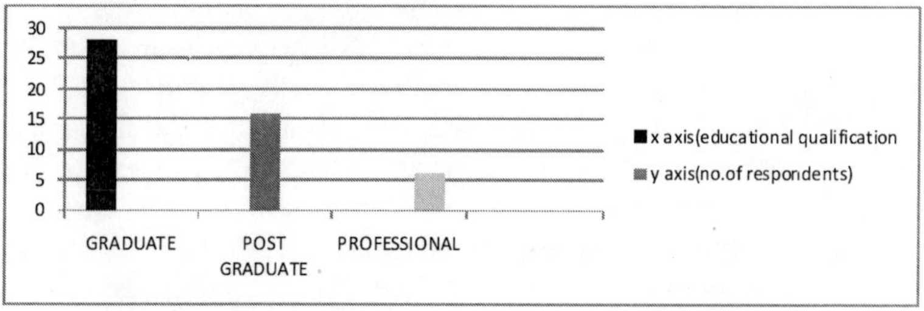

Overall all the respondents are literate with the minimum years of education being twenty with the maximum being twenty two.

Tool of the Present Study: Two standardized measuring instruments were used to measure the individual levels of spirituality and their creativity and innovation. The Spirituality Coping Strategy questionnaire is a 20 item questionnaire has two sections 1 and 2 and employs a 4-point response category.

The second questionnaire is "Creative Thought and Innovative Action" (Martin, 1990) comprises of 36 items with a six point rating scale.

In addition to these two questionnaires, the respondents' demographic data were also collected from the Information blank specifically designed for the purpose of the present study.

Method of data collection: The questionnaires were administered individually on each the respondents of the present study. Their responses were duly recorded for the analysis.

Findings

Pearson's correlation coefficient was the statistical tool employed in the study to examine the impact of spirituality (independent variable) on creative thought and innovative action (dependent variable) using SPSS.

Table 1: Pearson's Correlation Coefficient between Spirituality and Creativity and Innovation

	Creativity and innovation
Spirituality Pearson Correlation	.415**
Sig. (2-tailed)	.003
(N = 50)	

Note: ** denotes that the Correlation coefficient is significant at the 0.01 level (2-tailed)

Discussion and Conclusion

The findings of the present study, as presented in Table 1, seem to indicate the existence of a moderately strong positive relationship ($r = 0.415$, $p<.01$) between employee spirituality and their creativity in the workplace. Thus, according to the present findings, it appears that the higher the spirituality score of the employee, the higher is their creative potential. The magnitude of the association, however, is only moderate ($.3 < |r| < .5$).

This is in line with Krishnakumar and Neck (2002) where they found that the introduction of workplace spirituality can lead to benefits in the areas of creativity, honesty, personal fulfillment and commitment which ultimately lead to increased organizational performance. Firms with stronger feeling of spirituality allow employees to exercise stronger values and ethical beliefs in their workplace and empower them to show more creativity and flexibility at work (Mitroff and Denton, 1999).

The data of the present study therefore seem to indicate the presence of relatively strong and positive relationship existing between employee spirituality and their creative thinking and innovative actions in the work place. As the r^2 value of the Pearson's correlation coefficient ($r = 0.415$) that exists between employee spirituality and their creativity in the workplace is found to be 0.17

(square of the correlation coefficient of 0.415), we may say that about 17 per cent of the variability in employee creativity and innovation can be explained by the differences in their spirituality level.

The data of the present study thus refutes the null hypothesis and it may be said with reasonable assurance that there is positive correlation between workplace spirituality and creative thought and innovative action of employees.

Gone are those days when only financial capital added value to the organization. The so-called intangible aspects of individual behavior in the workplace seem to attract increasing attention today. Concepts like human resource capital and psychological capital are more readily recognized as potentially influential factors leading to the competitive advantage of a firm. Spirituality is one such new-age factor that is acknowledged as a factor critical for organizational success. Admittedly, spirituality is yet to be acknowledged as a factor critical for attaining sustainable competitive advantage of a firm. However, there is a spate of research conducted on spirituality in the recent time.(Benefiel, 2003; Krishnakumar and Neck, 2002; Ashmos and Duchon, 2000; Dehler and Welsh; 1994).The available research in this area seems to indicate that spirituality helps to reduce stress, brings in emotional stability important factors to attain creative thought and innovative action (Krishnakumar and Neck (2002). For all these, it is time the concept of spirituality be integrated into the ambit of modern management today. Successful companies like Hemlett-Packard, Ford Motor Company, World Bank, ATandT, Chase Manhattan Bank, DuPont, and Apple Computer, have brought in spirituality programmes into their management. No organization can survive for long without spirituality and soul (Sloan Management Review Article), as the recent research trend seems to indicate that spirituality leads to a better and more congenial organizational culture, which in turn may eventually lead to more conducive working atmosphere and a better ambience supporting employee creativity. One must find out ways of managing workplace spirituality without differentiating it from the other fields of management. Spirituality helps in bringing joy and a feeling of eternal bliss, the very same factors needed for creativity. For a long term organizational success, it is imperative that organizations learn how to foster spirituality in the workplace.

The present study strongly suggests that employers, management, human resource professionals, industrial personnel all must take a cautious note into the spiritual lives of employees and the richness of employee's aptitude for creativity and innovative actions. A number of rising articles and journals on the topic of spirituality show the interest in this topic among researchers demonstrating that implementing workplace spirituality will encourage the creativity and innovativeness of employees, which will, increase their productivity, and in turn lead to better o performance for the firm in terms of job satisfaction and organizational commitment. Workplace spirituality increases employees' motivation, morale and creativity due to decrease in burnout and stress. Employee's workaholism will be reduced to a great degree with the introduction of workplace spirituality thus reducing the pressure of work stress and thus enhancing organizational creativity. Creativity is essential for any business. With new technology coming in every day and changes in shifts in market firms needs to rethink about their products, services and hence creativity comes into play. Industries are now starting to recognize the importance of spiritual lives of employees and their creativity and innovative processes. Workplace spirituality understands that creativity is not limited within the hands of a few employees, but each and every employee has an aptitude for creativity and innovation. For the achievement of employees' creativity, various forms of workplace spirituality suggested to be practiced in the workplace should include optional morning prayers and evening prayers, arranging yoga sessions, designing appropriate places for individual/group meditation, initiating corporate chaplaincies. These will give employees opportunity for honing their cognitive and conative skills, better self awareness and heightened alertness, and most importantly, reduction of stress. With so much of stress around managers and employees should be motivated to take shelter under meditation, and undertake spiritual practices at work. Spirituality removes uncertainty from work and gives a peaceful mind by removing negative thoughts and this will increase creativity and innovative action in employees. Spiritual workplace allows employees creativity to flourish, tap their creative potential, unleash their innovative potential and practice the same in the organization. Organizations should encourage employees to express their spiritual feelings freely. Higher levels of employee spirituality will not only reduce stress, conflict, and absenteeism, but also enhance wellbeing, quality of life and work creativity and innovative action.

References

- A study of spirituality in the workplace (cover story) by Mitroff, Ian I. Denton, Elizabeth A Sloan Management Review. Summer 99, Vol. 40 Issue 4, p. 83-92.
- International conference on technology and business management March 24-26, 2014. Workplace spirituality an attribute of organizational culture. A new paradigm by Sangeetha Vinod, B. Sudhakar, Shweta Anand, Mrigya Malik, Syed Yaseen, Ahamed Abdur Rahman.
- Journal of Business and Economics Research – August, 2009, Vol. 7, No. 8, Professionals And Executives Support A Relationship Between Organizational Commitment and Spirituality In The Workplace by Eleanor Marschke, Nova Southeastern University, USA. Robert Preziosi,

Nova Southeastern University, USA. William Harrington, Nova Southeastern University, USA.

- Innovative Leader Vol. 9, No. 1, January 2000 Spirituality Can Impact Creativity by Roger A. Meyer, Ph.D.
- The Impact Of Workplace Spirituality And Employees' Wellbeing At The Industrial Sector: The Nigerian Experience by Emmanuel Majekodunmi Ajala Volume 13, No. 2, December 2013, The African Symposium (ISSN# 2326-8077)
- Morgan J.S. 1968 as cited in Martin L.P. "Inventory of barriers to creative thought and innovative action, The 1990 Annual: Developing human resources, University Associates, pp. 131 -141.
- Antony, S.D. (2012) The new corporate garage: where today's most innovative-and world changing thinking is taking place, HBR (September).
- Getzels, J.W. (1980) The psychology of creativity, presented at Carnegie Symposium on creativity, Inaugural meeting on the library of Congress Council Of Scholars, 19-20, November.
- Ritter, S.M., Baaren, R. Bvan and Dijksterhuis, A.J. (2011) Creativity: the role of unconscious processes in idea generation and idea selection, Thinking Skills and Creativity, 7 (1), pp. 21-27.

19

Talent Management and Development in Indian Industry

Priyanka Anand and Puja Chhabra Sharma

A Review of Literature

Purpose: To explore and understand the development of Talent Management in Indian people intensive organizations, conduct a review of existing Literature, identify need for research and gaps, formulate a proposal for further study.

Findings: The exploratory research revealed the Indian organizations vision and integration of the process. Talent management is an important element of the development process for the employees and it is perceived to be an organization wide practice. The process of effective management of the talent pool leads to enhanced employee engagement, reduced attrition and proportionately increased the average tenure of employees. The processes and content of talent management has contributed in varying degrees to development and growth of employees. Most Indian organizations have established the process and are in the stage of formulating the process of Talent Management. However few organizations have been able to establish a clear difference between HR practices and Talent Management. Research clearly revealed that Indian organizations were ripe to adapt robust talent management processes, these organizations also saw the benefit in these processes.

Originality/value: The review of literature probes the following aspects: The perception of talent management in successful Indian organizations, the recognition and growing acceptance of this process and the practices being followed. Talent management is widely adopted by MNC's operating in India, however most Indian organizations are either adopting the practice or in the process. Is talent management and off shoot of HR processes or is it an independent developmental process? Does talent management create a competitive advantage for an organization and enhance employee engagement? Talent management reduces poaching and enhances succession planning. Some of the aspects mentioned above are explored and evaluated through secondary information and data which is available.

Abstract: In the role of business Partner, HR leaders work closely with senior management to attract, hire, develop and retain talent. Yet the skills shortage presents both socio-economic and cultural challenges as talent crosses borders. Thus, in view of workforce trends such as shifting demographics, global supply chains, the aging workforce and increasing global mobility, forward-looking organizations must rethink their approach to talent management to best harness talent. By doing so, they will be positively positioned to succeed in a highly competitive marketplace. In addition, organizational culture, employee engagement and leadership development have a significant impact on talent retention. Taking these factors into consideration, an integrated approach to talent management offers a pathway toward sustaining outstanding business results. The research is conducted to explore and review the studies on Talent Management Practices and identify need for further study as well as any gaps that require to be explored. It is perceived that a lot the concept has attracted a lot of attention from industry practitioners and academicians however intensive study in India is the need of the hour.

It is perceived that organizations recognize the importance of Talent Management and its benefit to the employees. However organizations are also faced with perceptual barriers from Employees, it is felt that identification of talent from an existing workforce creates unhealthy competition and differentiates within the organization. The segregation of employees leads to demoralization of employees and further reduces the level of motivation to perform.

Keywords: Talent Management, Employee's Lifecycle, Human Resource Management, Talent retention, Talent Development.

Introduction to the topic: Global economy has created a more complex and dynamic environment in which most firms must learn to compete effectively to achieve sustainable growth. Workforces around the world have become larger, increasingly diverse, more educated, and more mobile (Briscoe, Schuler and Claus, 2009; Friedman, 2005). This global environment has not only changed the way business is conducted, it has also created the need for organizations to manage their workforces in a global context. As a consequence, the notion of a "global workforce" has received extensive discussion recently (Briscoe, Schuler and Claus, 2009; Collings, Scullion and Dowling, 2009; Scullion and Collings, 2006). Talent management is a mission critical process that ensures organizations have the quantity and quality of people in place to meet their current and future business priorities. The process covers all key aspects of an employee's life cycle "selection, development, succession and performance management. Although, many organizations have begun to recognize the important role talent plays in their success few are managing talent strategically. Leaders need to identify and invest in critical talent that provides a platform for success growth and new opportunities. The increasing fluidity of global labor markets, shifting workforce demographics and changes in the nature of work make it more difficult to attract, engage and retain the critical talent that creates value for the organization (Cheese et al 2008). Talent Management is the additional management, processes and opportunities that are made available to people in the organization who are considered to be 'talent' (Blass 2007). Talent drives performance and teams with the best people perform at a higher level. Leading organizations know that exceptional business performance is driven by superior talent. People are the difference. Talent management is the strategy (Taleo 2010). As the skill shortage bites, keeping hold of your best people is becoming all out war. Talent Management is not a Buzzword: it is a process of attracting and retaining people and companies practicing it are winning. The war of talent, reverse brain drain and a competitive global workforce has caused a change in the perspective of companies the world over. Talent management is emerging as the new trend across all industries. Contrary to the belief that is a makeover to the age old HR practices and procedures. Companies are investing huge amounts on training and developing of employees. The severe competition urges companies to hire wisely and smartly. The availability of the global workforce broadens the horizon and makes it imperative for companies to be focused on clear cut strategies to retain their best talent. The survey conducted on IT, FMCG, Telecom, Entertainment and Banking industry revealed the widespread awareness and knowledge of this fast growing trend. The companies are either adopting or have adopted Talent Management practices to train, retain and motivate their workforce. The opportunity and need to further explore the concept arises from the findings. The rise in level of Job satisfaction and retention needs to be studied.

Although the origins of talent management can be traced back to 1865(Simonton, 2011) and to the fields of arts/entertainment management, sports management literature, and early education, interest in talent management in the business context came in the 1990s with the ground breaking study entitled "The War for Talent," by McKinsey (Michaels, Handfield-Jones, and Axelrod, 2001). This study, reflecting the high tech boom times of the late 1990s,suggested that demand for talented employees exceeded the available supply, thus leading to the problem of talent shortage. Several HR practitioners and consultants recognized the importance of this trend, and as a result, several excellent studies were done in subsequent years by human resource practitioners and consultants to examine talent shortages(Tarique and Schuler, 2010). As a consequence of this, the phrases "talent acquisition, retention and management" and "attracting, retaining, and developing talent" become popular among human resource management community. Global talent management was widely accepted by *human resource practitioners, consulting firms and professional associations*(e.g., Boston Consulting Group, McKinsey and Company, Hay Group, Watson Wyatt Worldwide, Heidrick and Struggles, Korn/Ferry, Lominger International, Society for Human Resource Management, World Federation of People Management Associations, Manpower Inc., Economist Intelligence Unit, The Chartered Institute of Personnel and Development, the American Council on International Personnel). Building on this excellent work, academics recently started to examine the talent management phenomena more closely in the last few years.

Meaning of Talent Management: Talent management literature reveals a degree of debate as to the conceptual boundaries of the topic. Indeed, Aston and Morton (2005: 30) noted that there "...isn't a single consistent or concise definition" of talent management. Notwithstanding this criticism, Lewis and Heckman (2006) identified three key streams of thought around the concept of talent management. For those who merely substitute the label talent management for human resource management. Studies in this tradition often limit their focus to particular HR practices such as recruitment, leadership development, succession planning and the like. The contribution of this literature is relatively limited beyond the strategic HR literature, as it largely amounts to re-branding of HRM. A second strand of literature emphasizes the development of talent pools focusing on "projecting employee/staffing needs and managing the progression of employees through positions" (Lewis and Heckman, 2006: 140). Studies in this tradition typically build on earlier research in the manpower planning or succession planning literature. While adopting a relatively narrow focus, studies in this tradition at least provide a degree of differentiation as to what talent management is vis-à-vis HRM. The third stream focuses on the management of talented people. This literature argues that all roles within the organization should be filled with "A performers", referred to as "top grading" (Smart, 1999) and emphasizes the management of "C players", or consistently poor performers, out of the organization (Michaels, Hadfield-Jones and Axelrod, 2001). While the third approach is highly influential, we recognize limitations to this approach and argue it is neither desirable nor appropriate to fill all positions within the organization with top performers. Equally, if the talent management system is applied to all of an organization's employees (i.e. including poor performers as well as top performing employees), it is difficult to differentiate talent management from conventional human resource management.

In addition to the above three streams of thought about talent management, we recognize and add an emerging fourth stream which emphasizes the identification of key positions which have the potential to differentially impact the competitive advantage of the firm (Boudreau and Ramstad, 2005; Hulesid et al., 2005). The starting point here is identification of key positions rather than talented individuals. This latter approach informs our theoretical development. In this regard our theoretical orientation resonates with Boudreau and Ramstad's (2007) differentiation between talent management as a decision science and traditional HR plans and strategies. Therefore, as noted above, we view an organizational talent management strategy as activities and processes that involve the systematic identification of key positions which differentially contribute to the organization's sustainable competitive advantage, the development of a talent pool of high potential and high performing incumbents to fill these roles, and the development of a differentiated human resource architecture to facilitate filling these positions with competent incumbents and to ensure their continued commitment to the organization. Our definition is premised on the idea that the starting point for any talent management system should be the systematic identification of the key positions which differentially contribute to an organization's sustainable competitive advantage. This is consistent with an increasing recognition that there should be a greater degree of differentiation of roles within organizations, with a greater focus on strategic over non-strategic jobs (Becker and Huselid, 2006), or between those organizational roles which promise only marginal impact vis-à-vis those which can provide above-average impact (Boudreau and Ramstad 2007). This is in contrast to the extant situation in many organizations where over-investment in non-strategic roles is common (Boudreau and Ramstad, 2008; Huselid, Beatty and Becker, 2005). Talent management (TM) has become imperative in the face of today's business challenges. Companies are increasingly realizing that successful TM is the key to high performance.

By assessing available talent, placing the right people in their best roles and finally retaining them organizations can survive and thrive in today's increasingly complex markets. Survey conducted by Mc Kinsey and co. observed that 54 per cent senior managers don't spend enough time on talent management. The study aims at exploring the TM practices in Indian corporate. TM practices considered for the study includes recruiting and staffing, competency management,leadership development and assessment, performance management, compensation and succession planning. Effectiveness of talent management practices is examined through a talent management outcome scale consisting of Absenteeism, Turnover and Productivity as variables. For the purpose of the study, Data were collected from executives and non executives working in different manufacturing and service sectors of India. Co relation and regression analysis was conducted to examine the influence of TM practices on the dependent variable i.e., TM outcome. The result suggests that some of the practices are very important while others less important. Recruiting and staffing, competency management, leadership development and assessment, performance management are found to correlate least with absenteeism,whilst compensation and succession planning appeared to be more strongly related with absenteeism. Leadership development and assessment, performance management,compensation and succession planning are strongly related with turnover, whilst recruiting and staffing,competency management are found to correlate least with turnover. Competency leadership development and assessment, performance management are strongly related with productivity, whilst compensation and succession planning and recruiting and staffing correlate least productivity.

Literature Review

One of the major topics of research in global talent management has been around the notion of talent shortages (Manpower Group Talent Shortage Survey 2011), and the implications of talent shortages on the practice of human resource management in multinational organizations (Collings and Mellahi, 2009; Farndale, Scullion, and Sparrow, 2010; Scullion, et al., 2010; Stahl, et al., 2012; Vaiman, et al., 2012). Ironically the topic of global talent management is prevalent in times of economic prosperity as well as in times of economic uncertainty and economic and financial recession (Tarique and Schuler, 2010). There is considerable evidence that shows even in recent poor economic conditions organizations worldwide are having difficulty managing talent across a wide range of positions (McCauley and Wakefield, 2006). The recent *Manpower Talent Shortage Survey* (2011, p 2); Researchers from IBM and HCI surveyed 1,900 professionals in 2009 from over 1,000 public- and private-sector companies, from a range of industries, geographies and organizational sizes. Respondents scored their companies in 30 specific competencies, which fell into six key practices of talent management: strategy development, attracting and retaining, motivating and developing, deploying and managing, connecting and enabling, and transforming and sustaining.

Trends in Industry: Companies with high scores across the board were more likely to have strong financial performance, based on reported change in operating profits between 2003 and 2006. Companies with Integrated Talent Management strategies have reduced their employee turnover and increased their sales and profits. The war for talent clearly has cooled in the early stages of the 21st century, dampened by economic doldrums and concerns with global security, the real battle to attract, develop, motivate, and retain talent is going to heat up considerably. The pressure for performance on each employee has increased manifold. This exerts an influence on the companies to hire an exceptionally talented workforce. Global consistency in a company's talent evaluation processes is important, because for mobility to succeed, line managers need to feel confident that employees transferring into their units from other parts of the organization meet the same standards that their own people do. Moreover, company support and training is vital to the promotion of diversity. HR managers stressed the need for expatriates to learn more about the culture of the countries they transfer to than just the local language. "If you have to choose," explained one HR director, "it's more important to have an open-minded leader than to have someone with the right language skills." In our view the key implication of the research is that companies should focus hard on rotating talent globally across divisions and geographies. Not only will this rotation support the development of company talent, it will also promote greater cultural awareness and diversity. First, companies should balance make-versus-buy decisions by using internal development programs to produce most — but not all — of the needed talent, filling in with outside hiring. Second, firms can reduce the risks in forecasting the demand for talent by sending smaller batches of candidates through more modularized training systems in much the same way manufacturers now employ components in just-in-time production lines. Third, companies can improve their returns on investment in development efforts by adopting novel cost-sharing programs. Fourth, they should seek to protect their investments by generating internal opportunities to encourage newly trained managers to stick with the firm. Taken together, these principles form the foundation for a new paradigm in talent, talent-on-demand system. The environment for most organizations today is global, complex, dynamic, highly competitive, and extremely volatile, and is likely to remain so for years to come. In addition to these external conditions, most organizations are also facing several global challenges including those related to: talent flow; the managing of two generations of employees, viz., older or mature workers and younger workers; and a shortage of needed competencies. One major result of these challenges for organizations is that they have to be global and that they have to be systematic in managing their human capital if they wish to have any hope of gaining and sustaining a competitive advantage in the years ahead. Many human resource practitioners and consultants (HR professionals) are now recognizing this, especially those that operate globally, the multinational enterprises.

Origin of Talent Management: Since a group of McKinsey consultants coined the phrase the *War for Talent* in 1997 (see Michaels et al., 2001; Axelrod et al., 2002), the topic of talent management has received a remarkable degree of practitioner and academic interest. This relatively recent emphasis on talent management represents a paradigm shift from more traditional human resource related sources of competitive advantage literature such as those that focus on organizational elites, including upper echelon literature (Hambrick and Mason, 1984; Miller, Burke and Glick, 1998), and strategic human resource management (SHRM) (Huselid et al., 1997; Schuler, 1989; Wright and McMahon, 1992) towards the management of talent specifically suited to today's dynamic competitive environment. While the context may have shifted significantly since the latter part of the last century, the notion of talent management remains important.Talent Management is a process of attracting and retaining human capital, and companies practising it are winning. The organizations trying to set up talent management process, the essential guide to managing talent but real success comes when we engage the hearts and minds of individuals. Individuals joining an organisation need to feel that they are valued and that their contribution will make a difference. The new paradigm is talent management, which focuses on developing and retaining good people. Companies that are known to practice talent management have a better chance of attracting recruits at all levels. One of the challenges they face, is to identify and develop the next generation of talent. *Talent is now the key to strategic success, but is conversely getting harder to find and easier to lose. In tackling these issues, every organization must deal with a world of change and variability The paper drills down into how to embed and sustain talent power. It explains the importance of understanding and measuring how talent contributes to an organization's performance and goes on to examine the other capabilities and processes required to ensure that talent is not just retained, but is also actively multiplied. Talent is defined as an ability or quality possessed by a person in a particular field or activity In business it is also recognized as the only true and sustainable competitive advantage. As the criticality of attracting and retaining the best people has increased, so has the necessity to manage talent holistically on a unified and business-centric talent management platform. Talent management is evolving to become a series of complex HR processes combined to make sure you have the right staff, in the right role, doing the right things. Originality/value — Talent management is emerging as a fundamental element of business management. With this in mind, this feature will look at the need for talent management and how organizations need to adapt their mindset and processes if they are to attract and retain the next generation of talent.*

Current issues in TM in India: The process of Talent management is being widely adopted and adapted by large organizations. With the concept of a global workforce the process and policies of Talent Management are being used the world over. The narrowing of borders, free and fast flow of information has transformed these processes into a globally accepted phenomenon. The adaptation of this process in organizations brings forth major challenges, beginning with:

- Identification and assessment of talent during acquisition and during the tenure in the organization
- Grooming the talent pool
- Maintaining high level of engagement throughout the tenure
- Retention of talent pool
- Maintaining an adequate bench strength

Organizations are facing numerous challenges in the effort to make talent management and effective and accepted process for the entire workforce. This process leads to accelerated growth and development for an organization and an employee. However it also propels an employee to work harder and put in more work to increase the level of achievement. (Boston Consulting Group Report 2010)

Identification and Acquisition of Talent

Talent identification is evaluating what the organization has (Supply) versus its needs (Demand) in terms of abilities, skills, knowledge, experience, numbers and commitment. Talent identification primarily aims at :

- Translating organizational vision into goals and mapping the required level of capacities and competencies to achieve goals

  Assessment of talent to profile the level of capacities and set of competencies possessed within the organization.

  Gap analysis and identification of development path for internal talent
- Acquiring talent other than those available internally from the external market.

A Major retail giant in India has taken the following initiatives for talent acquisition:

- All organized retail and big stand alone store manpower mapped. Survey undertaken to understand consumer behaviour and link it to key attributes for potential hires.
- Creation of level wise compensation ranges for scientific lateral hiring and fitment.
- Source of acquisition of talent used are job portals (71 per cent), Employee referrals (26 per cent) and Head hunting (3 per cent).
- Establish a scientific approach to hiring and position HR as a Business Partner.

Talent Development

Talent development requires development of available talent in the organization and development of potential talent available in external talent supply source. Internal development of talent is ensured through identification of skill gap and developing them through skill training and development programs. Talent development requires corporate India to give more emphasis to restructure the external talent supply source.

Talent Retention

Talent retention is critical to talent management. The challenge of TM is more aggravated with the increasingly high attrition. All global industries including Indian corporates are struggling hard to retain the talent. The true impact of loss talent is often unclear to management. When talent walks out the door there are 4 broad categories of costs that the organization has to bear, separation costs (e.g. costs of exit interviews, separation pay) vacancy costs (e.g. costs of additional overtime, part-time staff) replacement costs (e.g. testing, recruitment, interviewing, travel and moving, training) and performance differential costs (e.g. customer dissatisfaction,loss business).With this background in view, talent retention is of vital importance. People have needs and these needs vary with changing times and situations. Achieving this requires a talent retention strategy which addresses the 5 major elements shown in figure 2. The organization needs to make specific plans to create a total retention package that is valued by their identified talent pool It certainly pays to be skilled in India. That of course is true everywhere, but the difference between skilled and unskilled labor in India is particularly striking.

Objectives for managing Talent

1. Strategic Intervention for Talent Retention and Development.
2. To build a sustained pipeline of hi potential talent for leadership and critical positions.
3. To further develop an organization of growth and rewards.
4. To promote Employee Engagement in the organization.

Challenges: Organizations are facing few challenges while developing talent management processes:

- The Company's have had to invest time and resources for concept selling on the need and scope for talent management which led to creation of a talent pool in the organization.
- The focus on cross business movements are very strong however, operational challenges are experienced initially. Implementation of

development plans for employees also absorbed a lot of time and resource.

- The different levels across the organization need to build these plans accordingly, to facilitate growth and tracking.
- Another major challenge faced by the organizations is fast growing rate of attrition due to new entrants in the business leading to excessive poaching of employees.
- This poses a problem for organizations as the market competition has increased and requires the organizations to build a stronger internal pool of Talent.

Need for Further Study and Gaps in Literature

Anticipated workforce changes and cost-effective ways to access talent are key to the next generation of talent management. Predictive workforce monitoring will lead to effective strategic talent decision-making. Factors such as flexible talent sourcing, customized and personalized rewards, distributed and influential leadership, and unified and compassionate workplace cultures will be important for successful talent management. Companies will increasingly utilize different types of employment relationships, and nonstandard employment models will continue to evolve. The review of literature revealed the need for intensive study into Indian Organizations following Talent Management Practices in India; It was observed that there is a lack of available literature on various Multinational Organizations located in India. The companies are widely following TM practices however much information was not available. It is also important to study the Impact of TM practices on ROI or organizational success or effective functioning. The gaps in literature were seen in seeking the above information. Given the high level of interest in the concept of talent management over the past decade, it is somewhat paradoxical that it remains relatively poorly defined and lacking in theoretical underpinning. This review of the current body of literature suggests that from a theoretical point of view, the area of talent management is in its infancy and a significant degree of theoretical advancement is required. The contribution of this paper is twofold; to develop a clear and concise definition of strategic talent management, and .propose a theoretical model of strategic talent management. In doing so we draw insights from a number of discreet literature bases; The paper aims to aid future research in the area of talent management though (1) helping to clarify the conceptual boundaries of talent management and (2) providing a theoretical framework which can help in framing their research efforts in the area. Additionally, it should aid managers in engaging with some of the issues they face with regard to talent management. This paper thus represents the elucidation of a research agenda in the area of talent management. While there have been some useful theoretical contributions to date (see Boudreau, and Ramstad, 2007; Cappelli, 2008), heretofore the theoretical foundations of talent management have been relatively sparse. If talent management is to gain more mainstream acceptance then the theoretical foundations which underpin it must be advanced. Our definition of strategic talent management—as activities and processes that involve the systematic identification of key positions which differentially contribute to the organization's sustainable competitive advantage, the development of a talent pool of high potential and high performing incumbents to fill these roles, and the development of a differentiated human resource architecture to facilitate filling these positions with competent incumbents and to ensure their continued commitment to the organization—emphasizes the identification of pivotal positions as the point of departure for strategic talent management systems. For an organization to fully exploit the potential of their internal talent, they must first identify those positions within the organization which have the potential to differentially impact on performance. It is only then that the emphasis shifts to filling those positions. In this regard we argue that the key is the development of a talent pool of high potential and high performing employees to fill these pivotal positions. Finally, we point to the requirement to support both of these stages with a differentiated HR architecture to maximize the potential for exploiting the talent pools. We propose that organizations which apply strategic talent management systems in this way will achieve improved performance. However, rather than suggest that strategic talent management leads directly to these firm level outcomes, we introduce a number of mediating variables to reflect the significant of attitudes and behaviors of the organization's talent pool in achieving this outcome. These variables recognize the importance of the talent pool in achieving financial performance.

Conclusion

The process of talent management definitely has a lot advantages and it is a good motivator for the employees. These processes are helping organizations retain their workforce and also generate high potential in the existing workforce. The process of talent management should not create a feeling of disparity and differences in the organization. The high level of poaching by competitors makes addressing growth needs and charts for all employees imperative. Companies should also create learning environments for employees. The talented employees always yearn for an extra challenge at work and look forward to accelerated opportunities for growth and development. Many organizations are using talent management for their employees, but most of them have not formalized the arrangement yet. The service intensive industries have adapted willingly however the nonprofit organizations do not relate to the concept. Knowledge intensive companies focus on employee development and collaboration. These organizations rely heavily on the edge they can develop with people. The financial service firms rely more on attracting and retaining talent. Retailers apply a lot of talent management practices; their business strategy is closely linked to their work strategies. Government agencies and education firms are less likely to be enlightened by these practices. Public sector firms should also adapt these practices so that the sense of sedation at work is diluted. The relation of high profits and talent management is already recognized.

References

- Aberdeen Group Inc./Human Capital Institute. (2009). *Retaining talent: Retention and succession in the corporate workforce;* Boston: Author.
- Berger.A. Lance and Berger.R.Dorothy(2010);The Talent Management Handbook: Creating A Sustainable Competitive Advantage By Selecting, Developing, And Promoting The Best People;Mcgraw-hill; London
- Briscoe, D., Schuler, R., and Claus, E (2009). *International Human Resource Management 3e*, Routledge: London
- Boston Consulting Group (2007) *The Future of HR: Key Challenges Through 2015.* Dusseldorf, Boston Consulting Group.
- Cappelli Peter(2008);Talent Management for the Twenty-First Century; Harvard Business Review, Mar2008, Vol. 86 Issue 3, p. 74-81, 8p.
- Cheese, Thomas and Craig (2008); The Talent Powered Organization: Strategies for Globalization, Talent management and High performance; Kogan Page, London.
- Currie, G., Tempest, S. and Starkey, K. (2006) "New careers for old? Organizational and individual responses to changing boundaries", *International Journal of Human Resource Management,* 17, 755-74. Delery, J.E. and Doty, D.H. (1996) "Models of theorizing in strategic human resource management: tests of universalistic, contingency, and configurational performance predictions", *Academy of Management Journal*, 39, 802-35.
- Collings, D., Scullion., H., and Dowling, P. (2009). Global staffing: a review and thematic research agenda. *The International Journal of Human Resource Management*, 20: 1251–1269.
  - Collison, J. (2005, June). *2005 future of the U.S. labor pool survey report.*

- Alexandria, VA: Society for Human Resource Management.
- Dell, D., and Hickey, J. (2002). *Sustaining the talent quest.* New York: The Conference Board.
- Fegley, S. (2011, January). *2011 talent management survey report.*
- Alexandria, VA: Society for Human Resource Management.

- Guthridge et al(2008); Why multinationals struggle to manage talent; McKinsey Quarterly, 2008, Issue 4, pp. 10-13, 4p.
- Lawler, III, E. E. (2010, Summer). From human resource management to organizational effectiveness. *Human Resource Management, 44*, 22 165-169.
- Lepak, D.P and Shaw, J.D. (2008) "Strategic HRM in North America: looking to the future", *International Journal of Human Resource Management*, 19, 1486-1499.
- Meglino, B.M., Ravlin, E.C. and Adkins C.L. (1989) "A work values approach to corporate culture: A field test of the value congruence process and its relationship to individual outcomes", *Journal of Applied Psychology*, 74, 424-432.
- Morton, L. (2010, January). *Integrated and integrative talent management: A strategic HR framework;* New York: The Conference Board.
  - Morton, L. (2009). *Talent management value imperatives: Strategies for execution.* New York: The Conference Board.
  - Morton, L. (2005). *Talent management value imperatives: Strategies for execution.* New York: The Conference Board.
  - Morton, L. (2005). *Talent management value imperatives: Strategies for execution.* New York: The Conference Board.
  - SHRM HR Glossary, www.shrm.org
- Smilansky, J. (2006) *Developing Executive Talent: Best practices from global leaders,* Chichester, John Wiley. Smith, C. A., Organ, D. W., and Near, J. P. (1983) "Organizational citizenship behavior: Its nature and antecedents", *Journal of Applied Psychology*, 68, 653–663.
- Somaya, D. and Williamson, I.O. (2008) "Rethinking the 'war for talent", *MIT Sloan Management Review,* 49, 4, 29-34.
- Sparrow, P. (2007) "Globalization of HR at function level: four UK-based case studies of the international recruitment and selection process", *International Journal of Human Resource Management,* 18, 845 – 67.

- Towers Perrin. (2013). *Working today: Understanding what drives employee engagement.* Retrieved February 14, 2006, from www.towersperrin.com
    - Tucker, E., Kao, T., and Verma, N. (2012). *Next-generation talent management: Insights on how workforce trends are changing the face of management.* Retrieved January 26, 2006, from www.hewitt.com
- http://www.airtel.in/wps/wcm/connect/106f0f804a5628afa41eb59a61245127/Annual-Report-2007-2008
    - Vaiman, V., Scullion, H., and Collings, D. (2012). Talent management decision making. *Management Decision, 50*(5), 925-941.
    - van der Heijden, J. A. V., van Engen, M. L., and Paauwe, J. (2009). Expatriate career support: predicting expatriate turnover and performance. *International Journal of Human Resource Management, 20*(4), 831-845.
    - Van Loo, J., De Grip, A., and De Steur, M. (2001). Skills obsolescence: causes and cures. *International Journal of Manpower, 22*(1/2), 121.
    - Watson, S. (2008). Where are we now? A review of management development issues in the hospitality and tourism sector. *International Journal of Contemporary Hospitality Management, 20*(7), 758-780.
    - Wayne, J. H., and Casper, W. J. (2012). Why does firm reputation in human resource policies influence college students? The mechanisms underlying job pursuit intentions. *Human Resource Management, 51*(1), 121-142.
    - Wickham, M., and O'Donohue, W. (2009). Developing employer of choice status: Exploring an employment marketing mix. *Organization Development Journal, 27*(3), 77-95.
    - Williamson, O.E. (1981). The Economics of Organization: The Transaction Cost Approach. *American Journal of Sociology, 87*(3), 548-577.
    - Wright, P. M., and McMahan, G. C. (2011). Exploring human capital: putting 'human' back into strategic human resource management. *Human Resource Management Journal, 21*(2), 93-104.
- http://www.airtel.in/wps/wcm/connect/about+bharti+airtel/Bharti+Airtel/About+bharti+airtel/?WCM
- http://www.ddiworld.com/DDIWorld/media/whitepapers/ninebestpracticetalentmanagement_wp_ddi.pdf

- http://www.taleo.com/researcharticle/what-talent-management
- http://www.shrm.org/research/articles/articles/documents/0606rquartpdf.pdf
- www.shrm.org/about/.../global%20tm%20lit%20review-final.docx (2009)
- http://www.academia.edu/2589589/Effectiveness_of_Talent_Management_in_India (2015)
- http://www.forbes.com/sites/sylviavorhausersmith/2012/07/31/talent-management-is-risk-management-in-india/ (2015)
- http://articles.economictimes.indiatimes.com/keyword/talent-management (2015).

20

Strategies for Effective Cross Cultural Communication for Honing Managerial Efficiency and Building Creative and Innovative Work Culture

Pratibha Kumari Singh, Indu Prabha Pathak & Jyoti Sharma

Abstract

Bygone are the days when organizations were dominated by mono cultural or homogeneous teams only. Today, the trends of liberalization, privatization, globalization, along with technological advancements have led to unprecedented changes in work environment and thus, have disrupted the old work culture and homogeneous concept of teams in organizations. In the 21st century, the work culture in organizations has thus become more dynamic, complex, volatile, unpredictable and diverse than ever before. In this global economy with no physical boundaries, employees are joining organizations from diverse cultures, different backgrounds, different geographical locations with different attitudes, behaviors, values and belief systems, to be a part of the team with specific objectives and goals. Amidst this, at times the mangers and the team leaders of the heterogeneous teams, find themselves fixed in the unsolicited cultural conflicts while leading the team members of different nationalities, different cultures with varied time zones.

Therefore, while cultural diversity poses a great thereat to managing effective communication in the heterogeneous teams on the one hand, the dynamic culture also leads, at times, to the nipping of growth and development of creative and innovative work culture in the organizations on the other. However, if dealt properly, the cross cultural conflict could be resolved by allowing the team leaders and managers to engage in meaningful cross-cultural communication with the members of their team. Moreover, the same communication tool could also be used by the team leader for cross pollination of creative ideas among the members of heterogeneous team. Therefore, understanding the nuances of cross cultural communication at macro level and micro level along with honing of this skill has become a critical point for the managers and leaders for the socio-economic –political and global health of their organizations and for building creative and innovation workforce in their organizations.

Hence, keeping the above context in mind the objectives of this paper have been identified as 1) to highlight the importance of cross cultural communication in the 21st century; 2) ways to hone the cultural competence and sensitivity among the team leaders and managers for improving their managerial efficiency and; 3) to use this cross cultural communication as an effective tool in building creative and innovative work force in the organizations for producing greater results and enhanced productivity.

***Key Words**: Cross Cultural Communication, conflict, cultural competence, high- and low-context cultures.*

Introduction

In the 21st Century, trends like globalization, technological advancements, rising environmental issues, democratic use of mass media and social media, global networking, and unprecedented fast connectivity in the world have made the world much closer than ever before. While organizations from across the globe are working together and are engaging in global collaborations on one hand, these global trends have also lead to scarcity of 'critical new skills' and their 'uneven distribution' around the world, however, on the other, changing the entire nature of the 21st century workforce according to Global Human Capital Trends Report, 2014, and studies by (Wakefield 2001, Baker and Grower, 2010, Langdon, McMenamin, and Krolik, 2002). According to this report, these trends have not only forced the nations and organizations of the world to be more interdependent on one another but have also lead to development of multigenerational workforce for enhanced productivity in the globalised world. Nations and their organizations are thus keeping constant focus on developing global understanding with greater force for effective businesses and socio-economic and political interactions with particular emphasis on developing cross cultural competency and cross cultural intelligence among their employees to avoid communication debacle.

While such global trends are increasing due to faster connectivity and diminishing of physical boundaries among various nations, they are also leading to identity of common grounds of interactivity among the diverse cultures. Amidst such trends, organizations are hiring and involving employees from other nations and thus concept of creating heterogeneous teams are becoming more frequent in workforce, than the homogeneous teams unlike before. With these global shifts, nations and organizations are thus focusing to understand the intricacies of cross cultural communication, the knowledge of which will not only give them competitive edge in global business environment, but will also enable them to use strategies and innovative practices in their organizations for creating rich culture, and will help them to enhance their business productivity.

However, mere acquaintance with the basics of communication and barriers to effective communication will not lead to successful results of these teams, therefore, if the team leaders and managers of the heterogeneous team will be well versed in the cross cultural communication and will be trained to develop cultural sensitivity, competence and intelligence, they will, then be expected to add value and better understanding to their overall project. Keeping this hypothesis in mind, this research, hence aims at finding the answers to these questions (a) why cross cultural communication is an important skill to be honed in the 21st century, (b) how cultural competency and intelligence can be inculcated in the leaders and their team mates through cross cultural training for enhanced productivity and better results (c) and how this cultural diversity could be used as a tool to enrich work culture and bring effective results in overall performance of the heterogeneous teams.

Literature Review: Culture and Cross Cultural Communication

Before moving further and finding answers to the above questions, it is important to understand the nuances of culture first; what is cross cultural communication, second; and brief history of its origin, third.

In order to define and understand culture, the inventory (table 1.1), which is not exhaustive, has been given below.

Definition and Description of Culture

Definition and description	*Source*
"Culture is communication and communication is culture."	Edwart T Hall, 1959
"It is the collective programming of the mind which distinguishes the members of one group or category of people from another."	Geert Hofstede, 1991

"Culture is a fuzzy set of attitudes, beliefs, behavioral norms, and basic assumptions and values that are shared by a group of people, and that influence each member's behavior and his/her interpretations of the "meaning" of other people's behaviour."	Spencer-Oatey, 2000
Culture is that which gives people a sense of who they are, of belonging, of how they should behave, and of what they should be doing. It provides a learned, shared, and interrelated set of symbols, codes, and values that direct and justify human behavior.	Harris and Moran, 1987
Culture is a phenomenon that has bound societies which share similar beliefs, norms, attitudes and notions of mindsets together and it plays a major role in shaping and governing the behavior of people, thus Cross cultural communication where people belonging to diverse cultures being in communication with each other needs to be effective in order to facilitate business firms to achieve their business objectives.	Dinuk Arseculeratne and Rashad Yazdanifard

Table 1.1

While the inventory given above defines culture, the studies given below show the impact of culture on organizations, their communication flow and their work culture. According to Hofstede (1980) there are two kinds of cultures: culture and National culture, which differs when it comes to values and practice. Values come from the experience of life, while practices come from social experience: working. In another study by Rufei He and Jianchao Liu, culture has been shown to influences people's way of thinking and behaving and result in different understandings toward vision and purposes of firms. Their study employs a qualitative approach in a single case study of Swedish company and its subsidiary in China. Moreover, the findings of this study indicate that the barriers of communication come from the national culture's influence on the work place and behaviors of people with different identity. (Liu, 2010) Hence, different characteristics of culture result in thinking, understanding and communicational diversity. These diversities obstruct organizational development and management more or less. Adler and Graham (1989) in their study refer to Mishler (1965, p.517) and argue that "The greater the cultural differences, the more likely barriers to communication and misunderstandings become."

Based on theses definitions and descriptions we can say that culture refers to the way we look at the things, make impressions and perceive the things. And therefore, the way we behave and respond to certain situations result from our own deep rooted culture and cultural conditioning. Our values, beliefs, traditions and convictions are shaped by our culture. Communication is thus deeply affected by our culture and this definition that, "Culture is communication and communication is culture" by Edwart T Hall is appropriate to quote here (Hall, 1959, p. 186).

With such cultural conditioning, communication with other nations, organizations and employees from different nations indeed becomes a challenge. Mere knowledge of communication would not add to the deeper understanding of the nuances of culture at micro and macro level therefore employees and managers need to be good at cross cultural communication which refers to the ability of successfully communicating with the members of other culture or community to foster and form meaningful relationship. It is communication across culture and across boundaries.

Now understanding culture and cross cultural communication, it is important to have a look at the genesis of this field, cross cultural communication, as an area of academic study. Although, the subject of intercultural communication as a field of study was introduced in the seminal publication, *The Silent Language* by Edward T Hall in 1959, however, its genesis could still be traced back to the collaborative endeavour of Edward T Hall, the Anthropologist and linguist George L. Trager at the Foreign Service Institute in the 1950s. After him, there were many scholars and researcher who defined culture and cross cultural communication.

However, the origin of cross cultural communication as a field of study grew in its dimension, understanding and popularity due to insights from the fields of anthropology, psychology, sociology and linguistics as shown in figure below.

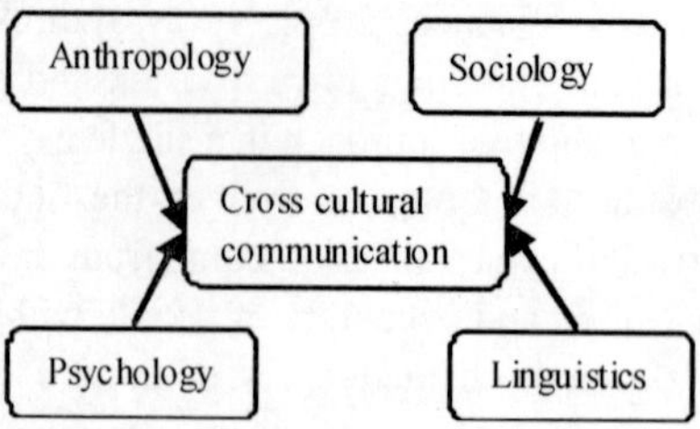

Figure 1.1

Source: Authors

Based on the studies above, it can be said that the impact of culture is highly pertinent on people, organizations and the entire nation. And this impacts their values, perceptions, ideologies, communications and work ethics at home and in organizations. It is obvious to come across intercultural encounters in a multinational organization, thus. This cultural conditioning may act as a blind fold when the managers and leaders communicate with the members of their teams. The employees may face cultural shock when they are not well versed in the cross-cultural communication.

However, if the leaders and managers are familiar with this cultural conditioning of their teammates well in advance, they can understand and analyze and well predict the conflicts arising out of such situations. Therefore, the organizations must take the onus to train their leaders and managers in gaining cross cultural competency and intelligence and must explain them first, the importance of cross cultural communication and its relevance in the 21st century diverse workforce set up.

Importance of Cross Cultural Communication

In order to meet the first objective of the research, the authors present the studies examined below to highlight the importance of cross cultural communication since it has become one of the most important aspects in a newer world where economical strength supersedes military prowess, and therefore, in order to gain access to new markets and sustain business with them how it pays richly to be sensitive towards the cultural differences and perceptions in 21st Century workforce.

In a study done by S. Krishna, Sahay and Welsham, on the importance of Cross cultural communication for a period of five years, through in-depth case studies and with a particular empirical focus on outsourcers in North America, Western Europe and Japan to software suppliers of India, the primary conclusion was that "Particular societies tend to have distinct ways of working, and they can prove problematic when attempting cross-border collaboration." This conclusion was substantiated with the example that, "Indian software companies have found they need to approach communication with U.S. and Japanese clients in very different ways. U.S. client companies normally work with extensive written agreements and explicit documentation, reinforced with frequent and informal telephone and email contact. In contrast, Japanese clients tend to prefer verbal communication, more tacit and continuously negotiated agreements, and less frequent but more formal use of electronic media." The second conclusion at which they arrived was regarding cultural norms of behavior, attitude towards authority and language issues which can prove to be quite challenging if not addressed properly. (S. Krishna, April 2004)

Highlighting the importance of Cross cultural communication in 21st century, Hilton says "Companies that are successfully able to communicate cross culturally have a competitive advantage because they can devote more time and resources to conducting business and less time on internal and external communication issues (Hilton, 2007) whereas Thakkar and Matthews opine that " Communication is necessary for individuals to express themselves and to fulfill basic needs. The same holds true for businesses, governments, and countries." According to them "Without the ability to communicate and understand each other, there would be chaos. Communication that is based on cultural understanding is more apt to prevent misunderstandings caused by personal biases and prejudices." (Thakkar, 2012)

Furthermore, Yajun Xie puts focus on China while elaborating on the value addition created by an understanding of cross border and cross cultural differences. As per the author, "those workers who are ready to admit, understand, and respect the cultural differences of other nations and are ready to take helpful steps, have a great advantage in performing tasks in a multicultural environment. Intercultural management should not be considered as a marginal area but as a significant area for international as well as purely national companies, if they want to succeed in the demanding competitive environment." (Xie, 2013) Every enterprise should pay enough attention to cross- cultural barriers and resort to the most suitable method for predicting, avoiding, and resolving the conflicts caused by these cross-cultural barriers suggests study by (Tufte PA, 2003).

In their journal article on developing usable cross cultural websites, Minochad, Frenchc and Changc state that people differ across regional, linguistic and country boundaries and user requirements are strongly influenced by their local and cultural perspective. For this purpose firstly they introduce the concept of cultural attractors to define the interface design elements of the website that reflect the signs and their meanings to match the expectations of the local culture. The paper then discusses a number of cultural models that can assist cross-cultural developers. An issue that concerns cross-cultural developers is the validity of cultural models derived from other disciplines. One approach is to undertake local website audits to identify the elements that are indigenous to sites in the target culture. The alternative is to predicatively apply theoretical models such as Hofstede when proposing designs. In respect of tools for design that successfully translate requirements in to usable solutions, a theoretical approach is to apply the limited but developing cross-cultural guidelines, whereas a practical approach would require effective prototyping. The same issues are mirrored in evaluation strategies: either test prototypes with real users in the target culture, or evaluate against cross-cultural heuristics. For significant international projects it is likely that tools and techniques selected from across all three underpinning issues will be necessary for effective design. (Shailey Minochad, 2004)

Additionally, the importance of cross-cultural communication within the constraining framework of cultural stereotypes and cultural differences, which can be, in the long run, softened or dissipated by placing them into the proper context and using them adequately has been pointed out in a research paper by Eugenia Irimias. (IRIMIA[a], 2011)

In another article the author defined major types of cultural barriers and provided empirical evidence of their occurrences. The research findings also suggest that cross-cultural interactions or work in a multi-cultural environment can be a determinant of job satisfaction. Functioning in such an environment affects development of competence and influences satisfaction of the need for fulfillment. (Ma³gorzata Rozkwitalska, November 2010)Whereas Through a qualitative study, based on a grounded theory approach, Ellen Eun Kyoo Kim identifies issues that concern ESL customers in intercultural service encounters. The findings suggest that the language barrier generates negative emotional and cognitive responses, and prevents ESL customers from taking certain actions such as seeking necessary information or complaining about service failures. (Ellen Eun Kyoo Kim)

Cross-cultural communication confronts us with limits to our perceptions, our interpretations, and our evaluations. Cross-cultural perspectives tend to render everything relative and slightly uncertain. Entering a foreign culture is tantamount to knowing the words without knowing the music, or knowing the music without knowing the beat. Our natural tendencies lead us back to our prior experience: our default option becomes the familiarity of our own culture, thus precluding our accurate understanding of others' cultures. (Adler N. J., 1991)

While the studies above explain the importance of cross cultural communication and its relevance, the studies by (Marquardt and Horvath, 2001) bottom lines that managing diverse culture, cultural differences, and cross cultural conflicts has become the most common challenge of multicultural teams. Thus, Shenkar and Zeira, (1992), through their study reveal that cultural differences among team members can cause conflict, poor performance and misunderstanding. In fact, besides the heterogeneous team members, if the Managers are from different cultures, they too are likely to interpret and respond differently to the same strategic issues or team tasks because they have distinct perceptions of environmental opportunities and threats and internal strengths and weaknesses.

The studies, therefore, presented above highlight that that managers and team leaders need to understand the importance of cross cultural communication in present century, knowledge of which will facilitate the leaders and managers to lead, direct, supervise best and bring best results from the their heterogeneous teams.

Therefore it is important to develop the knowledge of cross cultural communication among the team leaders and managers to address the common challenges faced by their multicultural teams. Managers working on multicultural teams must be competent cross cultural communicators in order to work effectively with people from different cultural backgrounds. The next segment, thus deals with the training and honing of cross cultural skills in managers and team leaders for improving their cultural competence and sensitivity, meeting the objective two of the research.

Ways to hone the Cross Cultural Communication and Cultural Competency among the Team Managers and Team Leaders

While employees from different cultures come with different set of beliefs, perceptions, thoughts and values, organizations too offer them set of their multi-dimensional and multi-level cultural concept. Thus, for managers and team leaders it is important to be well-versed with their organizational cultures and they should also be ready to create and innovate this culture with their leadership style. Although, this in itself is another field of research, however, for the present paper, the authors just want to underline that the employees and the leaders work at various cultural level. And therefore, for the present study, Cross cultural training, which is one of the effective ways to hone the cross cultural communication among the team leaders and managers, has been studied. This training aims at three vital aspects.

First, maintenance of self mental health, psychological well being, stress reduction and fostering feelings of self confidence among the team leaders; second, honing of skills required to make better relationships with host nationals; and third, honing cognitive skills and correct perception of the host environment and its social systems.

For the research purpose twenty-nine papers have been studied, out of which, ten examined the relationship between cross-cultural training and the development of greater feelings of well being and self confidence (Dege,1981; Fernandez,1986; Mcgarthy, 1984; Neimeyer, Fukuyama, Bingham, Hall and Mussenden,1986; O Brien and Plooij,1976; O'Brien, Fielder and Hewett,1970; PSI Associates,1982; Randolph, Landis and Tzeng 1977; Salisbury, 1971; Worchell and Michell,1972) and all ten found a positive relationship.

Nineteen of the twenty-nine studies examined the relationship between cross cultural training and skills related to fostering relationships with the host nationals.

The results revealed that cross cultural training prepares the individuals to adjust more rapidly in the new culture and to be more effective in their new roles. A total of nine studies examined the relationship between cross cultural training and adjustment (Befus, 1988; Earley, 1987; Gudykunstetal.,1977; Mitchell et al, 1972; Newbold et al,1982; O, Brien, Fieldler, and Hewett, 1970; Salisbury,1971; Stenkalk and Taft,1979; Worchell and Mitchell,1972). All nine studies found a positive relationship between cross cultural training and adjustment.

Furthermore, the studies also revealed that cross cultural training also enhances the performance of the individuals who are sent overseas or in to a multicultural setting. Fifteen of the 29 studies examined the relationship between cross cultural training and performance and 11 of the 15 studies found a significant relationship between cross cultural training and performance. Studies by Earley (1987), Worchell and Mitchell (1972), Lefley (1986) and O,brien et al (1970) all used independent measures of performance, and all found a significant and positive relationship between training and performance.

These studies showed that cross cultural training also enables the individuals to learn both content and skills reducing misunderstandings and inappropriate behaviours.

Thus, the development of cross-cultural skills in trainees has been a major objective in the evaluation studies reviewed here. The link between possessing these skills and subsequent success in overseas assignments has been demonstrated elsewhere (for reviews see Brein and David, 1971; Church, 1982; Mendenhall and Oddou, 1985). The purpose here is to ascertain whether cross-cultural training can indeed foster the development of such skills in trainees. The skills needed to be successful in a new culture can be subsumed under three dimensions: (a) skills related to the maintenance of self (mental health, psychological well-being, stress reduction, feelings of self-confidence), (b) skills related to the fostering of relationships with host nationals, and (c) cognitive skills that promote a correct perception of the host environment and its social systems (Mendenhall and Oddou, 1985).

Explaining the dimension of the self of the 29 studies, 10 examined the relationship between cross-cultural training and the development of greater feelings of well-being and self-confidence (Dege, 1981; Fernandez, 1986; McGoarty, 1984; Neimeyer, Fukuyama, Bingham, Hall, and Mussenden, 1986; O'Brien and Plooij, 1976; O'Brien, Fiedler, and Hewett, 1970; PSI Associates, 1982; Randolph, Landis, and Tzeng, 1977; Salisbury, 1971; Worchel and Mitchell, 1972), and all 10 found a positive relationship. In examining the validity of the findings of these studies, two points should be noted. First, all 10 studies relied on self-report measures of variables related to the self dimension (e.g., O'Brien and Plooij, 1976). This approach may have inflated the relationship between training and the self dimension dependent variables because of common method variance problems. However, studies by Worchel and Mitchell (1972), Salisbury (1971), and O'Brien and Plooij (1976) included control groups and found significant differences in pre- and posttest measures of self-confidence between the experimental and control-group subjects. Second, despite the fact that studies utilized control groups in an individual to use interaction skills that transcend those that are effective when dealing with others from one's immediate in-group (Adler, 1986; Mendenhall and Oddou, 1985; Torbiorn, 1982). Thus, the development of cross-cultural skills in trainees has been a major objective in the evaluation studies reviewed here. PSI Associates, 1982; Randolph, Landis, and Tzeng, 1977; Salisbury, 1971; Worchel and Mitchell, 1972), and all 10 found a positive relationship. Studies also revealed that Cross cultural interaction brings people together who have different patterns of behaving and believing and who have different cognitive blueprints for interpreting the world (Triandis, Vassiliou, Tanaka and Shanmugam,1972)

Earley and Erez (1997) posit that the cornerstone of successful cross cultural management is "knowing thyself". Particularly (a) self enhancement, the desire to maintain a positive self image,(b) self growth, the desire to feel competent in the face of challenge, and (c) Self consistency, a desire to experience coherence in their lives.

Besides developing cross cultural communication among the team leaders and managers, it is equally important to hone their cultural competence which refers to the skill sets, knowledge pool and capabilities that enables an individual to adapt effectively in the cross cultural environments. Based on the research this cross cultural competence is divided into three categories (a) International Business, (b) Workplace diversity and (c) Intercultural communications.

A study of Gertsen, 1990 (p. 346) defined cultural competence as the ability to function effectively in another culture consisting of three independent dimensions: (a) An Affective dimension (personality traits and attitudes); (b) Cognitive dimension (how individuals acquire and categorize cultural knowledge); and (c) Communicative behavioural dimension (being an effective communicator)

The success of cross cultural communication depends on these factors primarily. Intercultural competence implies three factors: attitude, skills and knowledge. Although intercultural competence can be taught but the personality factors also play an important role. In order to be culturally competent an individual would have to possess a strong personal identity, have knowledge of and faculty with the beliefs and values of the culture, display sensitivity to the affective processes of the culture, communicate clearly in the language of the given cultural group, perform specially sanctioned behavior, maintain active social relations within the cultural group, negotiate the institutional structures of that culture and his knowledge dimension.

Therefore, globally competent managers are expected to be well versed in adapting to living in other cultures and to be skillful in working with people from many cultures simultaneously, they should learn about many foreign cultures, perspectives, tastes, trends, technologies and approaches to conduct business and must know how to interact with foreign colleagues as equals. Here the knowledge of high-context communication and low-context communication is of paramount importance, ignorance of which may truly mar the accelerating growth of the business and project at work.

Hofsted refers to two different types of cultural knowledge, culture-general and culture specific.

Culture general knowledge- It includes a general knowledge of the complex environment in which international business operates and a general knowledge of cultural differences.

Culture specific knowledge- It focuses on specific knowledge about another culture information regarding geography, economics, politics, law, history, custom and hygiene.

Deresky stressed the concept of cultural convergence, the shifting of individual management styles to accommodate the styles used in other environments and total elimination of parochialism, stereotyping and ethnocentricism in managing multinational operations. He also laid stress that in order to learn International Business Etiquette, Managers must appreciate value and respect cultural differences. In order to do so they should develop a better understanding of the behavioural patterns. Moreover, Deresky (2006) also noted that the ability to conduct cross cultural negotiations cannot be overstated, which places global managers in a position to learn the complexities associated with cultural nuances and values. International Business Etiquette, thus requires the ability to adapt to different national processes, patterns and acculturations. To achieve a desirable result in international negotiations global managers should be adequately grounded in intercultural communication. Another study by Chaney and Martin (2011) explains that in high contexts cultures such as Japan, meaning is conveyed through body language, pauses, rephrasing as much as in the words used at negotiation meetings whereas in a high- context culture of the United States, meaning is conveyed mainly through spoken words. In cross cultural communication both the verbal and nonverbal communication is equally important. Mixed messages also create some difficulty for international managers. For example in the United States, direct eye contact is expected and is seen as a measure of honest, trustworthiness and reliability. Conversely in China and in some parts of Africa direct eye contact is considered rude and inappropriate. Therefore it is imperative for international managers to build a sound intercultural communication. Effective intercultural communication largely determines the success of international transactions or the performance and productivity of a culturally diverse work force. Being aware and sensitive to the cultural differences is the key to establishing good business relationship. The example of Walmart is worth mentioning here. Walmart's culture of always smiling at customers was perceived as flirting. Because of a number of cultural missteps Walmart had to leave the German market place. In the wake of globalization cultivating cross cultural awareness and skills and developing multicultural mindset by managers will lead to sustainable growth in international business.

Apart from etiquette, examination of cultural behaviour and values are also vital to hone the cross cultural communication. Two studies were conducted in this regard. Study 1 examined the relationship between individual's cultural values, self concept and argumentative behaviour. Study two tested actual communication behaviours in intra cultural and intercultural situations. It was categorized in to four possible cultural profiles: (a) Vertical collectivism, (b) Horizontal collectivism, (c) Vertical individualism, (d) Horizontal individualism.

Research indicates that the polarity that emerges from the most sophisticated mapping of culture to date falls along the broad cultural profiles of V-C and H-I (Smith and Bond, 1999). In short verticality is conceptually equivalent to the power distance dimension, whereby the positive correlation between power distance and collectivism suggests that V-C and H-I may be the dominant cultural profiles around the world (Triandis, 1995). Vertical collectivists see themselves as member of in group acknowledging that members are different in terms of status. V-C cultures typically have social systems that do not reflect values of individual freedom and/or equity (Rokeach, 1973). Horizontal individualists have high freedom of choice and highly independent nature. H-I cultures believe in the values of equality and individual freedom. Communication style and cultural values are linked together by various scholars. In low context cultures messages are basically conveyed by verbalization. However in high context cultures a great deal of the meaning is implicit. Words convey only the small part of the message. L-C and H-C communication are linked to individualism and collectivism respectively.

Argumentativeness is also considered as an important cultural construct. It is constructive as it attacks the given position on a given issue. It is related to work place success. Suzuki and Rancer (1994) found members of collectivistic Japanese and Korean cultures less argumentative than members of individualistic North American culture. This knowledge also plays an important role in any cross cultural communication.

Cognitive consistency behaviour is also important in cross cultural communication. The theory posits that individuals change their behaviour when there is a discrepancy in their views and behaviour. Attempts to influence other's attitudes, standards or behaviour to maintain consistency is called inconsistency reduction behaviour. In contrast people who are comfortable with other's views and behaviours are called inconsistency – support behaviour. Studies have shown cultural effects in cognitive consistency behaviours. Iwao (1997) and Iwao and Triandis (1993) found Japanese participants exhibited inconsistency support behaviours. In contrast Americans change another person's opinions to maintain consistency between their privately held and their publically expressed views. Greeks did not change another person's views. All these factors play an important role in cross cultural communication.

In continuation, Language training remains a significant dimension in cross cultural communication. This language comprises both verbal and non verbal communication. Gudkynst and Kym (2003) suggest that meaning cannot be transmitted in normal communication between individuals, primarily because of the ambiguity in the language spoken. The language is largely dependent upon cultural factors described as language of context, time and space, as explained below.

Language of Context: It remains the major component of cross cultural communication. Phelan (2008) suggests context is, "Information that surrounds a communication and helps convey the message." High and low context cultures are mention worthy here. In high context cultures the messages are highly coded and implicit. Japanese, Chinese and many Arab countries are the cultural example of it. On the other hand in low context cultures communication is mostly done through spoken words. United States, Swiss and Scandinavian countries are example of it.

Language of Time: The second cultural factor is the language of time which Phelan (2008) suggests is a nonverbal communication referred to as either monochronic or polychromic. In monochronic cultures time schedules are wisely used. For example in U.S. time is considered as money. In polychromic cultures people place more importance to personal involvement rather than meeting the deadlines. In Latin America certain cultures ranks time as being of less importance.

Language of Space: Phelan defines the non verbal communication of space as "the study of the way that people use physical space to convey messages" .He describes four types: (a) Intimate distance: confidential communication, (b) Personal distance: Family and close friends, (c) Social distance: Business transactions and (d) Public distance: speaking to a group.

U.S.is often referred as non contact society. In contrast, Latin American and Eastern cultures are contact societies, meaning that they enjoy close proximity to others while engaged in conversation. It goes without saying that the in depths studies of these languages may hone cross cultural communication among team leaders and managers. Moreover, these trained leaders, understanding the intricacies of language, culture and communication will be better equipped to handle the cultural conflict and will use their dynamic workforce as a creative workshop for brainstorming and ideating new concepts and initiatives. The next, section, which address the final objective of the paper, thus shows how leaders can use cross culture communication as a tool in building creative and innovative work force.

Use of Cross Cultural Communication as an Effective Tool in Building Creative Work Culture

The working of different brains from different parts of the world could be exciting initially, but it can also daunting and conflict leading due to diverse cultural backgrounds of the team. However, organizational researchers (Jackson et al., 1995; Lawrence, 1997; Snow et al., 1996) scrutinizing the performance of the multi cultural teams argue that workforce diversity could indeed add to team performance and increase organizational effectiveness and efficiency (Cox, 1993; Kirchmeyer and McLellan,1991; Tung, 1993) thus culturally trained and sensitive managers and leaders can look diversity as an idea generative factory and can use communication as an effective tool in finding out and executing the best ideas in their groups.

Dinuk and Arseculeratne in their study bring forth a very important observation that Communication system acts as link in transmitting values and norms associated with different cultures in an organization. Since the communication system holds the key to transcending the differences in cultures an MNC would regard its communication system as a mechanism to transfer knowledge. This mechanism has to bring about clarity and cohesion to sustain the organizational fabric so that it functions smoothly without being disrupted by cross cultural differences. (Dinuk Arseculeratne)

As per RD Jenifer and Dr. Raman, understanding cultural differences is one of the most significant skills for firms to develop in order to have a competitive advantage in international business. Understanding of cultural diversity is the key to effective cross-cultural communications. It impacts free trade policies, localization and standardization strategy decisions, advertising, brand effectiveness, business relationships, international business management, international marketing, international negotiation, and consumer behavior, staffing, industrial relations, interpersonal relationships, negotiation, and teambuilding. Cross-cultural communication presents a fine opportunity to foster global peace and prosperity. It may also present unpleasant consequences if not well managed. Many problems arise in our workplace today as a result of the barriers cultural diversity imposes on cross cultural communication. (R. Delecta Jenifer, 2015).

The cultural diversity of a team has many benefits, including the variety of perspectives, skills and personal attributes that multicultural team members contribute to an organization (Maznevski, 1994). Ethnically diverse groups generate more ideas of higher quality in brainstorming tasks (McLeod and Lobel, 1992). Culturally diverse teams outperform homogeneous teams at identifying problems and generating solutions (Watson et al., 1993). By employing multicultural teams, companies make significant gains in productivity (Townsend et al. 1998). For example, culturally diverse teams of a multi-branch financial services organization report higher levels of financial profitability than their culturally homogeneous counterparts (Ng and Tung, 1998). Mobilizing the energy and synergy of people from various cultures working as a team can lead to more creative approaches to the problems and challenges faced by corporate teams (Marquardt and Horvath, 2001).

Thus, we can say that studies above highlight that diversity creates opportunities for better exchange of thoughts and ideas among team members which further leads to enhanced productivity. In heterogeneous teams, cross cultural communication, thus comes not only as a potent tool in the hands of mangers and team leaders with the help of which they can express themselves better and build trust among their team members, but it can also allow them greater opportunities to create understanding, cohesiveness and effective communication among their team members so as to build an environment of companionship wherein team members can feel confident to express their perspectives and ideas, and share their skills for organizational advancement and growth, much better.

Conclusion

Based on the studies done above, authors conclude that in the changed and diverse workforce of 21st century, it is important for organizations to understand the need of cross cultural communication, lack of which may not only ruin their business practices but may also mar their reputation. Moreover, organizations should take regular initiative in training their team leaders and managers in cross cultural communication and ensure their cultural competency and sensitivity so that they are well equipped to handle the conflicts and challenges of the changed work force. These trained leaders will not only be able to understand the crisis, challenges, demands and needs of their team members, but will also be able to foster and nurture relationship with their team mates for healthy work culture. These managers and leaders should generate trust and mutual understanding among the team member which will act as a cohesive element in the workforce. Moreover, these trained leaders and managers will also be able to use the diversity of their heterogeneous teams in providing better solutions to the problems and idea generation for creativity and innovative practices. Cultural awareness by the team leaders will build international competencies and will enables them to become more globally sensitive.

References

- Adler, N. (1986). *International dimensions of organizational behavior*. Boston, MA: Kent.

- Adler, N. J. (1989). Cross-Cultural Interaction: The International Comparison Fallacy?. *Journal of International Business Studies*, 20 (3), 515-537.
- Adler, N. J. (1991). *International Dimensions of Oganizational Behavior* (2nd ed.). Boston: MA: PWS-KENT Publishing Company.
- Adler, Nancy J. and Graham, John L., Cross-Cultural Interaction: The International Comparison Fallacy? (September 1989). *Journal of International Business Studies,* Vol. 20, Issue 3, pp. 515-537, 1989.
- Barker, R.T., and Gower, K. (2010). Strategic application of storytelling in organizations.
- Toward effective communication in a diverse world. *Journal of Business Communication,* 47, 295-312.
- Tung, R.L. (1993), Managing cross-national and intra-national diversity, *Human Resource Management,* Vol. 32, No. 4, pp. 461-477.
- Brein, M., and David, K.H. (1971) Intercultural communication and adjustment of the sojourner. *Psychological Bulletin*, 76, 215-230.
- Chaney, L.H. and Martin, J.S. (2011). *Intercultural business communication* (4th ed.). Upper Saddle River, NJ: Pearson Prentice Hall.
- Church, A. T. (1982) Sojourner adjustment. *Psychological Bulletin,* 91, 540-571.
- Cox, T., Jr. (1993). *Cultural diversity in organizations: Theory, research and practice.* San Francisco: Berret-Koehler.
- Dege, D.B. (1981, May 21-25) Format and evaluation of the cross-cultural component of a foreign teaching assistant training program. Paper presented at the meeting of the International Communication Association, Minneapolis.
- Dinuk Arseculeratne, R.Y. Barriers to Cross Cultural Communication and the steps needed to be taken for a MNC to Succeed in the Global Market. Kuala Lumpur, Malaysia.
- Dresky, H. (2006). *International management: Managing across borders and cultures.*
- Pearson/Prentice-Hall Publishing: Upper Saddle River: NJ
- Early, P.C. (1987) Intercultural training for managers: A comparison of documentary and interpersonal methods. *Academy of Management Journal,* 30, 685-698.
- Earley, C.P. and Erez, M. (Eds.) (1997): *New Perspectives on International Industrial/Organizational Psychology* (pp.192-242).
- Ellen Eun Kyoo Kim, A. S. (n.d.). *The Impact of Language Barrier and Cultural Differences on Restaurant Experiences*:A Grounded Theory Approach.

- Fernandez, T.M. (1986, Oct 9-11) Guide design: Sensitivity to black-white interactions when giving nursing care. Paper presented at the 15th Annual Conference of the International Society for Individualized Instruction, Atlanta.
- Gertsen M., (1990). *Intercultural competence and expatriates*, Oslo Business school.
- Gudykunst, W. B., Hammer, M. R., and Wiseman, R. L. (1977) An analysis of an integrated approach to cross-cultural training. International Journal of Intercultural Relations, 1, 99-110.
- Gudykunst, W. B., and Kim, Y. Y. (2003). *Communicating with Strangers,* 2nd ed. Boston: McGraw Hill
- Global Human Capital Trends. (2014). *Engaging the 21st Century Workforce.* Deloitte University Press.
- Harris PR, Moran RT (1987). *Managing Cultural Differences. (2nd ed)*. Houston: Gulf.,
- Hall, E., T. (1959). *The Silent Language.* New York: Doubleday.
- Hall, E. T. (1976). *Beyond culture.* New York, NY: Doubleday.
- Hilton, G. (2007). *Becoming culturally fluent.* Communication World , 24(6) 34-36.
- Hofstede, G. (1980). Culture's consequences: International differences in work-related values. Beverly Hills, Cal., and London: Sage Publications.
- Hofstede, G. (1991). *Cultures and Organizations: Software of the Mind.* London: McGraw-Hill.
- Iwao S (1997). Consistency orientation and models of social behavior: is it not time for west to meet east? *Japanese Psychological Research* 39(4): 323–32.
- Iwao S and Triandis HC (1993) Validity of auto- and heterostereotypes among Japanese and American students.Journal of Cross-Cultural Psychology 24(4): 428–44.
- IRIMIA[a], E. (2011). Behavioural Stereotypes in Intercultural Communication. Acta Universitatis Sapientiae, Philologica, 3, 2 , 167-174.
- Jackson, S.E., May, K.E. and Whitney, K. (1995) 'Understanding the Dynamics of Diversity in Decision-making Teams', in R.A. Guzzo and E. Salas (eds) Team Effectiveness and Decision Making in Organizations, pp. 7–61. San Francisco: Jossey-Bass.
- Kirchmeyer, C. and McLellan, J. (1991), Capitalizing on Ethnic Diversity: An Approach to Managing the Diverse Workgroups of the 1990s. CAN J ADM SCI, 8: 72–79

- Lefley, H. (1985). Impact of cross-cultural training on black and white mental health professionals. *International Journal of Intercultural Relations*, 9, 305-318.
- Lawrence, B.S. (1997). Perspective: The Black Box of Organizational Demography, *Organizational Science* 8: 1–22.
- Liu, R. H. (2010). Barriers of Cross Cultural Communication in Multinational Firms- A Case Study of Swedish Company and its Subsidiary. Halmstead: *Halmstad School of Business and Engineering.*
- Langdon, D.S., McMenamin, T.M., and Krolik, T. J. (2002). U.S. labour market in 2001: Economy enters a recession. Monthly Labor Review, 125, 3-33.
- Ma³gorzata Rozkwitalska, P.G. (November 2010). Barriers of Cross-cultural Interactions According to the Research Findings. *Journal of Intercultural Management*, Vol. 2, No. 2 , 37–52.
- Maznevski, M.L. (1994) Understanding our differences: Performance in decision making groups with diverse members. *Human Relations* 47(5) 531–552.
- McGroarty, M. (1984, March 6-1) Design and evaluation of cross-cultural workshops for ESL teachers and administrators. *Paper presented at the annual meeting of Teachers of English to Speakers of Other Languages, Houston.*
- McLeod, P.L., and Lobel, S.A. (1992). The effect of ethnic diversity on idea generation in small groups. *Academy of Management Annual Meeting Best Papers Proceedings, 227-231.*
- Mendenhall, M., and Oddou, G. (1985). The dimensions of ex-patriate acculturation. *Academy of Management Review*, 10, 39-47.
- Marquardt, M. J. and Horvath, L. (2001). *Global Teams: How Top Multinational Span*
- *Boundaries and Cultures with High-Speed Teamwork.* Palo Alto, CA: Davis-Black.
- Neimeyer, G. J., Fukuyama, M.A., Bingham, R.P., Hall, L. E., and Mussenden, M. (1986). Training cross-cultural counselors: Comparison of the pro-counselor and anti-counselor trial models. *Journal of Counseling and Development*, 64, 437-439.
- Newbold, R.C. III., Carrol, J.G., Hartman, M.E., Mitchell, H.E., and Story, M. R. (1982). A training program in medical communications for foreign native medical graduates. *Project for the Educational Commission for Foreign Med-ical Graduates, ERIC ED 219010-HE015252.*

- Ng, E.S.W., and Tung, R.L. (1998). Ethno-cultural diversity and organizational effectiveness: A field study. *International Journal of Human Resource Management,* 9(6), 980–995.
- O'Brien, G.E., Fiedler, F.E., and Hewett, T. (1970). The effects of programmed culture training upon the performance of volunteer medical teams. *Human Relations,* 24, 209-231.
- O'Brien, G.E., and Plooij, D. (1976). *Development of cultural training manuals for medical workers with Pitjantjatjara aboriginals*. In G. E. Kearney and D. W. McElwain (Eds.), Aboriginal cognition (pp. 383-396). New Jersey: Humantic Press.
- Phelan, S. (2008). Cross-cultural communication and negotiations. Retrieved January 18, 2015 from *http://faculty.unlv.edu/phelan/MGT480/Lecture %205.ppt#258, 1, cross-cultural communication and negotiations.*
- PSI Associates, Inc. (1982). Peace corps stateside teacher training for volunteers in Liberia (Vol. 1) *Evaluation report.* (Contract No. 82-042-1003) Washington, DC: Peace Corps.
- Randolph, G., Landis, D., and Tzeng, O.C. (1977). The effects of time and practice upon culture assimilator training. *International Journal of Intercultural Relations,* 1, 105-119.
- R. Delecta Jenifer, D.G (2015). CROSS CULTURAL COMMUNICATION BARRIERS IN WORKPLACE . *International Journal of Management* (IJM), ISSN 0976 – 6502(Print), ISSN 0976 - 6510(Online) , 332-335.
- Rokeach M. (1973). *The Nature of Human Values*. New York: Free Press.
- Salisbury, L. (1971). *College orientation program for Alaskan natives: COPAN-education for survival. University of Alaska at Fairbanks, Institute of Social, Economic, and Government Research.*
- S. Krishna, S.S. (April 2004). Managing Cross Cultural Issues in Global Software Outsourcing. *Communication Of the ACM* (Vol 47, Number 4) .
- Shailey Minochad, T.F. (2004). A process model for developing usable cross-cultural websites. *Interacting with Computers* 16 , 63-91.
- Shenkar, Oded and Zeira, Yoram, Role Conflict and Role Ambiguity of Chief Executive Officers in International Joint Ventures (March 1992). *Journal of International Business Studies*, Vol. 23, Issue 1, pp. 55-75, 1992.
- Smith PB and Bond MH (1999) *Social Psychology Across Cultures.* Boston: Allyn and Bacon.

- Snow, C.C., Snell, S.A., Davison, S.C. and Hambrick, D.C. (1996). Us Transnational Teams to Globalize your Company, *Organizational Dynamics* 32(4): 20–32.
- Spencer-Oatey, H. (2000). *Culturally Speaking : Managing Rapport through Talk across Cultures.* London, Continuum.
- Steinkalk, E., and Taft, R. (1979) The effects of a planned inter-cultural experience on the attitudes and behaviors of the participants. *International Journal of Intercultural Relations*, 3, 187-197.
- Suzuki S. and Rancer A.S. (1994) Argumentativeness and verbal aggressiveness: Testing for conceptual and measurement equivalence across cultures. 61: 256–79.
- Thakkar, L.C. (2012). The Impact of Globalization on Cross-Cultural Communication. Globalization , *Education and Management Agendas*, 325-340.
- Torbiorn, I. (1982). *Living Abroad.* New York: Wiley.
- Townsend, A.M., DeMarie, S.M., and Hendrickson, A.R. 1998. Virtual teams: Technology and the workplace of the future. *Academy of Management Executive,* 12(3): 17–29.
- Triandis, H.C., (1995). *Individualism and Collectivism.* Boulder: Westview.
- Triandis, H.C., Vassiliou, V., Tanaka, Y., and Shanmugam, A. (Eds.) (1972). *The analysis of subjective culture.* New York: Wiley.
- Tufte PA, J.A. (2003). Introduktion till samhällsvetenskaplig metod. Malmö, Sweden: Liber AB.
- Wakefield, R.I. (2001). Effective public relations in the multinational organization. In R.L. Heath (Ed.), *Handbook of public relations* (pp. 639-647). Thousand Oaks, CA: Sage.
- Watson, W.E., Kumar, K., and Michaelsen, L.K. (1993). Cultural diversity's impact on interaction process and performance: comparing homogeneous and diverse task groups. *Academy of Management Journal*, 36, 590–602.
- Worchel, S., and Mitchell, T.R. (1972) An evaluation of the effectiveness of the culture assimilator in Thailand and Greece. *Journal of Applied Psychology*, 56, 472-479.
- Xie, Y. (2013). Review Cross-cultural communication barriers between staff in overseas-funded enterprises and management strategies for overcoming them. *Journal of Languages and Culture*, 44-48.

21

Factors Affecting Expectations of Gen Y at the Workplace: A Study of Delhi/NCR

Gaurav Wadhwa and Pulkit Gupta

Abstract

An innovative generation of employees is getting ready to enter the workforce with new expectations. The entrance of Generation Y into the workforce seems to have begun a certain level of commotion in the workplace, as employers scramble to find out information about them. Gen Y is *incredibly sophisticated, technology wise, racially and ethnically diverse and is strongly affected by the rapid expansion in TV channels, satellite radio, the Internet, e-zones, etc.* ***The ways in which these expectations will affect the processes and methods that organizations attract and retain these employees, is an increasingly popular discussion among managers as they try to understand generational differences among new, younger employees. It is against this background that this study has been conducted. This paper is a primary study conducted in NCR to analyse the expectations of Gen Y has upon entering the workplace.*** *A sample of 70 respondents was taken for the purpose of the study and administered a questionnaire developed on a five-point Likert-scale. The main objectives of this study were to analyse the Gen Y expectations on the following parameters – job profile, work environment, remuneration, monetary rewards, workplace flexibility and employee development. The study was carried out during the month of August 2014 in a few higher education institutions in NCR* *among students who will be seeking employment after the commencement of their course.*

Key words: Generation Y Expectations, Job Profile, Work Environment, Remuneration, Monetary Rewards, Workplace Flexibility, Employee Development

Introduction

With the emergence of Generation Y into the workforce, many employers are seeing the personality and cultural differences that exist between Generation Y and the other Generations. Generation Yers, also known as Millennials and Nexters, are the children of Baby Boomers who are born between 1980 and 1995. (Trunk, 2007; Alexander and Sysko, 2012; Shaw and Fairhurst, 2008) The arrival of Gen Y, has forced the organizations to re-strategize how to attract and retain star performers as their competitive advantage in a steadily dwindling labor market. The statistics show that by the year 2020, India will have the highest percentage of employable workforce in the world. And with Indian towns emerging as a talent centre, India will be a source of 500 million trained workforces by the year 2020.

To better understand Gen Y, we first look at the preceding age group, Generation X, to determine how the two generations differ from one another and how these differences affect the work atmosphere. Generation X is usually described as the generation following the baby boomers and born between 1961 and 1979. The term is based on a novel by Douglas Coupland, Generation X: Tales for an Accelerated Culture (1991), a book about young adults trying to discover themselves in society. Terri Nagle (1999) describes Generation X as, "the most ignored, misunderstood, and disheartened generation that our country has seen in a long time." This generation grew up during the beginning of the technology era. Home computers and the internet became widely used by households everywhere. Generation X grows into a generation who values education, hard work, and the power of money. These characteristics are quite different than Generation Y. Generation Y is widely known as the generation born between 1980 and 2000. This generation is confident, independent, and goal-oriented. Although, technology advances began in the Gen X era, Generation Y was born into technology and often knows more about the digital world than their teachers and parents. The enhanced technological knowledge has launched this generation into an era that is accessible everywhere to anyone. They are networked, collaborative and highly social, expecting to be constantly connected to their social networks, within and beyond company boundaries, and to work within a sociable environment with other people.

Objectives of the Study

- To analyze the Gen Y expectations from their workplace.
- To study the factors affecting Gen Y expectation from their future workplace.

Literature Review

Through an overview of selected studies an attempt has been made to study the various factors affecting the expectations of the Generation Y with respect to the workplace.

Generation Y is known as the Millennials and the age range of Generation Y varies. There is substantial debate regarding the boundaries of this generation. Literature defines the beginning of Generation Y as early as 1977 and as late as 1981 and ending as early as 1994 and as late as 2002 (CRS 2008; Erickson 2008; Karefalk, Petterssen and Zhu 2007; Hagevik 1999; Robert Half International 2008; The New Strategist 2006). In India, they make up the more than half of the population. Despite the large potential workforce, not all are 'employment ready' and so their talents are in short supply. With about half of India's one billion people under the age of 25, Generation Y in India is the world's largest. Positioned in a time of exciting and rapid economic growth in the country, they are keen to participate in the country's future and success. The country's recent parliament elections saw a huge turnout of Generation Y population, demonstrating their ambition to take the country forward.

Tulgan and Martin (2001) eloquently describe about the Generation Yers that these are people with new confidence, upbeat and full-esteem. Second, people of this generation are most education – minded among all generations in the history. Third, Generation Y is the generation of people who are paving the way for a more outspoken and tolerant society in the world. And last, the generation is leading a new wave of volunteerism. Tulgan (2009) is of the view that on each step of the way, people of this generation are looking for a work situation that they can incorporate into the kind of life they have desired and are building for themselves. These people are grown up in a highly supervised, coached environment and are highly rewarded by their parents; there are fewer chances that they will trust the "system" or the functions of the organization to take care of them over a period of time and thus less likely to make any immediate sacrifices in exchange of the promise of long term benefits and rewards (p. 10).

Volkert (2012) studied the behavior of employees and presents the view that there is no one-size-fits-all solution when it comes to situation in which a company wants to create a work environment which will help to keep the best employees. Members of the cohort known as "Generation Y or Millennials" differ considerably from the Baby Boom or Generation X employees, particularly in their behaviors towards the work and their expectations from employers. Espinoza, Ukleja, and Rusch (2010) suggest the work-life balance as one of the most celebrated values of the 'Millennial' generation. It means that they want the meaningful work (p. 50). Tulgan (2009) presents the nine proven strategies in order to manage the generation Y employees, outlined below:

- Hire them with the right message
- Get them up to speed quickly and turn them into knowledge workers
- Practice in loco parentis management. Take a strong hand
- Help them in understanding their role and responsibilities in the company and where they fit in your picture
- Get them to care about great customer service
- Teach them how to manage themselves
- Teach them how to be managed by you
- Retain the best of generation Y one day at a time
- Build the next generation of leaders

Gen Y tends to favour an inclusive style of management, dislike slowness, and desire immediate feedback about performance (Francis-Smith, 2004). It is a truly global generation, socially conscious and volunteer-minded, and positioned to be the most demanding generation. If treated professionally, it is likely to act professionally.

Gen Y is likely to perform best when its abilities are identified and matched with challenging work that pushes it fully. Speed, customization, and interactivity two-way non-passive engagement is likely to help keep Gen Y focused (Martin and Tulgan, 2004). Technically able, highly informed and confident, but lacking direction, Gen Y is more likely to rock the boat than any prior generation (Johns, 2003). Gen Y is likely to equate job satisfaction with a positive work climate, flexibility, and the opportunity to learn and grow more than any prior generation.

Compared with other generations, Gen Y tends to have less respect for rank and more respect for ability and accomplishment. It is likely to turn down more pay in order to do work it feels is meaningful at a company where it feels appreciated (Alati, 2004). Gen Y tends to value respect, and want to earn it. Acknowledgement and freedom to perform as it finds best tend to matter to Gen Y, too (Dealing with Your New Generational Mix, 2004).

Benchmarking is a technique that uses quantitative or qualitative data to make comparisons between different organizations or different sections of organizations. Benchmarking is usually treated as a continuous process in which organizations periodically measure, challenge, and improve their practices. A term now often used to describe performance assessment is benchmarking which seeks to assess the competences of an organization against "best in class" employees. To build and sustain Gen Yer's engagement in the organization as much as possible this HRM technique is used.

Based on the above review of literature, a primary study was conducted among students to understand the factors affecting their workplace expectations.

Research Methodology

This study has been conducted in Delhi NCR among undergraduate and post graduate students. The sample size of the study is 70. A survey questionnaire was developed based on the review of literature, titled, "Survey of Workplace Expectations of Gen Y". The questionnaire had two sections namely: Section I: Demographic profile, Section II: 20 statements on a five point Likert's scale. The parameters used for the purpose of the study included- *job profile, work environment, remuneration, monetary rewards, workplace flexibility and employee development.* The study was carried out in higher education institutions in NCR among students. The questionnaire was administered personally. All the responses were found to be complete in all respects and hence used for analysis. Data collected for the study was analyzed by using SPSS.

Results and Discussion

The frequencies were calculated for the purpose of checking the numbers in each category. Tables 1 to 3 give the relevant details. 52.86 per cent of the respondents were in the age group 21-23 years. 48.57 per cent of the respondents were in first year of their study and 48.57 per cent of the respondents were in the third year of their study. 52.8 per cent of the respondents were male whereas the rest were female.

Table 1: Age Group of the Respondents

Age Group	Frequency	Per cent
18 – 20	27	38.57 per cent
21 – 23	37	52.86 per cent
24-26	6	8.57 per cent
Total	**70**	**100.00 per cent**

Table 2: Year of Study of Respondents

Year of Study	Frequency	Per cent
1st Year	34	48.57 per cent
2nd Year	2	2.86 per cent
3rd Year	34	48.57 per cent
Total	**70**	**100.00 per cent**

Table 3: Gender of Respondents

Year of Study	Frequency	Per cent
F	33	47.1428571
M	37	52.8571429
Total	**70**	**100**

Factor analysis with principal component extraction was applied with varimax rotation to understand the factor loadings across the components. Cronbach's alpha was obtained to test the reliability of the data. The varimax rotation clubbed the items on 5 components, and using the Rotated Matrix Component Table, the Factor Loadings were derived (Table 4). Total Variance Explained in the above for the 4 factors is 63.86 per cent (Cumulative). The Cronbach's á value 0.726, which exceeded the minimum standard of .7, suggests and confirms about the reliability of the measures. From the 20 items, the following 5 dimensions were derived: ***Student Expectations, Work-related clarity, Rewards and Benefits, Work-life Balance, Employee Development.***

Table 4: Factor loadings for expectations of Gen Y

Student Expectations	*Factor Loadings*
I should know what my company expects from me.	0.761
I should feel a sense of accomplishment in my job.	0.672
Regular training opportunities must be provided by my company.	0.613
Adequate opportunities to use my skills and abilities should be there in my company.	0.591
My compensation should correspond to my skills.	0.529
I should be provided with leave facilities as per the norms.	0.509
Work-related clarity	
My company should clearly convey its mission to its employees.	0.818
I should have the tools and resources that I need to do my job.	0.736

The amount of work expected of me by my company should be reasonable.	0.457
My goal should be clearly communicated to me by my manager.	0.445
Rewards and Benefits	
I should be provided with health benefits by my company.	0.766
My company should reward me for achieving my goals	0.697
My organization should provide me the option of flexible work time.	0.579
Work-life Balance	
My company should not force me to stay back after working hours if I complete my work on a timely basis.	0.870
I would like to have the option of work from home in my company.	0.843
Employee Development	
My company must consider my personal goals.	0.874
I would like to work for a company that rewards seniority over merit.	0.718
I will join a company only if development opportunities are there.	0.601
Job rotation must be done after regular intervals in my organization.	0.468
Item dropped (low factor loadings)	
For me money is an important criterion for job.	0.044

Extraction Method: Principal Component Analysis. Rotation Method: Varimax with Kaiser Normalization.

Based on the above study, it can be seen that the organizations must understand the characteristics of this generation and their perceptions and desires regarding work and career. The survey results from graduate and post graduate students interested in public service provide insight into the preferences, perceptions, and attitudes of potential Generation Y employees. "Gen Y expects work related clarity, reward and benefits, work life balance and self-development from their employers." A major challenge which faces organizations is how to attract, engage, and retain Gen Y who, because of their experiences and attitudes toward work, is markedly different from other generations in their workplace needs and expectations.

Recommended Future HR Strategies for Managing Generation Y

Looking at the factors that affect the expectations of Gen Y, the following strategies are proposed:

From Organisation's perspective

- Organisation culture is the key

- Good corporate responsibility reputation
- Organization's commitment to the environment

From Job perspective

- Inculcate Flexibility in Jobs
- Provide opportunities for specialization and development
- Assign challenging assignments
- Give competitive and lucrative compensation
- Provide a launch pad for International career and overseas trips
- Flexibility for transition between jobs.

From Leadership's perspective

- Encourage competency development – for future needs
- Facilitate speed induction and integration through mentors
- Provide a collaborative and participatory work environment
- Encourage empathetic leadership through constant feedback, coaching and mentoring
- Allow for flexible and personalized work environments
- Develop binding communication
- Create customized career paths

References

- Crocker (June 2010). Generaton Y in Workplace: Managing Challenges. *The Journal of Human Resource and Adult Learning* , Vol. 6, Num. 1.
- Hodges. (June 2008). Coping With Different Generations In The Workplace Elena Comperatore. *Journal of Business and Economics Research* .
- Sean Lyons. Generation Ys Psychological Traits, Entitlement and Career Expectations. University of Guelph.
- Martin and Tulgan (2006). Managing the Generation Mix.
- Saxena and Jain (2012). Managing career aspirations of Gen Y. Grater Noida, India: Mangalmay Institute of Management and Technology.
- Sky Brown, Michael Collins, Christopher Gallerson, Grady Giffin, Jon Greer, Ray Griffith, Emily Johnson, Kate Richardson (2009). Generation Y In Workplace.
- NAS. (2006). Generation Y: The Millennials – Ready or Not, Here They Come.
- Yan, Sophia (2006). Understanding Generation Y. The Oberlin Review, 8 December.

22

Employee Engagement in Global Economy

Sambhavna Dogra

Abstract

Human capital plays crucial role in organizations sustainability. To retain competent workforce is the key to face competition. But the employees need to be engaged. Engagement is all about motivating employees to do their best. An engaged employee gives his company his 100 per cent. Engagement requires a two-way relationship between employer and employee. The quality of output and competitive advantage of a company depend on the quality of its people. In actual meaning we can say that Employee engagement is a powerful retention strategy. The purpose of studying employee engagement under the different organisations is to understand the relationship between employee engagement and attrition, absenteeism and low quality work. The survey ought to find out the level of Employee Engagement and to identify the key drivers which influence the level of engagement. This study has exposed to various components of employee engagement. The paper has extracted the behaviour pattern of employees towards their work through primary data. This study will help organizations to improve employee engagement and reduce attrition.

Key Words: *Employee engagement, job satisfaction, sustainability, Productivity.*

Introduction

Employee engagement is the level of commitment and involvement an employee has towards their organization and its values. An engaged employee is aware of business context, and works with colleagues to improve performance within the job for the benefit of the organization. The objective of this topic for study is to analyze the cause of failure of companies to engage their employees and to recommend the solution for better future. Literature has mentioned that companies are struggling to engage workforce. This is a worldwide issue. Gallup research shows that only 13 per cent of employees around the world are actively engaged at work, and more than twice that number are so disengaged they are likely to spread negativity to others. The study on an Employee Engagement required a detailed view of an employee. This study is conducted in the company named Power Grid Corporation of India limited. (PGCL)

Conceptual Background

Employee engagement is a positive attitude held by the employees towards the organization and its values. It also define as a measurable degree of an employee's positive or negative emotional attachment to their job, colleagues and organization which profoundly influences their willingness to learn and perform at work.

Employee commitment and engagement is measured by following three primary behaviours

(Source: Gallup studies, 2005)

Say, Stay and Strive.

'Say' is evidently achieved if the employee consistently speaks positively about the

organisation to co-workers and refers potential employees and customers.

'Stay' refers to the employee's intensive desire to be a member of the organisation, despite opportunities to work elsewhere.

'Strive' indicates an extra effort and behaviours that contribute to business success.

As organizations globalize and become more dependent on technology in a virtual working environment, there is a greater need to connect and engage with employees to provide them with an "organizational identity". Employee engagement plays a greater role in the current era where every contribution by each of the employee counts. Employee engagement programmes throw light into the success of the company in engaging its employees in the productive activities. Engagement Is Linked To Three Essential Forces In The Organization - Attrition, Productivity and Profitability. Engagement is important for managers to cultivate given that disengagement or alienation is central to the problem of workers' lack of commitment and motivation. Some of the advantages of Engaged employees are engaged employees will stay with the company, be an advocate of the company and its products and services, and contribute to bottom line business success; they will normally perform better and are more motivated. Today, employee engagement has become a critical element for business performance and success because we are working in a scenario where virtual work spaces are a reality. The organizations now days take all reasonable steps to ensure that they have engaged workforce like organizing birthday bashes, talent shows, sports activities and many other things. They want their employees to be committed to their work fully besides all the above activities they also make sure that the employees have role clarity, get all the material and equipment they require to perform their work efficiently etc. The employee must feel that there is somebody in the organizations who cares for him and wants his success and growth. In all this we referring to the 12 questions that Gallup uses for studying the engagement level of employees in the organization.

Gallup is an organization that studies the engagement level of the employees by studying following statements:

1. I know what is expected of me at work.
2. I have the materials and equipment I need to do my work right.
3. At work, I have the opportunity to do what I do best every day.
4. In the last seven days, I have received recognition or praise for doing good work.
5. My supervisor, or someone at work, seems to care about me as a person.
6. There is someone at work who encourages my development.
7. At work, my opinions seem to count.
8. The mission or purpose of my company makes me feel my job is important.
9. My associates or fellow employees are committed to doing quality work.
10. I have a best friend at work.
11. In the last six months, someone at work has talked to me about my progress.
12. This last year, I have had opportunities at work to learn and grow.

Lterature Review

Basically, Literature review of Employee Engagement covers both Private and Public Sectors.

The first review study is about Employee Engagement – Maximizing Organizational Performance which examines that Engagement is a two-way process between employees and an organization. Therefore, an engaged workforce is achieved when there is a high number of employees whose hearts and minds are aligned to both the job that they do and the organization that they work for. To maintain the integrity of this engagement measure, Right Management does not calculate engagement using a mean or average. A person is only described as "engaged" if he or she responds positively to all engagement questions. This ensures that the analysis provided is able to differentiate between employees who respond to half of the items negatively and half positively and employees who respond moderately to all items, which can mask the true reality. For example, when assessing health, you can't claim that an individual who answered the majority of questions positively (e.g., diet, exercise, and stress) is healthy if he or she answered one negatively (e.g., smoking). It is powerful information for business leaders to know what proportion of their workforce is engaged to both the organization and their jobs, versus what proportion is engaged to just the organization or just their jobs. If employees are engaged only to their job or profession, then they will not be aligned to organizational goals and strategy. If employees are engaged to the organization but not their job, they will be aligned to organizational goals but will find it difficult to do their jobs well and to deliver extra discretionary effort in the work that they do.

Driver analysis can be conducted to determine the key drivers of engagement for each employee segment, providing a solution for how an organization engages employees with their jobs and the company.

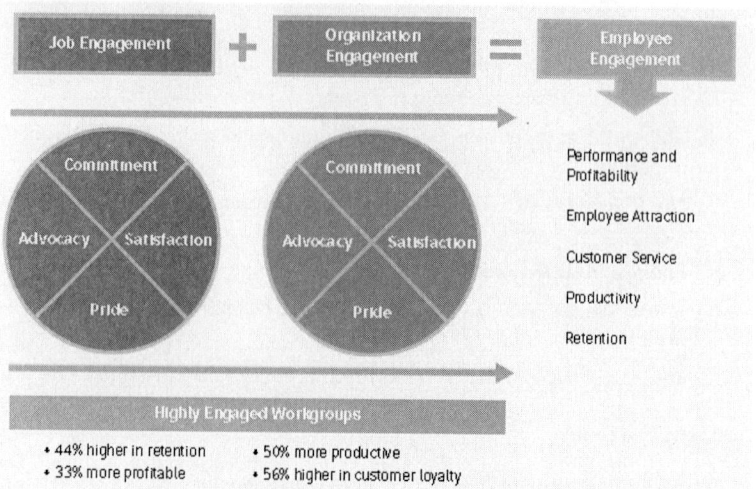

Fig.

The review of this study is mostly focusing upon the above figure which shows that the job engagement and organization engagement combine together with each and every work then they can get fully employee engaged with their job and performance.

Another research is done by Aloganandа and Oza in 2008. They both explain that "when they work with clients in bad times then it is one of the challenges which dread the most". They focus on things like strategy and cost – cutting while retreating into their offices. This study introduce that threats to companies are coming from the outside in. It is particularly at this time that the leadership team in the organization needs to communicate authentically, walk the talk and learn, in essence, lead from the inside out. According to their experience, they mentioned some principles which are key to employee engagement in a downturn.

Like: We do as we say, where the explains that as on the basis of part of Edger Schein breakthrough work on learning and culture , he had pointed out that people in organizations face survival anxiety and learning anxiety. Learning anxiety accounts for a good portion of resistance to change – most of the people chooses not to learn because its means changing what we value or risking failure or being judged. He rather acidly also pointed out that unfortunately organizations choose to address this issue by increasing survival anxiety : either an employee learns to do things or he loses his job. According to him, learning happens under coercion overshadows the fear of learning. In a downturn, survival anxiety doesn't have to be created. It is even truer that coercion is still not the best way to go, and that an exploitative approach of creating anxiety in people while stretching them on the work tasks which can be counterproductive. So, in order to build employees engagement in these times, companies first need to communicate candidly and clearly about current situations of each and every employee if times are difficult and profits are plunging. In such situations, leaders should convey specific actions that the company is taking to address these issues. The way a company behaves in a crisis is remembered for a long time. Work with clients as well as documented evidence suggests that companies that communicate honestly and then try to make amends as best they could to employees, whose lives and jobs were affected in downturns, are able to show greater employee engagement and loyalty over a longer period of time. So do as we do, where Apart from communicating regularly and acting consistently, the leadership team should also focus on creating an environment of psychological safety so that people can pick up new skills without the fear of falling. According to the authors, times of hardship can also be times in which people can be motivated to give the best they have to offer. According to this research, the basic premises of employee engagement do not change in difficult times, while employees want security, they also seek challenge and growth. In these times, organizations need people to learn faster than ever. Learning teams are powerful way to address multiple needs, both for the organization and the employees. Many communities of practice are a very effective tool in uncertain times: people have willingly shared the anxieties when coping with new situations as well as actively learnt from each other. These communities of practice also foster innovation and which in turn helps companies tide over crisis.

Another research is done by Babu (2007). He explains that Employee first, customers second is the new dimension which strengthens the concept of employee engagement. Business leaders are not simply saying that "our people are our most important asset", they are actually beginning to mean it too. Employee engagement is about building a truly great relationship with the workforce. People are the most important and valuable asset of every organization. Organization should prefer to maximize wealth through maximizing their human capital. It is a paradox that the valuable human resources are given less importance and attention during the wealth maximization process. A nation with abundance physical resources will not be benefited unless the human resources are effectively deployed. Basically, the study reviews that the success of any organization lies in employee engagement and involvement. Employee engagement leads to sharing of ideas among team members and boost the morale and innovative capabilities of employees. Engagement is much more than attraction, retention and commitment. Job involvement is a 'Cognitive or belief state of Psychologically Identification'. Job involvement is a thought to depend on both need saliency and the potential job and how far to satisfy these needs. Thus, job involvement results from a cognitive judgement about the need satisfying capabilities of the job. Jobs in this view are tied to one's self image. Engagement differs from job, as it is concerned more with how the individual employee engages themselves during the performance of their job. Therefore, the researcher has made an attempt to study the various factors contributing for employee engagement and involvement in the current scenario. Employee engagement approaches for new employees begin from the selection or recruitment stage by selecting the right person and giving a realistic job preview, organizing strong induction and orientation programme, providing rigorous training and development programme consisting of technical skills, soft skills, leadership development etc along with updating the employee about the current trends which will help in increasing their performance.

Another Research is about growing recognition, the need to evolve an engagement strategy to keep employees engaged and aligned with an organisation's mission. **He mainly focuses** on the need to implement this across five levels. This study reveals the traditional HR metrics to measure employee turnover rate, average time to open positions and total hours of training provided are unable to predict organisational performance. It emphasised the importance of tapping employee skills by proper job design methods, showing commitment to employees by recognising their contributions, offering job security and creating opportunities for advancement. The study also highlights that workload design should ensure good work-life balance for employees and their engagement needs to be tracked regularly. There have been various noteworthy definitions of employee engagement. Gallup, a leading performance management consulting firm, defines it as 'the individual's involvement and satisfaction with as well as enthusiasm for work.' The Hay Group defines it as 'a result that is achieved by stimulating employees' for their work and directing it towards organisational success.' After going through this study, it is obvious then that organisations should give importance to employee engagement and an engagement strategy needs to be implemented across five levels. The **first level** is concerned with the employees' dignity and competence, and the organisation's duty in respecting these. The **second level** focuses on facilitating employees with suitable equipment, systems and a conducive environment. At the **third level**, trustworthy relationships with employees should be nurtured through an inclusive approach. The **fourth level** is concerned with showing the organisation's commitment towards employee engagement by capturing the voice of employees proactively. At the **fifth level**, the organisation needs to work towards providing employees with the right sense of responsibility and purpose. Perhaps all these steps would lead to the creation of an engaged workplace where employees are aligned with the organisational values, mission and objectives.

Another Research is done by kahn (1990) and Holbeche and Springett (2003) which has revealed that employee engagement has been conceptualised in many different ways. There is no single agreed definition and research has shown that, however engagement is defined, it is a multi-faceted construct. The existence of various conceptualisations makes the state of knowledge around employee engagement difficult to determine, as each piece of research is undertaken under a different protocol, using different measures of engagement under different circumstances. Despite this potential problem, a similar pattern was found by all regardless of the country or context where the research was undertaken; the highest numbers of employees were found in the 'not engaged' category. This finding is disappointing, although perhaps not very surprising, and clearly many people do not enjoy going to work and gain little meaning from what they do for a living. People's perceptions of meaning with regard to the workplace has connections with how engaged they are and their level of performance. Findings suggest people seek more meaning in their day-to-day work than they do in their personal lives. This implies employers should be seeking to make work meaningful by finding out what matters to their employees, especially since evidence suggests that meaningfulness impacts not only on the individual, but also on the bottom line. Research has also suggested a connection between employee engagement and business results, eg the Gallup Organisation cite numerous examples of increased corporate profitability due to increased employee engagement. Looking more broadly, the evidence surrounding levels of engagement worldwide paints a negative picture; in Japan and Singapore levels of engagement are as low as 9 per cent, and levels of those 'not engaged' are as high as 82 per cent in Singapore and Thailand. Such findings indicate that one size does not fit all when it comes to motivating employees to engage with their company and work. This is in part due to differences in culture, values, politics, management styles and the economy. Those managing across borders must be fully aware of what leads to engagement in the countries in which they are operating; antecedents of engagement which work in the host country may have no effect, or the opposite effect, in other countries. There is clear evidence in the psychological literature of the effect of individual differences on work performance. Kahn (1990) suggested that individual differences shape a person's nature, which in turn, affects their ability to personally engage or disengage in all or some types or role performances. Furthermore, perception and personality have been suggested to be key influences on how individuals respond, thus shaping and directing how engaged they are. Evidence also suggests that employee engagement is related to emotional experiences and wellbeing. Researchers have found that emotional factors are linked to an individual's personal satisfaction and the sense of inspiration and affirmation they get from their work and from being part of their organisation. However a considerable number of employees agree that their company is not a good place to work, suggesting they are emotionally unhappy, whilst others argue emotions should not be allowed to flow free, and that employees are more productive when their emotions are managed.

Research Methodology

Objectives:

- To study Employee Engagement practices in PGCL
- To analyze the Behavior, Viewpoint and attitude of the employees.
- To explores the key drivers of employee engagement in PGCL
- To explore the concept of employee engagement and the view point of critics.
- To understand and quantify the major engagement factors among the contractual workforce.

Type of the research: The method was Descriptive research.

Operational Definition: Employee engagement is a positive attitude held by the employees towards the organization and its values. It also define as a measurable degree of an employee's positive or negative emotional attachment to their job, colleagues and organization which profoundly influences their willingness to learn and perform at work.

Data Collection: There are 3 methods widely used for gathering data viz. Survey, Observation and experimentation of these the most popular and widely used is the Survey and Observation Method.

Sample size = 50 Employees

Scope of the research:

- This study uncovers the priority of PGCL.
- The deeper investigations study the employee engagement level in PGCL.
- On the basis of this study employee engagement action plan can be developed for strategic implementation.

Limitation of the research:

- Many respondents were not interested to fill questionnaire due to time constraints.
- The responses of the entire questionnaire cannot be considered very accurate because some of the respondents were hesitant in lending the desired information.
- Though every precaution has been taken while analyzing the data, yet, a few errors are bound to appear.
- Due to time constraint the sample was restricted to 50 employees.
- Employees are not ready to fill the questionnaire properly. They were just doing the formality with wrong response because many of them don't want to share their thoughts with others.

Findings and Anyalsis:

Analysis

Table 1: Demographic data of respondents

Age	*Number of Respondents*	*Percentage*
Less than 30	8	16 per cent
30 – 40	14	28 per cent
40 – 50	7	14 per cent
Above 50	21	42 per cent

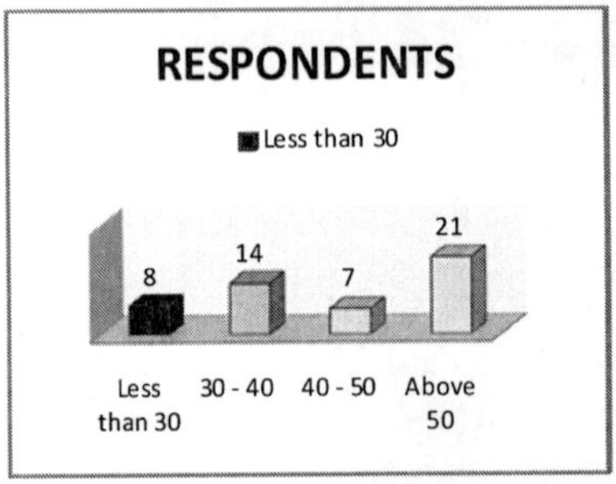

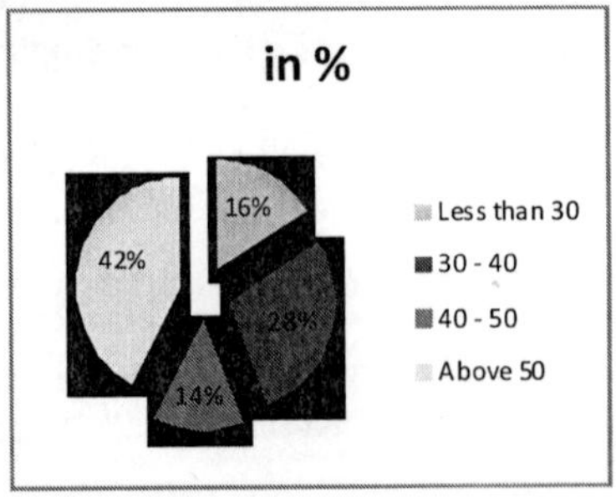

The analysis shows that 16 per cent of the employees are at the age of less than 30, 28 per cent of the employees are at the Age Group between 30-40, 14 per cent of the Employees are at the Age Group between 40-50, and finally 42 per cent of the Employees are at the Age Group of Above 50.

Table 2. Employee Tenure

Tenure in number of years	*Number of employees*	*(%)*
0 - 1 years	1	2 per cent
1 - 3 years	4	8 per cent
3 - 5 years	9	18 per cent
5 - 10 years	9	18 per cent
Above 10 years	27	54 per cent

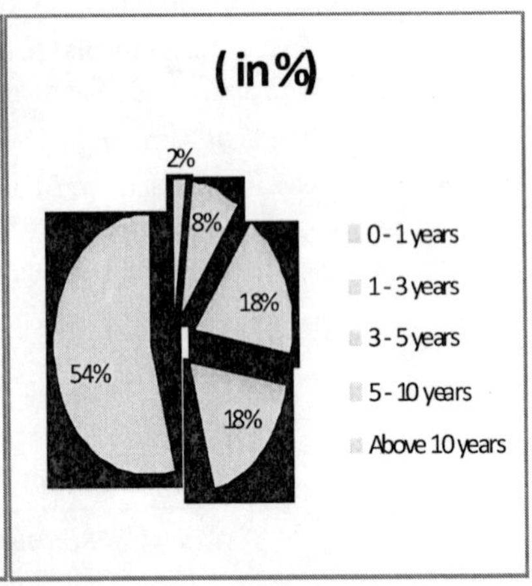

The analysis shows that 2 per cent of the employees fall into 0 – 1 years of tenure, 8 per cent into 1 – 3 years, 18 per cent into 3 – 5 years, 18 per cent in 5 – 10 years and 54 per cent in above 10 years i.e. 25 years.

Table 3: Gallup Q12 items Gantt chart

Gallup Q12 items	Sample Size	Strongly Agree 1%	2%	3%	4%	Strongly Disagree 5%	Mean (Average) Score
Q1) I know what is Expected of me at work.	50	18	28	2	1	1	0.89
Q2) I have the materials and equipment I need to do my work right.	50	14	24	2	8	1	1.09
Q3) At work, I have the opportunity to do what I do best.	50	24	17	4	3	2	0.92
seven days, I have received recognition or praise for good work.	50	8	25	9	4	4	1.21
at work seems to care about me as a person.	50	16	25	5	3	1	0.98
Q6) There is someone at work who encourages my development.	50	15	26	1	3	3	0.97
Q7) My opinions and ideas seem to	50	14	23	9	4	-	1.03
Q8) The Mission/Purpose of my company makes me feel my work is important.	50	19	19	7	2	2	0.96
Q9) My Co-workers are committed to doing quality work.	50	12	30	5	1	2	1.36
Q10) I have a best friend at work.	50	15	19	6	5	5	1.16
months, someone at work has talked to me about my progress.	50	10	25	5	6	2	1.09
Q12) In the last year, I have had opportunities to learn and grow.	50	12	27	4	5	2	1.08

The above table is showing the total number of responses to each and every particular questions. The next column is showing the average mean score of all responses with Gantt chart, the grand mean of the above responses is 1.06.

Overall result

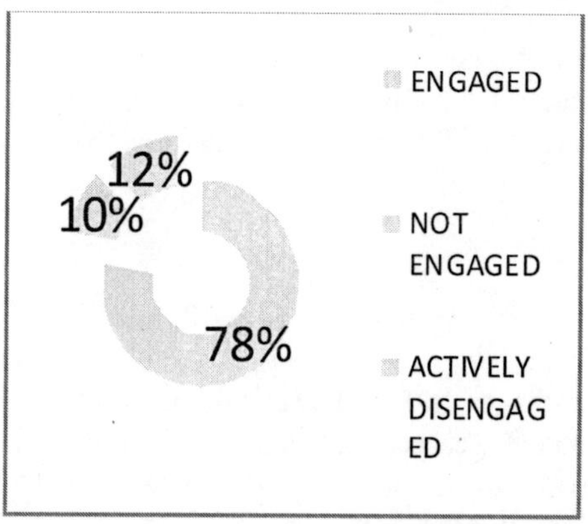

The analysis shows that 78 per cent of the employees of Power Grid are engaged, 10 per cent of the employees are not engaged and 12 per cent of the employees are actively disengaged.

Even if I had the opportunity to get a similar job with another organization, I would stay with POWER GRID.

Table 4

Options	*Response*
Yes	43
N	3
Not Sure	4

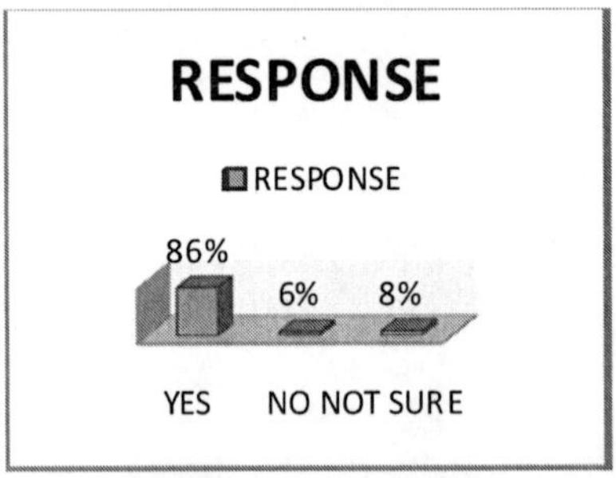

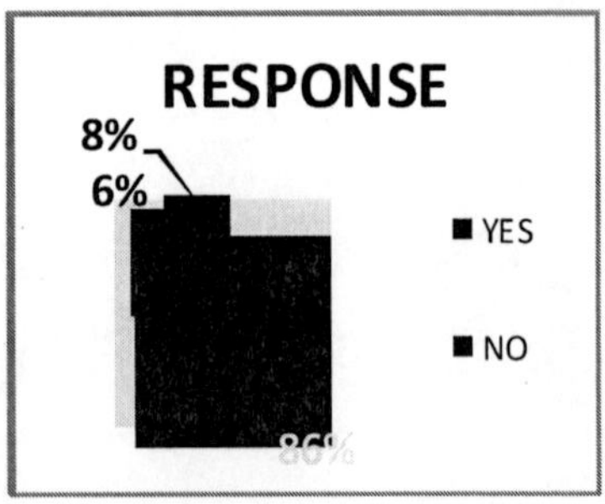

The analysis shows that 86 per cent of the employees are ready to stay with the power grid at this kind of situations because of good work environment, secured job and comfortable., but only 6 per cent are not ready for the same, and 8 per cent of the employees are not sure about this in the future because they want to see a opportunity first then on the basis of that they will decide what to do.

Analysis

As we already mentioned that, 78 per cent of the employees were engaged in PGCL. The research above is powerful - not only for organizations seeking to ensure their financial success, but for those seeking to harness their people power.

Findings

According to our survey on the basis of Q12 (12 questions of the Gallup Organisation), In India, most of the employees are not engaged but except few Organisation's like Power grid. In Power grid, most of the employees are Engaged i.e. 78 per cent. Reasons are Good work environment, Materials and Equipment are provided to them for completion of their work, Self – efficiency, Employee Retention is there in Power grid.

- Engagement levels correlate with business performance.
- Measuring Engagement tells us how well we are doing in the competition for talent.
- Driving Engagement levels higher improves our ability to attract, motivate and retain talent and so generates value from our human capital investment.

Our study has consistently shown that Employee Engagement is a lead indicator of lag business metrics, such as customer loyalty, productivity, and profitability. So why do many business leaders continue to think of engagement as a "nice-to-have" and fail to bring these key numbers to the table when regularly monitoring business performance, developing business strategy or preparing budgets? There is evidence that organizations are including engagement targets (along with retention and absenteeism) in their business plan as the "people" measure in a balanced scorecard approach. Some organizations are also including engagement scores in managers' individual performance targets. Sounds good, but often the systems don't support the behaviour. For example, when a manager achieves or exceeds a financial target but fails to deliver on engagement, he or she is often still considered a "high performer" and rewarded. The message is that engagement is "nice to have" but not essential to the organization's success, so managers continue to deliver short-term financial results regardless of the impact on engagement. Business leaders need to better understand the impact of engagement on their success. Executives need to act and behave in ways that reinforce its importance. A compelling way to achieve this is to model the exact financial impact that engagement has on productivity, customer, retention, absenteeism and financial results. This is achieved through creating and analyzing a unified database containing productivity data, customer data, HR data, and financial data for similar groups, e.g., stores, teams, locations. This creates a business case that is hard to ignore.

Recommendation

After observing and getting the result of the survey, we recommend the Power grid to conduct the feedback from employee in every month or week regarding their job, performance level and their work accomplishment to gather the information of the each particular issue that they are facing during their task. We also recommend the company to work upon their some of the hygiene environmental changes and the result is that they are start working upon it.

Conclusion

Employee Engagement is the buzz word term for employee communication. It is a positive attitude held by the employees towards the organization and its values. It is rapidly gaining popularity, use and importance in the workplace and impacts organizations in many ways. Employee engagement emphasizes the importance of employee communication on the success of a business. An organization should thus recognize employees, more than any other variable, as powerful contributors to a company's competitive position. While going through different reviews, we also considered that Engagement is a two-way process between employees and an organization.

The organization attempts to engage employees who return a level of engagement to the employer. Research, however, has revealed that engagement is more complex than this, and can be directed by employees in one of two ways (or both). The first is the level of engagement employees have with their career or profession, and the other is the engagement employees feel toward their employing organization. Therefore employee engagement should be a continuous process of learning, improvement, measurement and action. Engaged employees lead to increased productivity, retention, customer loyalty and profitability. Inspite of the above mentioned, the study reveals that the Employee engagement matters, but the extent to which it can lead to a step-change in organisational performance is uncertain. In particular, even where there is a clear vision and understanding of what needs to be done, there can be significant barriers to effecting 'change on the ground', **for example** if staff are generally opposed to change or if the capacity to implement change is limited by resource constraints Some of the approaches aimed at improving employee engagement can significantly increase employee engagement (as measured by staff surveys) and, in turn, this can have a measurable impact on HR variables such as retention and staff sickness. Review is demonstrated that yet considerable research hasn't been carried out about for indentifying influential factors on Employee Engagement at work which is an urgent need of today's people and organizations. We would hence conclude that raising and maintaining employee engagement lies in the hands of an organization and requires a perfect blend of time, effort, commitment and investment to craft a successful endeavour. Increasing employee engagement is highly dependent on leadership and establishing two-way communication where people's work and views are valued and respected. Thus these are the ways in which any organisation can work towards better employee engagement without incurring high costs.

Scope for the further research.

References

- Dessler, J., (2010), Applications from Human resource Management.
- First Break all the Rules – by Marcus Buckingham and Curt Coffman, (2005), Applications from Gallup Organization.

- Q12 Survey implementation Guide, (2005), Applications by Gallup Organization.
- Meta analysis research of Gallup Q12 survey.
- Employee Engagement in the public sector report, (2007), Applications from Scottish Executive Social Research.
- Employee Engagement in Times of Uncertainty report by Padmaja Aloganandа (leads Mercer's Human Capital business in India) and Anuradha Oza (senior associate in the Human capital India team).
- Engagement and Involvement of Employees in Private Sectors banks in Chennai – with special references to ICICI bank report by Dr. R. Suresh Babu (Assistant Professor, Department of Commerce, Patrician College of Arts and Science, Chennai) (2013), applications from Indian journal of Applied research.
- Engaging employees, Trust and Loyalty report by Kaushik Mukherjee.
- Coffman C. (2000). Is Your Company Bleeding Talent? How to become a true "employer of choice". The Gallup Management Journal, 2000. The Gallup Organization, Princeton, NJ.
- Coffman, C., and Gonzalez-Molina, G. (2002). Follow this Path: How the world's greatest organizations drive growth by unleashing human potential. New York Warner Books, Inc.
- Gallup, "Gallup Study: Engaged Employees Inspire Company Innovation," 2008,retrieved March 20, 2009, from http://gmj.gallup.com/content/24880/ Gallup- Study- Engaged-Employees-inspire-Company retrieved on 10th Dec,2011.
- The Gallup Organization, (2005), Employee Engagement: The Employee side of human sigma equation.
- Robinson, D., Perryman. S. and Hayday.S. (2004). The Drivers of Employee Engagement. Institute for employment studies.
- Robinson, D., Hooker, H., and Hayday S. (2007). Engagement: The Continuing Story.
- The Gallup Organization. http://www.gallup.com/home.aspx. Accessed June 4. 2009.

WEBSITES

- Community insights-https:/www.citehr.com/
- www.management-issues.com
- Building great workplaces by JRA

- http://www.powergridindia.com
- https://q12.gallup.com/Public/en-us/Features
- https://ceplb03.hewitt.com/
- http://www.fundoodata.com/mnc_companies.php?andpageno=2&tot_rows=4146&total_results=4153&no_of_offices=0
- http://www.grotal.com/Delhi/Multinational-Companies-C44/
- http://www.managementparadise.com/lusimaity/documents/9360/summer-internship-project-hr-mba-mms-human-resources-internship-report-on-recruitment/
- http://www.powergridindia.com/_layouts/PowerGrid/User/ContentPage.aspx?PId=76&LangID=english
- https://q12.gallup.com/Public/en-us/Features
- https://ceplb03.hewitt.com/
- http://www.siescoms.edu/
- http://www.custominsight.com/employee-engagement-survey/sample-survey-items.asp
- http://www.fundoodata.com/advance_search_results.php?&new_industry_id%5B%5D=1&level_id=1&city_id=16&criteria=1&search_type=1731673190&startW=M
- http://www.myopinionatbesix.com/besixsurvey/media/besix-survey/pdf/4.-employee-engagement-the-key-to-improving-performance.pdf

ANEXTURE 1

QUESTIONNAIRE

Q12 SURVEY TO MEASURE EMPLOYEE ENGAGEMENT

As part of our research, we (Aparna Sethi and Sambhavna), Gurgaon conducting a study to measure levels of Employee Engagement in Power Grid Corporation of India Limited. Kindly spare some of your valuable time and fill up the questionnaire.

I hereby confirm that:

1. This questionnaire is only for learning and analysis purpose.
2. The data collected shall be kept confidential.

1. **Department:** ____________________
2. **Age:** _______ **years**
3. **Designation and Level :** ____________________
4. **For how many years you have been at the current Level:** _________years
5. **Place of Posting:** ____________________
6. **Home Town:** ____________________
7. **Number of years of Service in Power Grid** :

a. 0-1 years ☐
b. 1-3 years ☐
c. 3-5 years ☐
d. 5-10 years ☐
e. Above 10 years ☐

8. **How many Transfers occurred during your tenure:** _______________

| -------------------|-------------------| -------------------|-------------------|

(1)	(2)	(3)	(4)	(5)
S.DISAGREE	**DISAGREE**	**NOT SURE**	**AGREE**	**S.AGREE**

QUESTION	**RESPONSE (1/2/3/4/5)**	
Q1) I know what is Expected of me at work.		
Q2) I have the materials and equipment I need to do my work right.		
Q3) In the last seven days, I have received recognition or praise for good work.		
Q4) There is someone at work who encourages my development.		
Q5) My opinions and ideas seem to matter.		
Q6) I have a best friend at work.		
Q7) In the last Six months, someone at work has talked to me about my progress.		
Q8) My supervisor at work seems to care about me as a person.		

Q10) The Mission/Purpose of my company makes me feel my work is important		
Q11) My Co-workers are committed to doing quality work.		
Q12) At work, I have the opportunity to do what I do best.		

- Even if I had the opportunity to get a similar job with another organization, I would stay with POWER GRID. **Please tick (√) mark your response below and Point reason thereof:-**

YES ☐ NO ☐

Reasons:-

1. ____

2. ____

3. ____

4. ____

5. ____

23

Behavioural Interventions in Psychosocial Adjustments of Adolescent Girls with Anxiety

(With Special Reference to Delhi-NCR Region)

Sarbani Chowdhury and Tania Shaw

Abstract

Adolescent girls form precious human resource of our country. Adolescence is a very crucial period in every girl's life that sets the stage for a healthy and productive adulthood and reduces the likelihood of health problems in later years. Even though, women empowerment is largely discussed, but women's' mental health has always been a neglected area. ***Mental Health*** *is a level of psychological well-being, or an absence of mental disorder.* ***Adolescence,*** *the critical phase of life (10-19 yrs) is a period of major physical, physiological, psychological and behavioural changes in changing pattern of social interactions and relationships. It is also an age of impulsivity accompanied by vulnerability, influenced by peer groups and media that results in changes in perception and practice (Sunitha, and Gopalkrishna, 2014). The study focuses on exploring the relationship between anxiety in 100 adoscent girls who suffered due to inter-personal relationship and identity crisis and the effect of interventions in combating this anxiety. The study focuses on exploring the relationship between anxiety in 100 adolescent girls who suffered due to interpersonal relationships and identity crisis.* ***Anxiety*** *is an unpleasant state of inner turmoil, often accompanied by nervous behaviour.* ***Sample*** *was chosen from the universe of 325 adolescent girls and developing effective interventions for them.* ***Interventions*** *could be psychosocial therapy, cognitive behaviour therapy, interpersonal therapy, behaviour therapy and psychoanalytically oriented therapy. But the researcher chose* ***cognitive behaviour therapy*** *(CBT) and* ***Interpersonal therapy*** *(IPT) for addressing the problems of adolescent girls. CBT focuses on cognitive distortions present in the patients and IPT addresses interpersonal problems. Fifty (50) anxious adolescent girls received intervention therapy, which included cognitive behavioural therapy (CBT) and interpersonal psychotherapy (IPT) - and for the remaining 50 girls, the control group, behavioural family intervention was applied. Family members of the control group were given psycho-education about the sensitivity of anxious girls. The parents of this group of girls were helped to understand various problems the girls were facing and how the proposed supportive behavioural intervention will alleviate these problems. The study revealed that introducing cognitive (CBT) and (IPT) as the supportive interventions were very promising interventions in combatting anxiety and preventing relapse. This was further proved by t-test which found that therapeutic interventions brought about significant decline in anxiety level. It was observed, since the respondent's anxiety level reduced significantly, they could perform their daily activities in much relaxed, composed and matured manner. Investment in adolescent girls is linked with achievement of nearly every developmental goal of the millennium. It helps to break cycles of poverty, as when due to anxiety girls drop out of school, the price to pay is their lost potential. They are married off early and begin child bearing at ages when they are not ready to be mothers. If we are truly aspire to achieve the stated goal of an ambitious sustainable transformation and development, adolescent girls' mental health needs must be given the utmost attention.*

Keywords*: Adolescence, Anxiety, Mental Health, Cognitive Behaviour Therapy, Interpersonal Therapy.*

Introduction

WHO identifies adolescence as the period in human growth and development that occurs after childhood and before adulthood, from ages 10 to 19. It represents one of the critical transitions in the life span and is characterized by a tremendous pace in growth and change that is second only to that of infancy. Biological processes drive many aspects of this growth and development, with the onset of puberty marking the passage from childhood to adolescence. The biological determinants of adolescence are fairly universal;

however, the duration and defining characteristics of this period may vary across time, cultures, and socioeconomic situations. This period has seen many changes over the past century namely the earlier onset of puberty, later age of marriage, urbanization, global communication, and changing sexual attitudes and behaviours. Anxiety affects boys and girls more or less, equally during childhood. But adolescent girls are much more vulnerable to anxiety than boys. Anxiety is a psychological and physiological condition that causes feelings of fear and worry. For the most part, anxiety is a normal response to stressful or tense situations. Anxiety motivates us to plan ahead and push through tough times. Anxiety and fear are different emotional responses. Fear produces an overwhelming need to escape while anxiety creates feelings of stress and nervousness in response to uncontrollable and unavoidable perceived threats. Excessive and constant anxiety can transform moments of worry into full-fledged disorders. Some amount of anxiety is normal, but excessive amounts are irrational and unjustified. Many people with anxiety disorders perceive threats that are not grounded in reality.

There have been some recent changes to the classification of anxiety disorders. Consistent with the previous version of the Diagnostic and Statistical Manual of Mental Disorders (DSM-IV), DSM-5 includes the following anxiety disorders: *Specific Phobia, Gneralised Anxiety Disorder, Social Anxiety Disorder (formerly Social Phobia), Panic Disorder and Agoraphobia.* Key changes in DSM-5 include: (i) *Agoraphobia* has been classified as a stand-alone diagnosis (i.e., no longer linked to the presence or absence of panic disorder), (ii) *Separation Anxiety Disorder* and selective mutism have been re-classified as anxiety disorders (rather than in a section for 'disorders usually first diagnosed in infancy, childhood or adolescence') and (iii) *Obsessive-Compulsive Disorder*, post-traumatic stress disorder and acute stress disorder are, respectively, grouped under obsessive-compulsive and related disorders, and trauma-related and stressor-related disorders (i.e., no longer included within the anxiety disorders category). Existential anxiety is a philosophical term used to describe the anxiety associated with the freedom and responsibility of choice. People with this type of anxiety might experience excessive difficulty and apprehension when making decisions. *Test or Performance Anxiety* causes people to feel apprehension when expected to perform in a competitive situation. Many people with test or performance anxiety feel physical symptoms of dizziness and nausea in competitive situations in school or at work.

Generally, this type of anxiety causes people to underperform. *Social Anxiety* creates a feeling of nervousness as a response to social interactions. Many people experience social anxiety as young children. Most people outgrow this condition by the time they reach adulthood. Social anxiety is abnormal when it affects adults. *Trait Anxiety* refers to a situation when anxiety becomes a part of a person's character. For people with trait anxiety, moments of irrational or excessive worry are the norm as opposed to the exception. Other types of anxiety include panic disorder, agoraphobia, general phobias, social anxiety disorder, post-traumatic stress disorder, and obsessive compulsive disorder. *Generalized Anxiety Disorder* is a condition that results from unnecessary worry about everyday life. People with generalized anxiety disorder never seem to stop worrying about health, money, family, employment, school, or something else. In the majority of situations, the worrying is unwarranted and excessive. Eventually, the condition escalates out of control, and unrealistic feelings of worry dominate every aspect of daily life. In many situations, anxiety is normal and justifiable. In fact, some experts say that a certain level of anxiety is necessary to facilitate performance in competitive situations. If you anticipate a stressful situation, anxiety can keep you motivated to persevere through.

Anxiety is a problem when you're worrying is abnormal, out of place, and excessive. If you are always stressed and unnecessarily afraid of everyday situations, you may suffer from an anxiety disorder. In no situation should anxiety become a dominant feeling. When your anxiety becomes out of control, treatment and counselling are available to help relieve symptoms. Physical symptoms of anxiety include heart palpitations, fatigue, nausea, chest pain, stomach aches, and headaches. Other symptoms include trembling, sweating, and pupillary dilation. You may not notice your physical symptoms, especially if your emotional symptoms are overwhelming. Most importantly, symptoms that interfere with an adolescent girl's daily routine are her attendance at school, the capacity to participate in normal peer activities etc. Suicidal risk is the key issue in adolescent girls with anxiety which is very important in the assessment of her mental health status that interfere with her ability to participate in normal activities, which may occur with prolonged panic disorder or social phobia.

The assessment of anxiety also includes whether the adolescent girl had a suicide plan, the extent to which the adolescent girl feels hopeless about herself and her situation, the availability of lethal instruments in her custody, the capacity of the family to provide support and ensure the safety of the child. Even though anxiety is highly prevalent in adolescent girls, they do not seek help in regular health care. The main aim of the present study is to examine the efficacy of preventive interventions to combat anxiety symptoms. A secondary objective is to gain insight into how the intervention works and for whom it works best. Some parents feel adolescent girl's behaviour is an extension of normal fears and worries. In severe situations they may find their daughters as being very disabled psychologically and hope that underlying, unexpressed trauma or fear can be understood and resolved before she becomes more anxious. In such cases, it helps parents to understand that anxious symptoms are not usually related to hidden trauma, but generally represent the reaction of a sensitive adolescent girl who feels stressed at current situation.

Interventions for Combating Anxiety:

The first goal of intervention was to reduce the stress that is perceived by and adolescent girl. This often involves helping the family understand that engaging into conflict with respect to the girl's avoidant behaviour worsens the situation. Anxious behaviour generally lessens when girl exposes herself to the avoided and feared situation and remains in that situation until the feeling of anxiety diminishes. This exposure needs to be repeated until the situation no longer invokes anxiety. Being able to confront the feared situation may require that the adolescent girl learns self-soothing or anxiety releasing strategies such as deep breathing, muscle relaxation or self-talk. For anxious girls, encouragement to reengage in normal activities also helps to combat anxiety.

Cognitive Behaviour Therapy (CBT):

CBT holds a unique status in the field of mental health. It focusses on the cognitive distortions, which include selective attention to negative aspects of the circumstances. The goal of this therapy is to alleviate depressive episodes by identifying negative cognitions and develop alternative, flexible and positive way of thinking; rehearse new cognitive behavioural responses.

Interpersonal Psychotherapy (IPT):

Interpersonal Psychotherapy (IPT) is a time limited treatment that encourages the patient to regain control of mood and functioning typically lasting 12-16 weeks. IPT has been adapted for the treatment of depressed adolescents (IPTA). To address developmental issues most common to teenagers such as separation from parents, development of romantic relationship and initial experience with death of a relative or a friend. IPTA helps adolescent identify and develop more adaptive methods for dealing with interpersonal issues associated with the onset or maintenance of their depression. The interventions explore the pattern that leads to self-destructive action and beliefs that direct the anxious thoughts. The adolescent girls were encouraged to monitor and write down the thoughts that pop into their minds. This allows the Clinical Psychologist and the girls to search for the thinking patterns that can cause them to have negative thoughts, which can lead to negative feelings and self-destructive behaviour. Treatment also helped the adolescent girls to identify more adaptive method for dealing with interpersonal issues associated with the onset of anxiety. A 14-week treatment involved primarily individual sessions with the adolescent girls. Parents were also asked to participate in a few sessions to receive education about anxiety, to address any relationship difficulties that may be occurring between the adolescent and her parents.

Literature Review

Anxiety is a fundamental emotion that at certain levels serves adaptive functions such as motivation, protection, and survival (Moore et al., 2010). Childhood fears, worries, and anxieties must be considered in their developmental context and only become a problem if they persevere and cause serious personal distress, hinder development or education, or greatly interfere in familial or social relationships. Nevertheless, even subthreshold levels of anxiety in children can result in considerable impairment and may necessitate attention and treatment (Moore et al., 2010). Approximately 1 out of 11 teenagers is diagnosed with anxiety severe enough to be considered a disorder, with girls being more likely to develop an anxiety disorder than boys. Common anxiety symptoms can affect people at any age tend to increase during the adolescence (Davis et al, 1995). As per the relaxation and stress reduction workbook (Martha, et al., 2008), anxiety occurs in both genders, but by the teenage years, girls are much more at risk than boys. Before puberty, the prevalence of mood disorders is about the same in boys and girls i.e. 3 to 5 per cent. But by mid-adolescence girls are more than twice as likely to be diagnosed with a mood disorder as boys, with the prevalence at adult levels, 14 to 20 per cent (Steingaurd, 2014). Some teenagers with anxiety disorders can also develop mood disorders or eating disorders. Some teenagers who experience persistent anxiety may also develop suicidal feelings or engage in self-destructive behaviours; these situations require immediate attention and treatment.

Anxious teens may also use alcohol and drugs to self-medicate or self-soothe or develop rituals in an effort to reduce or prevent anxiety. A worried teenager performs less well in school, sports, and social interactions. Too much worry can also result in a teenager's failing to achieve to her potential. A teen that experiences a great deal of anxiety may be overly conforming, perfectionistic, and unsure of her. In attempting to gain approval or avoid disapproval, she may redo tasks or procrastinate.. The anxious youngster often seeks excessive reassurance about her identity and whether she is good enough (Anxiety disorder resource centre by American Academy of Child and Adolescent Psychiatry). A large, national survey of adolescent mental health reported that about 8 per cent of teen's ages 13-18 have an anxiety disorder, with symptoms commonly emerging around age 6. However, of these teens, only 18 per cent received mental health care. The Child/Adolescent Anxiety Multimodal Study (CAMS), in addition to other studies on treating childhood anxiety disorders, found that high-quality cognitive behavioural therapy (CBT) given with or without medication, can effectively treat anxiety disorders in children. One small study even found that a behavioural therapy designed to treat social phobia in children was more effective than an antidepressant medication. Anxiety disorders vary from teenager to teenager. Symptoms generally include excessive fears and worries, feelings of inner restlessness, and a tendency to be excessively wary and vigilant.

Even in the absence of an actual threat, some teenagers describe feelings of continual nervousness, restlessness, or extreme stress. In a social setting, anxious teenagers may appear dependent, withdrawn, or uneasy. They seem either overly restrained or overly emotional. They may be preoccupied with worries about losing control or unrealistic concerns about social competence. Teenagers who suffer from excessive anxiety regularly experience a range of physical symptoms as well. They may complain about muscle tension and cramps, stomach aches, headaches, pain in the limbs and back, fatigue, or discomforts associated with pubertal changes. They may blotch, flush, sweat, hyperventilate, tremble, and startle easily. Anxiety during adolescence typically centres on changes in the way the adolescent's body looks and feels, social acceptance, and conflicts about independence. When flooded with anxiety, adolescents may appear extremely shy. They may avoid their usual activities or refuse to engage in new experiences. They may protest whenever they are apart from friends. Or in an attempt to diminish or deny their fears and worries, they may engage in risky behaviours, drug experimentation, or impulsive sexual behaviour.

There is strong evidence that panic disorder occurs in children and adolescents and that its clinical presentation in this population is similar to that found in adults (Moreau and Weisman, 1992). More common in girls than boys, panic disorder emerges in adolescence usually between the ages of fifteen and nineteen. Feelings of intense panic may arise without any noticeable cause or they may be triggered by specific situations, in which case they are called panic attacks. A panic attack is an abrupt episode of severe anxiety with accompanying emotional and physical symptoms (American Academy of Child and Adolescent Psychiatry).

Women were considerably more likely to have panic disorder and to have an earlier age of onset than males. Occurrence of DSM-IV panic attacks was strongly related to the subsequent development of various forms of mental disorders—not only panics disorder and agoraphobia. The conditional probability in those with panic attacks to develop other forms of mental disorders was 63 per cent in males and 40 per cent in females. (Reed and Wittchen, 1998) Women were considerably more likely to have panic disorder and to have an earlier age of onset than males.

During a panic attack, the youngster may feel overwhelmed by an intense fear or discomfort, a sense of impending doom, the fear he's going crazy, or sensations of unreality. Accompanying the emotional symptoms may be shortness of breath, sweating, choking, chest pains, nausea, dizziness, and numbness or tingling in his extremities. During an attack, some teens may feel they're dying or can't think. Following a panic attack, many youngsters worry that they will have other attacks and try to avoid situations that they believe may trigger them. Because of this fearful anticipation, the teen may begin to avoid normal activities and routines.

Phobias: Many fears of younger children are mild, passing, and considered within the range of normal development. Some teenagers develop exaggerated and usually inexplicable fears called phobias that centre on specific objects or situations. These intense fears can limit a teenager's activities. The fear generated by a phobia is excessive and not a rational response to a situation. The objects of a phobia usually change as a child gets older. While very young children may be preoccupied with the dark, monsters, or actual dangers, adolescents' phobic fears tend to involve school and social performance. In a study done by (Spence et al, 2000), 50 children with social phobia as their primary diagnosis were randomized to one of three conditions; treatment with no parental involvement, CBT with parent involvement or a wait list control group, utilizing an integrated cognitive-behavioural therapy (CBT) that involved social skills training, graded exposure and cognitive restructuring. The two treatment groups reported greater reductions in children's social and general anxiety impairment when compared to the control group. Both treatment groups (parent involved and parent not involved) maintained treatment effects or showed improvement at the 12 month follow up (Carla et al, 2009).

Several studies have revealed an increase in school avoidance in middle-school or junior-high years. With school avoidance, excessive worries about performance or social pressures at school may be at the root of the reluctance to attend school regularly. This leads to a cycle of anxiety, physical complaints, and school avoidance.

The cycle escalates with the worsening of physical complaints such as stomach aches, headaches, and menstrual cramps. Visits to the doctor generally fail to uncover general medical explanations. The longer a teenager stays out of school, the harder it becomes for him to overcome his fear and anxiety and return to school. He feels increasingly isolated from school activities and different from other kids. Some youngsters are naturally more timid than others, as their bodies, voices, and emotions change during adolescence, they may feel even more self-conscious. Despite initial feelings of uncertainty, most teens are able to join in if given time to observe and warm up. In extreme cases, called social phobia, the adolescent becomes very withdrawn, and though he wants to take part in social activities, he's unable to overcome intense self-doubt and worry.

Gripped by excessive or unreasonable anxiety when faced with entering a new or unfamiliar social situation, the adolescent with social phobia becomes captive to unrelenting fears of other people's judgment or expectations. She may deal with her social discomfort by fretting about hher health, appearance, or overall competence. Alternatively, she may behave in a clowning or boisterous fashion or consume alcohol to deal with the anxiety. Because so much of a teenager's social life gets played out in school, social phobia may overlap with and be hard to distinguish from school avoidance. Some teens with social phobia may try to sidestep their anxious feelings altogether by refusing to attend or participate in school, Classroom and academic performance falls off, involvement in social and extracurricular activities dwindles, and, as a consequence, self-esteem declines (American Academy of Child and Adolescent Psychiatry). Some teens may experience such a high level of anxiety that they cannot leave the house. This disorder, agoraphobia, seems to stem from feelings about being away from parents and fears of being away from home rather than fear of the world. In fact, a number of children who demonstrate severe separation anxiety in early childhood go on to develop agoraphobia as adolescents and adults.

A 6-year, multi-site, randomized controlled trial sponsored by the National Institute of Mental Health (NIMH) to examine the relative efficacy of various treatments aimed at reducing symptoms of anxiety disorders (separation anxiety disorder, social phobia, and generalized anxiety disorder) in children and adolescents aged 7-17 years was conducted by (Ginsburg, 2014). Results indicated that treatment was effective in reducing anxiety symptoms in nearly 81 per cent of children treated with combination therapy, 60 per cent of those treated with CBT, and 55 per cent of those treated with sertraline. All treatments were significantly more effective than placebo and combination therapy was superior to both CBT and sertraline alone. This comparative treatment trial confirms that SSRI, CBT, and especially their combination, are effective treatments that may offer hope to youth suffering from anxiety disorders and may alter the life trajectory of affected individuals. For GAD and other anxiety disorders, cognitive behavioural therapy (CBT) is the well-researched treatment and usually the treatment of choice due to the positive research evidence. Individual (e.g., Kendall, 1994; Kendall et al, 1997; Kendall and Hud, 2008), group (e.g., Barrett, 1998); and family-centred (e.g., Barrett, Dadds, and Rapee, 1996; Silverman et al, 1999; Rapee, 2000; Shortt, et al, 2001; Lumpkin, et al, 2002).

Controlled clinical trials by (Kendall, 1994), (Kendall and Southam-Gerow, 1996) and (Barrett, Dadds, and Rapee, 1996) have demonstrated that childhood anxiety can be effectively treated with an individually administered cognitive-behavioural intervention. CBT treatments have received strong empirical support for treating childhood anxiety. A series of other studies have demonstrated the efficacy of family CBT conducted in a group format (Cobham, Dadds, and Spence, 1998; Manassis et al., 2002; Mendlowitz et al., 1999; Rapee, 2000; Silverman et al., 1999; Shortt, Barrett, and Fox, 2001; Toren et al., 2000). For example, a ten-session family-based group cognitive-behavioral intervention (FRIENDS) for anxious children was developed and evaluated in Australia (Barrett and Turner, 2004). The program integrates core elements from a cognitive-behavioural perspective (exposure, relaxation, cognitive restructuring, problem solving, self-reward, relapse prevention) with useful strategies from family therapy and interpersonal approaches (e.g., establishment of social support network, conflict management). The theme running through the program is the enhancement of skills and competencies to handle anxiety provoking situations. A FRIEND is an acronym for each of the skills taught: F—Feeling worried? R—Relax and feel good; I—Inner thoughts; E—Explore plans, N—Nice work so reward yourself; D—don't forget to practice; and S—Stay calm, you know how to cope now. In fact, individual CBT, group CBT, and group CBT with parents have all been deemed "probably efficacious" in the treatment of childhood anxiety disorders (Silverman, Pina, Viswesvaran, 2008; Flannery-Schroeder, 2004).

CBT can be delivered in two modes: individual therapy and group therapy. Seventy-one Puerto-Rican adolescents and youth (13- to 17-years-old) diagnosed with major depressive disorder, dysthymia, or both disorders were evaluated. Participants were recruited from a university psychological service centre. Data were collected from participants at baseline, post treatment, and 3-month follow-up on depressive symptoms, self-concept, self-esteem, social adjustment, family emotional involvement, social abilities, and behaviour problems. Data on parent involvement was collected from the parents of participants. The researchers found that IPT-A significantly reduced depressive symptoms at post-test compared with the control group. IPT-A had an effect size (Cohen's d) of 0.73 on depressive symptoms. Self-esteem and social adaptation scores also significantly increased at post-test for participants in the IPT-A group when compared with the control group. IPT-A did not have a significant impact on family emotional involvement or on behavioural problems at post-test. At the 3-month follow-up, attrition for the IPT-A group was high (53 per cent) and the wait-list group could no longer serve as a control because they became eligible for treatment at 12-weeks; as such, no follow-up analyses were conducted (Mufson, et al., 1999).

The group receiving IPT-A had lower levels of depressive symptoms post-treatment than the control group. In addition, significantly more patients receiving IPT-A recovered from their depression than patients in the control group (75 per cent versus 46). Treatment group members were also rated as less depressed by the treating clinicians than control group members post-treatment, and more treatment group members were reported as improved by the clinicians. IPT-A did not have an impact on suicidality or global functioning. Participants receiving IPT-A scored significantly higher on overall social adjustment functioning, functioning with their friends, and functioning in dating relationships than the control group. The treatment and control group scores did not differ for school functioning or family functioning. The group receiving IPT-A scored significantly higher on positive problem-solving orientation and rational problem-solving than the control group. Looking at the subscales of the rational problem-solving scale, IPTA-A participants also scored higher on functioning in generation of alternatives, and solution and verification. Meanwhile, no differences existed between the two groups on the subscales of negative problem-solving orientation, impulsivity/ carelessness, and avoidance style (Mufson, 2004).

IPT warrants further efficacy examination, particularly in economically disadvantaged and minority women, for a number of reasons. IPT is a well-established and efficacious treatment for depression (Cuijpers et al., 2011). It is well suited for impoverished mothers of infants because strengthening and expanding their relational network given possible social isolation may be particularly salient. The importance of providing social support is further highlighted by the strong association between poverty and single mother households (US Census Bureau, 2006–2010). The STAR*D depression treatment trial found that single women were less likely to remit compared to married or cohabiting women, suggesting the importance of social support for remission (Pilowsky et al., 2008; Trivedi et al., 2006) and further highlighting the need for a relational treatment for depression in a population with high rates of single mothers. Although cognitive behaviour therapy is also an efficacious treatment for depression, it may be less efficacious when provided to populations with histories of trauma (Lewis et al., 2010). Thus the researchers chose to provide IPT along with CBT in this clinical trial.

Rationale of the Study

The adolescent girls of today are the future of our country .When their mental health is perfect they can bring innovations in planning to bring success in various industrial strategies. Hence the topic was selected by the researcher. Delhi NCR was selected to do this study as mental status of adolescent girls from all the cultures and economic backgrounds could be easily studied.

Objectives of the Study

1. To study the impact of Behavioural Interventions (CBT and IPT) in case of anxious adolescent girls.

2. To study the impact of Psycho-Education given to the parents of adolescent girls with anxiety.
3. To find new vistas of research in the same arena.

Hypothesis: The present paper attempt to explore the significance of behavioural interventions in psychosocial adjustments of adolescent girls with anxiety with the following null hypotheses:

H_1: There is no significant impact of behavioural interventions (CBT and IPT) on the anxiety level of the adolescent girls.

H_2: There is no significant impact of Psycho-Education given to the parents of anxious adolescent girls.

Methodology

The Study: The study is exploratory in nature, as it is done for the purpose of gaining insights and discovering whether the behavioural interventions (CBT and IPT) help the anxious adolescent girls to reduce their anxiety and to also look for other interventional therapies as well which can also help to better the mental status of these girls.

The Design: Researcher has chosen Correlational Research Design as the variable 'behavioural intervention' is having a positive correlation on the other variable the 'anxiety' in adolescent girls. So increase or decrease in one variable corresponds to the increase or decrease in the other variable. So a positive correlation is present in between two variables.

The Sampling and Sample: Convenience sampling has been done by the researcher for the study, where 100 respondents were selected because of their convenient availability and proximity to the researcher.

The Tools: T-Test's effect size compliments its statistical significance, describing magnitude of differences between the control group and the group of adolescent girls, which underwent behavioural interventions (CBT+IPT). Surveys were conducted over a period of one month on hundred anxious adolescent girls aged between 13-18 years, who had anxious thought, also had thought of committing suicide. Semi-structured interviews and questionnaires and standardized psychological tests (HAM-A) were conducted. Out of hundred, fifty girls were given Cognitive Behaviour Therapy (CBT) and Inter Personal Psychotherapy (IPT). 14 sessions were conducted of both the therapies for the rest of the fifty anxious girl's reduction of stress in Parent-Child Relationship was emphasised. Parent were made to understand that encouraging the adolescent girls by giving a listening ear to them and their problems, will help them to overcome anxiety.

Results and Findings

The study revealed that those fifty anxious adolescent girls who received

CBT and IPT for 14 weeks were found very relaxed than the control group of fifty girls whose parents were given Psycho- Education about vulnerability and sensitivity of anxious girls.

Table- 1: Anxiety Level of 50 Adolescent Girls

Calculations	*Before Treatment*	*After Treatment*
	25	09
	26	11
	30	15
	27	07
	28	07
	29	10
	26	13
	27	12
	19	13
	20	12
	21	11
	18	10
	25	15
	20	05
	20	03
	20	10
	26	10
	20	08
	19	02
	21	12
	20	04
	21	06
	19	08
	20	10
	22	12
	26	09
	27	08
	27	11
	28	10
	20	05
	19	04
	18	03

	26	01
	19	04
	19	02
	27	03
	26	02
	28	02
	29	08
	28	09
	20	10
	20	12
	19	13
	19	15
	21	11
	22	08
	23	09
	24	09
	27	07
MEAN	23.02	8.52
STANDARD DEVIATION	3.674180181	3.905073623
T-TEST		5.51676E-25

Interpretation: The difference in the mean of anxiety level of 50 adolescent girls before and after the treatment of (CBT+IPT) is very significant. Statistically also it is proved that the treatment has brought remarkable improvement in the mental health of the adolescent girls as the anxiety level of the girls have reduced significantly. From the results of the T-TEST=5.51676, we can very easily reject the null hypothesis (H_1), which states that treatment i.e. behavioural Interventions (CBT and IPT) had no significant impact on the anxiety level of the adolescent girls. Whereas the second null hypothesis i.e. (H_2) is accepted as it shows not much significant impact of Psycho-Education given to the parents of adolescent girls with anxiety in the improvement of their mental health and to combat anxiety. Hence, we can say that the treatment (CBT+IPT) has got a clear advantage over the Psycho-Education given to the parents of the anxious adolescent girls.

Discussions

The anxious adolescent girls were continued to be monitored for suicidal thoughts and behaviour for six months. Those girls who received only parental encouragement could overcome some anxiety but were significantly more likely to relapse as the opinion they had about themselves was a good evidence of their beliefs for example- it was found that they definitely remembered the person who ignored them in a crowd rather than the appreciations or the encouragements they received. This is also supported by statistical findings. The difference of mean of the anxiety level of control group girls, who do not receive treatment and the mean of the anxiety level of the same group of girl after their parents received psycho education is not significant. The result of the T-TEST is also not significant enough to ignore the null hypothesis, which proves the parental psycho education does not bring much change in the anxiety level of the girls. The girls who underwent CBT learnt new behaviours, new ways of thinking and new ways of coping with events often involving particulars skills. These 50 adolescent girls could identify dysfunctional thoughts and by learning to think positively about their experiences, their behaviour changed. They started looking at life as a glass which was half filled rather than half empty.

In a recent study published in May 2014, in the same line, cognitive bias modification versus CBT, in reducing adolescent social anxiety it was found : (i) In the short run (6 months follow-up) participants in the CBT condition showed a larger reduction in social anxiety symptoms than participants in the control condition, and a similar trend was evident in the CBM condition, with effect sizes in the small to moderate range, (ii) In the long run (12 months follow-up) the control condition eventually showed a similar reduction in social anxiety symptoms as both active conditions, (iii) After CBT, adolescents reported a stronger decrease of test anxiety compared to the no-intervention control group, (iv) From post-test to 12 months follow up the CBM group showed a stronger decrease of negative automatic associations than both the CBT and the no-intervention control group. In general (Sportel, 2014) they also received Interpersonal Psychotherapy (IPT) along with CBT for 14 weeks which was a structured treatment. Anxious adolescent girls were taught, problems solving strategies for the key relationships in their lives, primary areas of interpersonal difficulty. The girls were held to find solutions to deal with problems adapting to new circumstances. They were taught exploring patterns of thinking that lead to self-destructive actions and the beliefs that direct these thoughts they can modify pattern of thinking to improve coping.

They were asked to schedule positive activities into their daily calendars in order to increase the amount of pleasure they experience. They learnt how to change or restructure negative thought patterns, in order to interpret their environment in a less negative biased way. These girls showed very positive changes after the therapy which included clarification, supportive listening, roleplaying, communication-analysis and encouragement. The interpersonal therapy taught patients new communication skills, helps them to develop insight into how they communicate their needs, and helps them to establish more functional social support networks all leading to improving interpersonal functioning. The clinical psychologist then reviews the progress made in therapy and give as much as positive feedback to the adolescent girl as is genuinely possible. A review of the problems identifying in the interpersonal inventory and progress in dealing with these, as well as reviewing was conducted. A summary of positive changes that the patient has made in improving her communication and in developing an improved social support network should also be undertaken. Credit for the change is ascribed primarily to the girl. The therapies (CBT+IPT) successfully brought down the anxiety level of the adolescent who underwent the interventions.

This is also supported by statistical findings. The mean of anxiety level of 50 adolescent girls was found to be 23.02 and the mean after the girls underwent therapies was 8.52 which represent significant difference and a substantial decline in their anxiety levels. The T-TESTS result 5.51676 is also significant and the null hypothesis can easily be rejected. In the line of above findings (Kendall et al., 2010) found that not all adolescent participant experience ideal outcomes after the treatment of CBT and IPT. The idea behind empirically supported treatment has been found to be effective. Considering the treatment of anxiety in youth and the six-site study of 488 youth with anxiety disorders (Walk up et al., 2008) and other comorbid conditions (Kendall et al., 2010) 60 per cent of CBT treated youth were found to have "very much improved " or " much improved" outcomes following treatment. Though such a response rate was comparable to that produced by medications and significantly better than pill placebo, not all youth outcome were of such a favourable magnitude and not all respondents went forward without other difficulties.

Conclusions

Based on first objectives, the current study showed that our early CBT and IPT interventions have a beneficial effect in terms of reducing anxiety in adolescent girls. In case of second objective, it showed not much significant impact of Psycho-Education given to the parents of adolescent girls with anxiety in the improvement of their mental health and to combat anxiety. It would be hence important for future researchers to test the relative efficacy of the various behavioural interventions. On the basis of such findings, the optimal combination of effective interventions could be selected, which in turn might help to improve further the efficacy of maintaining better mental health of girls, as a tool to prevent the generation and/or persistence of anxiety symptoms.

Suggestions

This research is only the beginning to articulate the mental health problems of the adolescent girls of Delhi NCR region; furthermore the specific aetiologies of behavioural and psychological problems are many a time unknown. For example- there was difficulties in finding about various negative events and circumstances happening and prevailing at home of the adolescent girl suggesting the need for complex and multi component programs. Sample to be studied should have been larger and required extended and preferably thorough follow up once a week.

Recommendations

When the parent expects too much "adult-like behaviour" from a girl, the essential problem does not lie in her. In such cases parents also need to be counselled. It is not possible for the respondents to always think positively, rather we all experience life events that have negative features and they should be able to accept these inevitabilities. One could not be thinking only positive thoughts when in severe difficult situations. There are times when a negative or two are quite reasonable. It is rather teaching these girls to bring reduction in negative thinking that would be a rational expectation as the outcome of the intervention.

Implications

By treating the mental health of adolescent girls with behavioural interventions, the researcher had tried to work towards building up future capital asset of the country as it is them who are significant contributors to a brighter tomorrow of our country. An adolescent girl's mental health is highly vulnerable and usually overlooked in national and international developmental spheres. Working towards ending the negligence in this sphere will end the hobbles for developmental progress globally and would be a dynamic strategy for sustainability.

Bibliography

- Barrett, P. M.; Sonderegger, R. and Xenos, S. (2004). Using friends to combat anxiety and adjustment problems among young migrants to Australia: A National Trial. *Clinical Child Psychology and Psychiatry.*
- Carla, A.; Hitchcock, B. A.; Chavira, D. A.; and Stein, M. B. (2009). Recent Findings in Social Phobia among Children and Adolescents. *Journal of Psychiatry Related Science,* 46(1): 34–44.
- Costello, E. J.; Mustillo, S.; Erkanli, A.; Keeler, G. and Angold, A. (2003). Prevalence and development of psychiatric disorders in childhood and adolescence. *General Archives of Psychiatry*, 60, 837-844.

- Craske, M. G., and Zucker, B. (2002). Prevention of anxiety disorders: A model for intervention. *Applied and Preventive Psychology*, 10, 155-175.
- Cuijpers P., Geraedts A. S.; Oppen P.; Andersson G.; Markowitz J. C. and Straten A. (2011). Interpersonal psychotherapy for depression: A meta-analysis. *American Journal of Psychiatry*, 168, 581–592.
- Dahl, R. E. (2004). Adolescent brain development: A period of vulnerabilities and opportunities. Keynote address. In R.E. Dahl and L. P. Spear (Eds.), Annals of the New York Academy of Sciences: Vol. 1021. Adolescent brain development: Period of vulnerabilities and opportunities (pp. 1-22). *The New York Academy of Sciences,* New York.
- Davis, M., Robbins-Eshelman, E., and Mckay, M. (1995). The relaxation and stress reduction workbook. New Harbinger, Oakland, California.
- Esther, B. Maaike, (2013). Department of Psychiatry, in PLOS, DOI, 10. 1371.
- Hankin, B. (2008). Rumination and depression in adolescence: Investigating symptom specificity in a multi wave prospective study. *Journal of Clinical child and Adolescent Psychology*, 37,701-713.
- Hazen E, Schlozman S, Beresin E. (2008). Adolescent psychological development: A review. *Paediatri c Review.* May; 29(5): 161-168.
- Kendall, P. C. (1994). Treating anxiety disorders in children: Results of a randomized clinical trial. *Journal of Consulting and Clinical Psychology*, 62, 100-110.
- Kendall, P. C.; Flannery-Schroeder, E.; Panichelli-Mindel, S. M.; Southam-Gerow, M.; Henin, A. and Warman, M. (1997). Therapy for youths with anxiety disorders: A second randomized clinical trial. *Journal of Consulting and Clinical Psychology*, 65, 366-380
- Kessler, R. C.; Avenevoli, S.; Merikangas, K. R. (2001). Mood disorders in children and adolescents: *An epidemiologic perspective. Biological Psychiatry*, 49: 002-1014.
- Kessler, R. C.; McGonagle, K. A.; Zhaos, S.; Nelson, C. B.; Hughes, M.; Eshelman, S.; Wittchen, H. U.; Kendler, K. S. (1994). Lifetime and 12-month prevalence of DSM-III-R psychiatric disorders in the United States. Results from the National Co morbidity Survey. *Archives General Psychiatry,* 51(1): 8-19.
- Lewinsohn, P., Rohde, P. (1993). The cognitive- behavioural treatment of depression in adolescents: Research and suggestions. Panic disorder in children and adolescents: A review (6):177-183.

- Moreau, D., Weissman, M. M. (1992). Panic disorder in child and adolescent. *American Journal of Psychiatry*. 149 (10): 1306- 1325.
- Martha, D., Elizabeth, R. E. and Matthew, McKey. (2008). **The Relaxation and Stress Reduction Workbook, New Herbinger, Oakland, USA.**
- Mufson, L. (2004). A randomized effectiveness trial of interpersonal psychotherapy for depressed adolescents. *Archives of General Psychiatry, 61*, 577-584.
- Mufson, L.; Dorpa, K. P.; Wickramaratne, T.; Nomura, Y.; Olson, M. and Weissman, M. M. (1999). Efficacy of interpersonal psychotherapy for depressed adolescents. *Archives of General psychiatry, (61), 577-584.*
- Reed, V.; Gander, F.; Pfister, H.; Steiger, A.; Sonntaq, H.; Trenkhalder, C.; Hundt, W.; Wittchen, H.U. (1998). To what degree the Composite International Diagnostic Interview (CIDI) correctly identifies DSM-IV disorders: Testing validity issues in a clinical sample. *International Journal of Methods in Psychiatric Research; 7(3), 142-155.*
- Ron, J. Steingaurd, (2014). Mood disorder and teen age girls. Child and Mine Institute.
- Rossello, J. and Bernal, G. (1999). The efficacy of cognitive-behavioural and interpersonal treatments for depression in Puerto Rican adolescents. *Journal of Consulting and Clinical Psychology, 67*, 734-745.
- Silverman, W. K.; Pina, A. A. and Viswesvaran, C. (2008). Evidence-based psychosocial treatments for phobic and anxiety disorders in children and adolescents. *Journal of Clinical Child and Adolescent Psychology, 3 (7), 105–130.*
- Spence, S. H.; Donovan, C.; Brechman-Toussaint, M. (2000). The treatment of childhood social phobia: The effectiveness of a social skills training-based, cognitive-behavioural intervention, with and without parental involvement. *Journal of Child Psychology, 41(6):713-26.*
- Sportel, D. E.; Nauta, M. H. (2014). Department of Psychiatry, University Medical Centre Groningen, University of Groningen, Netherland.
- Singh, Sunita and Gururaj, Gopal Krishna (2014). Review Article: Health Behaviours and problems among young people in India: cause for cousin and call for action. *Indian Journal of Medicinal Research,* 140, 185-208.
- Walkup, J.; Albano, A.; Piacentini, J.; Birmaher, B.; Compton, S.; Sherrill, J. (2008). Cognitive behavioral therapy, sertraline, or a combination in childhood anxiety. *The New England Journal of Medicine,* (359), 2753–2766.

Appendix

1. QUESTIONNAIRE

A. SOCIO ECONOMIC PROFILE:

A1. General Profile

a) Name:

b) Address:

c) Occupation:

d) Age:

e) Religion:

A2. Educational Qualification

a) Illiterate

b) Schooling

c) Degree

d) Any other

A3. Type of family

a) Nuclear

b) Joint

A4. No. of family members:

A5. Details of family members:-

Sl. No.	*Name*	*Relationship with The Respondent*	*Age*	*Sex*	*Education*	*Occupation*

B. Expenditure Pattern:

B1. What is the monthly income of the father?

B2. Family income per month.

B3. What is your average monthly household expenditure?

C. Interaction of the adolescent girl with her father:

(Answer with yes or no, unless stated otherwise)

C1. Do you feel comfortable sharing your failures, feelings with your father?

C2. Do you feel comfortable discussing the various changes taking place in your body during adolescence?

C3. Do you feel comfortable introducing your peer group to your father?

C4. Does your father behave in a democratic manner?

C5. Do you get enough support from your father?

C6. If no, what is the reason?

(a) Lack of interest

(b) Lack of time

(c) Lack of attention

(d) Any other

D. Interaction of the adolescent girl with her mother:

(Answer with yes or no, unless stated otherwise)

D1. Do you feel comfortable sharing your failures, feelings with your mother?

D2. Do you feel comfortable discussing the various changes taking place in your body during adolescence?

D3. Do you feel comfortable introducing your peer group to your mother?

D4. Does your mother behave in a democratic manner?

D5. Do you get enough support from your mother?

D6. If no, what is the reason?

(e) Lack of interest

(f) Lack of time

(g) Lack of attention

(h) Any other

E. Interaction of adolescent girls with peer group:

E1. Does the peer group accept you as a leader?

E2. Do your peers include you in all group activities?

E3. Does your peer group takes your opinion in all the activities?

E4. Are you excluded from participating in various activities?

F. Interaction of adolescent girl with her neighbors:

F1. Do you take part in the neighborhood activities actively?

F2. Are you a social recluse?
F3. Are you looked up to in your neighborhood?
F4. Are you considered to be a role model in the neighborhood?
G Body weight and shape:
G1. Are you satisfied with your body weight and shape?
G2. Does your body shape make you feel inferior?
G3. Do you compare yourself to or wish to look like models?
H. Social Security:
H1. Do you feel confident to venture out of the house for tuition purposes after dark?

2. Hamilton Anxiety Rating Scale (HAM-A)

Source: **Hamilton, M. (1959). The assessment of anxiety states by rating. *British Journal of Medical Psychology; (32), 50–55.***

Rating Clinician-rated

Administration time 10-15 minutes

Main purpose to assess the severity of symptoms of anxiety

Population Adults, adolescents and children

Scoring

Each item is scored on a scale of 0 (not present) to 4 (severe), with a total score range of 0–56, where <17 indicates mild severity, 18–24 mild to moderate severity and 25–30 moderate to severe.

Commentary

The HAM-A was one of the first rating scales developed to measure the severity of anxiety symptoms, and is still widely used today in both clinical and research settings. The scale consists of 14 items, each defined by a series of symptoms, and measures both psychic anxiety (mental agitation and psychological distress) and somatic anxiety (physical complaints related to anxiety). Although the HAM-A remains widely used as an outcome measure in clinical trials, it has been criticized for its sometimes poor ability to discriminate between anxiolytic and antidepres-sant effects, and somatic anxiety versus somatic side effects. The HAM-A does not provide any standardized probe questions. Despite this, the reported levels of inter-rater reliability for the scale appear to be acceptable.

Versions

The scale has been translated into: Cantonese for China, French and Spanish. An IVR version of the scale is available from Healthcare Technology Systems.

Additional references

Maier W, Buller R, Philipp M, Heuser I. The Hamilton Anxiety Scale: reliability, validity and sensitivity to change in anxiety and depressive disorders. J Affect Disord 1988; 14 (1):61-8.

Borkovec T and Costello E. Efficacy of applied relaxation and cognitive behavioral therapy in the treatment of generalized anxiety disorder. J Clin Consult Psychol 1993; 61(4):611-19

Address for correspondence

The HAM-A is in the public domain.

Hamilton Anxiety Rating Scale (HAM-A)

Below is a list of phrases that describe certain feeling that people have. Rate the patients by finding the answer which best describes the extent to which he/she has these conditions. Select one of the five responses for each of the fourteen questions.

---

0 = Not present, 1 = Mild, 2 = Moderate, 3 = Severe, 4 = Very severe.

1. Anxious mood *0 1 2 3 4*
Worries, anticipation of the worst, fearful anticipation, irritability.

2.Tension *0 1 2 3 4*
Feelings of tension, fatigability, startle response, moved to tears easily, trembling, feelings of restlessness, inability to relax.

3.Fears *0 1 2 3 4*
Of dark, of strangers, of being left alone, of animals, of traffic, of crowds.

4.Insomnia *0 1 2 3 4*
Difficulty in falling asleep, broken sleep, unsatisfying sleep and fatigue on waking, dreams, nightmares, night terrors.

5. Intellectual *0 1 2 3 4*
Difficulty in concentration, poor memory.

6. Depressed mood *0 1 2 3 4*
Loss of interest, lack of pleasure in hobbies, depression, early waking, diurnal swing.

8. Somatic (sensory) *0 1 2 3 4*
Tinnitus, blurring of vision, hot and cold flushes, feelings of weakness, pricking sensation.

9. Cardiovascular symptoms *0 1 2 3 4*
Tachycardia, palpitations, pain in chest, throbbing of vessels, fainting feelings, missing beat.

10. Respiratory symptoms *0 1 2 3 4*
Pressure or constriction in chest, choking feelings, sighing, dyspnea.

11. Gastrointestinal symptoms *0 1 2 3 4*
Difficulty in swallowing, wind abdominal pain, burning sensations, abdominal fullness, nausea, vomiting, borborygmi, looseness of bowels, loss of weight, constipation.

12. Genitourinary symptoms *0 1 2 3 4*
Frequency of micturition, urgency micturition, amenorrhea, menorrhagia, development of frigidity, premature ejaculation, loss of Libido, impotence.

7. Somatic (muscular) *0 1 2 3 4*

Pains and aches, twitching, stiffness, myoclonic jerks, grinding of teeth,

13 Autonomic symptoms *0 1 2 3 4*

Dry mouth, flushing, pallor, tendency to sweat, giddiness, tension unsteady voice, increased muscular tone.

14 Behaviour at interviw *0 1 2 3 4*

Fidgeting, restlessness or pacing, tremor of hands, forrowed brow, strained face, sighing or rapid respiration, facial polar, swallowing etc.

24

Regional Disparity in FDI Inflows and Inclusive Growth in India

Rachna Madan & Jitender Bhandari

Abstract

Since liberalization, Indian economy has been attracting colossal FDI inflows and developed as the most favored venture destination for foreign investors. Nonetheless, investigation of FDI statistics shows immense difference in FDI distribution among Indian states. The essential target here is to comprehend the progress of development in the nation which is bringing about regional disparity and propose measures for assuaging the issue. This paper analyses the comprehensive database on FDI inflows subsequent to the early 1990s to address two noteworthy issues identified with FDI and regional growth in India in the post structural reform period. Initially, we break down the location decisions of foreign investors. The confirmation shows that the amassing of FDI in a couple of moderately propelled regions may have kept FDI impacts from spreading over the Indian economy. Second, we assess whether the connection between FDI and economic growth has gotten to be stronger in the fallout of changes. Various categories of FDI are for sure emphatically related with per capita income growth crosswise over Indian states. Then again, it is just for the wealthier states that FDI seems, by all accounts, to be connected with higher growth. FDI is therefore prone to increment regional income disparity in India. This paper tries to evaluate the reasons for the skewed dispersion of FDI among states. An understanding of such factors will support

Indian government to detail approaches for impartial growth of FDI inflows and for inclusive growth.

Keywords: *FDI inflows, regional disparity, location decisions, inclusive growth.*

Introduction

In the period of globalization and financial amalgamation, foreign direct investment (FDI) has risen as a standout amongst the most essential types of capital flows to developing nations. FDI is frequently favored over different types of capital flows by the policy makers as it is thought to be of a more steady nature furthermore it doesn't structure as a part of the host nation's external debt stock. Aside from constituting a mode of fund, FDI likewise has a tendency to upgrade economic growth through spill over of innovation and learning in the host nation. There is, in any case, substantial imbalance in the circulation of FDI flows within the developing market and emerging economies. While a few nations like China, India and Brazil have pulled in main part of the FDI flows, the vast majority of the others have neglected to accomplish the same.

FDI flows to India pulled up in the 1990s, after the economic reforms and liberalization of the FDI policies. According to the IMF's Global Financial Stability Report, April 2012, India has developed as one of the significant beneficiaries of FDI flows among the developing business economies in the last few years. Arrangement of FDI flows to India uncovers that throughout the years automatic route has developed as the most imperative channel of FDI flows to India, emulated by reinvested earnings and securing of shares. FDI through government approval route, then again, has declined over time, which is in accordance with the policy reforms. The sectoral composition of FDI to India has experienced critical changes following the 1990s. The greater part of the FDI flows in the pre liberalization period were steered towards the manufacturing sector. In the late years, nonetheless, a great part of the FDI flows have moved into the services sector.

Economically propelled states, destination wise have pulled in the lion's share of FDI flows to India. The top six Indian states, *viz*., Maharashtra, Delhi, Tamil Nadu, Karnataka, Gujarat and Andhra Pradesh together represented more than 70 per cent of FDI equity flows to India during the period April 2000 to July 2013 reflecting different indications of FDI concentration at the state level. The FDI policy in India was liberalized in the early 1990s as a part of economic reforms to pull in the foreign capital furthermore to exploit the advantage of the spillover of innovation and knowledge. It is, in this manner, crucial to get maximum advantage from the FDI flows and guarantee that the climbing FDI flows don't prompt an increment in regional disparity.

In perspective of this, an endeavor has been made in this paper to inspect the real reasons influencing regional distribution of FDI flows to India. In light of the discoveries, the paper additionally makes an endeavor to list out the conceivable strategy suggestions for the national and the state governments.

Literature Review

A genuinely strong amassing of FDI in moderately few locations can be watched both across and inside host nations. Models of location decision by foreign investors have tended to different variables that may help clarify the absorption of FDI across and inside host nations. The theoretical beginning stage normally is that foreign firms settle on a specific area taking into account expected profitability. Therefore, location decisions rely on upon how the qualities of one specific spatial unit and its geographic surroundings influence firms' profits with respect to the attributes of other spatial units. Central point forming these decisions incorporates expected interest for a firm's products, the supply of obliged inputs, factor costs, and the infrastructure availability. Moreover, past location decisions by the foreign investors figure unmistakably on the rundown of FDI determinants and have gotten specific consideration in the recent observed literature.

From the earlier contemplation on more particular speculations include extensive ambiguity relying upon the level of regional disaggregation and the kind of FDI (Alegria 2006; Blonigen et al. 2007). For example, it may seem obvious that the size and purchasing power of local markets induce more foreign investors to enter a location. This hypothesis is most reasonable in a cross-country context and as long as FDI is purely horizontal. The motive of market access may also shape the distribution of horizontal FDI across fairly large spatial units in major host countries such as US or Indian states. Local demand should matter less, however, when location choices relate to smaller spatial units such as Indian districts, or when FDI is motivated by vertical specialization. Conversely, the surrounding market potential might become more important with smaller spatial units being analyzed. Similar ambiguity prevails with regard to the costs of production. The relevance of wage costs, on which previous literature focuses, is highly sensitive to small alterations in the conditioning information set in cross-country studies according to the Extreme Bounds Analysis of Chakrabarti (2001). According to the World Bank's Investment Climate Assessment, survey respondents complained about serious skill shortages in various Indian states (World Bank 2004). Majumder (2008) stresses persistent regional disparities with respect to education. Majumder also provides extensive evidence on substantial variation in the regional quality of infrastructure, particularly with regard to financial infrastructure. Regional disparities in the quality of infrastructure appear to have widened in the post-reform era. Local skills and efficient infrastructure can be expected to be important regional pull factors of FDI even though FDI-related outsourcing may primarily involve labor that is relatively low skilled from the country of origin's point of view. Feenstra and Hanson (1997) have clearly demonstrated that the corresponding labor demand of foreign investors qualifies as relatively high skilled in lower-income host countries such as or India.

Dunning (1998) discussed that the locational preferences and strategies of MNEs towards FDI have significantly changed between 1970 and 1990s. He identified certain instrumental developments in the world economy in relation with the locational preference decisions of MNEs during this period. The increasing knowledge component in manufacturing goods, increase in share and demand for professional and skilled workers in labor force, increase in share of expenditure in IT sector reflect a major development in the growth of intellectual capital. Increasing significance of the non-material knowledge intensive assets was the result of growth in service sector, particularly knowledge and information oriented services. The location of creation and use of these knowledge intensive assets have been increasingly influenced by the presence of immobile clusters of complementary value-added activities. Clustering benefitted firms in similar and related activities in many forms like localized support facilities, specialized factor inputs and distribution networks. This gave rise to "alliance capitalism" in which the key shareholders in wealth sharing process need to collaborate more actively and purposefully with each other. There were also many evidences where MNEs were increasingly seeking locations which offer the best economic and institutional facilities for core competence to be efficiently utilized. Fourth, the renaissance of market economy and the consequent changes in the macroeconomic policies and macro-organizational strategies of many national governments have also contributed significantly to the economic and political risk assessment of FDI by MNEs.

Since the last two decades the agglomeration factor has proved to be a vital factor in formulating the locational preferences for FDI. Agglomeration economies emerge when there are some positive externalities in collocating near other economic units due to presence of knowledge spill overs, specialized labour markets and supplier network (Krugman, 1991). Several studies focusing on emerging economies statistically proved that foreign investors favour locations that could minimize information costs and offer agglomeration economies (He Canfei, 2002). Incentives offered by state government like tax abatements, job credits, grants, sales tax abatements, job training, infrastructure subsidies and loan guarantees play a significant role in attracting the investment inflows (Fisher and Peters, 1998).

Morris (2007) argued that in a country like India, the regions with the metropolitan cities have an advantage in headquartering the country operation of MNEs and so attracted a huge share of FDI inflows. Nunnenkamp and Stracke (2007) found significant positive correlation of FDI with per capita income, per capita bank deposits, telephone density, and standard of education, population density and per capita value added in manufacturing in India. On the other hand FDI was negatively correlated with state population and had insignificant effect of availability of electricity and unemployment rate.

Goldar (2007) found that the variables influencing the locational decisions of local company plants all around likewise influence the area choice of outside multinational ventures.

His examination of plants situated in 100 noteworthy urban communities in 17 separate states uncovered that city size is an imperative figure setting up locational inclination. States with metropolitan urban areas had an ideal impact catching the point of interest in "headquartering" the nation operations of MNEs. Accessibility of talented skilled laborers, the current investment climate and accessibility of urban conveniences in urban communities had a solid impact.

Siddharthan (2006) found that the determinants of regional conveyance of FDI flows are truly comparative for India and China. In both the nations a huge share of FDI streams to generally developed districts, while other regions poor in physical, social and institutional framework got a little impart from the entire pie. In India states which are moderately developed and located at key seaside area get high impart of FDI inflows. In addition, the areas accepting high FDI inflows were the districts with high domestic investment.

Lall and Mengistae (2005) in their study on business environment, clustering and plant location in the Indian cities using firm level data from 2003 round of Investment Climate Survey, India, found local business environment to have a strong effect on locational preferences. Predatory enforcement of business regulation is a big setback for investment plans in a region and prevalence of such activities decreases interest of foreign investors in the region. Better access to finance, better infrastructure facilities and availability of land attracted firms to invest in the region. Firms were also attracted by the agglomeration economies from clustering of firms for dependent industries therefore new firms will prefer to locate their activities in a region where their line of business is already established.

Aggarwal (2005) found rigid labor laws to be one of the major impediments in FDI inflows. The effect of labor cost and market rigidities are more pronounced for export oriented market rather than domestic market. He also pointed out the importance of export processing zone in deciding location for investment. Statistical evidences from the study suggested that infrastructure, human development and regional development were also important in attracting higher FDI both in export and domestic market sectors.

Ramachandran and Goebel (2002) assessed why Tamil Nadu has emerged as one of the most favored investment destination in India. He cited several advantages like political stability with proactive government policy framework, investor friendly and transparent decision making process, sufficient availability of power, abundance of skilled and professional labor, sound diversified industrial infrastructure, harmonious industrial relations, high quality of work culture, highly cosmopolitan composition and high proportion of English speaking population which makes Tamil Nadu as one of the best locations to invest in India. FDI inflow in Tamil Nadu is heavily dominated by the IT sector.

Atri Mukherjee (2011) has dissected real determinants bringing on regional divergence in FDI inflows to Indian states. Her examination demonstrates that variables like business sector size, size of industrial and service base and agglomeration impacts have positive effect on FDI inflows. Then again the effect of taxation and cost of labor is negative. She argues that as more similar firms in the related fields of business cluster, to reduce their production costs significantly with increased competition at the supplier end as well as specialization and division of labor and benefiting from the industrial linkages. Firms in related fields of business cluster together, their costs of production may decline significantly (firms have competing multiple suppliers, greater specialization and division of labor result Hakan Yilmazkuday 2010).

According to Singh J. (2010) the FDI inflows, in general, show an increasing trend during the post-reform period. Furthermore, country-wise comparison of FDI inflow also indicates that FDI inflow into India has increased considerably in comparison to other developing economies in the recent years. India opened up its economy and allowed MNEs in the core sectors as a part of reform process in the beginning of 1990s. Since then it has captivated a big share of FDI inflows among the developing countries and has become one of the worthwhile investment locations for the foreign investors. Thus, the study indicates that the FDI inflows into India responded positively to the liberalization measures introduced in the early 1990s and since the inception of the economic reforms in India in 1991, the role of foreign investment in the growth process has been recognized by the policy makers. The FDI coming from abroad has played a vital role in expediting the economic growth process by strengthening domestic investment. It is examined from vari-ous issues of World Investment Report that while in 2002, FDI flows expressed as percentage of gross fixed capital formation stood at 3.0 per cent in India, the same has increased to 9.6 per cent in 2008.

Singh, Shikha (2009) study describe that foreign direct investment (FDI) policies play a major role in the economic growth of developing countries around the world. Attracting FDI inflows with conductive policies has therefore become a key battleground in the emerging markets. The prospect of new growth opportunities and outsized profits encourages large capital inflows across a range of industry and opportunity types. And this has led to competition among the states in formulating flexible policies and providing incentives to woo private investors to invest more and more. In the light of the above the paper highlights the trend of FDI in India after the economic reforms, sector-wise and country-wise share of FDI, the manner in which FDI has affected the growth of Indian states. Various factors, which play a significant role in attracting FDI into a particular state, are also examined. Efforts made by the state governments in order to attract maximum FDI are also studied.

Bajpai and Sachs (2002) found that the reform-oriented states have performed better in attracting domestic and foreign investment, software exports, 100 per cent export-oriented units, and in some of the social sector indicators. These states are the fastest growing states during the post-reform period. Larger private investment, smaller government and better state-level institutions were found to be positively associated with growth performance (Purfield, 2006). The states that implemented liberalization policies particularly in the factor markets, and promoted good institutions were found to have performed better than the others. Kochhar et al. (2006) observed that the states with weaker institutions and poorer infrastructure experienced lower income and industrial growth.

Embodiment of FDI Theories

Extensive literature has been developed to explain the anomaly of FDI, its motives, driving forces and consequences. Due to the nature of the subject there is no general theory that would explain FDI occurrence, the perception of FDI stretch over various disciplines ranging from international economics, economic geography, international business and management. For illustrative purposes, the following section presents the evolution of FDI theory.

Internalization Theory

As developed in the 1970s by British economists Peter Buckley and Mark Casson, Internalization theory, however, asks why a firm organizes the international transaction within its own boundaries and not via the market. Internalization theory explains that FDI occurs when the transaction costs are high and it makes sense that international production is internalized within the firm. Transaction costs are the costs of entering into a transaction, that is, those related to monitoring, negotiating and entering into a contract. A firm must decide whether it is profitable to own and operate its own facility overseas or should enter into a contract with a foreign firm to do this through a franchise, licensing or supply agreement. Methods of internalization include creating patents, copy rights, technical know-how.

Product Life Cycle Theory

As developed in the 1960s by Raymond Vernon and Lewis T.Wells, international product life cycle theory explains that the production of a product shifts to different categories of countries through the different stages of the product life cycle. According to this theory, the international product life cycle consists of three stages: New Product, Maturing product, Standardized product.

In the initial stage of **new product** market, a firm develops and introduces an innovative product in response to the perceived need in the domestic market. It is then exported to other developed markets in the **maturing product** stage since the demand for the product grows as the consumer recognizes its value. As competition increases in these markets, manufacturing units are set up to satisfy the domestic and foreign demand. In stage three, the **standardized product** stage, the market for the product stabilizes and competition further intensifies, manufacturing units are set up in developing countries to lower the production costs and labor costs. As a result, the product begins to be imported into the innovating firm's home market.

John Dunnings Eclectic Theory/OLI Model

The theory aims to explain the extent and pattern of international production, i.e. production financed by FDI and undertaken by MNEs. This theory endeavors to explain that FDI reflects both international business activity and business activity internal to the firm. The paradigm asserts that, at any given moment of time, this will be determined by the configuration of three sets of forces:

Ownership advantage: The firm must own some unique competitive advantage that beats the disadvantages of competing with foreign firms on their home ground. This advantage may be a brand name, the benefits of economies of scale, ownership of proprietary technology.

Location advantage: Undertaking the business activity must be more profitable in a foreign location than undertaking it in a domestic location. Foreign locations may be more attractive because of lower land prices, tax rates, better and cheap availability of skilled or unskilled labor.

Internalization advantage: The firm benefits more from controlling the foreign business activity than from hiring an independent local company to provide the service because supervising and monitoring the contractual performance of the local company is expensive when the firm's reputation could be threatened by bad behavior by the local company.

Institutional Theory

According to DiMaggio and Powell (1983), "Institutional theory argues how organisations are constrained by institutional belief systems, norms, conventions and rules shared by relevant members of their environment. Subsequently, to attain authenticity and respectability around critical institutional factors, for example, customers and governments, MNEs imitate the institutional standards and desires to accomplish fit, or get isomorphic. The theory verifies a company's competitive advantage credited upon a level of legitimacy in their respected markets that is required to access precarious resources, needed for survival and growth. It emphasized on political and social considerations which goes beyond "Internationalization Theory" based on efficiency and cost. This theory stands mainly on three pillars, also regarded as the legitimacy pressures:

- ***Regulatory Pillar:*** Focused widely upon the "explicit regulative processed such as rule setting, monitoring and sanctioning activities.
- ***Cognitive Pillar:*** Discusses the broadly shared cognitive structures by which performers of an organizational field or general individual infer and make sense of their world.
- ***Normative Pillar:*** Refers to communal understandings and meanings formed by national values, culture, norms, and belief system followed in a nation.

New Trade Theory

As proposed by David Ricardo, his "Comparative Advantage" hypothesis serves that each region has the competence to specialize in either products or services that they handle at an opportunity cost than other nations (Tabarrok, 2008). Following came the extended version of this hypothesis, known as "The Hecksher-Ohlin-Samuelson (HOS)" trade model which expressed that the two elements of production "capital and work" creates a net gain for all nations. On the other hand, the primary perspective that was disregarded in this hypothesis was the determinants of the competitive advantage. "The New Trade Theory" founded by Paul Krugman in 1979 recommended that trade can assists nations gain economies of scale which builds the scale of production and diminishes expenses and costs. Alongside, the New Trade Theory could be acknowledged as an alternate motivation behind why trade might be helpful and a major awareness in globalization. Case in point, France and Germany offer loads of stuff to one another despite the fact that they have a comparable atmosphere and assets. Like if there should be an occurrence of assembling colossal jets, only Germany is more capable enough to prepare them due to tremendous economies of scale involved though France has the limit of generating particular sort of machine apparatuses needed to make an air craft. Accordingly, France imports the air craft while Germany imports all the obliged apparatuses. Additionally, Germany dominates in the export business sector of air craft since they have a sustainable competitive advantage over other nations.

Oerview of FDI Inflows in India:

Graph 1: FDI Inflows during Pre Liberalization Period

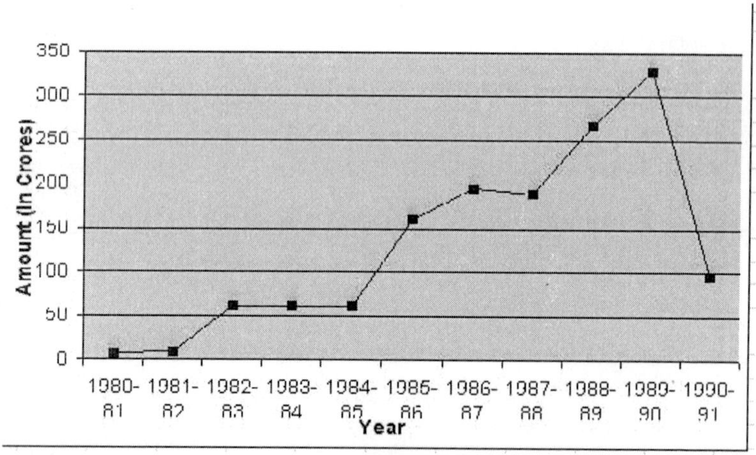

Graph 2: FDI Inflows during Post Liberalization Period

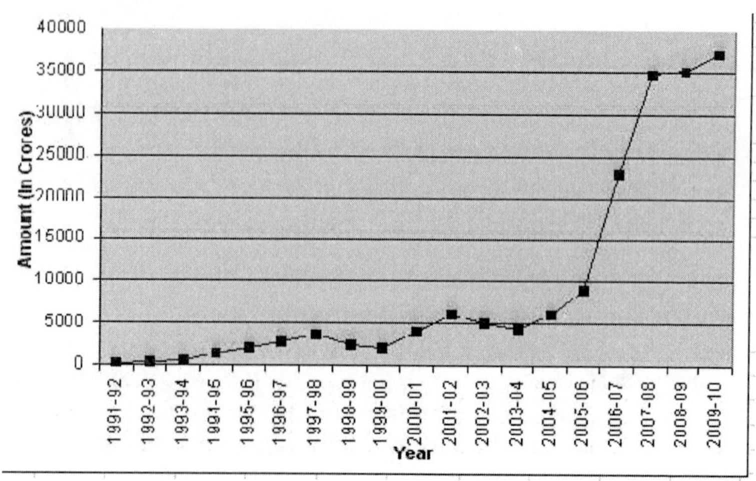

Graph 3: FDI Inflows in India

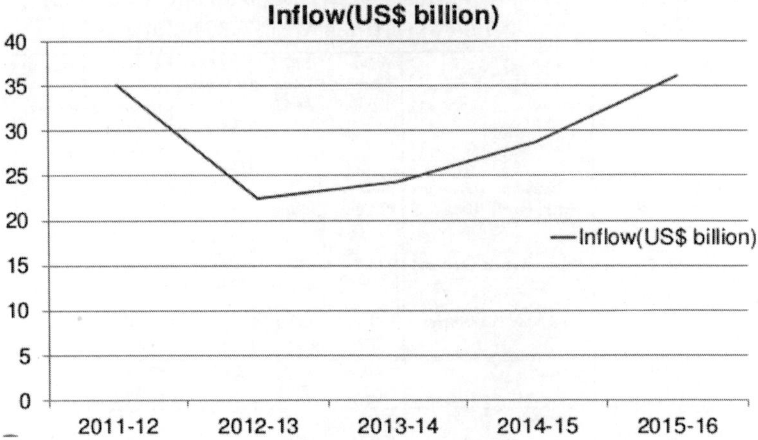

Source: Various issues of SIA, GOI (2015-16 estimated)

Since liberalization, the FDI inflow to the country has increased many folds. It has increased from 2463 US$ million in 2000-2001 to 18,749 US$ million in 2013-14. The above graphs (graph 1,2 and 3) show that FDI inflows into India before 1991 was minimal, later substantial increase in the volume of FDI inflows into India was observed during the Post Liberalization period.

Regional Distribution of FDI Inflows:

During financial integration and in the globalization era, FDI has emerged as one of the most important forms of capital flows to developing countries. Despite the fact that after liberalization, India developed as one of the prime speculation areas for foreign investors, however the real concern lies in the dispersion of FDI. The spatial imbalance of FDI is one of the real reasons of climbing regional inequalities.

Graph 4: Regional Inequalities in FDI Inflows in India.

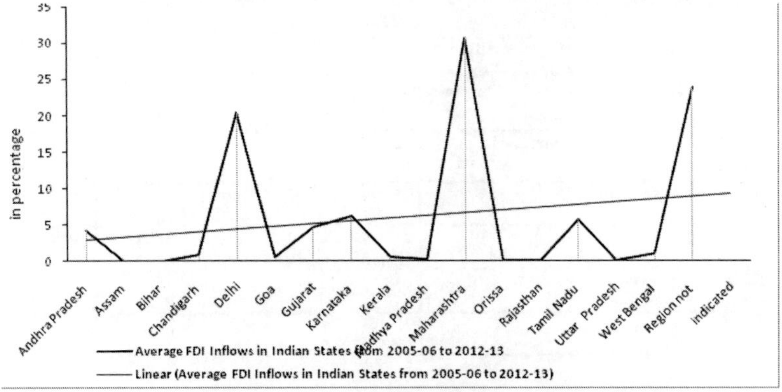

Table1. Statement on RBI's Regional Offices (With States Covered) Received FDI Equity Inflows (1) (from April, 2000 to July, 2013):

S. No.	RBI? s - Regional Office(2)	State covered	2011-12 (April - March)	2012-13 (April - March)	2013-14 (April- July, 2013)	Cumulative Inflows (April ? 00 - July „ 13)	%age to total Inflows (in terms of US$)
1	MUMBAI	Maharashtra, Dadra and Nagar Haveli, Daman & Diu	44,664 (9,553)	47,359 (8,716)	8,059 (1,410)	301,553 (64,746)	32
2	NEWDELHI	Delhi, Part of Up and Haryana	37,403 (7,983)	17,490 (3,222)	4,018 (708)	172,599 (37,002)	18
3	CHENNAI	Tamil Nadu, Pondicherry	6,711 (1,422)	15,252 (2,807)	5,586 (990)	58,397 (12,071)	6
4	BANGALORE	Karnataka	7,235 (1,533)	5,553 (1,023)	3,770 (661)	53,215 (11,446)	6
5	AHMEDABAD	Gujarat	4,730 (1,001)	2,676 (493)	1,369 (234)	40,469 (8,884)	4
6	HYDERABAD	Andhra Pradesh	4,039 (848)	6,290 (1,159)	1,660 (297)	38,551 (8,265)	4
7	KOLKATA	West Bengal, Sikkim, Andaman and Nicobar Islands	1,817 (394)	2,319 (424)	5888 (104)	11,092 (2,409)	1
8	CHANDIGARH`	Chandigarh, Punjab, Haryana, Himachal Pradesh	624 (130)	255 (47)	90 (16)	5,654 (1,217)	1
9	BHOPAL	Madhya Pradesh, Chattisgarh	569 (123)	1,208 (220)	693 (116)	5,480 (1,113)	0.6
10.	KOCHI	Kerala, Lakshadweep	2,274 (471)	390 (72)	268 (47)	4,589 (958)	0.5
11	PANAJI	Goa	181 (38)	47 (9)	43 (8)	3,597 (779)	0.4
12	JAIPUR	RAJASTHAN	161 (33)	714 (132)	40 (7)	3,364 (692)	0.4
13	KANPUR	Uttar Pradesh, Uttranchal	635 (140)	167 (31)	50 (9)	1,665 (356)	0.2
14	BHUBANESHWAR	Orissa	125 (28)	285 (52)	60 (11)	1,677 (352)	0.2
15	GUWAHATI	Assam, Arunachal Pradesh, Manipur, Meghalaya, Mizoram, Nagaland, Tripura	5 (1)	27 (5)	0 (0)	348 (78)	0
16	Patna	Bihar, Jharkhand	123 (24)	41 (8)	1 (0)	191 (38)	0
17	Region Not Indicated(3)		53,851 (11,399)	21,833 (4,004)	13,635 (2,436)	233,868 (49,930)	25.0
SUB. Total			165,146 (35,121)	121,907 (22,424)	39,931 (7,053)	936,311 (200,335)	100.00
18	RBI'S-NRI Schemes (from 2000 to 2002)		0	0	0	533 (121)	-
Grand Total			165,146 (35,121)	121,907 (22,423)	39,931 (7,053)	936,844 (200,456)	-

(1) Includes equity capital components only.

(2) The Region-wise FDI inflows are classified as per RBI?s - Regional Office received FDI inflows, furnished by RBI, Mumbai.

(3) Represents, FDI inflows through acquisition of existing shares by transfer from residents to non residents. For this, RBI Regional wise information is not provided by Reserve Bank of India

Source: www.data.gov.in

From the graph 4 and the table 1 given above it is observed that the Indian states such as, Maharashtra, Karnataka, Tamilnadu, Delhi, Gujarat and Andhra Pradesh together accounted for more than 70 per cent of FDI equity flows to India during the period 2005-06 to 2013-14, Maharashtra alone accounted for 32 per cent and Mumbai in Maharashtra alone attracted most of FDI inflows. Maharashtra was followed by New Delhi with 18 per cent, Tamilnadu with 6 per cent, Karnataka with 6 per cent, Gujarat and Andhra Pradesh with 4 per cent each. The states attracted lowest FDI inflows are Goa, Odissa, Assam, Arunachal Pradesh, Manipur, Meghalaya, Mizoram, Nagaland, Tripura, Bihar and Jharkhand. This study is committed to investigate the systems of locational inclination received by Multinational Enterprises (MNEs) and approach changes that can be accomplished keeping in mind the end goal to manage this issue. The capital cities of the states attracted majority of FDI inflows of the respective states. It is observed that despite tax and other fiscal concessions, FDI flow is concentrated only in few states, further only in few cities of these states.

What attracted FDI?

Maharashtra launched the New Industry, Trade and Commerce Policy 1995, with the objective of integrating different sectoral development schemes into a cohesive plan for overall development, and for promoting the private sector in development. Tamil Nadu has followed a liberal industrial policy to make the industrial climate attractive for domestic and foreign private investment. It has focused on strengthening its industrial and social infrastructure. Karnataka has taken a series of reforms, focusing mainly on progressive industrial policy, industrial infrastructure development, transport and communication network, water and power supply, effluent treatment, and development of human resources. Private sector has been encouraged to invest in high technology industries. The reforms in Gujarat have been primarily focused on privatization and restructuring of state-owned enterprises, promoting private sector participation and investment in physical and social infrastructure development, tariff and duty rationalization in the power sector, and fiscal policies including tax and expenditure.

Table2. State Wise Per Capita Gross State Domestic Product at Current prices (2005-06 to 2013-14)

State/UT	In crore - 2005-06	In crore - 2006-07	In crore - 2007-08	In crore - 2008-09	In crore - 2009-10	In crore - 2010-11	In crore - 2011-12	In crore - 2012-13	In crore- 2013-14
Andhra Pradesh (undivided)	255941	301035	364813	426765	476835	583762	662592	754409	854822
Arunachal Pradesh	3755	4108	4810	5687	7474	9018	10396	11817	13491
Assam	59385	64692	71076	81074	95975	112688	125820	141621	162652
Bihar	82490	100737	113680	142279	162923	203555	243269	296153	343054
Chhattisgarh	53381	66875	80255	96972	99364	119420	144382	163461	185060
Goa	14327	16523	19565	25414	29126	33605	43255	42407	NA
Gujarat	244736	283693	329285	367912	431262	521519	594563	670016	NA
Haryana	108885	128732	151596	182522	223600	260621	298786	339451	383911
Himachal Pradesh	27127	30274	33963	41483	48189	57452	64957	73710	82585
Jammu & Kashmir	29920	33230	37099	42315	48385	58073	68185	77558	87319
Jharkhand	60901	66935	83950	87794	100621	127281	135618	151655	172773
Karnataka	195904	227237	270629	310312	337559	410703	455212	519109	582754
Kerala	136842	153785	175141	202783	231999	263773	307906	349338	NA
Madhya Pradesh	124276	144577	161479	197276	227557	263396	311670	372171	450900
Maharashtra	486766	584498	684817	753969	855751	1049150	1175419	1323768	1476233
Manipur	5718	6137	6782	7397	8254	9137	11083	12484	NA
Meghalaya	7265	8625	9735	11617	12709	14583	17199	18296	21045
Mizoram	2971	3290	3816	4577	5260	6388	6890	8363	NA
Nagaland	6588	7257	8075	9436	10527	11759	13859	15676	17749
Odisha	85096	101839	129274	148491	162946	197530	214583	255459	288414
Punjab	108637	127123	152245	174039	197500	226204	256374	285165	317054
Rajasthan	142236	171043	194822	230949	265825	338348	403422	459215	513688
Sikkim	1993	2161	2506	3229	6133	7412	8907	10473	12377
Tamil Nadu	257833	310526	350819	401336	479733	584896	667202	744859	854238
Tripura	9826	10914	11797	13573	15403	17868	20982	23855	NA
Uttar Pradesh	293172	336317	383026	444685	523394	600286	685292	782285	890265
Uttarakhand	29968	36795	45856	56025	70730	83969	97858	107868	122433
West Bengal	230245	261682	299483	341942	398880	460959	528316	612701	700117
Andaman & Nicobar Islands	2044	2538	2990	3480	4120	4343	4994	5633	6150
Chandigarh	10185	12276	13669	15334	17577	20014	22826	25046	29076
Delhi	115374	135584	157947	189533	217619	252753	296957	348221	401576
Puducherry	7977	8335	9251	10050	12304	13092	14661	16769	21061
All-India GDP(2004-05 base)	3390503	3953276	4582086	5303567	6108903	7248860	8391691	9388876	10472807

Source: www.data.gov.in, www.planningcommission.nic.in

Table3. State Wise Per Capita GSDP Growth over previous year in Percentage

State/UT	*2006-07*	*2007-08*	*2008-09*	*2009-10*	*2010-11*	*2011-12*	*2012-13*	*2013-14*
Andhra Pradesh (undivided)	17.62	21.19	16.98	11.73	22.42	13.5	13.86	13.31
Arunachal Pradesh	9.4	17.09	18.23	31.42	20.66	15.28	13.67	14.17
Assam	8.94	9.87	14.07	18.38	17.41	11.65	12.56	14.85
Bihar	22.12	12.85	25.16	14.51	24.94	19.51	21.74	15.84
Chhattisgarh	25.28	20.01	20.83	2.47	20.18	20.9	13.21	13.21
Goa	15.33	18.41	29.9	14.61	15.38	28.72	-1.96	NA
Gujarat	15.92	16.07	11.73	17.22	20.93	14.01	12.69	NA
Haryana	18.23	17.76	20.4	22.51	16.56	14.64	13.61	13.1
Himachal Pradesh	11.6	12.19	22.14	16.17	19.22	13.06	13.48	12.04
Jammu & Kashmir	11.06	11.64	14.06	14.34	20.02	17.41	13.75	12.59
Jharkhand	9.91	25.42	4.58	14.61	26.5	6.55	11.83	13.93
Karnataka	15.99	19.1	14.66	8.78	21.67	10.84	14.04	12.26
Kerala	12.38	13.89	15.78	14.41	13.7	16.73	13.46	NA
Madhya Pradesh	16.34	11.69	22.17	15.35	15.75	18.33	19.41	21.15
Maharashtra	20.08	17.16	10.1	13.5	22.6	12.04	12.62	11.52
Manipur	7.33	10.51	9.07	11.59	10.7	21.3	12.64	NA
Meghalaya	18.72	12.87	19.33	9.4	14.75	17.94	6.38	15.03
Mizoram	10.74	15.99	19.94	14.92	21.44	7.86	21.38	NA
Nagaland	10.15	11.27	16.85	11.56	11.7	17.86	13.11	13.22
Odisha	19.68	26.94	14.87	9.73	21.22	8.63	19.05	12.9
Punjab	17.02	19.76	14.32	13.48	14.53	13.34	11.23	11.18
Rajasthan	20.25	13.9	18.54	15.1	27.28	19.23	13.83	11.86
Sikkim	8.43	15.96	28.85	89.93	20.85	20.17	17.58	18.18
Tamil Nadu	20.44	12.98	14.4	19.53	21.92	14.07	11.64	14.68
Tripurâ	11.07	8.09	15.05	13.48	16	17.43	13.69	NA
Uttar Pradesh	14.72	13.89	16.1	17.7	14.69	14.16	14.15	13.8
Uttarakhand	22.78	24.63	22.18	26.25	18.72	16.54	10.23	13.5
West Bengal	13.65	14.45	14.18	16.65	15.56	14.61	15.97	14.27
Andaman & Nicobar Islands	24.17	17.81	16.39	18.39	5.41	14.99	12.8	9.18
Chandigarh	20.53	11.35	12.18	14.63	13.86	14.05	9.73	16.09
Delhi	17.52	16.49	20	14.82	16.14	17.49	17.26	16.18
Puducherry	4.49	10.99	8.64	22.43	6.4	11.98	14.38	25.59
All-India GDP(2004-05 base)	16.6	15.91	15.75	15.18	18.66	15.77	11.88	11.54

Source: www.data.gov.in, www.planningcommission.nic.in

Economic Inequalities in Indian States-Gross State Domestic Product and FDI:

With the economic growth in terms of GDP, the inequalities also increased in Indian states. It can be observed from the Table 2 and 3 that some states have been able to grow at phenomenal growth rate, while others lagged behind the all India growth rate. The states with higher FDI inflow have higher gross state domestic product than the low FDI inflow states. There is a positive relationship between economic growth and FDI inflows. It further fosters growth in the developed states but widens the regional disparity.

Table 4. Sectors Attracting Highest FDI Equity Inflows:

Ranks	*Sector*	*2011-12 (April-March)*	*2012-13 (April-March)*	*2013-14 (April-July, 2013)*	*Cumulative Inflows (April ? 00-July? 13)*	*% age to total Inflows (In terms of US$)*
1.	SERVICES SECTOR **	24,656 (5,216)	26,306 (4,833)	5,770 (1,021)	178,046 (38,255)	19 %
2.	CONSTRUCTION DEVELOPMENT: TOWNSHIPS, HOUSING, BUILT-UP INFRASTRUCTURE	15,236 (3,141)	7,248 (1,332)	2,092 (359)	103,141 (22,439)	11 %
3.	TELECOMMUNICATIONS (radio paging, cellular mobile, basic telephone services)	9,012 (1,997)	1,654 (304)	66 (12)	58,798 (12,868)	6 %
4.	COMPUTER SOFTWARE & HARDWARE	3,804 (796)	2,656 (486)	1,244 (215)	54,019 (11,906)	6 %
5.	DRUGS & PHARMACEUTICALS	14,605 (3,232)	6,011 (1,123)	5,453 (1,002)	54,333 (11,320)	6 %
6.	CHEMICALS (OTHER THAN FERTILIZERS)	18,422 (4,041)	1,596 (292)	2,069 (354)	42,567 (9,235)	5 %
7.	AUTOMOBILE INDUSTRY	4,347 (923)	8,384 (1,537)	3,576 (637)	42,746 (8,932)	4 %
8.	POWER	7,678 (1,652)	2,923 (536)	1,199 (208)	37,336 (8,043)	4 %
9.	METALLURGICAL INDUSTRIES	8,348 (1,786)	7,878 (1,466)	1,090 (190)	35,904 (7,697)	4%
10	HOTEL & TOURISM	4,754 (993)	17,777 (3,259)	694 (123)	33,954 (6,755)	3 %

Note: (i) ** Services sector includes Financial, Banking, Insurance, Non-Financial / Business, Outsourcing, R&D, Courier, Tech. Testing and Analysis

Source: www.data.gov.in

Effect of Agglomeration on FDI Inflows:

The industries want to set up their organizations in the regions where physical foundation is sufficiently accessible and thus, the related businesses would float framing bunches in that area. These industry groups bring about geological territories or districts specializing in specific activities. This bunching of firms, which is otherwise called the "agglomeration" impact has risen as an essential determinant in the territorial dispersion of FDI streams inside a nation amid the most recent two decades. Comparable pattern was followed in India, industry groups were framed from the earliest starting point of industrialization. Places, for example, Bangalore have come up as a aftereffect of this grouping in the service and IT sector. The vicinity of agglomeration economies is reflected regarding earlier presence of foreign investors, former concentration of assembling plants and number of undertakings in a region.

India's trade openness increased inequality among states: After 1991 trade liberalization, coastal regions have been privileged relative to interior regions. The southern states have always had enormous seaports and a dynamic coastline which has always welcomed foreign traders and travelers. Besides, South India has many other inherent qualities. Guha (2007) established that the good practice of English, the good quality of sub national governments and of local education made this region even more attractive for Indian and foreign firms. Jayanth (2007) observed that Indian firms, from Tata and Reliance Industries to the Mahindras and the Mittals that positioned in the past in the northern parts of the country have been moving into New Delhi or into South India since 1991. Indian industrialized clusters have emerged since 1991 and are now concentrated in the three clustered regions: the region of capital New Delhi, in Mumbai in the state of Maharashtra and in Chennai, Bangalore in the states of Karnataka and Tamilnadu.

Challenges Ahead

Foreign and domestic investors can support from keenly contributing to inclusive growth in host economies. Inclusive growth can empower bigger segments of the local population to become consumers, in turn, growing the size of local markets. Hence, it makes good quality business sense to recommend training to people who might turn out to be prospective customers, creative workers or suppliers. Moreover, it would also make good logic for foreign companies to engross local suppliers to the extent that possible in their supply chain. FDI can also add to inclusive growth in the course of implementation of inclusive business models and the execution of responsible business practices or corporate social responsibility.

Conclusion

Inclusive Growth refers to growth that is assessed and shared impartially by all segments of society. India's inclusion into the global economy is certainly connected to growing regional disparities. Regional disparities embody a development confront. The diligence of large disparities may facade a threat to a country's territorial integrity and affects its political harmony. FDI is favored over all other capital flows in the world. FDI is preferred as it is a non debt financial capital. The constructive attributes of FDI are notionally perfect, but when it comes to ground realities these are moderately true. Nonetheless, many economies are persuaded over by the FDI's encouraging attributes. The governments contend with each other by announcing various concessions and incentives to draw FDI. However, even though the profoundly laden concessions and incentives by host economies, FDI does not move evenly into all the regions. There is a soaring degree of absorption of FDI inflows in few regions, which leads to high regional disparity in FDI inflows amongst the states. If states develop the governance, bring lucidity, eliminate corruption, make available basic infrastructure and build their state more energetic and pulsating, the FDI inflow will enhance the growth of the respective states. Both the public and private sectors have a role to play in making FDI inclusive.

References

- Aggarwal, A. (2005). The Influence of Labour Markets on FDI: Some Empirical Explorations in Export Oriented and Domestic Market Seeking FDI across Indian States. Global Conference on Business and Economics, Oxford University, London. (2005).
- Aggarwal (2007). FDI in India and its Growth Linkages, Annual Report submitted by NCAER to DIPP, Ministry of Commerce and Industry, GOI, 2009.
- Algeria, R. (2006). Countries, Regions and Multinational Firms: Location Determinants in the European Union. London School of Economics, mimeo.
- Blonigen, B.A., Davis, R.B., Waddell, G.R. and Naughton, H.T. (2007). FDI in Space: Spatial Autoregressive Relationships in Foreign Direct Investments. *European Economic Review*, 51(5), 1303-1325.
- Buckley, P. J., and Casson, M. C. (1976). The future of the multinational enterprise. London: Macmillan.
- Buckley, P. J., and Casson, M. C. (1981). The optimal timing of a foreign direct investment. *The Economic Journal,* 91(361), 75–87.
- Business.mapsofindia.com. 2014. Challenges facing larger FDI. Retrieved from http://business.mapsofindia.com/india-retail-industry/fdi/challenges-facing-larger.html.
- Chakrabarti, A. (2001). The Determinants of Foreign Direct Investment: Sensitivity Analyses. Kyklos, 54(1), 89-113.

- DiMaggio, P.J., and Powell, R. (1983). The iron cage revisited. Institutional isomorphism and collective rationality in organizational fields. *American Sociological Review*, 48, 147-60.
- Dunning, J.H. (1998). Location and the Multinational Enterprise: A Neglected Factor? *Journal of International Business Studies,* 29(1).
- Dunning, J.H. (2001). The Eclectic Paradigm as an envelope for economic and business theories of MNE activity. *International Business Review*, 9(2), 163-190.
- Fact Sheet on FDI, Dec (2013) Report- Department of Industrial Policy and Promotion, Ministry of Commerce and Industry, Government of India.
- Fisher, P. S., and Alan H. Peters. (1998). Industrial Incentives: Competition among American States and Cities. Kalamazoo, MI: W.E. Upjohn Institute for Employment Research.
- FDI Intelligence Report (2013) retrieved from http://www.fdiintelligence.com/Custom/Special-Reports/fDi-Report-2013
- Feenstra, R.C. and Hanson, G.H. Hanson (1997). Foreign Direct Investment and Relative Wages. *Journal of International Economics*, 42(3-4), 371-393.
- Global Investment Trends Monitor. (2014). UNCTAD. Retrieved from http://unctad.org/en/PublicationsLibrary/webdiaeia2014d1_en.pdf.
- Goldar, B. and Aggarwal, S.C. (2005). Trade Liberalization and Price-Cost Margin in Indian Industries. *The Developing Economies*, 43(3), 346-373
- Guha, R. (2007). The Better Half, Outlook India Magazine.
- He, C.F. (2002). Regional Decentralization and Location of Foreign Direct Investment in China. *Post-Communist Economies,* 18(1).
- Hill, C. and Jain, A (2009). International Business: Competing in the Global Marketplace. 6th edition, McGraw-Hill.
- Hill, C. Global Business Today, Chapter 12, 6th edition, (411-435). New Trade Theory.
- Jayanth, V. (2007). Why the South attracts, The Hindu.
- Kochhar, K., U.Kumar, R.Rajan, A. Subramanian, and I. Tokatlidis (2006). India's pattern of Development: What happened, what follows? *Journal of Monetary Economics*, 53(5), 981-1019.
- Krugman, Paul. (1991). Increasing Returns and Economic Geography. *Journal of Political Economy,* 99(3).
- Krugman, P. (2008). The conscience of a Liberal. Retrieved from http://krugman.blogs.nytimes.com/2008/10/15/about-the-work/?_r=2.
- Lall, S.V. and Mengistae, T. (2005). Business Environment, Clustering and Industry Location: Evidence from Indian Cities. World Bank Policy Research, Working Paper No.3675.
- Majumder, R. (2008). Infrastructure and Development in India: Interlinkages and Policy Issues. Jaipur (Rawat Publications).
- Mukherjee, A. (2011). Regional Inequality in FDI Inflows to India: the problems and the prospects. Reserve bank of India Occasional Papers, 32(2).

- Nunnenkamp, P. and Stracke, R. (2007). Foreign Direct Investment in Post-Reform India; Likely to work wonder for Regional Development? Kiel Working Paper No.1375.
- Purfield (2006). Mind the Gap – Is Economic Growth in India leaving some states behind? IMF Working Paper, WP/06/13, International Monetary Fund, Washington, D.C.
- Planning Commission State Plans retrieved from http://planning commission.nic.in/plans/stateplan/sdr_maha/ch-6-14-02-05.pdf
- Ramachandran, V. and Geobel, J. (2002). Foreign Direct Investment in Tamilnadu: Review and Comparison across Host Sights. Centre for International Development, Harvard University.
- Sach, D.Jeffrey, Bajpai, N. and Ramiah, A. (2002). Understanding Regional Economic Growth in India. Centre for International Development, Working Paper No. 88, Harvard University.
- Sebastian, M. (2007). A Study of the Regional Determinants of Foreign Direct Investments in India and the case of Gujarat. Indian Institute of Management (Ahmedabad). Working Paper No. 2004/03/07.
- Siddharthan, N.S. (2006). Regional Difference in FDI Flows: China – India Comparison. Institute of Economic Growth.
- Singh, J. (2010). Economic Reforms and Foreign Direct Investment in India: Policy, Trends and Patterns. Retrieved from http://papers.ssrn.com/sol3/papers.cfm?abstract_id=1765804.
- Singh, J. (2010). Economic reforms and foreign direct investment in India: policy, trends and patterns. *The IUP Journal of Financial Economics,* 8(4), 59-69.
- Singh, S. (2009). Foreign Direct Investment (FDI) and Growth of States of India. Retrieved from http://papers.ssrn.com/sol3/papers.cfm?abstract_id =1324058.
- Tabarrok, A. (2008). What is New Trade Theory? retrieved from http://marginalrevolution.com/marginalrevolution/2008/10/what-is-new-tra.html.
- UNCTAD (2013) World Investment Report 2013 retrieved from http://unctad.org/en/publicationslibrary/wir2013_en.pdf.
- Vernon, R. (1966). International investment and international trade in the product cycle. *Quarterly Journal of Economics,* 190-207.
- World Bank (2004). India: Investment Climate Assessment 2004: Improving Manufacturing Competitiveness. Washington, D.C. (The World Bank).
- Yilmazkuday, H. (2010). Agglomeration and Trade: State-Level Evidence from U.S. Industries. *Journal of Regional Science.*
- Economic Survey, Government of India. Various Years.
- FDI Factsheets and other publications of Department of Industrial Policy and Promotion (DIPP), Government of India. Various Years.
- Secretariat of Industrial Assistance, SIA: News letters, Ministry of Industry, Government of India, New Delhi. Various Years.

25

Innovative Practices in the Convergent World of Indian e-tailing

Asif Ali Syed & Asma Khan

Abstract

India is fast catching up with the global phenomena, that world is fast shrinking into a Global Village because of Internet and other communication mediums. Internet has brought nearly the entire world just a click away from us. The retail industry canvass and the rules of the game in retailing are fast changing because of the advances of Information technology. Besides a tremendous increase in online shopping over the past few years, e-tailing in India is still a partly success and a failure story. Internet holds many virtues that can be turned favorable for the domestic retail industry including a higher customer penetration, increased distinguishability, and expedient operations.Not only big cities are driving the online scene in India but also the demand supply gap in tier 2-3 cities is adding up to e-tailing because of non-availability of products and services of branded goods.The current web-based models for e-tailing are in part of an embryonic phase preceding an era of rapid transformation, challenge, and opportunity in Indian retail market. The growth of Internet has enabled the new retail format of the virtual retailer to emerge and forced the existing retailers to consider e-tailing model of retailing as well. This paper attempts to provide a clear picture about the e-tailing environment in India as well as the global market. It explores various issues, opportunities and attempts to draw an effective e- tailing strategy in India based on extensive literature reviewed and factors assimilated on e tailing models from Indian and global studies. Technology adoption models like Theory of Planned Behaviour, Theory of Planned Behaviour (TPB), Technology Adoption Model (TAM), Diffusion and Innovations theory (DIT) and Unified Theory of Acceptance and Use of Technology (UTAUT) have been studied and applied in the Indian and global context to analyze the changing typology of e-consumers. This study focuses on a conceptual analysis about innovative practices in e marketing and e-tailing. The contributions of the findings would attempt to assist policy makers, e-marketers and provide an insight for further research exploring the gaps in this important social and commercial economic discipline which impacts each and everyone of us.

Keywords: *e-consumerism, customerization, e-pace, e tailing, and e marketing*

Introduction

World has experienced a complete change in the virtual world from the age of ARPANET to the current age of technically advanced, customized and much more user friendly online environment. According to ASSOCHAM projections, e-commerce in India will reach a value of US$56 million in just 10 years' time. In the late 1990's and early 2000's, several e-tailing sites like rediff.com, indiaplaza.com and bazee.com were launched in India. However, the real game changing entry in this domain was that of Flipkart in 2007 post that a multitude of new players have entered the space. According to A.T. Kearney Global Retail E-Commerce Index for Market Opportunity in Global Retail E- Commerce, India fails to rank under top 30 developed and developing countries. E-tailing is still a very small part (0.1 per cent) of overall retail in India but

it is projected to grow at a rapid pace to reach 7-8 per cent of the total Indian retail market by 2020.It is estimated that the $2.3 billion e-tailing market in 2014 will reach 3 per cent of Indian retail or $32 billion by 2020 (Technopak, 2014). Internet access is anticipated to grow and reach 800 million users by 2020.All the big markets like China and the US, developed as Desktop markets, but India is being developed as a mobile market (Google's report, 2014). The country's growing Internet-habituated consumer base, which will comprise 180 million broadband users by 2020, a burgeoning class of mobile Internet users and a large dynamic consuming class will drive this growth.According to Motiwal Securities report, E-commerce in India is a $11 billion market, and is estimated to reach $20 billion by 2015, growing at a CAGR of 37 per cent over 2013-15.According to Google's annual online shopping growth trends report dated Nov., 2014 done in collaboration with Forrester Research, India willhave 100 million online shoppers including 40 million women, by 2016. India's online retail industry will grow at a healthy 50-55 per cent CAGR to Rs 504 billion by 2015-16 (CRISIL report, 2014). India is witnessing the same e-pacethat USA witnessed a decade back where the giant retailers were forced to incorporatee-marketing methods for customer relationship management. Thus this transformation in India also will start in the near future where the retailers mark business growth through online rather than traditional outlet.

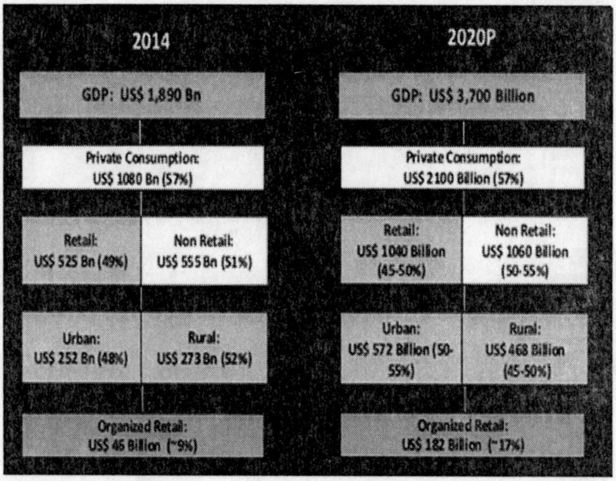

Figure 1.1: 2014 v/s 2020 E-tail projections

(***Source:*** Technopak Analysis Report, 2014)

Internet Users as % of Population

Year	US	UK	China	India
2005	68%	70%	9%	2%
2008	74%	78%	23%	4%
2011	70%	85%	38%	10%
2014	87%	90%	46%	19%

Figure 1.2: Worldwide Comparison of Internet users' population

(Source: Technopak Analysis Report, 2014)

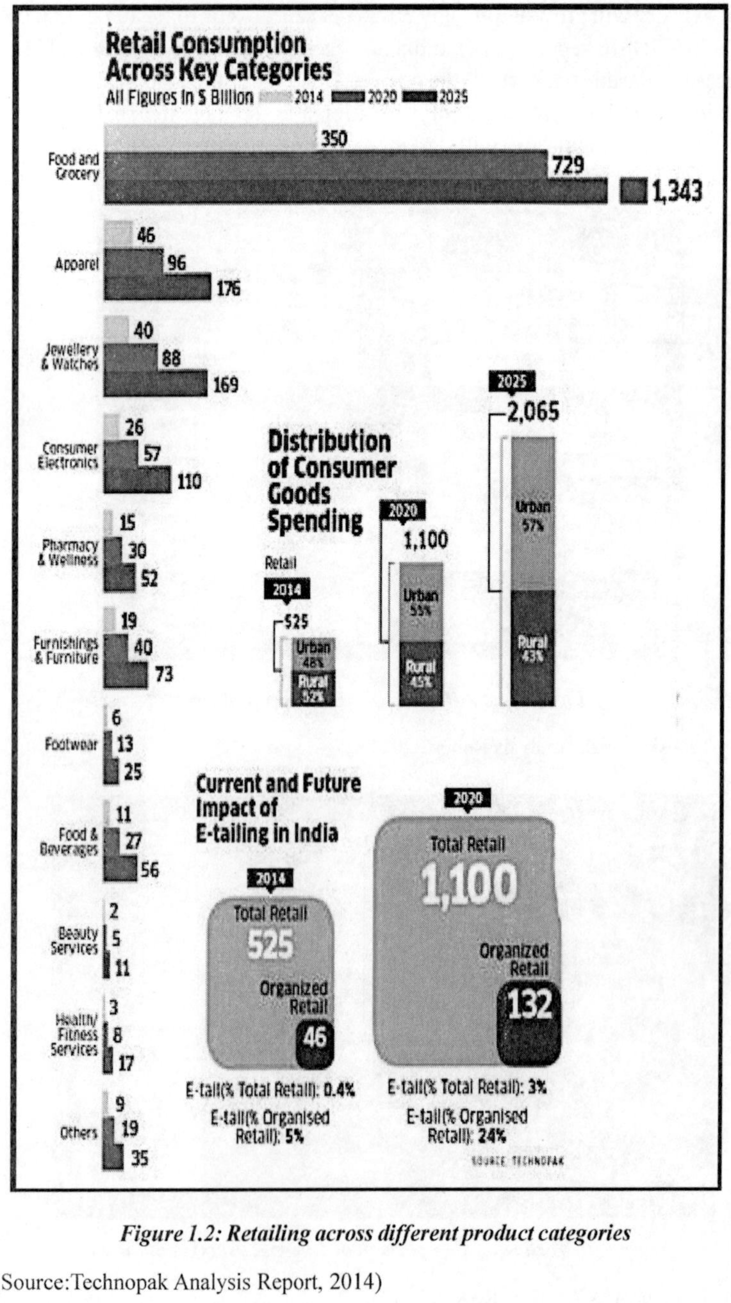

Figure 1.2: Retailing across different product categories

(Source:Technopak Analysis Report, 2014)

Need and Scope of the Study

Wang (2002) has defined e-tailing as the selling of goods and services to the consumer market via the internet. Singla et al. explained e-shopping where consumers perform an exchange through a computer based interface while buyer's computer interact with digital retailer to buy any thing over internet. According to Na Li and Ping Zhang (2002), online purchasing behavior is the process of purchasing products or services via the Internet. India is a country of diverse traditions and culture. Indian consumers show various kinds of buying behaviour patterns that are yet to be studied carefully in case of online shopping. Online retailing is still at a very nascent stage in India and still is an unorganized sector with the third party business model and without proper big brand based e-retail market. This paper therefore delves into the details of e-tailing scenario worldwide and attempts to provide a conceptual understanding of the factors that influencethe buying behaviour of Indian online consumers by using Technology adoption models like TRA, TPB, TAM and DIT.The study analysesthe current innovative practices in e-marketing and e-tailing. The contributions of the findings would attempt to assist policy makers and e-retailers in formulating strategies to target potential online consumers.

Emerging Global Scenario

Against a background of moderate economic growth, an achievement-oriented society is established worldwide. In many of the developed economies, such as Australia, France or the United Kingdom, social contrasts have increased. Hyper-connectivity of the future will take on the added dimension of the industrial Internet – where objects are connected to and communicate with other objects. It will amplify the impact of consumer Internet on e-commerce. With the help of WTO and LPG, trade barriers across the borders have been delimited thereby creating dynamism and innovative flair of IT as the main driving forces behind the global economy. Consumers are living in a highly developed digital culture (Christof E. Ehrhart, Deutsche Post DHL, 2014). A middle class with a comparatively strong purchasing power has developed worldwide for the first time. This has been accompanied by a shift in values, with the focus on leisure time rather than on work. Self-fulfillment and individual lifestyles have become significant than success in one's job. International lifestyle communities mainly set the latest trends and thereby impact the consumer shopping habits. Small, innovative online retailing platforms serve the different communities, while large online retailers and platforms take care of the mainstream market. Stationary retailing is principally focused on "experience" shopping.

The global economy is growing moderately with only slight fluctuations in the economic cycle. The engine of growth is centered on Asia mainly by the national economies of India, Indonesia and China. Indian and Indonesian economy is booming while the Chinese economy continues to grow steadily. The European Union has regained economic stability following radical structural reforms in the southern Eurozone countries.Youthof Asiawill be setting the global trendsespecially where the use of technology(in stores is concerned, for example Google Glasses or chips integrated into products(JurgenGerdes, 2014). On the other hand, traditional forms of shopping, such as night markets, will begin to disappear in the medium term with(the exception of travel destinations, where they will continue to attract tourists (Christof E. Ehrhart, Deutsche Post DHL, 2014).

Globally, the merger of stationary retailing and e-commerce has made major advances. So-called Everywhere Commerce is now widespread. E-consumers can obtain a clear impression of any product by the use of smartphones, tablets, laptops and pervasive interfaces in public places. Shopping is possible anytime and anywhere by the help of innovative e-tailing practices.Evaluation of purchase and search patterns by various e-marketing researchers has helped the e-tailers to understand the consumer mind-set. This also provides information about highly personalized consumer profiles that companies may use to apply customerization. Thus, e-tailers may deliver good quality products, service and individualpromotional messages. International e-tailing is still in the hands of just a few global players, while at regional and domestic levels small players have set up joint venturesfor providing supplementary services, for instance the assembly or installation of goods.

Since China, India and other emerging countries are posting higher levels of growth than Germany, US, Australia and other countries with a longer history of industrialization, the gap in income levels is gradually closing.An aspirational middle class with good income is emerging in many Asian countries. Because of the huge difference in incomes of the high and low class, the wealthy and the less well-off lead increasingly separate lives. The social extremes is clearly seen in the growing ghettoization of major cities of the world including developed countries like United States, France, U.K., etc. Although tariff barriers to world trade have continued to decline, environmental, climate-related directives and international patent disputes are still having a negative impact on e-commerce. Various industrial environmental drivers like demographic, economic, socio-cultural, political, legal and environmental forces need to be analyzed conspicuously for making e-tailing a success story in developing nations.

Important Models

Various studies on e-tailing have used different technology adoption models like Theory of Reasoned Action (TRA), Theory of Planned Behaviour (TPB), Technology Adoption Model (TAM), Diffusion and Innovations theory (DIT) and Unified Theory of Acceptance and Use of Technology (UTAUT) to analyze the factors that influence online retailing and e-consumers. E-marketing tactics often require a detailed study on typology of online consumers for creating an effective e-tailing strategy. Media Matrix and McKinsey(Hamilton, 2000) examined online shopper typology and classified them into six categories:

- Simplifiers-Net users who are impatient but lucrative.
- Surfers -Consummate browsers who spend 32 per cent time online.
- Connectors-New internet users who may also prefer brick-mortar brands.
- Bargain shoppers-Consumers who wish to bargains and enjoy finding good deals.
- Routine followers–Information addicts.
- Sportsters- E-consumers who visit sports and entertainment sites.

Kau, Tang and Ghose (2003) studied the Asian online consumers and categorized them into six e-consumer classes:

- On-off shoppers-Online shoppers who collect information from internet but shop offline.
- Comparison shoppers-These consumers compare product features, brand, prices, offers etc. before making the real purchase.
- Traditional shoppers-Consumers that buy only from retail stores and don't surf internet for information.
- Dual shoppers- Consumers who prefer to compare brands and product features and seek information online,however they are not particularly deal prone.
- e-Laggards-They have less interest in pursuing information from the Internet.
- Information surfers:Consumers wholove and click on banner ads frequently and also use internet for information along with having an online purchase experience.

Evaluating the customer's attitude towards online shopping and the factors influencing it can assist the e-marketers and managers to plan appropriate strategies and gain profit (Halimi, et al, (2011). Theory of Reasoned Action

(Ajzen and Fishbein, 1975) suggests that behaviour is determined by behavioural intention, which in turn is a function of the individual's attitude toward the act and the subjective norms.

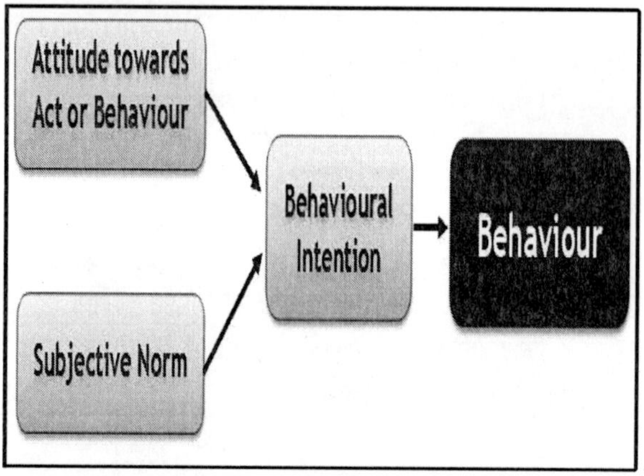

Figure 3.1: Theory of Reasoned Action

Source: Fishbein and Ajzen, (1975). Belief, attitude, intention, and behavior: An introduction to theory and research, MA: Wesley.

Theory of Planned Behaviour (Ajzen, 1985) proposes that behaviour is determined by behavioural intention, which in turn is a function of the individual's attitude toward the act, the subjective norms and perceived behavioural control.

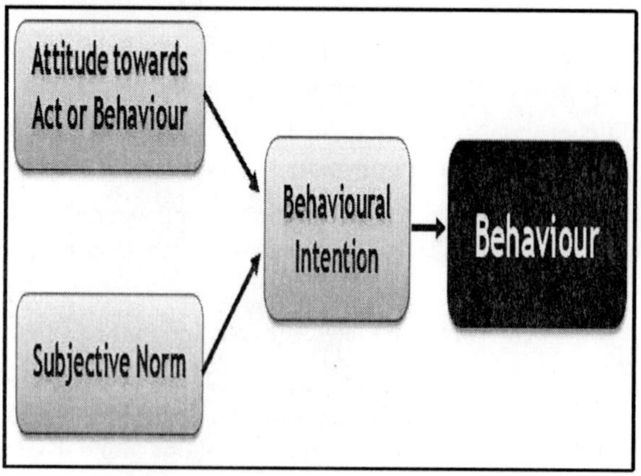

Figure 3.2: Theory of Planned BehaviourSource: Ajzen (1985). From intentions to action: A theory of planned behavior. In J. Kuhl and J. Beckman (Eds.) Action-control: From cognition to behavior, Heidelberg: Springer, 11-39

TAM (Davis,1989) comprises of the perceived usefulness and the perceived ease of use, which determine about positive or negative behavior for a new technology.

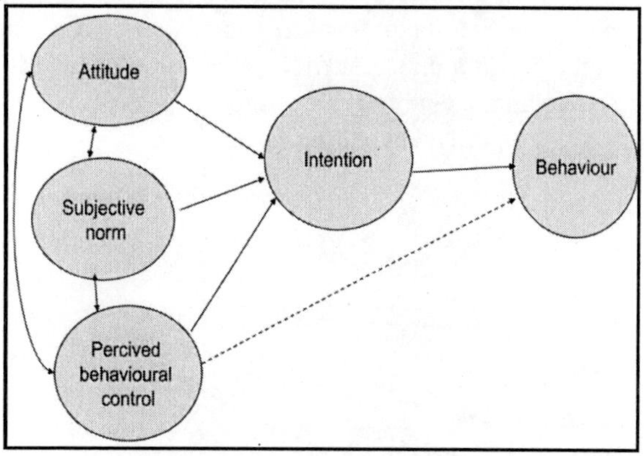

Figure 3.3: Technology Adoption Model (Davis, 1989)

Source: Davis, F.D., Bagozzi, R.P., and Warshaw, P.R. (1989). User acceptance of computer technology: a comparison of two theoretical models, Management Science, 35(8), 982-1003.

Diffusion of Innovations theory (Rogers, 1995) suggests that the adoption of a new idea is a process whereby some people adopt innovations easily than others and those who adopt an innovation early have different characteristics than the ones who adopt an innovation later. The adopters were divided into 5 types: Innovators, Early adopters, Early majority, Late majority and Laggards.

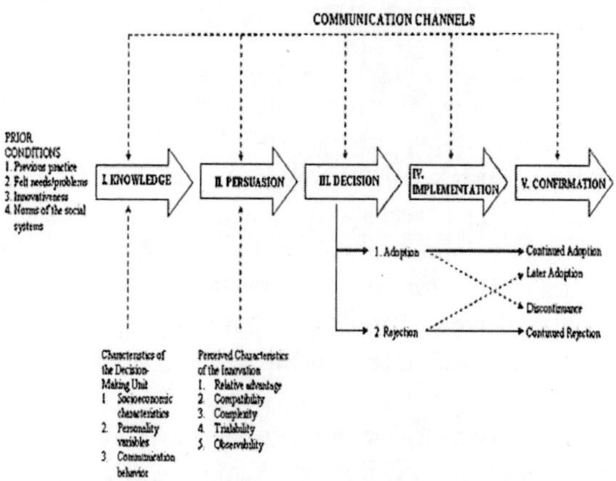

Figure 3.4: Diffusion of Innovations Model (Rogers, 1995)

Source: Rogers, E.M. (1995), Diffusion of Innovations. New York: The Free Press. (Original publication 1962)

Unified Theory of Acceptance and Use of Technology (UTAUT) (Venkatesh, Morris, Davis and Davis, 2003) holds that four key constructs: performance expectancy, effort expectancy, social influence facilitating conditions; being the first three direct determinants of usage intention and behavior, and the fourth a direct determinant of use behavior. Gender, age, experience, and voluntariness of use are posited to moderate the impact of the four key constructs on usage intention and behavior.

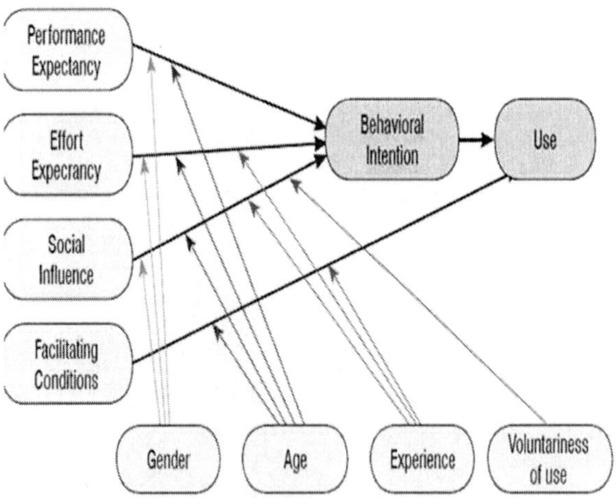

Figure 3.5: Unified Theory of Acceptance and Use of Technology

Source: Venkatesh, V., Morris, M.G., Davis, F.D., and Davis, G.B. "User Acceptance of Information Technology: Toward a Unified View," MIS Quarterly, 27, 2003, 425-478.

The critical success factor for e-tailers is to know their customers well.The ability to gather as much data as possible about consumers, and to analyze and interpret it accurately, allows e-marketers to always be one step ahead with the help (of predictive purchasing technologies.

To enhance consumer satisfaction and purchase intentions, online stores should start improving the reliability dimensions, such as capability of delivering products as promised, providing up-to date and accurate information, and strengthening the security of online transactions. (Lee and Lin, 2004). Online retail players have a scope to focus on new product delivery models and payment mechanisms, since customers are facing problems with the options available Ernst and Young (2012). Moreover, e-tailers should continue to offer customer with wide range of products rather than selling one or two items. Consumers expect varieties and alternatives including promotions, vouchers and discounts which may intrigue them to purchase online (Vegiayan, et al, 2013). Karve, Sunil (2014) hinted that India's big retail companies should start with virtual 3D online shopping.

E-Tailing in India

Business is now changed from commerce to E-commerce and retailing to internet retailing.According to Hoffman et al (2005), marketing communication model is driven by hypermedia computer aided environment promotese-marketing on a large scale. Email marketing, blogs, Pay per Click, affiliate marketing, banner advertisements are different forms of Internet marketing.India is witnessing a massive digital revolution. Broadband subscription rates of 3G and 4G services increased penetration of mobile internetwhich has led to an ever-increasing number of "netizens" and consequently broadened the country's internet horizons. Internet has become an integral part of this growing population segment in order to connect with friends through various social networking sites, accessing emails, buying air, rail, movie tickets or ordering food. The changing lifestyles of the country's urban population have also to an increase in online shopping. India is on the verge of an Internet boom with a projected user base of 330 million to 370 million by 2015, which will be the second largest in the world, and the largest in terms of incremental growth (McKinsey and Company report).

India has witnessed an accelerated consumption of digital products over the last few years, which has led to growth of e-commerce. Today's shopper is tech-savvy with almost black belt certification in researching product and pricing. Concept of research via social sites and given their continued influence and time spent by consumers in these communities, it appears to be a divide between community and commerce as just significant number of customers take advantage of social sites for research. Large e-tailers have adopted an aggressive M&A strategy just like Flipkart and Myntra.com in which they acquire specialty e-tailers for an increment in product and service offerings in their existing portfolio and achieve economies of scale. Due to the success stories of big e-tailers like Flipkart, this sector has attracted large FDI's and has also interested various other investors. 2014 has witnessed flurry of deals in this sector and $1.6 billion (9700 crores) has been pumped in across 24 deals as compared to that of about $553 million (3300 crores) investment across 36 deals in the year 2013 (Venture Intelligence report).

Large fundraises by industry leaders like Flipkart, Snapdeal and the entry of investors like Singapore's sovereign wealth fund GIC have boosted investors confidence. Their growth stories are heating up and have occupied space in every day newspapers.Indian online population has overcome different mental barriers as socio-cultural conservativeness, feel and touch buying behavior, insecurities regarding payments on internet etc. and is accepting e-retailing model in a very fast way. online users'impulse buying behavior has increased the revenue earned from Indian e-tail market which led to a positive effect on country's economy, govt. revenues, urban and rural development, industrial growth and employment opportunities (Ghosh,2014).

With the median age of 26 years, India has a fast growing young population. According to a report by NCAER on the 'Indian Youth', the population between 13-35 years was 459 million in 2009 and is projected to reach 574 million by 2020. This young population uses technology the most and is one of biggest consuming age group (Manyika and Cabral et al, 2013). Social media has given a boost tothis trend.Despite country's diverse population, disposable income has increased in India and is expected to increase at the rate of 8.5 per cent per annum till 2015. The number of workingwomenand the size of working middle class are also increasing. Indian Consumers have larger disposable incomes, greater purchasing power and less time to spend on daily shopping. This will lead people to buy daily goods online rather than waste time and fuel to shop from a supermarket.

Brick and mortar retailers are identifying the opportunities offered by e-commerce in India and have started toopen online stores. Big Bazaar through Futurebazaar.com, Shoppers Stop through Shopperstop.com, Wills Lifestyle through Shopwillslifestyle.com and TATA's Croma through Cromaretail.com have been trying to take advantage of the online shopping wave. A Bain report states that going online has become a must for physical retailers also, especially to win new and retail critical customers. Such an integrated omni-channel strategy is also expected to enhance the offline experience.

Urban areas account for a majority of e-commerce where internet penetration is much higher as compared to the rural areas in India.

However, this should in no way signify the inability of the villages to contribute in the digital commerce market of India. SREI SAHAJ e-Village Limited, a subsidiary of SREI Infrastructure Finance Limited, has launched one of the largest IT projects in rural India with an investment of about \$160 million. This IT infrastructure project aims to establish about 250,000 Common Service Centres (CSCs) (website) in the numerous villages of West Bengal, Bihar, Orissa, Assam, Uttar Pradesh and Tamil Nadu and over 27,000 have already been established (website). These CSCs will serve as a bridge between the rural India and the world thereby enabling services like e-governance, e-learning and even e- commerce and will service a rural population of over 210 million people (Mohanti, 2008). Such initiatives in the country may build a tremendous platform for the growth of e-tailingin future. Online retailing in India is still in its infancy stage and the policy makers need to organize and channelize it properly and overcome the barriers in order to make it a success story.

Internet retailing has emerged as an attractive alternative to traditional brick and mortar stores offering a number of advantages such as high speed of transaction, more number of selections and prices, convenience, time and space neutrality, fun and enjoyment (Ruchi, Ashish and Gupta, 2009). Osterwalder and Pigneur (2002) believe that it is vital for companies to understand, communicate and share, change, measure, simulate and learn more about the different aspects of e-business in their firm.

The firms can therefore redefine customer relationship by incorporating information strategy. Trust and Loyalty constitutes a very important factor in enhancing customer relationship especially in virtual world. Sawney (2008) has identified various performance indicators critical to success of online retailing. Some of them include ease of navigation, quick loading times, accurate product/service delivery system, clear transaction policies, online interactivity between buyer and seller, transaction safety, and transaction privacy.

Madlberger (2006) identified various exogenous and endogenous factors responsible for buying behaviour of online shopping in a multi-channel environment. The exogenous (independent of the retailer) factors primarily include perceived convenience, perceived security and consumer's attitude towards catalogue shopping. On the other hand, attitude towards e-shopping is the only endogenous factor influencing online shopping behaviour.

Gender and other socio- demographic factors can moderate the relation between exogenous and endogenous variables. In the Indian context, Prasad and Aryasri (2009) have explored the determinants of shopping behaviour such as convenience, customer service, trust, web store environment and web shopping enjoyment and examined the impact of these parameters on online buying behaviour. Kiran et al. (2008) identified the factors affecting online buying behaviour in India, along with the effect of online advertisements. Product information and reliability were found as the key contributing factors to e-tailing adoption.

Various studies have found different types of factors that contribute to online shopping but none of them have done a combined analysis of different attributes of online buying behaviour of consumers. This study aims to bridge this gap and attempts to present a detailed study on factors influencing online purchase intentions of consumers. In this study, the parameters that lead to online purchase intention are divided into three broad categories based upon TPA,TRA, TAM DIT and UTUAT as shown in figure 4.2.

Customer-centric factors, website-related factors and perceived risk factors were found to cast a joint influence on internet shopping behaviour of e-consumers. E-marketers need to analyze the individual impact of these factors during online purchases in order to create innovative e-marketing strategies.

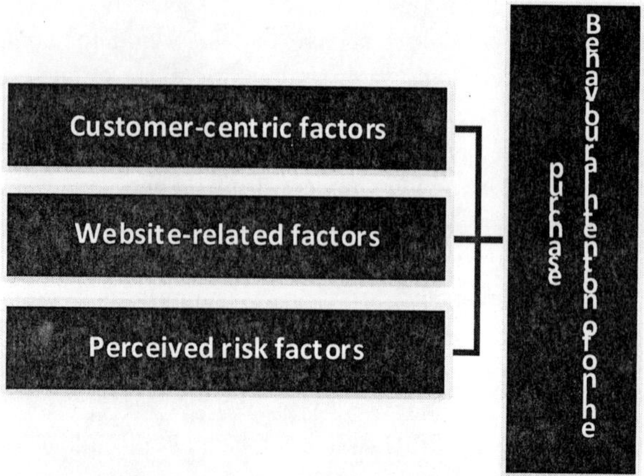

Figure 4.1: Impact of online buying behaviour factors on behavioural intention of online purchase

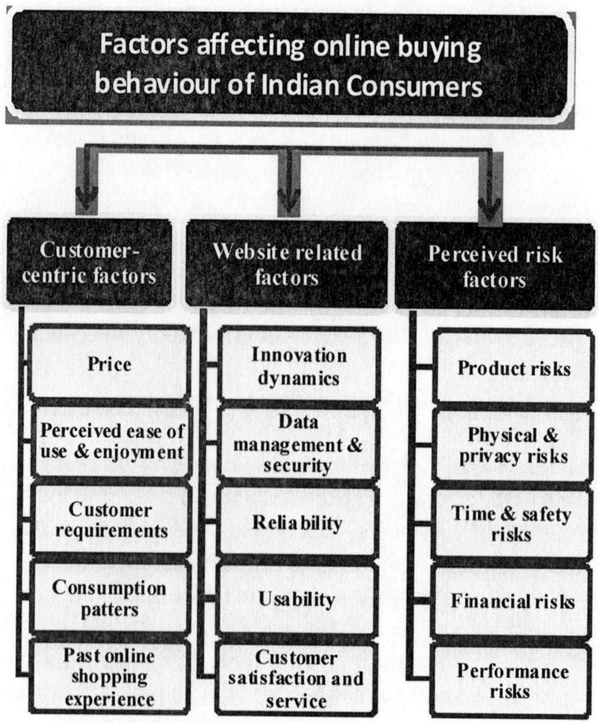

Figure 4.2: Factors affecting online buying behaviour of Indian consumers

Emerging E-Tailing Strategies in the Indian Context

Organized retailing has many hurdles to overcome, such as rise real estate prices, lack of viable store locations, overhead costs, pilferage, lack of trained manpower and many more. Internet retailing, on the other hand, is accessible even through a smartphone, saves time, energy and fuel for the e-consumers and demands no expensive real estate investment for expansion. Recent changes in lifestyles, consumer requirements and consumption patterns along with a rise in internet and credit cards penetration pave way for the growth of e-tailing in India. It becomes imperative for internet retailers to understand the online buying behaviour of consumers and assuage the customer anxiety with respect to online purchasing. By taking proper measures, customer concerns regarding transaction security, financial thefts, identity thefts, privacy and product authenticity could be alleviated easily. For instance, offering secured online payments; escrow service, better return policies and exciting discounts could help reducing apprehensions revolving around shopping online. (Nayyar and Gupta, 2009).

Several indicators like product quality, shopping experience, service quality, website features,risks involved in online shopping, price usability activity. Perceived usefulness and perceived ease of use of technology that depends on experience, control, computer playfulness, computer anxiety etc. have played a vital role determining online buying behaviour. These factors in conjunction with the consumer traits mould the consumer attitude towards purchase. The transition from positive attitude of online shopping towards actual intention to e-purchase depends upon certain factors like trust, product features and previous online shopping experiences. Perceived risks associated with online shopping have a critical effect on e-consumer's decision making. Consumer risk perceptions involve the privacy and security of personal information, data management and security, online transaction systems' security and the uncertainty of product quality. In the virtual environment, a consumer cannot physically check the product quality before making an actual purchase, or inspect the safety and security of sending sensitive personal and financial information like credit card details to a third party on the internet whose conduct and motives may be hard to predict. Website design characteristics serve the purpose of providing adequate and easy to comprehend information, ease of completing transaction, reliability and personalization features. Consumers prefer to shop online with the brands they trust. Brand equity is found to be affected by the following web purchase related factors in many studies: privacy, security, brand name, word-of-mouth, online experience and information quality. By carefully exploring these variables in formulating e-marketing strategies, e-marketers can foster brand loyalty and eventually gain competitive advantage. For making adequate strategic, technological, and marketing decisions to increase customer satisfaction, as well as improving web site design of virtual stores, a deeper understanding of consumers' motivations and limitationsto shop online is of major importance to e-tailers.

Online vendors should design such website portals that may offer more interactive options and provide a sense of emotional attachment andenjoyment along with the detailed information about their offerings to gain recognition among Indian online users. Transparent business termsand conditions with special emphasis on privacy and data security by adopting radical technologies will definitely gain consumers trust. Durability and efficiency of the online products should be crosschecked by the e-tailers before making deliveries. Special promotional offers, sales and discounts may attract price sensitive Indians more towards online shopping. Effective and quick after sales service will decrease the post-purchase dissonance of Indian consumer and might even encourage them for repetitive purchases. Indian E-commerce portals should use simple designsby avoiding technical complexities and provide user-friendly portals with pertinent and crisp product or service descriptions, thus decreasing general conventional mental blockages of Indian online users with respect to internet usages (Ghosh, 2014).

In future, Indian E-retail portals should include local language contents to attract Indian consumers specially the rural ones. All E-commerce portals should adopt cash on delivery option as price sensitive Indians will definitely prefer than other online payment options. The Indian government should provide online shopping model with better infrastructures.Cyber laws should be enforces appropriately and defined more clearly in order to discourage the cyber crimes, which in turn will solve trust issues of online Indian consumers. E-marketers should avoid too many small suppliers; instead they should opt for fewer big retailers and evade third party business models. Indian government should provide better physical infrastructures and transport facilities across the country to curtailthe logistic problems and delivery issues of Indian online retailers. E-tailers should focus on quality reliabilities and deliver innovative products.E-marketers can meet high customer expectancies by offering continuously updated information on the company, its products/ services, answers to frequently asked questions (FAQs), special offers, etc. Furthermore, the e-tailer may inform its online customers about inventory status, delivery options, timeframe, and payment conditions.

E-tailers should use multiple information sources toincrease their credibility. Providing both traditional and online communication channels is a necessity.All online portals should have a dedicated 24/7 customer care centers to solve the problems of consumers instantly.

Policymakers should frame proper legal rules for e-tailing industryand encourage a healthy competitive environment.E-tailers should try to curb down competition by limiting the number of alternatives available for consumers bydecreasing the delivery and overhead costs. By providing same-day delivery and specific day or time delivery options to customers and concentrating on returns management and Cash-on-delivery (COD) servicesmay attract and hold the interest and trust of e-consumers. Sensitive return of goods and refund of money policies bye-tailers will definitely generate trust among Indian consumers. E-tailers can also work on CRM by training delivery personnel to take customer feedback. Proper advertising of online portals should be managed by e-retailers for attracting potential new customers and retaining existing buyers.Many e-retailing experts (e.g. Jeff Bezos, founder of Amazon.com) say that a firm should spend moreon improving delivery performancesrather than advertising. Also, it is difficult for a competitor to duplicate a superior distribution system than to copy a competitor's advertising campaign. An e-tailer can differentiate itself by designing a better and faster delivery system. There are three levels of differentiation (Jian, Rosenbloomg, 2004). The first is reliability: some e-tailers are more reliable in their on-time delivery, order completeness, and order-cycle time. The second is resilience: some e-tailers are better at handling emergencies, product recalls, and answering inquiries. The third is innovativeness: some e-tailers create better information systems, introduce bar coding and mixed pallets, and in other ways help the customer.

Usage of innovative techniques like customerization, mobile marketing, etc. may hold the interest ofinternet users.E-tailers should try to minimise the payment gateway errors with the help of the concerned Indian banks to build trust regarding online payments among conventional and price cynical Indians. While skills like speed, product differentiation, innovation, and branding have the ability to transmute core operations and practices to this new medium which might make the difference between success and failure. Retailers need to assess the viability of such anevolution, and look into the synergies of using the new channel of e-tail. e-tailers, on the other hand, need to revisit some basic retail functions, and develop further competencies in the areas of merchandising and demand forecasting(Rao,1999).The information generated by members of an e-tailer's virtual community provides valuable feedback on the quality of existing fulfillment and after-sales services. Hence, virtual communities serve as a live test-field where e-tailers can get in touch with the consumers, continue to content them, and hold their loyalty and trust. Certain techniques such as a "rules engine" that can drive personalization based on information from the database are critical to satisfy individual customers. Additional retention strategy includes the possibility of carrying out online andoffline product simulation and testing, the availability of after-sales service and advice, the handling of returned goods as well as possible financing schemes. By doing so, customer relationships as well as the e-tailer'sreputation can be strengthened and revenues could be increased.

E-tailing is an integrator of technology, logistics, and infrastructure, and creates a relatively efficient marketplace for vendors and consumers. At present, the Indian e-tailing market is incapable to play the role of an efficient integrator. Given the fact that the current share of corporatized retail is under 10 per cent, and that the domestic venture capital industry is still in its infancy, policymakers will need to seek a rapprochement with investment and expertise from overseas players. Indian government needs to facilitate the growth of an ecosystem conducive to e-tailing and should include the following measures:

- Opening up of e-tailing for international capital and knowledge infusion.
- Enhancing infrastructure fora wireless data access and broadband connectivity all over the country.
- Innervating B2C logistics and warehouse capability building.
- Implementing a proper Taxation policy on e-products and services.
- Capital deployment in B2C logistics, domestic air cargo services, and warehousing industries.
- E-tailing adoption as a key growth driver by retailers and consumer product companies.
- Promoting entrepreneurshipfor creatinginnovative technology, analytics and packaging solutions.
- Building sustainable and Indian-specific e-tailing business models, especially in wholesaling and distribution.
- Aiming for "best in class" capabilities across the e-tailing value chain to compete in the global arena.

Case Study of Flipkart and Myntra Merger and Acquisition

Flipkartstarted with online bookstore similar to Amazon but now it sells products across all categories, including fashion and electronics. White goods and furniture are also sold on it.It hit the billion-dollar milestone in annual gross merchandise value last month.Subsequently, Fashion, which delivers over 35 per cent in operating margin, is among the most contested categories in e-commerce and has seen the emergence of players like Jabong, Fashionara and Limeroad and even web-only brands like Yepme and Zovi. Flipkartmoved to market place model in Feb. 2013 where third party merchants sell goods to consumers through Flipkart'swebsite. It allows e-commerce companies to scale up faster, save storage and other inventory related cost as merchants hold the products. For Flipkart, setting up a huge fashion vertical means boosting margins, because fashion has the highest 35 to 40 per cent sales among all products sold online. Myntra has big plans with its private brands like Anouk, Dress berry and Roadster, which promise margins as high as 60 per cent. Myntra will continue to operate as a separate brand, and its founder Flipkart will bring in its competencies in customer service and technology. However, the companies will not integrate the back end. The two teams will also function distinctly.Marking the biggest coalition in the e-commerce space in India, Flipkart and fashion e-tailerMyntra jointly expose their vision to capture more than 50 per cent e-market share by strategic alliance. As Flipkart's annualized sales crossed over 6,100 crore a year ahead of it's target, it had estimated to reach the billion dollar mark for gross merchandise value by 2015; on the other hand Myntra's revenue was about 1,000 crore in the previous financial year. Myntraseems to follow China's biggest e-retail model Alibaba.com and intends to double its revenue in this financial year by expanding its seller's base. Myntra has about 100 sellers on board and plans to increase this number to 1,000 by fiscal end. The strategy of Flipkart is to invest around 600 crore in its fashion business in coming years to combat with global rivals like Amazon and eBay Inc. The current deal appears to be a win-win situation for both companies, and could be the making of a giant company, better positioned to address India's growing demand for online retail. This merger and acquisition of Flipkart and Myntra will contribute to the progression of Indian economy that will lead it to become a global player in E- commerce.

E-Tailing Prospects in India

E-tail industry is set to benefit driven by investments from various private enterprises and venture capital firms in India.A demand fore-shopping is going to exist, from people who value its convenience and know about its ability to supply unusual items to distant markets.The potential of India's E-tailing will continue to remain untapped if a mindset of exclusion and seeing E-tailing as a "passing fad" creeps in. Being different from retail, etailingrequires a different mindset and fresh thinking from the policy makers as well as the private sector. For designing an effective E-tailing strategy in India, it is important to understand the needs and demands of individual customers. Successful E-tailing is concerned with high velocity, flexible systems and procedures, extremely high service levels, and full electronic connections to the trading community (Rakesh, 2014). In order to develop the right E-tailing strategy, following five points need online vendors' attention: prompt delivery, supply chain, demand nature, reverse logistics, and accuracy.

E-tailing can provide employment to 1.45 million people by 2021. It has the prowess to act as a catalyst and support the growth of new skills and industries.It will open up international markets for the SME sector and can become an important facilitator for the growth of the telecom and domestic air cargo industries. It will also help in reducing inventory costs and help the companies in achieving economies of scale.Online retailing will play a crucial role in bringing sustainability and economic viability to many facets of the economy. It will provide both direct and indirect employment as well as support infrastructure industries like logistics, telecom, etc. by creating demand. The growth of B2B, C2C and B2C market segment would reposition and have a geometric growth. It will stimulate entrepreneurship by providing business opportunities to merchandise vendors and service providers, and reduce transaction costs (tax leakages, distribution costs, etc.) by providing accessibility to quality products / solutions in an efficient manner.E-tailing will basically help in generating employment, facilitating growth of allied industries, promote entrepreneurship and reduce transaction costs.In order to support small business enterprises government can introduce variable tax levy for online and offline purchasing and selling considering the interest of both the types of retailers. Good customer relations, interaction, enhanced after sale service, proper redressal of complaints and customization could serve as the survival strategies in the intense competitive online national as well as international market.

Conclusion

This paper attempts to provide a conceptual insight about the e-tailing scenario in India. It provides an in-depth study of the factors that contribute towards online buying behaviour of Indian consumers by the use and application of Technology Adoption Models. Also, this study presents a set of innovative practices that could be used by e-tailers in the convergent world of online retailing in India.

It was found that customer-centric factors (price, perceived ease of use and enjoyment, customer requirements, consumption patterns and past online buying behaviour), website related factors (innovative dynamics, data management and security, usability, reliability and customer satisfaction) and perceived risks (financial, time, safety, physical, privacy, performance and product risks) positively or negatively cast an impact on buying behaviour of online purchase intention of consumers. E-tailing strategies like providing secure online transactions, enhancing website usability and reliability, improving delivery performance and after sales service could be used by online vendors to gain e-consumers credibility and maintain brand equity. It was also observed that the growth of e-tailing would lead to a boost in country's economy and provide employment opportunities. The study suggests that e-marketers should focus upon the factors that influence consumers to go for online shopping which in turn would help them to improve their customer relationships by meeting the consumer demands as per their interests.

Scopefor Future Studies

This study attempts to present a detailed view about the existing e-tailing scenario in Indian as well as global context by analyzing the various attributes that lead to online buying behaviour of Indian consumers. The factors highlighted in this study may not be enough for other countries. So, this study could be further extended to find out the variables that influence the global online consumers..Finally analyzing all the pros and cons a set of recommendations had been made in this paper to overcome the challenges for online shopping in Indian scenario to achieve the desired success in near future. Also, the study provides a few e-tailing strategies that may not be applicable to the international e-retail market. Further researches may focus on the global e-tailing business models and provide strategies for the same. The present study may provide basis for future studies. This study paper may be proved as a productive guideline for online marketers and policy makers to attract more new Indian online users towards online transactions. E-retail researchers may further explore directions and gaps identified in this paperfor researching the Indian e-markets.

References

- Lee,G.G and Lin, H. F. "Customer perceptions of e-service quality in online shopping" International Journal of Retail and Distribution Manage- ment 2005,Vol. 33, No. 2, pp. 161-176.
- Technopak: E-tailing in India: unlocking the potential (2014)
- CRISIL, "CRISIL Opinion", E-tail eats into retail, CRISIL RESRACH, February, 2014
- Balachandran, V and Sakthivelan, S.M (2013) "Impact Of Information Technology On Entrepreneurship (e-Entrepreneurship)" Journal of Business Management and Social Sciences Research (JBM&SSR), Vol 2, No.2, pp. 10-14.
- Bajpai A, Wen C, Lee (2014) Online buying behavior: A cross-country study between India and Taiwan I.J.R.F.M. 4: 23-46.
- Vegiayan, K. D., Ming, C. W., and Harun, M. L. O. (2013). "Online Shopping and Customer Satisfaction in Malaysia" International Journal of Marketing Practices, Vol. 1, No., pp 43-51
- Ranganathan, C., and Ganapathy, S. (2002). Key dimensions of business-to-consumer web sites. Information and Management, 39(6), 457-465.

- SajjadNazir, ArsalanTayyab, Aziz Sajid , Haroonur Rashid , IrumJaved (May 2012) "How Online Shopping Is Affecting Consumers Shoping Behavior in Pakistan?" IJCSI International Journal of Computer Science Issues, Vol. 9, Issue 3, No 1 pp 486-495.
- Liebermann, Y. and Stashevsky S, "Perceived risks as barriers to Internet and e-commerce usage" Qualitative Market Research: An International Journal, Vol 5, No. 4, pp 291-300, April 2005
- Khitoliya. P. (2014) "Customers Attitude and perception towards online" PARIPEX Indian Journal of Applied Research Vol. 3, Issue 6, pg no. 36-39 1.
- Zhou L, Dai L, Zhang D (2007) Online shopping acceptance model – a critical survey of consumer factors in online shopping Journal Of Electronic Commerce Research 8: 41-61.
- Lina Z, Dai L, Zhang D (2007) Online shopping model – a critical survey of consumer factors in online shopping Journal Of Electronic Commerce Research 8: 1-42.
- A.T. Kearney, Inc. (2004), Emerging Priorities for Global Retailers, Chicago: A.T.Kearney, Inc. Marketing and Communications.
- Mathwick, C., Malhotra, N.K. and Rigdon, E. (2002), "The effect of dynamic retail experiences on experiential perceptions of value: an Internet and catalog comparison", Journal of Retailing, Vol. 78 No. 1, pp. 51-60.
- Menon, S. and Kahn, B. (2002), "Cross-category effects of induced arousal and pleasure on the Internet shopping experience", Journal of Retailing, Vol. 78 No. 1, pp. 31-40.
- Moon, J. W. and Kim, Y.-G. (2001), "Extending the TAM for a World-Wide-Web context", Information and Management, Vol. 38 No. 4, pp. 217-30.
- O'Cass, A. and Fenech, T. (2002), "Web retailing adoption: exploring the nature of Internet users web retailing behavior", Journal of Retailing and Consumer Services, Vol. 10 No.3:323-333, 2013.
- Oliver, T.A. and Shapiro, F. (1993), "Self-efficacy and computers", Journal of Computer-Based Interactions, Vol. 20 No. 1, pp. 81-5.
- Parasuraman, A. and Zinkhan, G.M. (2002), "Marketing to and serving customers through the Internet: an overview and research agenda", Journal of the Academy of Marketing Science, Vol. 30 No. 4, pp. 286-95.
- Ratchford, B.T., Talukdar, D. and Lee, M.-S. (2001), "A model of consumer choice of the internet as an information source", International Journal of Electronic Commerce, Vol. 5 No. 3, pp. 7-21.

- Kumar R, Bakshi G (2012) A study of Indian online consumers and their buying behaviour IJRESS 2: 267-270.
- Reinhardt, A. and Passariello, C.W. (2002), "E-commerce starts to click", Business Week, No. 3796, p. 56.
- Shim, S., Eastlick, M.A., Lotz, S.L. and Warrington, P. (2001), "An online prepurchase intentions model: the role of intention to search", Journal of Retailing, Vol. 77 No. 3, pp. 397-416.
- Kim, C., W. Zhao,and K. H. Yang (2008), "An empirical study on the integrated framework of e-CRM in online shopping: evaluating the relationships among perceived value, satisfaction, and trust based on customers' perspectives",Journal of Electronic Commerce in Organizations, Vol. 6 No.3: 1-19.
- Kim, J. and J. Park (2005), "A consumer shopping channel extension model: Attitude shift toward the online store", Journal ofFashion Marketing and Management, Vol. 9 No.1:106-121.
- Kim, J.-H., M. Kim, and S. J. Lennon, (2007) "Information components of apparel retail web sites: Task relevance approach", Journal of Fashion Marketing and Management, Vol. 11 No.4:494-510.
- Kim, S. and G. Garrison,(2008) "Investigating mobile wireless technology adoption: An extension of the technologyacceptance model", Information Systems Frontiers Vol. 11 No.3:323-333.
- Ku, E. C.S. (2012), "Beyond price: How does trust encourage online group's buying intention?", Internet Research, Vol. 22, No.5:569-590.
- Lee., H.-H. and J. Kim(2008) , "The effects of shopping orientations on consumers' satisfaction with product search andpurchases in a multi-channel environment", Journal of Fashion Marketing and Management, Vol. 12 No.2:193-216, 2008.
- Lepoutre, J. and A. Heene (2006), "Investigating the impact of firm size on small business social responsibility: A criticalreview", Journal of Business Ethics, Vol. 67 No.3:257-273.
- Liao, S.-h., P.-H Chu, Y.-J. Chen, and C.-C. Chang (2012), "Mining customer knowledge for exploring online group buyingbehavior", Expert Systems with Applications, Vol. 39 No.3: 3708-3716.
- LifewinOnline group-buying market survey (2013), Retrieved from http://life.trendgo. com.tw/ epaper /5738, 2013.
- (Lin, H.-F (2007), "The role of online and offline features in sustaining virtual communities: an empirical study", InternetResearch, Vol. 17 No.2:119-138.

- López, C., F. J. Molina, and H. Bouwman, (2008) "An assessment of advanced mobile services acceptance: Contributionsfrom TAM and diffusion theory models", Information and Management, Vol. 45, No.6:359-364.
- Market Intelligence and Consulting Institute (2011), A analysis of online shopping behavior in Taiwan. Retrieved fromhttp://mic.iii.org.tw/aisp/pressroom/ press01_pop. asp?sno =243&type1=2.
- Matsuo, T. (2009) "A reassuring mechanism design for traders in electronic group buying", Applied Artificial Intelligence, Vol. 23, No.1:1-15.
- Park, C. and J.K. Jun (2003), "A cross-cultural comparison of Internet buying behavior: Effects of Internet usage, perceivedrisks, and innovativeness", International Marketing Review, Vol. 20, No.5:534-553.
- W., N. Robertson, and L. McQuilken (2012), "A novel romance: The Technology Acceptance Model with emotional attachment", Australasian Marketing Journal, Vol. 19, No.5: 223-229.
- Pookulangara, S., J. Hawley, and G. Xiao (2011), "Explaining multi-channel consumer's channel-migration intention usingtheory of reasoned action", International Journal of Retail and Distribution Management, Vol. 39, No.3:183-20.
- Ryu, K., H. Han, and T. H. Kim (2008), "The relationships among overall quick-casual restaurant image, perceived value,customer satisfaction, and behavioral intentions", International Journal of Hospitality Management, Vol. 27, No.3:459-469.
- Sanayei, A., A. Shaemi,and H. Jamshidi (2011), "An Analysis of the factors affecting customers satisfaction and trust inmobile banking", Interdisciplinary Journal of Contemporary Research In Business, Vol. 3, No.7:440-452.
- Shen, J., "Social comparison, social presence, and enjoyment in the acceptance of social shopping websites" (2012), Journalof Electronic Commerce Research, Vol. 13, No. 3: 198-212.
- Shen, J., and L. B. Eder (2009), "Exploring intentions to use virtual worlds for business", Journal of Electronic CommerceResearch, Vol.10, No. 2: 94-103.
- A.D. Miyazaki and A. Fernandez (2001), Consumer perceptions of privacy and security risks for online shopping. The Journal of Consumer Affairs 35(1): 27-44.

- W.R. Swinyard and S.M. Smith (2003), Why people don't shop online: A lifestyle study of the Internet consumer. Psychology and Marketing 20(7): 567-597.
- S.M. Lee, J. Choi, and S-J. Lee (2004), The Impact of a Third-Party Assurance Seal in Customer Purchasing Intention. Journal of Internet Commerce 3(2): 33-51.
- Y. Xia, Z.U. Ahmed, S. Stone, C.S. Wei, C.L. Eng and H.L. Lian (2008), Determinants of consumers' perceptions and attitudes towards assurance seals for Internet marketing: an Asia Pacific marketing perspective. International Journal of Internet Marketing and Advertising 4(2/3): 156-178.
- A. Bhatnagar, S. Misra and H.R. Rao (2000), "On risk, convenience, and (Internet shopping behavior," Communications of ACM 43(11): 98-105.
- Leonard S. (2011) A Journey of Exploration into the World of of E-Marketing and Independent Publishing, Bud Werner Library, Steamboat Springs, CO.
- Richa D. (2012) Impact of demographic factors of consumers on online shopping behaviour : a study of consumers in India I.J.E.M.S. 3: 43-52.
- Singhi A, Shukla A (2012), " Retailing: Consumer purchase decision", National Conference On Emerging Challenges For Sustainable Business, ISBN - 978-93-81583-46-3.

26

Factors Influencing E-Commerce Adoption in India

Ashamayee Mishra

Abstract

The internet has created a new medium for communication and commerce for businesses. It is hard to imagine a business working without using a computer. The internet performs as a marketplace for getting sellers and buyers together to conduct sales as a form of transaction. The World Wide Web provides an inexpensive, easy and fast way to interact with customers, suppliers and business. The advent of internet based E-Commerce offers considerable opportunities for large and smallfirms across to expand their customer base enter new products and rationalize their businesses by competing in the global economies.Ecommerce is new concept in India, and is growing at a good pace. So, it will grow only in future.There is relevance of e-commerce and the opportunity of its growth in developing countries, it is important to understand national factors that affect e-commerce adoption.There has been a significant growth of e-commerce in developed countries in the last two decades and more recently in developing countries.There are many ecommerce players in India and several booming up daily. Many are working on marketplace model and many are working as private label brands. Different initiatives are being taken in India for the adoption and development of E-Commerce in every sector of today's era.

Key Words: *E-Commerce, Opportunity, Relevance, Factors and Adoption.*

Introduction

The usage of Internet is increasing and moving roundthe world during the last decade. Today, computers and the internet have become an integral part of modern societies. For communication and commerce for businessesthe internet has created a newmedium. It is hard to imagine a business working without using a computer.

The internet performs as a marketplace to bring sellers and buyers together for conducting sales as a form of transaction, being a communication medium, the world wide web provides an inexpensive, easy and fast way for interacting with customers, suppliers and other businesses and a company's web presence helps enhance credibility, gather feedback, improve customer service and facilitate business process (Chen et al., 2003).

The internet can create a direct link between the members of the members of the industries and consumers, and also websites can provide information about the services and create an instant conformation response to an inquiry (Braun, 2006).

The advent of internet based E-Commerce offers considerable opportunities for large and small firms across the globe to expand their customer base enter new products and rationalize their businesses by competing in the global economies.

E-Commerce can be defined as any economic or business activity that uses Information Communication Technology (ICT) based applications to enable the buying and selling of products and services and to facilitate the transaction of business activities between and among businesses, individuals, governments or other organizations (Fink and Disterer, 2006). This includes using ICTs to strengthen a company's internal operations, such as logistic, procurement and human resource and contract management, information and data management, communication functions, and to facilitate the flow of products between businesses and consumers, e.g., marketing, ordering, payment, delivery and searching for suppliers (Mclovor and Humphreys, 2004). Adoption of E-Commerce offers a great opportunities to SMEs(Small Medium Enterise) to gain greater global access and reduced transaction costs, provide substantial benefits via improved efficiencies and raised revenues; facilitates access to potential customers and suppliers, productivity improvements, customization of products and services and information exchange and management (UNCTAD,2002).

E-Commerce is a process of trading goods, information or services via computer networks including the internet over website (Jantarajaturapath and Ussahawanitchkit, 2009; Silveira, 2003). E-Commerce is changing the way business is conducted throughout the world and provides a lot of opportunities to improve the performance of businesses. E-Commerce is not just about buying and selling products only. It covers information for customer inquiry on products and information, Price comparison. Therefore, E-Commerce has a direct impact on business owners, suppliers, and customers. The rapid change of environment such as internet, computer and communication technology including infrastructure enable E-Commerce to allow SME to streamline their business process, enhance customer service and offer new channel to customers (Chang, 2003). IT competence, organizational support and trust and security are antecedents of Ecommerce adoption vie competitive.

As a major regional trading, manufacturing, and services hub in Asia, India's future competitiveness and economic development prospects are signicantly affected by the development of e-commerce on a global scale.

Electronic commerce or simply e-commerce, which relies on various information and communication technologies (ICT), has the potential to improve trade efficiency around the globe and to integrate developing countries into the global economy (UNCTAD 1999). As a result, there has been a significant growth of e-commerce in developed countries in the last two decades and more recently in developing countries (Chowdhury 2003).

Most technologies, including e-commerce were developed in Western countries that have very different backgrounds to those of developing countries. The success of technology adoption is heavily dependent on how it is used by the adopters and this in turn is affected by the fit between the technology and the adopters (Unhelkar 2003).

In the globalization era, understanding the adoption of ICT, including e-commerce by developing countries is becoming important to improve its adoption success. This, in turn, enables developed countries to trade with developing countries more efficiently. At this stage, there are still a limited number of studies on the adoption of e-commerce technologies by developing countries (Chowdhury 2003).

It includes activities such as servicing customer online, collaborating with business partners and exchanging business documents within an organization over the Internet or other private networks. Because of its broad coverage, e-commerce is often referred to as e-business (Barness and Hunt 2001).

With the availability of the Internet and the popularity of the World Wide Web to access the Internet, e-commerce has grown significantly in the last few years (Turban et al. 2006).

According to WTO (2002) the Internet is revolutionizing the distribution of tourism information and sales. An increasing proportion of Internet users are buying on–line and tourism will gain a larger and larger share of the online commerce market (Wang, and Cheung, 2004). Obviously, the Internet is having a major impact as a source of information for tourism (Buhalis and Schertler, 1999).

Farooq Ahmed (2001) reported that the enormous flexibility of the internet has made possible what is popularly called e-commerce which has made inroads in the traditional methods of business management. All the facets the business tradition with which we are accustomed in physical environment can be now executed over the internet including online advertising, online ordering, publishing, banking, investment, auction and professional services. E commerce involves conducting business using modern communication instruments: telephone, fax, e-payment, money transfer systems, e-data interchange and the internet. The WTO has recognized that commercial transactions can be broken into 3 stages. 'The advertising and searching stage, the ordering, and payment stage, and the delivery stage.'

Factors Influencing e-commerce Adoption

To explore the relevance of e-commerce and the opportunity of its growth in developing countries, it is important to understand national factors that affect e-commerce adoption. A number of such factors have been identified from the literature as summarized in the Figure. The figure also demonstrates the influence of each factor on other factors. These factors will be used in developing a research model of EC adoption by developing countries in a later stage of the study, combined with other factors identified at various levels including industry and organizational levels.

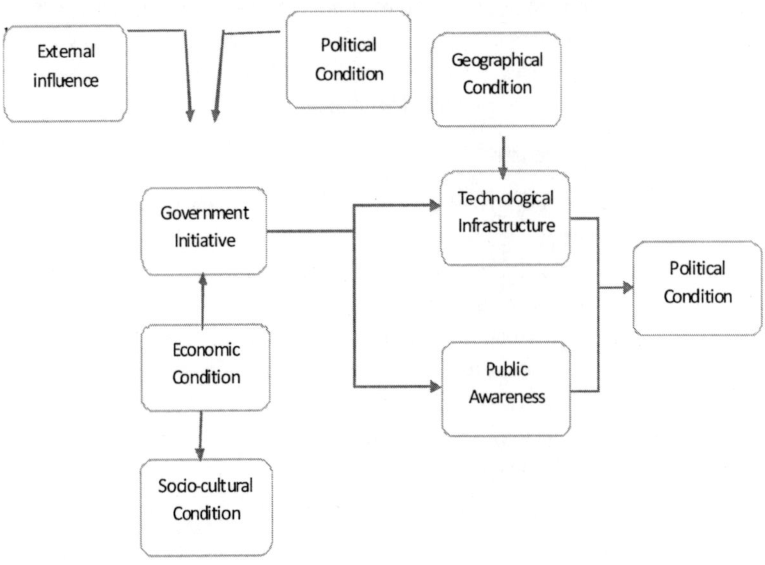

Figure. Factors Affecting e-commerce Adoption

Government Initiatives

In the adoption of e-commerce and other ICT in general Government initiative plays an important role (Molla 2005). They can be preferred in terms of promotion of ICT usage, education and the establishment of adequate regulatory framework for e-commerce which also includes taxation and tariff for revenue generated through e-commerce and Intellectual Property protections. The country's political condition, economic condition, and external influence from other countries are certain factors that affect Government initiative.

Political Condition

A key factor for e-commerce growth is the situation of Politics. In a country with an unstable political condition, it is less likely that government will give enough attention, if any, on e-commerce development (Dedrick et al. 1995).

Economic Condition

For adoption of E-Commerce, a major driver is Economic condition which is also widely recognized. The GDP and income per capita are common indicators for the economic condition of a country. Countries with unfavorable economic condition are not likely to be involved in e-commerce and since e-commerce relies on technology infrastructures are relatively expensive for many developing countries (Dedrick et al. 1995). The socio-cultural condition of a country will also be affected with the economic condition.

Technology Infrastructure

E-commerce success relies heavily on a number of technology infrastructures. Firstly, telecommunication infrastructures are required to connect various regions and parties within a country and across countries (Molla 2005). The cost of accessing the infrastructures also influences the growth of e-commerce. E-commerce also relies on efficient logistic infrastructures within a country. Its growth further requires the establishment of reliable and secure payment infrastructures to avoid frauds and other illegal actions (Boerhanoeddin2000). The overall technology infrastructure development of a country relies heavily on the economic and geographical conditions of the country.

Geographical Condition

Geographical condition of a country can be a motivation or barrier to technology infrastructure development. In countries that consist of many small islands, technology infrastructures can be difficult to develop. On the other hand, the need for having such infrastructure is also significant for effective communication and trading among the widely spread parties (Boerhanoeddin 2000; Minges 2002).

Socio-cultural Condition

The adoption of e-commerce also depends on the cultural and social environment. In some countries, people consider shopping as a recreation, and therefore, B2C e-commerce is difficult to nurture (Boerhanoeddin 2000). Likewise, the level of education, the availability of IT skills, the level of penetration of personal computers and telephone within the society affect the growth of e-commerce (Raffa et al. 2002).

Public Awareness

A lack of awareness of the use and potential benefits of ICT can also hinder the growth of e-commerce (Molla 2005, Jennex et al. 2004). In some developing countries, many people are only aware of limited e-commerce applications such as chat, email and browsing websites (Minges 2002). As a result, many organizations have not considered exploiting the potential of e-commerce to improve their business operations.

External Influence

The growth of e-commerce in a country is also influenced by other countries. For example, the reputation of credit card frauds in some countries caused blockages of several IP addresses by a number of commercial sites from different countries. This situation can cause those countries to be expelled from global business transactions and hence, limit the usefulness of e-commerce (Hidayat 2004).

There are many ecommerce players in India and several booming up daily. Many are working on marketplace model and many are working as private label brands. Yet, major ecommerce players in India are Flipkart , myntra , jabong , ebay , yebhi , infibeam , amazon.in etc. They are improving the quality of their services and using new techniques in ecommerce. Competition among these players is taking the whole ecommerce industry in positive direction. Major Players are: 1. Flipkart 2. Myntra 3. Ebay 4. Jabong 5. Infibeam 6. Yebhi 7. Amazon India 8. Pepperfry 9. Croma 10. Zovi 11. MakeMyTrip 12. Yatra.com 13. Golbibo 14. Redbus.in 15. IRCTC

Important Factors Affecting E-commerce

The factors that affect the E-Commerce is vital in its adoption. It can be counted as follows:

- ***Successful Campaigns of Marketing:*** It focuses on the technologies resulting with high touch marketing. It includes internet marketing referring marketing through e mail viz, defining the reach, direct e-mail, language translation specifically for global market, outsourcing e-mail marketing. It also focuses on web-based promotions like click rewards, point-based rewards, discounts, virtual coupons and so on. Online advertising is also a part of this aspect i.e., web page banner ads, registration with search engines, pop-up boxes, alliances with advertising/game dot com companies, etc.
- Successful System of Customer Relationship Management (CRM) : This system involves algorithms and statistical tools like SAS, SPSS, Group/rank customers by profitability, sales, number of visits per week, expenditure per visit, retention forecast, etc.. This also include online tracking, online survey, and online registration. Technology interactivity is also vital viz., effective and attractive web site (HTML), managing customer database is essential, smooth communication between client's browser and server etc.
- Safe And Secured Online Monetary Transaction: Online monetary transactions happens safely and in a secured manner. This transactions are possible through Electronic Debit, Micropayments, E-payments in B2B transactions, E-billing in B2C, Online banking etc.

E-commerce in India

E-Commerce provides significant opportunity for developing countries like India. E-Commerce in India is still in initial stage, but even the most-pessimistic projections indicate a boom. It is believed that low cost of personal computers, a growing installed base for Internet use, and an increasingly competitive Internet Service Provider (ISP) market will help fuel E-Commerce growth in Asia's second most populous nation. This makes India a real attractive market for e-commerce. To make a successful e-commerce transaction both the payment and delivery services must be made efficient. There has been a rise in the number of companies' taking up e-commerce in the recent past. Major Indian portal sites have also shifted towards e-commerce instead of depending on advertising revenue. Many sites are now selling a diverse range of products and services from flowers, greeting cards, and movie tickets to groceries, electronic gadgets, and computers. With stock exchanges coming online the time for true e-commerce in India has finally arrived. On the negative side there are many challenges faced by e-commerce sites in India. The relatively small credit card population and lack of uniform credit agencies create a variety of payment challenges unknown in India. Delivery of goods to consumer by couriers and postal services is not very reliable in smaller cities, towns and rural areas. However, many Indian Banks have put the Internet banking facilities. The speed post and courier system has also improved tremendously in recent years. Modern computer technology like secured socket layer (SSL) helps to protect against payment fraud, and to share information with suppliers and business partners. With further improvement in payment and delivery system it is expected that India will soon become a major player in the e-commerce market.

While many companies, organizations, and communities in India are beginning to take advantage of the potential of e-commerce, critical challenges remain to be overcome before e-commerce would become an asset for common people. India's ecommerce industry is on the growth curve and experiencing a spurt in growth. The Online Travel Industry is the biggest segment in ecommerce and is booming due largely to the Internet-savvy urban population. The other segments, categorized under online non-travel industry, include e-Tailing (online retail), online classifieds and Digital Downloads (still in a nascent stage). The online travel industry has some private players such as Makemytrip, Cleartrip and Yatra as well as a strong government presence in terms of IRCTC, which is a successful Indian Railways program. The online classifieds segment is broadly divided into three sectors; Jobs, Matrimonial and Real Estate. Mobile Commerce is also growing rapidly and proving to be a stable and secure supplement to E-Commerce due to the record growth in mobile user base in India, in recent years. Growth drivers and barriers are present in equal measures for new E-Commerce ventures.

E-Commerce market in India has a wonderful growth. The market was worth about $3.8 billion in 2009, it went up to $12.6 billion in 2013. The e-retail market in 2013 was worth about $ 2.3 billion. About 70 per cent of India's e-commerce market is related to travel. India has close to 10 million online shoppers and is growing at an estimated 30 per cent growth rate, with global growth rate of 8-10 per cent.

Electronics and Apparel are the biggest categories in terms of sales.

Some of the key drivers in E-Commerce of India can be pointed out as follows:

- Increase in broadband internet and 3G penetration.
- Rise in the standards of living and upward growth in usage of mobile even among middle class with high disposable incomes.
- Wide product range is available as compared to what is available at the shops.
- Busy lifestyles, urban traffic congestion and lack of time for offline shopping creates interest towards online shopping.

- Lower prices as compared to the brick and mortar retail driven by disintermediation and reduced inventory and real estate costs.
- Usage of online classified sites, with more consumer buying and selling second-hand goods has increased.
- Evolution of the online marketplace model with sites like Flipkart, Jabong, Snapdeal, Myntra, Homeshop18, Infibeam etc. creates revolution in the market.

As per data retrieved, overall e-commerce market is expected to reach around $24 billion by the end of 2015 with equal contribution from online travel and etailing. In e-commerce one of the biggest segment can be referred to the mobile and DTH recharge with nearly 1 million transactions daily by operator websites.

Objective of the Study

To know about the ecommerce in brief.
To focus on the influence of E-Commerce in India.
To understand various factors affecting the adoption of e-commerce.
To refer the opportunity involved with ecommerce.
To study the growth of e commerce

Scope of Study

This study has a much wider scope. Ecommerce is new concept in India, and is growing at a good pace. So, it will grow only in future. By applying the findings and recommendations of this study, ecommerce in India can be improved. It will help India to build world class ecommerce ventures like Amazon and Ebay.

Hypothesis

H_0: Because of growth in E-Commerce adoption, there can be positive influence on India.

H_1: Because of relevance of E-Commerce adoption, there comes opportunities and success.

H_2: The greater the technological upliftment, the stronger the relationship between E-Commerce adoption and success.

H_3: If E-commerce is adopted, then the customer awareness increases.

H_4: The greater the support of organizational factors, the higher the adoption of E-Commerce will be.

H_5: Because of increasing adoption of E-Commerce, there can be increase in trust and security.

H_6: If the competitive pressure grows, then the adoption of E-Commerce grows.

Methodology

The study focuses on the adoption of E-Commerce. The influence of the factors involved in the adoption of E-Commerce is vital and thus data are collected and then interpreted to understand the study.

The data of the study were collected from the primary sources with the help of questionnaire from certain organizations that have adopted and even adopting E-Commerce recently. Selected organization were provided with structured questionnaire and were collected after duly filled in by them. In certain cases direct personal and telephonic interviews were also conducted with the help of the structured questionnaire.

Books, Journals, Thesis and Websites related to E-Commerce for broad study of the subject as secondary source of data.

Data Analysis and Interpretation

The data is analyzed on the basis of the answers redeemed based on the structured questionnaire. The data is then interpreted with the help of chi-square test to understand the level of significance with 5 per cent Degree of Freedom.

Formula of Chi-Square Test,

$$\chi^2 = \Sigma[(O - E)^2 / E]$$

H_0: Because of growth in E-Commerce adoption, there can be positive influence on India.

	Strongly Satisfied	*Satisfied*	*Can't say*	*Dissatisfied*	*Strongly Dissatisfied*	*Total*
A	6	5	2	2	2	17
B	8	4	1	1	3	17
C	5	3	3	4	1	16
D	7	4	3	3	1	18
E	6	6	2	2	1	17
	32	22	11	12	8	85

Chi-Square test-1:

Sl.No.	*Observation (O)*	*Expectation (E)*	*O-E*	*(O-E)2*	*(O-E)2/E*
1	6	3.4	2.6	6.76	1.988235
2	8	3.4	4.6	21.16	6.223529
3	5	3.4	1.6	2.56	0.752941
4	7	3.4	3.6	12.96	3.811765
5	6	3.4	2.6	6.76	1.988235
6	5	3.4	1.6	2.56	0.752941
7	4	3.4	0.6	0.36	0.105882
8	3	3.4	-0.4	0.16	0.047059
9	4	3.4	0.6	0.36	0.105882
10	6	3.4	2.6	6.76	1.988235
11	2	3.4	-1.4	1.96	0.576471
12	1	3.4	-2.4	5.76	1.694118
13	3	3.4	-0.4	0.16	0.047059
14	3	3.4	-0.4	0.16	0.047059
15	2	3.4	-1.4	1.96	0.576471
16	2	3.4	-1.4	1.96	0.576471
17	1	3.4	-2.4	5.76	1.694118
18	4	3.4	0.6	0.36	0.105882
19	3	3.4	-0.4	0.16	0.047059
20	2	3.4	-1.4	1.96	0.576471
21	2	3.4	-1.4	1.96	0.576471
22	3	3.4	-0.4	0.16	0.047059
23	1	3.4	-2.4	5.76	1.694118
24	1	3.4	-2.4	5.76	1.694118
25	1	3.4	-2.4	5.76	1.694118
					29.41176

$\chi^2 = 29.411$ (Calculated Value).

$\chi^2 = 36.414$ (Tabulated Value; Here the degree of freedom = 25-1=24 on 0.05)

Since the Calculated value of χ^2 is less than the tabulated value, it is not significant. Hence, the null hypothesis can be accepted by 5 per cent level of significance and we may conclude that the experimental result supports the theory of the study.

H$_1$: Because of relevance of E-Commerce adoption, there comes opportunities and success.

	Strongly Satisfied	*Satisfied*	*Can't say*	*Dissatisfied*	*Strongly Dissatisfied*	*Total*
A	5	7	3	3	2	20
B	7	5	3	1	0	16
C	3	4	4	3	1	15
D	5	4	5	2	2	18
E	6	5	3	1	1	16
	26	25	18	10	6	85

Chi-Square test-2:

Sl.No.	*Observation (O)*	*Expectation (E)*	*O–E*	*(O–E)²*	*(O–E)²/E*
1	5	3.4	1.6	2.56	0.752941
2	7	3.4	3.6	12.96	3.811765
3	3	3.4	-0.4	0.16	0.047059
4	3	3.4	-0.4	0.16	0.047059
5	2	3.4	-1.4	1.96	0.576471
6	7	3.4	3.6	12.96	3.811765
7	5	3.4	1.6	2.56	0.752941
8	3	3.4	-0.4	0.16	0.047059
9	1	3.4	-2.4	5.76	1.694118
10	0	3.4	-3.4	11.56	3.4
11	3	3.4	-0.4	0.16	0.047059
12	4	3.4	0.6	0.36	0.105882
13	4	3.4	0.6	0.36	0.105882
14	3	3.4	-0.4	0.16	0.047059
15	1	3.4	-2.4	5.76	1.694118
16	5	3.4	1.6	2.56	0.752941
17	4	3.4	0.6	0.36	0.105882
18	5	3.4	1.6	2.56	0.752941
19	2	3.4	-1.4	1.96	0.576471
20	2	3.4	-1.4	1.96	0.576471
21	6	3.4	2.6	6.76	1.988235
22	5	3.4	1.6	2.56	0.752941
23	3	3.4	-0.4	0.16	0.047059
24	1	3.4	-2.4	5.76	1.694118
25	1	3.4	-2.4	5.76	1.694118
					25.88235

χ^2= 25.882 (Calculated Value).

χ^2=36.414 (Tabulated Value; Here the degree of freedom = 25-1=24 on 0.05)

Since the Calculated value of χ^2 is less than the tabulated value, it is not significant. Hence, the null hypothesis can be accepted by 5 per cent level of significance and we may conclude that the experimental result supports the theory of the study.

H_2: The greater the technological upliftment, the stronger the relationship between E-Commerce adoption and success.

	Strongly Satisfied	*Satisfied*	*Can't say*	*Dissatisfied*	*Strongly Dissatisfied*	*Total*
A	4	7	3	2	1	17
B	4	6	3	1	2	16
C	3	5	4	3	3	18
D	5	7	5	2	1	20
E	6	5	2	1	0	14
	22	30	17	9	7	85

Chi-Square test-3:

Sl.No.	*Observation (O)*	*Expectation (E)*	*O–E*	*(O–E)²*	*(O–E)²/E*
1	4	3.4	0.6	0.36	0.105882
2	7	3.4	3.6	12.96	3.811765
3	3	3.4	-0.4	0.16	0.047059
4	2	3.4	-1.4	1.96	0.576471
5	1	3.4	-2.4	5.76	1.694118
6	4	3.4	0.6	0.36	0.105882
7	6	3.4	2.6	6.76	1.988235
8	3	3.4	-0.4	0.16	0.047059
9	1	3.4	-2.4	5.76	1.694118
10	2	3.4	-1.4	1.96	0.576471
11	3	3.4	-0.4	0.16	0.047059
12	5	3.4	1.6	2.56	0.752941
13	4	3.4	0.6	0.36	0.105882
14	3	3.4	-0.4	0.16	0.047059
15	3	3.4	-0.4	0.16	0.047059
16	5	3.4	1.6	2.56	0.752941

17	7	3.4	3.6	12.96	3.811765
18	5	3.4	1.6	2.56	0.752941
19	2	3.4	-1.4	1.96	0.576471
20	1	3.4	-2.4	5.76	1.694118
21	6	3.4	2.6	6.76	1.988235
22	5	3.4	1.6	2.56	0.752941
23	2	3.4	-1.4	1.96	0.576471
24	1	3.4	-2.4	5.76	1.694118
25	0	3.4	-3.4	11.56	3.4
					27.64706

χ^2=27.647(Calculated Value).

χ^2=36.414 (Tabulated Value; Here the degree of freedom = 25-1=24 on 0.05)

Since the Calculated value of χ^2 is less than the tabulated value, it is not significant. Hence, the null hypothesis can be accepted by 5 per cent level of significance and we may conclude that the experimental result supports the theory of the study.

H_3: If E-commerce is adopted, then the customer awareness increases.

	Strongly Satisfied	*Satisfied*	*Can't say*	*Dissatisfied*	*Strongly Dissatisfied*	*Total*
A	6	5	2	2	1	16
B	7	6	3	1	0	17
C	5	7	4	2	3	21
D	5	4	3	3	2	17
E	6	5	2	1	0	14
	22	30	17	9	7	85

Chi-Square test-4:

Sl.No.	*Observation (O)*	*Expectation (E)*	*O–E*	*(O–E)²*	*(O–E)²/E*
1	6	3.4	2.6	6.76	1.988235
2	5	3.4	1.6	2.56	0.752941
3	2	3.4	-1.4	1.96	0.576471
4	2	3.4	-1.4	1.96	0.576471
5	1	3.4	-2.4	5.76	1.694118
6	7	3.4	3.6	12.96	3.811765

7	6	3.4	2.6	6.76	1.988235
8	3	3.4	-0.4	0.16	0.047059
9	1	3.4	-2.4	5.76	1.694118
10	0	3.4	-3.4	11.56	3.4
11	5	3.4	1.6	2.56	0.752941
12	7	3.4	3.6	12.96	3.811765
13	4	3.4	0.6	0.36	0.105882
14	2	3.4	-1.4	1.96	0.576471
15	3	3.4	-0.4	0.16	0.047059
16	5	3.4	1.6	2.56	0.752941
17	4	3.4	0.6	0.36	0.105882
18	3	3.4	-0.4	0.16	0.047059
19	3	3.4	-0.4	0.16	0.047059
20	2	3.4	-1.4	1.96	0.576471
21	6	3.4	2.6	6.76	1.988235
22	5	3.4	1.6	2.56	0.752941
23	2	3.4	-1.4	1.96	0.576471
24	1	3.4	-2.4	5.76	1.694118
25	0	3.4	-3.4	11.56	3.4
					31.76471

$\chi^2 = 31.765$ (Calculated Value).

$\chi^2 = 36.414$ (Tabulated Value; Here the degree of freedom = 25-1=24 on 0.05)

Since the Calculated value of χ^2 is less than the tabulated value, it is not significant. Hence, the null hypothesis can be accepted by 5 per cent level of significance and we may conclude that the experimental result supports the theory of the study.

H_4: The greater the support of organizational factors, the higher the adoption of E-Commerce will be.

	Strongly Satisfied	*Satisfied*	*Can't say*	*Dissatisfied*	*Strongly* Dissatisfied	*Total*
A	6	5	3	2	1	17
B	4	6	4	1	1	16
C	5	6	3	2	2	18
D	6	5	2	3	2	18
E	7	4	2	2	1	16
	28	26	14	10	7	85

Chi-Square test-5:

Sl.No.	*Observation (O)*	*Expectation (E)*	*O–E*	*(O–E)²*	*(O–E)²/E*
1	6	3.4	2.6	6.76	1.988235
2	5	3.4	1.6	2.56	0.752941
3	3	3.4	-0.4	0.16	0.047059
4	2	3.4	-1.4	1.96	0.576471
5	1	3.4	-2.4	5.76	1.694118
6	4	3.4	0.6	0.36	0.105882
7	6	3.4	2.6	6.76	1.988235
8	4	3.4	0.6	0.36	0.105882
9	1	3.4	-2.4	5.76	1.694118
10	1	3.4	-2.4	5.76	1.694118
11	5	3.4	1.6	2.56	0.752941
12	6	3.4	2.6	6.76	1.988235
13	3	3.4	-0.4	0.16	0.047059
14	2	3.4	-1.4	1.96	0.576471
15	2	3.4	-1.4	1.96	0.576471
16	6	3.4	2.6	6.76	1.988235
17	5	3.4	1.6	2.56	0.752941
18	2	3.4	-1.4	1.96	0.576471
19	3	3.4	-0.4	0.16	0.047059
20	2	3.4	-1.4	1.96	0.576471
21	7	3.4	3.6	12.96	3.811765
22	4	3.4	0.6	0.36	0.105882
23	2	3.4	-1.4	1.96	0.576471
24	2	3.4	-1.4	1.96	0.576471
25	1	3.4	-2.4	5.76	1.694118
					25.29412

χ^2=25.294 (Calculated Value).

χ^2=36.414 (Tabulated Value; Here the degree of freedom = 25-1=24 on 0.05)

Since the Calculated value of χ^2 is less than the tabulated value, it is not significant. Hence, the null hypothesis can be accepted by 5 per cent level of significance and we may conclude that the experimental result supports the theory of the study.

H_5 : Because of increasing adoption of E-Commerce, there can be increase in trust and security.

	Strongly Satisfied	*Satisfied*	*Can't say*	*Dissatisfied*	*Strongly Dissatisfied*	*Total*
A	6	7	4	2	1	20
B	7	5	2	1	1	16
C	6	5	3	1	1	16
D	6	4	4	2	1	17
E	5	6	2	1	2	16
	30	27	15	7	6	85

Chi-Square test-6:

Sl.No.	*Observation (O)*	*Expectation (E)*	*O–E*	*$(O-E)^2$*	*$(O-E)^2/E$*
1	6	3.4	2.6	6.76	1.988235
2	7	3.4	3.6	12.96	3.811765
3	4	3.4	0.6	0.36	0.105882
4	2	3.4	-1.4	1.96	0.576471
5	1	3.4	-2.4	5.76	1.694118
6	7	3.4	3.6	12.96	3.811765
7	5	3.4	1.6	2.56	0.752941
8	2	3.4	-1.4	1.96	0.576471
9	1	3.4	-2.4	5.76	1.694118
10	1	3.4	-2.4	5.76	1.694118
11	6	3.4	2.6	6.76	1.988235
12	5	3.4	1.6	2.56	0.752941
13	3	3.4	-0.4	0.16	0.047059
14	1	3.4	-2.4	5.76	1.694118
15	1	3.4	-2.4	5.76	1.694118
16	6	3.4	2.6	6.76	1.988235
17	4	3.4	0.6	0.36	0.105882
18	4	3.4	0.6	0.36	0.105882
19	2	3.4	-1.4	1.96	0.576471
20	1	3.4	-2.4	5.76	1.694118
21	5	3.4	1.6	2.56	0.752941
22	6	3.4	2.6	6.76	1.988235

23	2	3.4	-1.4	1.96	0.576471
24	1	3.4	-2.4	5.76	1.694118
25	2	3.4	-1.4	1.96	0.576471
					32.94118

$\chi^2 = 32.941$ (Calculated Value).

$\chi^2 = 36.414$ (Tabulated Value; Here the degree of freedom = 25-1=24 on 0.05)

Since the Calculated value of χ^2 is less than the tabulated value, it is not significant. Hence, the null hypothesis can be accepted by 5 per cent level of significance and we may conclude that the experimental result supports the theory of the study.

H_5 : If the competitive pressure grows, then the adoption of E-Commerce grows.

	Strongly Satisfied	*Satisfied*	*Can't say*	*Dissatisfied*	*Strongly Dissatisfied*	*Total*
A	5	7	4	2	1	19
B	6	6	2	1	1	16
C	5	5	4	2	1	17
D	6	4	3	2	1	16
E	4	7	2	2	2	17
	26	29	15	9	6	85

Chi-Square test-7:

Sl.No.	*Observation (O)*	*Expectation (E)*	*O–E*	*(O–E)²*	*(O–E)²/E*
1	5	3.4	1.6	2.56	0.752941
2	7	3.4	3.6	12.96	3.811765
3	4	3.4	0.6	0.36	0.105882
4	2	3.4	-1.4	1.96	0.576471
5	1	3.4	-2.4	5.76	1.694118
6	6	3.4	2.6	6.76	1.988235
7	6	3.4	2.6	6.76	1.988235
8	2	3.4	-1.4	1.96	0.576471
9	1	3.4	-2.4	5.76	1.694118
10	1	3.4	-2.4	5.76	1.694118
11	5	3.4	1.6	2.56	0.752941

12	5	3.4	1.6	2.56	0.752941
13	4	3.4	0.6	0.36	0.105882
14	2	3.4	-1.4	1.96	0.576471
15	1	3.4	-2.4	5.76	1.694118
16	6	3.4	2.6	6.76	1.988235
17	4	3.4	0.6	0.36	0.105882
18	3	3.4	-0.4	0.16	0.047059
19	2	3.4	-1.4	1.96	0.576471
20	1	3.4	-2.4	5.76	1.694118
21	4	3.4	0.6	0.36	0.105882
22	7	3.4	3.6	12.96	3.811765
23	2	3.4	-1.4	1.96	0.576471
24	2	3.4	-1.4	1.96	0.576471
25	2	3.4	-1.4	1.96	0.576471
					28.82353

χ^2 = 28.823 (Calculated Value).

χ^2 =36.414 (Tabulated Value; Here the degree of freedom = 25-1=24 on 0.05)

Since the Calculated value of χ^2 is less than the tabulated value, it is not significant. Hence, the null hypothesis can be accepted by 5 per cent level of significance and we may conclude that the experimental result supports the theory of the study.

Findings

According to the study conducted and the data interpretation done, the findings can be listed as follows:

- The growth in E-Commerce adoption can influence the growth and development of the country with positive and valuable influence in the economy of India.
- Adoption of E-Commerce plays a relevant role in creating opportunities and success in the business.
- The involvement of the relation of adoption of E-Commerce with the success rate increases with the upliftment and enhancement in the technology as it leads towards techno-era.
- The awareness towards the organizational products and details can be increased and go high among the customers.
- The advancement and growth in the adoption of Ecommerce can be increased with the support of the organizational factors.

- Trust and security is very vital which is needed to be focused, can increase more with the adoption of E-Commerce in the organization.
- It is also can be pointed that pressure in the competition can create growth in the E-Commerce adoption.

Suggestion

So, it can be suggested that the growth of E-Commerce which can create opportunity should focus on the clarity, understanding, awareness and competition within the organization and even towards the customer. This can help the organization to grow and achieve a height in the competitive market with influence in economy. Technological upliftment and development steps should be taken and need to be accepted as well as technology friendliness needs to be created so that t can be acquired easily both by the employees and even by the customers.

Conclusion

Thus it can be concluded that influence of E-Commerce has become very vital for the growth of the organization with focus to the country. Considerable Opportunities for large and small firms across prefers with the advent of internet based E-Commerce offers to expand their customer base enter new products and rationalize their businesses by competing in the global economies. Ecommerce is new concept in India, and is growing at a good pace. Though the sector has witnessed tremendous growth and is expected to grow a lot of e-commerce ventures have faced extreme pressure to ensure cash flows. So, it is in the growth stage and will grow in future as well. There is relevance of e-commerce and the opportunity of its growth in developing countries, it is important to understand national factors that affect e-commerce adoption.

Reference

- Barnes, S. and hunt, B.; 2001; E-Commerce and V-Business: Business models for global success (pp.1-4). Oxford; Boston: Butterworth-Heinemann.
- Chowdhury, A. "Information technology and productivity Payoff in the Banking Industry: Evidence from the Emerging Markets", Journal of International Development, (15:6), 2003.
- Dedrick, J., Goodman, S.& Kraemer, K. "Little Engines that could: Computing in Small Energetic Countries", Association of Computing Machinery, (35), 1995, pp. 21-26.
- Hidayat, Indonesia Kampiun Cyberfraud: Pemerintah Jangan Diam Saja, detiki-Net,2004, available at: http://jkt1.detiknet.com/

index.php?fuseaction= deti.read&tahun=2004&bulan= 3&tgl= 19&time=179&idnews=11625&idkanal=110

- Minges, M. Kretek Internet: Indonesia Case Study, 2002, available at: http://www.apjii.or.id/dokumentasi/id_cs.pdf
- Molla, A. Exploring the Reality of e-Commerce Benefits Among Businesses in a Developing Country, University of Manchester, Precinct Centre, Manchester, 2005, UK, available at: http://www.sed.manchester.ac.uk/idpm/publications/wp/di/index.htm
- Turban, E.et al. Electronic Commerce: A Managerial Perspective, 2006, Prentice Hall.
- Unhelkar, B., "Understanding the Impact of Cultural Issues in Global e-Business Alliances", 4th International We-B Conference, 24-25 Nov, 2003, Perth, Western Australia.
- UNCTAD- United Nation Conference on Trade and Development. "Can Electronic Commerce be an Engine for Global Growth?" Electronic commerce and the integration of developing countries and countries with economies in transition, International Trade, 19-23 July 1999, Geneva.
- Buhalis, D., and Schertler, W., 1999, Information and Communication Technologies in Tourism, ENTER'99, Springer-Verlag, Wien-New York, ISBN321182580.
- Chang, Kuo-chung, Joyce Jackson, and Varun Grover. "E-Commerce and Corporate Strategy: An Executive Perspective" Information and Management 40, 7 (2003): 663-75.
- Jantarajaturapath, Palan, and Phapruke Ussahawanitchkit. "E-Commerce Competencies and Success of Thai E-Commerce Firms: A Mediating of Multi-Channel Retailing Advantage." (2009).
- Siveira, and Giovani J.c da. "Towards a Framework for Operations Management in E-Commerce." International Journal of Operations & Production Management 23, 2 (2003): 200
- Farooq ahmed 2001, electronic commerce: an indian perspective; international journal of law an d information technology; Vol.9, No.2, 2001; pp. 133-170.
- Fink, D., and Disterer, G. (2006). International case studies: To what extent is ICT infused into the operations of SMEs? *Journal of Enterprise Information Management, 19*(6), 608-624.
- Chen, S.C. and Dhillon G.S. (2003); "Interpreting dimensions of customer trust in E-Commerce"; Information Technology and Management, (4); pp. 303-318.

- UNCTAD (2002), "Building Confidence: Electronic Commerce and Development", United Nations, New York.
- www.ecommercetimes.com
- www.wikipedia.com
- www.ecomomictimes.com

27

It is up to you now! Rise of Green Consumerism: A Study of Automobile Sector in India

Bhavya Soni & Sana Rehman

Consumer demand has got the world into the current mess, now it has to get us out again.

Abstract

The rapid economic growth in the past years have witnessed increasing consumers' consumption worldwide causing environmental deterioration through over-consumption and utilization of natural resources (Chen and Chai, 2010). It is anticipated that if the current trend of economic growth and irresponsible consumption pattern continues, the environment degradation would worsen (Ramlogan, 1997).

On a global level, there is an increased awareness of global warming and adverse climate conditions and as a result there is a spur in interest toward environmental protection and sustainable development. A general deterioration in the physical environment is driving individuals and organizations to implement changes for improving the current state of the environment. As such, shift towards more sustainable consumption patterns is required and it is important to increase people's environmental awareness and consciousness.

People, as consumers, can reduce their impact on environment and make a positive difference through their purchasing decisions. The belief is that the consumer's environmental concern is one of the determinants of their "green buying" behaviour i.e., buying and consuming products that are environmentally beneficial (Mainieri et al., 1997). Consumers must inform themselves about major environmental problems and then, by being cross-informed through product labelling, they should only select environmentally benign products and green life-styles to match their new consumption tastes.

The idea of green consumerism is very much important in this decade to popularize among all sections of society to save the planet Earth. World over, economic development has come at the cost of environment only. Global warming, an outcome of greenhouse gas emission, is the price the world pays for it's over ambitious automobile growth. It is a movement to encourage people to buy products which are considered as environmental friendly. It refers to recycling, purchasing and using eco-friendly products that minimize damage to the environment.

Green consumerism is based on public awareness of pressing environmental issues. Green consumerism can be described as either a highly democratic strategy to save the planet or exploitative marketing, depending on who you are talking to. As a strategy to save the planet it confronts the mass of consumers in industrialised countries and in effect says: "it is up to you".

This article is an attempt to thrust the idea of green consumerism and look at the other side of green marketing from the perspective of consumers; not producers. It will also try to understand the awareness level and readiness of Indian consumers in automobile sector towards green products.

Introduction

The rapid economic growth in the past years have witnessed increasing consumers' consumption worldwide causing environmental deterioration through over-consumption and utilization of natural resources (Chen and Chai, 2010). It is anticipated that if the current trend of economic growth and irresponsible consumption pattern continues, the environment degradation would worsen. The consequences of environmental degradation are global warming, depletion of stratospheric ozone layer, pollution of sea and rivers, noise and light pollution, acid rain and desertification (Ramlogan, 1997).

On a global level, there is an increased awareness of global warming and adverse climate conditions and as a result there is a spur in interest toward environmental protection and sustainable development. A general deterioration in the physical environment is driving individuals and organizations to implement changes for improving the current state of the environment. As such, shift towards more sustainable consumption patterns is required and it is important to increase people's environmental awareness and consciousness.

People, as consumers, can reduce their impact on environment and make a positive difference through their purchasing decisions. The belief is that the consumer's environmental concern is one of the determinants of their "green buying" behaviour i.e., buying and consuming products that are environmentally beneficial (Mainieri et al., 1997). The rising numbers of consumers who prefer and are willing to buy eco-friendly products are creating opportunity for businesses that are using "eco-friendly" or "environmental friendly" as a component of their value proposition.

Environmentally responsible or "green" marketing refers to the satisfaction of consumer needs, wants, and desires in conjunction with the preservation and conservation of the natural environment.

Green consumerism is based on public awareness of pressing environmental issues. Green consumerism can be described as either a highly democratic strategy to save the planet or exploitative marketing, depending on who you are talking to. As a strategy to save the planet it confronts the mass of consumers in industrialised countries and in effect says: "it is up to you". Consumer demand has got the world into the current mess, now it has to get us out again. Consumers must inform themselves about major environmental problems and then, by being cross-informed through product labelling, they should only select environmentally benign products and green life-styles to match their new consumption tastes.

The growing social and regulatory concerns for the environment lead an increasing number of consumers to consider green issues. In particular, this trend has major and complex implications on the technological strategy of an automobile company and on its product innovations. Even though it is increased eco-awareness of Indian customers during the past few decades, there are some barriers to the diffusions of more ecologically oriented consumption and production styles.

The idea of green consumerism is very much important in this decade to popularize among all sections of society to save the planet Earth. World over, economic development has come at the cost of environment only. Global warming, an outcome of greenhouse gas emission, is the price the world pays for it's over ambitious automobile growth. It is time to encourage people to buy products which are considered as environmental friendly. It refers to recycling, purchasing and using eco-friendly products that minimize damage to the environment.

It is very important to establish the growth of green consumerism in India, particularly in the number of consumers who deliberately go green when it comes to the means of transport they buy.

This is a study that endeavors to identify and mark the highlights, drivers, and barricades for green consumerism in unique milieu of Indian Electric Automobile sector.

Literature Review: Talk in Academia

Businesses across the globe are bestowed with the responsibility of promoting sustainable development thereby preserving the rare natural resources to meet the needs of the forthcoming generation. Changes in the condition of natural resources and their long term negative impact has led to some realization about human responsibility towards nature. This realization has led to development of eco-friendly consumption patterns among consumers.

Grunert (1993) reported that about 40 per cent of environmental degradation has been brought about by the consumption activities of private households. The need for eco-friendly products is gradually increasing on account of persistent raise in the concern for environment related issues. Fortunately, eco-friendly consumption and spending patterns has led the marketers to understand the eco-friendly attitude of the consumers and come up with the marketing mix which preserves environmental resources and at the same time deliver value added products and services (Chitra, 2007). Some of the greatest challenges faced by these firms are changes in consumer preferences for the eco-friendly products, suspicion of eco-friendly advertising claim, unfavourable consumer perception of eco-friendly products and the high cost invested in developing eco-friendly products (Chen and Chai, 2010).

Green marketing is considered as one of the major trends in modern businesses (Kassaye, 2001; McDaniel and Rylander, 1993; Pujari and Wright, 1996).

Environmental ecological or green marketing are similar terms used in

Literature is a way to use the environmental benefits of a product or service to promote sales. Belz and Peattie (2008) stated that green marketing and environmental marketing in the late 1980's focused on green consumers who would be willing to pay premium prices for more environmentally friendly products. Many consumers choose products that do not damage the environment over less environmental friendly products, even if they cost more. With green marketing, advertisers focus on environmental benefits to sell products such as, electric and less emission vehicles, energy-efficient light bulbs, and environmentally safe detergents. Green marketing encourages consumers to use eco-friendly products and manufacturers to develop more environmental beneficial products.

If a product has a low environmental impact, it is regarded as an eco-friendly product. Mainieri et al., (1997) define eco-friendly products as ecologically safe products that can facilitate the long term goal of protecting and preserving our natural habitat. Pickett-Baker and Ozaki (2008) suggest that eco-friendly products should be supplied by companies with a reputation for reducing environmental impacts from their manufacturing processes.

Most researchers (Dunlap and Van Liere, 1978; Weigel and Weigel, 1978) relate pro-environmental concern to environmental protection. Pro-environmental concern is conceptualized as a general attitude that reflects the extent to which the consumer is worried about the threats to the environment (Alhassan, 2007). Recent studies suggest that the concern for the environmental problems is high (Mainieri*et al.,* 1997). Marketers and researchers seek to explore if pro-environmental concerns among consumers is predictive of any green buying behaviour.

Green buying can be defined as purchasing and consuming products that are benign towards environment (Mainieri et al., 1997). Some studies suggest that there is a positive relationship between environmental concern and green buying behaviour (Arbuthnot and Lingg, 1975). Although past research indicates that the consumers are concerned with the environment, marketers have found that consumers are price-sensitive when it comes to buying green (Mandese, 1991). Also, consumers' willingness to pay more for eco-friendly products is not always indicative of their green buying behaviour. For example, consumers who recycle waste may not want to buy products made from recycled material. Pickett-Baker and Ozaki (2008) suggest that an individual who is concerned about environment does not necessarily purchase eco-friendly products. The pro-environmental concern among consumers is likely to lead to green buying behaviour.

As consumers attitudes towards eco-friendly products continue to evolve, green marketing continues to be an issue of global interest. Laroche et al., (2001) suggests that there has been an increase in the number of individuals who are willing to pay more for environmentally friendly products. In 1991, environmentally conscious individuals in America were willing to pay 15-20 per cent (Suchard and Polonsky, 1991) as compared 5-10 per cent in 1989 (Coddington, 1990). Consumers are willing to help out environment and engaging in green buying could be one such compensatory behaviour. Concerns about environment are making consumers to contribute to the environment positively. This could be the reason for consumers engaging in green buying behaviour.

Also, marketers and researchers seek to explore if pro-environmental concern among consumers is predictive of their any green buying behaviour. Researchers (Dunlap and Van Liere, 1978; Weigel and Weigel, 1978) relate pro-environmental concern to environmental protection. Pro-environmental concern is conceptualized as a general attitude that reflects the extent to which the consumer is worried about the threats to the environment (Alhassan, 2007). Recent studies suggest that the concerns for the environmental problems is high (Mainieri*etal.,* 1997), suggesting a likely increase in green buying behaviour.

The concept of environmental friendly or eco-friendly products is not new. Since ages, the conservation ethics have been an inseparable part of Indian thought, traditions, and day-to-day consumption. Nikhil Mirashi andDeepti Gupta in DOCC, AERF (2008-09) project reports that since last few decades, the mad quest for the material end and economical progress in India and abroad has become identical with the exploitation of nature in all its appearances. Despite the continued growth of environmental movement all over the world, it has yet to make its impact on the Indian consumers. As a result, it is vital to explore how consumers in India view the environmental issues, and how they behave, especially in their green buying towards environmental friendly products.

Green Consumerism: An Electric Automobile Industry Perspective

Enhancing the quality of life is the ultimate objective and the driving force behind many of the critical decisions we take. However, for this to happen, we as a community need to shift from individualistic mindsets and take responsibility for the environment we live in. It is only then that we would see holistic improvement.Against the backdrop of environmental concerns and depleting resources, it is imperative not only to preserve what's left but find new alternatives to drive engines of growth in the economy. The effort, however, requires a collaborative approach by the government, regulatory authorities industry, R&D institutions and the community.

As a nation of keen minds, the answer lies in innovation, which has always been the force behind powerful changes in our times. This has been recently proven at the Asian Wall Street Journal awards. Out of the twelve finalists short-listed for the Asian Innovation Awards five of them were Indians, recognised for their inventions that improve the quality of life or productivity. These included an electric walking stick, modified pulley and energy efficient electric vehicles amongst others.The most sustainable invention recognised for applying technology to a strong business model and commercial potential has been the electric vehicles (EVs). EVs are the long-term solution to

India's urban pollution and planning problem.Rise in economic activity and population has led to a tremendous demand in the transport sector especially in urban India. By 2020, India's population in cities is expected to grow five-fold to a staggering 200 million while pollution is expected to grow by seven times. With this tremendous growth has emerged a very critical issue of keeping air and noise pollution in urban areas under control.

The Indian market for electric cars is still nascent. Electric cars are expected to account for close to 5 per cent of the Indian car market, or 175,000 cars, by 2017. Auto majors such as Mahindra and Mahindra, Tata Motors, Maruti Suzuki, Hyundai and Hero Electric are assessing the electric car market.

Most international electric car brands haven't been launched in India, primarily because of the high duty structure, lack of component supplies, and insufficient suppliers for charging such vehicles.

By 2020, about 20 million cars, or 5 per cent of automobiles, globally are expected to run on electricity.

If we can have three lakh Electric Vehicles on the roads by 2020, including three-wheelers, cars, and scooters, this could result in a reduction of over 16 lakh metric tons of CO, NOx and HC by 2020, savings of over Rs. 3700 crores in foreign exchange and significant health costs savings. EVs are zero polluting, easy to handle and have low running and maintenance costs. Small electric buses, three wheelers and electric scooters are ideal for city mobility in India but it could take between 5 and 10 years before they become viable for commercial use. Many local auto manufacturers such as REVA, Mahindra and Mahindra and Eko Scooters are embarking on alternate fuel transportation programs to combat air pollution in India.

Apart from being environment and user friendly, there are several other reasons for alternate fuel cars to flourish in India. Firstly, electricity for EVs can be produced from various sources for which India has natural resources and does not need to depend on the import of oil. Although, EVs will not replace LPG, CNG or petrol and diesel for intercity use, the infrastructure required for EVs in the form of electricity distribution infrastructure is already available in all our cities and minimum costs are required to install additional.

Green buyers, of course, have been around for a long time, but until recently they were only a discriminating few. The birth of the modern green consumer movement is usually dated at around the time the newly-released Brundtland Report was generating heightened awareness of the global ecological crisis. In 1987 a British company called The Body Shop won the UK "Company of the Year" Business Enterprise Awards. The Body Shop was then "riding high on a wave of green consumerism" as an outlet for "cruelty-free, minimally packaged, natural ingredient soaps". It was expanding at the rate of 20 new outlets a year and its extraordinary success helped to inspire several authors to quickly assemble popular guides to both green economics and green consuming. Green discrimination by consumers was thereafter quickly established as an essential ingredient of the business culture's plan to save the planet.

As green consumerism took off in early 1989 the popular media fell over each other in the rush to inform the public about their new responsibility to consume with green discrimination. Numerous articles appeared featuring environmental/consumer experts with trolleys full of supermarket purchases offering advice on exactly what form this discrimination should take. Lists of supposedly good and bad products were presented.

With the green shopping year in full stride even, The Bulletin, a magazine directed to the business community, got so caught up in the general enthusiasm they published an article with a front cover pointer announcing, "Shopping with a conscience. At last, a guide to who's behind the products Indians buy. Do you really want to give your money to companies that pollute, that make excessive profits, experiment on animals, and mistreat their employees? Now you have the power ..."

Was there a genuine consumer revolution under way? Perhaps. A manufacturer of hamburger packaging called Ozone Packaging took out newspaper advertisements to advertise "The Hamburger That Saved the World. You don't have to change the way you live to do the right thing by the environment. Keep on eating hamburgers. But make sure they come in Ozone take-away packaging."

Spurred into action McDonalds went one better advertising "Our Packaging Has Changed. It's A Wrap. .... McDonald's will continue to pursue the most environmentally sound operating practices and procedures possible to protect the global environment on which we all depend."

In automotive sector, Chevrolet came up with the idea of an electric vehicle being a new face in industry representing low emission, environment friendly, low operating cost car. High level business conferences were organised to discuss the situation. In 1989 it sure looked as if the suits were dressing themselves in green.

In India, government, business organizations and consumers are triad for green consumerism in India. Government of India has already taken initiative by imposing many rules and regulations regarding environmental preservation across the country, like imposing the use of CNG buses and auto rickshaws in cities like Delhi, Ahmadabad etc. to curb pollution. This calls for automobile makers to stick to the environmental norms and also come up with some new innovative technologies, which are environment friendly. The manufacture, sale and use of recycled plastic bags for storing, carrying or packaging food items has been banned in Kerala and a few other states like Andhra Pradesh, Delhi, Himachal Pradesh including Meghalaya also has banned the use of polythene bags. The Government of India has also launched the Eco-labeling scheme known as Eco-Marks. The Scheme was launched with a view to provide an incentive for manufacturers and importers to reduce the detrimental impact of the products, assist consumers to become environmental friendly in their daily lives. However it is unfortunate that not a single product in the Indian market bears an Eco-Mark (R. Marvin M, 2012).

Many business organization mainly in corporate sector have started incorporating green activities however these activities are done as a part of either a corporate social responsibility or as a part of corporate sustainability. Royal Dutch Shell operated LNG Plant in Hazira which is one of the company's largest ventures in India is completely a green business. Hero Honda has been consistently been working towards the elimination of harmful substances such as asbestos and hexavalent chromium from its products. JK Tyres developed eco-friendly tyres and launched them on the world environment day on June 5, 2002.

Government and business organizations have already started their initiatives in the greening process. In India, a very few consumers are green conscious. They seek green goods like ayurvedic medicines, natural dyes, natural textiles, bio-fertilizer, bio-pesticides, organic foods, herbal cosmetics etc. The demand and knowledge about green products and services is very less among the Indian consumers. It is also believed that whatsoever little demand exists in the market exists out of the reason of the economy that it provides and not out of the environment friendliness of the consumer (Tikoo, 1998).

Considering the bad impacts on environment, environmentalism is a major concern and firms are forced to adopt environmental friendly market practices such as developing and marketing products which are recyclable, more fuel efficient, less polluting, bio-degradable and reusable. Government and NGO's have to play an important role on marketing green ideas more intensively to make people more aware and knowledgeable about environmental issues and problems, so that there will be a new breed of green minded consumers to keep themselves healthy as well as there will be a great contribution to preserve our planet healthy for our next generations.

Research Methodology

250 questionnaires were distributed to a conveniently generated sample of a highly and semi-educated segment of general population across the country in various states including Jaipur, Chandigarh, Ludhiana, Delhi, Pune, Mumbai, Banglore, Kolkata, Patna.

The questionnaire is structured as follows. The first part contained 9 dichotomous questions with Yes and No as two possible responses and 2 multiple choice questions. These questions measured general consumers' knowledge about environmental issues, awareness of eco-friendly products, trust in performance of eco-friendly products and their willingness to pay more for such products.

The second part of the questionnaire consisted of a 5-point scale, used to explore and assess pro-environmental concerns and any potential effect of such concerns on consumers' green buying behavior. The survey scale consisted of 10 items of which 5 items were adapted from Roberts and Bacon's (1997) Ecologically Conscious Consumer Behaviour (ECCB) scale. Scores on the scale items varied from a low of 1 (strongly disagree) to a high of 5 (strongly agree), with disagree, neutral, and agree as interval points.

The final part of the questionnaire consisted of 3 open ended questions to explore and assess various other factors such as drivers and other barricades to green consumerism.

The questionnaire also included general demographic questions such as age, gender, and education.

Research Interpretations

- Research identifies that the Indian consumers in urban and semi-urban areas have high degree of awareness about electric and eco-friendly automobile and their affirmative impact on sustainable future.
- As a majority of Indian consumers are comparatively poor, their choice of products is naturally chiefly influenced by price. Other issues, such as environmental impact, play little role in their choice of products. As environmentally friendly products usually cost more, only consumers with higher purchasing power are willing to pay the premium price because of their concern for environment.
- They have come across pieces of information about such products through various individual and mass sources that will chip in the noble cause to save the environment and promoting action for sustainable development.
- It evidently shows the infancy stage of the electric automobile sector and its impact on consumer decision making process.
- The consumer acquaintance about such products is still extremely superficial.
- There is no strong brand positioning, awareness and identification in the minds of consumers to evoke them about electric automobile during consumers' decision making process.
- It also underlines the low quality perception about offerings in mind of consumers.

- It underlines the key perceptual barricade in the intensification of electric automobile industry in India. The Indian consumers perceive electric vehicle technology as substandard.
- Indian consumers are not enthusiastic to pay more than existing alternatives available in the market.
- It also finds the fact that Indian consumers are denying the products with adverse effects on the environment.
- They are not willing to take initiative and inspire others about the issue and limited to themselves only regarding this issue.
- Role of Government:
    - o Tax Benefits
    - o Free Services
    - o Infrastructure Development: Recharge points at precise distances
    - o Facilitate electric vehicle development through Research and Development assistance
    - o Awareness campaigns
    - o Benefits in Licensing and Land Permissions to customers
    - o Benefits in Licensing and Land Permissions to companies
- Major Barricades:
    - o More maintenance cost
    - o Shorter life period
    - o Slow speed Poor power and pick up
    - o Lack of safety measures
    - o Handling problems
    - o Not suitable for longer drives
    - o Lack of infrastructure
    - o Reliability of technology
- Major current and potential drivers:
    - o Sufficient speed reducing chances of accidents
    - o Lesser running cost
    - o Eco friendliness
    - o Rapid increase in fuel prices
    - o Longer charging support
    - o Battery recycling
    - o Ease of charging

Conclusion

There are significant indications that environmental issues will grow in importance over the coming years and will require imaginative and innovative redesign and reengineering of existing marketing efforts on the part of many businesses. Solutions to environmental problems can be characterized into roughly three categories: ethical, legal, and business (economic and technological). Long-term sustainability of the planet is likely to require some rather distinct changes in the ethical behaviour of its human population. Barring a crisis, these changes will probably be a long time coming. Legislation is a useful tool for effecting social change; it has a tremendous advantage over moral persuasion in terms of speed and efficacy of implementation, although its results are not always as intended. In the short term, business solutions—the enlightened self-interest of commercial enterprises finding new ways to incorporate technology and carry on exchanges with greater concern for heretofore unprized environmental goods and services—offer particular promise. Green consumerism and the promotion of responsible consumption are part of that solution.

One hopes, however, that the trend does not change for the worse. Let us avoid the same mindless development path as pursued in past that has caused the earth to warm up, the glaciers to recede, the forests to vanish, the rivers to dry up, and the air to be rendered unbreathable.

Let the green Indian consumer be an example for the world.

References

- http://www.newsallyear.com/growth-of-green-consumers-in-india/2255/
- http://www.referenceforbusiness.com/encyclopedia/Gov-Inc/Green-Marketing.html#b
- http://theshillongtimes.com/2012/03/15/the-rise-of-green-consumerism/
- https://sites.google.com/site/richardgosden/green-consumerism
- http://www.emergent-ventures.com/docs/Consumer-Going-Green.pdf
- http://www.psbresearch.in/pdf/imagepower-green-brands-survey.pdf
- http://www.triplepundit.com/2010/06/2010-green-brands-survey-what-do-green-consumers-want/
- http://www.wpp.com/wpp/press/press/default.htm?guid={7d135945-e34d-456b-a209-b27156624ce7}
- http://articles.economictimes.indiatimes.com/2011-06-27/news/29709214_1_esty-environmental-partners-green-products-green-quotient
- http://ezinemark.com/a/growth-of-green-consumers-in-india/

28

Customer Relationship Management in Organised Retail Sector

Narinder Tanwar

Abstract

Customer Relationship Management (CRM) is the need of hour for the business world in today's competitive scenario. For every business house either it is manufacturing or service to attract a customer and then to sell the product/service may by the first important step but if any organization wants to survive in the market over a longer period of time then it becomes very important to maintain mutual relationships with its customers. Customer relationships management strategies allow an organization to put the customer right at the center of the organization and then framing each and every strategy around the customer portfolio. The article covers different aspects of customer relationship management (CRM) related to organized retail sector, which include understanding the concept of CRM, its strategic approach, its process approach and various benefits which an organization derives by using customer relationship management strategies. The retailer and customer relationship is favourable for organizations to flourish in any economic condition and for customers to receive quality products and services. Therefore, the right Customer Relationship Management Strategies practiced is able to create a strong relationship with customers and at the end of the day it will creates loyal customers. This will subsequently increase company's profitability regardless of economic condition. Operational Excellence is the most effective CRM Strategies that led to customer loyalty in retail industry. Whereby, product leadership less used by the retailer in CRM strategies. The researcher believes that the customer felt that they need to trust the company first before they can really commit and be loyal to the company. The retail sector in many ways such as by using various CRM strategies as a guideline to conduct business to achieve organizational goals and at the end of the day, creating customer loyalty, results in mutual benefits of both organization as well as the customer.

Today, no organization is secure unless its every action is processed through the customer's eyes. The so-called typical customer no longer exists, and companies have been learning this lesson the hard way. Until very recently, business was more concerned about the "what's" than about the "who's." In other words, companies were focused on selling as many products and services as possible, without regard to who was buying them. But the baby boomers came of age and competition burgeoned. Consumers are having more choices than ever before about where to do their banking, their grocery shopping, and their vacationing. Today's businesses are facing fierce and too aggressive competition while operating in both domestic and global markets. Traditional marketing methods have failed to deliver results in recent times and companies are forced to invent new methods of interacting with customers to reduce costs and gain market share and more importantly to retain the customers and make them loyal to company. According to Court (2004) in an article in the McKinsey Quarterly: "Twenty years ago, big companies used one advertising spot on three television networks to reach 80% of the US population; now they need up to 20 messaging and media programmes to the same reach".

Keywords: Customer Relationship Management; Organized Retail Stores; Customer Trust; Customer Satisfaction; Customer Loyalty

Customer Relationship Management (CRM)

CRM is a business approach that integrates people, processes, and technology to maximize the relations of an organization with all types of customers. CRM helps in understanding the customer better, which enable organizations to effectively customize their products and service offerings according to the customer needs in order to retain customers and increase customer's loyalty and satisfaction. Many organizations are embracing customer relationship management strategies to reap benefits such as enhanced revenues and high profits.

The diverse and uncertain environment has forced organizations to restructure themselves in order to enhance their chances to survival and growth. The restructuring efforts have included, among others, the emergence of the "new paradigm" which is commonly referred as Customer Relationship Management (CRM).

Customer Relationship Management business strategy places the customer at the center of the organizations' universe. Relationships in today's world are more important than anything else which an organization wishes to maintain with their associations and it has become even more and more important to sustain them to be rewarding forever.

The situation was summed up well by Pine, Peppers, and Rogers (1995) in the Harvard Business Review article titled "Do You Want to Keep Your Customers Forever?" wherein they argued that: "Customers, whether consumers or businesses, do not want more choices. They want exactly what they want - when, where, and how they want it - and technology now makes it possible for companies to give it to them."

Customer relationship management (CRM) is a term which is not only used by business organizations today to maintain such good relationships with their present and old clients and associates but the terminology is now being used by almost any type of organization to create a beneficial environment for them and all in today's era of competition. CRM has played an ever increasing and important role in the growth of all such organizations those have developed a sense of understanding towards customer service and satisfaction and implementing CRM. According to Sheth and Sisodia (1995), the purpose of relationship marketing is to enhance marketing productivity by achieving efficiency and effectiveness.

Strategic Approach of CRM

Greenleaf and Winer (2002) have explained CRM as, "Customer Relationship Management is a business strategy to select and manage customers to optimize long-term value". CRM strategy helps organizations to serve the customer on an individual basis, to enjoy a long-term relationship and to get rid of barriers and distortions created by non-value adding intermediaries. It also helps to reduce marketing costs, target specific customers by focusing on their needs, track the effectiveness of given marketing action, maximizing life-time value of customers, and increasing their loyalty towards the organization. CRM has the power to help organizations quickly and directly improve customer satisfaction. CRM is an added dimension to ensure that what the customer expects is consistent with what the organization is prepared to deliver.

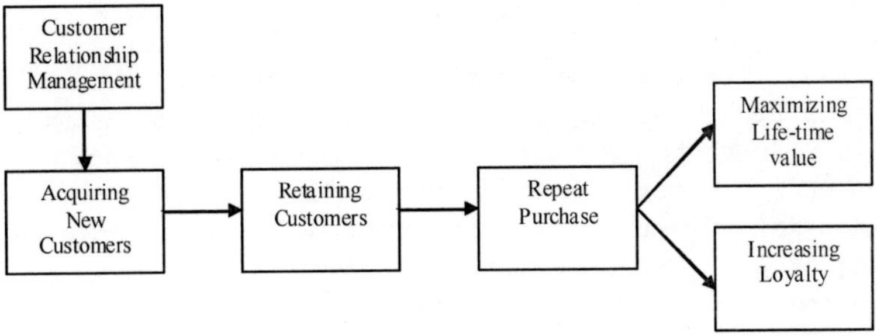

(Figure 1: Basic CRM Strategy)

The basic proposition of a CRM strategy is based on the age-old idea that knowledge, understanding, and serving the customer is the best method developing a sustainable competitive advantage. But building a sustainable and successful relationship with a large customer base is not the easiest thing to do and carries a direct impact on many core operational processes. CRM focuses on understanding the needs and desires of the customers and is achieved by placing these needs at the heart of the business by integrating them with the organization's strategy, people, technology, and business processes (Fox, Stead, 2001). At the heart of a perfect CRM strategy is the creation of mutual value for all the parties involved in the business process. It is about creating a sustainable competitive advantage by being the best at understanding, communicating, and delivering values to the existing customers in addition to creating and keeping new customers. It addresses to the changing needs of the customers by developing products and services that continuously seek to satisfy the lifestyle and need patterns of individual customers. Organizations tend to acquire a structure around customer segments and not on the basis of product lines to deliver customer satisfaction.

CRM is a corporate level strategy, focusing on creating and maintaining relationships with customers. An effective CRM system is able to identify factors important to clients, promote a customer oriented philosophy, adopt customer based measures, develop end-to-end processes to serve customers, provide successful customer support, handle customer complaints, track all aspects of sales, create a "holistic" view of customers' sales and service information. The long-term success of an organization depends mainly on how well it attracts and retains a large customer base. Managing relationships with customers is very important for organizations since improved relationships increase business value. CRM helps in leveraging information regarding customer behavior to achieve high levels of customer satisfaction, retention, and loyalty all resulting in improved profitability.

CRM focus on how to make the business approach more customers focused. CRM aims to increase the profitability of the customer portfolio which comprises many elements, for example: customer acquisition, price, cost to serve, cross sales (further sales to the same customer), up sales (the customer makes greater use of the same product or service), number and size of transactions, expected value of loss and longevity. Cao and Gruca (2005) have pointed out that attempts at cross-selling and up-selling will encounter adverse conditions when the firm has not chosen the right customers. So, companies must focus on profitable customers to ensure success through CRM initiatives. CRM is just about value added services. Alignment of present business according to customer needs is the success of CRM.

Process Approach of CRM

Peppers and Rogers (1993) in their book "One to One Marketing" predicted the demise of mass marketing and emphasized the fact that business organizations must stress more on customer relationships and less on products. They argued "you will not be trying to sell a single product to as many customers as possible. Instead you will be trying to sell a single customer as many products as possible - over a long period of time, and across different product lines". They recommended the following methodology for practicing relationship marketing. In the first step, organizations must identify the customers individually and understand their behaviors. This includes their needs, habits, and desires. In second step, details of customers are used to segment them. The third step advocates initiating the interaction with the customers and developing a relationship. Customers and organization may interact with each other using a number of channels and this knowledge is fed into the business strategy. In order to maintain customer life cycle, the relevant client dialog must be captured and customized for best possible future action. Ultimately the vision is to build a 'one to one' enterprise such that most valuable customers are treated differently by providing customized products and services.

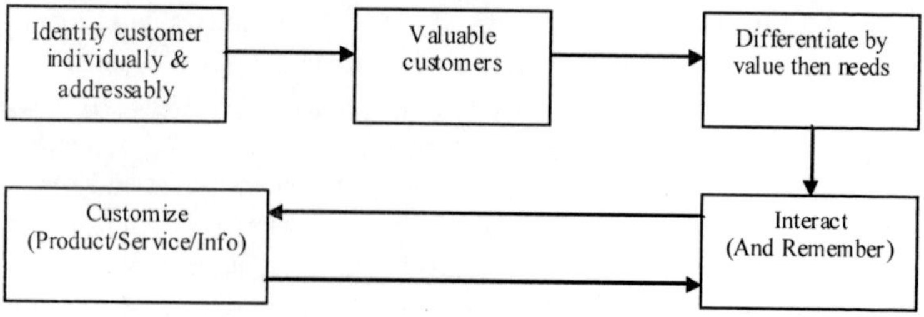

(Figure 2: Peppers & Rogers Methodology)

(***Source:*** Don Peppers and Martha Rogers (1993), 'One to One Marketing'.)

CRM life cycle begins with the integration of front office systems and the centralization of the customer-related data. The benefits of this phase include improved front office efficiency and productivity. In this phase, the customer data has to be collected in detail and maintained properly. Customer profile regarding demographics, socio-economic and lifestyle characteristics of customers has to be collected. Based on collected data, analysis of customer begins to understand behavior, identify the pattern of buying and trends, and discover causal relationship. The out of this is strategic business decision. Business processes and organizational structures are refined based on the improved customer understanding gained through analysis.

Retail Industry in India

Retailing is the largest private industry in the world, with total sales of $ 6.6 trillion World over the retail sector is not only the oldest but also one of the most advanced users of the technology. Retailing is also India's largest industry accounting for over 10% of the country's GDP and round 8% of the employment (CII-Mckinsey report). Retailing in India is gradually inching its ways towards becoming next booming industry. The Indian retailing industry is highly fragmented with 97% of its business being run by the unorganized retailers such as the traditional family run stores and corner stores. Organized retailing, however, is at a very nascent stage though its share is expected to rise to 10%-12% in the coming year constituting roughly 14 per cent of the total retail market..The figure is much higher for the U.S. & U.K. and relatively higher too for neighboring Asian countries like China, South Korea, Indonesia, Philippines, Thailand and Malaysia. (Vedamani G. Glbson "Comprehensive policy vital", The Hindu survey of Indian Industry 2007). According to India Retail Report 2009 organized retail has touched around Rs. 230000 cr. in 2010 while the global retail business is around $08 Trillion. Over 50 of the Fortune 500 companies are retailers. In this modern era Indian retailing industry is eyeing the global retail players. Indian retail industry is one of the fastest developing industries which have inculcated modern techniques, exclusive retail outlets, emergence of retail chains etc. Large Indian players like Reliance, K Rahejas, Bharti, and ITC are making significant investment in this sector, leading to the emergence of big retailer who can bargain with suppliers to reap the benefits of economies of scale.

The emergence of Retail in India is cause for success of Indian organized retail sector. With the help of modern management techniques we will become the specialist Retailers in future. We know that the relationship between the Retailer & customer is very close than other chains of distribution. India is a nation of shopkeepers. We can see more than 16 million plus retail outlets in India, and India has highest density of retail outlets in the world. Retail Industry in India is at present estimated to be more than US $ 250 billion. On that part of organized retailing is estimated 3.5% i.e. $ 7.47 billion. By the year 2015 the industry is expected to achieve a business of US $ 23 billion in organized retail. The share of organized trade in retailing in India was quite more than 4% in 2005 but in China it was between 7-8% in 1996 and 17% in 2003. At present USA is biggest retail market with 85% share of organized trade in retailing and then after there is Malaysia with 55% plus, Thailand with 40%plus , Brazil with 35%plus, Russia with 33%plus, Indonesia with 30%plus, Poland with 20%plus, China with 17% plus & India with 6% plus only.

CRM & Organized Retailing

Retailing is one of the oldest businesses that human civilization has known. It acts as an interface between the producer and consumer, improves the flow of goods and services and raises the efficiency of distribution in an economy. For a strong, stable and consistently growing economy, a well-organized and efficient retail sector is a must. Most of the developed and even emerging economies had adopted the organized retail long ago and percentage share of organized retail in total retailing has increased over the years. However, India, a land of self-sufficient villages, has continued to rely primarily on small, close to home shops. It is only off-late with pick-up in pace of urbanization and rising disposable incomes that the country started to take a few steps towards the organized retailing. A good progress has been made in the last few years, and the retail industry is off late being hailed as one of the sunrise sectors in the economy. Interestingly, for many years, retailers have been administering surveys to their customers to measure both their overall level of satisfaction and their opinion of various details of their store experience, service and merchandise provided at organized retail outlets but they are not able to retain all their customers by providing solutions to them. Satisfying customers is one of the main objectives of every business. Businesses recognize that retaining the existing customers is more profitable than having to win the new ones to replace those lost. Management and marketing theorists underscore the importance of customer satisfaction for a business's success and using customer relationship management strategies can be very much significant in achieving this success. Customer satisfaction is the key factor in the success of any retail business and therefore it is very important to measure it and to find out the factors that affect which affect customer satisfaction.

Products are easy to copy but services are harder to match. Therefore, the role of CRM strategies has become highly significant in establishing better relationship with customers. It increases profitability of the retail business in different ways such as:

- Increased Sales

- Customer Lifetime Value (CLV) and Profitability
- Increased Margin:
- Increased Response Rate
- Improved Customer Satisfaction Ratings
- One-to-One Marketing
- Decreased Marketing Administrative Costs

Organized retail segment has been growing at a blistering pace, exceeding all previous estimates. According to a study by Deloitte Haskins and Sells, organized retail has increased its share from 5 per cent of total retail sales in 2006 to 8 per cent in 2007. The fastest growing segments have been the wholesale cash and carry stores (150 per cent) followed by supermarkets (100 per cent) and hypermarkets (75- 80 per cent). Further, it estimates the organized segment to account for 25 per cent of the total sales by 2011. This paper focuses on identifying the antecedents and determinants of customer relationship management in organized retail sector. Different parameters of CRM have been identified after discussion with customers and experts in the field and the same has been presented in this paper.

Literature Review

In the present day's retail business, ensuring customer satisfaction in delivering the right product and service to the end-users is the major concern for the future growth of the organization. In the present study an attempt is made to find out the customer satisfaction during purchase in retail outlets based on customer survey. (Das Prasun, 2009). Literature on customer satisfaction is voluminous and spans several areas such as marketing, management and accounting. For example, numerous papers use the ACSI (American Customer Satisfaction Index) to study customer satisfaction at the company, industry and macroeconomic levels. This paper focuses only on customer satisfaction studies that are related to retailing and does not survey the literature that studies the design of satisfaction survey instruments, as there is no control over survey design. Iacobucci et al. (1994, 1995) provide precise definitions of service quality versus customer satisfaction. They contend that service quality should not be confused with customer satisfaction, but that satisfaction is a positive outcome of providing good service. Ittner and Larcker (1998) provide empirical evidence at the customer, business-unit and firm- level that various measures of financial performance (including revenue, revenue change, margin, return on sales, market value of equity and current earnings) are positively associated with customer satisfaction. However, in the retail industry they find a negative relationship between satisfaction and profitability which may be because benefits from increased satisfaction can be exceeded by the incremental cost in retail. Sulek et al. (1995) find that customer satisfaction positively affects sales per labor hour at a chain of 46 retail stores.

Anderson et al. (2004) find a positive association between customer satisfaction at the company level and Tobin's q (a long-run measure of financial performance) for department stores and supermarkets. Babakus et al. (2004) link customer satisfaction to product and service quality within retail stores and find that product quality has a six significant impact on store-level profits. Research on customer satisfaction usually views employees as facilitators of the sales process who are critical to improving the conversion ratio, by providing information to the customers on prices, brands, and product features and by helping customers to navigate store aisles, finding the product and even cross-selling other products. The unique feature of the retail store execution problem is that it combines the factory and the sales components, but this stream of literature focuses only on the latter. As stated by Mendoza et al. (2006) the CRM concept has evolved in such a way that nowadays it must be viewed as a strategy to maintain a long-term relationship with the customers. Michael et al.(2005) suggested that companies have to move in accordance to the customer behavior if they want to thrive in coming world. They have to come along with new customer loyalty programmes and build more comprehensively among partners and vendors, enabled by technology, to bring mutually beneficial relationships. According to Peppers and Rogers (1999) In some organizations, CRM is simply a technology solution that extends separate databases and sales force automation tools to link sales and marketing functions in order to improve targeting. Other organizations consider CRM as a tool specifically designed for one-to-one customer communications, only responsibility of sales/service, call centers, or marketing departments.

Ramanakumar, KPV (2008) writes about the Customer Relationship Management or Relationship Marketing. He refers to all marketing activities directed towards establishing, developing and maintaining relational exchanges successfully. According to V. Ramanathan (2008), Customer Relationship Management is an emerging tool that enables retail marketers to maintain their presence in the dynamic market environment. In early days CRM was the tool preferred by the manufacturers in order to motivate and retain retailers. Now retailers are applying this very same tool in order to retain customers. Both KPV Ramanakumar and V. Ramanathan bring certain CRM strategies into lime light being followed in the retail sector. They mention certain CRM strategies like personalization strategies, communication strategies like "Stay in Touch", "Inform Customers About the New Arrival", "Reward Strategies like offer tangible reward, discounts offers etc. Pahuja, Anurag opines that customer relationship management encompasses certain characteristics aspects. He says that business necessity regardless of whether one sells to end - consumer or to enterprise customers. According to Pradeep K Deb (2009), customer loyalty programs are the in - thing in today's retail world and Foodlands in Mumbai is one of the pioneers in this field in western India. He further gives the reaction of the a typical consumer that "privilege cards or special offers are nothing but retail trade gimmicks and the consumer ends up spending more by availing themselves of the offer". According to Sreekumar P (2009), for implementing any CRM initiative or special loyalty offers, Lifetime Customer Value is the most important criteria.

Objective of the Study

The purpose of carrying out this research was to identify the antecedents and determinants of customer relationship management strategies in organized retail sector.

Research Methodology

The research design of the study is exploratory cum descriptive. The research is exploratory due to the fact that the field of organized retail has not been deeply touched by the earlier researcher. Therefore, in this case, extensive preliminary work needs to be done to gain familiarity with the phenomena in the situation to understand what is occurring, before developing a model and setting up a rigorous design for comprehensive investigation. The study is descriptive because the area of research that has been chosen by the researcher explains the attributes, which are associated with implication of customer relationship management strategies in the field of organized retail. To fulfill the objective of the study a questionnaire was prepared for customers visiting retail outlets. The questionnaire was put forwarded to respondents/customers (N = 140) visiting different organized retail outlets (Reliance Mart, Vishal Mega Mart, SRS Value Bazar). In the questionnaire respondents were asked to indicate their opinions on a five-point likert scale and the results are presented in the form of Table. The research has been carried out in Faridabad which has emerged as a prominent center for organized retail. Further, to solve the purpose of the study both descriptive as well as inferential statistical techniques were applied. In the descriptive, Means and Standard Deviation were calculated and to test the significance level of the difference between Means of the criterion variables Karl Pearson's Coefficient of Correlation (r) were applied.

Results of Survey

From the literature review and discussion with experts in the field, various antecedents & determinants of customer relationship management in organized retail have been identified and a questionnaire was prepared. The questionnaires were put forwarded to respondents visiting retail outlets and observations are presented in Table 1.1.

Table 1.1: Antecedents and Determinants of CRM in Organized Retailing (Number of Respondents = 140)

S. No.	Variables	Mean Scores	Standard Deviation
1.	Product range	3.74	1.081
2.	Price range of products	4	1.155
3.	Layout of products	3.69	1.229
4.	Accessibility/location of retail store	3.84	1.051
5.	Quality of personnel service	3.77	1.103
6.	Quality of self service availability	3.4	1.353
7.	Billing facility	3.53	1.32
8.	Equipments/bags to carry products	3.37	1.31
9.	Mode of payment	3.27	1.318
10.	Time consumption at entrance/exist points	3.62	1.337
11.	Parking facility	3.66	1.146
12.	Point/product schemes on additional purchase	3.87	1:.16
13.	Interior of retail store	3.66	1.225

Source: Computed on the basis of Field Data

It may be noted that out of different practices used by the retail outlets to establish better relationship with the coustomers price range of products has the top value (Mean = 4.00, Std. Dev. = 1.155), and then point/product schemes on additional purchase (Mean =3.87, Std. Dev. = 1.160), accessibility/location of retail store (Mean = 3.84, Std. Dev. = 1.051), quality of personnel service (Mean = 3.77, Std. Dev. = 1.103), product range (Mean = 3.74, Std. Dev. = 1.081), layout of products (Mean = 3.69, Std. Dev. = 1.229), parking facility (Mean = 3.66, Std. Dev. = 1.146), interior of retail store (Mean = 3.66, Std. Dev. = 1.225), time consumption at entrance/exit points (Mean = 3.62, Std. Dev. = 1.337), billing facility (Mean = 3.53, Std. Dev. = 1.320), quality of self service availability (Mean = 3.4, Std. Dev. = 1.353), equipments/bags to carry products (Mean = 3.37, Std. Dev. = 1.31), and mode of payment (Mean = 3.27, Std. Dev. = 1.318).

Standard deviation value of some of the CRM strategies used by retail outlets such as product range (1.081), accessibility/location of retail store (1.051), quality of personnel service in retail store (1.103), qualified and experienced staff (1.155) indicate that there is consistency in the opinions of respondents, where as in case of quality of self service availability (1.353), time consumption at entrance/exit points (1.337), mode of payment (1.318) there is divergence of opinion among the respondents.

Customers (N=140) were asked to indicate their opinion about various CRM strategies used by organized retail outlets to attract and retain them. From responses it has come out that about 71% customers feel that retails store are having a wide range of products offer to them. As competition is growing in marketplace so it is important that a variety of products should have been offered to customers. Nearly 4/5th of the customers are in agreement that retail stores keep a wide range of products with wide range of prices as customers want that product/s should be made available in different varieties and prices. About 78% customers stated that retail outlets are approachable and it is also visible that due to increased competition in marketplace especially in organized retail focus has been given to make the location convenient for customers. About 3/4 customers agreed that in retail outlets the staff is well trained and they answer the queries raised by customers very well.

Nearly 63% students stated that product layout is well arranged and thus resulting in a satisfied self-service experience. About 65% customers have praised the billing system in retail outlets as we all know that technology has become an integral part of every sector today so is the retail sector. Most of the respondents have agreed on the growing importance of technology. Nearly 3/5th customers have revealed that they are provided equipment/bags to carry products. As revealed by respondents retail outlets generally provide trolley to carry products and make it a better buying experience for customers. Nearly 65% of the respondents are in agreement that there is a proper arrangement made by retail outlets on entrance and exit points and thus resulting in less time consumption at these points. Retail outlets know that generally it frustrates customers if it takes long time on entrance or exit. Therefore, sufficient number of staff members is deployed at these points. Around 75% respondents have stated that generally there are some schemes offered in these retail outlets on a particular amount of shopping. Even the retail stores know that offering schemes to customers is one of the better ways to attract and retain them. Nearly 68% customers stated that retail stores focus on interior. When a customer enters in a retail store he/she interacts with the interior first. So, retail stores focus on this aspect to make a better shopping experience for customers. From the result of survey, it is evident that in most of the cases response of customers is positive and this is due to the reason that organized retail outlets are well aware of the fact usage of such CRM strategies will help in maintaining better relationships with customers and developing a better brand image in the marketplace.

In the study, at attempt has also been made to gain insight into major CRM strategies used by retail outlets to have connected approach with customers. To identify a relationship among the means values of CRM determinants and average of key CRM determinants coefficient of correlation has been calculated and results are presented in Table 1.2.

Table 1.2: Relationship Between Determinants of CRM and Average of Key CRM Determinants in Organized Retailing (Number of Respondents = 140)

S. No.	Variables	Mean Scores	Standard Deviation	r value
1.	Product range	3.74	1.081	0.942**
2.	Price range of products	4	1.155	0.983**
3.	Layout of products	3.69	1.229	0.954**
4.	Quality of personnel service	3.77	1.103	0.978**
5.	Interior of retail store	3.66	1.146	0.952**
6.	Point/product schemes on additional purchase	3.87	1.16	0.972**

Notes: r-value indicates value of Karl Pearson's Coefficient of Correlation.
** indicates Correlation is significant at 1% level.
Source: Computed on the basis of Field Data

Higher value of 'r' (Towards +1.000) indicates that such variables are more focused by the retail outlets while less value of 'r' (Towards 0.0) indicates that such variables are less focused for establishing better relationships with customers. The test results indicate that there is significant and positive correlations in relation to various CRM strategies used by stores such as price range of products (r = 0.983), focus more on providing point/product schemes to customers on additional purchase (r = 0.972), quality of personnel service (r = 0.978), vast variety of products in the store (r = 0.942), layout of products (r = 0.954), and interior of retail store (r = 0.952).

Conclusion

According to a research by Reichheld and Sasser in Harvard Business Review, 5% increase in customer retention can increase profitability by 35% in banking business, 50% in insurance and brokerage, and 125% in the customer credit card market. Therefore, banks are now stressing on retaining customers and increasing market share. The primary value of CRM is its potential as a customer retention tool. Customer relationship management is an important and valuable tool in various service sectors such as hospitality, banking, insurance etc. but an equally important tool for the retail sector as well. Today, customers are having lots of options as there is so much competition in the market. Therefore adopting customer relationship management practices will surely help retail outlets to retain customers. Furthermore it is highly important to understand that customer relationship management does not enable a quick win. It is a long-term approach that has to be adopted at a strategic level. Whilst the value of customer relationship management has been identified by organizations, they are yet to look at the bigger picture and understand all of associated benefits that would enable their business strategies to be successful. Those responsible for delivery are perhaps the most informed about these strategic benefits yet the transformation is long-drawn-out process. The competencies required to deliver these customer benefits are: to deliver on its service promise, integrate products and service channels effectively, customize products & service and their respective prices, create opportunities for cross selling and delivery mechanisms for the onward promotion of these products and services and reduce the gestation period to market by allowing quick and effective introduction of new products and services.

References

- Reichhed, Frederick F. and Phil Schefter, 'E-Loyalty: Your Secret Weapon on the Web,' Harvard Business Review, 78(7), 2000, pp. 105-113.
- Shapiro, B., K. Rangan, R. Moriaty and E. Ross, 'Manage Customers for Profits (not just sales),' Harvard Business Review, 65(9): 1987, pp. 101-108.
- Dyche, Jill, 'The CRM Handbook - A Business Guide to Customer Relationship Management,' Pearson Education, 2007.
- Rey, B., 'The Paradigm of CRM,' Marketing Mastermind, 2007, pp. 54-56.
- Michael Levy, Baston, Aweitz and Ajay Pandit, 'Retail Management,' 6thEdition, Tata McGraw Hill, 2007.
- Shainesh, G., Sheth, N. Jagdish, 'CRM - A Strategic Perspective,' Macmillan India Ltd., 2007.
- Light, B., 'A Review of the Issues associated with Customer Relationship Management Systems,' in proceedings of Ninth European Conference on Information Systems - ECIS 2001, Association for Information Systems, Bled, Slovenia, 2001, pp. 1232-1241.
- Ang, Lawrence, and Ben Taylor, 'Managing Customer Profitability Using Portfolio Matrices,' Journal of Database Marketing & Customer Relationship Management, 12(4): 2005, pp. 298-304.
- Cao, Yong and Thomas S. Gruca, 'Reducting Adverse Selection through Customer Relationship Management,' Journal of Marketing, 69(4): 2005, pp. 219-229.
- Leszinski, R., F. A. Weber, R. Paganoni and T. Baumgarten, 'Profit in Your Backyard,' McKinsey Quarterly, 4: 1995, pp. 119-127.

- Goldenberg, B., 'What is CRM? What is an e-customer? Why you need them now?,' in Proceedings of DCI Customer Relationship Management Conference, Shared Insights, Boston, USA, June 2000, pp. 27-29.
- Ciborra, C., and Failla, A., 'Infrastructure as Process: The Case of CRM,' IBM, Oxford University Press, 2000.
- Court, David C., 'A New Model of Marketing,' McKinsey Quarterly, 4: 2004, pp. 4-6.
- Greenleaf, Eric and S. Russell Winer, 'Putting the Customer Back into Customer Relationship Management (CRM),' Advances in Consumer Research, 29(1): 2002, pp. 357-360.
- Pine, B. Joseph, II, Don Peppers, and Martha Rogers, 'Do You Want to Keep Your Customers Forever'? Harvard Business Review, 73(2): 1995, pp. 103-114.
- Seth J.N. and R. S. Sisodia (1995), 'Improving Marketing Productivity in' in J. Heilbrunn (Ed.) Encyclopedia of Marketing for the Year 2000, Chicago: American Marketing Association/NTC.
- Chen, I., and Popovich, K., 'Understanding Customer Relationship Management (CRM): People, Process, and Technology,' Business Process Management Journal, 9 (5), 2003, pp. 672-688.
- Zeithaml, V., R. Rust, and K. Lemon, 'The Customer Pyramid: Creating and Serving Profitable Customers,' California Management Review, 43(4): 2001, pp. 118-142.
- Raman, V. Venkata, and G. Somayajulu, 'Customer Relationship Management - A Key To Corporate Success,' Excel Books, 2003.
- Sumner, M., 'Critical Success Factors in Enterprise Wide Information Management Systems,' Proceedings of the Americas Conference on Information Systems, Milwaukee, WI, 1999, pp. 232-234.
- Diyan Kishore, 'Lure of Huge Consumer Base,' The Hindu, 2007, pp 285-289.
- Gibsn G., 'Modern Retailing Comprehensive Policy Vital,' The Hindu, 2007, pp 281-284.
- Pahuja Anurag & Verma Rajesh, 'Customer Relationship Management Need of the Hour,' Marketing Mastermind, January 2008, pp 26-29.
- Banerjee Arindam (2002), 'Roadmap for Successful CRM Implementation,' Indian Management, July 2002, pp 48-52.
- Benjamin Appiah - Kubi & Andrews, K. D., 'Towards a successful customer relationship management: A conceptual framework,' African

Journal of Marketing Management ,Vol. 2(3), 2010, pp 037-043

- Keith A. R, & Eli Jones, 'Customer relationship management: Finding value drivers,' Industrial Marketing Management, vol. 37, 2008. pp 120-130.
- Kenyon, J., & Vakola, M., 'Evolving the customer relationship management paradigm in the retail industry,' International Journal of Customer Relationship Management, 3(4), 2001, pp 313-332.

29

Inclusive Marketing: An Innovative Marketing Tool to Attain High Industrial Growth and achieve High Market Share in Service Industry

Tanuja Singh & M.S.Khan

Abstract

The purpose of this research is to exploit the opportunities in service industry of India and develop a strategic marketing tool for achieving high industry growth rate and high market share in Service Industry. The services sector has been the major growth levitate of the Indian economy with the highest sectoral contribution in India's Gross Domestic Product. However, in recent quarters, in alignment with general slowdown of the economy, the growth of services sector has also obstructed. The bottom of pyramid that includes the largest but the poorest socio-economic population of India constituting more than 2.5 billion people that live on less than $2.50 contributing 30 per cent of India 's income and consumption day in India. Aiming to make these people productive and to raise their purchasing power and living standards to turn them into buyers and customers from an economic demand outlook is the objective of Inclusive marketing in Service Industry.

Inclusive marketing revolves around Reach, Engage and Create which can link the Bottom of Pyramid with Service Sector to attain a glorifying growth in Service Industry. Inclusive markets are open markets that offer choices and opportunities to the poor and other excluded groups as producers, consumers and employers. Inclusive markets thus create jobs and affordable goods and services needed by the Bottom of Pyramid. Inclusive Marketing is an approach that looks at the poor not only as consumers but also as producers. This approach offers promise to add economic value to goods and services contributed by the poor. Indigent get right price for their produce and face immense challenges in accessing markets. This research paper is based on an extensive secondary research of the current market scenario and latest trends in Service Sector of India and the role of inclusive marketing as a strategic marketing tool to increase the growth and market share of service industry. There is therefore an imminent need to look for innovative ways of integrating Service Sector with bottom of pyramid through inclusive marketing approaches.

Keywords : *Inclusive Marketing; Inclusive Markets; Service Sector; Bottom of Pyramid; Marketing tools; Strategic Marketing.*

Introduction

The economy of India hold tenth position in the world by nominal GDP and stands third by purchasing power parity (PPP). In economic contribution its manufacturing industry has held a constant share; service sector has been the fastest-growing part of the economy - which includes information technologies, telecom, software, infrastructure and construction, tourism and travel, trade & banking etc. Major portion of India's GDP is contributed by Service sector with a 57 per cent share in GDP at factor cost (at current prices) in 2013-14. Services-sector GDP growth has been higher than that of overall GDP during 2000-01 to 2013-14. Services in India are emerging as influential sector in terms of contribution to national and states incomes, trade flows, employment etc. India has the second fastest growing services sector with its Compound Annual Growth Rate (CAGR) at 9.0 per cent and china at 10.9 per cent, during the last 11-year period from 2001 to 2012. Service sector has maximum contribution of 64.8 per cent in India's GDP followed by Industries and Agriculture at 21.5 per cent and 13.7 per cent respectively. Now connecting this Service Sector contribution to Agriculture depended Rural Population is the objective of this research study. Accepting the fact that agriculture dependent population is India is close to 70 per cent that makes agriculture a way of life for rural people is one the least experimented area or rather a neglected sector with huge potential to utilize the vast population in various job profiles.

On contrary, the service sector with mere 30% depended population is contributing highest. If a few characteristics of Service sector are incorporated in Agriculture sector, we can see the revolutionary economy in a short span of time.

Aim of Study: Aim of this research paper is to suggest the measures for development of Bottom of Pyramid through Inclusive Marketing which will trigger the rural population employability contribution towards Economy.

Objectives of the Study

- To suggest the measures to uplift the contribution of declining service sector in GDP.
- To utilize the population at the Bottom of Pyramid and create Job Market.
- To develop Inclusive Markets for Inclusive Development in Rural India.

Literature Review

India's services sector which was growing at a steady rate of over 10 per cent since 2005-06 has shown despondent performance in the last three years. The pliability of services growth witnessed even during and in the aftermath of the 2008 global recession has started declining, though the growth of services sector is still higher than that of other sectors. While the slowdown in mining and manufacturing and mining sectors directly affected some services like transportation services (shipping, ports, railways), communications, and other services were affected by the income effect with slowdown in growth global income and domestic incomes.

There has been an unprecedented growth in services across all countries in the recent years. While in the developed countries this is seen as a continuation of the economic transformation. Both from the demand as well as the supply factors are responsible for rise in the services sector. The unprecedented growth in services of India is not new; it has been coincided by a declining share of the primary sector (agriculture) and secondary (industry) sector over the years. The share of services at factor cost is increased from 33.5 per cent in 1950-51 to 55.7 per cent in 2011-12 and to 56.9 per cent in 2012-13 in India's GDP.

In spite of its growing share in the total GDP, a serious discrepancy between the share of services in total GDP and the correlated share of services in total employment is visible. While the contribution of the service sector in GDP increased from 34 per cent in 1970s to 54 per cent in 2010?11, in total employment the share of services sector employment changed from 15 per cent in 1972?73 to merely about 26.67 per cent per cent in 2009?10. It was due to this a large section of workers remained in primary sector (rural agriculture). There are some dissimilarity within the services sector with regard to the contribution of different subsectors to employment and GDP.

Research Methodology

Statement of Problem: 70 per cent of rural population of India i.e., 83.3 Crore of people out of total population of 121crore are dependent on traditional agricultural practices and living obsolete way of life. Where the contribution towards GDP from this population is merely 15 per cent as compared to Service sector with 25.3 per cent employability rate and 58.84 per cent contribution in GDP. This rural population which is distributed in 6, 40,867 Villages of India constitutes the Bottom of Pyramid. This bottom of pyramid is the most neglected areas by corporate and business organizations. Inspite of several government efforts we are still lacking behind in finding a concrete solution this problem.

Scope of Study: The suggestions of Research can be Implemented in 6, 40,867 Villages of India in collaboration with Micro Finance Institutions, SHG and Independent Inclusive Market teams. 70 per cent of rural population will benefit from this in terms of entrepreneurship, employment, self dependence and increased per capita income. This will also dwindle the Rural to Urban migration.

Data Collection Method: This research paper is based on an extensive secondary research by analyzing different research papers, journals, articles, government reports, consultancies reports and research organization's projected numbers.

Strategic Marketing Tool: Inclusive Marketing

Inclusive marketing: This is a new concept which goes much beyond Bottom of Pyramid which looks at the poor not only as consumers but also as producers/suppliers of goods and services. This approach extends assurance to add economic importance to goods and services contributed by the poor. Therefore poverty can be impacted positively. In India ITC's E-choupal is a model example of inclusive marketing. Its business model ensures that farmers as producers get desirable value for their produced goods and services. Once their incomes are increased the model then utilize the same channel that was created for acquiring, produce to propel relevant goods and services required by the farmers as consumers. Through the development of reverse distribution channels, the corporates and Government needs to come together to promote inclusive marketing and grow the size of the rural pie rather than companies fighting with each other to grab share of the limited pie.

It is noticeable that Rural India is the largest segment of the Indian market and companies are targeting to be the service provider for the same. Companies are now benchmarking against rural because the latter is bigger in size. It was visible that rural marketing got dominated by its on in the recent developments in the country. But now the time is calling to give an attention to the Population falling under Bottom of Pyramid.

Rural Marketing and Social Marketing are already well studies and exploited also they have proved to be big business opportunities for corporates and therefore still continue to earn the exceptional attention by government and corporates. Currently in the thread line there is a much needed call to upgrade the standard of Rural India; therefore there is a need to deepen the roots to reach this enormous population constituting the Bottom of Pyramid.

There is a need to develop the Inclusive Markets for this section of population. Though inclusive marketing is not a well developed idea in the market but it will be cresting a standalone status very soon. Simply because 650Miliion of population each earning less than a 1$ collectively accounts to 30% of the India's Consumption - is the reason to why Inclusive Marketing is still at an Introducer Stage. But this population represents 165 billion dollar market in India. Consequently not astonish, that not many companies have been able to unbolt the potential of this low income market. The actual challenge is that though the total market is vast, the per capita income is a meagerly Rs 35 per day. Like other marketing approaches glance at the poor as consumers only, it cannot be anticipated to increase their incomes nor reduce poverty. The challenge for social sector is to increase the income level of the millions of poor occupied in the handlooms, handicrafts, dairy and other related sectors. Professional marketing support is lacking with these promotional agencies and hence is unable to help the poor get better value for products made by them. Here 'Inclusive Marketing's an approach that comes into focus which looks at the poor not only as consumers but also as producers. With a promise to add economic value to goods and services contributed by the poor this approach offers support to this huge mass of population.

Contribution of Marketing for the poor : Indian Government poverty reduction programs treat poor as beneficiaries who need a liberal dose of subsidies and grants for their income generating practices, so government assume that poor are unable to help themselves. But this traditional approach has not resulted in sustainable solutions because activities collapse as the funding is withdrawn. But on the other hand with a market based approach government can focuses on the poor as consumers and also producers and on competence that can make markets more inclusive, competitive and efficient so that Bottom of Pyramid can benefit from them. This market oriented approach recognizes that only sustainable solutions can be mounted to fulfill the needs of the 650 million poor in the country. The Corporates use marketing as an effective tool to initially understand the needs of consumers and then extend appropriate products and services to fulfill their need at reasonable prices. This effective marketing tool can be used to help increase income level of the poor and empower them. Involving poor in the free market system: India with an impressive growth of 7-8% GDP is witnessing a significant improvement in physical infrastructure such as warehousing, road connectivity, transport, tele-connectivity and IT, has opened up many new opportunities for the people. But Bottom of Pyramid does not benefit from it as it is not integrated into the market economy. Like in Labor Market, two third of the labor force constitute Bottom of Pyramid segment. They earn very low wages and do not get permanent work. Recent market studies have identified Retail, Construction, Healthcare and Tourism as high growth sectors. Millions of workers can be absorbed by these organized sectors alone provided their skills are updated at higher income levels and better employment benefits.

India's fastest growing services sector which contributes to 60% of total GDP if provides Bottom of Pyramid population with employment opportunities the contribution of service sector will be effected more positively. Like plumbers, electricians, domestic servants and other service providers living in urban slums, if they form themselves into marketing collectives they can negotiate better rates for their services and earn a better living. They can also aim at providing their services to large contractors and builders in an organized way and thus enter the organized sector of the economy. The swift spread of Information Technology will also promise greater inclusion of the poor in the market as they can now access the market information beforehand which was earlier represented as reserve of the rich and powerful. Like the poor can now access prices of commodities in different agricultural -markets (Mandis) through the new innovative, transparent electronic exchanges or receive this information through SMS on mobiles.

The case of AMUL is an excellent example of milk production by millions of individual dairy farmers and processing and marketing centrally under the strong AMUL brand. Corporates also stand to gain by engaging with the poor as they can get skilled manpower for their flourishing businesses and aggregated supply of raw materials and other produce.

Solution to Poverty-Inclusive Marketing: The gap between rich and poor has only widened since economic reforms were set in motion in 1991, and the absolute numbers of poor has not declined significantly. Extra efforts will therefore be needed to have to enhance the incomes of the poor by using inclusive marketing approaches like Public -Private Partnership, Micro-Finance Model, which will offer benefits to all stakeholders. Such equitable, market based models are expected to be sustainable as they utilize the best strengths of each partner. Considering inclusive marketing as a part of market development strategy will result in higher business growth as Bottom of Pyramid will sound for rising income level which will translate to higher business growth for companies and also can help empower the poor economically.

ITCs e choupal and Project Shakti that was co created by HUL with MART are examples of accomplishing PPP models. Like in Project Shakti, the Self Help Group women benefit because of the additional income they earn from this business, where the company market and sell their brands to remote villages which were not possible earlier because of high distribution costs. This has helped the government in achieving its objective of reducing poverty by creating more livelihoods and NABARD has benefited because the loan off take has gone up. The Rural Business Hubs of the government like HP Rasoi Ghar and Dhristee IT kiosks are some new initiatives that have enhanced the practice of inclusive marketing. Micro-finance model is one of the PPP initiatives that are successful in achieving the scale and sustainability because of the active involvement of the different stake holders - the poor themselves, governments, financial institutions and NGO's.

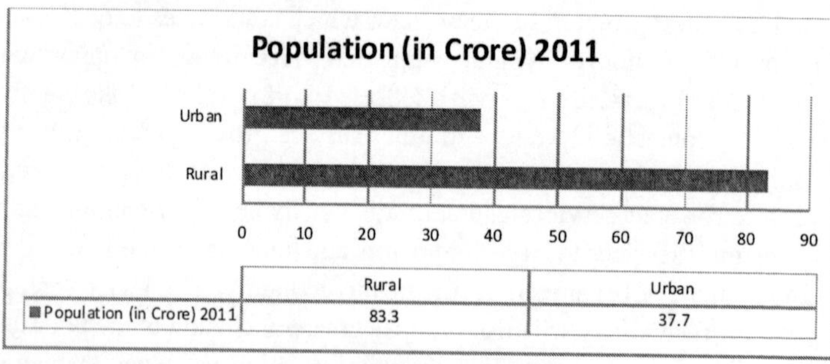

Data Analysis *Fig. 1. Population of India in*

Source: Census India 2011

Rural - Urban Distribution: 68.84 per cent and 31.16 per cent.

Figure1. In 2011 Rural population is 83.3 Crore as compared to urban population. This shows that more people are residing in Rural Area and this population is mainly dependent on Agricultural Activities.

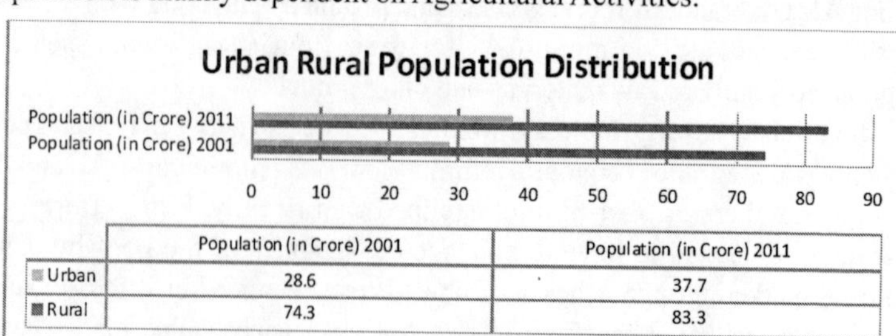

Fig. 2. Urban Rural Population Distribution

Source: Census India 2011

Figure2. There is a significant rise in population from 2001 to 2011 both in Rural India and Urban India both. This rising population calls for potential growth solutions.

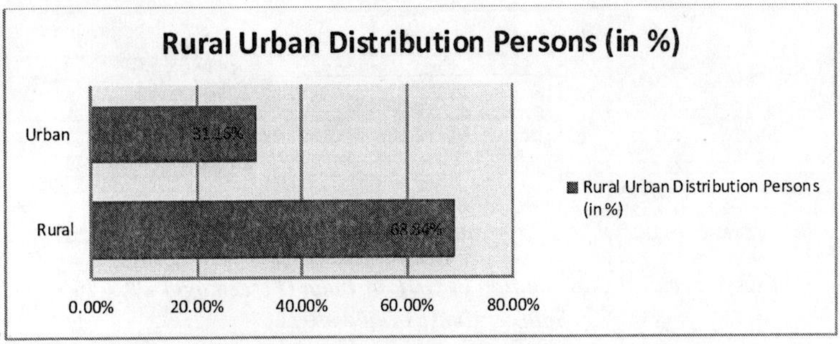

Fig. 3. Rural Urban Distribution Persons (in per cent)

Source: Census India 2011

For the first time since Independence, the absolute increase in Population is more in urban areas that in rural areas:

- Rural - Urban distribution: 68.84 per cent and 31.16 per cent
- Level of urbanization increased from 27.81 per cent in 2001 Census to 31.16 per cent in 2011 Census
- The proportion of rural population declined from 72.19 per cent to 68.84 per cent

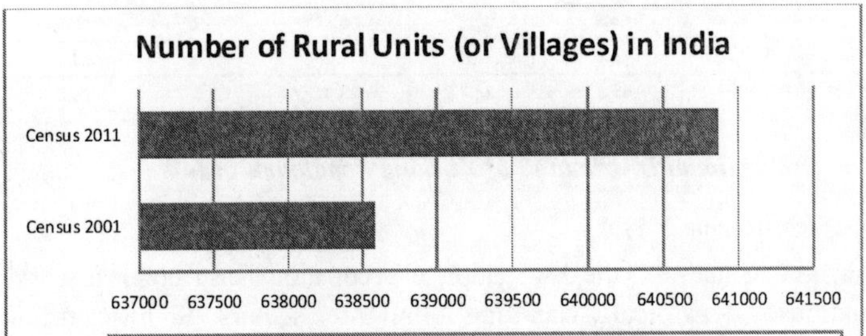

	Census 2001	Census 2011
Series1	638588	640867

Fig. 4. Number of Rural Units (or Villages) in India

Source: Census India 2011

Figure 4. From 2001 to 2011 there is a significant increase in number of villages of India from 638,588 to 640,867. These increasing number of Village units along with increasing population calls for attention and sustainable development to at least meet their requirement.

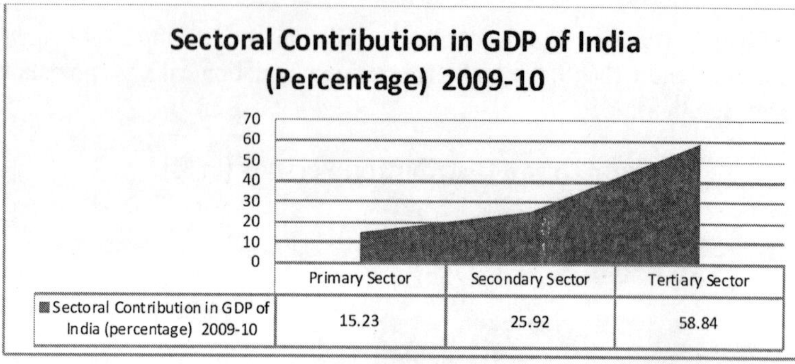

Fig. 5. Sectoral Contribution in GDP of India (Percentage) 2009-10
Source: Census India 2011

Figure 5: Sectoral Contribution of Service sector is Maximum in Indian Economy with a contribution of 58.84 per cent, followed by secondary sector with 25.92 per cent contribution and least by Primary sector at 15.23 per cent which includes the people constituting Bottom of Pyramid.

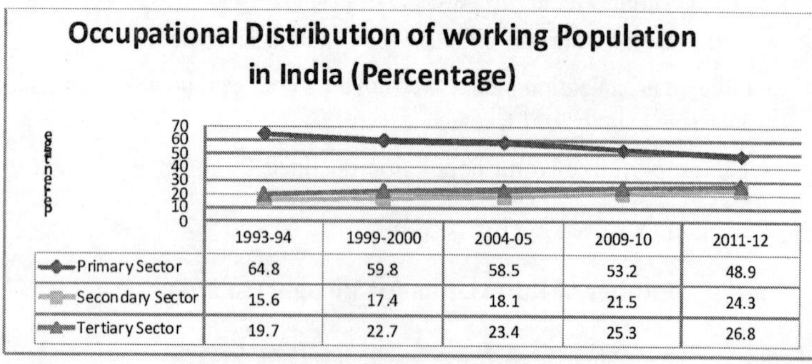

Fig. 6. Occupational Distribution of Working Population in India (Percentage)

Source: Census India 2011

Figure6. Since 1993 the distribution of Occupational distribution is working populations is dynamically changing for all three sectors. Significant fall in Primary sector from 64.8 % to 48.9% calls for attention towards the progressive development in this sector. Service sector being the most promising sector for the economy has shown significant rise from 19.7% to 26.8% after LPG reforms.

Out of the total of 1210.2 million population in India, the size of Rural population is 833.1 million (or 68.84% of the Total Population)

- Urban population 377.1 million (or 31.16%)
- During 2001 - 2011 the population of the country increased by 181.4 million

- Increase in Rural areas: 90.4 million
- Increase in Urban areas: 91.0 million

Findings and Recommendations

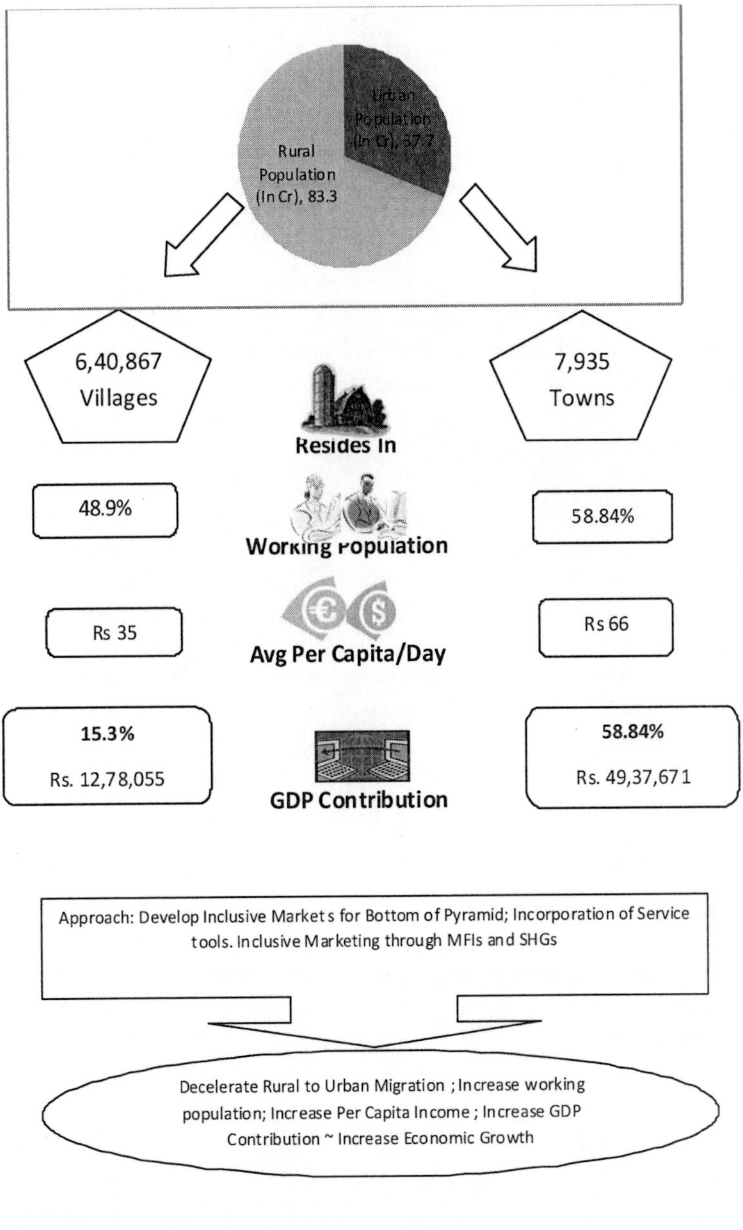

The Bottom of the Pyramid Stands for the most thronged group of people with an income of less than 2 dollars per day. There are different various ways of grouping but according to the most wide-extending grouping, four billion people fill the major area and live at the bottom of the pyramid. Most of the economic activities in India target the one fourth of the population that lies in the top of the pyramid. The remaining four billion people are ignored and neglected in all the performing economic activities. And the produced goods can't reach the mass market in appropriate conditions. Therefore, there is a scenario for completely neglected population, while goods and services are developed for the other. The concern is to targeting the first group and ensures that they exploit these services as well. That is the Poor who are concluded as consumers and also producers should get the access to goods and services produced by multinational companies.

Conclusion

Inclusive markets are markets that extend choices and opportunities to the poor (and other excluded groups) as wage earners, producers and consumers. Inclusive markets thus create jobs and affordable goods and services needed by the poor. Together disadvantaged groups as customers on the demand side and hardworking entrepreneurs from different levels of the value chain on the supply side. To give a simple definition we can say that inclusive markets produce with the poor, for the poor, including disabled people too. The underprivileged group is comprised of people who can't have access to goods and services and those to whom these are not made available. Business model aiming to make these people productive and to raise their living standards and purchasing power to turn them into buyers and customers from a demand outlook will be an innovative approach by Inclusive Marketing.

It is lucrative to develop business with the poor and to produce services, oriented towards them as this will prosper the company and society both. Inclusive Marketing is about reach, engage and convert the Bottom of Pyramid into producers as well as consumers.

Acknowledgement

I am grateful to my supervisor Dr.M.S.Khan, who gave me moral support and guided in different matters regarding the topic, he had been very kind and patient while suggesting me the outlines of this Research. Without his guidance and support this research would not have been possible. I thank him for his overall supports.

References

- Kashyap.P .Demystifying Rural Market(2011,Ocotober).Retrieved from http://martrural.com/wp-content/uploads/2014/08/MART-Sir-talks-20th-year-1.pdf
- India Budget 2013-14.(2014,December 27). Retrieved from http://indiabudget.nic.in/es2013-14/echap- 10.pdf
- Economic Forecasts (2014, December). Retrieved from http://www.tradingeconomics.com/india/forecast
- 60 per cent of rural India lives on less than Rs 35 a day (2012, May 4).Economic Times. Retrieved from http://articles.economictimes.indiatimes.com/2012-05-04/news/31559329_1_rural-areas-mpce-nsso-survey.
- Contribution of the primary sector to the national income in India (2014, (November) Retrieved from http://www.quora.com/contribution-of-the-primary-sector-to-the-national-income-in-India.
- Census of India 2011 (2011,July). Retrieved from http://censusindia.gov.in/2011-prov-results/paper2/data_files/india/Rural_Urban_2011.pdf
- T.S. Papola and Sahu.P (2012, March) Growth and Structure of Employment In India. Retrieved from http://isidev.nic.in/pdf/ICSSR_TSP_PPS. pdf
- https://ipec.gspia.pitt.edu/Portals/7/Papers/Aprita%20Mukherjee.pdf
- Indian Economic Survey 2013-14 Key Highlights (2014, July) Retrieved from http://www.kpmg.com/IN/en/services/Tax/FlashNews/India-Economic -Survey-2013-14%E2%80%93Key-Highlights.pdf
- India: Distribution of gross domestic product (GDP) across economic sectors from 2003 to 2013 (2015,January) Retrieved from http://www.statista.com/statistics/271329/distribution-of-gross-domestic-product-gdp-across-economic-sectors-in-india/
- Chand, S. (2014, December) Important Changes in Composition of National Income. Retrieved from http://www.yourarticlelibrary.com/economics/what-are-the-important-changes-in-composition-of-national-income/3050.
- Kaur.G, Bordoloi.S &Rajesh.R (2008) An Empirical Investigation of the Inter-Sectoral Linkages in India. Retrieved from http://www.rbi.org.in/Scripts/bs_viewcontent.aspx?Id=2107.
- Dalvi.A (2014, December) Indian economy and sectorial contribution. Retrieved from http://www.slideshare.net/ammardalvi/indian-economy-and-sectorial-presentation.

- Retrieved from http://www.mea.gov.in/articles-in- indian-media.htm?dtl/23611/Economic +Survey +2014+ India+ has+ second+ fastest+growing+services
- Interrelationship between Primary, Secondary and Tertiary Sectors (2008, November 21 Retrieved from http://ortho-neity.blogspot.in/2008/11/interrelationship-between-primary.html
- Service Sector in India report by Indian Brand Equity Foundation (2014, November). Retrieved from http://www.ibef.org/industry/services.aspx
- NIOS.Economics (2015, January) Ch.10. Sectoral Aspects of Indian Economy. Retrieved from http://www.nios.ac.in/media/documents/sececocour/english/chapter-20.pdf.
- Jain, V. and Saini, B. IJRIM Volume 2, Issue 11 (November 2012) Contribution Of Rural Marketing in the Inclusive growth of India. Retrieved from http://www.euroasiapub.org/IJRIM/nov2012/9.pdf

30

Exhibition Marketing—A Sustainable Business Practice: An Indian Perspective

Vinod Kumar & Rajiv Kumar

Abstract

Exhibition marketing is a PR initiative by corporate sector which require considerable capital investment to innovate, launch, promote and market the products and services within the entire business chain and industry at large. The basic objective of participation in exhibitions is public and social welfare by providing a common platform to industry and academia at a low cost which otherwise would not have been possible, while achieving the mutually profitable relationships for all stakeholders in different industries. The exhibition industry has a huge economic and social impact on business, the benefits of exhibition industry are quite high and it offers a unique marketing medium to participants. In order to sustain in this competitive world, we are required to provide customer value, satisfaction, mutually beneficial deals, international participation, innovative products and services & single window mechanism etc. Corporate have understood the power of exhibitions as one stop solution and sustainable business practice covering the entire supply chain not only at national but also at international level. Therefore we are focusing upon what this Indian exhibition industry all about, its participants, its categories, advantages, and its future, acting as a sustainable business practice in this competitive environment.

Keywords: Exhibition Industry, tradeshows, trade fairs, exhibitions, marketing

Background Connecting Sustainability and Exhibitions

Sustainable marketing is about a balanced approach to economic activity, environmental responsibility (reuse, recycle and reduce) and social progress referred to as triple bottom line for (3ps) people, planet and profit. Sustainable marketing is the adoption of sustainable business practices that creates better business, better relationship and a better world (www. sustainablemarketing. com); exhibitions are the best place for the achieving the above mentioned objectives at a lower cost. Therefore Author of this chapter has taken exhibition marketing as a sustainable business practice in India, which has a positive social and economic impact. During the past decade, the Indian Exhibition Industry has been the choice of corporate sector and performed an important economic function for our nation to share, grow, educate, network and improve relationship including buying and selling of products and services. There are several objectives to participate in exhibitions for different players involved in the supply chain management process including customers. As a sustainable business practice, participating in exhibitions helps in several ways such as: Optimizing performance, CRM, Financial sustainability, growth reduce carbon foot print etc. Therefore, let's understand what exhibitions are all about, its participants, advantages, sustainability, and its future with industry examples:

2. Definitions of Exhibitions

Exhibition is a service circulation process in social reproduction for the smooth social mobility of goods. It is a social service activity that delivers and exchanges information through visual display under certain time and space conditions in accordance with the social needs so as to allow viewers to make purchases and sales, investment decisions, or to learn and soon (Xiaoming, 2012).

Kumar & Meenakshi (2010) explains that exhibition is the only promotional tool that brings buyers, sellers and the competitors in a commercial setting. Exhibitions are usually designed to create a form of mass hysteria and attract lot of media attention which helps in attracting more customers. Exhibitions are very expensive and there is a lot of expenditure in logistics.

Gaur & Saggere (2009) defines Exhibitions as presentation of goods and services at a common location for the purpose of either sale or display which may be commercial in nature or may be a non commercial display of rare arts, ancient artifacts or other skills.

Karunakaran (2009) mentions core concept in exhibitions is presentation of goods and services at a common location for the purpose of display and sale.

Kazmi & Batra (2009) defines a trade fair or exhibition is a temporary exhibit, generally held at some interval in a major city. Brieter & Milman (2006) describe Exhibitions and Trade shows are synonymously used with the basic meaning of exhibiting the products and services.

Exhibitions are not only an event that presents and showcases a set of new products but also an event that provides several activities, performances, entertainment and other dynamic activities for the exclusive purpose of achieving the different goals of an organization. Exhibitions are impermanent and time sensitive marketing event organized by an individual or corporation where several activities takes place like direct marketing, personal selling, test marketing, product display and launch, sales promotion, publicity, channel development, trade development, networking, information, knowledge, education, performances, relationship building etc. (Alles, 1989).

Exhibitions are gatherings where entire businesses chain performs business related activities on a relatively low cost per contact basis. Researcher says technically exhibition has a broader meaning than trade show (Browning & Adams, 1988).

3. Exhibitions - A Sustainable Platform to Deal

Purandeswari (2013) describes that Exhibition Industry can be a powerful and effective tool for improving the standard of living of people by creating a huge number of jobs and stimulating growth in a wide range of sectors. What's required is a public private partnership to ensure that exhibitions cover the length and breadth of the country bringing benefits to maximum number of people.

Singh (2013) mentions that Exhibition Industry in India, holds great opportunities for companies to generate business through quality networking. The only thing we require is right infrastructure, regulatory body and government support. Also, there is a lack of talent and hence, skill management is required in the exhibition industry in India.

Rittichainuwat & Mair (2012) through his research paper in consumer travel exhibitions explains the importance of exhibitions and major factors that motivates visitors to attend these exhibitions. These factors are purchasing, ongoing information search, networking, educational activities and low entrance fees. However, many people may envision an exhibition as simply quiet place where new products are displayed.

Blythe (2002) reports that Exhibitions are considered a universal marketing tool that helps in achieving organizational objectives and improve market size i.e. existing and potential customers. Rice & Almossawi (2002) reports that consumers are willing to participate in exhibitions therefore domestic and international exhibitions are going greater in numbers. McCabe (2001) discusses that Exhibition Industry provides various options such as promotional opportunities, channel development, potential to make and execute business contracts etc. Bonoma (1983) argue about the potential of exhibitions as a marketing tool that not only help in product launches, latest state of the art technical advancements but also provide direct marketing opportunities and a platform for personal selling.

4. Indian Exhibition Industry: Who does what?

Chapman (1987) describes there are number of players involved in the Exhibition Industry which are put together as a hand with five fingers and a thumb. Exhibitors are considered the thumb. Show organizers are the first finger. The thumb pays most of the invoices. Show organizers with a team of managers gather the audience. The other fingers of this hand serve both of us and collectively, we reach out to serve the visitors.

The following are the participants in the Exhibition Industry:

1. Exhibitors
2. Show organizers
3. Stand designers and fabricators
4. Consultants and advertising agencies
5. Show service contractors
6. Logistics companies
7. Facility managers &
8. Industry associations
9. Government
10. General Visitors
11. Business Visitors
12. Consumers, Users, Customers

These are natural alliances. The exhibitors in the industry are actually dependent upon stand designers and fabricators for their branding and marketing motives and infrastructure development as well. They know each other very well and understanding the requirements or objectives in hand. Show organizers regularly work with facilitating agencies and infrastructural teams to achieve customer satisfaction. Logistics team is responsible for all the movement within the exhibition and support exhibitors and other participants from all parts of the world.

5. Advantages of Exhibitions

Attendance at an exhibition helps visitors in number of ways like: Collecting information on new products, view particular products, observes companies, and makes contacts (Rosson & serinhaus et al.,1995); reduce cognitive dissonance after making a purchase (Godar & O'Connor, 2001); and collect information for future purchases (Munuera & Ruiz, 1999).

Herbig, O'Hara & Palumbo (1997) mentioned Exhibition provide advantages such as product launch, publicity, promotion, CRM, marketing intelligence and research and improvement of corporate morale. Trade Shows were regarding important marketing communication tool yet there are few studies that have examined the effectiveness of this medium. This might be due to difficulty of isolating the various factors involved in successful promotion, the great variety of types of exhibitions or well established attitudes on the part of exhibitors and non exhibitors (Blythe, 1999).

Sharland & Balogh (1996) indicated that Trade Shows offer an excellent environment for non selling activities such as information exchange, relationship building, and channel partner assessment there its not just sales revenue that make sense for companies to participate. (Gopalakrishna, Lilien, Williams & Sequiera. 1995; Kerin and Cron, 1987) have explained Exhibitions Industry represent major sales promotion opportunities for B2B and B2C segment. Companies have lakhs or crores of rupees as a budget on exhibition participation, identifying prospects and converting them into final customers through personal selling, introducing new or modified products, testing new products, launching new products and servicing existing and potential customers (Waugh, 1995)

6. Sustainability and Exhibitions:

Developing a sustainable business is about balancing financial, social and environmental priorities. Sustainable marketing services, involves the following five key elements:

(a) Embed sustainable business practices into your business strategy through SMART objectives
(b) Deliver marketing activities that create ongoing growth through right segmentation, branding, collaborations, permission marketing and CRM etc.
(c) Promote and grow business through implementing marketing plan, marketing strategies and branding strategies
(d) Influence other businesses to adopt sustainable business practice through policy guidelines
(e) Minimize the use of resources in your day to day business operations through undertaking activities such as using recycled paper, environment friendly inks, online communications, virtual communications etc.

(As per Wikipedia) Sustainable event management (also known as event greening) is the process used to produce an event with particular concern for environmental, economic and social issues. Exhibition industry is focusing upon these sustainable marketing initiatives mentioned above. (Schueneman, 2012) White sheets and brochures for exhibitors' products and services are increasingly offered electronically while participants navigate their trade show experience with a mobile app built for the show - design and build one app or hand out 10,000 maps. The advantage is clear. Even the displays themselves are potentially greener with companies offering eco-friendly booths made from recycled material for purchase or rent. Green meeting industry council (GMIC) in discussions with the United States Environmental Protection Agency (US EPA) developed a set of voluntary sustainability standards incorporated into APEX, or the Accepted Practices Exchange, an initiative of the Convention Industry Council (CIC). There are nine "sectors" at the core of the Sustainable Meeting Standards. These nine sectors encompass the entire footprint of a trade or consumer event:

1. Transportation
2. Onsite Office
3. Meeting Venue
4. Food & Beverage
5. Exhibits
6. Destinations
7. Communications
8. Accommodations
9. Audio-Visual

Within each sector, eight impact areas are targeted:

1. Staff and environmental policy
2. Communications
3. Waste
4. Energy
5. Air Quality
6. Water
7. Procurement
8. Community Partners

The UK events industry took the global lead on sustainable management practices when it launched the British Standard 8901 standard in late 2007 to give organizers, venues and suppliers a means of delivering events more sustain ably through management strategies, evaluation, reporting, communication and training. Although sustainability disciplines like BS8901 are being adopted, widespread take-up of it and other sustainability measurements will come down to cost, Wellman claimed. ISO20121 has been created and implemented by an international committee of event and standards experts.

Therefore, as per Author of this chapter, a lot is happening into exhibition industry and participants are considering it as a platform to grow economically and socially while maintaining good environmental practices. The author has described how exhibitions have been considered a sustainable marketing initiative or practice in the next section with the help of industry examples of sustainability.

7. What the Future Holds for Indian Exhibition Industry

Bhatia (2013) explains that Indian Exhibition Industry is one of the fastest growing Industries. Talking about the noticeable trends in the coming years, Joji George (MD, UBM India Pvt. Ltd.) Points out, a significant trend that we see is the focus on building more effective onsite experiences. Adding to the same, Darryl Dasilva (CEO, MMI India Pvt. Ltd.) Says, Business have already realized the importance of exhibitions and are actively participating in shows pertaining to their domain. Both (George & Dasilva) feel that the key to success in the coming times will be the state of the art venues, single window clearance and easy movement of exhibitions thus every stage is important from start to finish in Exhibition Industry and each team has to work hand in hand and coordinate well for success of the show. Therefore, exhibitions will never loose its charm till the time its generate ROI, customer value, environmental welfare, social welfare, economic welfare and mutually beneficial relationship. At last, Exhibitions will continue to be a sustainable marketing tool for all the participants of exhibition industry.

8. Exhibition Industry: Examples of sustainable Practices

Varathan Anbu, CEO Bangalore International Exhibition Centre (India) February 2014: "Sustainability, Competiveness and Inclusiveness have been an integral part of the BIEC journey. The design and construction of BIEC has been in line with the best practices of Sustainability, which has enabled us to become a 'Green' venue. Continuing with these efforts, we have embarked on the path of environmental management through the application of ISO 14001 principles effective from 2013. We have been partnering with stakeholders i.e. Clients, Service Providers and Industry for creating awareness of sustainable practices in Exhibitions in India. Our endeavor has been to have an inclusive and focused approach which can make the industry truly green".

GL events Group has adopted a global strategy for sustainable development, spearheaded by three programmes: Think Green (environmental issues), Think Local (societal issues) and Think People (labour and employee-related issues), all contributing to daily advances, highlighted by the quantitative data published in our "Corporate Social Responsibility" report.

(UFI, Sustainable development) Claude Membrez, Managing Director of Palexpo (Switzerland), January 2014: "Palexpo has been on a sustainable development path for some 25 years. We switched to electricity from renewable sources in 1989 and began sorting out our waste in 1992. We get our heat from a nearby plant. A share of our energy is produced on our own roof which hosts the largest photovoltaic unit in Switzerland. Yet, there is more than this to sustainability: by also focusing on the social side of our activity, it provides a very powerful tool to thoroughly improve our overall practices. When acting to preserve the planet for future generations, the fairness of the working conditions is paramount. Ultimately, sustainability is about creating a race to the top."

Figure 2 - Sustainability development at palexpo

Source: Sustainable development at Palexpo. Retrieved September 26, 2014 from http://www.palexpo.com/en/Palexpo/Developpement/Developpement.php.

9. Conclusion

Exhibitions have several objectives to participate, however the primary purpose is to encourage business interactions. As the size of scope of exhibition in India is getting larger and more entertainment activities are being added, therefore its not just business visitors who are interested to attend the exhibition but also the general public as well is interested to experience a gamut of activities while attending exhibitions. Thus, exhibitions are considered to be most effective and sustainable marketing medium to survive in this competitive world as exhibitions just not only ensures the presence of entire supply chain within specific industry but also provide several opportunities at low cost to the entire society and nation at large. Therefore the author of this study has emphasized upon exhibition industry, & its advantages to corporate while gaining value, satisfaction and providing welfare to public, society and economy at large through this medium of communication. The future of exhibition industry is quite bright however with the advent of internet and other technological innovations its very easy to get information at the click of a button but it is very difficult to meet the entire industry face to face at one go including customers, as in case of physical exhibitions rather being virtual, however virtual practices are being followed for environmental welfare with the help of technology. Therefore, exhibitions will never loose its charm till the time its generate ROI, customer value, environmental welfare, social welfare, economic welfare and mutually beneficial relationship. At last, Exhibitions will continue to be a sustainable marketing tool for all the participants of exhibition industry.

References

- Alles, A. (1989). Exhibitions: A key to effective marketing (2nd edn). Southampton, The camelot press, 1 - 2.
- Bhatia, N. (2013, April 25). Indian exhibition industry - what the future holds. The Economic Times, p. 17.
- Blythe, J. (1999). Visitor and exhibitor expectations and outcomes at trade exhibitions. Marketing Intelligence and Planning, 17 (2).
- Blythe, J. (2002). Using trade fairs in key account management. Industrial Marketing Management, 31, 627-635.
- Brieter, D., & Milman, A. (2006). Attendees' needs and service priorities in a large convention centre: Application of the importance performance theory. Tourism Management, 27, 1364 - 1330.
- Browning, J. M., & Adams, R. J. (1988). Trade shows: An effective promotional tool for the small industrial business. Journal of Small Business Management, 26 (4), 31 - 36.
- CEIR (1994). A guide to the U.S. exposition industry. Center for exhibition industry research.
- CEIR (1996). The power of exhibitions II: Summary results: What successful exhibitors do to get results. Bethesda MD, Center for exhibition industry research.

- Chapman, E. Jr. (1987). Exhibit marketing. Singapore, McGraw-Hill Book Co., 253 - 254.
- Cherunilam, F. (2009). Industrial marketing: Text and cases (2nd edn.). Mumbai, Himalaya publishing house pvt. Ltd., 177 - 178.
- Convention Industry Council (CIC): About the standards. Retrieved September 26, 2014 from http://www.conventionindustry.org/standardspractices/APEXASTM/AboutAPEXASTM.aspx.
- Datta, D., & Datta, M. (2010). Advertising & sales promotion. Delhi, Vrinda publications (P) Ltd. 617.
- Exhibition News - Being sustainable. Retrieved September 26, 2014 from http://www.exhibitionnews.co.uk/featuredetails/98/being-sustainable.
- Gaur, S. S. & Saggere, S. V. (2009). Event Marketing Management. Noida, Vikas publishing house pvt. Ltd., 85.
- Godar, S. H., & O' Connor, P. J. (2001). Same time next Year: Buyer trade shows motives. Industrial Marketing Management, 30, 77 - 86.
- Gopalkrishna, S., Lilien, G. L., Williams, J. D., & Sequeria, J. K. (1995). Do trade shows pay off? Journal of Marketing, 59 (3), 75 - 83.
- Herbig, P., O'Hara, B., & Palumbo, F. (1997). Differences between trade show exhibitors and non exhibitors. Journal of Business and Industrial Marketing, 12 (6), 368 - 382.
- Karunakaran, K. (2009). Marketing management: Text and cases in Indian context (2nd edn.). Mumbai, Himalaya publishing house pvt. Ltd., 392.
- Kazmi, S., & Batra, S. K. (2009). Advertising & sales promotion (3rd edn.). New Delhi, Excel Books, 606.
- Kerin, R. A., & Cron, W. L. (1987). Assessing trade show functions and performance: An exploratory study. Journal of Marketing, 51 (3), 87 - 94.
- Kumar, A., & Meenakshi, N. (2010). Marketing management. Noida, Vikas publishing house pvt. Ltd., 427 - 430
- Munuera, J. L, & Ruiz, S. (1999). Trade fairs as services: a look at attendees objectives in Spain. Journal of Business Research, 44 (1), 17 - 24.
- Purandeswari, D. (2013, April 25). Exhibition industry, crucial for India's growth. The Economic Times, p. 15.
- Rice, G., & Almossawi, M. (2002). A study of exhibitor firms at an Arabian gulf trade show: Goals, selection, criteria and perceived problems. Journal of Global Marketing, 15 (3/4).

- Rittichainuwat, B., & Mair, J. (2012). Visitor Attendance motivations at consumer travel exhibitions. Tourism Management, 33, 1236 - 1244.
- Rosson, P. J., & Serinhaus, F. H. R. (1995). Visitor and exhibition interaction at Industrial trade fairs. Journal of Business Research, 32, 81 - 90.
- Schueneman, T. (2012). Green Meetings: International sustainability standards for the convention and exhibition industry. Retrieved September 26, 2014 from http://www.triplepundit.com/2012/12/green-meetings-international-sustainability-standards-convention-exhibition-industry.
- Singh, V. (2013, April 25). Indian exhibition industry - paving the way forward. The Economic Times, p. 17.
- Sustainability guidelines for the Singapore MICE industry. Retrived September 26, 2014 from http://www.yoursingapore.com/content/dam/mice/en/whysingapore/PDF/STB_sustainability_guidelines_manual_november_2013.pdf.
- Sustainable development at Palexpo. Retrieved September 26, 2014 from http://www.palexpo.com/en/Palexpo/Developpement/Developpement.php.
- Sustainable marketing. Retrieved September 26, 2014 from http://www.sustainablemarketing.com.au/what-is-sustainable-marketing
- UFI: The Global association of exhibition industry. Sustainable development. Retrieved September 26, 2014 from http://www.ufi.org/Public/Default.aspx?Clef_SITESMAPS=105&Clef_SITESMAPS=666.
- Waugh, T. A. (1995). Trade show can create good leads. The CPA Journal, 65 (11), 14.
- Wikipedia, the free encyclopedia. Sustainable event management. Retrieved September 26, 2014 from http://en.wikipedia.org/wiki/Sustainable_event_management.
- Xiaoming, L. (2012). An economic analysis of the specialization and marketization of convention and exhibition industry. International Business and Management, 5 (1), 86 - 92.

31

Quality of Services and Customer Loyalty: A Study of Private Banks in Delhi and NCR Through Servqual

Esha Jain & Manish Madan

Abstract

Aim of Study: The main aim of study is to explore various dimensions of service quality in the services provided by private banks, to determine the significant relationship between the service quality dimensions and the customer satisfaction and also to determine the relationship between customer satisfaction and loyalty towards the private banks of Delhi and NCR.

Research Objectives:The broad objectives of study are to identify the factors of service quality dimensions, to analyze various service quality dimensions of services offered by the private banks, and to find the significant relationship between the customer satisfaction and loyalty.

Research Methodology: The study is explorative in nature. A systemized and organized study was done to reach the desired objectives of the study. The responses obtained from the respondents using services offered by the private banks in Delhi and NCR are analyzed using various statistical techniques. This study is restricted to users of private banks in Delhi and NCR. The importance of this study is that it displays the relationship between various service quality dimensions,and customersatisfaction with their loyalty to the bank.

Significance of Study: As far as the significance of the study is concerned, the significance of the study lies in the fact that in the last few years the service provided by private banks has been deteriorated and that leads to the dissatisfaction among the customer and their loyalty.

Key Words: Service Quality, SERVQUAL, Customer Satisfaction, Customer Loyalty, Private Banks.

Introduction

This study is an in-depth empirical investigation that seeks to compare consumer expectations to perceptions in the delivery of service within private banks in the Delhi. It has as its aim to develop a useful instrument to evaluate service quality by comparing consumer expectations to their perceptions of delivered service. An additional purpose is to determine bank chief executive officers' ability to predict consumer expectations in the area of service delivery.The main findings of the research built upon and extended the research by Ittner and Larcker (1996) which noted that the three prime components of customer satisfaction revolved around three specific antecedents-perceived quality, perceived value, and customer expectations, the study strongly reinforced and confirmed the importance of the three antecedents.

Indian banking isthe lifeline of the nation and its people. Banking has helped indeveloping the vital sectors of the economy and usher in a new dawn ofprogress on the Indian horizon. Thesector hastranslated the hopes andaspirations of millions of people into reality.But to do so, it has had to controlmiles and miles of difficult terrain, suffer the indignities of foreign rule and thepangs of partition. Today, Indian banks can confidently compete with modernbanks of the world.

Service quality is an approach to manage business processes in order to ensure full satisfaction of the customers which will help to increase competitiveness and effectiveness of the industry. Quality in service is very important especially for the growth and development of service sector business enterprises. It works as an antecedent of customer satisfaction. With the increase of the importance of service sector in the economy of Bangladesh, the measurement of service quality became important. ISO standards are one of the measurement tools of service quality, where quality is defined as the totality of features and characteristics of a product, process or service. Private Banks dealing in retail banking Industry is consequently put into lot of pressures due towards increase in global competition. Different strategies are formulated to retain the customer and the key of it is to increase the service quality level. Typically, customers perceive very little difference in the banking products offered by private banks dealing in services as any new offering is quickly matched by competitors.

Numerous researchers and scientific associations have tried and are trying to define the concept of quality based on different aspects. It is safe to say, however, that as of this day we do not have one uniform definition. Quality is objective and subjective at the same time, it can only be generalized to a limited degree, among its factors there are specifications, which can be measured; and others, that only can be appraised, quality can mean a technical-efficiency level and any departure there from (condition), it has perceivable use effects and effects that the purchaser does not consciously perceive.

Service Quality

Service quality is considered an important tool for a firm's struggle to differentiate itself from its competitors (Ladhari, 2008). The relevance of service quality to companies is emphasized here especially the fact that it offers a competitive advantage to companies that strive to improve it and hence bring customer satisfaction. Service quality has received a great deal of attention from both academicians and practitioners (Negi, 2009) and services marketing literature service quality is defined as the overall assessment of a service by the customer (Eshghi et al., 2008).(Ghylin et al., 2008) points out that, by defining service quality, companies will be able to deliver services with higher quality level presumably resulting in increased customer satisfaction. Understanding service quality must involve acknowledging the characteristics of service which are intangibility, heterogeneity and inseparability, (Parasuraman et al., 1985; Ladhari, 2008). In that way, service quality would be easily measured. In this study, service quality can be defined as the difference between customer's expectation for service performance prior to the service encounter and their perception of the service received. Customer's expectation serves as a foundation for evaluating service quality because, quality is high when performance exceeds expectation and quality is low when performance does not meet their expectation (Asubonteng et al., 1996). Expectation is viewed in service quality literature as desires or wants of customer i.e., what they feel a service provider should offer rather than would offer (http://thesis.binus.ac.id/Doc/Bab2/Bab%202_20-12_BI.pdf) (Parasuraman et al., 1988). Perceived service is the outcome of the customer's view of the service dimensions, which are both technical and functional in nature (Gronroos, 1984). The customer's total perception of a service is based on his/her perception of the outcome and the process; the outcome is either value added or quality and the process is the role undertaken by the customer (Edvardsson, 1998).(Parasuraman et al., 1988) define perceived quality as a form of attitude, related but not equal to satisfaction, and results from a consumption of expectations with perceptions of performance. Therefore, having a better understanding of customers attitudes will help know how they perceive service quality in grocery stores. (Negi, 2009) suggests that customer-perceived service quality has been given increased attention in recent years, due to its specific contribution to business competitiveness and developing satisfied customers. This makes service quality a very important construct to understand by firms by knowing how to measure it and making necessary improvements in its dimensions where appropriate especially in areas where gaps between expectations and perceptions are wide. In the context of grocery stores, we are not only interested in learning more about the factors associated to service quality perceived by customers and how service quality is measured but also provide a direction for improvement of service quality in order to bring customer satisfaction.

Banking Industry in India

The Indian banking industry has its foundations in the 18th century, and has had a varied evolutionary experience since then. The initial banks in India were primarily traders' banks engaged only in financing activities. Banking industry in the pre-independence era developed with the Presidency Banks, which were transformed into the Imperial Bank of India and subsequently into the State Bank of India. The initial days of the industry saw a majority private ownership and a highly volatile work environment. Major strides towards public ownership and accountability were made with nationalization in 1969 and 1980 which transformed the face of banking in India. The industry in recent times has recognized the importance of private and foreign players in a competitive scenario and has moved towards greater liberalization.

The banking sector in India is on a growing trend. It has vastly benefitted from the surge in disposable income of individuals in the country. There has also been a noticeable upsurge in transactions through ATMs, and also internet and mobile banking. Consequently, the different banks, viz public, private and foreign banks have invested considerably to increase their banking network and thus, their customer reach.

The banking industry in India has the potential to become the fifth largest banking industry in the world by 2020 and third largest by 2025 according to a KPMG-CII report. Over the next decade, the banking sector is projected to create up to two million new jobs, driven by the efforts of the RBI and the Government of India to integrate financial services into rural areas. Also, the traditional way of operations will slowly give way to modern technology.

The Indian banking sector is fragmented, with 46 commercial banks jostling for business with dozens of foreign banks as well as rural and co-operative lenders. State banks control 80 percent of the market, leaving relatively small shares for private rivals.

Banks have opened 7.73 crore accounts under the Pradhan Mantri Jan Dhan Yojana (PMJDY) till November 19, according to Ms Snehlata Shrivastava,

Additional Secretary, Department of Financial Services, Ministry of Finance, Government of India. Of the 77.3 million accounts, public sector banks have opened 62.1 million accounts with a total balance of Rs 4,946.03 crore (US$ 802.64 million), and have distributed RuPay debit cards to around 43 million accounts.

Total banking sector credit is anticipated to grow at a CAGR of 18.1 per cent to reach US$ 2.4 trillion by 2017. The total banking assets in India touched US$ 1.8 trillion in FY13 and are anticipated to cross US$ 28.5 trillion in FY25

Literature Review

YEAR	AUTHOR	FINDINGS
1998	Moala	Study aimed at measuring the quality of banking services provided by commercial banks of Jordan, from the point of view of the banks customers, where the study found that the actual level of banking services quality is low compared with the level of quality expected by customers in their banking services. The study recommended that the departments of commercial banks should adopt programs to develop and improve the quality of their services.
1998	Horstmann	He stated that there is a strong and positive relationship between customer satisfaction and loyalty.
2001	Newman	He found that the separation of service quality management and marketing management caused major problems in adequately satisfying the banking customers.
2001	Ryals and Payne	They noted that there was a need to tie information technology with marketing strategies to build long-term customer relationships. Another finding disclosed that CRM is more advanced in the financial services area than any other industry segment.
2003	Zarour	Study aimed at measuring the impact of the quality and price of services provided by banks to customer's satisfaction of the industrial sector in Jordan, the study found a relationship between industrial company's satisfaction, and dimensions of quality banking services, and the prices of these services. The study recommended banking departments to improve the quality of services and prices.

2006	Al-Mahiaoi	The concept quality of service is standard for a match between the actual performances of service with customer expectations for this service.
2008	Al-Mahiaoi	Satisfaction of the customer can be seen in the feelings of joy or resentment, after obtaining the service, resulting from the comparison between the actual and expected performance for the customer
2011	Mohsan	He stated that unsatisfied customer can banish more business from the organization than ten highly satisfied customers do.
2012	Tee	They found a significant positive relationship between customer satisfaction and customer loyalty. Other several studies have indeed found satisfaction to be a leading factor in determining loyalty.

Table 1: Contribution of Researchers

Broad Objectives of Study

The broad objectives of study are as follows:-

1. To explore the various services offered by private banks in Delhi and NCR
2. To establish a relationship between the service quality dimensions and satisfaction of customers.
3. To establish a relationship between customer satisfaction and loyalty of customers towards private banks.

Hypotheses of Study

The following Hypotheses were formulated as follows:-

Here HO represents Null Hypothesis and HA represents Alternative Hypothesis.

Hypothesis 1:-

H01: There is no significant relationship between service quality dimensions and customer satisfaction in banking services.

HA1: There is significant relationship between service quality dimensions and customer satisfaction in banking services.

Hypothesis 2:-

H02: There is no significant relationship between overall service quality and customer satisfaction in banking services.

HA2: There is significant relationship between overall service quality and customer satisfaction in banking services.

Hypothesis 3:-

H03: There is no significant relationship between customer satisfaction and loyalty in banking services.

HA3:There is significant relationship between customer satisfaction and loyalty in banking services.

Research Methodology

Research Design

The research design is explorative in nature. In order to collate the responses, 7- point likert's scale from strongly disagree to strongly agree is employed. The responses obtained from the respondents are analyzed using the Regression analysis. The test of significance is done with the help of t - test and ANOVA. This study is restricted to respondents utilizing banking services provided by private banks in Delhi and NCR. The importance of this study is that it focuses on investigating the impact of various service quality dimensions on the satisfaction of customers using banking services provided by private banks of Delhi and NCR.

Sources of Data

To cater the need of the research, the researchers have used primary data through self-constructed structured Questionnaire and as far as the secondary data is concerned that was obtained from web sites, journals etc. to explore the significance of various dimensions of service quality on the satisfaction of customers using banking services.

Data Collection Technique

Primary data were collected from respondent using banking services provided by private banks of Delhi and NCR. There were 245 respondents from various places in Delhi and NCR used for this study. Structured questionnaire was constructed to interview the respondents using banking services provided by private banks of Delhi and NCR. The responses of the respondents are measured on Likert'sseven point scale (ranging from strongly disagree to strongly agree).

Sampling Technique

As far as the sampling technique is concerned, purposive probability sampling is used to collect data.

Statistical Tools Used

IBM SPSS 20 (Statistical Package for the Social Sciences), for data analysis and as far as for hypothesis testing the statistical tools used is regression analysis and for the reliability the cronbach's alpha was calculated and sample adequacy was tested on KMO and Bartlett's Test.

About the Questionnaire

The questionnaire is divided into four parts consisting of 32 questions in all. The first part of the questionnaire consisting of issues related to the demographic profile of the respondent. It included the age, gender, educational background and frequency of use of the respondents. The second part of the questionnaire was concerned with the questions used to assess the expectations of customers in terms of service quality of the private banks. Similarly third part of the questionnaire was concerned with the questions used to assess the perception of customers about service quality of the private banks. The fourth part of the questionnaire contains questions related to the loyalty of the customers.

Data Analysis and Interpretation

Reliability Analysis

	Reliability Statistics	
Cronbach's Alpha	**Cronbach's Alpha Based on**	**No. of Items**
	Standardized Items	
0.834	0.819	26

Table 2: Reliability Statistics

In order to check the reliability of the questionnaire, the Cronbach's Alpha test was applied. The value of Cronbach's alpha is found to be 0.834. As the value of Cronbach's Alpha is more than 0.6, which considers the data to be reliable for hypothesis testing.

Validity Analysis

KMO and Barlett's Test

Kaiser-Meyer-Olkin Measure of Sampling Adequacy.		0.826
Bartlett's Test of Sphericity	Approx. Chi-Square	6982.240
	Df	529
	Sig.	0.000

Table 3: KMO and Barlett's test of Sphericity

From table 3, it is found that the value for Kaiser-Meyer-Olkin Measure of Sampling Adequacy was more than 0.6, and it is 0.826 also Bartlett's Test of Sphericity has significance value less than 0.05 at 5 % level of significance.

Gap Analysis

The difference between the Expectations and Perceptions of Customers is the GAP score which is then averaged. Respondents were advised to put a value between 1 and 7 against each statement twice; one for expectations and another for perceptions. Then the gap between gap score is calculated and averaged as given below:

Step 1:- Designing SERVQUAL Instrument

EXPECTATIONS		**PERCEPTIONS**		**GAP SCORE**
Tangibles	**E**	**Tangibles**	**P**	**E-P**
E1Private Banks has modern looking equipment.	6.5	**P1** Private Banks has modern looking equipment.	5.4	1.1
E2 The physical facilities at private banks are visually appealing.	6.8	**P2** The physical facilities at private banks are visually appealing.	3.9	2.9
E3 Employees at private banks are neat in appearance.	6.8	**P3**Employees at private banks are neat in appearance.	4.5	2.3
E4 Materials associated with the services is visually appealing at aprivate banks.	5.7	**P4**Materials associated with the services is visually appealing at aprivate banks.	4.1	1.6
Total	**25.8**		**17.9**	**7.9**
Average Gap Score of Tangibles [Total of Gap Score/4]				**1.97**

Reliability	E	Reliability	P	E-P
E5 When private banks promise to do something by a certain time, they do so.	5.8	**P5**When private banks promise to do something by a certain time, it does so.	4.3	1.5
E6 When a customer has a problem;private banks show a sincere interest in solving it.	6.1	P6 When a customer has a problem; private banks show a sincere interest in solving it.	4.1	2.0
E7 Private banks perform the services right the first time.	5.8	**P7** Private banks perform the services right the first time.	3.8	2.0
E8Private banks provide the service at the time they promise to do so.	6.5	**P8**Private banks provide the service at the time they promise to do so.	4.4	2.1
E9 Private banks insist on error free records.	6.8	**P9** Private banks insist on error free records.	5.2	1.6
Total	**31.0**		**21.8**	**9.2**
Average Gap Score[Total of Gap Score/5]				**1.84**

Responsiveness	E	Responsiveness	P
E10 Employees of privatebanks tell customers exactly when services will be performed.	6.8	**P10**Employees of private banks tell customers exactly when services will be performed.	4.7
E11 Employees of privatebanks give prompt service to customers.	6.4	**P11**Employees of private banks give prompt service to customers.	4.8
E12 Employees of private banks always willing to help customers.	6.4	**P12**Employees of private banks always willing to help customers.	4.8
E13 Employees of privatebanks never be too busy to respond to customers' requests.	6.1	**P13**Employees of private banks never be too busy to respond to customers' requests.	3.5
Total	**25.7**		**17.8**
Average Gap Score (Total Of Gap Score/4)			

Assurance	E	Assurance	P	E-P
E14 The behavior of employees in private banks instills confidence in customers.	6.1	**P14**The behavior of employees in private banks instills confidence in customers.	3.9	2.2
E15 Customers of privatebanks feel safe in transactions.	5.8	**P15**Customers of private banks feel safe in transactions.	4.2	1.6
E16 Employees of private banks are consistently courteous with customers.	5.8	**P16**Employees of private banks are consistently courteous with customers.	3.9	1.9
E17 Employees of privatebanks have the knowledge to answer customers' questions.	6.4	**P17** Employees of private banks have the knowledge to answer customers' questions.	4.2	2.2
Total	**24.1**		**16.2**	**7.9**

Average Gap Score(Total of Gap Score/4)				**1.98**
EMPATHY	**E**	**EMPATHY**	**P**	**E-P**
E18 Private banks give individual attention to customers.	6.8	**P18**Private banks give individual attention to customers.	4.1	2.7
E19 Private banks have operating hours convenient to all their customers.	6.4	**P19**Private banks have operating hours convenient to all their customers.	3.2	3.2
E20 Private banks have employees who give customers personal attention.	5.6	**P20**Private banks have employees who give customers personal attention.	3.2	2.4
E21 Private banks have their customers' best interests at heart.	6.1	**P21**Private banks have their customers' best interests at heart.	3.1	3.0
E22 The employees of private banks understand the specific needs of their customers.	6.5	**P22**The employees of private banks understand the specific needs of their customers.	3.5	3.0
Total	**31.4**		**17.1**	**14.3**
Average Gap Scores(Total of Gap Score/5)				**2.86**

Table 4: Servqual Model

Gap scores for different categories as calculated in Servqual Model is average to compute unweighted average score given below:

Categories	Gap Scores
Average score for Tangibles	1.97
Average score for Reliability	1.84
Average score for Responsiveness	1.98
Average score for Assurance	1.98
Average score for Empathy	2.86
Total	**10.63**
Average (Total/5) Un-weighted score	**2.126**

Table 5: Average Scores

This is the extension of the SERVQUAL score and is only required if weighted score is calculated. Putting weights against each of the five dimensions is critical because the amount of weight represents the relative importance of the dimensions to the customer. The questionnaire has a separate page asking each respondent to put relative weight against each dimensions. The points against each of the dimensions are totaled and averaged to normalize it. Total 100 points has been allocated among these dimensions as stated below that have been calculated considering respondents' viewpoint on it:

Dimensions	Points
The appearance of the private banks Physical Facilities, Equipment, Personnel,and Communication Materials(Tangibles).	14
The private bank's ability to perform the promised service dependable and accurately(Reliability).	24
The private bank's willingness to help customers and provide prompt service(Responsiveness).	22
The knowledge and courtesy of the private bank's employees and their ability to convey trust and confidence(Assurance).	28
The caring, individual attention the private bank provides its customers (Empathy)	12
Total	**100**

Table 6: Ranks

Weighted Scores

DIMENSIONS	Un-weighted score(step2)		Weights(step3)	=Weighted
Tangibles	1.97	X	0.14	= 0.275
Reliability	1.84	X	0.24	= 0.441
Responsiveness	1.98	X	0.22	= 0.435
Assurance	1.98	X	0.28	= 0.554
Empathy	2.86	X	0.12	= 0.343
Total Weight Score				**2.048**

Table 7: Calculation of weighted Scores

Finally, the score should be analyzed to find out the weak area where more attention is required. The gap score indicates the extent of gap in service quality .The higher the gap score is the more is the dissatisfaction.

Dimensions	Expecta-tions	Percep-tions	Total Gap Score (E-P)	Average Gap Score	Weightings (w)	Weighted
Tangible	25.8	17.9	7.9	1.97	0.14	0.275
Reliability	31.0	21.8	9.2	1.84	0.24	0.441
Responsiveness	25.7	17.8	7.9	1.98	0.22	0.435
Assurance	24.1	16.2	7.9	1.98	0.28	0.554
Empathy	31.4	17.1	14.3	2.86	0.12	0.343
Total						**2.048**

Table 8: Overall Weights Scores

The dimension Empathy has highest average gap score 2.86. But after the adjustment with weights, the score is 0.343 which is not the greatest score anymore. This proves that the weight has a significant implication. Individually, the customers are somewhat dissatisfied in this Category, but they believe that it should have less weight at the time of calculating aggregated score. On the basis of weighted score, the dimension Assurance got the highest score (0.554). It means that the performance of the bank in this category is not up to the mark. The bank should pay sufficient attention to all of the sub categories under this dimension to better the service.

Hypotheses Testing

Correlation Results of Service Quality Dimensions and Customer Satisfaction

According to the Table 9, there is a significant positive relationship between the five dimensions of service quality and customer satisfaction, the highest correlation is between Responsiveness and customer satisfaction (0.805); followed by Tangibility (0.792), Empathy (0.779) and assurance (0.741) respectively.

Dimensions	Customer Satisfaction	Tangibility	Reliability	Responsiveness	Assurance
Tangibility	0.792	-	-	-	-
Reliability	0.649	0.651	-	-	-
Responsiveness	0.805	0.578	0.349	-	-
Assurance	0.741	0.629	0.724	0.682	-
Empathy	0.779	0.618	0.662	0.628	0.736

Table 9: Correlation between Service Quality Dimensions and Customer Satisfaction

The weakest correlation is between reliability and customer satisfaction (0.649). Because the correlation was positive, service quality and customer satisfaction is positively related, which means the better service quality was the higher customer satisfaction. Accordingly, the most important service quality dimension that affects customer satisfaction is Responsiveness, which goes to prove that Responsiveness perceived as a dominant service quality followed by tangibility. Thus, we can conclude that there is significant relationship between the service quality dimensions and the customer satisfaction. Thus in case of hypothesis 1, null hypothesis is rejected and the alternative hypothesis is accepted. Thus, there is significant relationship between service quality dimensions and customer satisfaction in banking services.

Regression Analysis

Model	Unstandardized Coefficients		Standardized	t	Sig.
	B	S.E.	Beta		
Constant	- 0.118	0.074		- 1.429	0.284
Tangibility	0.048	0.027	0.048	2.250	0.083
Reliability	0.043	0.079	0.043	0.787	0.478
Responsiveness	0.170	0.141	0.159	1.148	**0.022***
Assurance	0.141	0.052	0.139	3.024	**0.034***
Empathy	0.725	0.149	0.734	4.707	**0.014***
R^2	0.924				
Adjusted R^2	0.913				
F	18.584				

Table 9: Regression analysis between overall Service quality and customer satisfaction

From Table 9, it is indicated that Empathy, Responsiveness, and Assurance dimension of service quality have a significantinfluence on customers' satisfaction at 95% confidence level. Conversely, reliability and tangibles dimension have no significant influence on customers' satisfaction. The significant service quality factors have been included for the establishment of the function. The established regression function is:

$$Z = -0.118 + 0.048 \times 1 + 0.043 \times 2 + 0.170 \times 3 + 0.141 \times 4 + 0.725 \times 5$$

The regression results indicate all the service quality dimensions (tangibility, reliability, responsiveness, assurance and empathy) combined significantly influence the satisfaction of customers. The value of R2 is 0.924 and adjusted R2 of 0.913 indicates 91.3% of the variance in customer satisfaction can be predicted by the service quality offered by the private banks.

Thus from the above regression analysis, it is clear that there is significant relationship between overall service quality and the customer satisfaction.

Regression Analysis - Customer Satisfaction and Loyalty

Model	Unstandardized Coefficients		Standardized	t	Sig.
	B	S.E.	Beta		
Constant	- 0.118	0.074		- 1.429	0.284
Tangibility	0.048	0.027	0.048	2.250	0.083
Reliability	0.043	0.079	0.043	0.787	0.478
Responsiveness	0.170	0.141	0.159	1.148	**0.022***
Assurance	0.141	0.052	0.139	3.024	**0.034***
Empathy	0.725	0.149	0.734	4.707	**0.014***
R^2	0.924				
Adjusted R^2	0.913				
F	18.584				

Table 10: Regression Analysis - Customer Satisfaction and Loyalty

The table 10 displays the relationship between customers satisfaction with their loyalty to the bank. In order to test the relationship, linear regression is used. The overall satisfaction of customers seems to have statistically significant and positive effect on their loyalty. The adjusted R2 of 0.684 indicates 68.4% of customer satisfaction is associated with their loyalty. This indicates customer satisfaction plays an important role in enhancing customer loyalty in private banks of Delhi and NCR. Thus there is significant relationship between customer satisfaction and loyalty in banking services.

Conclusion

The objective of the study was to assess the service quality of private banks and its impact on customer satisfaction as well as study also indicated the relationship that exists between customer satisfaction and their loyalty. It was being observed that the average scores of service quality dimensions were between 3.2 and 6.8. Thus it can be concluded that there is a need of improvements of service quality on all the five service quality dimensions, especially the dimensions of Responsiveness and Empathy. It is also concluded that there is a significant relationship between all service quality dimensions and the customer satisfaction. Also there is a strong positive correlation between the service quality dimensions and the customer satisfaction towards private banks of Delhi and NCR. It is also concluded that there is strong relationship between the customer satisfaction and the customer loyalty. The overall satisfaction of customers seems to have statistically significant and positive effect on their loyalty. The adjusted R2 of 0.684 indicates 68.4 % of customer satisfaction is associated with their loyalty. This indicates customer satisfaction plays an important role in enhancing customer loyalty in private banks of Delhi and NCR. Thus there is significant relationship between customer satisfaction and loyalty in banking services.

Limitations

The study has covered only limited number of variables leading to satisfaction of customers towards private banks. The satisfaction of customers differs from one person to another depending upon the kind of services they want to avail. One person can be satisfied on one aspect and other may not on that. As the study is subjective, although lot of care has been taken to involve variables related to study, but may be some gaps can exist. The study can be done on larger samples and more diversified manner in terms of demographic and regions to make it more effective. Also although this research provides some significant insights into service quality in Delhi and NCR banking industry, there is still a chance to extend the findings to gain a more comprehensive understanding of the nature of banking services.

Scope of Further Research

The future research may highlight the service quality in banking in total, comparative analysis on SERVPERF scores in different types of banks and comparative analysis on SERVQUAL and SERVPERF scores in banking industry. The future research may be directed to analyze the application of SERPERF to other service industries by incorporating other dimensions of service quality.

References

- Al-Mahiaoi, Q. (2006).Service Quality Management Concepts, Processes and Applications.Dar El Shorouk, Amman, Jordan, 52.
- Altai, K., and Ra'ad, I. (2008).Total Quality Management.Al-yazji scientific publishing house, Amman, Jordan, 153.
- Asubonteng, P., McCleary, K.J., and Swan, J.E. (1996). SERVQUAL Revisited: A Critical Review of Service Quality. The Journal of Services Marketing, 10(6), 62-81.
- Edvardsson, B. (1998). Service Quality Improvement. Managing Service Quality, 8(2), 142-149.
- Eshghi, A., Roy, S.K., and Ganguli, S. (2008). Service Quality and Customer Satisfaction: An Empirical Investigation in Indian Mobile Telecommunications Services. Marketing Management Journal, 18(2), 119-144.
- Ghylin, K.M., Green, B.D., Drury, C.G., Chen, J., Schultz, J.L., Uggirala, A., Abraham, J.K., and Lawson, T.A. (2006). Clarifying the Dimensions of Four Concepts of Quality. Theoretical Issues in Ergonomics Science, 9(1), 73-94.
- Gronroos, C. (1982). A Service Quality Model and its Marketing Implications.European Journal of Marketing, 18(4), 36-44.
- Horstmann R (1998). Customer Satisfaction and Loyalty: An Empirical Assessment in the Service Industry. J. Appl. Manage. Entrepreneurship. 4, 39 -54.
- Ladhari, R. (2008). Alternative Measures of Service Quality: A Review. Managing Service Quality, 18(1), 65-86.
- Moala, N. (1998).Measuring the Quality of Banking Services Provided by Commercial Banks of Jordan.Faculty of Administrative Sciences studies, folder # 25(2), 353 - 373.
- Mohsan, F. (2011). Impact of Customer Satisfaction on Customer Loyalty and Intentions to Switch: Evidence from Banking Sector of Pakistan.International Journal of Business Social Science, 16(2), 39 - 48.
- Negi, R. (2009). Determining Customer Satisfaction through Perceived Service Quality: A Study of Ethiopian Mobile Users. International Journal of Mobile Marketing, 4(1), 31-38.
- Newman, K. (2001). Interrogating SERVQUAL: A Critical Assessment of Service Quality Measurement in a High Street Retail Bank.International Journal of Bank Marketing, 19(3), 126-139.

- Parasuraman, A., Zeithaml, V.A., and Berry, L.L. (1985). A Conceptual Model of Service Quality and Its Implication. Journal of Marketing, 49, 41-50.
- Parasuraman, A., Zeithaml, V.A., and Berry, L.L. (1988). SERVQUAL: A Multi-item Scale for Measuring Consumer Perceptions of the Service Quality. Journal of Retailing, 64(1), 12-40.
- Ryals, L. and Adrian, P. (2001). Customer Relationship Management in Financial Services: Towards Information-Enabled Relationship Marketing.Journal of Strategic Marketing, 9, 3-27.
- Tee (2012). The Effects of Service Quality, Customer Satisfaction on Re-patronage Intentions of Hotel Existing Customers. International Journa Management Administrative Science, 8(1), 23-31.
- Zarour, G. (2003).The Impact of the Quality and the Price of Services Provided by Banks on Customers Satisfaction of the Industrial Sector in Jordan.Unpublished Master thesis, Amman Arabic University for graduate studies.

32

Influence of Digital Marketing Strategies on Children

Vijita Singh Aggarwal & Shefali

Abstract

Children constitute an important target market segment and this has prompted researchers & marketers to direct their attention to study the influence of marketing strategies on children. In the past the main commercial place to sell to children through advertisements is Television but the trend has now changed with the advancement of technology. Digital marketing is advancing very rapidly, and is on the edge to reach a vital tipping point in the very near future. Hence, Marketers are using various digital marketing techniques to sell their products and services to the children of different ages. The research focuses on types of digital marketing strategies used by marketers to target children and how they influence children in their purchasing decision. An observational study along with the secondary research has been done on children to conduct research. Findings suggest that Advergames, online ads,social media sites, banner ads, mobile advertisements, etc. are various marketing strategies used by marketers to tempt the children to purchase their products and services. These strategies direct the child's attention and builds brand preference, likings ,intention and choice which ultimately affect the children buying behavior.

Keywords: *Internet,Advertising,Digital marketplace*

Influence of Digital marketing strategies on children

In today's market the immortal line "The child is the father of man" holds a new meaning. According to the report by Anusha & K.R. Balasubramanyam (2010) "The consumption driven child is the father of man". They concluded that some million of kids below the age of 15 are India's most conspicuous customers, picturing not for just toys, clothes etc. but also counseling their parents on big ticket purchases .Children constitute an important target market segment and this has prompted researchers & marketers to direct their attention to study the influence of marketing strategies on children.

Children are attracted towards the strategies used by marketers to promote their products and it ultimately affects the buying behaviour of children. Changing technology, family structures, family income, purchasing power, parents' education etc are changing the parents and child's perspective of purchasing. In the modern media environment children usually spend most of their leisure time in playing games, watching TV, surfing on the internet which makes them more critical and knowledgeable. Thus leading to changes in purchasing preferences and intentions. In the past the main commercial place to sell to children through advertisements is Television but the trend is now changed with the advancement of technology.The commercial sites are new marketplace for children which includes advergames,viral marketing,mobile ads,social media marketing,banner ads on websites and product placements(A common sense media research brief 2014).With the help of these strategies companies are successful in developing one to one relationship with children so as to market the products .With this background it becomes important to study future consumers. (H.Skaar, 2009), defines children as much more active, competent and powerful.The business of marketing kids online is booming.Most of the internet sites are designed for children and teens which use advertisement as a medium of communication.

(C.Montgomery, 2000)The internet provides various ways for children to interact and to exchange information with the stuff placed on the website by making use of their personal media devices.Idit Harel, expert in this field concluded this attitude of children with the phrase "High tech is now my tech."

Due to the increase in the spending power of children, marketers are entering into the marketplace by utilising the unique and new characteristics of the internet (i.e. advertising, website content) to make them aware about the brand and also to cultivate brand loyalty at the early stage of their development. In this new era of digital culture,several innovative methods are adopted by the marketers to promote brand loyalty along with the generation of profit. Hence, Marketers be inclined to concentrate on "newer commercial strategies" such as "product placement, peer-to peer marketing, cross-promotion and viral and online marketing" (Buckingham, 2007, p. 21).Allison Ellis ,General manager of

Foxkids.com says that kids spend 30 min per online session of fox site with their products like games, hidden treasure etc. Similarly Candystand.com is a very good integration of product as well as of games. (Businessweek,2001)Yet, in the midst of this expanding digital marketplace, still have little knowledge of just how these new forms of marketing are influencing child and their behaviour.

Hence, the research focuses on types of digital marketing strategies used by marketers to target children and how they influence children in their purchasing decision

Digital Marketing strategies to Influence Children

Intensive digital marketing campaigns are an integrated set of digital practices designed to engage children and youth continuously. The six concepts that constitute unique features of digital media and marketing are Ubiquitous connectivity, Engagement, User-generated Content, Personalization, Social graph and Immersive environments. (Montogomery K) (C. Montgomery, 2000)

The most common website used not only by children but also by their parents are now created by digital marketers (such as Headbone Interactive, MaMaMedia, and Girl Game) which is acting as a webspace for children.This webspace includes common chat rooms, contests, games, downloadable art etc to interact and to improve the skills of children bycreating curoisity of knowing more. The study done by Clarke and svanaes, 2012 explained the child engagement with the digital technology at a younger stage. (Kathryn.C. Montogomery, 1999). The Mama Media site is one of hundreds of "destinations" created for children on the Internet. Marketers and advertisers on the websites offer a richness and diversity of experiences to the children. They create website content according to the needs of children. Digital media is having deep impact on the learning and development of children. Advertising, marketing and selling to children are significant strategies in the kid space of World Wide Web. Montgomery, 2000) .

Banner ads are the flashing brand names at the top of websites in which advertisers link branded environment with the games, puzzles, contests to engage children for long time. (Thompson, 1999). In his paper call the children of this digital era as Digital kids, Interactive kids and teen power. In Digital marketing, it is easy to collect personal information about the children attitude and behaviour by offering them incentives such as games, surveys, discounts and prizes etc. Direct marketing which is offline is now possible online for data collection where the response is fast with various free emails and discounts. (Montgomery & Pasnik, 1996). To boost the purchases by children, companies are using variety of strategies, including the creation of digital wallets, in which the parents deposit money into the child's online account with the help of credit cards. (Thompson, 1999). Many companies are using classrooms in the schools as a site for promoting online sales (Manning, 1999)

Cowburn and Boxer (2007) A study of food marketing promotions on Australian children related websites found that marketers promote products in the kid space and link them with the games, competition, prizes etc., to attract children. Similar analysis of 119 food product websites and 196 websites on Australian children done by (Jones et al., 2008)

(Winkler and Buckner, 2006)Digital marketing promotes product directly through the advertisements on the websites which provides information about the product and nutrition. Along with the various opportunities on the websites, downloadable games and activities are available to interact with the promotional material to enhance the brand attitude of children. Puzzles, Packages, downloadable material etc are used by marketers to increase the purchasing of product by positioning the product in the minds of children and teenagers.

Chester and Montgomery (2008, p. 14) content present on website having product pitches and cartoon spokes character persuades the future consumers to spend their leisure time with them. (Schumann, 2004) The ads containing favourite cartoon characters of children influence them and direct their attention to the product and develop a positive attitude towards product. These kinds of ads persuade them to buy the product along with the development of critical evaluation and consumption skills (Acuffand Reiher 1997; Guber and Berry 1993).

(Henry & Story, 2009) A research analysis proves that advergaming are available on 85 per cent and interactive content on 92 per cent of websites.55 per cent of websites feature brand mascots, celebrities, cartoons and children who consumes that product along with colourful brand logo. Kids clubs and online stores to purchase specific merchandise for the children. These all kinds of marketing techniques change the perception of child towards the product, build brand recognition, instills brand loyalty. Brand immersion is the main motive of advertisers to cultivate in children by use of advergames. In case of food marketers, several promotional strategies such as incentives, tie-ins, sweepstakes, contests are used to enhance the brand value.

As a result of exposure to the ad in game, positive brand attitude has formed as playing game is the main focus of attention at that time which ultimately leads to the feeling of association and evaluation in the child. Marketers use various tools to promote sales on their website in which children could participate such as sweepstakes, prize offerings to stimulate the behaviour of brand purchase, word of mouth etc. (Moore & Rideout, 2007). Brand associations are created by advertisers with the use of endorsements by animated brand icons and play an important role in children buying process. (Priya, Baisya, & Sharma, 2010)

Games are having at least one brand identifier to promote brand loyalty among the children. The interactive and changing features of Internet play a predominant position than television to influence children purchasing habits.

An advergame is used to place the product in the minds of children (Culp, Robert A. Bell, & Diana Cassady, 2010)

(Rust, 1986) Definition, association and proposition are the levels of understanding through which children are able to differentiate among commercials. Product placement is the fast growing advertisement technique used nowadays in children films but parents believe it to be unethical which make the parents decision separate from children decision taking. (Hudson, Hudson, & Peloza, 2008)

In a virtual world,product placement and product integration in the advertisement or game involves a character which promotes the product virtually in the marketplace. (Cain, 2011).

Advergames provides children the branded environment having fun experience (Bailey, Wise et al. 2009). These games are very effective in catching the attention of children because they are in long term contact with these games (Mallinckrodt and Mizerski 2007; Dahl, Eagle et al. 2009; Culp, Bell et al. 2010; Hernandez and Chapa 2010). They are argued to be influential as they are helpful in building brand memory and loyalty along with positive emotional bonding (Lee, Choi et al. 2009; Purswani 2010).

Nowadays social networking sites are very popular such a Facebook.A research on Australian children revealed that one in three 9-16 old children have facebook account and one in five 9-12 year olds. Almost 65% of 9-16yearold have social networking profiles which are increasing day by day (Green, Hartley et al. 2011). Facebook and twitter allows the children to interact with each other,to exchange ideas and information,to recognise brands through variety of techniques including peer to peer,viral,user generated content and mobile marketing etc. It explains the ubiquitous nature of social media marketing (Chester and Montgomery 2008). In India it is estimated that around 5 per cent of the 37 million Facebook users are between 13 and 15 years old, and 7 per cent are between 16 and 17 years old (Socialbakers.com 2011). A comparison between online ads and mobile ads has been made and concluded that mobile ads are very much effective in attracting customers (Miller and Washington 2011). Social networking sites (SNS) create great opportunities for children and young people to maintain friendships and develop relationships (Clarke, 2009). Location based advertisement is also one of the digital marketing method adopted by companies to generate impulse buying behaviour in adolscents by reducing the time period between exposure and consumption (Montgomery, 2013) and(Calvert 2008).

The famous names in the world of social media marketing are burger king and Pepsi who restructure their marketing approach and started focusing on social media. They are having millions of fans on face book which uses social marketing campaigns to market products and services (Montgomery, 2013) Social media is seen as mainly significant, and the opportunities for customization, personalization, user generated content, sharing and interaction offered is considered to be a important and dynamic vehicle for healthy messages (Brennan, Dahl et al. 2010).

Results and Findings

Digital media is becoming an increasingly integrated part of children's lives globally, and digital marketing in one form or another will be part of their online experience. Following are the digital marketing strategies extracted from the literature review used by marketers to influence children buying behaviour.

Advergames

The games made by a firm with the objective to promote its brands .It is a virtual tool used by marketers having company logos or product images which involves user with the branded items by the method of playing. It is one of the digital marketing techniques often used by children for longer period of time and share fun experience to brand identification. It also has positive emotional investment (Moore & Rideout, 2007) reinforces the brand's credibility, and potentially motivates the young person to buy more products (Johnson, 2012). As a result of exposure to the ad in game, positive brand attitude has formed as playing game is the main focus of attention at that time which ultimately leads to the feeling of association and evaluation in the child. It also influences children's brand preferences towards product.

Social Networking sites and Cross Promotions

Embedded advertising is one of the main objective of social networking sites includes placing ads on sites such as on facebook,twitter to interact and to maintain relationship with children and teens. This type of technique helps marketers to promote their products effectively. Facebook and twitter allows the children to interact with each other,to exchange ideas and information,to recognise brands through variety of techniques including peer to peer,viral,user generated content and mobile marketing etc. It explains the ubiquitous nature of social media marketing (Chester and Montgomery 2008).

Advertising to children and teens continues to rely heavily on cross-promotional tie-ins with popular cartoon characters, sports stars, and Hollywood celebrities persuades the future consumers to spend their leisure time with them.(Schumann, 2004)The ads containing favourite cartoon characters of children influence them and direct their attention to the product and develop a positive attitude towards product. These kinds of ads persuade them to buy the product along with the development of critical evaluation and consumption skills (Acuffand Reiher 1997; Guber and Berry 1993).

Mobile and location based marketing - Mobile as an advertising platform encompasses many areas including mobile display ads, in-app advertising,video, gaming, SMS, QR codes, search and location based marketing. The mobile advertising to children and teens is another digital marketing technique to influence children .It is very beneficial and easily accessible method to target children. As with online advertising, the content is interactive. Mobile advertising can be targeted to young people more narrowly than other online advertising, since it can track their locations in relation to specific retail outlets or fast-food venues (Montgomery, 2013) .It is proved that Younger consumers ages 12-17 are the heaviest mobile video viewers, watching 7 hours 13 minutes of mobile video a month (Nielson, 2011) Marketers believe that this exposure to branded content on a mobile device is "a great way to create significant lifts in brand affinity, brand recall and future purchase intent" (Ting, 2008).

Other Techniques

Videogames, contests, downloadable branded products on websites etc tempts children to hand over contact information for future marketing (Moore & Rideout, 2007). These websites are having branded items for a child to download, screensavers or for printing to be used in the real world. The other technique of the digital world is Branded app which is just like branded website through which children and teens interact with the firm and its products by the help of special offers such as coupons. Product placement is the fast growing advertisement technique used nowadays in children films.

Viral marketing: It is one more digital marketing strategy which persuades children to post branded greetings to their friends and invite them to visit company website. Various suggestions are available on the website like sending a postcard or challenging a friend to play to interact with the children. (Montgomery, 2000) Banner ads are the flashing brand names at the top of websites in which advertisers link branded environment with the games, puzzles, contests to engage children for long time. Kids clubs and online stores to purchase specific merchandise for the children.These all kinds of marketing techniques change the perception of child towards the product, build brand recognition, instills brand loyalty. Brand immersion is the main motive of advertisers to cultivate in children by use of advergames.

Influence of digital marketing on children-This literature review has focused on digital marketing and advertising targeted to children who influence their attitude and create positive emotional bonding with the product. Following are the results which shows how digital marketing affects and influence children behaviour.

Attention- Online advertisements attracts the attention of children which influence their attitude with the positive feeling (Chebat et al. 1992).Animated spokes-characters are typically large, colorful, action-oriented, and are accompanied by silly voices and sound effects. The character is often the focus of the commercial and are having attention catching ability related to the message (Wartella and Ettema 1974) Watt and Welch 1983; Welch and Watt 1982). (Schumann, 2004) The ads containing favourite cartoon characters of children influence them and direct their attention to the product and develop a positive attitude towards product. These strategies are very effective in catching the attention of children because they are in long term contact with the online games.

Recognition-Digital marketing strategies targeted at children increase brand recognition. Cartoon spokescharacter, animated cartoons, celebrities etc invoke visual brand recognition as today's children has limited reading abilities (Henke 1995; Mizerski 1995), and recognition ability typically increases with age.Social media marketing allows children torecognise brands through variety of techniques including peer to peer,viral,user generated content and mobile marketing etc.

Association-These strategies evoke the feeling of association between children and the product. As a result of exposure to the ad in game, positive brand attitude has formed as playing game is the main focus of attention at that time which ultimately leads to the feeling of association and evaluation in the child. Brand associations are created by advertisers with the use of endorsements by animated brand icons and play an important role in children buying process. (Priya, Baisya, & Sharma, 2010)

Preference-While research findings show that young children can ex-hibit high levels of character/product recognition, association, and preference with these kinds of techniques. Digital media is all the time more interactive and allows for active engagement with the promotional material. Rather than merely exposing the consumer to the brand or product, digital marketing creates environments where children can interact with the brand, create emotional connections and integrate it into their social relationships. Advergames are very popular with children which influence children's brand preferences.

Intention and Choice

Kids clubs and online stores to purchase specific merchandise for the children. These all kinds of marketing techniques change the perception of child towards the product, build brand recognition, instils brand loyalty.Digital marketing foster emotional and unconscious choices in children when they are able to understand the persuasive message of advertisement (Montgomery, Grier et al. 2011).

Conclusion

The whole research revolves around the digital marketing strategies and their influence on children. Advergames, online ads,social media sites, banner ads ,mobile advertisements etc are various marketing strategies used by marketers to tempt the children to purchase their products and services .These strategies direct the children attention and builds brand preference, likings, intention and choice which ultimately affects the children buying behaviour. The research has some limitations as secondary research has been done. Various factors such as age, gender and their engagement with digital advertising has not been taken into consideration during research. Effect of digital marketing techniques on Social, cultural, minority and ethnic groups is the future area of research.

References

- Bailey, R., K. Wise, et al. (2009). "How Avatar Customizability Affects Children's Arousal and Subjective Presence During Junk Food-Sponsored Online Video Games." Cyberpsychology and Behaviour 12(3): 9.
- Brennan, R., S. Dahl, et al. (2010). "Persuading young consumers to make healthy nutritional decisions." Journal of Marketing Management 26(7-8): 21.
- Cain, R.M. (2011). Embedded advertising on television: Disclosure, deception, and free speech rights. Journal of Public Policy and Marketing, 30(2). Retrieved from http://www.marketingpower.com/AboutAMA/Pages/AMA%20Publications/AMA%20Journals/Journal %20of % 20Public%20Policy%20Marketing/TOCS/SUM_2011.2/embedded _advertisement.aspx
- Clarke, D.B., and Svanaes, S. (2012). Digital marketing and advertising to children: A Literature review. Advertising Education forum.
- Culp, J., Robert A. Bell, and Diana Cassady. (2010). Characteristics of Food Industry Web Sites and Advergames targeting Children. Journal of Nutrition Education and Behaviour.
- Dahl, S., L. Eagle, et al. (2009). "Analyzing advergames: active diversions or actually deception: An exploratory study of online advergames content." Young Consumers: Insight and Ideas for Responsible Marketers 10(1): 14.
- Green, L., J. Hartley, et al. (2011). Risk and safety for Australian children on the internet. London, EU Kids Online, London School of Economics.

- Henry, A.E., and Story, M. (2009). Food and Beverage Brands That Market to Children and adolscents on the Internet: A content analysis of branded websites. Journal of Nutrition Education and Behaviour.

- Hernandez, M., D. and S. Chapa (2010). "Adolescents, advergames and snack foods: Effects of positive affect and experience on memory and choice." Journal of Marketing Communications 16(1-2): 10

- Lee, M., Y. Choi, et al. (2009). "Playing With Food: Content Analysis of Food Advergames." The Journal of Consumer Affairs 43(1): 26

- Mallinckrodt, V. and D. Mizerski (2007). "The effects of playing an advergame on young children's perceptions, preferences, and requests." Journal of Advertising 36(2): 14.

- Miller, R.K. and K. Washington (2011). Consumer Behavior 2012, Richard K. Miller and Associates.

- Montgomery, K.C. and J. Chester (2011). Digital Food Marketing to Children and Adolescents: Problematic Practices and Policy Interventions, Public Health and Law Policy.

- Calvert, S. (2008). "Children as Consumers: Advertising and Marketing." Future of Children 18(1): 20.

- Montgomery, K.C., Grier, S.A., Chester, J., and Dorfman, L. (2013). The digital food marketing landscape: Challenges for researchers. In J.D. Williams et al. (Eds.), Advances in Communication Research to Reduce Childhood Obesity (221-242). New York: Springer.

- Nielsen. (2011, June). Trends in advertising spend and effectiveness. Retrieved from http://www.nielsen.com/content/dam/corporate/us/en/reportsdownloads/2011-Reports/TrendsAd Spendan Effectiveness_Spreads.pdf

- Moore, E.S., and Rideout, V.J. (2007). The Online Marketing of Food to Children: Is It Just Fun and Games? Journal of Public Policy and Marketing, , 202-220.

- Priya, P., Baisya, R. K., and Sharma, S. (2010). Television advertisements and children's buying behaviour. Marketing Intelligence and Planning, 151-169.

- Purswani, G. (2010). "Advergames, their use and potential regulation." Asia Pacific Public Relations Journal 11: 7.

- Socialbakers.com (2011). "India Facebook Statistics, Penetration, Demography." Retrieved 24/01, 2012, from www.socialbakers.com/facebook-statistics/ india#chart-intervals.
- Ting, R. (2008, September 8). Want a deeper connection? Apps are where it's at: marketers go beyond text alerts, mobile websites to take advantage of phones' capabilities and offer richer, more-engaging experiences. Advertising Age. Retrieved from http://adage.com/article/print-edition/a-deeper-connection-apps/130698.

33

Relationship to Experience - The Changing Face of CRM

Sumeet Malik & Nidhi Choudhry

Abstract

CRM is being adopted widely by business now despite the criticism by some practitioners and academics initially. This paper looks at some of the reasons why eCRM tools are gaining popularity across industry as firms look for competitive advantage. It looks at some of the popular cloud based CRM tools and compares them. Finally, an effective CRM program is only possible if the firms include CRM in their strategic vision or DNA. Zappos or Amazon is often cited for their strong CRM precisely because they have built the organizations on excellent customer experience. The paper concludes that to gain competitive advantage through CRM, firm need to include all the stakeholders in their vision for great customer experience.

Keywords - *CRM, eCRM, Amazon, Zappos, Freshdesk, Zendesk, CRM and Sales.*

Introduction

Customer Relationship Management (CRM) is not a new concept in business practice now and already adopted by a majority of firms in some form or other. Kennedy (2006) defines CRM as "about identifying a company's best customers and maximizing the value from them by satisfying and retaining them". There has been some scepticism from both practitioners and academics about the efficacy of CRM. Some academics have questioned its very existence, calling it a fundamentally flawed concept because CRM ignores the reality that many customers do not want to engage in relationships. According to them people simply don't have the time, interest or emotional energy to form relationships with a wide variety of products and services. (Dowling 2002). Some practitioners have called it an over-hyped technology and empirical studies have been unable to determine the extent to which CRM investment contributes to firm's performance (Boulding et al. 2005).

The increasing adoption of CRM aligns with the research that a properly implemented, company-wide CRM initiative will truly save company money, increase revenue, and grow customer loyalty (Larson, Rebecca 2009). Firms worldwide, as they come out of recession are looking at eCRM to gain an edge over competition. The estimates of CRM Industry revenues have been revised higher. In 2008, it was estimated that CRM Industry would be worth 16 Billion USD by 2016 but recent estimates by Gartner Research have pegged it to 36 Billion USD by 2017.

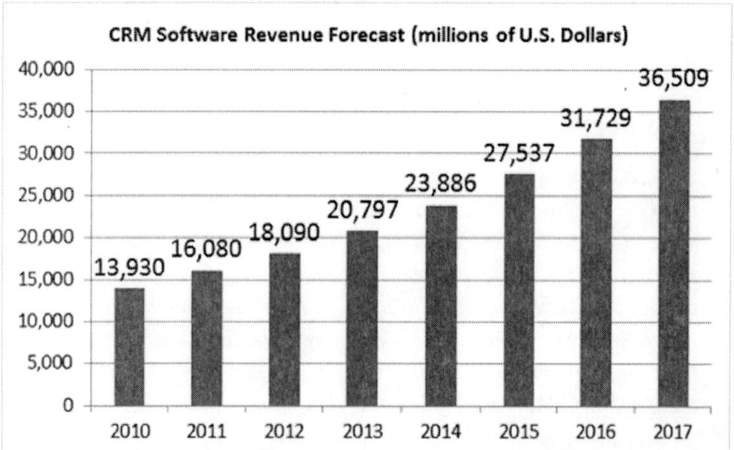

Source: Gartner

It is also no surprise that the market leader is Salesforce, a SaaS (Software as a Service) Vendor with 16 per cent market share.

For many of the digital service and product start-ups new web-based CRM tools have been a boon. Not only there is a lot of choice for CRM tools but also the investment required in CRM technology for fledgling start-ups who are on a tight-budget has come down as competition between Software as a Service (SAAS) CRM providers has intensified. A lot of the pricing plans start with a small (Zendesk) or no monthly costs (Freshdesk) along with zero investments in Data Storage and Analysis. This has allowed firms to start their CRM vertical with even one employee. This is the similar story of Jeff Bezos who, in Amazon's early days, used to provide customer support himself and that led him to build Amazon's often cited strong customer orientation.

Worldwide CRM Software Spending By Vendor, 2013
Market Size: $20.4B: 13.7% Growth Over 2012

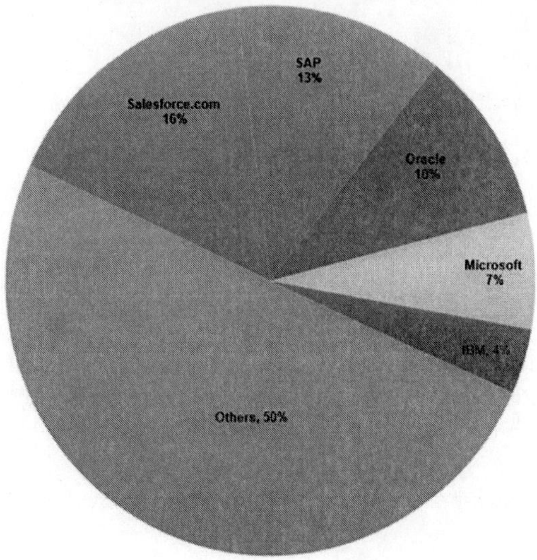

Source: Gartner

Current Trends

The web-based CRM tools not only help in Customer Support but also help the process of sales. Tools like Zopim (on Online Chat tool) and Freshdesk (Ticketing CRM tool) address the needs of potential customers. Zopim allows you to online observe a visitor and study her behaviour. Salesperson can see which page the visitor landed on and referral page, how much time is the visitor spending on a page or if the visitor is clicking to the sales page as intended, etc. It then allows the sales representative to start chat with the visitor at the time the representative feels that the customer needs more information for a sale to happen. For example the sales representative can start a conversation with the visitor if the representative feels a particular visitor is taking too much time on the sales page or is jumping from one page to another quickly. Another advantage of chat tools is that they provide multi-language support which means that the potential customer can ask question in her native language and the Support/Sales Representative can answer back in English with the tool doing the translation at both ends.

A recent study by Marketing Charts has found out that majority of Small and Medium Businesses are using CRM software for Lead Generation, Email Marketing and Sales Forecasting.

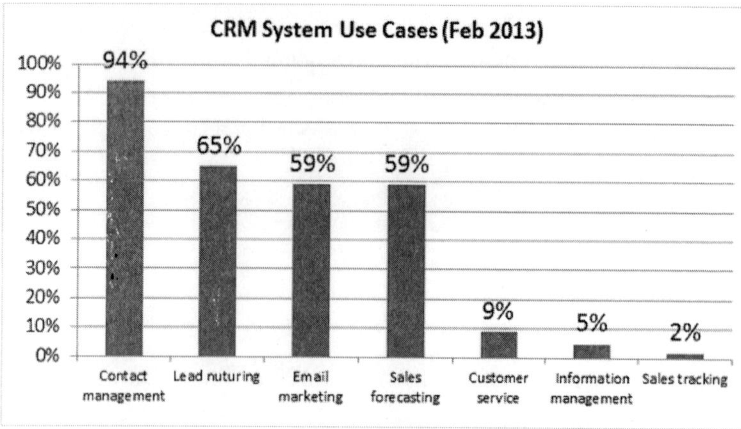

Source: Marketing Charts

Another advantage the cloud-based CRM tools give is that of mobility. Since the data is stored on cloud, it can be accessed using smart phones or tablets through compatible applications. A sales or customer support representative can reply to tickets or chat with potential customers out of their smart phones allowing extra sales support time. This helps sales representatives reach sales quota increase companies revenues.

From Relationship to Experience

Although the choice of CRM tools and the price of technology is coming down yet measurable returns from IT investment programs rarely arise from a narrow concentration on IT alone, with the most successful programs combining technology with the effective organization of people and their skills (Bharadwaj 2000; Piccoli and Ives 2005). Therefore, it is not just sufficient for firms to build and invest in their IT infrastructure but to also build their employees' skills and motivation. Zappos.com, an online retailer that has made a name for itself in its exceptional customer service also boasts of a quirky culture where employees bond over their varied interests through company's events and outings. One of the company's 'Ten Commandments' is 'to build a positive team and team spirit'. Tony Hsieh, the founder of Zappos says in his book that he was left very influenced after his first rave party experience where he saw the participants dancing facing the DJ instead of dancing with each other. He felt that with people can act as a tribe over shared purpose 'The entire room felt like one massive, united tribe of thousands of people. I felt a sense of experiential epiphany. Everyone in the room had a shared purpose,' he writes. 'We were all contributors to the collective rave experience.' (Tony Heish)

Customer Satisfaction, which is one the major goals of CRM, is directly co-relational to how employees feel about the organization. If employees feel that the organization stresses on achieving quality, they will feel committed to providing quality service to customers leading to superior customer satisfaction. And if the organization has a high technology adoption, employees adopt various mentioned tools quickly for sales and CRM processes. Thus to effectively implement CRM tools and applications to gain competitive advantage companies need to involve all the stakeholders and align them with the vision of creating an organization that is known for its customer experiences.

Bibliography

- Bharadwaj, A.S. (2000) A Resource-Based Perspective on Information Technology Capability and Firm Performance: An Empirical Investigation, MIS Quarterly (24:1): 169-196.
- Boulding, W., Staelin, R., Ehret, M., and Johnston, W. (2005) A Customer Relationship Management Roadmap: What is Known, Potential Pitfalls, and Where to Go, Journal of Marketing (69:4): 155-166.
- Danaher, P.J., Conroy, D.M., and McColl-Kennedy, J.R. (2008) Who Wants a Relationship Anyway?: Conditions When Consumers Expect a Relationship With Their Service Provider, Journal of Service Research, (11:1): 43-52.
- Dowling, G.R. (2002) Customer Relationship Management: In B2C Markets, Often Less is More, California Management Review (44:3): 87-103.

Gartner Study

- http://www.forbes.com/sites/louiscolumbus/2014/05/06/gartners-crm-market-share-update-shows-41-of-crm-systems-are-saas-based-with-salesforce-dominating-market-growth/
- Kennedy, A. (2006). Electronic customer relationship management (eCRM): opportunities and challenges. Irish Marketing Review, 18(1/2), p. 58-69.
- Larson, Rebecca, "The Future of Customer Relationship Management" (2009). Faculty Publications and Presentations. Paper 7.

Marketing Charts:

- http://www.marketingcharts.com/wp/online/6-in-10-smbs-using-their-crms-for-email-marketing-26767/
- Piccoli, G., and Ives, B. (2005) IT-Dependent Strategic Initiatives and Sustained Competitive.
- Advantage: A Review and Synthesis of the Literature, MIS Quarterly (29:4): 747-777.
- Tony Hsieh Delivering Happiness: A Path to Profits, Passion, and Purpose.

34

How Social is Your Bank !

Yukti Bajaj & EktaPandey

Abstract

Positive economy growth has led to boom in Indian banking sector. With an expansion spree and enormous competition in the banking industry it is necessary to connect with each and every potential customer. This increasing demand has paved the way for use of social media in the banking service industry.

With social media banks have been able to reach customers in a more personal way that goes beyond what their traditional advertising is able to do. It is a new form of customer relationship building, branding, and online marketing tool tremendous growth of banking industry is expected. Without social media there is no doubt that bank's relationship with customers has never been closer and positive word of mouth has never been stronger. In the banking industry, it has been a matter of worry that how social sites like Facebook, Twitter etc. will ensure customer security. Even though few bank are struggling on how to get started in the social media space.

The suggested study aims to understand the various social networking sites which are popularly incorporated in banks. A close analysis of selected private sector banks in context of social networking in India is also done. Data analyzed is collected from published reports and articles of various banks. Official websites of selected banks are also used to generate authenticity in data.

Research study proposed aims to do a descriptive analysis of the relevant data.

It is expected that the use of social networks in financial service industry would continue to expand in the future so it became relevant to see the potential issues involved and understand the lacunas related to its use.

Keywords: *Banking Industry, Social Media, Customer Relationship Management, Financial Service Institution*

Introduction

With the invention and development of Internet, communication has evolved as a revolutionary platform. Earlier, people had multiple modes of communication to choose from including: telephones, E-mail, instant messaging and text messaging. The Internet has evolved from being just a means to facilitate data towards a medium of communication through social media. The term 'Social media' can be split into two parts: social and media; where being social means interaction or networking and media is considered as a communication tool. Thus, social media are the platforms that help users interact and build up relationships. With the rapid development of technology, people can keep in touch with the rest of the world via these platforms. Twitter, Facebook, LinkedIn, etc. are most commonly used examples of social media. (Eisenberg, 2008)

Social Media has touched many aspects of life. It also changed the way we do business, especially in marketing industry. In comparison with old media such as print and broadcast, new media allows marketers to promote products and spread messages to their customers in a very short period of time. (Hambleton).

Evolved in past two decades, social media in marketing has changed the prospective and beliefs of the marketers as well as the consumers. Now marketers prior to design the marketing policy keep the power of social media in their mind.The advent of social media led to yet another innovative idea in the minds of marketers called as 'Social Media Marketing'.

Social media marketing is a term defining marketing via social networks, such as online communities, networks, blogs and other marketing tools to create awareness amongst their potential customers. Some common social media marketing tools are Twitter, Facebook, LinkedIn, Flickr, Orkut and YouTube.

Since, the first aim of any business is to be known amongst their target audience, these networking sites are used for creating relationships between the business organisations and target audience, for publicizing its products, increasing its sales and handling customer service. The main aspects of Social media marketing involve:

- Creating a buzz and attracting readers with catchy and impressive messages. This buzz spreads through the Internet through contact between users who in turn pass it on to their own contacts. Within moments, these messages spread like wild fire.
- Secondly, it allows all loyal customers of a brand or company to come together, interact with one another and communicate their liking for that brand or its products. Hence, these online conversations over these networking sites bring together the current as well as potential customers. Their loyalties in turn lead to word of mouth promotion of one's brand on one hand and increases awareness amongst other potential customers. Not only this, this simple networking or marketing on social media outlets help websites gain an online presence quickly. Thus, businesses reach their target audience regardless of which part of the world they reside.

Social media is dramatically impacting the banking industry, as most banks have established a presence on various social sites. Barclays Bank, Citigroup, Inc., HSBC, NatWest and others all engage on social media through Twitter, Facebook, Google+, LinkedIn, etc. With approximately two billion people using social media around the world, banks are seriously considering to engage with customers on social channels. Nowadays, customers expect the companies to listen, respond and offer services through social media. Hence, banks are not simply establishing a presence on social media but also use social channels to deliver faster and more effective customer service and customized financial advice; share financial offers and upcoming events; offer knowledge about regulations; and provide a feedback mechanism about banking products and services.

Literature Review

In recent years huge amount of research has been done on social media marketing and its role in the financial sector. The following literature review attempts to demonstrate the ranking of banks on the basis of performance in social media marketing.

In June, 2014, David Hazarika and Supratik Nag conducted a research "How Banks Can Use Social Media Analytics to Drive Business Advantage", published in Cognizant Insights 20-20. The report indicated that social media is like a double edged sword - on one hand, it raises the question of security and privacy threats for banks and their customers, while on the other hand, it definitely generates enormous value. It stated the fact that social media is all about the customer experience hence, banks need to develop their social media strategies around the customer in order to have enhanced customer loyalty, revenues and profitability.

Also, there has been witnessed a shift in the industry from "customer service" to "customer engagement," requiring a two-way mode of communication.

To enhance their engagement capabilities, banks should develop deeper understanding of customer behaviour, sentiments and needs by using social analytics. The study led to identification of more benefits than risks involved in using social media hence, stressed that banks must balance the risks and rewards associated with use of social media.

As per the report a successful social media strategy relies on the critical factors given as below:

- Development of a vision and needed organizational support for embracing social media strategy.
- Define the scope and objectives for the social media strategy.
- Determine the right metrics for measuring the effectiveness of the strategy.
- Draft a robust risk mitigation plan before actual engagement in social platforms.
- Understand the regulatory requirements to be observed on the social path
- Integration of technology and infrastructure for advancement and achievement of business objectives.
- Cultural assimilation of the social strategy in the organization
- Achieve customer centricity through the social strategy.

Adding to the knowledge the paper by RajibChanda and Steve Zaorski, titled "Social Media Usage in the Financial Services Industry: Toward a Business-Driven Compliance Approach", (2013) showed that irrespective of the business purpose for which a financial firm uses social media, it is high time that firms should adopt written social media policies. Social media as a method of communication is highly prevalent today; firms cannot simply excuse and state that they do not use social media.

The study identifies four major purposes for usage of social media by financial service firms and stress edit as a useful framework for considering the issues involved.

It showed that social media use by the financial services industry is prevalent and is expected to grow as the social networks continue to expand and become further entrenched in the public's online consciousness.

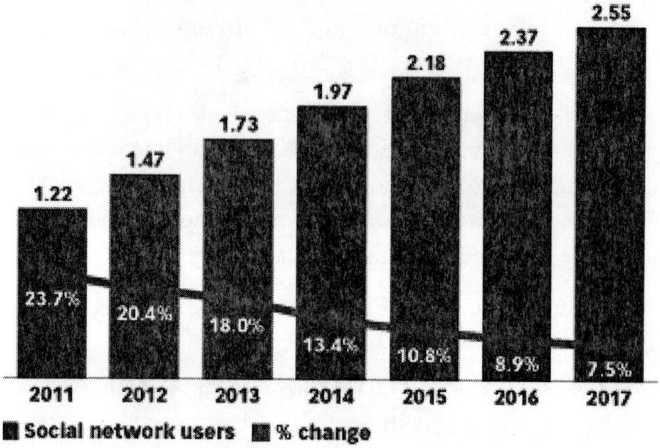

Figure 1: Trend Showing Growth of Social Media Users.

Source : eMarketer, http://www.emarketer.com/Article/Social-Networking-Reaches-Nearly-One-Four-Around-World/1009976 accessed on 23-02-15.

However, the industry has lagged behind its corporate peers, likely due to regulatory concerns. The author suggested that the purposes behind financial firm's intent to use social media must be considered instead of using regulatory concerns as an excuse to avoid it. Moreover, firms with clear business purpose in mind, not only leads to effectiveness in online interactions, but also a better understanding of the risks involved.

The authors not only identified four major purposes for financial services firms to use social media, but also explained the issues involved and potential pitfalls that can be avoided. The financial sector being the most regulated sector has been slower to adopt social media than other corporate peers.

Nonetheless, according to a 2011 Social Ware study of financial advisers in North America, as of September 2011 more than 84 % of such advisers use social media for business purposes.This percentage is a marked increase from the 60 % of advisers who used social media in 2010. Among the 84 % who used social media for business purposes, approximately 65 % stated that they used social media every day, ranging from at least ?ve minutes to one hour of usage.

This rapid increase in the social media adoption by the financial services industry seems to have happened due to three favourable factors:

1. Technological advancements (e.g., wide use of smart phones, such as Apple's i-Phone and Google's Android);
2. Increased comfortableness of customers with new technologies and channels (e.g., online and mobile banking); and
3. A more predictable regulatory environment.

Financial firms focus on managing relationships and building trust with their customers, prospecting for new clients and talented employees and Social media has enough potential to do so. Moreover, this acceleration is also due to the explosion of social media usage by the adult population generally; a recent report shows that an estimated 91 % of adults use social media regularlyand online social networking now accounts for nearly one in every ?ve minutes spent online globally. Including the financial services industry, we believe the specific purpose for adopting social media will most likely fall into one of four categories: Branding or advertising; to form and mobilize a community or group; to take advantage of the live search capabilities facilitated by social media platforms; and to provide efficient and cost-effective customer service.

The authors discussed each purpose, along with the risks and regulations that affect financial services companies as they try to achieve the respective purposes. In thecase, 'Social Media in Banking Industry" (May, 2011), published in business, economy and finance by InRev Systems, comparative analysis of various banks was done on the basis of different criterions. The

Social Media Grades showed the activeness of banks in the social media space Calculated on a scale of 5. For this purpose, the interactivity level of the banks in Facebook, Twitter, LinkedIn, YouTube and Blogs were considered. The bank's presence on any social networking sites was represented by number of channels. HDFC Bank was ranked as one of the most prominent private sector bank in India using social media as a way of connecting and engaging with customers as per the social Media Grades.

Not only has this, HDFC leveraged the power of twitter for both customer engagement and notification along with more than 12307 followers in LinkedIn. "Indian Banking Industry Social Media Case Study" retrieved from http://simplify360.com Published in business (Jan 07, 2011), the social media reach of each individual bank was searched over the internet and were scored on various parameters on the basis of statistical analysis. Banks were categorized into National Banks and Private Banks. Moreover, based on their scores, Banks were plotted against each other to measure their engagement level across social media communities (channels). Twitter, Face book, LinkedIn, Blogs, You tube etc were used .According to number of channels, HDFC and ICICI had a highest score of 5.14 whereas American express scored the highest as per the level of interactivity. On an overall basis, HDFC ranked to be the most social private sector bank in India.

Research Objective

This paper attempts to cover three broad issues:

(a) To study the role of social media marketing in banking sector

(b) Comparative analysis of Performance of Indian private sector banks on the basis of Social Media Marketing.

(c) Give suggested measures to improve their performance

Research Methodolgy

The research design used to achieve the desired objectives is Descriptive research design. The data is collected using secondary data sources. Published papers, articles and web sources of relevance are used to generate data. The target group studied is Nationalized Banks. The sample consists of Private sector banks and its Indian branches only.

Research Findings

Banking industry is on expansion spree as the economy is growing. The role of social media has increased in both the government and private Indian banks. The use of social media to stay in touch with their customers is a common thing now-a-days. As per the figure 2 which shows the results of a study done to see the interactivity level (Y axis) and the number of social channels (X axis) of the Indian private sector banks, the graph clearly indicates that almost all high customer banks use social media by any one of the following channels. Social channels surveyed were Facebook, LinkedIn and Twitter etc. Amongst these the highest social friendly bank as per the given statistics is HDFC Bank, showing presence across 8 social channels. Its presence is quiet prominent on Facebook, LinkedIn, Twitter, Youtube& its official blog. HDFC surpassed other banks in leveraging social media both in terms of number of channels used as well as customer engagement.

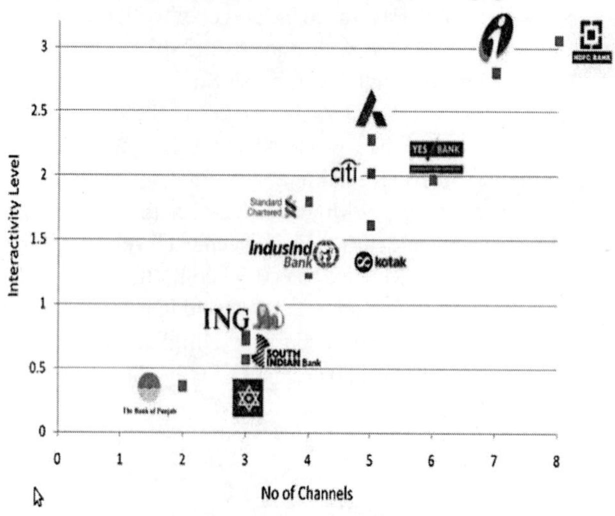

Figure 2: Relationship Between Social Media Usage and Private Banks

Source : 'Why HDFC Is No.1 Among Indian Banks For Social Media Practice. (n.d.). Retrieved from http://www.digitalvidya.com/blog/why-hdfc-is-no-1-among-indian-banks-for-social-media-practice/

Banks	No of Channels	Social Grades
HDFC BANK	8	3.06
ICICI BANK	8	2.81
AXIS BANK	5	2.28
CITI BANK	5	2.02
YES BANK	6	1.97
KOTAK MAHINDRA	5	1.62
STANDARD CHARETERED	4	1.8
INDUS IND BANK	4	1.24
ING VYSYA BANK	3	0.79
SOUTH INDIAN BANK	3	0.72
KARNATAKA BANK	3	0.57
BANK OF PUNJAB	2	0.36

The Social Media Grades shows how active the banks are in the social media space

Calculated on a scale of 5, the interactivity level of the banks in Facebook, Twitter, LinkedIn, YouTube and Blogs are taken into consideration

No of channels represents the bank's presence in any social networking sites

Social Media Grades for the Private Sector Banks in India

Figure 3: Social Grading of Banks.

Source:'Why HDFC Is No.1 Among Indian Banks For Social Media Practice. (n.d.). Retrieved from http://www.digitalvidya.com/blog/why-hdfc-is-no-1-among-indian-banks-for-social-media-practice/

Figure 3 shows the social ranking of various banks on the social channels. Grades indicate the activeness of banks on the respective social channels used.

Analysing the data the results show the private banks adopted the individual social channels for the following purposes as mentioned channel-wise below.

Facebook used as a Social Media Channel in Banks

The most common social media channel used now-a-days is Facebook. It provides platform not only for promotion of banking products but also understanding the customers and receiving their feedbacks. In addition to the above uses, HDFC provides recent financial news and puzzles based on financial terms on Facebook to enhance customer engagement.

Twitter used as a Social Media channel in Banks

Just like Facebook, Twitter is also used by banks for providing relevant information, sharing new products and interesting puzzles for customer engagement.

Youtube and LinkedIn used as Social Media Channel in Banks

Banks post their commercials regularly on Youtube for promotion. ICICI the second most social bank in India uses Youtube in a better way than HDFC for marketing purposes. HDFC still needs to leverage this channel.

LinkedIn is used by banks for displaying their products and getting recommendations from the customers. Not only this, the presence of banks on LinkedIn helps the users to extract company stats and employee information. HDFC Bank's company page on LinkedIn has more than 13,000 followers.

Conclusion

In the light of evidences it is clear that use of social media can dramatically increase the market of banking services. Moreover it will also impact how the bank's conduct product and service design, risk management, business forecasting and customer education.

The banks can benefit in numerous fronts by overcoming the risks associated with social media.

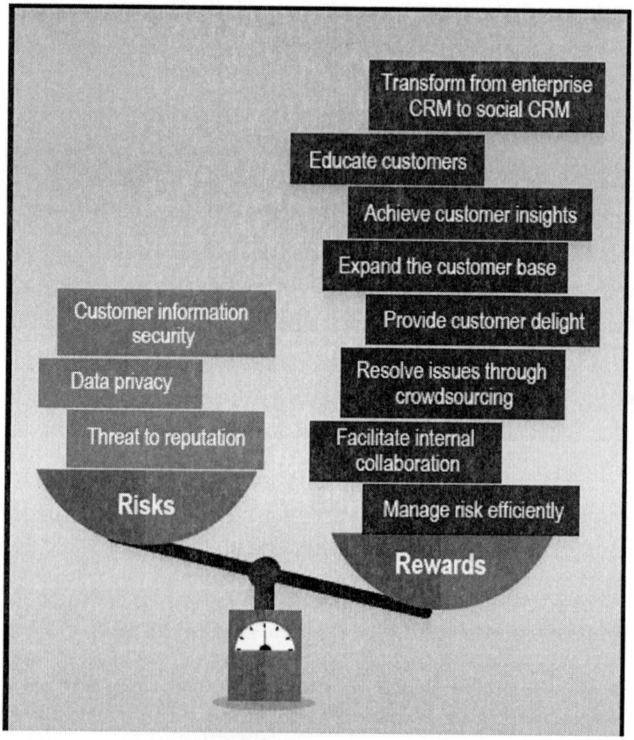

Figure 4: Risk - Reward analysis of use of social media in Banks

Source : 'How-Banks Can Use Social Media Analytics To Drive Business Advantage' Article Retrieved 02,2015, from http://www.cognizant.com/InsightsWhitepapers/How-Banks-Can-Use-Social-Media-Analytics-To-Drive-Business-Advantage.pdf

Banks using customer data for mortgage, wealth management, etc. are more successful as they generate a more holistic view of their customers' experiences. Moreover customer data gives information to customize suitable products and services by knowing important dates of customers, such as birthdays, anniversaries, etc. Moreover, keeping an eye on posts and comments of bank customers on social media provides with an idea of customer perception regarding their services. Social media also helps in increasing the reach geographically to the customers by using apps in mobile devices.

Moreover, social media channels also contain information of competitors' services. Close monitoring this information helps bank to understand the consumer needs and demand. It also informs about the customer reaction to competitive offerings. This helps in adapting strategies that lead to increased customer satisfaction.

Social media can be used to engage customers to discover solutions to business problems. It will give a feeling of belongingness to the customer.

In addition to adding value to customers, employees can use social media to share information to boosting workforce and help in knowledge dissemination.

To conclude this paper the data suggests ample evidence to say an effective social media channel can make the bank more customer friendly but also increases its accessibility and responsive to customers. In a world where customer is King, providing the right information as and when desired to customers increases customer satisfaction and elevate the bank's popularity.

References

- Chanda, R., and Zaorski, S. (2013). Social Media Usage in the Financial Services Industry: Towards a Business-Driven Compliance Approach. Journal of Taxation and Regulation of Financial Institutions, 26(5). (2011), Chanda R., Social_Networking_Leads_as_Top_Online_Activity_Globally
- Eisenberg, B. (2008). 'Understanding and aligning the value of social media', Future Now, Retrieved 02-20-2015, from http://www.grokdotcom.com/2008/11/07/understanding-and-aligning-the-value-of-social-media/
- (2015),e-Marketeer, Article Retrieved 02, 2015, from http://www.emarketer.com/Article/Social-Networking-Reaches-Nearly-One-Four-Around-World/1009976 accessed on 02-23-15.
- Hambleton, D. (2011.). Enzine Articles. Retrieved 9 -18- 2011, from http://ezinearticles.com/?How-Have-Social-Media-Platforms-Changed-The-Market-Paradigms-Of-Traditional-Industries?&id=6389273

- 'How-Banks Can Use Social Media Analytics To Drive Business Advantage' Article Retrieved 02,2015, from http://www.cognizant.com/InsightsWhitepapers/How-Banks-Can-Use-Social-Media-Analytics-To-Drive-Business-Advantage.pdf
- (2010, 10). Impact Of Social Media On Marketing Industry Researchomatic. Retrieved 10 , 2010, from http://www.researchomatic.com/Impact-Of-Social-Media-On-Marketing-Industry-42755.html
- (2013, 10). Impact of social media marketing.StudyMode.com. Retrieved 10, 2013, from http://www.studymode.com/essays/Impact-Of-Social-Media-Marketing-39824194.html
- (2012), IBM Software, Grasping the Power of Social Networking for Financial Services available at http://smcapture.com/ documents/Power%20of%20Social % 20Networking%20for%20 Financial%20 Services.pdf.
- (2011), Press Release, It's a Social World: Social Networking Leads as Top Online Activity Globally, Accounting for 1 in Every 5 Online Minutes (comScore, Dec. 21, 2011), available at http:// www.comscore.com/Press_Events/Press_ Releases/2011/12/
- (2011),Social Media Use by Financial Advisors, Social Ware Retreived23-02-15 from http://www1.socialware. com/rs/socialware/images/2011%20Financial%20Advisor%20Survey-Executive%20Summary.pdf.
- (2011, 02). Study on Social Media Marketing. StudyMode.com. Retrieved 02, 2011, from http://www.studymode.com/essays/a-Study-On-Social-Media-Marketing-574224.html
- (2012), SEC Risk Alert, supra note 1; FINRA, Regulatory Notice 11-39, supra note 1; FINRA, Regulatory Notice 10-06, supra note 1.
- (2013, 1). Social Media Marketing Researchomatic .Retrieved 1 , 2013, from http://www.researchomatic.com/Social-Media-Marketing-153368.html
- (2015), Social Media in Indian Banking available on http://www.slideshare.net/bexdeep/social-media-in-indian-banking-industry accessed on 20-02-15
- (2015), Social Media Banking available on http://www.slideshare.net/bexdeep/socia-media-banking-inrev?related=8 accessed on 02-20-2015
- (2015), 'Why HDFC Is No.1 Among Indian Banks for Social Media Practice' Article Retrieved 02,2015, from http://www.digitalvidya.com/blog/why-hdfc-is-no-1-among-indian-banks-for-social-media-practice/

35

CSR and Brand Image at Amul: Exploring the Relationship

Kanika Mahajan

Abstract

This case is about Amul, which has been able to enhance its brand image through corporate social responsibility. The paper is about what brand is and how CSR helps in enhancing brand image. Amul's CSR activities have been discussed here. It is based on the secondary data collected through various web sources. The key findings of this paper are that through CSR, Amul has been able to enhance its brand. Amul has taken up many CSR initiatives like Tribhuvandas Foundation, Swarnjayanti Gram Swarozagar Yojana, tree plantation activities, blood donation campaign, rural sanitation campaign etc. Also its organizational structure is sensitive towards CSR as it believes that technology and capital are replicable inputs but not the human capital. Since men are the basis for achieving the CSR, the Amul lays emphasis on their development also.

Keywords: *CSR, Brand Image, Amul, Agri-business*

Conceptual Background

Kotler and Armstrong (2001) defined a brand as "a seller's promise to deliver a specific set of features, benefits, and services consistent to the buyers". He also stated that branding has become such a strong force today that hardly anything goes unbranded.

A brand is a complex symbol and can convey up to six levels of meaning, in terms of attributes, benefits, values, culture, personality and user. This connects well with CSR as it reflects the core values that a company wishes to develop and engage with and communicate to its stakeholders. It has been observed that corporate branding has, over time, broadened its reach to include delivering the brand's promise to the full range of stakeholders both inside and outside the firm. This in turn has meant that new approaches to CSR, involving employee, community, and stakeholder engagement, blended seamlessly with this idea of enterprise branding. On the ground, reality of CSR management indicates that there are usually several activities, involving various actors, going on. However, to build a mature CSR framework that will support a coherent brand building exercise, it is important to consider how these activities interrelate and support each other. Research shows that conventional management systems fail to question and guide organisations towards a more responsible social and environmental performance. Many of the conventional systems enable organisations to manage their social and environmental impacts but rarely do they provide any guidance on how far or how fast the organisation needs to go to become sustainable.

Review of Literature

Barnett (2007) proposed the insight that the impact of CSR on firm value depends on the ability of CSR to influence stakeholders in the firm. Drawing upon this proposal, Servaes and Tamayo (2013) proposed an indirect link and focused on one of the key stakeholders, consumers. The pair suggested that one of the most necessary conditions for CSR to modify consumer behaviour and, hence affect firm value, is consumer awareness of firm CSR activities. They argued that consumers are less likely to respond to CSR activities, even if they are aware of them, if the CSR activities are not aligned with the firm's reputation as a responsible citizen. The view of the company's stakeholders is the most important when it comes to assessing the role of CSR activity in brand management and improvement. One can assess this view in a variety of scenarios. The most common one is a crisis scenario. Janney and Gove (2011) have studied whether a company's CSR initiatives helped it when dealing with the corporate governance scandals. They looked at the stock option backdating scandal that shook Wall Street some years back and found out "firms with enhanced overall reputations for CSR are partially buffered from scandal revelations. Studies have indicated that CSR could help companies become more resilient not just to climate change risks, but also to negative information about the company. Bhattacharya and Sen (2004), have described this as "consumers' motivations to downplay or minimize negative information about a company (e.g, in the event of crises) that they perceive to be socially responsible is a key reason why investing in CSR is akin to "building a reservoir of goodwill." It is a well-documented fact that consumers might not be willing to pay higher prices for greener products but they will more likely purchase goods from firms that are more socially responsible. According to Servaes and Tamayo (2013), the problem is that consumers are often not aware of a firm's CSR activities and this which limits the extent to which CSR reputation actually makes a difference in customers' decisions. A 2010 McKinsey global survey's shows that 76 per cent of executives believe that CSR contributes positively to the long term shareholder value and 55% of executives agree that sustainability helps their companies build a strong reputation.

CSR is being increasingly considered as a strategic branding tool and can become a market differentiating strategy. Moreover CSR is now considered as an important attribute of corporate branding. Amul's CSR mixed business model makes it a sustainable strategy for corporate brand building. It safeguards the beneficiaries from the labour exploitation. Since farmers are paid on the basis of the quality of milk they supply, it ensures quality food products by Amul reducing chances of getting blamed for sub-standard food products. (Wang & He, 2014) This case provides a road map for designing CSR sensitive organizational structure in agri-business where entire value chain from procurement of raw material to production and selling of finished agri-products is involved. This aspect would be particularly useful for new ventures and farmers' organizations. The case of Amul demonstrates that beneficiary driven CSR programmes are more sustainable, and hence an important lesson for practicing managers to build a sustainable brand.

Amul: The Company Background

Amul is one of India's most iconic brands. It's a dairy cooperative based in the town of Anand, in Gujarat state and was born out of the so-called "white revolution" which turned India into the world's largest milk producing country. The company is most known for butter and milk, but produces dozens of products from frozen yogurt to paneer. With $2 billion in revenue, the brand is as recognizable across India as Coca-Cola and has begun exporting products to the Indian communities in UAE, Singapore and elsewhere. The brand is managed by the Gujarat Cooperative Milk Marketing Federation (GCMMF) which is owned by more than 3 million small farmers in the state of Gujarat, all of whom benefit directly from the company's successes. What's even more interesting is how the milk collection system is structured to benefit even folks with a single cow.

The seeds of this unusual saga were sown more than 65 years back in Kaira, a small town in the state of Gujarat in western India. Over six decades ago the life of a farmer in Kaira was very much like that of farmers anywhere else in India. His income was derived almost entirely from seasonal crops. Many poor farmers faced starvation during off-seasons. Their income from milch buffaloes was undependable. The milk marketing system was controlled by contractors and middlemen. As milk is perishable, farmers were compelled to sell their milk for whatever they were offered. Often they had to sell cream and ghee at a throwaway price. They were in general illiterate. But they could see that the system under which contractors could buy their produce at a low price and arrange to sell it at huge profits was just not fair. This became more noticeable when the Government of Bombay started the Bombay Milk Scheme in 1945. Milk had to be transported 427 kilometers, from Anand to Bombay. This could be done only if milk was pasteurized in Anand.

After preliminary trials, the Government of Bombay entered into an agreement with Polsons Limited to supply milk from Anand to Bombay on a regular basis. The arrangement was highly satisfactory to all concerned - except the farmers. The Government found it profitable; Polsons kept a good margin. Milk contractors took the biggest cut. No one had taken the trouble to fix the price of milk to be paid to the producers. Thus under the Bombay Milk Scheme the farmers of Kaira District were no better off ever before. They were still at the mercy of milk contractors. They had to sell their milk at a price the contractors fixed. The discontent of the farmers grew. They went in deputation to Sardar Patel, who had advocated farmers' co-operatives as early as 1942. Sardar Patel reiterated his advice that they should market their milk through a co-operative society of their own. This co-operative should have its own pasteurization plant. His advice was that the farmers should demand permission to set up such a co-operative. If their demand was rejected, they should refuse to sell their milk to middlemen. Sardar Patel pointed out that in undertaking such a strike there should be some losses to the farmers as they would not be able to sell their milk for some time. If they were prepared to put up with the loss, he was prepared to lead them. The farmers' deputation readily accepted his proposal. Sardar then sent his trusted deputy, Mr. Morarjibhai Desai, to Kaira District to organize milk co-operative - and a milk strike if necessary. Mr. Desai held a meeting in Samarkha village on January 4, 1946. It was resolved that milk producers' co-operative societies should be organized in each village of Kaira District to collect milk from their member-farmers. All the milk societies would federate into a Union which would own milk processing facilities. The Government should undertake to buy milk from the Union. If this wasn't done, the farmers would refuse to sell milk to any milk contractor in Kaira District.

The Government turned down the demand. The farmers called a 'milk strike'. It lasted 15 days. Not a drop of milk was sold to the milk merchants. No milk reached Bombay from Anand, and the Bombay Milk Scheme almost collapsed. After 15 days the milk commissioner of Bombay, an Englishman, and his deputy visited Anand, assessed the situation and accepted the farmers' demand. This marked the beginning of the Kaira District Co-operative Milk Producers' Union Limited, Anand. It was formally registered on December 14, 1946. Its objective was to provide proper marketing facilities for the milk producers of the district. The Union began pasteurizing milk in June 1948, for the Bombay Milk Scheme-just a handful of farmers in two village co-operative societies producing about 250 liters a day. An assured market proved a great incentive to the milk producers in the district. By the end of 1948, 432 farmers had joined village societies, and the quantity of milk handled by the Union had increased to 5000 liters a day. In the early stages, rapid growth brought in its wake serious problems. Their solution provided the stimulus for further growth. For example, as the co-operative movement spread in the district, it was found that the Bombay Milk Scheme could not absorb the extra milk collected by the Union in winter, when buffaloes yielded an average of 2.5 times their summer yield. Thus by 1953, the farmer-members had no regular market for the extra milk produced in winter. They were again forced to sell a large surplus at low rate to middlemen.

The only remedy was to set up a plant to process the extra milk into products like butter and milk powder. The logic of this step was readily accepted by the Government of Bombay and the Government of India, except for a few doubting Thomases. The government of India helped the Union to get financial help from UNICEF and assistance from the Government of New Zealand under the Colombo Plan. Technical aid was provided by F.A.O. A Rs. 50 - lakh factory to process milk powder and butter was blueprinted. Its foundation stone was laid by the then President of India the late Dr. Rajendra Prasad on November 15, 1954. The project was completed by October 31, 1955, on which day the late Pandit Jawaharlal Nehru, the then Prime Minister of India, declared it open. The new dairy provided a further fillip to the co-operative movement among milk producers. The union was thus enabled to organize more village co-operative societies and to handle more and more milk each year. This event also brought a breakthrough in dairy technology as the products were made processing buffalo milk for the first time in the world. Kaira Union introduced the brand "Amul" for marketing its product range. The word "Amul" is derived from Sanskrit word 'Amulya' which means 'priceless' or precious'. In the subsequent years Amul made cheese and baby food on a large commercial scale again processing buffalo milk creating a history in the world.

1964 was the turning point in the history of dairy development programme in India. Late Shri Lal Bahadur Shastri, the then Prime Minister of India who visited Anand on 31s October for inauguration of Amul's Cattle Feed Plant, having spent a night with farmers of Kaira and experiencing the success wished and expressed to Mr Kurien, then the General Manager of Amul that replicating Amul model throughout our country will bring a great change in the socio-economic conditions of the people. In order to bring this dream into reality, 1965 The National Dairy Development Board (NDDB) was established at Anand and by 1969-70 NDDB came out with the dairy development programme for India popularly known as "Operation Flood" or "White Revolution". The

Operation Flood programme, even today, stands to be the largest dairy development programme ever drawn in the world. This saw Amul as model and this model is often referred in the history of White Revolution as "Anand Pattern". Replication of "Anand Pattern" has helped India to emerge as the largest milk producing nation in the world.

Type	Cooperative
Industry	Dairy / FMCG
Founded	1946
Headquarters	Anand, Gujarat, India
Revenue	US$3.1 billion (2013-14)
Employees	750 employees of Marketing arm; The real pool consists of 3 million milk producer members
Slogan	The Taste of India
Website	www.amul.com
Logo	Amul The Taste of India

Figure 1: About Amul (Anand Milk Union Limited)

Source: http://en.wikipedia.org/wiki/Amul

The Amul Model

To meet with the CSR it is expected that a business in its entire procurement-production-processing-marketing chain should focus on human development involving the producer, the worker, the supplier, the consumer, the civil society, and the environment. Indeed, a very tough task. Most businesses would certainly flounder in not being able to achieve at least one or many of those expectations. But Amul has shown the way.

The Amul Model of dairy development is a three-tiered structure with the dairy cooperative societies at the village level federated under a milk union at the district level and a federation of member unions at the state level. Due to this movement, the country's milk production tripled between the years 1971 and 1996. Similarly, the per capita milk consumption doubled from 111 gm per day in 1973 to 222 gm per day in 2000. The Amul model has helped India to emerge as the largest milk producer in the world. More than 15 million milk producers pour their milk in 1,44,500 dairy cooperative societies across the country. Their milk is processed in 184 District Co-operative Unions and marketed by 22 State Marketing Federations, ensuring a better life for millions. Amul is a three tier co-operative organization. The first tier is the co-operative society at the village of which; milk producers are voluntary members, managing the co-operative through a democratically elected 9-member managing committee, and doing business by purchasing milk from members and selling it to the district level co-operative. There are more than 11,000 co-operatives in villages of Gujarat. The second tier is the district co-operative that processes milk into milk products, markets locally and sells surplus to the state co-operative for national and international marketing. There are 12 district co-operatives each being managed by a 15-member board elected by the college comprising the nominated representatives or chairmen of the village co-operatives. Third tier is the state level co-operative — the Gujarat Co-operative Milk Marketing Federation (GCMMF) responsible for national and international marketing of milk and milk products produced and sold to it.

The GCMMF is managed by the board democratically elected by and from amongst the chairmen of the district co-operatives. The entire three-tier structure with the GCMMF at its apex, is a unique institution because it encompasses the entire chain from production of raw material to reaching the consumer with the end product. Every function involves human intervention: 23.60 lakh primary milk producers; 35,000 rural workmen in more than 11,400 village societies; 12,000 workers in 15 dairy plants; 750 marketing professionals; 10,500 salesmen in distribution network and 600,000 salesmen in retail network. Accumulation of human capital is sine qua non for the development and growth of any enterprise or economy. The GCMMF is sensitive towards CSR. It believes that technology and capital are replicable inputs but not the human capital. Since men are the basis for achieving the CSR, the GCMMF lays emphasis on their development also.

The dairy cooperatives have been able to maintain democratic structure atleast at the grass-root level with the management committee of the village level unit elected from among the members in majority of the villages. The dairy cooperatives have also been instrumental in bridging the social divide of caste, creed, race, religion and language at the villages, by offering open and voluntary membership. This CSR-sensitive organizational structure has made a huge impact on millions, as can be seen in Table 1 and Figure 2.

Table 1: The Stakeholders and the Capacity

Number of Producer Members	6,80,962
Number of Village Dairy Cooperative Societies	1206

Total Milk Handling Capacity	4.5 Million litres per day
Milk Collection (Daily Average)	1.8 Million litres
Milk Drying Capacity	100 Mts per day
Whey Drying Capacity	60 Mts per day
Cattle Feed Manufacturing Capacity	1200 Mts per day

Source: www.amul.com

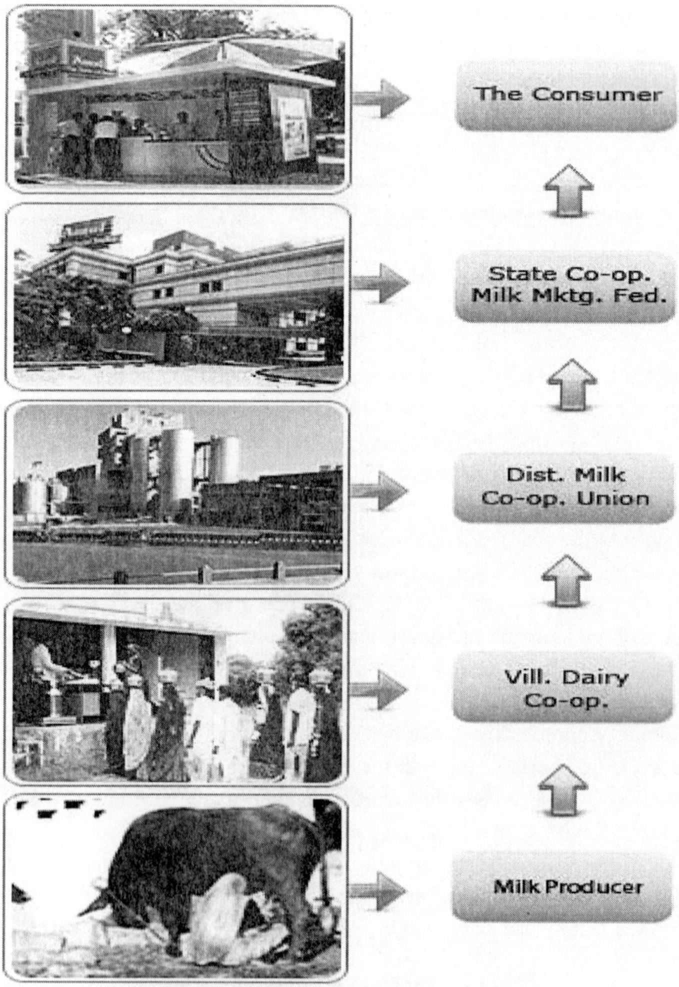

Figure 2: The Amul Model of Dairy Development

Source : www.amul.com

CSR-Sensitive Business Philosophy

The first step towards discharging the CSR is the business philosophy of the GCMMF. It is two-fold: one, to serve the interests of milk producers and second, to provide quality products to consumers as value for money. Evolution of an organisational system has ensured that the corporate social responsibility towards the primary milk producers, village and the ecological balance is fulfilled. The milk producers are paid for their milk in accordance with market forces and realisation of value for their produce. Invariably the price paid to the member-producers in Gujarat is higher by 15 per cent than the national average.

CSR Orientation to Distributors and Retailers

The GCMMF has identified the distributors and retailers are its important link in its vendor supply chain. Through surveys the GCMMF found that 90% of the distributors do not get any opportunity of exposure to latest management practices. The GCMMF realised that it was a corporate social responsibility to strengthen the core business processes of its distributors so as to keep them in mainstream business and compete with those with formal training in management. The GCMMF has developed and trained all its distributors through Value-Mission-Strategy Workshops, competence building, Amul Yatra, Amul Quality Circle meetings, computerisation, and electronic commerce activities.

CSR-Oriented Staff

The GCMMF hires and trains people to take advantage over its competitors. It has developed in-house modules for training and competence building to improve and upgrade of their knowledge; communication skills to understand the customer, be responsive to customer requirements, and communicate clearly for trouble shooting of problems. They are expected to be courteous, friendly, respectful, and considerate to the customer. To improve the credibility and trustworthiness of the managers it is important they perform consistently and accurately every time and at all times. The structure of salary and perquisites is altogether different. The first and foremost the staff must get satisfaction from the job they. They are recognised for their contribution.

Amul as a Brand

Amul has been adjudged as India's 'Most Trusted' food and beverage (F&B) brand, according to The Brand Trust Report, India Study (BTR)-2013. The brand is owned by Gujarat Cooperative Milk Marketing Federation (GCCMF). There were a total of 123 brands listed in the category. Climbing 56 ranks over its last year, Amul has also become India's 22nd Most Trust among all brands, the report said. Amul is also the largest exporter of dairy products in the country. Amul is available today in over 40 countries of the world. Amul is exporting a wide variety of products which include whole and skimmed milk powder, cottage cheese (Paneer), UHT milk, clarified butter (Ghee) and indigenous sweets. The major markets are USA, West Indies, and countries in Africa, the Gulf Region, and SAARC neighbours, Singapore, The Philippines, Thailand, Japan and China, and others such as Mauritius, Australia, Hong Kong and a few South African countries. Its bid to enter the Japanese market in 1994 did not succeed, but it plans to venture again. There are many reasons which has led to the Amul becoming a trusted brand like the quality it offers, well managed supply chain, advertisement policies and the most important is CSR initiatives.

CSR Initiatives of Amul

Amul Relief Trust : A devastating earthquake (Richter scale 7.9) hit Gujarat on 26th January 2001. The epicentre of the quake was located in Kutch district. It caused death of thousands of people, tens of thousands were injured, hundreds of thousands were rendered homeless and damage of billions of Rupees was done. GCMMF formed a specific organization named "Amul Relief Trust" (ART) under the Chairmanship of Dr. V. Kurien in 2001 with a donation of Rs. 50 Millions for reconstruction of the school buildings damaged in the 2001 earthquake in the Kutch area.

Tribhuvandas Foundation : Tribhuvandas Foundation is an Integrated Rural Health & Development Programme of Amul. Inspired by the great success of round the clock health care services to the livestock of dairy farmers of Kaira, Shri Tribhuvandas Patel, the Founder Chairman of Amul felt the need of such a service to the rural populace too as he could learn and experience the afflictions brought to them by absence of medical services in rural villages of Kaira. The Foundation derives its uniqueness from the fact that it is a need-based programme for villagers and is run by the villagers themselves. It fulfills the basic health care needs of the villages. Apart from providing primary treatment for various common ailments, the Foundation is also actively involved in promoting preventive health practices. It is headquartered at Anand with sub-centers spread over the district Anand and Kheda. The Foundation has a dedicated Team of Medical Officers, Nurses, Administrative staff, Dais (Traditional Birth Attendants) and Village Health Workers to provide various services. It also provides continuous training and retraining to Village Health Workers who are chosen from villages with the help of the Dairy Co-operative Societies. The Foundation has pioneered in large scale implementation of the concept of 'Safe Delivery Kit' in India ensuring a hygienic and safe delivery of pregnant mother. In association with Sankara Eye Hospital, the Foundation has helped in performing 2000 surgeries free of cost for the vision impaired patients.

Tribhuvandas Foundation has become one of Asia's largest community healthcare service providers covering more than 700 villages. The Foundation still strives to extend its services to as much villages as possible.

Swarnjayanti Gram Swarozgar Yojana (SGSY) : The Swarnjayanti Gram Swarozagar Yojana is a holistic self-employment programme for the rural poor of India. The basic objective of the programme is to bring below poverty line families above poverty line by providing them in generating assets to become self-employed. The purchase of assets is facilitated through a mix of government subsidy and bank credit.

Tree Plantation : Alarmed by the climate change and global warming and their understanding of that dairy farming like agriculture is dependent on nature, farmers of Kaira took an oath on 15th August, 2007, after the flag hoisting ceremony, to plant a sapling and ensure that it grew into a tree. Then individually they planted sapling on their own at their identified locations like their farm, near their home, on farm bunds, etc. This marked the beginning of a silent new revolution to bring a green carpet on Gujarat and India. In the year 2007, 21,000 saplings were planted by the farmers in Kaira of which 10,000 plants have survived. In the following year 2008, they planted more than 5,05,000 saplings of which 1,79,000 have survived. In 2009, third year of their movement, more than 13,51,000 saplings have been planted.

Blood Donation : Amul in association with the Indian Red Cross Society aim to inspire, encourage and initiate humanitarian services to minimize, alleviate and prevent human suffering at all times to contribute for "Humanity to Peace". Towards this objective Amul initiated blood donation campaign since 1987. Blood donation camps are organized regularly in rural areas through Village Dairy Co-operative Societies. Similarly camps are organized in Amul Dairy Campus wherein employees and their family members join in donating blood. In addition, Amul organizes donation of blood on emergency. Amul has made a trend in donating blood to the society.

Dairy Demonstration Farm : A Dairy Demonstration Farm (DDF) has been set up at Mogar to demonstrate scientific methods of dairy farming. The project envisages encouraging the farmers to use high yielding animals and modern aids to increase milk production. The Union provides technical support to milk producers on Scientific Animal Husbandry practices and also facilitates loan disbursement from banks to the needy by guaranteeing the loan repayment on behalf of farmers. The Dairy Demonstration Farm is generating overwhelming interest in milk producer members because of its success and viability.

Amul Scholarships : To encourage outstanding children of farmers in pursuing higher studies Amul introduced scholarship schemes in 1992. The children are given scholarships for pursing Diploma, Graduation, Post-Graduation and Doctorate. Every year the outstanding children are identified from the villages and scholarships are provided to fulfill their dream of achieving academic excellence. This effort has motivated greatly children to excel in their studies and spread education in rural areas.

Rural Sanitation Campaign : Amul Dairy has launched a novel scheme for total rural sanitation and set a target for itself whereby not a single milk producer will attend to nature's call in the open. The Dairy with the support of District Rural Development Agency (DRDA) will provide interest free loans to its milk producers in Anand and Kheda districts to set up 'pucca' toilet blocks, which will not only help women milk producers avoid embarrassment but will also ensure hygiene. In five years' time, dairy wishes to achieve the target of providing 100 per cent toilet facilities in all villages where Amul has a milk society.

Leaders of Indian industry could contribute significantly to corporate social responsibility by adopting the methodology followed by Amul, World Bank Country Director Onno Ruhl said at an orientation workshop on CSR (corporate social responsibility) being organised by the Department of Public Enterprises in partnership with the World Bank. He recalled that Amul had pioneered inclusive growth through work with dairy farmers at grass-root level, changing lives, enhancing income, empowering women and at the same time reaping benefits to the business.

Achievements

The effort to provide green cover to the earth was also acknowledged when the state level apex body of Gujarat Dairy Cooperatives GCMMF received four successive prestigious "SRISHTI's G-Cube Award" in 2007, 2008, 2009 and 2010 for Good Green Governance in the "Service Category." Further, "Amul Green" movement has also been awarded by International Dairy Federation for best environment initiative in the "Sustainability Category" during the 4th Global Dairy Conference held at Salzburg Congress Center, Austria in 2010. These CSR initiatives have helped Amul actually become a global brand.

Conclusion

CSR has plays a very important role in building a brand as it enhances the organisation's reputation. CSR is associated with a greater intention to consume the company's products, greater intention to seek employment with the company, and also greater intention to invest in the company. By adopting CSR sensitive organizational structure and taking up number of CSR initiatives Amul has also benefitted from CSR which is one of the important factors that has contributed in making Amul a successful brand.

References

- American Marketing Association (2005): Dictionary of Marketing Terms.
- Barnett, ML (2007) Stakeholder influence capacity and the variability of financial returns to corporate social responsibility, Academy of Management Review, 32:794-816.
- Bhattacharya and Sen (2004), Doing better at doing good: When, Why, and How Consumers Respond to Corporate Social Initiatives, California Management Review, Vol. 47, No. 1.
- http://www.amuldairy.com/index.php/about-us/history [Accessed on February 22, 2015].
- http://archive.financialexpress.com/
- http://archive.financialexpress.com/news/corporate-social-responsibility-the-amul-way/112172.
- http://www.amuldairy.com/[Accessed on February 22, 2015].
- http://www.business-standard.com/article/companies/amul-india-s-most-trusted-food-beverage-brand-report-113021300399_1.html.
- http://www.marketingpower.com.
- Janney, J. and Gove, S. (2011), Reputation and Corporate Social Responsibility Aberrations, Trends, and Hypocrisy: Reactions to Firm Choices in the Stock Option Backdating Scandal (November 2011). Journal of Management Studies, Vol. 48, Issue 7, pp. 1562-1585, 2011.
- Kotler, P. and Armstrong, G. (2001) The Principles of Marketing, New Jersey; Pearson.
- Servaes and Tamayo (2013) The Impact of Corporate Social Responsibility on Firm Value, Management Science 59(5), pp. 1045-1061.
- Wang and He (2014), Brand Management in Emerging Markets: Theories and Practices, 2014, IGI Global, USA.

36

Innovations in Dairy Industry of Haryana: An Overview

Rupa & Rajiv Kumar

Abstract

Haryana is one of the major producers of dairy products of India. Dairying contributes lots in the economic development of Haryana state. Haryana state occupies a prominent place for high breed livestock wealth and a home town of precious breed of buffalo i.e., 'Murrah' and cow i.e., 'Hariana'. Haryana, with 660 grams of availability of milk per capita per day, ranks at number two in the country as against the national average of 232 grams. The main objective of this study is to trace the scenario of Haryana dairy industry with critical examination of innovations run by govt. of Haryana. This study also finds out problems and prospects of Haryana dairy industry. In order to make the Haryana a model State in the dairy sector, a lot more has to be done for promoting dairy development in coming decades.

Introduction

Haryana came into existence on 1 November 1966 as a newly created state. At present Haryana is one of the wealthier states of India and had the second highest per capita income in the country at 119,158 in the year 2012-13 and 132,089 in the year 2013-14. The state is divided into four divisions for administrative purposes: Ambala, Rohtak, Gurgaon and Hisar. Within these there are 21 districts, 58 sub-divisions, 80 tehsils, 50 sub-tehsils and 125 blocks. Haryana has a total of 154 cities and towns and 6,841 villages. Haryana is one of the most progressive states of Republic of India. People rear and breed cattle as a subsidiary occupation.

Table 1

Divisions	***Districts***
Ambala	Ambala, Kaithal, Kurukshetra, Panchkula, Yamuna Nagar
Gurgaon	Faridabad, Palwal, Gurgaon, Mahendragarh, Mewat, Rewari
Hisar	Bhiwani, Fatehabad, Jind, Hisar, Sirsa
Rohtak	Jhajjar, Karnal, Panipat, Rohtak, Sonipat

Dairy farming is also an essential part of the Haryana economy. Milk and milk products form an essential part of the local diet. There is a saying Desaan main des Haryana, jit doodh dahi ka khaana, Haryana holds a special place in the field of milk production and it is truly known as the 'Milk

Pail' of the country as 80 per cent of the State milk comes from buffaloes alone. Haryana, with 660 grams of availability of milk per capita per day, ranks at number two in the country as against the national average of 232 grams. There is a vast network of milk societies that support the dairy industry. The National Dairy Research Institute at Karnal, and the Central Institute for Research on Buffaloes at Hisar are most prestigious and important institutions for the development of new breeds of cattle.

The State is proud to be the home town of one of the best buffalo breeds of the world i.e., 'Murrah'. Buffalo has also been recognized to be the animal of the 21st Century and thus, systematic improvement of buffaloes for milk production of the country is a topic to be proud. There is a great demand of this high yielding breed not only from within but outside the country as well. Most of the States procure breeding stock from Haryana for upgradation of their low producing buffaloes. The State is quite conscious of conserving, improving and fast multiplying this unique genetic stock of buffaloes by promoting breeding activities in the State.

Haryana Dairy Policy

The various programmer launched in the State has been to adopt the Anand pattern of Milk Co-operatives. Under this system, all the functions of dairying like milk procurement, processing and marketing are controlled by the Milk Producers themselves. It has three tier system comprising milk Producers Societies at the village level, Milk Producers Co-operative Union at the district level and the state Milk Federation as an apex body at the State level came into existence on April 1,1977. Its authorized share capital is Rs.4000 lacs. It was established with the primary aim to promote economic interests of the milk producers of Haryana particularly those belonging to weaker sections of the village community by procuring and processing milk into milk products and marketing thereof by itself or through its unions. In furtherance of the above objects, the Federation undertakes a number of activities such as establishment of milk plants, marketing of milk products of the Milk Unions. It also extends technical guidance to the Unions in all spheres of personnel, technical, marketing and financial management as well as makes them quality conscious, through use of modern methods of laboratory testing of various products.

Government of Haryana vide notification dated 12/13 January, 2000 constituted the Haryana Livestock Development Board to promote breeding and development of livestock specially cattle and buffaloes in the State by undertaking activities relating to and necessary for improving livestock production and productivity. Later on vide notification dated 12.04.2001 the Government enacted an act titled the Haryana Murrah Buffalo and Other Much Animal Breed (Preservation and Development of Animal Husbandry and Dairy Development Sector) Act, 2001 with the objective to provide for improvement of the genetic stock of the milch animals specifically the prime breed 'Murrah' and local breeds like 'Sahiwal' and 'Hariana' to improve the skills and technology in the dairy farming and for taking steps for the development of Animal Husbandry and Dairy Development Sectors and to constitute the Haryana Livestock Development Board to achieve this objective.

Organisations for dairy development

Haryana Animal Husbandry and dairy development administration This has been playing a significant role in making dairying work on modern commercial lines. The major trust of policies and programmes of the State Government has been concentrated on the following strategies.

(i) To achieve growth rate more then 6-7 to 10 per cent in animal husbandry and dairy sector.

(ii) To increase individual animal productivity.

(iii) To make Murrah Buffaloes to the Animal of 21st Century.

(iv) Global export of Murrahs Germplasm as Triple purpose animals.

(v) Quality Breeding Improvement Services.

(vi) Veterinary Health and Disease Control.

(vii) Feed and Fodder production.

(viii) Human Resource Development.

(ix) Publicity and Extension.

Department of Animal Husbandry and Dairy, Haryana The main objective of animal husbandary department is:

1. To provide quality breeding services to enhance productivity.
2. Upgradation and conservation of indigenous breeds.
3. Quality control of Feed, Milk and Milk products.
4. Veterinary Extension, Education and Training.
5. Promotion of Dairying for self-employment.
6. Special livestock production programme for social upliftment.

Haryana livestock development board

Dairydevelopment Programme

Under this programme, the Board's mandate is to provide self employment opportunities to the un-employed youth through dairy profession. The department is providing training facilities to the un-employed youth and conducting 21 days' Dairy Training of the Milk Producers so as to create awareness about the Scientific methods and techniques/management in the field. Beneficiaries are being imparted training free of cost at various District Head Quarters about Modern Dairy Technology, Dairy Management, Feeding and Breeding of Milch Animals and production of clean and wholesome milk.

Haryana Dairy Development Cooperation Federation Ltd.

The Dairy Corporation was formed in 1970 which continued active functioning till 31.03.1977. The Haryana Dairy Development Cooperative Federation Ltd. (HDDCF) is engaged in procurement and processing of milk and manufacturing of milk products under the famous market brand "Vita". A range of Vita Products is including 250 No. of milk and milk products distributor, Institutions, Defence Units, Districts Jails and 354 No. of milk booth network to provide good quality liquid milk & milk products to the general public. Vita milk products are known for their quality and good taste not only in Haryana but entire Northern Region. The sale of Vita products also contributes to the economic upliftment and welfare of farmers of Haryana.

Developments of Dairy in Haryana State

Live Stock Population

Haryana is a rural prominent state. About 80% of state income come from agriculture and animal husbandry. In villages almost two in one family has cow or buffalo for milk. These milk can be used for their consumption or for sale. As per Survey of National dairy development Board Livestock Census-2007, Livestock population of the State is 3564 thousand including 662 thousand cows. Total 2,799 Veterinary Institutions spread over the entire State. On an average, there is one Veterinary Institution for every three villages in the State. In addition to this 1,145 ILDCs (Integrated Livestock Dev. Centres) have been established in PPP (private public partnership) mode to provide animal breeding facilities in equal number of villages.

Milk Production

The milk production in the State during the year 2012-13 was 70.40 lakh tonne. The per capita per day milk availability in the State for the year 2012-13 was 747 grams, which is the second highest in the country.

Table 2

Year	Estimated Milk Production in Haryana	Milk Production in India	Growth in Haryana Production (%)	Growthin India Production(%)
1999-2000	4.7	78.3		
2005-2006	5.3	97.1	13%	24%
2010-2011	6.3	121.8	19%	25%
2012-2013	7	132.4	11%	9%

ANIMAL HUSBANDRY AND DAIRYING DEPARTMENT, HARYANA
Statement showing Progress made during 2006-07 to 2012-13

Table 3

Item	Units	2006-07	2007-08	2008-09	2009-10	2010-11	2011-12	2012-13	
Milk Production	Lacs M.T.	53.67	54.51	57.45	60.06	62.67	66.61	70.40	-
Per Capita avail. Per Day	Grms	624	622	668	673	680	708	747	-

Pricing Milk Products

The Dairy Co-operatives in Haryana has procured 3.40 lakh milk per day during the period 1.4.2013 to 31.12.2013. The rate of milk has been increased Rs 385 to Rs 510 per kilo fat.

Innovations in Dairy Industry

Haryana Dairy has introduced insurance scheme for those farmers who are committed members and are pouring milk continuously for the last 3 years. The farmers will be insured for Rs 1 lakh for which they will have to pay Rs 10 only. Under the scheme, 26,000 milk producers have been insured.

Gujarat based Sabarkantha District Co-operative Milk Producers Union Limited (SDCMPUL), popularly known as Sabar Dairy has started operation of its new plant in Rohtak, Haryana.

In order to improve the genetic merit of livestock, special attention is being given towards conservation, multiplication and improvement of indigenous germplasm such as Murrah breed of buffaloes and Hariana and Sahiwal breeds of cows. The owners of recorded high milk yielding Murrah buffaloes are to be awarded cash incentive ranging from Rs 5,000 to Rs 25,000 which has been raised to Rs 10,000 to 30,000 depending on the peak milk yield for the year 2013-14 (to be given in the year 2014-15).

The Veterinary Institutions are being provided all essential veterinary medicines and life-saving drugs. For providing specialised veterinary services, the State has established veterinary polyclinics at strategic locations. So far, 5 Polyclinics have been established at Sirsa, Bhiwani, Sonipat, Rohtak and Panchkula.

A new scheme "Mukhya Mantri Gramin Dudharu Pashudhan Suraksha Yozna" has been launched in the year 2013-14 to provide compensation to the farmers in the eventually of 44sudden death of milch animals in the State and a budgetary provision of Rs 4 crore under plan scheme has been made for the year 2014-15.

Constraints Hampering the Optimum Output

A critical appraisal of the dairy development efforts done by Haryana govt. reveals that these programs are facing following constraints which hampered the optimum output of the these programmes:

1. The productivity of animals for milk in quite low which is one of the major constraints in dairy development. The farmers rear un-producing animals due to social and other factors. Poor animal management has led to poor performance of animals and lesser economic returns. There is lack of scientific knowledge among the farmers
2. Inadequate health coverage is another problem . It is evident from the number of veterinary hospitals are not adequate.
3. The institutional and service infrastructure created at different levels could not be utilized sufficiently and effectively. Today, dairying is a highly technical activity, present study revealed that very limited number of people has been trained in dairy farming in the State.
4. The human resource requirement and availability in respect of veterinary personnel, to meet the development need, is not available at desired levels.
5. The dairy farmers who wanted to setup high tech commercial dairies frequently been harassed by the Bankers and the amount sanctioned under loan scheme has not been found adequate.

6. The dairy cooperative network has not been able to procure adequate quantity of milk to the total milk production in the State. The dairy cooperative network in the State has been facing various organizational and administrative problems and shortage of staff at various levels.
7. With the rise in industrialisation in Haryana, there is a tremendous reduction of grazing land. Along with this, today, villagers with even a small piece of land have begun cultivating crops. This has subsequently resulted in dairy farmers having to buy fodder from the market instead of getting it for free from the grazing fields.
8. Fixing the right price for milk is urgently required for dairy farmers to have a profitable dairy business. This could help them modernise dairy production and cattle rearing, and help buy more cattle. Eventually the right milk price can allow the dairy farmers of Haryana to have decent earnings and a better life.

Concluding Observations

The present critical study of various dairy development programmes in the State of Haryana reveals that the financial, operating and many other types of assistance to dairy farmers have now been looked after by different separate agencies, mostly operating in isolation. In absence of a clear sense of directions and proper supervision and coordination, the dairy development programmes tend to lose their original perspect to enhance the earning levels of dairy farmers.

The net outcome has been in the form of unproductive and inadequate utilization of resources coupled with duplicacy of efforts due to lack of proper coordination at various level between State Department of Animal Husbandry & Dairying Development and the Dairy Cooperative Network in the State as well as other agencies. In order to make the Haryana a model State in the dairy sector, a lot more has to be done for promoting dairy development in coming decades.

References

- Armstrong, G., Farley, H., Gray, J., and Mark, D. (2004) .Marketing health enhancing foods: implications from the dairy sector. Marketing Intelligence & Planning, 23(7), 705-719.
- Chawla, A., Chawla, N,. and Pant, Y.(2009). Milk and Dairy products in India-Production, Consumption and Exports. Hindustan studies and Services Ltd.Retrievedmarch ,2013fromhttp://www. technology park.com/marketplace/ reports/ hs_milkreport_intro_toc_sep09. pdf
- Indian Dairy and Products Annual, Gain report (2012), retrieved March 22, 2013 from http://www.thefarmsite.com/reports/contents/inddoct12. pdf
- Indian Dairy Industry, IUF Dairy division, Retrieved March 21,2013, from http://cms.iuf.org/sites/cms.iuf.org/files/Indian % 20Dairy % 20 Industry. pdf.

- Karmakar, K., & Banerjee, G.(2006). Opportunities and challenges in the Indian Dairy industry. Technical digest, 9, 24-27.
- Milk and dairy products, Agribusiness handbook, retrieved march 21, 2013 from https://www.responsibleagroinvestment.org/sites/responsibleagroinvestment.org/files/FAO_ Agbiz % 20hand book_ Milk_ Dairy % 20Products. pdf
- Milk and Dairy Sector, Retrieved April 20, 2013, from www.dsir.gov.in/reports/ittp_tedo/agro/AF_Animals_Milk_Dairy_Intro.pdf
- National dairy development board website. Retrieved 23 march, 2013 from http://www.nddb.org/English/Pages/default.aspx
- Rathore, Bhavna, (2006), The Indian drinks industry 2006: Management briefing: Milk and dairy based beverages. Just Drinks, 17.
- Rathore, Bhavna.(2006). Milk and dairy based beverages. The Indian drinks industry 2006, 17.
- Smith, N (1999). A study of milk marketing by selected dairy companies in port Elizabeth. Paper for master degree fulfillment.
- Mallikarjun, K. (2009-10). A study on consumer awareness of nandini milk and milk products and impact of promotional activities in creating brand awareness. school of management studies. banglore, Indian academy: 1-124.
- John, S., & Senith, S.(2012). A study on relationship between income level and branded milk. European Journal of Business and Management, 4(8), 133-140.
- Prague.(2013). The competitive environment in the dairy industry and its impact on the food industry. Agris on line papers in economics and informatics. 5(2), 89-102.
- Mani.(2012). A macro to micro study on the history of milk cooperatives across the globe. Shiv shakti international journal in multidisciplinary and academic research.2(1)
- http://www.nddb.org/English/Pages/default.aspx
- http://www.vitaindia.com/objectives.php
- http://pashudhanharyana.gov.in/html/statistics.htm
- http://www.icar.org.in/en/animal-science.htm

37

LIPC: Logistics Information Platform on Cloud

Shivani Dubey & Sunayana Jain

Abstract

Cloud computing provides numerous opportunities and value-added capabilities for logistics organizations in order to remain competitive and be successful, however, there are conflicting viewpoints regarding cloud viability. Logistics information platform serves hundreds of thousands of customers in more than hundred countries. The logistics companies are expanding to help their customer achieve lower latency and higher throughput and to ensure that their data resides only in the region they specify. Logistics information platform has complexity which involves the relevant interest in long term development of many departments and enterprises. The logistics companies should improve the logistics informatization policies and regulations, improve the environment of logistics development and speed of the logistics infrastructure. This paper focuses on the overall framework of logistics information platform and introduces and analysis the logistics information platform on cloud (LIPC), which establish a logistics information interchange, data exchange to meet the business requirements of the various types logistics information platform.

Keywords: *Logistics Information Platform, Cloud Computing, Logistics Information Platform on Cloud (LIPC)*

I. Introduction

Logistics use new advance information technologies and equipment and takes the goods from suppliers to receive accurate, timely, accurate, secure, quality and quantity of rationalization, door to door service mode and service processes. It is the management of the flow of resources, between the point of origin and the point of destination in order to meet some requirements. The resources managed in logistics can include physical items as food, materials, equipment, liquids and staff as well as abstract items as information, particles and energy. The logistics of physical items usually involves the integration of information flow, material handling, production, packaging, inventory, transportation, warehousing and oftentimes security. Furthermore the complexity of logistics can be modeled, analyzed, visualized and optimized by dedicated simulation software. Minimizing time and use of resources are common goals. Logistics appears with the emergence of commodity products, with the development of commodity products, so logistics is an ancient traditional economic activity. However, this traditional logistics system has a big problem, platform, it toward more diversity on the service scope and improves a greater scope of information exchange. Logistics information management is a unified planning and organization of logistics information resources, and controls logistics information collection, processing, storage, retrieval, transfer and application reasonably. So that coordinated the logistics supply chain, achieved information shared and interaction, reduced information redundant and errors, assisted decision support, improved customer relationship, eventually realize a height unified in information, funds, business and logistics, and achieve the purpose of improving the competitiveness of supply chain of the logistics. Quality of logistics information platform is the demand for logistics can enjoy faster, cheaper services, improve its efficiency or quality of life.

II. Logistics Information Platform

Logistics information platform can enable enterprise to actively respond to the market and business activities through the information fast, accurate and real time flow in the logistics system. The information of each subsystem is extracted and stored in the database of logistics information platform, which can effectively integrate various existing logistics information resources. The platform supports and provides guarantee for the rapid development of logistics industry. Logistics information platform can be improved for the transparency of the logistics operation, reduce logistics information exchange links, shortens the cycle of logistics operation, reduce operating cost and logistics service level. Logistics enterprises establish long term partnership with multiple logistics agencies through the logistics information platform, which is very important to improve the utilization rate of a large number of idle logistics resources to realize the logistics scale benefits. There are so many functions of Logistics Information Platform:

- Logistics Information Collection
- Logistics Information Processing
- Logistics Information Management
- Logistics Information Storage
- Logistics Information Query
- Online Trading

The main important function of logistics information platform is integrating various information resources to complete the data exchange, improve the data sharing and the information transformation. Each information system send public data to the platform following specific rules, and the platform deal with those data and store them, then provide services using those data. Logistics Information Platform can be described 3C model in paper, which describes 3 functionalities which contains content, connectivity and business, content refers to the release of logistics information and construction of logistics knowledge, connectivity mainly refers to the exchange of logistics data, focusing on data transmission, the core of business aspects is of online trading, logistics tracking and query.

Governments, research institutions and logistics business need timely access to foreign-related logistics information to understand the logistics dynamical domestic and international, and conduct cross border logistics business interaction. Therefore, logistics information platform is very necessary, which is an important for the development of the logistics information platform. The logistics information platform builds a unified platform for network data processing and business systems connecting domestic and foreign platforms, thus making the domestic logistics companies joint track with foreign logistics platforms, realizing data exchange; providing accurate, rapid and comprehensive domestic and international logistics information and other related value- added business services; developing inter-regional co- operation of logistics, which will be play a significant role in promoting multi faceted, multi-level and wide-ranging cooperation and exchanges on domestic logistics enterprises and foreign enterprises.

III. Cloud Computing

Cloud computing includes virtualization services, ranging from those operating internally to a large enterprise, to outside firms that manage major computing and data handling tasks, to those providing small-scale services from centralized providers. Cloud computing can offer individual organizations many benefits in addition to productivity increases.

These include:

- Functionality: the economies of scale of cloud services mean that providers are able to make significant investments in the functionality of their products.
- Mobility: increased capacity to work from a mobile device is a key reason for some organizations in acquiring cloud services. Cloud services have enabled a new wave of mobile applications and virtualized work environments, accessible on any device, anywhere.
- Scalability: cloud services enable an individual or company to access computer services on a pay-as-you-go basis, with the flexibility to scale up and down as needed for little marginal cost.
- Strong security: cloud service providers can offer small business better security, reliability and access to the latest upgrades than would otherwise have been possible through traditional in-house solutions.

IV. History of Cloud Computing Based Logistic Information Platform

In 2010, Yu Huafeng built a cloud logistics information platform from the cloud computing infrastructure services, platform services and cloud federal services by discussing the application of cloud computing in the logistics information platform [8]. In 2011, Guo Shi-jun explored the impact of cloud computing to Internet of things intelligent logistics system in China and puts forward the architecture and operational framework of Internet of things intelligent logistics system [9]. In 2011, Cai Guo-ping also analyzed the logistics enterprise's business process and the existing problems. In 2012, Lin Yun put forward an innovation model of logistics service oriented to supply chain called logistics cloud service (LCS).And also proposed the business architecture and technology architecture, the discussed key technologies and problems for implementing LCS [10]. In 2012 Xun W also proposed the cloud logistics-based One-stop Service Platform for logistics center has been put forward. Through a unified, centralized, intelligent management and operation of cloud logistics platform, we can provide the supply chain users with comprehensive, fast and efficient logistics services [11]. The other studies about the cloud computing have also provides basis and reference model for cloud logistics service mode research. Huang Shen-quan put forward the meta-modeling framework for cloud service supporting evolution, presented the formal definition of meta-meta-model and the conceptual model of cloud service. Based on the research, he presented the evolution process model of cloud service [12]. Kaewpuang R proposed that a service oriented cloud can be built and program using Microsoft Windows server and program using Microsoft CCR/DSS, presented the architecture of this service oriented cloud [13]. Cheng Y analyzed information flow and capital flow, the transactions on hardware-class, software-class, product class and capability-class CSs by considering the multi-layer of logistics and the characteristics of different cloud services (CSs) [14]. Christoph A presented a core feature of the platform, In this paper, a service repository as a single point of truth coping with the complexity of miscellaneous service descriptions and models. Central idea behind this repository is the integration of different specialized service models and the construction of a comprehensive model, which supports direct implementation of services as concrete logistics tasks [15]. These research works are mainly in view of the construction of logistics information platform. According to IBM, a top multinational IT consulting corporation, the use of cloud computing will be more than double until 2014 (Berman et al., 2012). Through the survey, they discovered that 72 per cent of the participants had already piloted, adopted or substantially implemented cloud technologies and 90 per cent of the respondents expected to have done so in three years. More specifically, the number of respondents whose companies have substantially implemented cloud is expected to grow from 13per cent today to 41 per cent in three years [16].

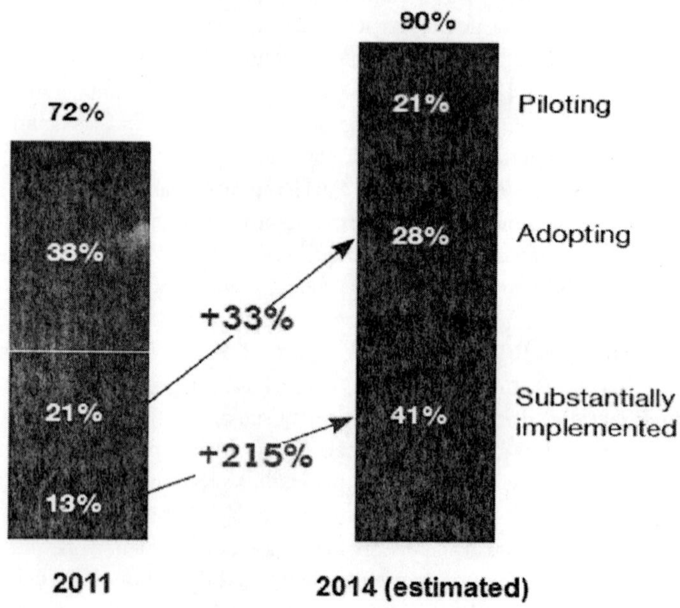

Figure 1: Level of Cloud Computing (IBM Institute for Value, 2011)

Cloud logistics service system is not effectively yet and has not set up this type of any logistics information platform model. In the study of cloud service, though the cloud services is studied from the perspective of cloud services architecture and built parts of the service models, but it has not constructed logistics information system of cloud systemically for specific characteristics of the cloud logistics. Cloud Computing helps users decrease their investments for their own IT infrastructure. So it is very beneficial for small and medium enterprises. In this paper, we propose to design a logistics information platform on cloud computing. Any logistics firm can access this platform as service and no need to buy their own IT infrastructure.

V. Logistics Information Platform on Cloud (LIPC)

LIPC is to integrate the resources of the whole society so that the enterprises can achieve interconnection of information networks, can share the information resources to the society, can make full use of all resources in the areas of economic and social development, reduce operational costs and increase social benefits.

LIPC helps companies to improve their service levels by coordinating the chain's partners (retailers, suppliers and distributors) that are playing a major role in demand forecasting. LIPC can gather information related to sales data via internet, perform basic analytics and consequently execute more accurate statistical demand forecasts for all the logistics partners. This platform can operate database, which contains multiple data about different suppliers, creating significant benefits for companies that deal routinely with thousands of them. Consequently, companies are able to choose their suppliers depending if they can provide the appropriate information according to the specifications and time limits.

LIPC has open standard system platform, software services and these services are not concentrated in one place, but located in different servers across tens of thousands of. it has also virtualization which enables users to various resources in the cloud anywhere using different terminals to access information without the need to understand the specific situation of logistics resources and the calculation process. This platform has different functions like data collection, calculation, update, configuration management, dynamic control and transmission as well as business development, and other functions. In LIPC, an information can be easier to collect and flow, and significantly reduce the cost of logistics information management system on the basis of the cloud computing technologies. The studies in cloud based platform about logistics are still less, it has not yet been able to build cloud applications business architecture for the cloud logistics. So building the logistics information platform on cloud is very necessary.

VI. Applications of LIPC

Logistics companies use cloud computing which has facilities of transmission technology, distribution technology, storage technology, automation and other expertise to support the pattern of the modern logistics equipment and technology. There are some new applications where LIPC can be used:

- Agricultural Platform: Government investment in the information distribution is very inadequate and producer cannot pay more attention on the information distribution, so low degree of information sharing hampered the process of the construction of agricultural information. Now Cloud computing establishes information network services platforms in agricultural industry for qualitative upgrading of information [17].
- GPS/GIS platform: It is based on geographic information to support GPS/ GIS information support platform, set data access and system interface, vehicle location, route information and personal information [18].
- Smart Logistics platform: it is an application which includes continuous vehicle fleet tracking, container goods control, and asset management, or other location-based services [19].
- Sensor platform: Wireless Sensor Network is an information source is enabler for a new type of logistics, which uses static best before dates into account using information acquired during storage and transport [20].

VII. Conclusion

Cloud computing attracts more countries and enterprises with its powerful advantages and market potential, the feasibility and applicability of whose application are also exploring in various logistics industries. LIPC will bring greater opportunities to the information platform development and also be the inevitable choice to achieve modernization and informatization in logistics industries. Government should be aware that it will be a long exploring process in the weak infrastructure and information distribution, where the application difficulties are hard to imagine. Government and logistics industries should pay attention on this type of platform, raise awareness, and especially provide strong support in platform construction, resource integration and service capabilities.

References

- H. G. wu and s. Dunn. Environmentally Responsisle Logistics Systerms [J]. International Journal of Physical and Logistics Management, 1995,25(2):20

- Jean-paul Rodrigue, Brian slack, Claude comtois. Green logistics[M]. Published in A.M. Brewer, K.J. Button and D.A.Hensher (eds), 2001:141-145.
- Limin Jia, Zhigang Liu, Yong Qin, Minghua Zhao, Lijun Diao, Research on Construction of Urban Logistics information Platform, proceeding of International Conference on Electrical and Information Technologies for Rail Transportation (EITRT 2013), Vol.1, 2013
- S.L. Deng, "Port Logistics Information Platform,"China Communications Press, Beijing, 2007.
- Z.Y. Liu and Y.Q. Hu, "Sutdy on Logistics Information Platform Architecture," Chinese Journal of Management, Vol. 2, 2005.
- Zhen Yu, Gui-Cheng Shen, Bing-Wu Liu, Research on Architecture of Logistics Public Information Platform, Intelligent Information Management, 2012, 4, 396-400
- Information Economy Report 2013, The Cloud Economy and Developing countries, United Nations Conference on Trade and Development, UNCTAD, United Nation Publication, ISSN 2075-4396
- AMIR V.D., SAYED? GHOLAM H T, RAJKUMAR B., An effective architecture for automated appliance management system applying ontology, based cloud discovery[C]//IEEE/ACM International Conference on Cluster, Cloud and Grid Computing, 2010: 104-112.
- Bian Wen-liang, Logistics information network: building and operation [M]. Social sciences academic press,2008. (In Chinese) BIAOS, A hybrid algorithm for partner selection in market oriented cloudcomputing[C]//International Conference on Management and Service Science. 2009:1-4.
- Bosona, T.G. and Gebresenbet, G. Cluster building and logistics network integration of local food supply chain. Biosystems Engineering, 2011,108(4):293-302.
- Cai Guo-ping, Cloud computing technology and its application in the design and operation of the electronic commerce logistics[J]. Wuyi University.2011. (In Chinese)
- Christoph Augenstein, André Ludwig, Bogdan Franczyk. Integration of Service Models -Preliminary Results for Consistent Logistics Service Management[C]. 2012 Service Research and Innovation Institute Global Conference, 2012.pp.100-109.
- CUI Ai-ping, LIU Wei, Study on Capabil ity Coordination in Logistics Service Supply Chain with Options Contract[J].Chinese Journal of Management Science,2009.02. (In Chinese)

- Guo Shi-jun, Luo Ting, Qing Tai-ping, The Internet of things intelligent logistics system based on cloud computing[J]. 2011(12):115-117.(In Chinese)
- Holtkamp, B., Steinbuss, S. Gsell, H. et al. Towards a logistics cloud. Semantics Knowledge and Grid (SKG), Proceedings of 2010 Sixth International Conference on Semantics Knowledge and Grid (SKG 2010). 2010, 305 - 308.
- CUI Ai-ping, LIU Wei, Study on Capability Coordination in Logistics Service Supply Chain with Options Contract[J].Chinese Journal of Management Science,2009.02. (In Chinese)
- Yanxin Zhu, Di Wu and Sujian Li, Cloud Computing and Agricultural Development of China: Theory and Practice, IJCSI International Journal of Computer Science Issues, Vol. 10, Issue 1, No. 1, January 2013.
- Eirini Aivazidou, 2 Antonios Antoniou, 3 Konstantinos Arvanitopoulos 4 Agorasti Toka 4, Using Cloud Computing in Supply Chain Management: Third-Party Logistics in the Cloud, 2nd International Conference on Supply Chains, 2013.
- Guo Shi-jun, Luo Ting, Qing Tai-ping, The Internet of things intelligent logistics system based on cloud computing[J]. 2011(12):115-117.(In Chinese)
- Abel Avitesh Chandra and Seong Ro Lee, A Method of WSN and Sensor Cloud system to Monitor Cold Chain Logistics as Part of the IoT Technology, International Journal of Multimedia and Ubiquitous Engineering Vol. 9, No. 10 (2014), pp. 145-152

38

Finally Medicines are Affordable: Success Story of Innovative Public Procurement Model

Ekta Pandey

Abstract

Health of highest attainable standards is a fundamental right and access to affordable medicines is an integral part of it. World has made monumental advances in healthcare yet every year millions of people die due to lack of life-saving medicines. The issue of accessibility and affordability of essential medicines is today a global concern, more so critical in case of developing and underdeveloped nations.

In India approximately 4% of gross domestic product is spent on health care. Out of this contribution about 70-80% of health care expenditure is on drugs . One of the key barriers to accessing health services is the cost of medicines. Thus ensuring access to affordable medicines is essential for health of citizens and sustainable development of the Indian economy.

The proposed research focuses on the economic burden of the society due to expenditure on medicines. The aim is to collect information for evidence based decision making by doing cost analysis of medicines and to find out innovative methods of financing to provide increased access to affordable medicines.

The cost analysis will include a comparative study of retail prices and public procurement rates of Tamil Nadu Medical State Corporation of selected extremely essential and commonly used drugs. Based on the study results, the aim is to collect information for evidence based decision making and suggest policy recommendations if required, to reduce the expenditure on medicines.
Keywords: *Affordable Medicines, Cost Analysis, Public Procurement, Centralized Procurement, TNMSC Model.*

1. Introduction

Medicines are scientific innovations which have saved a lot of lives and greatly reduced burden of many diseases. The success story of Indian pharmaceutical has unfortunately not reflected in improved health status of the citizens. Though India is called "The pharmacy of the globe" but ironically 50 to 65 per cent of people do not have regular access to essential medicines .

The key impediments to treatment are low purchasing power, high medicine prices and poor availability critically in developing nations due to inadequate public healthcare funding, inefficient supply chain management system, poor governance and lack of accountability.

In countries like India where majority of the population buys its medicines and is not provided state insurance, so even a single illness episode exposes the family to a high risk of impoverishment.

The ultimate goal of healthcare system is to improve the population health along with providing risk protection and thereby enhancing the consumer satisfaction. Financial mechanism has a critical role in healthcare systems of all the countries.

1.1 Medicine Expenditure Financing Mechanism in India

Health systems collect revenue by tax based financing which includes both direct tax and indirect tax and public sector involving Central and State Government along with many autonomous public sector bodies, Insurance based financing which includes social health insurance, private insurance, community based health insurance, Out of pocket expenditure and Donor financing While all the methods have their own advantages and shortcomings, relying solely on any single method is usually not advisable.

Tax based health financing followed in a few counties along with social health insurance system is considered to be the most equitable and efficient method of financing as they work on the principles of insurance supported by three pillars of prepayment, risk pooling and cross subsidization. On the other hand household expenditure is considered to be quiet inefficient. Countries where major source of health financing comes from out-of-pocket there is disproportionately higher payment from low income people than the high income people, (inequity) both in terms of the access and the ability to pay.

In India only 4% of gross domestic product is spent on health care as is shown in Figure 1.

The government contribution to the public health system is around 1% Gross Domestic Product and the rest is majorly contributed by private expenditure.

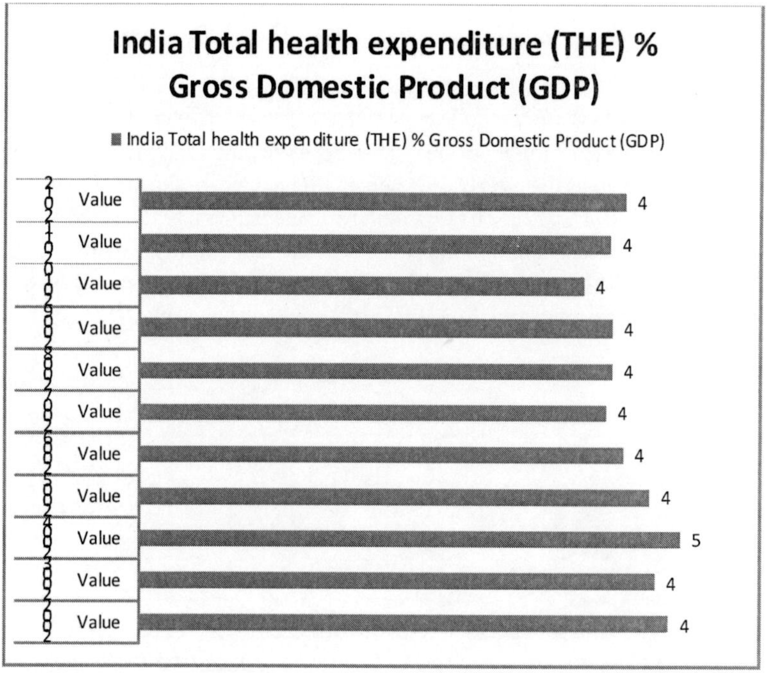

Figure 1: Pattern of Indian Total Health Expenditure as a Percentage of GDP from 2002 to 2012

Source 3: NHA 2012, Global Health expenditure database, WHO available on http://apps.who.int/nha/database/ViewData/Indicators/en as accessed on 21-02-2015.

Out of the total health expenditure in India the contribution of households is around 67% of total health expenditure . While rest 33% is done by State and Central Government as shown in Figure 2.

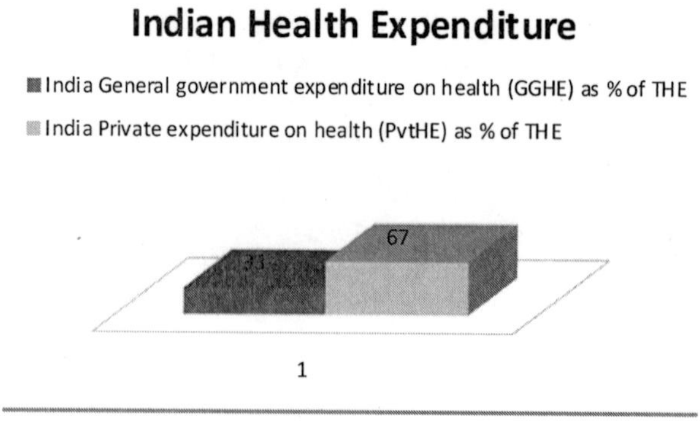

Figure 2: Indian Health Expenditure Mechanism in 2012.

Source3: NHA 2012, Global Health expenditure database, WHO available on http://apps.who.int/nha/database/ViewData/Indicators/en as accessed on 21-02-2015

Household expenditure on health has been growing at nearly 14% overall, and research shows that nearly 66.4 percent of health care expenditure was on drugs during 2011-2012 , . The expenditure on medicines has decreased around 5% in rural areas and approximately 3% in urban India, from 2004-05 to 2012. Surprisingly the expenditure on medicines was higher approximately 69% in the rural India as compared to 63% in urban areas during 2011-2012.

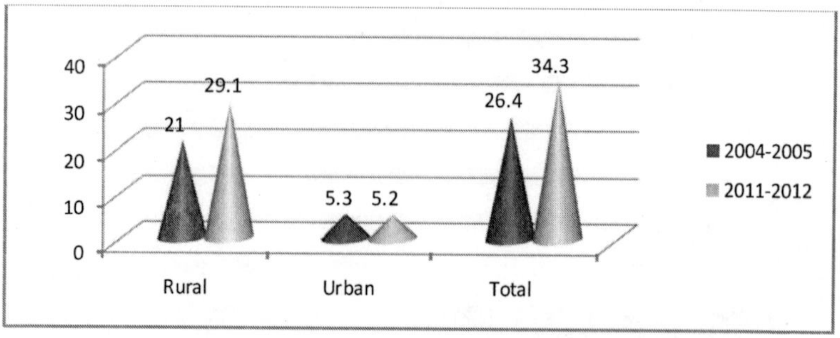

Figure 3: Expenditure on Medicine as Percentage of Total OOP Expenditure on Health in Rural and urban areas of India During 2004-05 and 2011-12.

Source 4,5 Selvaraj, S. et al India Infrastructure Report 2013-14

NSSO Report, CES Data 68th Round.

As previously discussed a health system is considered inefficient if it is not adequately funded by the Government. As Indian healthcare majorly relies on out of pocket expenditure, the chances of catastrophic expenditure increases in our country's scenario. Most of the people either do not avail treatment as they cannot afford it or if they consume the health services they are pushed below poverty lines.

Moreover the effects of medicine expenditure are worse on poor and rural population and this leads to widening of gap between rural and urban population leading to inequity in health. This is clearly illustrated in figure 4 given below.

It is even more ironical India being the "Global Pharmacy of South" 2 supplying generic drugs to many countries is unable to provide drugs to many of its citizens.

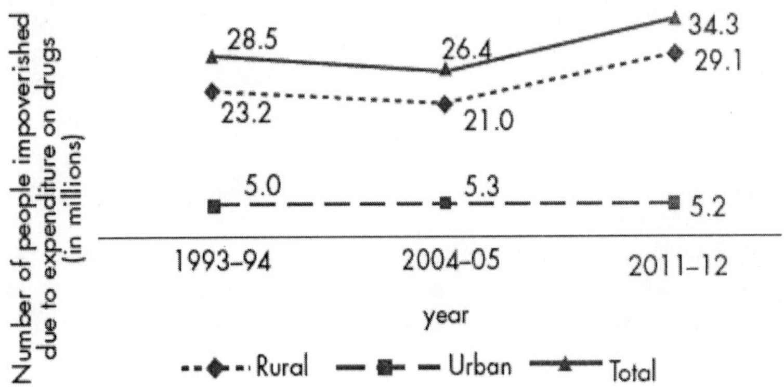

Figure 4: Medicine Expenditure leading to impoverishment in India.

Source 4,5 Selvaraj, S. et al India Infrastructure Report 2013-14

NSSO Report, CES Data 68th Round.

Recognizing the emerging problem of providing equitable and affordable medicines many innovative models of procurement were adopted in various states of India. One of these models of public medicine procurement revolutionized the Indian health system by its successful innovative ways.

1.2 Tamil Nadu Medical Services Corporation Limited

Tamil Nadu Medical Services Corporation Ltd., (TNMSC) was established under the Companies Act, 1956 in July, 1994 and the functionality begun from January, 19956. The main objective was to ensure availability of all essential medicines in the Government hospitals and Medical Institutions in Tamil Nadu state by streamlining medicine procurement, storage and distribution system.

The TNMSC does the procurement, storage and supply of medicines and drugs, surgical items and sutures to various primary health centers and government hospitals of Tamil Nadu.

2. Literature Review

Medicines are scientific innovations which have saved a lot of lives and greatly reduced burden of many diseases. Evidences indicate expenditure on medicines is quite high. Medicines are the second biggest expenditure item after personnel . Though it is a matter of grave concern throughout the world but it becomes crucial in developing country like India where pharmaceutical market is dominated by the private sector along with absent or weak social health insurance systems.

As stated by Lu et al. in The World Medicine Situation Report, 2011 the per capita expenditures on medicine in 2005-2006 was approximately US$ 7.61 in low-income countries and it was around US$ 431.6 in high-income countries with some variation with different income groups. The rate of change in pharmaceutical expenditure as compared with 1995 statistics showed greater increase in middle- and low-income countries. Provision of medicines to patients is one of the key functions of efficient health system. Rising health care costs, inelastic nature of healthcare demand and limited resources has made it mandatory to make efficient allocation of scarce resources. Sound decisions based on cost analysis are the basis of health policy formulation.

The situation of expenditure on medicines in various states is depicted in Figure 5 given below. Though increasing the public expenditure on health would improve the situation but it is seen to be ineffective without a sound supply chain and logistics management system.

Name of states	*Overall expenditure on healthcare 2010–11 (Rs Lakh)*	*Drug expenditure as % of healthcare expenditure*
Assam	8,635	5.0
Bihar	13,350	7.0
Gujarat	15,431	7.6
Haryana	6,090	5.5
Kerala	24,861	12.5
Maharashtra	20,882	5.2
Madhya Pradesh	12,213	9.3
Punjab	1,545	1.0
Rajasthan	3,854	1.5
Uttar Pradesh	31,481	5.3
Jharkhand	2,716	3.4
West Bengal	21,403	6.8
Andhra Pradesh	23,458	10.0
Karnataka	14,831	6.3
Tamil Nadu	43,657	12.2
Himachal Pradesh	1,122	1.9
Jammu & Kashmir	4,550	4.3
Central Government	253,368	15.0
Total	503,447	13.0

Figure 5: State-wise Expenditure on Medicines During 2010-11

Source : 4 Selvaraj, S. et al India Infrastructure Report 2013-14.

In India the pharmaceutical prices have increased many-fold due to various policy regimes. The trend line of price changes in medicines as compared to other commodities from 1993-2011 is shown in Figure 6.

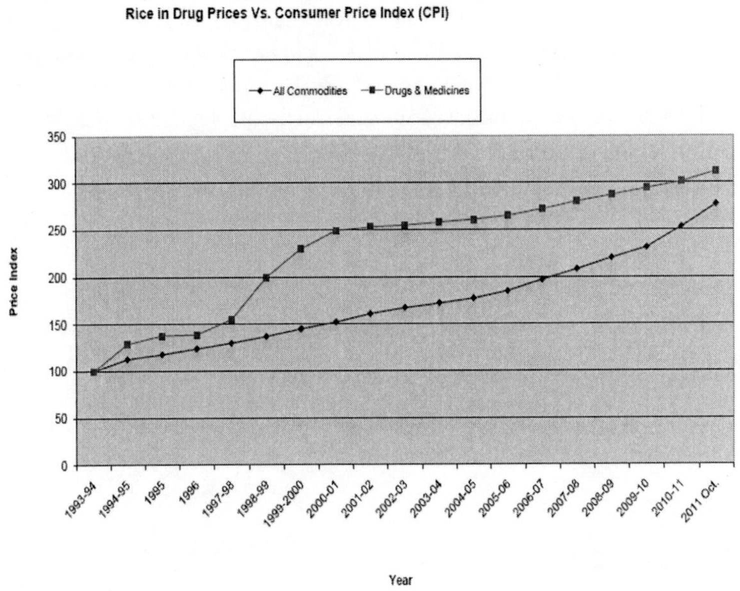

Figure 6: Trend line Showing Medicine Prices and other Commodity Prices from 1993 -2011

Source : HLEG Secretariat, Aggregated data from Respective Monthly Bulletin of Reserve Bank of India, Mumbai

A procurement system is efficient if the medicines are procured comes under the category of NLEM (National List of Essential Medicines), both the quality as well as quantity are optimum and the procurement is done at lowest possible prices. Moreover an accurate demand and forecasting method is of utmost importance in healthcare to avoid acute shortage as well as wastage of medicines.

A model is based on the principle of transparency is the key to success in public procurement of medicines. Based on these norms many states adopted innovative public procurement models to ensure ready availability of affordable medicines and drugs at government hospitals.

Rajasthan and Tamil Nadu followed a centralized procurement system with decentralized distribution, while Chhattisgarh followed a decentralized system of procurement.

The Tamil Nadu Medical Services Corporation (TNMSC) started in 1994, is now a pioneer of the drug procurement system in India. The TNMSC model supplies medicines free of cost at the public hospitals. TNMSC has adopted a complete transparency through a passbook-based supply system supported by computerized management. Drug warehouses have been set up in headquarters of all districts, from where supplies given to the public health facilities. Drug Distribution Management System (DDMS) of each district warehouse is connected to the head office and whole process of issue and receipt of medicines has been computerized. This has not only made it time effective but also has reduced wastage and stock-outs. On the similar lines of TNMSC model the Rajasthan Medical Services Corporation (RMSC) was established in 2011 to replicate its success. RMSC is also a centralized procurement system with decentralized distribution system.

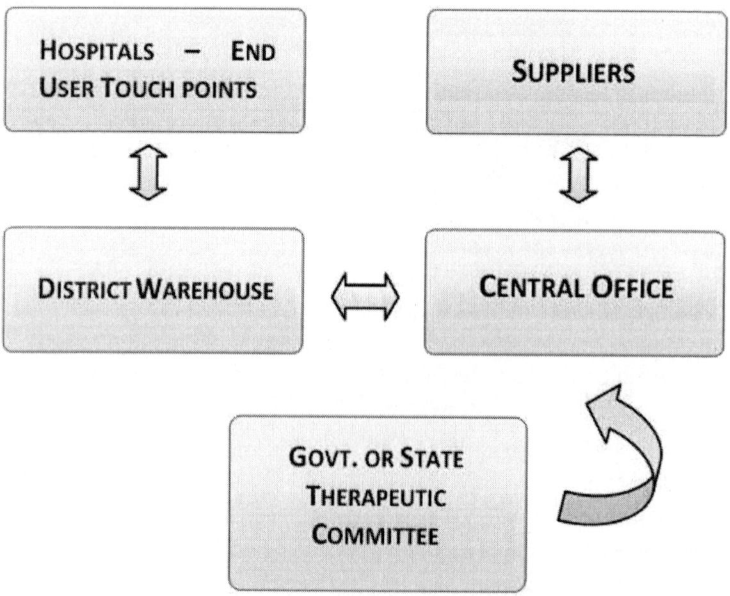

Figure 7: Centralized Drug Delivery System of TNMSC model

Source : Article on Public Healthcare - Paving the way for a Cost Efficient Drug Procurement & Distribution System from website http://tejas.iimb.ac.in/articles/17.php accessed on 22-01-15

While these centralized models were working well, Chhattisgarh adopted a decentralized procurement system at district level. This model could not utilize the advantage of economies of scale in pooled procurement of centralized systems. Clarity in documentation was also absent leading to several compounded problems.

3. Methodology

The aim of this study is to undertake an independent evaluation of the difference in the prices of the selected basket of medicines at public procurement prices of TNMSC and RMSC and market prices. The study was grounded in access to medicines framework and the approach was from the dual perspective of market prices and public procurement prices at TNMSC and RMSC. The ultimate goal of this research is to suggest measure to reduce expenditure on medicines used in the treatment.

3.1 Objectives of the Study:

- Assess the cost of medicines. Analyze the difference between retail prices of pharmaceuticals in the open market and the procurement rates of TNMSC and RMSC.
- Recommend relevant policy options to reduce the out of pocket expenditure on medicines based in the light of findings.

3.2 Research Design

Type of study: Cost analysis - Partial Economic evaluation study (Analytical Research)

3.3 Statistical and Conceptual Tools

This section describes the terms that were adopted in the study.

Maximum Retail Price (MRP): The price at which the product shall be sold in retail and which include all taxes levied on the product.

Price to Retailer (PTR): The price to retailer is the price of a medicine at which it is sold to the retailer and is presumed to include duties but not local taxes.

Cost: The total resources consumed in producing a good or service. It represents the sum of the value of the inputs in production - land, labor, capital and enterprise.

Price: The amount of money that consumers have to give up to purchase an item.

Cost Analysis: Cost analysis is a partial economic evaluation that helps in the estimation of the comparative costs of alternative treatments or healthcare programmes.

Microsoft Excel and STATA software is used to analyze the dataset of NHA on health expenditure as given in who website. The mean of MRP is calculated as given in IMS health data and mean procurement prices are calculated from TNMSC procurement tender to analyze the price differences of a unit of selected medicine.

3.4 Sources of Data

The data collected and analyzed is secondary data from published literature from refereed journals. Economic evaluation articles are analyzed. The document guidelines of government on medicine procurement have been evaluated from various health reports. National Health accounts latest statistics on health expenditure in India has been taken from World Health Organization website.

Price documents / tenders of drugs procured were accessed from the official website of TNMSC (www.tnmsc.com) RMSC (http://rmsc.nic.in/background.html). Approved medicine procurement rates were only taken from published tender documents. TNMSC and RMSC are public enterprises established under Company's Act, 1956.

4. Research Findings

The Tamil Nadu Medical Service Corporation (TNMSC) was set up in 1994, is a pioneer in a system of procurement and distribution. The design of the system helps to contain costs of drugs to a large extent. There is a centralized drug procurement system followed by a distribution system supported by a decentralized system of drug management. It is clearly seen to ensure maximum efficiency and transparency TNMSC uses a 'two-envelope system'. The first phase has technical bidding. Once companies pass technical bid they are allowed to fill the second tender of financial bid. To ensure quality the contracts awarded to Good Manufacturing Practices (GMP) compliant manufacturers only and that too, with a minimum ceiling of annual turnover.

The result of the efficiency of centralized public procurement and decentralized distribution of medicines is clearly shown in Table 1.

Table 1: Comparison of TNMSC Procurement Prices and MRP of Selected Medicines is Shown.

Generic Name of Drug (1)	Dosage (2)	Unit (3)	MRP printed on pack/strip (4)	TNMSC prices (5)	TNMSC Price/ MRP (5/4)
Albendazole Tablets	400mg	10 Tablets	250	4.55	54.94
Alprazolam Tablets	0.5 mg	10 Tablets	14	0.51	27.45
Amlodipine Tablets	2.5 mg	10 Tablets	23	0.41	56.01
Atorvastatin Tablets	10mg	10 Tablets	65	2.1	30.95
Citizine Tablets	10mg	10 Tablets	35	0.49	71.42
Diazepam Tablets	5mg	10 Tablets	18	0.55	32.72

Source : Article on the need to cut pharma super-profits available at http://

Albendazole medication is a broad-spectrum antihelmenthic and is used for the treatment of a variety of parasitic worm infestations. The Albendazole tablet costs Rs 250 in retail market. While the same medicine was procured at Rs 4.55 in TNMSC prices which shows the price is fifty four times higher in retail market as compared to public procurement prices.

Alprazolam tablets are short-acting psychoactive drugs. The MRP of Alprazolam tablets is Rs 14,while it costs 50paise in TNMSC procurement model. Again a stark price difference is seen as MRP of Alprazolam is twenty seven times higher than TNMSC prices.

Amlodipine is a medication used to lower blood pressure and prevent chest pain. The MRP of these tablets is Rs 23, while it costs 41 paise in TNMSC procurement model. MRP is fifty six times higher than TNMSC prices.

Atorvastatin is a member of the drug class known as statins which are used primarily for lowering blood cholesterol. This helps to prevent events associated with cardiovascular disease. The tablet Atorvastatin costs Rs 65 in retail market. While the same medicine was procured at Rs 2.1 in TNMSC prices which shows the price is thirty times higher in retail market as compared to public procurement prices.

Cetirizine is a second-generation antihistamine used in the treatment of hay fever. The MRP of Citrizine tablets is Rs35, while it costs 49paise in TNMSC procurement model. Again a stark price difference is seen as MRP of Citrizine is seventy one times higher than TNMSC prices.

Diazepam is used to treat a wide range of conditions, including anxiety, panic attacks, insomnia and seizures. The tablet Diazepam costs Rs 18 in retail market. While the same medicine was procured at 55paise in TNMSC prices which shows the price is thirty two times higher in retail market as compared to public procurement prices.

5. Conclusion & Recommendation

The centralized medicine procurement system especially of Tamil Nadu state has clearly demonstrated its superiority over the other systems of procurement of medicines. Public procurement is seen as a promising option to bring economies of scale and affordability in medicines. But there is always a need to ensure transparency in the whole system.

However, considering the stark difference in prices of retail market and public procurement in the same medicines it is worth the effort to invest in promoting and sustaining the centralized procurement of medicines.

The two phased bidding system will help in better implementation and transparency of the procurement. To avoid bottlenecks an internet portal should be developed and a common link should be maintained between the suppliers and warehouse. The drug delivery saves a lot of manual entry time.

A decentralized system is vulnerable to wastage of time and money. There are more chances of making mistakes and increased rate of corruption and pilferage is seen in these systems. In contrast, a centralized, procurement system provides maximum quality control of procured drugs with minimum costs.

However, the centralized system should ensure transparency and high audit of quality as well as finances to avoid corruption to percolate in the system. The suppliers should be given a complete delivery schedule in order to eliminate stock-outs and maximize the installed capacity usage. Further, the supply chain management is completely controlled by e-governance. With the help of an internet portal a common link is maintained between the suppliers and warehouse. The supplier enters all the critical information including batch number and expiry date etc of the medicines in the portal. These details are verified at the warehouse, and the drug delivery is approved. This prevents stock out and saves manual entry time.

As India aims to provide universal health coverage, it becomes mandatory to achieve equity in health. To realize the Millennium Development Goal 8-E that aims to ensure access to essential affordable medicines by 2015 globally we need to eliminate irrational use of drugs and ensure centralized procurement of medicines.

Referencing

- Lu, Y.et al., (2011), The world medicines situation 2011: medicine expenditures. Geneva: WHO.
- National Health Accounts, India 2004-2005, A report by National Health Accounts Cell, Ministry of Health and Family Welfare ,Government of India (In collaboration with WHO India Country Office).
- National Health Accounts, India 2012, A report by National Health Accounts Cell, Ministry of Health and Family Welfare ,GOI (In collaboration with WHO India Country Office), Global Health expenditure database available on http://apps.who.int/nha/database/ViewData/Indicators/en as accessed on 21-02-2015.
- NHA 2012, Global Health expenditure database, WHO available on http://apps.who.int/nha/database/ViewData/Indicators/en as accessed on 21-02-2015.
- NSSO Report (2014), A Report by Ministry of Statistics and Programme Implementation, CES Data 68th Round. available on http://mospi.nic.in/Mospi_New/site/inner.aspx?status=3&menu_id=31 as accessed on 21-02-2015.
- Rajasthan Medical services Corporation website www.tnmsc.com accessed on 21-02-15.

- Rajasthan Medical services Corporation Approved rate list (Drug) from website http://rmsc.nic.in/background.html accessed on 10/04/ 2014.
- Selvaraj, S (2005), Access to Essential Medicines and Drugs, Background Papers of the National Commission on Macroeconomics and Health, Ministry of Health and Family Welfare.
- Selvaraj, S. et al, (2014), India Infrastructure Report 2013-14, Access to Medicines, Medical Devices and Medicines, Chapter available on http://www.idfc.com/pdf/report/2013-14/Chapter-12.pdf as accessed on 21-02-2015.
- Tamil Nadu Medical Services Corporation Ltd. (TNMSC website), available on http://www.tnmsc.com/tnmsc/new/html/aboutus.php accessed on 22 February 2015.
- Tara S. et al. (2014), ' Public Healthcare - Paving the way for a Cost Efficient Drug Procurement & Distribution System' available on http://tejas.iimb.ac.in/articles/17.php accessed on 22-02-15.
- "The need to cut pharma super-profits" article (2015), available at http://infochangeindia.org/
- public-health/analysis/the-need-to-cut-pharma-super-profits.html accessed on 21-02-15.
- World Health Organisation (WHO). 2004. 'The World Medicine Situation', http://apps.who.int/medicinedocs/ pdf/s6160e/s6160e.pdf, accessed on 20 -02-2015.

Note

- Selvaraj, S (2005), Access to Essential Medicines and Drugs, Background Papers of the National Commission on Macroeconomics and Health, Ministry of Health and Family Welfare.
- World Health Organisation (WHO). 2004. 'The World Medicine Situation', http://apps.who.int/medicinedocs/ pdf/s6160e/s6160e.pdf, accessed on 28 March 2014.
- National Health Accounts, India 2012, A report by National Health Accounts Cell, Ministry of Health and Family Welfare ,GOI (In collaboration with WHO India Country Office), Global Health expenditure database available on http://apps.who.int/nha/database/ViewData/Indicators/en as accessed on 21-02-2015.
- Selvaraj, S. et al India Infrastructure Report 2013-14,Chapter 12: Access to Medicines, Medical Devices and Medicines.

5. NSSO Report, CES Data 68th Round.

   2 World Health Organisation (WHO). 2004. 'The World Medicine Situation', http://apps.who.int/medicinedocs/ pdf/s6160e/s6160e.pdf, accessed on 28 March 2014.

6. WHO 2004 The World Medicine Situation WHO/EDM/PAR/2004.5 Geneva. World Health Organization

7. Lu, Y., Hernandez, P., Abegunde, D., & Edejer, T. (2011). The world medicines situation 2011: medicine expenditures. Geneva: WHO.

8. Budget Documents, Government of India 2010-11 (Centre and respective states)

9. HLEG Secretariat, Aggregated data from Respective Monthly Bulletin of Reserve Bank of India, Mumbai

10. Article on Public Healthcare - Paving the way for a Cost Efficient Drug Procurement & Distribution System from website http://tejas.iimb.ac.in/articles/17.php accessed on 22-01-15.

11. Rajasthan Medical services Corporation website www.tnmsc.com accessed on 21-02-15.

12. Rajasthan Medical services Corporation Approved rate list (Drug) from website http://rmsc.nic.in/background.html accessed on 10/04/2014.

13. Article on the need to cut pharma super-profits available at http://infochangeindia.org/public-health/analysis/the-need-to-cut-pharma-super-profits.html.

39

Trends in Education in 21st Century: An Overview

Monika Khurana & Neelam Vohra

Abstract

Education in 21st century has changed and is more challenging. Selection in higher education is largely based upon prior academic performance and we don't understand that the newer education demand is to justify decision-making and innovation. In 21st century our businesses and universities must be designed to foster innovation that has come from individuals. Students of twenty first century will have to think out of the box, must develop interdisciplinary and critical thinking and problem solving skills. Thus, the present article overviews education in 21st century and its trends.

Keywords: *higher education, trends, e- learning, learning techniques*

Introduction

The twenty-first century has posed newer challenges and frontiers for educational professionals. Students need latest twenty-first century skills, using the pedagogy of the new century 1. This pedagogy a shift from "teacher centered" teaching, which is perceived as leading to superficial and shallow learning, to "student centered" teaching methods which are considered as leading to deep and significant learning.

With the increased rise in the international schooling system, where the demographic mix of nationalities there, the move from a multicultural education stance to that of an intercultural understanding offers a more dynamic approach to learning2. This leads students to be responsible global citizens where a commitment to peace, justice, understanding and co-operation are the consequences of the education system. Across the world the implementation of a multicultural education program has offered schools a platform to build awareness around a country's specific national identity. This view of multicultural education focused on providing understanding the culture of the people of the land and this philosophy purports improved student acceptance and possible action will occur as they develop a deeper appreciation and respect for others3.

The words "twenty-first century" star in many of the titles of many education studies. The twenty-first century is more challenging and to deal with its challenges, the student must be equipped with different set of abilities, which the educational system should provide.

Higher Education

Higher education has traditionally been defined in terms of two goals: instruction and research. In the past, these have been seen as very different aspects. Research done mainly by faculty and graduate students is the process whereby we increase the world's knowledge. Instruction, which involves all students, is the process whereby we transfer some subset of that knowledge to individuals. For this we must prepare all students, not just professional scholars, to embark on a lifetime of learning and discovery which means that our students will not simply be passively absorbing subject matter but be more like researchers actively exploring their environment. The reason for higher education is simple i.e. to prepare students, predominantly young adults, for future success. Success can be defined in many ways: the ability to pursue and advance in the career of one's choice, to contribute meaningfully to one's community and the ability to pursue an "intellectual life".

Students are admitted largely based on prior academic performance. Decisions are based predominantly on 2 factors: grade point average (from previous school) and standardized test scores (SAT Reasoning Test etc). Grade point average (GPA) and test scores are reflections of a student's ability to master content and, to some extent, utilize content in limited technical ways.

In the higher education, the single-minded approach on using GPA and standardized test scores to categorize student capabilities leads to a self-fulfilling cycle. We give admission to students who will perform well in the classroom and we hire faculty who are comfortable with a content-delivery-centered instructional model. When students perform well, we claim that we have been responsible stewards of our young generation. We propagate this model because we rarely expand our horizons as educators and we don't understand that the newer education demand is to justify decision-making and innovation.

The Relationship Between Higher Education and Business in 21st Century

The world is in passage from the industrial age to the information age. The key economic resources in the world will be rather knowledge, individual innovators, and information4. Emerging technologies will give us the ability to explore and create knowledge as never before. This has enormous implications for us as individuals and for our institutions especially our colleges and universities, which will have to take on especially heavy responsibilities.

Globally in business, we are moving from a hierarchical order to one of interdependence. Not long ago the United States of America stood unchallenged at the top of the world's economic hierarchy. The global economy functions like a biological ecosystem and an unbalance in one sector can affect the whole. Our businesses and universities must be designed to foster innovation which has always come from individuals. There is a dangerous time lag built into even the most successful institutions. They are created at one time in response to some particular opportunity in a given historical context. And then as the context shifts, the institution finds itself carrying excess baggage that is no longer useful. Organizations in 21st century can thrive only by reinventing themselves through refocusing on individuals. Individuals in 21st century will need to have tremendous flexibility to be able to move from one industry to another. Those who are best prepared to do that will be the most successful. Over-specialization and a limited perspective can be a dead-end trap. Students today cannot count on finding one smooth career path because jobs that exist today will change radically (by the millions) tomorrow.

Trends in Higher Education

Internet age and Distance Learning

Trends in higher education outline a strategy for successful implementation of innovations in educational delivery. Decreasing classroom time wastage and evolving critical thinking in students in order to solve problems are focus areas5. This generation students have grown up with interactive technologies such as computers and videogames. There is increasing prevalence of mobile technology in the form of handheld devices as smart phones and iPods. These students rarely read newspapers, learn by doing, and gravitate toward group or other activities that include a social component. They have little tolerance for traditional modes of information exchange exemplified by the word "lecture". In response to these changes, electronic learning (e-learning) is being implemented more frequently, creating new and exciting opportunities for educational institutions and students5.

Learning environments used in on-campus education have been the standard for education delivery. This embraces the traditional classroom environment in which instruction is either instructor- or student-centered. Over the time, distance education has evolved as a means for meeting the needs of individuals who could not access on-campus teaching. As this concept spread, it was realized that the distance between the student and instructor was not only geographical, but also pedagogical and psychological. This distance was coined as a "transactional distance". In the 21st century, online learning has decreased transactional distance and has led to transformations in distance education.

The opportunities offered by e-learning do not come without challenges. The fact is that e-learning is expensive to develop: instructors need to be trained, material needs to be created, assessments must be developed, help desks or online support materials must be established, electronic office hours must be held.

Implementation of New Learning Techniques

Changing teaching practice is difficult. One of the reasons is that faculty members often feel fully occupied with their existing teaching, research, and service duties. Faculty members often are reluctant to adopting a student-centered (as opposed to an instructor-centered) approach because they feel student-centered approaches would negatively affect the content and rigor of the course or simply because they may lose some measure of control.

Faculty members tend to teach the way they were taught, and most were taught with traditional lectures. Faculty members also tend to view lectures as an effective method of teaching. There is no argument that lecture is a good means to transmit information. In this information age, when information is easy to find, other teaching approaches are required to facilitate the skills students need to apply information, communicate, and reason. We should try to build a cooperative environment, involving the institution's members as active participants, support faculty development and effective leadership. As adult learners, the learning style of most faculty members requires information and a rationale for change in order to understand and accept a proposed change. The time required for investigation, questions, dialogue, and reflection is essential to facilitate this process. It is equally important that faculty members take responsibility and be prepared to implement a proposed change.

Conclusion

In 21st century student culture has been impacted tremendously by the digital revolution. These students have grown up communicating and sharing through the Internet. We should be poised to take advantage of the digital world for learning. Students of twenty first century must learn to think out of the box, must develop interdisciplinary and critical thinking and problem solving skills. They must know how to work collaboratively in a team, to inquire and analyze for which they must have written and oral communications skills

References

- Blouin RA, Riffee Wh, Robinson ET. Beck DE, Green C, Joyner PU, Persky AM, Pollack GM. Roles of Innovation in Education Delivery American Journal of Pharmaceutical Education 73 (8), 2009, Article 154
- Hovenga EJ and Bricknell L. Current and Future Trends in Teaching and Learning. Stud Health Technol Inform. 109, 2004, 131-42
- Madden J. Raising Student Achievement: The work of the Internationally Minded Teacher. International Journal of Innovation, Creativity and Change 1(4), 2014, 1-11
- Pinto A, Selvaggi S, Sicignano G, Vollono E, Iervolino L, Amato F, Molinari A, Grassi R. E-learning tools for education: regulatory aspects, current applications in radiology and future prospects. Radiol Med. 113(1), 2008, 144-57
- Sculley J. The Relationship Between Business and Higher Education: a Perspective on the 21st Century. Communications of the ACM 32(9), 1989, 1056-61.

40

Telemedicine: Beginning of e-Health Era

Kashmira Patel, Shivani Khandelwal, Ekta Pandey, & Yukti Bajaj

Abstract

India is an emerging prowess but despite this growth the nation lags behind not only developed nations but also many developing nations as far as global standards in healthcare. It was reported by World Bank that India looses around 6 per cent of its GDP in preventable illnesses and premature death.

Information technology has recently paved its way into Health Sector in India. Emergence of e-health seems have raised the hope in health industry not just by increasing the access but also making it affordable and quick.

The research paper aims to study the e-health initiatives, especially telemedicine in India. The aim is to understand the mechanism of operation of telemedicine and also to gather information on various state initiatives to provide e- health. The objective is to recommend policy initiatives for improvement of the current tele-health systems.

Keywords

e-health, Telemedicine, Telehealth, Information and communication technology

Background

Telemedicine is the delivery of medicine information from one part to another through electronic information and communications technologies to assist the health of people and to reach out the rural areas. Tele-health refers to broader remote services in health. It also includes remote non-clinical services. It broadly include video conferencing, the internet, store and forward imaging, streaming media, e-health including patient portal, remote monitoring of vital signs and nursing call centres.

The term e-health and Tele-health also differ from telemedicine. Telemedicine provide care only to remote clinical services but tele-health includes broader remote health care services and non-clinical services such as administration, continuing medical education and providing training. The term e-health is relatively new term for healthcare practice. The method is used in UK and Europe for electronic medical record and other component of health.

Telemedicine is growing rapidly in clinical medicine where the medicine information is exchanged through the internet for the purpose of providing health to none and to improve health where there is some. Telemedicine uses communication and information technologies for the delivery of medical care.

In olden days care at a distance was conducted via post but we are grateful to the modern technology that has evolved modern telemedicine. African villagers used to convey their messages through smoke signals so the villagers stay away from serious disease. And in 1900s people conveyed their messages through two-way radios. As modern telemedicine arrived the olden methods are gone.

Types of Telemedicine

Telemedicine can be broken into 3 concepts:

1. Real time
2. Store and forward
3. Home Health

1. ***Real Time:*** Real time telemedicine is simple as well as complex. The interaction take place only when there is presence of both the parties and the communication link which is between them allow a real time interaction. Equipment which is used in real time telemedicine is video-conferencing. These are the commonest form of technologies used in synchronous telemedicine.

2. ***Store and Forward:*** These are different then real time telemedicine. Store and forward does not require presence of both the parties at the same time. It acquire medical data (like medical images, bio signals etc.) and then transmit it to medical specialist for further assessment when offline. Dermatology, pathology and radiology are common specialist which is in asynchronous telemedicine.

3. *Home Health:* When the patient is kept under general observation in hospital after any surgical or medical procedure, the hospital is losing a valuable bed so the home health allows general observation and care of the patient. Equipment used are vital signs capture, video conference and patient stats can be reviewed and alarms are set from hospital nurses station.

Tools of Telemedicine

For the effective and efficient working of telemedicine, various tools are require for example telecommunication, telemedicine software and hardware platform.

Telecommunication tools involve satellite, lease line, ISDN (integrated service digital network), PSTN (public switched telephone network). Data is transmitted through telecommunication within large geographical areas.

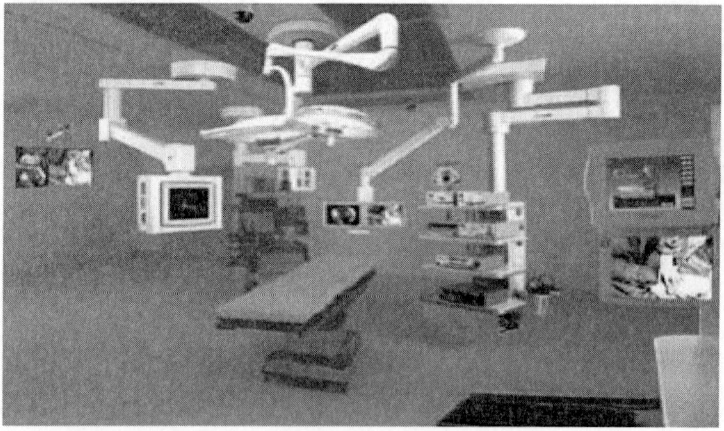

Fig. 1: Set up of telemedicine centre

Source: Mishra, S. Telemedicine, EMR & Report Connectivity. Retreived from http://www.telemedindia.org/eseminar/Telemedicine,%20EMR%20&%20 Remote%20Connectivity.pdf on 20-02-2015.

Telemedicine hardware involves the information technology equipments and video-conferencing kit for the visualization of data by the specialist.

The internal core on which telemedicine actually run are telemedicine software like ATNF of Apollo, VSee etc. These are the software working on storing the patient's data as per the need and maintaining records.

There are many tele- imaging tools which help in diagnosing the problem like digital ultrasound, digital mammography, digital transparency scanner, digital microscope, digital X-ray, digital ECG. This helps in direct acquisition of digital images. For good quality image transmission image database system, high speed network, super HD imaging system and video conference system are required. Tele-imaging has various field of scope:

- The primary basis of tele- imaging is for diagnosing the problem.
- Tele-follow up procedures can be done.
- Junior doctors require experience on various complex diseases and tele-education can also be provided.
- Various tele-CME and consultation programs can be done.

Literature Review

Indian healthcare industry is very big in worldwide where private sector provides almost 80% of healthcare services. In rural area it is difficult to retain specialist doctors due to lack of very basic facilities which usually de-motivate their work. Moreover, there is very less investment on building infrastructure for healthcare facilities in rural area. There are so many public private partnership models working in India towards providing services and enhancing growth. These PPP models help in bridging these gaps. Telemedicine is a very good example of PPP model in India which aims to provide effective healthcare services to poor people.

Main motive of telemedicine is to provide clinical support, overcoming geographical barriers and by using information and communication technologies (ICT) improve healthcare services which should be cost effective. Penetration of internet leads to rapid and easy utilization of telemedicine in developing countries. This leads to advancements in web based applications and multimedia approaches.

While all other hospital was in their initial stage of growth, Apollo hospital came up with the idea of telemedicine and started Apollo Telemedicine Networking Foundation (ATNF). This was started in between 1997. Their main focus was to provide healthcare services to rural and suburban India. ATNF system was a huge success which makes others to follow the same.

ATNF is a nonprofit organization with 106 centers in India and around nine outside the country. ATNF utilizes appropriate software and hardware to examine, monitor and treat a patient who is physically present at the other location. Today several data or solution for several diseases is present like radiology, cardiology, psychiatry, dermatology, neurology and ophthalmology. Apollo hospital is well established and patients come for treatment from all parts of the country. They use to review patients from far away.

ATNF has now developed new software for the transmission of MRI scans, ultrasounds, CT scans, x-ray films etc. which are viewed by the specialist at tertiary center. Interaction doesn't only take place in English but in also six other Indian languages. Medical records are kept in digital form and are called Electronic Medical Record (EMR).

In 1999, department of space and Apollo hospital, Indian research space organization and government of India made VSAT available in a village hospital of aragonda and tele-consultations were provided through satellite technology from Apollo hospital, Chennai. Children with complex disease get the benefit of advice from experts and junior doctors got an opportunity to explore their experience in understanding rural problems. This method became a success in 2000 and more than 6000 villagers in the region had taken the advantage of telemedicine. ATNF had a very great role for the development of telemedicine in south Asia. Government of India started Apollo telemedicine in Africa with an aim of sharing tele-consultations with the doctors of Africa related to healthcare.

Research Methodology

The proposed research is a descriptive observational research design. The study is based on description and analysis of data collected by secondary sources. The sources include published research papers in journals, research articles and published reports.

Research Objectives

1. To analyze the uptake of e-Health policies and strategies in India.
2. To understand the mechanism of deployment of e-health in India,
3. To understand the use of telemedicine solutions in treatment in India,
4. To analyze the adoption of e-learning for health professionals and students,
5. To understand the collection, processing and transfer of patient information.

Results & Discussion

Telemedicine is widely used in isolated communities and remote areas where there is no knowledge about prevention of health. Telemedicine also work as a communication tool for general practitioner and a specialist in remote region.

The first interactive telemedicine system was developed and marketed by med phone corporation in 1989 for the purpose of diagnosing and treating patient requiring cardiac resuscitation in remote areas.

Patients are monitored in their home by using devices like blood pressure monitoring and sugar monitoring and data are transferred to the care giver and through way prevention steps are taken in emerging world. In fast growing developing country new telemedicine practises are emerging that is primary remote diagnostic visit. Through theses device the doctor examines the patient and treat them. This new technology promises to solve most of the health problems in country.

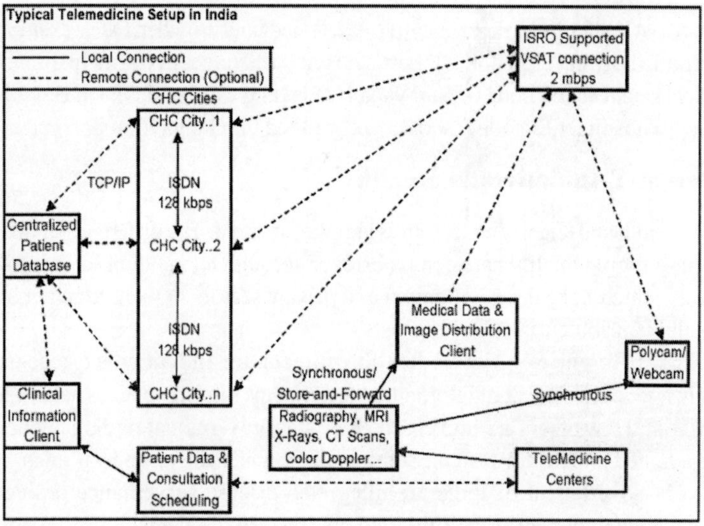

Fig. 2: Telemedicine service setup in India

Source: Pal, A., Mbarika, V. W. A., Cobb-Payton, F., Datta, P., & McCoy, S. (2005). Telemedicine diffusion in a developing country: the case of India (March 2004). Information Technology in Biomedicine, IEEE Transactions on, 9(1), 59-65.

Other E-Health Initiatives

Indian Space Research Organization (ISRO)-they had developed GRAMSAT (rural satellite) for the development of society. In collaboration with state government they had developed a huge telemedicine network along with sixteen telemedicine mobile units. It has established telemedicine network in many places like Karnataka, Bangalore, Orissa, Madhya Pradesh, Maharashtra, Andaman and Nikobar.

Ministry of Health and Family Welfare (MoH&FW), Government of India-it is working towards tele-consultancy, tele-education/training for the implementation of Integrated Disease Surveillance Programme. Recently it is decided to connecting all medical colleges under "National knowledge network" under central scheme of e-health.

Department of Information Technology (DIT), Ministry of Communication and IT (MCIT), Government of India is involved in initiation of many pilot schemes and their standardization. Funding of many telemedicine software are also done under this, for example mercury and Sanjeevani software by C-DAC.

Telemedicine by large hospitals-Sanjay Gandhi Postgraduate Institute of Medical Sciences (SGPGIMS) in 1999 started their telemedicine project and has a network of 27 national and international nodes. All India Institute of Medical

Sciences (AIIMS) is one more example of telemedicine provider. Other examples are Apollo hospital (150 nodes), Fortis hospital (20 nodes), Amrita Institute of medical sciences (69 nodes), Narayana Hrudayalaya (26 nodes), Dr. Balabhai Nanavati hospital (32 nodes) and recently added Sir Ganga Ram hospital etc.

Different E-Initiatives in Health

E-health and telemedicine is growing areas in India. The difference of urban and rural region quality care can be bridged through telemedicine. These are the way which links the government and private sectors to work together and actively contribute to various projects.

The different e-initiative health projects are Indian space research organization, department of information technology, ministry of external affairs, MHFW and few others are implemented by state government finding but none have adopted into health system. Some projects which are taken by ministry of health in government of India are integrated disease surveillance projects, national cancer network (ONCONET), national rural telemedicine network, national medicine college network and the digital medical library network. Various e - health initiative are: -

1. Electronic Medical Records and Hospital Automation

Most of the Hospital in India requires records to be maintained which is very difficult. Insurance sector is the one which needs the more accurate / efficient information. Electronic medical records and hospital automation can alone help to meet these challenges. The Apollo Hospital took initiative to build network called health highway. Health highway will be given as hosted solution by IBM and Apollo on market demand via pay per use model. It is available in open market for the development of knowledge base.

2. Department of Information and Technology (DIT), Ministry of Communication and Information Technology (MCIT), Government of India

The DIT has played major role in building and shaping the future of telemedicine in India. DIT has been taking parts at various levels from starting of pilot scheme to standardization of telemedicine in country. DIT has sponsored various projects of telemedicine they are SGPGI- Lucknow, AIIMS-new Delhi and PGIMER-Chandigarh. DIT has built more than 100 nodes all over India with state government. The telemedicine network in west Bengal is for diagnosis and monitoring of tropical disease. Some of the projects which are launched by DIT are oncology network for facilitator cancer care in Kerala and Tamil Nadu.

3. Indian Space Research Organization (ISRO)

ISRO established telemedicine pilot project in the country under GRAMAT (rural satellite) which are for the benefit of society. In collaboration with state government the telemedicine network consist of 382 hospitals out of which 306 are rural. District hospitals/health centres are connected to 51 super specialty hospitals which are in main state. Sixteen mobile telemedicine units are linked to this network. Andaman and Nicobar Island and Lakshadweep are connected to specialty hospital through satellite. With state government it helped Karnataka state telemedicine where the district hospital in state are linked in Bangalore and Mysore. ISRO has helped various states in establishing telemedicine pilot projects.

4. Ministry of Health and Family Welfare, Government of India

MOH and FW is working on integrated disease surveillance programme network which connects all district hospital to medicine colleges to provide them tele - consultation, tele-education/training of health professionals and to monitor disease. OncoNet Indian project will provide 27 regional cancer centres (RCCs) and 108 peripheral cancer centres (PCCs) hospital to national cancer control programme for those regions.

5. State Government

Every state wants to strengthen their health care facilities so the government of Orissa and Uttar Pradesh supported the networking of secondary hospital and linked them to SGPGIMS. Government of Chhattisgarh by the support of ISRO established wide premier hospital across country. Rajasthan state government has build up network between 6 state medical college and 32 district hospital and 6 mobile vans. Andhra Pradesh launches mobile clinics in villages to check blood pressure and diabetes. Gujarat launch telemedicine project to enhance quality of healthcare.

6. Telemedicine Initiative Undertaken by Large Hospitals: Academic / Public / Corporate

Many super specialty hospitals are taking initiative to establish telemedicine programmes with the help of government agencies or private agencies. Most of the telemedicine programmes have started long back and have completed a year. Sanjay Gandhi Post graduate Institute of Medical Sciences (SGPGIMS), Lucknow started telemedicine system in year 1999 with the coordination of government agencies. These SGPGI has connected 27 national and international nodes to carry out tele- education and tele- healthcare activities. All India Institute of Medical Science, New Delhi connected with Jammu and Kashmir. Haryana, Orissa, North East States network and PGIMER

In corporate sector Amrital Institute Medical of Sciences (AIMS) Kochi (69 nodes), Apollo hospital group (150 nodes), Asia heart foundation, Bangalore,

Mumbai (02 nodes), Fortis hospital (20 nodes), and Escort heart institute research centre (08 nodes) are the main player in theses sector.

Different State Initiatives in Telemedicine

Though India has different and varieties of health care facilities it is still considered to be low health care service in India. There are 90% of hospitals in cities and town and remaining 10% of hospitals in rural areas. And about 68% of population lives in remote areas and 32% lives in town/cities. Primary health care facilities in rural area is very low where as in town and cities it is very high .Though Government and private sector has taken many steps in health care facilities the rural and remote region still continue to suffer. The number of patients in the remote region can be reduced through proper advice/guidance from super specialist in cities. Many worldwide health care services programmes are being conducted through telemedicine technologies for the awareness and prevention of disease

Various state initiative in telemedicine are taken they are : -

Telemedicine in Kerela

Telemedicine and Telehealth education has been set up in Kerala using the technology which is developed under Department of Information Technology. The telemedicine and Telehealth network project will connect three speciality medical hospital at MCH, SCTIMST and the RCC and with four District and rural hospitals. These networks also conduct the programmes of continuing medical education for the people in the urban as well as rural region to upgrade the knowledge of advanced technology. Telemedicine Network has also established Cancer Net project in Kerala. This project is for cancer patient in Kerala and to provide them medical services which will help in early detection of cancer, treatment and pain relief to the patient. It even helps for the follow - up and continuity of care in peripheral hospital of Regional cancer centre. It has more than 3000 patients getting treated and consulted at the centre. It is easy for the patient to approach and there is affordable cost for the treatment.

Telemedicine in West Bengal

Telemedicine system in west Bengal is especially for tropical disease and they use the technology which are established by WEBEL and IIT Kharagpur. Telemedicine system is used for the diagnosis and monitoring of tropical diseases. They also help in diagnosing and monitoring skin and blood related tropical diseases. These further reduce the number of patients in the region. Telemedicine have established a system in school of tropical Medicine, Kolkata and two other District Hospital. Many people come for treatment purpose and for consultation and there are more den 800 patients who have undergone consultations. Telemedicine has updated their system and extended to other two referral hospital and four district hospitals.

Telemedicine in North Eastern States in India

North East State is a area where there are lot of remote regions and they have lack of quality health care facilities so it is very much important to take telemedicine initiative in theses state. Telemedicine started up in turnkey project in Kohima hospital in Nagaland. Two telemedicine centres were started which connects hospital in North-eastern states of Sikkim and Tripura with multi-specialty hospital. The North Eastern Council of India has planned scheme to cover 75 districts in 7 states through telemedicine.

Current Problems

Indian health industry is very complex where 70 per cent of rural area people do not access healthcare services because around 80 per cent doctor lives in urban or metropolitan area. There is a big unequal distribution which actually makes the industry more complex and hard to apply equally in all states and their respected areas. Some of the major problems are discussed below:

- ***Fear of New Technology:*** People don't like to adapt new technologies because of their traditional beliefs. Convincing them is itself is a big challenge. They lack confidence in telemedicine's outcome because it is based on data provided to the physician and on that basis She/he use to give advices to the patient without patient's physical presence in front.
- ***Subdivision of Language Locally:*** Language is a big problem in India. Particular state has its own language and beside that, various subdivisions of local languages is also there. This creates problem in developing and implementing single software all around the country.
- ***Unconvinced Doctors:*** Telemedicine is totally based on data provided where patient is not physically present. This may affect proper checkup level and also patient and doctor satisfaction. There are some diseases where doctor use to examine the patient by touching various symptom related parts of the patient's body and reach to the final problem, which is lacking in telemedicine.
- ***Basic Amenities:*** Telemedicine is a efficient way of providing healthcare services but it is not possible where there is no telecommunication, electricity etc. This service cannot change or help an area where even basic amenities are not present.

- ***Dependence on Human Work:*** It is solely dependent on the organization providing this service. Lack in motivated and well trained staff cannot help in improving health.
- ***Literacy Rate:*** There is a huge gap in literacy rates of different states of India. A state like Kerala has 93.9 per cent (year 2011) literacy rate whereas in Bihar it is as low as 63.8 per cent (year 2011). It is a very big challenge for people to adopt telemedicine easily due to lack of knowledge. The basic language of this software is English which is not understood by a large number of populations.

Conclusion & Recommendations

India is a country with many layers of religions, beliefs, culture and with huge demographic and social differences. It is very hard to provide healthcare services at all locations at affordable prices. Telemedicine can revolutionize the way of providing healthcare services to reach out at very poor area both by geographically and economically too.

Figure 3: A Surgical Treatment Session Conducted Using Telemedicine Set up.

Source: Mishra, S. Telemedicine, EMR & Report Connectivity. Retreived from http://www.telemedindia.org/eseminar/Telemedicine,%20EMR%20&%20Remote%20Connectivity.pdf on 20-02-2015.

There are several ways and areas where telemedicine can help to improve healthcare in India:

1. It can avail the high quality healthcare for underprivileged people where there are lots of geographical and economical barriers.
2. It will help in enhancing the equality for various medical services.
3. It will help in preserving the resources by cutting down the travelling time of both provider and patient. Immediate consultancy can be

provided for the patient who needs immediate attention which can be controlled on that geographical location too.

4. Patient centric care at hospitals include various cost other than patient's treatment cost like travel charges, waiting area for patient and relative, accommodation for relatives, food etc. Telemedicine can reduce these associated costs.

The need of the hour for Indian health sector is to provide universal health coverage to all the citizens. The pillars of universal health coverage rely on increasing access to health services, providing equitable and affordable health services. E-health is revolutionary step in health industry, so the time is right to tap the potential of telemedicine and information technology to achieve highest health standards.

References

- Ganapathy, K. and Ravindra, A. (2009). Telemedicine in India: the Apollo story. Telemedicine and e-Health, 15(6), 576-585.
- Mishra, S., Ganapathy, K., and Bedi, B. S. (2008). The current status of e-Health initiatives in India. Presentations made at making the e-Health connection: 13 July-3 August, 2008 Bellagio, Italy.
- Mishra, S.K., Singh, I.P., and Chand, R.D. (2011). Current status of telemedicine network in India and future perspective. Proceedings of the Asia-Pacific Advanced Network, 32, 151-163.
- Pal, A., Mbarika, V.W.A., Cobb-Payton, F., Datta, P., and McCoy, S. (2005). Telemedicine diffusion in a developing country: the case of India (March 2004). Information Technology in Biomedicine, IEEE Transactions on, 9(1), 59-65.
- Saxena, G. and Singh, J.P. (2009, December). E-medicine in India:- Hurdles and future prospects. In International seminar organized at The International Institute of Professional Studies.
- Mishra, S. Telemedicine, EMR and Report Connectivity. Retreived from http://www.telemedindia.org/eseminar/Telemedicine,%20 EMR%20&%20 Remote%20Connectivity.pdf on 20-02-2015.
- Bedi, B.S. Telemedicine in India: Initiatives and Perspective Retreived from http://www.oldagesolutions.org/publications/bedi_telemedicine_ india.pdf on 21-02-2015.